Better
Homes
and Gardens

Better Homes and Gardens®

ANNUAL•
Recipes
1999

Better Homes and Gardens® Books
Des Moines, Iowa

Pear Tree Wonders (page 309)

*E*ach *month, more than 34 million people read* Better Homes and Gardens® *magazine, and many of you automatically trust our food ideas will work for you. That's a reality check that gives food editors a tremendous sense of responsibility.*

Part of that responsibility means keeping up with what's happening in homes just like yours. Living and working in the heart of America—Des Moines, Iowa—makes that job easier because we share many of the same needs as you. Our homes and families are central to us. Our home kitchens contain ordinary appliances and cooking utensils.

Like you, we also lead active lives. I have a 1½-hour round-trip commute from home to work each day. Though past the kid-raising stage, my husband and I work a 200-acre farm and apple orchard while also caring for parents who live nearby. I love to cook, but the recipes I use must be easy, affordable, and healthful, as well as great tasting.

With both the century and millennium drawing to a close, Annual Recipes 1999 *has been an extra special labor-of-love. All of the food ideas have been tested to meet our highest personal and professional standards so that you and your family can enjoy them now and well into the new millennium.*

Happy Cooking! Happy New Millennium!

Nancy Byal

Nancy Byal
Executive Food Editor

The Editors

Richard Swearinger

*O*ur team of food experts is just like you. They're busy balancing work, family, home, and play. And they understand the challenges of "real life," including how to prepare eye-catching, delicious recipes, even on the go. Senior Food Editor Nancy Wall Hopkins—also our resident prop and photo styling guru—oversees the content of all our stories. And at home she's never idle with two bubbly little girls. Nutrition Editor Jeanne Ambrose, who likes to flavor dinner with herbs from her garden, contributes expertise in nutrition and creativity, as does family man and Associate Editor David Feder, shown here with his canine companion Peanut. Associate Editor Richard Swearinger, who has a hands-on role in story development and the

Nancy Wall Hopkins

David Feder

Jeanne Ambrose

Anna Anderson

Karen Pollock

Prize Tested Recipe contest, relishes time outside with his sons. Editorial Assistants Anna Anderson and Karen Pollock stay energized in their off hours by taking to the outdoors. Despite their diverse interests, our food editors share a passion for food. They love to prepare inviting dishes for their families. Chances are your favorite recipes were "taste-tested" by our editors and their families at home in addition to being guaranteed by the Better Homes and Gardens® Test Kitchen.

Vice President, General Manager: *Jamie L. Martin*

Better Homes and Gardens® Magazine

Editor in Chief: *Jean LemMon*
Executive Food Editor: *Nancy Byal*
Senior Editor: *Nancy Wall Hopkins*
Nutrition Editor: *Jeanne Ambrose*
Associate Editors: *David Feder, R.D.; Richard Swearinger*
Editorial Assistants: *Karen Pollock, Anna Anderson*

Meredith Publishing Group

President, Publishing Group: *Christopher M. Little*
Vice President, Consumer Marketing & Development: *Hal Oringer*

Meredith Corporation

Chairman and Chief Executive Officer: *William T. Kerr*

Chairman of the Executive Committee: *E. T. Meredith III*

Our seal assures you that every recipe in
Better Homes and Gardens Annual Recipes 1999 has been
tested in the Better Homes and Gardens® Test Kitchen.
This means that each recipe is practical and reliable, and meets
our high standards of taste appeal. We guarantee your satisfaction
with this book for as long as you own it.

All of us at Better Homes and Gardens® Books are
dedicated to providing you with the information and ideas you
need to create delicious foods. We welcome your comments
and suggestions. Write to us at: Better Homes and Gardens Books,
Cookbook Editorial Department, 1716 Locust Street, LN 112,
Des Moines, IA 50309-3023.

Cover photograph: Mile High Cranberry-Apple Pie *(page 269)*
Page 1: Lemon Cheesecake *(page 288)*
Page 2: Pear Tree Wonders *(page 309)*

*If you would like to order additional copies
of this book, call 800-439-4119.*

*Some of the images in this book are used by permission
of Zedcor, Inc., Tucson, AZ, from the 100,000 image and the
30,000 image DeskGallery® collections. 800-482-4567.*

© Copyright 1999 by Meredith Corporation, Des Moines, Iowa.
All Rights Reserved. Printed in the United States of America.
First Edition. Printing Number and Year: 5 4 3 2 1 03 02 01 00 99
ISSN: 1083-4451
ISBN: 0-696-20968-3

CONTENTS

When this symbol appears with a recipe, rest assured that you can prepare the dish—start to finish—in 30 minutes or less.

Any recipe that bears this low-fat symbol meets our guideline of having no more than 10 grams of fat per serving (see page 8).

This symbol is assigned to recipes that are both low in fat and can be prepared—start to finish—in 30 minutes or less.

The recipes that display this blue-ribbon symbol have earned top honors in our monthly Prize Tested Recipes contest.

NUTRITION INFORMATION

With each recipe, we give you useful nutrition information you easily can apply to your own needs. First read "What You Need" (below) to determine your dietary requirements. Then refer to the Nutrition Facts listed with each recipe. You'll find the calorie count and the amount of fat, saturated fat, cholesterol, sodium, carbohydrates, fiber, and protein for each serving. In most cases, along with the Nutrition Facts per serving, you'll find the amount of vitamin A, vitamin C, calcium, and iron noted as a percentage of the Daily Values. The Daily Values are dietary standards set by the Food and Drug Administration. To stay in line with the nutrition breakdown of each recipe, follow the suggested number of servings.

HOW WE ANALYZE

The Better Homes and Gardens® Test Kitchen computer analyzes each recipe for the nutritional value of a single serving.

◆ The analysis does not include optional ingredients.

◆ We use the first serving size listed when a range is given. For example: If we say a recipe "Makes 4 to 6 servings," the Nutrition Facts are based on 4 servings.

◆ When ingredient choices (such as margarine or butter) appear in a recipe, we use the first one mentioned for analysis. The ingredient order does not mean we prefer one ingredient over another.

◆ When milk is a recipe ingredient, the analysis is calculated using 2-percent (reduced-fat) milk.

WHAT YOU NEED

The dietary guidelines below suggest nutrient levels that moderately active adults should strive to eat each day. As your calorie levels change, adjust your fat intake, too. Try to keep the percentage of calories from fat to no more than 30 percent. There's no harm in occasionally going over or under these guidelines, but the key to good health is maintaining a balanced diet *most of the time*.

Calories:	About 2,000
Total fat:	Less than 65 grams
Saturated fat:	Less than 20 grams
Cholesterol:	Less than 300 milligrams
Carbohydrates:	About 300 grams
Sodium:	Less than 2,400 milligrams
Dietary fiber:	20 to 30 grams

LOW-FAT RECIPES

For recipes that meet our low-fat criteria, a main-dish serving must contain 10 or fewer grams of fat. For side dishes or desserts, the serving must contain 5 or fewer grams of fat. These recipes are flagged with a low-fat symbol.

JANUARY
Winter's Bounty

*C*alm those cold-weather cravings with the unexpected bounty of canned and frozen fruits and vegetables. They don't have to be garden-fresh to satisfy, and they pack a nutritional punch. Cozy up to vegetable-rich soups and main dishes like Catalan Chicken Chowder, Potato-Beet Soup, Spicy Corn Chowder, Mexican Lasagna, and Vegetable Pastitsio. Chase away the winter blahs with Asian-style Ravioli Duet swimming in an Onion-Herb Broth. Finish off your cravings with Just-Like-Mom's Cobbler—full of fruit and so easy.

30-minute recipes indicated in RED.
Low-fat and no-fat recipes indicated
with a ♥.
Photographs indicated in italics.
*Bonus recipe

VIETNAMESE CHICKEN NOODLE SOUP

Prep: 20 min. ◆ Cook: 10 min.

2 medium carrots, halved lengthwise and thinly sliced (1 cup)
¾ cup thinly sliced celery
2 cloves garlic, minced
1 Tbsp. cooking oil
3 cups water
2 14½-oz. cans reduced-sodium chicken broth
2 oz. rice sticks or vermicelli
1½ cups cubed cooked chicken
¼ cup thinly sliced green onions
2 Tbsp. bottled hoisin sauce
2 Tbsp. reduced-sodium soy sauce
Few dashes bottled hot pepper sauce
Thinly sliced green onions

1 In a large saucepan cook carrots, celery, and garlic in hot oil over medium-high heat about 4 minutes or until tender. Carefully add water and chicken broth. Bring to boiling. Add rice sticks or vermicelli; return to boiling. Cook, uncovered, 2 to 3 minutes or until noodles are tender. Stir in chicken, the ¼ cup green onions, hoisin sauce, soy sauce, and pepper sauce; heat through.

2 To serve, ladle soup into soup bowls. Sprinkle with additional thinly sliced green onions. Makes 4 or 5 main-dish servings.

Nutrition facts per serving: 273 cal., 9 g total fat (2 g sat. fat), 51 mg chol., 1,179 mg sodium, 25 g carbo., 2 g fiber, 22 g pro.
Daily values: 87% vit. A, 6% vit. C, 3% calcium, 10% iron.

PRIZE TESTED RECIPE WINNER

CATALAN CHICKEN CHOWDER

Prep: 10 min. ◆ Cook: 20 min.

This hearty dish gets attention whether for a weeknight supper or weekend get-together.

1 5-oz. pkg. saffron-flavored yellow rice mix
8 oz. skinless, boneless chicken breast halves, cut into bite-size pieces
½ cup chopped onion
1 clove garlic, minced
2 tsp. olive oil

◆◆◆

1 14½-oz. can diced tomatoes
1 14½-oz. can reduced-sodium chicken broth
½ of a 14-oz. can artichoke hearts, drained and quartered (about ¾ cup)
½ cup loose-pack frozen baby sweet peas
½ of a 7-oz. jar roasted red sweet peppers, drained and cut into strips

◆◆◆

2 Tbsp. toasted slivered almonds

1 Prepare rice according to package directions; set aside and keep warm. Meanwhile, in a large saucepan cook chicken, onion, and garlic in hot oil over medium-high heat about 5 minutes or until chicken is no longer pink.

2 Add undrained tomatoes, chicken broth, and artichoke hearts to chicken mixture. Bring to boiling; reduce heat. Simmer,

uncovered, 10 minutes, stirring occasionally. Add peas and red pepper strips. Cook for 3 to 4 minutes more or until soup is heated through.

3 To serve, ladle soup into soup bowls. Spoon a mound of cooked rice in center of each bowl. Sprinkle with almonds. Makes 4 main-dish servings.

Nutrition facts per serving: 321 cal., 10 g total fat (2 g sat. fat), 30 mg chol., 1,099 mg sodium, 42 g carbo., 4 g fiber, 19 g pro.
Daily values: 20% vit. A, 133% vit. C, 5% calcium, 23% iron.

FENNEL-POTATO SOUP

Prep: 35 min. ◆ Cook: 25 min.
Bake: 15 min.

The light and dark rye croutons can be made up to 1 week in advance and stored in a tightly covered container. (See the photograph on page 38.)

2 medium fennel bulbs (about 2 lb.)

◆◆◆

6 medium potatoes, peeled and cubed (about 2 lb.)
4 cups reduced-sodium chicken broth

◆◆◆

⅓ cup margarine or butter
½ cup all-purpose flour
½ tsp. caraway seed
½ tsp. pepper
2 cups buttermilk or milk
2½ cups chopped cooked chicken
1 recipe Rye Croutons (see page 11) (optional)

1 Wash fennel. Snip ¼ cup of the leafy tops; set aside. If desired for garnish, set aside additional leafy tops. Cut off and discard upper stalks of fennel. Remove any wilted outer layers; cut off and discard a thin slice from the base of fennel. Halve, core, and chop remaining fennel. (You should have about 4 cups.)

2 In a 4-quart Dutch oven combine fennel, potatoes, and chicken broth. Bring to boiling; reduce heat. Simmer, covered, for 15 to 20 minutes or until potatoes are tender. Drain, reserving broth. Set aside half the potatoes and fennel. Place remainder in a medium-size bowl; mash with a potato masher.

3 Meanwhile, in the same pot melt margarine or butter over medium heat. Stir in the flour, caraway seed, and pepper. Add buttermilk or milk. Cook and stir until slightly thickened and bubbly. Cook and stir for 1 minute more. Stir in the mashed potato mixture, the reserved chopped potatoes and fennel, reserved broth, reserved snipped fennel tops, and chicken. Cook and stir until heated through. If necessary, stir in additional broth to achieve desired consistency.

4 To serve, ladle soup into soup bowls. If desired, top each serving with Rye Croutons and reserved leafy tops of fennel. Makes 8 main-dish servings.

Rye Croutons: Cut 4 slices of ½-inch-thick light and/or dark rye bread into ¾-inch squares; set aside. In a large skillet melt ¼ cup margarine or butter. Remove from heat. Stir in ¼ teaspoon garlic powder. Add the bread cubes,

stirring until coated. Spread cubes in a single layer in a shallow baking pan. Bake in a 300° oven for 10 minutes; stir. Bake about 5 minutes more or until cubes are dry and crisp. Cool. Makes 3 cups croutons.

Nutrition facts per serving (without Rye Croutons): 334 cal., 13 g total fat (3 g sat. fat), 44 mg chol., 549 mg sodium, 36 g carbo., 16 g fiber, 20 g pro.
Daily values: 10% vit. A, 26% vit. C, 10% calcium, 8% iron.

POTATO-BEET SOUP

Prep: 15 min. ◆ Cook: 30 min.

A playful, colorful soup that's sure to brighten winter evenings.

2 **medium potatoes, peeled and cubed (¾ lb.)**
2 **leeks, coarsely chopped (⅔ cup)**
1 **Tbsp. olive oil**
4 **tsp. all-purpose flour**
2½ **cups chicken broth**
½ **tsp. dried basil, crushed**
½ **tsp. dried savory, crushed**
½ **tsp. dried tarragon, crushed**
½ **of a 16-oz. jar Harvard beets and their liquid (about ¾ cup)**

◆◆◆

½ **cup half-and-half, light cream, or whipping cream**
Fried potato strips (optional)

1 In a medium saucepan cook potatoes and leeks in hot oil over medium heat for 3 minutes. Stir in flour. Carefully add broth, basil, savory, and tarragon. Bring to boiling, stirring occasionally;

TEST KITCHEN TIP

THE BEST BROTHS

When a recipe calls for chicken, beef, or vegetable broth, you can use a homemade stock recipe or substitute commercially canned broth. Just remember that the canned varieties usually are saltier than homemade stocks, so hold off on adding extra salt until the end of cooking. Then, season to taste. Another option is to try a canned reduced-sodium broth. Bouillon cubes and granules diluted according to package directions may be used, but they also are saltier than homemade stocks.

reduce heat. Simmer, covered, about 20 minutes or until potatoes are very tender. Stir in beets. Cool slightly.

2 Place half of the mixture in a blender container or food processor bowl. Cover and blend or process until smooth. Transfer to a medium bowl. Repeat with remaining potato mixture. Return all of blended mixture to saucepan. Stir in half-and-half or whipping cream; heat through. If desired, top with fried potato strips. Makes 4 side-dish servings.

Nutrition facts per serving: 229 cal., 8 g total fat (3 g sat. fat), 12 mg chol., 582 mg sodium, 34 g carbo., 3 g fiber, 7 g pro.
Daily values: 4% vit. A, 17% vit. C, 6% calcium, 11% iron.

SPICY CORN CHOWDER

Prep: 10 min. ◆ Cook: 15 min.

For a fiery bowl of soup, use hot salsa.

½ tsp. ground cumin
½ tsp. chili powder
1 cup chicken broth
1½ cups loose-pack frozen whole kernel corn
1 cup frozen diced hash brown potatoes
½ cup chopped onion
½ cup chopped red or green sweet pepper

◆◆◆

2 oz. American cheese, cubed
¾ cup chunky salsa
1 cup half-and-half, light cream, or milk

◆◆◆

2 Tbsp. snipped fresh cilantro and/or snipped chives

1 In a large saucepan combine cumin and chili powder. Cook and stir over medium heat until spices are lightly toasted and aromatic. Carefully add chicken broth. Stir in corn, hash brown potatoes, onion, and sweet pepper. Bring to boiling; reduce heat. Simmer, covered, for 5 minutes.

2 Stir cheese into soup mixture. Cook and stir until cheese is melted. Stir in the salsa and half-and-half; heat through.

3 To serve, ladle chowder into soup bowls. Sprinkle with fresh cilantro and/or chives. Makes 4 main-dish servings.

Nutrition facts per serving: 248 cal., 12 g total fat (6 g sat. fat), 30 mg chol., 594 mg sodium, 31 g carbo., 2 g fiber, 9 g pro. *Daily values:* 29% vit. A, 72% vit. C, 14% calcium, 13% iron.

RAVIOLI DUET

An onion-herb broth accents these easy crab and butternut squash ravioli. (See the photograph on page 42.)

1 recipe Crab Rangoon Ravioli (see right)
1 recipe Butternut Squash Ravioli (see page 13)
1 recipe Onion-Herb Broth (see page 13)

◆◆◆

⅓ cup finely shredded Asiago cheese or Parmesan cheese
Fresh basil leaves (optional)

1 Prepare and cook the Crab Rangoon Ravioli and the Butternut Squash Ravioli. Prepare Onion-Herb Broth.

2 To serve, place about ⅓ cup of Onion-Herb Broth on each of 6 dinner plates or shallow bowls. Top each with 2 cooked Crab Rangoon Ravioli and 2 cooked Butternut Squash Ravioli; sprinkle with 2 to 3 teaspoons Asiago or Parmesan cheese. Garnish with basil leaves, if desired. Makes 6 main-dish servings.

Nutrition facts per serving: 219 cal., 8 g total fat (2 g sat. fat), 30 mg chol., 626 mg sodium, 25 g carbo., 1 g fiber, 12 g pro. *Daily values:* 19% vit. A, 8% vit. C, 9% calcium, 10% iron.

CRAB RANGOON RAVIOLI

Prep: 25 min. ◆ Cook: 5 min.

Pot sticker and wonton wrappers are found frozen or refrigerated in Asian markets or in many large supermarkets.

1 cup fresh or frozen lump crabmeat, thawed and drained (6 oz.)
½ of an 8-oz. tub cream cheese with chives and onion, softened
⅓ cup chopped leek
1 Tbsp. white wine Worcestershire sauce

◆◆◆

24 pot sticker or wonton wrappers (about 6 oz.)

1 In a small bowl stir together crabmeat, cream cheese, chopped leek, and Worcestershire sauce.

2 For each ravioli, place a rounded tablespoon of crab filling in center of a pot sticker or wonton wrapper. Brush edges with water and place a second wrapper over first, pressing to seal edges. Trim edges with fluted pastry wheel, if desired. Repeat with remaining wrappers and filling.*

3 In a 4-quart Dutch oven cook the ravioli, 6 at a time, in a large amount of gently boiling, lightly salted water 2 to 2½ minutes or until just tender. (Don't let water boil vigorously.)

4 Use a slotted spoon to remove ravioli. Place in a single layer on lightly greased baking sheet. Cover loosely with foil. Keep warm in a 300° oven up to 20 minutes. Serve with Butternut Squash Ravioli and Onion-Herb Broth (see recipes, below and right). Makes 12 ravioli.

*Note: If desired, place filled ravioli on foil-lined baking sheets. Cover and freeze, then place ravioli in freezer bags; seal, label, and freeze for up to 3 months. Cook frozen ravioli as above about 3 minutes or until just tender.

BUTTERNUT SQUASH RAVIOLI

Prep: 30 min. ◆ Bake: 50 min.
Cook: 5 min.

Using purchased pot sticker or wonton wrappers instead of making pasta from scratch cuts the fuss of making these tasty pillows.

½ **of a butternut squash, seeds removed (¾ lb.)**
⅓ **cup finely shredded Asiago cheese or Parmesan cheese**
⅛ **tsp. salt**
⅛ **tsp. freshly grated nutmeg or ground nutmeg**
⅛ **tsp. freshly ground pepper**

◆◆◆

24 **pot sticker or wonton wrappers (about 6 oz.)**

1 Place squash half, cut side down, in a shallow baking dish. Bake in a 350° oven for 30 minutes. Turn the cut side up. Bake, covered, 20 to 25 minutes more or until tender.

2 Spoon squash pulp into a mixing bowl, discarding skin. (You should have about 1 cup.) Add the Asiago or Parmesan cheese, salt, nutmeg, and pepper. Beat with electric mixer on low speed until smooth.

3 For each ravioli, place a rounded tablespoon of filling in center of a pot sticker or wonton wrapper. Brush edges with water and place a second wrapper over first, pressing to seal edges. Trim edges with fluted pastry wheel, if desired. Repeat with remaining wrappers and filling.*

4 In a 4-quart Dutch oven cook the ravioli, 6 at a time, in a large amount of gently boiling, lightly salted water 2 to 2½ minutes or until just tender. (Don't let water boil vigorously.)

5 Use a slotted spoon to remove ravioli. Place in a single layer on lightly greased baking sheet. Cover loosely with foil. Keep warm in a 300° oven up to 20 minutes. Serve with Crab Rangoon Ravioli (see recipe, page 12) and Onion-Herb Broth (see recipe, right). Makes 12 ravioli.

*Note: If desired, place filled ravioli on foil-lined baking sheets. Cover and freeze, then place ravioli in freezer bags; seal, label, and freeze up to 3 months. Cook frozen ravioli as above for 3 minutes or until just tender.

Ravioli Duet
(see page 12)

◆◆◆

Spinach-Mushroom Sauté
(see page 18)

◆◆◆

Sage-Olive Baguettes
(see page 18)

◆◆◆

Chocolate pound cake with fresh winter fruits

ONION-HERB BROTH

Start to finish: 10 min.

Browning the onions gives this broth a rich golden color.

1 **cup thinly sliced onion**
2 **cloves garlic, minced**
1 **Tbsp. margarine or butter**
1 **14½-oz. can chicken broth or vegetable broth**
2 **Tbsp. snipped fresh basil or 2 tsp. dried basil, crushed**

1 In a medium saucepan cook onions and garlic in margarine or butter over medium heat about 5 minutes or until onions are golden brown, stirring frequently. Add chicken or vegetable broth. Heat through, stirring occasionally. Stir in basil. Serve with Crab Rangoon Ravioli and Butternut Squash Ravioli (see recipes, page 12 and at left). Makes 2 cups.

Is Fresh Always Best?

It's time for a pop quiz: Which form of fruits and vegetables is more nutritious—fresh, frozen, or canned? Most of us would say "fresh," believing any other form of produce is nutritionally inferior. But decades of studies have brought to light little-known facts about canned and frozen produce.

Many canned and frozen vegetables and fruits rival fresh as sources of vitamins and minerals, according to research conducted at the University of Illinois for the Steel Packaging Council. All are excellent nutrient sources and preference is really a matter of personal taste.

Granted, just-picked fruits and veggies are still at the top of the nutrient heap, but such freshest-of-fresh produce rarely makes it to your dinner table. By the time fresh fruits or vegetables travel from field to supermarket to your home, two weeks may have passed. By then, your produce has lost a significant amount of nutrients.

Can Do

When compared by serving sizes, canned fruits and veggies meet or exceed the per-serving percentages of daily vitamin, mineral, and dietary fiber needs recommended by the U.S. Food and Drug Administration. In fact, some canned fruits and vegetables pack a nutrient punch that scores as high or higher than fresh and frozen, according to the University of Illinois study.

Green beans offer a good example of the differences between fresh, canned, and frozen produce, says Barbara Klein, Ph.D., the lead researcher in the Illinois study. "When fresh green beans are harvested, the vitamin C content begins falling immediately. A significant portion of this important vitamin is gone within 24 hours."

Actually, 58 percent of the vitamin C found in freshly picked green beans is lost within three days, Klein says. In comparison, the amount of vitamin C in

canned and frozen green beans diminishes by only 15 to 20 percent from the beans' just-picked state, according to Klein. That's because processing and packaging takes place within hours of harvest, thereby preserving more nutrients.

Frozen Assets

Frozen fruits and vegetables actually outshine fresh produce in many cases. In controlled testing, quick-frozen fruits and vegetables were compared with fresh fruits and vegetables exposed to air and fluorescent lighting (similar to that in supermarkets) for periods of time ranging from a few days to two weeks. Frozen produce retained more nutrients in all cases.

The longer harvested or cut fruits or vegetables are exposed to the elements—air, oxygen, light—the more their nutrients degrade. This can cause available vitamin amounts to fall by 50 percent or more by the time you get your produce home. And once home, the same fresh vegetables and fruit may sit in your refrigerator's vegetable drawer for yet another week.

"When discussing nutrient value, it's best to differentiate between 'retail-market fresh' produce and 'farmer's-market fresh' since large gaps can exist between the time of harvesting and retailing," Klein says.

Most commercially frozen fruits and vegetables undergo a treatment known as IQF—individual quick frozen. Foods prepared this way are washed, sorted, and graded. Then they're blanched, cooled, and, in seconds, frozen to -30°F. Kept at that temperature, IQF foods can last five years or more without changes in color, flavor, or nutrients. Since home freezers are not as cold as commercial ones, unopened frozen fruits and vegetables should be used within one year.

A Fresh Perspective

The concept of seasons for many fruits and vegetables is almost a thing of the past. Hydroponics, greenhouse "farming," plus the increased availability of imported produce enable us to enjoy such luxuries as fresh peaches in December and butternut squash in May.

Despite year-round availability of fresh produce, the process of getting these fruits and vegetables to your home requires time, travel, exposure to light and air, and sometimes long periods of storage. These factors speed up the loss of nutrients. That's when fresh produce can lose its nutrient edge over frozen and canned.

SEALED-IN SAFETY

Not only are canned and frozen vegetables as reliable as fresh in providing essential nutrients, the canned and frozen foods also may offer an added safety factor when it comes to preventing foodborne illnesses. Since commercially processed fruits and vegetables are packaged with a minimum of handling under strictly controlled conditions, they have less chance of meeting up with—and thus harboring—harmful microorganisms. The canning process and the blanching step done before freezing also helps to kill off many harmful organisms. However, not all frozen fruits are blanched.

BRINGING HOME THE BOUNTY

The processes of preparing and cooking fruits and vegetables at home further breaks down nutrients. This is true whether fresh, frozen, or canned. You'll get the most benefit out of your fruits and vegetables by practicing these four techniques:

◆ Minimize chopping. When more surface area is exposed, more nutrients are likely to be lost. Try using larger pieces for recipes.

◆ When possible, keep fruits and vegetables whole right up until the time you need to include them in a recipe. Remember, exposure to the elements—heat, air, light, and water—hastens the loss of nutrients.

◆ Cook fresh or frozen vegetables in a small amount of water only to the crisp-tender stage. They'll have more flavor plus a satisfying crunch. Cooking helps release minerals and phytochemicals, making them easier for your body to absorb. Overcooking leaches out those same nutrients, as well as the water-soluble vitamins.

◆ Use the leftover cooking liquid. You can incorporate cooking liquids into other recipes in place of water or broth.

5-A-DAY FACTS

Consumption of fruits and vegetables climbed only slightly over the last few decades. To figure out where you stand, here are some suggested servings of fruits and vegetables according to the National Cancer Institute's "5 A Day for Better Health." Aim for at least five servings.

◆ 1 medium fruit or vegetable (banana, orange, zucchini)
◆ ½ cup cut-up fresh, frozen, or canned fruit (with juice)
◆ 1 cup raw leafy vegetables
◆ ½ cup raw or cooked dark green and yellow vegetables
◆ ¾ cup (6 oz.) 100-percent fruit or vegetable juice
◆ ¼ cup dried fruit
◆ ½ cup cooked dried peas, lentils, or beans

FRESH TECHNOLOGY IN THE BAG

Consumers are tossing bags of precut salad mixes, vegetables, and fruits into their shopping carts at an incredible rate. But how do these favored time-savers stay fresh for up to 14 days? The answer is in the bag.

After being harvested, washed, and cut, the produce finds its way into a special "breathable" bag that reduces spoilage. This modified-atmosphere packaging (MAP) process replaces air with pure nitrogen (the air we breath is 78 percent nitrogen and 22 percent oxygen). The reduced oxygen content helps lengthen shelf life sans chemical preservatives. Studies have shown that modified-atmosphere-packaged produce reduces vitamin loss caused by exposure to air.

Since MAP uses a natural component, there are no labeling requirements. Some manufacturers use the term "modified-atmosphere packaging" on their product labels. Others include the words "ready-to-eat" or "triple-washed." Another clue: Look for crimp-bottomed, airtight sealed bags instead of plastic sheet wrapping or deli-style packaging. To get the longest shelf life possible from MAP produce, refrigerate immediately. Also, reseal and store any unused portions in the bag.

CABBAGE CASSEROLE

Prep: 20 min. ◆ Bake: 30 min.

This fresh-tasting side dish makes a tempting companion for roast pork or ham.

5 cups coarsely chopped
  cabbage
2 Tbsp. margarine or butter
2 Tbsp. all-purpose flour
1¼ cups milk
½ cup chopped yellow sweet
  pepper
½ cup shredded cheddar cheese
¼ cup chopped onion

◆◆◆

4 cups prepared crumbled corn
  bread

1 In a medium saucepan cook cabbage, covered, in a small amount of boiling, lightly salted water for 5 minutes. Drain and set aside. In the same pan melt margarine or butter. Stir in flour, ½ teaspoon *salt,* and ⅛ teaspoon *black pepper.* Add milk all at once. Cook and stir over medium heat until thickened and bubbly. Stir in sweet pepper, cheese, and onion. Stir until cheese is melted. Remove from heat.

2 Place 3 cups of the corn bread in a 2-quart casserole. Top with cabbage, sauce, and remaining corn bread. Bake, uncovered, in a 375° oven 30 to 35 minutes or until heated through. Makes 8 side-dish servings.

Nutrition facts per serving: 216 cal., 10 g total fat (4 g sat. fat), 14 mg chol., 548 mg sodium, 27 g carbo., 2 g fiber, 6 g pro.
Daily values: 8% vit. A, 34% vit. C, 11% calcium, 7% iron.

MEXICAN LASAGNA

Prep: 35 min. ◆ Bake: 1 hour

9 dried lasagna noodles

◆◆◆

3 cups chopped onions
1 Tbsp. olive oil

◆◆◆

2 14½-oz. cans diced tomatoes
  with basil, oregano, and
  garlic
1 15-oz. can black beans,
  rinsed and drained
1 15¼-oz. can whole kernel
  corn, drained
1 7-oz. jar roasted red sweet
  peppers, drained and
  chopped
1 Tbsp. snipped fresh cilantro
1 Tbsp. chili powder
2 tsp. ground cumin
1 15-oz. container ricotta
  cheese
2 cups shredded Monterey
  Jack cheese with jalapeño
  peppers (8 oz.)

◆◆◆

½ cup grated Parmesan cheese
  Snipped fresh cilantro

1 Cook lasagna noodles according to package directions. Drain and rinse with cold water; drain again. Set aside.

2 Meanwhile, in a large skillet cook the onions in hot oil until tender. Set aside.

3 In a large saucepan combine the undrained tomatoes, beans, corn, roasted red peppers, the 1 tablespoon cilantro, chili powder, and cumin. Bring to boiling; reduce heat. Simmer, covered, for 10 minutes. In a small bowl stir together the ricotta cheese and Monterey Jack cheese; set aside.

4 To assemble, in a 3-quart rectangular baking dish arrange 3 of the noodles. Top with 2 cups of the sauce, half of the onions, and half of the cheese mixture. Top with 3 noodles, 2 cups of the sauce, remaining onions, and remaining cheese mixture. Top with remaining noodles, remaining sauce, and Parmesan cheese.

5 Bake, covered, in a 350° oven 50 minutes. Uncover; bake 10 minutes more or until bubbly. Let stand 10 minutes before serving. Sprinkle with additional snipped cilantro. Serves 8.

Nutrition facts per serving: 441 cal., 18 g total fat (8 g sat. fat), 47 mg chol., 1,090 mg sodium, 50 g carbo., 6 g fiber, 26 g pro.
Daily values: 38% vit. A, 107% vit. C, 42% calcium, 30% iron.

VEGETABLE PASTITSIO

Prep: 35 min. ◆ Bake: 35 min.

Low in fat, this version of a popular Greek dish is a delicious entrée and side dish in one.

8 oz. dried elbow macaroni

◆◆◆

½ cup refrigerated egg product
½ tsp. ground nutmeg
2 cups fresh spinach leaves

◆◆◆

½ cup chopped onion
1 clove garlic, minced
1 Tbsp. chicken broth or water
4 tsp. margarine or butter
1 8-oz. can tomato sauce
1 cup loose-pack frozen whole
  kernel corn
1 cup cubed, cooked potatoes
¾ tsp. dried mint, crushed

½ tsp. dried oregano, crushed
¼ tsp. ground cinnamon
3 Tbsp. all-purpose flour
1½ cups fat-free milk
¼ cup grated Parmesan cheese

1 Spray a 2-quart square baking dish with *nonstick spray coating;* set aside. Cook pasta according to package directions; drain, reserving hot water. Rinse pasta with cold water; drain.

2 Combine pasta, egg product, ¼ teaspoon of the nutmeg, and ¼ teaspoon *salt.* Spread mixture evenly in prepared dish. Add spinach to reserved cooking water; let stand 2 minutes or until wilted. Drain; arrange atop pasta.

3 In a large nonstick skillet cook onion and garlic in broth and 1 tsp. of the margarine over medium heat 3 minutes or until onion is tender. Add tomato sauce, corn, potatoes, mint, oregano, cinnamon, ¼ teaspoon *salt,* and ¼ teaspoon *pepper;* cook and stir until heated through. Spread mixture over spinach.

4 In a saucepan melt remaining margarine. Stir in flour. Add milk all at once. Cook and stir until thickened and bubbly. Cook and stir 1 minute more. Stir in cheese and remaining nutmeg. Spread over vegetable mixture.

5 Bake, uncovered, in a 350° oven about 35 minutes or until top is firm. Let stand 5 minutes before serving. Makes 6 servings.

Nutrition facts per serving: 321 cal., 6 g total fat (2 g sat. fat), 5 mg chol., 602 mg sodium, 54 g carbo., 3 g fiber, 14 g pro. *Daily values:* 28% vit. A, 26% vit. C, 187% calcium, 22% iron.

PORK POCKET PIES

Prep: 1 hour ◆ Bake: 45 min.

(See the photograph on page 43.)

1 recipe Pocket Pie Pastry (see below right)
   ◆◆◆
1 recipe Skillet Gravy (see page 18)
8 oz. boneless pork sirloin, cut into ½-inch cubes
1 turnip, peeled and chopped (about 1½ cups)
1 cup peeled, cubed sweet potatoes (¾-inch cubes)
¾ cup chopped onion

1 Prepare Pocket Pie Pastry. Divide dough in half; divide each half into 4 equal portions. Form each portion into a ball. Cover and set aside.

2 Prepare Skillet Gravy. In a large bowl combine pork, turnip, sweet potato, onion, and ¼ teaspoon *salt.* Stir in Skillet Gravy.

3 On a lightly floured surface flatten 1 portion of dough (keep remaining dough covered until ready to use). Roll from center to edges into a 7-inch circle (⅛ inch thick). Place about ½ cup filling on half of the circle. Brush edges with water. Fold pastry over filling. Seal edges by crimping with a fork. Prick top of pastry several times with a fork. Repeat with remaining dough and filling.

4 Spray an extra-large, foil-lined baking sheet with *nonstick spray coating.* Place pies 1 inch apart on baking sheet. Bake in a 375° oven about 45 minutes or until golden brown. Serve immediately or wrap each pie securely

Vegetable Pastitsio (see page 16)
   ◆◆◆
Salad of torn romaine, thin onion slices, tomato wedges, and feta cheese drizzled with an herbed vinaigrette
   ◆◆◆
Lemon sorbet sprinkled with snipped fresh mint

in foil and keep warm in a 300° oven up to 1 hour. Makes 8 individual pies.

TO MAKE AHEAD

Place unbaked pies on a baking sheet; freeze. Transfer frozen pies to freezer containers. To serve, place frozen, unbaked pies on an extra-large, foil-lined baking sheet sprayed with nonstick coating. Bake, uncovered, in a 350° oven 50 to 55 minutes or until golden.

Pocket Pie Pastry: In a bowl combine 3 cups all-purpose flour, ¾ teaspoon baking powder, and ½ teaspoon salt. Using a pastry blender, cut in ½ cup shortening until the pieces are pea-sized.

Sprinkle 1 tablespoon ice water over part of mixture; gently toss with a fork. Push moistened dough to side. Repeat, using 1 tablespoon ice water at a time, until all dough is moistened (10 to 12 tablespoons water total).

Nutrition facts per pie: 359 cal., 18 g total fat (4 g sat. fat), 12 mg chol., 405 mg sodium, 42 g carbo., 3 g fiber, 9 g pro. *Daily values:* 35% vit. A, 12% vit. C, 4% calcium, 17% iron.

Skillet Gravy

Start to finish: 10 min.

This curry-flavored gravy adds rich flavor to the Pork Pocket Pies on page 17. Or, serve it over roasted pork.

2 Tbsp. margarine or butter
3 Tbsp. all-purpose flour
1 tsp. curry powder
1 cup vegetable broth or beef broth

1 In a medium skillet melt margarine or butter. Stir in flour and curry powder. Carefully add the broth all at once. Cook and stir over medium heat until thickened and bubbly. Use to prepare Pork Pocket Pies (see recipe, page 17). Makes about 1 cup.

Spinach-Mushroom Sauté

Start to finish: 20 min.

Portobellos and leeks take a gentle tumble in the skillet before the spinach is tossed into the pan to create this barely wilted vegetable side dish. (See the photograph on page 42.)

8 oz. fresh portobello mushrooms
2 medium leeks, cut into 1½-inch pieces
2 large cloves garlic, minced
4 tsp. margarine or butter
6 cups prewashed fresh spinach
2 cups coarsely shredded bok choy or Chinese cabbage
1 tsp. lemon-pepper seasoning

1 Cut mushrooms in half and slice. In a 12-inch skillet cook mushrooms, leeks, and garlic in

THE CLEVER COOK

PRESSING GARLIC

Save time by putting garlic cloves in your garlic press with the skin on. More garlic comes out and the skin doesn't get pushed through.

Julie Gottfried
Vallejo, California

margarine or butter over medium-high heat about 4 minutes or until tender and most of liquid has evaporated, stirring occasionally. Add spinach, bok choy or Chinese cabbage, and lemon pepper. Cook, covered, 1 minute or just until greens are wilted. Makes 6 side-dish servings.

Nutrition facts per serving: 64 cal., 3 g total fat (1 g sat. fat), 0 mg chol., 262 mg sodium, 8 g carbo., 4 g fiber, 3 g pro. *Daily values:* 43% vit. A, 43% vit. C, 7% calcium, 18% iron.

Ruby and Gold Grapefruit Cocktail

Start to finish: 25 min.

For a tempting predinner tickler, try this winter-fresh citrus dish.

1⅓ cups red grapefruit sections
1⅓ cups white grapefruit sections
4 tsp. rosemary-flavored oil or olive oil
½ tsp. cracked black pepper
Snipped fresh rosemary

1 In a medium bowl combine red and white grapefruit sections, rosemary oil or olive oil, and cracked pepper. Toss gently to coat. Divide evenly among 6 small bowls. Sprinkle with snipped rosemary. Garnish with *rosemary sprigs,* if desired. Makes 6 servings.

Nutrition facts per serving: 60 cal., 3 g total fat (0 g sat. fat), 0 mg chol., 1 mg sodium, 8 g carbo., 1 g fiber, 1 g pro. *Daily values:* 1% vit. A, 58% vit. C, 1% calcium, 1% iron.

Sage-Olive Baguettes

Prep: 20 min. ◆ Rise: 80-105 min.
Bake: 30 min.

From the comforts of home, treat your family to a delicious Mediterranean getaway. Start the aromatic adventure by stirring herbs and kalamata olives into the dough. (See the photograph on page 42.)

3½ to 4 cups bread flour or unbleached all-purpose flour
1 pkg. active dry yeast
½ tsp. salt
1¼ cups warm water (120° to 130°)
½ cup coarsely chopped, pitted kalamata olives
2 to 3 Tbsp. snipped fresh sage or 2 to 3 tsp. dried sage, crushed

◆◆◆

1 egg white, slightly beaten
1 Tbsp. water

1 In a large bowl stir together 1 cup of the flour, yeast, and salt; add warm water. Beat with electric mixer on low to medium speed for 30 seconds, scraping sides constantly. Beat on high speed for 3 minutes. Stir in the olives and sage. Using a wooden spoon, stir in as much of the remaining flour as you can.

2 Turn dough out onto lightly floured surface. Knead in enough remaining flour to make a stiff dough that is smooth and elastic (8 to 10 minutes). Shape dough into a ball; place in a lightly greased bowl, turning once to grease surface. Cover and let rise in a warm place until double in size (45 minutes to 1 hour).

3 Punch dough down; turn out onto a lightly floured surface; divide in half. Shape into balls. Cover; let rest 10 minutes. Meanwhile, lightly grease 2 baking sheets or 2 baguette pans; sprinkle with flour. Roll each portion of dough into a 14×5-inch rectangle. Starting from a long side, roll up, pinwheel style; seal well. Pinch ends and pull slightly to taper. Place, seam side down, on prepared baking sheets or in baguette pans.

4 In a bowl stir together egg white and water; brush some over loaves. Cover; let rise until nearly double in size (35 to 45 minutes). With a sharp knife, make 3 or 4 diagonal cuts about ¼ inch deep across tops of loaves.

5 Bake in a 375° oven for 20 minutes. Brush again with egg white mixture. Continue baking 10 to 15 minutes more or until bread sounds hollow when you tap the top with your fingers.

Immediately remove the bread from baking sheets or pans. Cool on a wire rack. Makes 2 baguettes (14 servings).

Nutrition facts per serving: 132 cal., 1 g total fat (0 g sat. fat), 0 mg chol., 103 mg sodium, 25 g carbo., 1 g fiber, 5 g pro. *Daily values:* 9% iron.

SALT-AND-PEPPER CRACKERS

Prep: 30 min. ◆ Bake: 15 min.

Corn tortilla flour can be found in most supermarkets or Hispanic markets. (See the photograph on page 42.)

1¾ **cups all-purpose flour**
¾ **cup corn tortilla flour or corn flour**
1 **Tbsp. sugar**
½ **tsp. baking soda**
¼ **tsp. kosher salt**
2 **Tbsp. butter**
1 **cup buttermilk**
◆◆◆
  Water
3 **to 4 tsp. freshly cracked dried green whole peppercorns, peppercorn mix, or black whole peppercorns**
2 **to 3 tsp. kosher salt**

1 Line a baking sheet with parchment paper; set aside. In a mixing bowl stir together the all-purpose flour, corn tortilla flour, sugar, baking soda, and the ¼ teaspoon kosher salt. Using a pastry blender, cut in butter until mixture resembles coarse crumbs. Make a well in center of flour mixture. Add buttermilk. Using a fork, stir until mixture can be shaped into a ball.

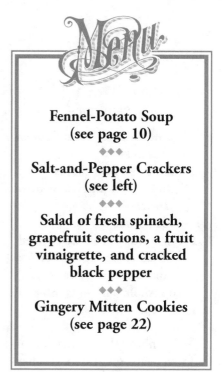

Fennel-Potato Soup
(see page 10)

◆◆◆

Salt-and-Pepper Crackers
(see left)

◆◆◆

Salad of fresh spinach, grapefruit sections, a fruit vinaigrette, and cracked black pepper

◆◆◆

Gingery Mitten Cookies
(see page 22)

2 Turn the dough out onto a lightly floured surface. Knead for 8 to 10 strokes or until dough is almost smooth. Divide dough into 6 portions. Roll each portion into a 9×6-inch free-form rectangle (⅛ inch thick). Use a pastry wheel or knife to cut rectangles into quarters. Using a fork, prick rectangles well. Place 1 inch apart on prepared baking sheet.

3 Lightly brush crackers with water. Sprinkle with peppercorns and the 2 to 3 teaspoons kosher salt; press into dough. Bake in a 375° oven about 15 minutes or until crisp. Remove from baking sheet to wire racks; cool. Store in airtight container at room temperature up to 1 week. Makes 24 oversize crackers.

Nutrition facts per cracker: 59 cal., 1 g total fat (1 g sat. fat), 3 mg chol., 247 mg sodium, 10 g carbo., 0 g fiber, 2 g pro. *Daily values:* 1% calcium, 4% iron.

WINTER TRAIL MIX

Start to finish: 20 min.

1 recipe Orange-Pecan Crunch
    (see below)
2 cups dried pear halves,
    halved lengthwise, or dried
    apricots
1½ cups sesame sticks
1 6-oz. pkg. chocolate-covered
    dried cherries, blueberries,
    and/or raspberries
1 cup whole hazelnuts (filberts)
1 cup coconut curls*

1 Combine the Orange-Pecan Crunch, pears, sesame sticks, cherries, hazelnuts, and coconut. Store in a cool, dry place for up to 1 week. Makes 8 cups (16 servings).

*Note: Coconut curls can be purchased at health-food stores, Asian markets, or large supermarkets.

Orange-Pecan Crunch: Line a baking sheet with foil. Butter foil; set aside. In a heavy 10-inch skillet combine 1½ cups pecan halves, ½ cup sugar, 2 tablespoons margarine or butter, and ½ teaspoon vanilla. Cook over medium-high heat, shaking skillet occasionally, but do not stir. When sugar begins to melt, reduce heat to low. Cook, stirring frequently, until sugar is golden brown. Quickly stir in 1½ teaspoons finely shredded orange peel. Immediately spread onto the prepared baking sheet. Cool; break up into bite-size pieces.

Nutrition facts per serving: 317 cal., 18 g total fat (4 g sat. fat), 4 mg chol., 139 mg sodium, 39 g carbo., 4 g fiber, 4 g pro. *Daily values:* 6% vit. A, 3% vit. C, 3% calcium, 7% iron.

JUST-LIKE-MOM'S COBBLER

Prep: 20 min. ◆ Bake: 30 min.

An easy batter poured over three kinds of fruit bakes into a memorable cobbler.
(See the photograph on page 39.)

2 cups dried golden plums
    and/or dried apricots,
    quartered
1 15-oz. can peach slices in
    heavy syrup
1 cup loose-pack frozen
    unsweetened marion-
    berries or blackberries,
    thawed
2 tsp. cornstarch
½ tsp. finely shredded orange
    peel
½ tsp. ground cinnamon
    ◆◆◆
1 cup all-purpose flour
½ cup sugar
2 tsp. baking powder
¼ tsp. salt
⅔ cup milk
2 Tbsp. margarine or butter,
    melted

1 In a 3-quart saucepan pour enough boiling water over dried plums and/or apricots to cover. Let stand 10 minutes; drain. In the same pan combine plums and/or apricots, peaches and their syrup, marionberries or blackberries, cornstarch, orange peel, and cinnamon. Cook and stir mixture over medium heat until slightly thickened and bubbly. Transfer hot filling to an ungreased 1½-quart deep casserole.

2 In a medium mixing bowl stir together flour, sugar, baking powder, and salt. Stir in milk and

melted margarine or butter until combined. Pour batter over the filling. Place baking dish on foil-lined baking sheet. Bake in a 400° oven for 30 to 35 minutes or until a wooden toothpick inserted in the center of topping comes out clean. Serve warm. Makes 6 to 8 servings.

Nutrition facts per serving: 355 cal., 5 g total fat (1 g sat. fat), 2 mg chol., 276 mg sodium, 78 g carbo., 6 g fiber, 5 g pro. *Daily values:* 40% vit. A, 17% vit. C, 15% calcium, 23% iron.

CHOCOLATE-HAZELNUT TORTE

Prep: 45 min. ◆ Bake: 1 hour
Chill: overnight

Grind nuts in small batches with a blender or food processor, but be careful: Nuts form a paste if ground too much.
(See the photograph on page 43.)

½ cup butter, softened
1½ cups granulated sugar
1 Tbsp. vanilla
6 eggs
10 oz. bittersweet or semisweet
    chocolate, melted and
    cooled
2 cups hazelnuts (filberts),
    finely ground
½ cup all-purpose flour
    ◆◆◆
1 recipe Chocolate Topping
    (see page 21)
    Fresh apricots, seeded and
    quartered, or fresh
    raspberries
3 Tbsp. sifted powdered sugar

1 Grease and flour an 8-inch springform pan. In a large mixing bowl beat butter with an electric mixer on medium to high speed for 30 seconds. Add granulated sugar and vanilla; beat until mixture is well combined. Add eggs, 1 at a time, beating well after each. With a rubber spatula, stir in chocolate, hazelnuts, and flour. Spoon batter into prepared pan.

2 Bake in a 350° oven about 1 hour or until a toothpick inserted near the center comes out fudgy, but not wet. Cool on wire rack (center may fall slightly). Cover loosely and chill overnight.

3 Before serving, let stand at room temperature 2 hours. Meanwhile, prepare Chocolate Topping. Spread over top of torte, allowing it to drizzle over sides. Just before serving, top with fresh apricots. Sift powdered sugar over apricots. Makes 16 servings.

Chocolate Topping: In a small saucepan combine 1 cup milk chocolate pieces and ½ cup half-and-half or light cream. Heat and stir over low heat until chocolate is melted. Remove from heat. Cool to room temperature.

Nutrition facts per serving: 413 cal., 26 g total fat (11 g sat. fat), 98 mg chol., 97 mg sodium, 43 g carbo., 2 g fiber, 7 g pro. *Daily values:* 12% vit. A, 1% vit. C, 6% calcium, 2% iron.

SNOWMEN COOKIES

Prep: 40 min. ◆ Chill: 3 hours
Bake: 6 min. per batch
Decorate: 15 min.

Marzipan Clay makes it easy to add accessories to these jolly cookies. (See the photograph on page 43.)

⅓ **cup butter**
⅓ **cup shortening**
¾ **cup granulated sugar**
1 **tsp. baking powder**

1 **egg**
½ **cup ground almonds**
1¾ **cups all-purpose flour**
♦♦♦
1 **egg white, slightly beaten**
1 **Tbsp. water**
  Coarse or granulated sugar
  Miniature semisweet
   chocolate pieces (optional)
♦♦♦
1 **recipe Marzipan Clay (see**
   right)
1 **recipe Quick Icing (see**
   below right)

1 In a large mixing bowl beat butter and shortening with an electric mixer on medium to high speed for 30 seconds. Add granulated sugar and baking powder. Beat until combined, scraping bowl. Beat in whole egg until combined. Beat in ground almonds and as much of the flour as you can with the mixer. With a wooden spoon stir in remaining flour. Divide dough in half. If necessary, cover and chill dough about 3 hours or until easy to handle.

2 On a lightly floured surface roll half the dough at a time to ⅛-inch thickness. Using 2½-, 3-, and 4-inch round cutters, cut 1 of each size circle for each snowman.

3 Place a 4-inch cutout on an ungreased baking sheet. Add the 3-inch cutout and then the 2½-inch cutout, overlapping the circles about ¼ inch to form the shape of a snowman. Allow about 1 inch space between snowmen on cookie sheet.

4 Combine the egg white and water. Lightly brush egg white-water mixture on cutouts; sprinkle with coarse sugar. If desired,

use miniature chocolate pieces to create eyes, mouth, and buttons.

5 Bake in a 375° oven for 6 to 8 minutes or until edges are firm and bottoms are lightly browned. Cool on cookie sheet 1 minute. With a large spatula, carefully transfer to a cooling rack. Use Marzipan Clay to decorate cookies. Makes 7 oversize Snowmen Cookies, each cookie big enough to split in half and share.

Marzipan Clay: Crumble half of an 8-ounce can almond paste into a small mixing bowl. Add 2 tablespoons softened butter. Beat with electric mixer on medium speed until combined. Add ½ cup sifted powdered sugar and 1½ teaspoons light-colored corn syrup. Beat until combined. Shape into a ball. Knead in ½ to 1 cup additional sifted powdered sugar until mixture is firm enough to hold its shape.

To tint, divide into small portions. Add enough food coloring paste or liquid food coloring to each portion to make desired color. Form into shapes. Use Quick Icing to attach shapes to snowmen. Or, wrap each portion of marzipan in plastic wrap; refrigerate up to 1 week.

Quick Icing: In a small bowl combine ½ cup sifted powdered sugar and 1 teaspoon water. Stir in additional water, a few drops at a time, until of a thick, drizzling consistency.

Nutrition facts per serving (2 servings per cookie): 293 cal., 16 g total fat (5 g sat. fat), 31 mg chol., 97 mg sodium, 35 g carbo., 1 g fiber, 4 g pro. *Daily values:* 6% vit. A, 5% calcium, 8% iron.

Gingery Mitten Cookies

Prep: 1 hour ◆ Chill: 3 hours
Bake: 10 min. per batch

Decorating Dough adds puffy bursts of color as it bakes right onto the cookies. (See the photograph on page 39.)

⅓ cup shortening
⅓ cup butter, softened
½ cup packed light brown sugar
½ tsp. baking soda
½ tsp. ground cinnamon
¼ tsp. baking powder
⅓ cup molasses
3 Tbsp. grated fresh ginger
1 slightly beaten egg
½ tsp. vanilla
2¾ cups all-purpose flour

◆◆◆

1 recipe Decorating Dough (see right)

1 In a large mixing bowl beat shortening and butter with electric mixer on medium to high speed for 30 seconds. Add brown sugar, baking soda, cinnamon, and baking powder. Beat until combined, scraping bowl. Beat in molasses, ginger, egg, and vanilla until combined. Beat in as much of the flour as you can with the mixer. With a wooden spoon stir in remaining flour. Divide the dough in half. Cover and chill dough about 3 hours or until easy to handle.

2 On a lightly floured surface roll half the dough at a time to ⅛-inch thickness. Using a 6-inch mitten cutter or cardboard pattern, cut cookies. If desired, use a bamboo skewer to press designs into dough. With a large spatula (or 2 smaller spatulas) carefully transfer cookie to an ungreased baking sheet. Decorate with colored Decorating Dough.

3 Bake in a 375° oven for 10 to 12 minutes or until edges are lightly browned. Cool on cookie sheet for 2 minutes. Carefully transfer to wire racks and let cool. Makes 12 cookies.

Decorating Dough: In a medium bowl beat 10 tablespoons butter (no substitutes) with electric mixer on medium to high speed for 30 seconds. Gradually add 1 cup all-purpose flour and 2 tablespoons light-colored corn syrup, beating on low to medium speed until smooth. Mixture should be the consistency of thick frosting.

Divide and tint the dough with food coloring paste. For Gingery Mitten Cookies (shown on page 39), we tinted ⅓ cup of dough red, ⅓ cup purple, and ⅓ cup yellow. Place Decorating Dough in decorating bags fitted with #6 tip.

Nutrition facts per cookie: 377 cal., 21 g total fat (11 g sat. fat), 57 mg chol., 220 mg sodium, 43 g carbo., 1 g fiber, 4 g pro. *Daily values:* 14% vit. A, 3% calcium, 16% iron.

Hot Caramel Chocolate

Start to finish: 15 min.

Sip this for a welcome warm-up. (See the photograph on page 39.)

⅓ cup sugar
⅓ cup unsweetened cocoa powder

How To Freeze Cookies

You can store cookies at room temperature up to three days. Store bar cookies tightly covered in a container or in their own baking pan.

Cookies with a frosting or filling that contains cream cheese must be stored in the refrigerator.

Most drop, sliced, bar, and shaped cookies freeze well. If the cookies are to be frosted or glazed, wait until they are thawed. Freeze cookies in layers separated by waxed paper. To thaw, let the cookies stand about 15 minutes in the container at room temperature.

⅓ cup water
6 milk chocolate-covered round caramels
6 cups milk, half-and-half, or light cream
Whipped cream (optional)

1 In a large saucepan combine sugar, cocoa powder, and water. Cook and stir over medium heat until sugar is dissolved. Add candies until melted. Stir in milk; heat through. Pour into mugs; top with whipped cream, if desired. Makes 6 servings.

Nutrition facts per serving: 213 cal., 7 g total fat (4 g sat. fat), 19 mg chol., 133 mg sodium, 29 g carbo., 0 g fiber, 10 g pro. *Daily values:* 15% vit. A, 3% vit. C, 29% calcium, 5% iron.

$\mathcal{F}$EBRUARY
Chocolate Cravings

IN THIS CHAPTER

Chocolate's the word for February. What better way to tantalize your Valentine than with a rich layered Chocolate-Raspberry Cheesecake? Or indulge in triple-chocolate decadence with an easy from-scratch Devil's Food Cake topped with Chocolate Cream Cheese Frosting and a decorative Chocolate Glaze. Get the family together for a cookie fest and bake Chocolate Chip Cookie Sticks or Our Best Basic Chocolate Chip Cookies—baked three ways. Who cares if the groundhog sees his shadow?

30-minute recipes indicated in RED.
Low-fat and no-fat recipes indicated
with a ♥.
Photographs indicated in italics.
***Bonus recipe**

BAKED BRIE
Prep: 20 min. ◆ Bake: 10 min.

When this favorite party appetizer first appeared in the 1980s, it was wrapped in a puff pastry or brioche crust. We've eliminated this tricky step and robed the cheese in tomato preserves and caramelized onions. Find tomato preserves next to the other jams and preserves in large supermarkets or specialty stores.

1 small onion, cut into thin wedges
2 tsp. margarine or butter
⅓ cup tomato preserves or mango chutney
½ tsp. snipped fresh rosemary or ¼ tsp. dried rosemary, crushed
⅛ tsp. crushed red pepper
◆◆◆
1 8-oz. round of brie cheese (about 4 inches in diameter)
◆◆◆
Assorted crackers or French bread slices (optional)

1 For caramelized onions, in a small saucepan cook onion in hot margarine or butter, covered, over low heat about 15 minutes or until tender and golden, stirring occasionally. Meanwhile, in a small bowl stir together the tomato preserves or chutney (cut up any large pieces of chutney), rosemary, and crushed red pepper.

2 Cut off and discard a very thin slice from the top of the brie to remove the rind. Place the round of brie in an ungreased 9-inch pie plate. Top with tomato or chutney mixture, then with caramelized onions.

3 Bake, uncovered, in a 325° oven for 10 to 12 minutes or until brie is softened and warmed but not runny. If desired, serve with crackers or bread slices. Makes 8 servings.

Nutrition facts per serving: 143 cal., 9 g total fat (5 g sat. fat), 28 mg chol., 191 mg sodium, 10 g carbo., 0 g fiber, 6 g pro. *Daily values:* 7% vit. A, 1% vit. C, 4% calcium, 2% iron.

WHEAT BERRY AND WILD RICE SALAD
Prep: 15 min. ◆ Cook: 1 hour
Chill: 4 to 24 hours

Make this nutty salad even more inviting by serving it in radicchio leaf cups.

3 cups water
1 cup wheat berries
¼ tsp. salt (optional)
½ cup brown and wild rice blend or long-grain and wild rice blend
◆◆◆
½ cup dried cranberries
¼ cup thinly sliced green onions
¼ cup nonfat or regular Italian salad dressing
1 Tbsp. snipped fresh basil or 1 tsp. dried basil, crushed
1 Tbsp. honey mustard
½ cup coarsely chopped pistachio nuts

1 In a medium saucepan bring the water to boiling. Stir in wheat berries and if desired, salt. Return to boiling; reduce heat. Simmer, covered, about 1 hour or until tender. Drain; set aside. Meanwhile, cook rice blend according to package directions, omitting the butter or margarine and salt.

2 In a medium bowl combine cooked wheat berries, cooked rice, cranberries, and green onions. In a bowl stir together dressing, basil, and mustard. Pour over salad mixture and toss to coat. Cover and chill salad for 4 to 24 hours. Just before serving, stir in pistachio nuts. Makes 8 side-dish or 4 main-dish servings.

Nutrition facts per main-dish serving: 378 cal., 9 g total fat (1 g sat. fat), 0 mg chol., 638 mg sodium, 69 g carbo., 4 g fiber, 10 g pro. *Daily values:* 1% vit. A, 5% vit. C, 3% calcium, 28% iron.

MEDITERRANEAN COUSCOUS SALAD
Start to finish: 25 min.
Chill: 4 to 24 hours

1 cup chicken broth
⅔ cup quick-cooking couscous
¼ cup finely chopped green onions
¼ cup oil-packed dried tomatoes, drained and chopped
◆◆◆
¼ cup olive oil
¼ cup lemon juice
¾ cup crumbled feta cheese with garlic and herbs (3 oz.)
½ cup kalamata olives, pitted and chopped
⅓ cup golden raisins
¼ tsp. ground cinnamon
¼ tsp. ground coriander
¼ cup snipped fresh parsley

1 In a small saucepan bring broth to boiling. Stir in couscous, green onions, and dried tomatoes.

Cover and remove from heat. Let stand 5 minutes. Fluff with a fork; turn mixture into a large bowl.

2 In a small bowl whisk together olive oil and lemon juice until slightly thickened; stir into couscous. Add feta cheese, olives, raisins, cinnamon, coriander, and parsley; toss to coat. Cover and chill for 4 to 24 hours. Makes 8 side-dish servings.

Nutrition facts per serving: 192 cal., 11 g total fat (3 g sat. fat), 9 mg chol., 266 mg sodium, 20 g carbo., 3 g fiber, 5 g pro. *Daily values:* 3% vit. A, 17% vit. C, 6% calcium, 4% iron.

24-HOUR VEGETABLE SALAD

Prep: 25 min. ◆ Chill: 2 to 24 hours

To get the best-looking layers, use a bowl that is taller than it is wide. (See the photograph on page 40.)

5 cups torn mixed salad greens
1 medium carrot
1 cup sliced fresh mushrooms
½ cup crumbled feta cheese (2 oz.)
½ cup coarsely chopped pitted kalamata olives
1 medium cucumber, halved, seeded, and sliced ¼ inch thick (1¾ cups)
¼ cup sliced green onions
◆◆◆
½ cup mayonnaise or salad dressing
¼ cup plain low-fat yogurt
1 tsp. finely shredded orange peel
½ to ¾ tsp. crushed red pepper
⅛ to ¼ tsp. ground black pepper
1 medium orange, peeled and sliced
¼ cup coarsely chopped walnuts

Menu

Roasted chicken
◆◆◆
24-Hour Vegetable Salad (see below)
◆◆◆
Whole wheat rolls
◆◆◆
Chiffon Pie (see page 36)

1 Place salad greens in a 2½- to 3-quart clear straight-sided bowl or soufflé dish. Peel carrot. Using a vegetable peeler, carefully cut carrot into long, paper-thin ribbons; set aside. Layer atop salad greens in the following order: mushrooms, ¼ cup of the cheese, olives, cucumbers, carrot ribbons, and green onions.

2 For dressing, in small bowl combine the mayonnaise or salad dressing, yogurt, orange peel, crushed red pepper, and ground black pepper. Spread dressing over top of salad, sealing to edge of bowl. Sprinkle with the remaining ¼ cup cheese. Cover salad tightly with plastic wrap. Chill for 2 to 24 hours.

3 Garnish with orange slices, walnuts, and, if desired, *orange peel strips.* Just before serving toss to coat vegetables. Makes 6 to 8 side-dish servings.

Nutrition facts per serving: 236 cal., 23 g total fat (5 g sat. fat), 16 mg chol., 268 mg sodium, 8 g carbo., 2 g fiber, 4 g pro. *Daily values:* 39% vit. A, 31% vit. C, 10% calcium, 8% iron.

30 MIN. LOW FAT

BLACK BEAN COUSCOUS

Start to finish: 20 min.

If there's any left over, add a splash of vinegar and oil and chill to convert this savory side into a simple salad.

1 Tbsp. olive oil
½ cup sliced green onions
½ cup chopped red or green sweet pepper
2 cloves garlic, minced
½ tsp. ground cumin
¼ tsp. salt
¼ tsp. paprika
¼ tsp. chili powder
⅛ to ¼ tsp. ground red pepper
◆◆◆
1 15-oz. can black beans, rinsed and drained
1 14½-oz. can vegetable or chicken broth
1 cup quick-cooking couscous
¼ cup snipped fresh cilantro

1 In a large skillet heat oil; add green onions, sweet pepper, and garlic. Cook and stir until vegetables are just tender but not brown. Stir in the cumin, salt, paprika, chili powder, and ground red pepper; cook and stir 1 minute more.

2 Carefully stir beans and broth into mixture in skillet. Bring to boiling; stir in couscous. Remove from heat. Cover and let stand for 5 minutes. Just before serving, stir in 3 tablespoons of the cilantro. Sprinkle remaining cilantro atop each serving. Makes 8 side-dish servings.

Nutrition facts per serving: 140 cal., 2 g total fat (0 g sat. fat), 0 mg chol., 412 mg sodium, 27 g carbo., 6 g fiber, 7 g pro. *Daily values:* 7% vit. A, 20% vit. C, 2% calcium, 7% iron.

PASTA PRIMAVERA

Start to finish: 35 min.

Feel free to substitute any combination of your favorite fresh vegetables; aim for about 4½ cups of cut-up vegetables before cooking. (See the photograph on page 41.)

- 6 oz. dried pappardelle, gemelli, or rotini pasta (about 2 cups)

♦♦♦

- 1 Tbsp. margarine or butter
- 2 cups broccoli florets
- 1 small red and/or yellow sweet pepper, cut into thin strips
- 1 cup peeled and cubed Jerusalem artichokes and/or celeriac
- 1 cup fresh or frozen pea pods
- 1 5-oz. container semisoft cheese with garlic and herbs
- ¼ cup milk
  Freshly ground black pepper

♦♦♦

- 2 Tbsp. coarsely chopped, toasted pine nuts or toasted cashews
- 1 oz. smoked provolone or smoked Gouda cheese, thinly shaved

1 Prepare pasta according to package directions. Drain well; keep warm.

2 Meanwhile, in a large saucepan or Dutch oven melt the margarine or butter. Stir in broccoli, sweet pepper, and Jerusalem artichokes and/or celeriac. Cook and stir over medium-high heat

LETTUCE SPICE UP YOUR SALADS

Mesclun has hit the mainstream! This French mixture of tiny greens that may include peppery arugula, chervil, chickweed, dandelion, and oak leaf lettuce once was considered to be solely the domain of the gourmet, but now is often available at large supermarkets. Its greatest boon is flavor; unlike the mildly flavored iceberg, these spicy herblike greens together have a distinct taste, which is nicely accented by a drizzle of vinaigrette.

for 5 minutes. Stir in pea pods. Cook, covered, for 1 minute more. Gently stir in semisoft cheese, milk, and cooked pasta. Season to taste with freshly ground black pepper.

3 To serve, divide pasta mixture among 4 bowls. Garnish each serving with pine nuts or cashews and shaved smoked provolone or smoked Gouda cheese. Makes 4 main-dish servings.

Nutrition facts per serving: 443 cal., 20 g total fat (9 g sat. fat), 38 mg chol., 328 mg sodium, 51 g carbo., 6 g fiber, 14 g pro. *Daily values:* 39% vit. A, 158% vit. C, 15% calcium, 30% iron.

GREEN GODDESS DRESSING WITH SEAFOOD SALAD

Start to finish: 25min.

Omit the seafood and you can enjoy this main dish salad as a side dish; it's especially tasty with unusual salad greens.

- 4 cups mesclun or torn mixed salad greens
- 1 medium fennel bulb, cut into very thin wedges (1½ cups)
- ½ cup sliced celery
- 6 oz. fresh or frozen peeled, cooked shrimp
- 6 oz. cooked lobster meat, cut into bite-size pieces

♦♦♦

- ¾ cup packed fresh parsley sprigs
- ⅓ cup mayonnaise or salad dressing
- 3 Tbsp. dairy sour cream
- 3 Tbsp. plain low-fat yogurt
- 2 Tbsp. sliced green onion
- 1 Tbsp. vinegar
- 1 Tbsp. snipped fresh basil or 1 tsp. dried basil, crushed
- 2 tsp. anchovy paste or 1 large anchovy fillet, cut up
- 1 clove garlic, halved
- 1 tsp. snipped fresh tarragon or ¼ tsp. dried tarragon, crushed

♦♦♦

  Borage flowers or other edible flowers (optional)

1 In a large salad bowl toss together salad greens, fennel, and celery. Top with shrimp and lobster; set aside.

2 For dressing, in a food processor bowl or blender container combine parsley, mayonnaise or salad dressing, sour cream, yogurt, green onion, vinegar, basil, anchovy paste or anchovy, garlic, and tarragon. Cover and process or blend until nearly smooth.

3 Drizzle ¼ cup of the dressing over salad. Toss gently. Top with edible flowers, if desired. Serve immediately. Pass remaining salad dressing. Makes 4 main-dish servings.

Nutrition facts per serving: 276 cal., 19 g total fat (4 g sat. fat), 127 mg chol., 440 mg sodium, 8 g carbo., 10 g fiber, 21 g pro. *Daily values:* 25% vit. A, 55% vit. C, 12% calcium, 20% iron.

SMOKED RIBS

Prep: 20 min. ◆ Chill: 6 to 24 hours
Grill: 1¼ hours

The indirect grilling method—which uses a drip pan under the food—eliminates flare-ups and prevents burning. It's a technique that's useful for many foods, including ribs and chicken.

  2 **Tbsp. sugar**
1½ **tsp. dry mustard**
  ¼ **tsp. paprika**
  ¼ **tsp. ground turmeric**
  ¼ **tsp. celery seed**
  4 **lb. pork loin back ribs or pork spareribs**
  4 **cups hickory or fruitwood chips**

◆◆◆

  1 **recipe Ginger Sauce (see right)**

TEST KITCHEN TIP

TESTING TEMPERATURE

To determine the temperature of the coals, carefully hold your hand, palm side down, above coals in the same location you plan to place the food for cooking. Count "one thousand one, one thousand two…" for as long as you can hold your hand there. Four seconds means coals are medium—just right for the Smoked Ribs (see left).

If you need to withdraw your hand after:

2 seconds, the coals are hot;
3 seconds, they're medium-hot;
4 seconds, they're medium
5 seconds, they're medium-slow;
6 seconds, they're slow.

1 For barbecue rub, combine sugar, dry mustard, paprika, turmeric, and celery seed. Rub mixture onto ribs. Cover and refrigerate ribs for 6 to 24 hours. At least 1 hour before cooking, soak wood chips in enough water to cover. Drain chips.

2 In a grill with a cover, arrange preheated coals around a drip pan. Test for medium heat above the pan. Sprinkle some of the drained wood chips over the coals. Pour 1 inch of water into the drip pan. Place ribs, meaty side up, on grill rack over drip pan but not over coals, or use a rib rack placed over the drip pan. Cover grill. Grill for 1¼ to

1½ hours or until ribs are tender, adding more coals and wood chips as necessary. During the last 10 minutes of cooking, brush generously with Ginger Sauce. Cut ribs into serving-size pieces. Heat and pass any remaining Ginger Sauce. Makes 6 servings.

■ OVEN DIRECTIONS ■

Place ribs, coated with barbecue rub, bone side up, in a shallow roasting pan. Bake in a 350° oven for 1 hour. Drain fat. Turn ribs meaty side up. Spoon some Ginger Sauce over ribs. Bake, covered, for 30 minutes more. Uncover and bake about 20 minutes more or until tender, brushing often with Ginger Sauce. If desired, add a few drops *liquid smoke* to the remaining sauce. Heat and pass remaining sauce.

Nutrition facts per serving: 343 cal., 20 g total fat (8 g sat. fat), 79 mg chol., 599 mg sodium, 20 g carbo., 0 g fiber, 20 g pro. *Daily values:* 3% vit. A, 6% vit. C, 3% calcium, 12% iron.

GINGER SAUCE

Prep: 5 min. ◆ Chill: 6 to 24 hours

  ½ **cup catsup**
  ¼ **cup packed brown sugar**
  3 **Tbsp. reduced-sodium soy sauce**
  3 **Tbsp. water**
  1 **Tbsp. grated fresh ginger or 1 tsp. ground ginger**

1 In a small bowl combine catsup, brown sugar, soy sauce, water, and ginger. Cover and refrigerate for 6 to 24 hours. Use to prepare Smoked Ribs (see recipe, left). Makes ⅔ cup sauce.

Menu

Asian-Style Turkey (see below center)

◆◆◆

Couscous sprinkled with cinnamon

◆◆◆

Steamed snow peas

◆◆◆

Warm pita bread wedges

FRUIT SALSA

Prep: 30 min. ◆ Chill: 8 to 24 hours

Serve as a dip with baked pita chips or as a sauce with Asian-Style Turkey (see recipe, right), seafood, fish, or pork. (See the photograph on page 40.)

1 cup chopped papaya or mango
1 cup finely chopped fresh pineapple
¼ cup finely slivered red onion
¼ cup slivered yellow, orange, and/or green sweet pepper
3 Tbsp. snipped fresh cilantro
1 tsp. finely shredded lime or lemon peel
2 Tbsp. lime or lemon juice
2 to 4 tsp. finely chopped fresh jalapeño pepper*
1 tsp. grated fresh ginger

1 In a medium bowl stir together the papaya or mango, pineapple, red onion, sweet pepper, cilantro, lime or lemon peel, lime or lemon juice, jalapeño, and ginger. Cover and chill salsa for 8 to 24 hours. Makes about 2¼ cups.

*****Note:** Because hot peppers contain oils that can burn your

eyes, lips, and skin, protect yourself when working with the peppers by covering your hands with plastic bags or plastic or rubber gloves. Be sure to wash hands thoroughly before touching your eyes or face.

Nutrition facts per 2-tablespoons salsa: 11 cal., 0 g total fat, 0 mg chol., 1 mg sodium, 3 g carbo., 0 g fiber, 0 g pro. *Daily values:* 17% vit. C.

ASIAN-STYLE TURKEY

Prep: 20 min. ◆ Marinate: 4 hours
Broil: 8 min.

Transform simple broiled poultry into gourmet fare by topping each serving with a spoonful of Fruit Salsa (see recipe, left).

¼ cup dry white wine
¼ cup orange juice
¼ cup soy sauce
2 Tbsp. water
1 Tbsp. rice vinegar
1 Tbsp. cooking oil
1 tsp. garlic powder
1 tsp. ground ginger

◆◆◆

1 lb. turkey breast tenderloins or skinless, boneless chicken breast halves

1 For marinade, in a 2-cup glass measure combine white wine, orange juice, soy sauce, water, rice vinegar, oil, garlic powder, and ginger.

2 Rinse turkey or chicken; pat dry. Cut lengthwise into thin strips. Place strips in a plastic bag set in a shallow bowl. Pour marinade over poultry; seal and turn bag. Marinate in the refrigerator for 4 hours.

3 Drain the poultry. Skewer strips accordion-style onto several wooden skewers. Place on the unheated rack of a broiler pan. Broil 4 inches from heat for 8 to 10 minutes or until no longer pink, turning once. Makes 4 servings.

Nutrition facts per serving: 132 cal., 3 g total fat (1 g sat. fat), 50 mg chol., 389 mg sodium, 1 g carbo., 0 g fiber, 22 g pro. *Daily values:* 4% vit. C, 1% calcium, 7% iron.

FUSION CHICKEN

Prep: 20 min. ◆ Cook: 20 min.

The watchword of '90s cooking has been "simplify," and that's what we've done with this quick main dish that's perfect for after-work meals. The chicken is browned, then quickly glazed with an Asian-style sauce, and served with a South American-inspired relish that has just two ingredients.

¼ cup water
3 Tbsp. hoisin sauce
2 Tbsp. peach preserves
1 Tbsp. sugar
2 tsp. soy sauce
4 medium tangerines or 2 large oranges
3 Tbsp. snipped fresh cilantro

◆◆◆

4 medium skinless, boneless chicken breast halves (about 1 lb. total)
1 Tbsp. cooking oil

◆◆◆

Shredded tangerine or orange peel (optional)

1 In a small bowl combine water, hoisin sauce, preserves, sugar, and soy sauce. Finely shred 1 teaspoon of peel from 1 of the tangerines or oranges. Add peel to hoisin mixture; set aside. Peel and coarsely chop tangerines or oranges; remove seeds. In a bowl gently toss chopped tangerines or oranges and cilantro; set aside.

2 Rinse chicken; pat dry. In a large skillet cook chicken in hot oil over medium heat for 3 to 5 minutes or until chicken is browned, turning once. Drain off fat. Carefully pour hoisin mixture over chicken. Bring to boiling; reduce heat. Simmer, covered, for 8 to 10 minutes or until chicken is tender and no longer pink.

3 Remove chicken from skillet. Boil sauce gently, uncovered, about 5 minutes or until reduced to ⅓ cup. Return chicken to skillet. Heat through, turning once to coat with glaze. Remove to individual serving plates or serving platter; spoon glaze over top. Sprinkle with additional tangerine or orange peel, if desired. Serve tangerine mixture alongside the chicken. Makes 4 servings.

Nutrition facts per serving: 270 cal., 8 g total fat (2 g sat. fat), 59 mg chol., 446 mg sodium, 27 g carbo., 2 g fiber, 23 g pro. *Daily values:* 8% vit. A, 43% vit. C, 3% calcium, 8% iron.

HAMBURGER PIE
Prep: 25 min. ◆ Bake: 30 min.
Stand: 5 min.

Use homemade or refrigerated mashed potatoes to make the top "crust" for this savory, vegetable-filled favorite.

¾ **cup shredded pizza cheese or Italian cheese blend**
2 **cups mashed potatoes,* or refrigerated mashed potatoes**

8 **oz. lean ground beef**
4 **oz. bulk sweet Italian sausage**
½ **cup chopped onion**
2 **cups sliced zucchini or yellow summer squash**
1 **14½-oz. can chunky pasta-style tomatoes**
½ **of a 6-oz. can (⅓ cup) tomato paste**
¼ **tsp. pepper**

◆◆◆

Paprika (optional)
Flat-leaf parsley

1 Stir ½ cup of the cheese into the potatoes; set mixture aside.

2 In a large skillet cook ground beef, sausage, and onion until meat is no longer pink and onion is tender; drain. Stir in squash, undrained tomatoes, tomato paste, and pepper. Bring to boiling. Transfer the mixture to a 2-quart casserole.

3 Spoon mashed potato mixture into a large pastry bag fitted with a large round tip. Starting at an end, fill in the center of the casserole with rows of the mashed potato mixture until the meat mixture is covered (see illustration, top right). (Or, spoon mashed potato mixture in mounds on top of hot mixture.) Sprinkle with remaining cheese. Sprinkle with paprika, if desired.

4 Bake in a 375° oven about 30 minutes or until mashed potato top is golden brown. Let stand 5 minutes before serving. Sprinkle with fresh flat-leaf parsley. Makes 6 servings.

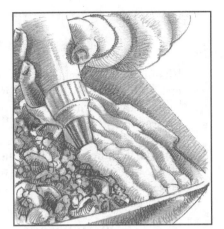

TO MAKE AHEAD

Prepare pie as directed at left, except after bringing meat filling mixture to a boil, divide evenly among six 10-ounce individual casserole dishes. Top with potatoes. Cover with plastic wrap; chill up to 48 hours.

To bake, remove plastic wrap; place casseroles in a 15×10×1-inch baking pan. Cover with foil. Bake in a 375° oven for 35 minutes. Remove foil. Bake, uncovered, 5 minutes more. Let stand 5 minutes before serving.

*Note: To make mashed potatoes, wash and peel 1 pound of potatoes. Cut into quarters or cubes. Cook, covered, in a small amount of boiling salted water for 20 to 25 minutes or until tender. Mash with a potato masher or beat with an electric mixer on low speed until lumps are gone.

Nutrition facts per serving: 254 cal., 12 g total fat (3 g sat. fat), 39 mg chol., 644 mg sodium, 21 g carbo., 3 g fiber, 16 g pro. *Daily values:* 8% vit. A, 47% vit. C, 2% calcium, 11% iron.

Vitamin E Extraordinary

Vitamin E is emerging as a health superstar. What makes vitamin E so interesting is that it poses a challenge to the doctrine that we can get all the nutrients we need solely from a healthful diet. Vitamin E, which before the 1920s was actually thought to be non-essential for humans, has been the subject of hundreds of research studies that point to its ability to help prevent heart disease, cancer, and a host of other disease complications.

Vitamin E's Many Roles

After more than seven decades of research, scientists know that vitamin E plays an important role as an antioxidant, works as an integral part of our immune system, and is a key component in the structure of our body's cells.

Vitamin E figures in the cancer equation, too. Population studies make a connection between low intake of vitamin E and higher risks for certain cancers, such as those of the prostate and breast. And this important compound doesn't stop there:

◆ In persons who have diabetes, high vitamin E intake can protect against diabetic complications, such as damage to small blood vessels.

◆ As an antioxidant, vitamin E can help with the prevention of visual disorders, such as macular degeneration and cataracts.

◆ Vitamin E appears to improve the immune response in the healthy elderly and may slow the progression of Alzheimer's disease.

◆ Vitamin E also may alleviate some of the stiffness experienced by arthritis sufferers.

The Heart of the Matter

Vitamin E leaped to the headlines a few years ago with two major investigations reported in the New England Journal of Medicine. One study, out of the Channing Laboratory in Boston, looked at information taken from over 80,000 female nurses, ages 34 to 69. The other, at the Department of Epidemiology, Harvard School of Public Health, looked at almost 40,000 male health professionals, ages 40 to 75. All participants were free of heart disease at the onset. When the volunteers' diets and vitamin supplement intakes were compared with the development of disease, those persons with an intake of at least 100 IUs of vitamin E a day had a 40 percent lower risk for heart disease.

Vitamin E helps more than just your heart—it protects your body against oxygen. This may seem strange since oxygen is essential for life, but it turns out that oxygen has something of a split personality. On the good side, oxygen helps build cells and power the heart. But on the bad side, oxygen has a tendency to form compounds that can contribute to the development of heart disease, cancer, and other degenerative diseases. This is where vitamin E and other antioxidants come into play: They all help keep oxidized fat cells in our body from wreaking havoc on the lining of our arteries.

Supplemental Advice

Key food sources of vitamin E include wheat germ, sunflower seeds, almonds, nuts, and nut and grain oils. Lesser amounts of the vitamin are found in peanuts and vegetables—especially asparagus, kale, spinach, and yams. Vitamin E also is abundant in fortified cereals and whole-grain products.

Can you get all the vitamin E you need from food? In the study reported in the New England Journal of Medicine, the reduction in heart disease risk wasn't evident unless individuals took at least 100 IUs of vitamin E every day. It can be difficult to get that much from food alone, even if your diet is a paragon of nutrition planning (see chart, page 31).

The United States Department of Agriculture's Recommended Dietary Allowances (RDAs) of 12 to 15 IUs were set up to help eliminate diseases of deficiency. Yet, vitamin E can provide a measure of protection against common ailments and age-related illnesses—a bonus beyond protecting against mere dietary deficiency.

If you're not getting the vitamin E you desire from your diet, you're better to get it from a pill than not at all. A vitamin E supplement won't make a poor diet better, but it can be an important ally to have in the battle against heart disease and cancer.

A daily intake of 100 IUs is suggested for disease-preventive benefit.

The Safety Question

Although vitamin E's apparent powers are noteworthy, it is not a panacea. Also, vitamin E deficiency is uncommon, occurring predominantly because of malnutrition or rare genetic conditions.

Toxicity from vitamin E also is rare. Subjects in studies who took more than 1,500 IUs a day for extended periods of time reported some gastric upset and nausea, and were at risk for deficiency of vitamins A and K. Also, overdosing on vitamin E can lead to subtle effects on the way blood clots.

One 1994 Finnish study of older males who smoked more than a pack of cigarettes a day for nearly 40 years indicated that vitamin E may slightly increase lung cancer risk, but the results were not conclusive. Also, previous studies revealed that smokers show sharply decreased amounts of vitamin E in their system. Unfortunately, details from the Finnish study have been reported out of context over the years, creating confusion about vitamin E's value.

Vitamin E's role as a major component in the body's cells and as a member of the immune system's SWAT team helps explain why low levels are associated with increased disease risk. It also supports the evidence that higher intakes decrease the risk for many health problems.

So, should we take vitamin E supplements? Taking 100 to 400 IUs of vitamin E per day in the form of a supplement might not be such a bad idea. Even amounts between 400 to 800 IUs per day are still considered safe, although not recommended. All supplements should be used with caution, as directed, and according to your physician's advice.

Individuals with blood coagulation disorders or those taking anticoagulation medications should be especially careful with vitamin E supplements. Consult your health professional if you have any health problems or questions.

—Ed Blonz is a syndicated columnist and the author of Power Nutrition, *published by Signet (1998). Dr. Blonz initially studied nutrition at the University of California, Davis, under Dr. Harold Olcott, one of the discoverers of vitamin E.*

COUNT AND AMOUNTS

Vitamin E content may appear on nutrition labels in either of two ways: The International Unit, or IU, is a measurement used with the fat-soluble vitamins A, D, E, and K. Newer and easier-to-understand terminology now expresses amounts for vitamin E in milligrams. The RDA for adult males is 10 milligrams, or 15 IUs. For adult females, the recommended amount is 8 milligrams, or 12 IUs.

ROMANCING THE VITAMIN

Vitamin E's roots are in romance. The original research had to do with fertility in animals. In fact,

vitamin E's chemical name, tocopherol (toe-CAW-fur-awl), comes from the Greek words *tokos* and *pherin,* meaning "to bear offspring." This early research triggered fad fame for vitamin E as a "love potion" for people, in spite of the lack of human studies in the matter.

But in an example of how science can come full circle, recent research has proven that vitamin E has more to do with romance—or at least reproduction—than previously believed. Studies now show that vitamin E can keep sperm cells from being damaged. Perhaps next Valentine's Day may find us presenting our loved ones with an elegantly wrapped package of wheat germ oil and sunflower seeds.

RIGHT TO THE SOURCE

Including some of the following foods in your daily diet can help you attain a goal of 100 IUs of vitamin E each day*:

1 oz. wheat germ oil	51 IUs
1 cup extra-fortified oatmeal	40 IUs
1 oz. sunflower oil	21 IUs
1 oz. shelled sunflower seeds	20 IUs
1 oz. soybean oil	20 IUs
1 oz. safflower oil	17 IUs
1 oz. corn oil	12 IUs
1 oz. whole almonds	10 IUs
1 medium sweet potato	9 IUs
1 oz. peanut oil	8 IUs
1 cup canned peaches	6 IUs
3 Tbsp. toasted wheat germ	4 IUs
1 cup cooked pasta	4 IUs
1 cup steamed asparagus	3 IUs
1 cup cooked Brussels sprouts	2 IUs

* Amounts approximate. Be sure to check the labels as vitamin E content can vary according to brand.

E AS IN EGG

Eggs aren't naturally a good source of vitamin E, but a team of researchers came up with the idea of enriching chicken feed with vitamin E in the hopes of changing that. These vitamin E-spiked eggs tend to cost a little more than the unfortified ones, but they do offer a good dietary source for vitamin E.

Each enhanced egg provides about 50 percent of the USDA's Recommended Dietary Allowance.

PEANUT BUTTER COOKIES

Prep: 25 min. ◆ Bake: 12 to 15 min. per batch

If miniature candy bars aren't available, cut regular-size bars into 1-inch squares.

- 1¾ **cups all-purpose flour**
- ½ **cup sugar**
- ½ **tsp. baking soda**
- ¼ **tsp. salt**
- ½ **cup butter**
- ½ **cup creamy peanut butter**
- ¼ **cup honey**
- 1 **Tbsp. milk**

◆◆◆

- 24 **miniature chocolate-coated caramel-topped nougat bars with peanuts**

1 In a large mixing bowl stir together flour, sugar, baking soda, and salt. Using a pastry blender, cut in the butter and peanut butter until mixture resembles coarse crumbs. Using a wooden spoon, beat in honey and milk until well combined.

2 For each cookie, pat 1 tablespoon of the dough into a 2-inch circle. Place 1 piece of candy in the center of the circle. Shape the dough around candy to form a 1½-inch ball. Place the balls 2 inches apart on an ungreased cookie sheet.

3 Bake in a 350° oven for 12 to 15 minutes or until edges are lightly browned. Transfer cookies to a wire rack and let cool. Makes 24 cookies.

Nutrition facts per cookie: 148 cal., 8 g total fat (3 g sat. fat), 11 mg chol., 125 mg sodium, 17 g carbo., 1 g fiber, 3 g pro. *Daily values:* 3% vit. A, 3% iron.

HISTORY OF CHOCOLATE CHIP COOKIES

Ruth Wakefield, owner of the Toll House Inn in Whitman, Massachusetts, created chocolate chip cookies in 1930. She was making a cookie named Butter Drop Dos that called for nuts when she discovered she had none. So she substituted chopped semisweet chocolate. She later added the nuts back into the recipe and created the cookie we love today.

CHOCOLATE CHIP COOKIE STICKS

Prep: 35 min. ◆ Bake: 28 min. Cool: 1 hour

Crisp and crunchy, these twice-baked treats are perfect dunkers for milk or coffee.

- ½ **cup shortening**
- ½ **cup butter, softened**
- 1 **cup packed brown sugar**
- ½ **cup granulated sugar**
- ½ **tsp. baking soda**
- 2 **eggs**
- 2 **tsp. vanilla**
- 2½ **cups all-purpose flour**
- 8 **oz. coarsely chopped semisweet chocolate (2 cups)**
- 1 **cup chopped walnuts, pecans, or hazelnuts (filberts) (optional)**

1 In a large mixing bowl beat the shortening and butter with an electric mixer on medium to high speed for 30 seconds. Add the brown sugar, granulated sugar, and baking soda. Beat mixture until combined, scraping the sides of the bowl occasionally. Beat in the eggs and vanilla until combined. Beat in as much of the flour as you can with the mixer. Using a wooden spoon, stir in remaining flour. Stir in the chopped chocolate and, if desired, walnuts, pecans, or hazelnuts.

2 Press dough evenly into a foil-lined 13×9×2-inch baking pan. Bake in a 375° oven for 22 to 25 minutes or until golden brown and center is set. Cool in pan on a wire rack for 1 hour.

3 Holding securely to the foil lining, gently remove cookies from pan and place on a cutting board, leaving the cookies on foil lining. Cut crosswise into 9×½-inch slices. Carefully place slices, cut side down, about 1 inch apart on an ungreased cookie sheet.

4 Bake in a 325° oven for 6 to 8 minutes or until cut edges are crispy. Carefully transfer cookies to wire rack and let cool (cookies will be soft). Makes 18 cookies.

Nutrition facts per cookie stick: 333 cal., 20 g total fat (8 g sat. fat), 37 mg chol., 98 mg sodium, 39 g carbo., 2 g fiber, 4 g pro. *Daily values:* 5% vit. A, 2% calcium, 11% iron.

CHOCOLATE CHIP COOKIES 3 WAYS

A few tweaks to the ingredients in chocolate chip cookies can dramatically change the outcome. Want a crispy, thin cookie? Use an all-butter dough. Because butter melts more quickly than shortening in a hot oven, the dough spreads. For a puffy cookie, use shortening to keep the dough from flattening. Get a softer cookie by sweetening it only with brown sugar. Combine brown with granulated sugar for a crisper cookie. Our tinkering resulted in three versions: Our Best Basic, Thin-and-Crispy, and Soft-and-Cakelike.

OUR BEST BASIC

Prep: 25 min. ◆ Bake: 8 to 10 min.
per batch

- ½ cup shortening
- ½ cup butter
- 1 cup packed brown sugar
- ½ cup granulated sugar
- ½ tsp. baking soda
- ¼ tsp. salt
- 2 eggs
- 1 tsp. vanilla
- 2½ cups all-purpose flour
- 1½ cups semisweet chocolate pieces
- 1 cup chopped walnuts or pecans

THIN-AND-CRISPY

Prep: 25 min. ◆ Bake: 10 to 12 min.
per batch

- 1 cup butter
- ¾ cup packed brown sugar
- ¾ cup granulated sugar
- ½ tsp. baking soda
- ¼ tsp. salt
- 1 egg
- 1 tsp. vanilla
- 2 cups all-purpose flour
- 1½ cups semisweet chocolate pieces
- 1 cup chopped walnuts or pecans

1 For Basic or Thin cookies, in a bowl beat shortening and/or butter on medium to high speed for 30 seconds. Add brown sugar, granulated sugar, baking soda, and salt; beat until combined. Beat in eggs or egg and vanilla until combined. Beat in as much of the flour as you can with the mixer. Using a wooden spoon, stir in remaining flour. Stir in chocolate pieces and nuts.

2 Drop by rounded teaspoons 2 inches apart on an ungreased cookie sheet. Bake in a 375° oven for 8 to 10 minutes for Basic cookies and for 10 to 12 minutes for Thin cookies or until edges are browned. Transfer cookies to a wire rack and let cool. Makes 60 cookies.

SOFT-AND-CAKELIKE

Prep: 25 min. ◆ Bake: 9 to 11 min.
per batch

- ½ cup shortening
- 1½ cups packed brown sugar
- 2 slightly beaten eggs
- 1 tsp. vanilla
- 2½ cups all-purpose flour
- 1 tsp. baking soda
- ½ tsp. baking powder
- ½ tsp. salt
- 1 8-oz. carton dairy sour cream
- 1½ cups semisweet chocolate pieces
- 1 cup chopped walnuts or pecans

1 For Cakelike cookies, in a bowl beat shortening and brown sugar on medium to high speed until combined. Add eggs and vanilla; beat until combined. Combine flour, baking soda, baking powder, and salt. Alternately add flour mixture and sour cream to shortening mixture, beating after each addition. Using a wooden spoon, stir in chocolate pieces and nuts.

2 Drop by rounded teaspoons 2 inches apart on an ungreased cookie sheet. Bake in a 375° oven for 9 to 11 minutes or until edges are browned. Transfer cookies to a wire rack and let cool. Makes 60 cookies.

Nutrition facts per Our Best Basic Chocolate Chip Cookie: 97 cal., 6 g total fat (2 g sat. fat), 11 mg chol., 38 mg sodium, 11 g carbo., 0 g fiber, 1 g pro. *Daily values:* 1% vit. A, 3% iron.

7-GRAIN CEREAL MUFFINS

Prep: 40 min. ◆ Bake: 12 min.

A hearty grab-and-go treat to tide you through the morning rush hour.

1   **cup seven-grain cereal**
1   **cup dried tart red cherries**
½   **cup packed brown sugar**
¼   **cup cooking oil**
1¼ **cups buttermilk**
1   **cup whole wheat flour**
1   **tsp. baking powder**
1   **tsp. ground ginger or**
    1 Tbsp. crystallized ginger,
    finely chopped
½   **tsp. baking soda**
½   **tsp. salt**
½   **tsp. ground nutmeg**

◆◆◆

1   **egg, slightly beaten**

1 Grease 12 muffin-top cups, six 3¼-inch (jumbo) muffin cups, or sixteen 2½-inch muffin cups. (Or, line standard muffin cups with paper bake cups.) Set aside. In a medium bowl combine seven-grain cereal, dried cherries, brown sugar, and oil. Pour buttermilk over mixture; let stand for 30 minutes. Meanwhile, in a large bowl combine whole wheat flour, baking powder, ginger, baking soda, salt, and nutmeg. Make a well in the center of dry mixture; set aside.

2 Stir beaten egg into buttermilk mixture. Add buttermilk mixture all at once to dry mixture. Stir just until moistened. Fill the muffin-top cups almost full or other muffin cups three-fourths full of batter.

3 Bake in a 400° oven about 12 minutes for muffin-top cups, about 20 minutes for 3¼-inch muffins, or 15 to 18 minutes for 2½-inch muffins or until golden. Cool on a wire rack 5 minutes. Remove from cups; serve immediately. Makes 12 muffin tops, six 3¼-inch muffins, or sixteen 2½-inch muffins.

Nutrition facts per muffin top: 160 cal., 5 g total fat (1 g sat. fat), 19 mg chol., 206 mg sodium, 26 g carbo., 2 g fiber, 3 g pro. *Daily values:* 7% vit. A, 5% calcium, 5% iron.

MONKEY BREAD

Prep: 1 hour ◆ Rise: 1½ hours
Bake: 35 min.

Use this yummy, pull-apart bread to introduce kids to the fun of baking. It can be prepared in individual muffin cups or a tube pan.

3¼ **to 3½ cups all-purpose flour**
1   **pkg. active dry yeast**
¼   **cup milk**
¼   **cup butter**
2   **Tbsp. sugar**
2   **Tbsp. light-colored corn**
    syrup
½   **tsp. salt**
¾   **cup mashed ripe bananas**
1   **egg**

◆◆◆

⅔   **cup chopped pecans**
1   **cup sugar**
¾   **tsp. ground cinnamon**

◆◆◆

⅓   **cup butter or margarine,**
    melted

◆◆◆

½   **cup caramel ice-cream**
    topping
2   **Tbsp. maple-flavored syrup**

1 In a large mixing bowl stir together 1 cup of the flour and

THE CLEVER COOK

MEASURE NOW, SAVE TIME LATER

When mixing up a batch of your favorite cookies or quick bread, measure a second set of dry ingredients, place in a self-sealing plastic bag, and label. Next time you make the recipe, all you have to do is add a few ingredients.

Melanie Flynn Kozinski
Dekalb, Illinois

the yeast. In a small saucepan heat and stir milk, the ¼ cup butter, the 2 tablespoons sugar, corn syrup, and salt just until warm (120° to 130°), and butter almost melts. Add milk mixture to dry mixture. Stir in bananas and egg.

2 Beat with an electric mixer on low speed for 30 seconds, scraping sides of bowl constantly. Beat on high speed for 3 minutes. Using a wooden spoon, stir in as much of the remaining flour as you can. Turn dough out onto a lightly floured surface. Knead in enough of the remaining flour to make a moderately stiff dough that is smooth and elastic (6 to 8 minutes). Place in a greased bowl; turn once. Cover; let rise until double (about 1 hour).

3 Generously grease ten 3¼-inch (jumbo) muffin cups or one 10-inch fluted tube pan. Sprinkle about half of the pecans in the bottoms of the 10 cups (about 1 teaspoon per muffin cup) or in bottom of tube pan; set aside. Combine the 1 cup sugar and cinnamon; set aside.

4 Punch dough down. Turn dough out onto a lightly floured surface. Roll out dough, forming a 10×6-inch rectangle; cut rectangle into sixty 1-inch pieces. Gently pull each portion of dough into a ball, tucking edges beneath. Roll each ball in the ⅓ cup melted butter, then roll in sugar-cinnamon mixture. Arrange 6 balls in each prepared muffin cup, smooth side down, or all the balls in prepared tube pan, stacking gently. Cover; let rise in a warm place until nearly double (30 to 40 minutes).

5 Sprinkle remaining pecans on top. Stir together caramel topping and maple-flavored syrup; drizzle on top. Bake individual breads in muffin cups in a 350° oven for 25 to 30 minutes or until light brown. Or, for whole loaf in fluted tube pan, bake 35 minutes or until bread is golden brown and sounds hollow when you tap the top with your fingers. Let stand for 1 minute. (If breads stand for more than 1 minute, the loaves will be difficult to remove from the muffin cups or tube pan.) Invert onto individual plates or a serving platter. Spoon any topping and nuts remaining in the cups or pan onto rolls or loaf. Cool 15 minutes. Serve warm. Makes 10 servings.

Nutrition facts per serving: 463 cal., 17 g total fat (7 g sat. fat), 50 mg chol., 289 mg sodium, 75 g carbo., 2 g fiber, 6 g pro. *Daily values:* 11% vit. A, 4% vit. C, 3% calcium, 16% iron.

BANANA-PECAN STREUSEL BREAD PUDDING

Prep: 20 min. ◆ Bake: 40 min.

1⅓ cups mashed ripe bananas
1 12-oz. can (1½ cups) evaporated milk
3 eggs, beaten
½ cup sugar
1 Tbsp. vanilla
1 tsp. ground cinnamon
¼ to ½ tsp. almond extract
2 large (5 oz.) croissants, cut or torn into 1-inch pieces

◆◆◆

¼ cup packed brown sugar
2 Tbsp. all-purpose flour
1 Tbsp. margarine or butter, melted
1 tsp. ground cinnamon
½ cup chopped pecans

1 Stir together first seven ingredients. Place croissant pieces in a lightly greased 2-quart rectangular casserole; pour egg mixture evenly over croissants. Press pieces into egg mixture to moisten.

2 Combine brown sugar, flour, margarine, and 1 teaspoon cinnamon. Stir in nuts. Sprinkle over croissant mixture. Bake in a 350° oven 40 to 45 minutes or until a knife inserted near center comes out clean. Let stand 30 minutes. Serve warm with *whipped cream or ice cream,* if desired. Makes 10 to 12 servings.

Nutrition facts per serving: 280 cal., 12 g total fat (5 g sat. fat), 93 mg chol., 141 mg sodium, 38 g carbo., 1 g fiber, 7 g pro. *Daily values:* 9% vit. A, 8% vit. C, 9% calcium, 8% iron.

PEANUT BUTTER MOUSSE

Prep: 35 min. ◆ Chill: 3 hours

¼ cup sugar
1 Tbsp. cornstarch
1 cup milk
¼ cup peanut butter-flavored pieces

◆◆◆

1 egg yolk, beaten
½ tsp. vanilla
1 cup whipping cream

1 In a saucepan combine sugar, cornstarch, and ¼ teaspoon *salt.* Stir in milk and peanut butter pieces. Cook and stir over medium heat until peanut butter pieces are almost melted and mixture is thickened and bubbly. Cook and stir 2 minutes more. Remove from heat. (All peanut butter pieces may not be melted.)

2 Stir half the milk mixture into egg yolk. Return to saucepan. Bring to gentle boil; reduce heat. Cook and stir, using a wire whisk, 2 minutes more. Remove from heat. Stir in vanilla. Pour into a medium bowl; cover surface with plastic wrap. Chill thoroughly. (Small flecks of chips may remain.) Beat whipping cream until soft peaks form. Fold whipped cream into chilled mixture. Spoon into dessert dishes; chill. Top with *chopped peanut butter and chocolate candies,* if desired. Serves 6.

Nutrition facts per serving: 241 cal., 18 g total fat (11 g sat. fat), 93 mg chol., 143 mg sodium, 16 g carbo., 0 g fiber, 4 g pro. *Daily values:* 25% vit. A, 1% vit. C, 7% calcium, 1% iron.

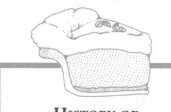

CHIFFON PIE

Prep: 1 hour ◆ Chill: 4 hours

If you wish to omit the tequila, replace it with an equal amount of orange juice.
(See the photograph on page 37.)

1 recipe **Pretzel Crust (see right)**

◆◆◆

3 envelopes **unflavored gelatin**
1 cup **cold water**

◆◆◆

1 cup **whipping cream**
1½ tsp. **vanilla**

◆◆◆

1⅔ cups **refrigerated or frozen egg product, thawed**
1⅓ cups **sugar**
½ cup **frozen lemonade concentrate, thawed**
4 tsp. **finely shredded lime peel**
½ cup **lime juice**
2 Tbsp. **tequila or orange juice**
Several drops green food coloring (optional)

◆◆◆

Glazed Shredded Lime Peel (see right) (optional)

1 Prepare and bake Pretzel Crust; set aside to cool.

2 For filling, in a small saucepan soften gelatin in the cold water. Cook and stir over low heat just until gelatin dissolves.

3 Meanwhile, in a chilled bowl combine whipping cream and vanilla. Beat with chilled beaters of an electric mixer on medium speed until soft peaks form. Keep chilled (do not hold longer than 30 minutes).

4 Remove gelatin from heat; transfer to a large mixing bowl. Stir in egg product, sugar, lemonade concentrate, lime peel and juice, tequila, and, if desired, green food coloring. Chill until mixture just begins to mound when spooned (see below), stirring occasionally (the gelatin sets up quickly, about 5 to 6 minutes).

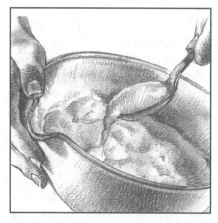

5 Beat gelatin mixture with an electric mixer on medium to high speed for 4 minutes. Immediately fold the whipped cream into gelatin mixture. Chill again until mixture mounds when spooned (about 1 to 2 minutes).

6 Spoon filling into Pretzel Crust. Loosely cover and chill for 4 to 6 hours or until firm. Garnish with Glazed Shredded Lime Peel, if desired. Serves 10.

Glazed Shredded Lime Peel: Shred the peel from 3 limes (you should have about 2 tablespoons peel). In a small bowl stir together 1 tablespoon water and 1½ teaspoons refrigerated or frozen egg product, thawed. Dip shredded lime peel in egg mixture. Remove from mixture using a fork and allow to drain; place on waxed paper, separating shreds of peel. Sprinkle evenly with 2 tablespoons sugar. Let dry in refrigerator on waxed paper 2 to 4 hours.

Nutrition facts per serving: 376 cal., 16 g total fat (9 g sat. fat), 49 mg chol., 399 mg sodium, 51 g carbo., 1 g fiber, 8 g pro. *Daily values:* 38% vit. A, 14% vit. C, 3% calcium, 7% iron.

PRETZEL CRUST

Prep: 10 min. ◆ Bake: 7 min.

⅓ cup **butter**
3 Tbsp. **sugar**
3½ cups **pretzels, coarsely crushed into ⅛- to ¼-inch pieces (1¼ cups crushed)**
1 **egg white (optional)**

1 Spray a 9-inch pie plate with *nonstick spray coating*. In a medium saucepan melt butter; stir in sugar. Add crushed pretzels, then egg white, if using (egg white gives a firmer but less crunchy crust). Toss to mix well. Spread evenly into prepared pie plate. Press onto bottom and sides to form a firm, even crust. Bake in a 350° oven for 7 to 9 minutes or until edge is lightly browned. Cool on a wire rack before filling.

Chiffon Pie (page 36)

Page 38: *Fennel-Potato Soup (page 10);* Top left: *Gingery Mitten Cookies (page 22)*
Top right: *Hot Caramel Chocolate (page 22);* Above: *Just-Like-Mom's Cobbler (page 20)*

Page 41: *Pasta Primavera (page 26)*
Left: *24-Hour Vegetable Salad (page 25)*
Below: *Fruit Salsa (page 28)*

Top: *Ravioli Duet (page 12) and Spinach-Mushroom Sauté (page 18)*; Above left: *Salt-and-Pepper Crackers (page 19)*; Above right: *Sage-Olive Baguettes (page 18)*

Top: *Pork Pocket Pies (page 17)*; Above left: *Snowmen Cookies (page 21)*; Above right: *Chocolate-Hazelnut Torte (page 20)*

Left: *Devil's Food Cake (page 45)*
Below: *Hot Fudge Sauce (page 46)*

DEVIL'S FOOD CAKE

Prep: 40 min. ◆ Bake: 30 min.
Cool: 1 hour ◆ Frost: 30 min.

*Measure to make sure your baking
pans are at least 1½ inches tall.
Shallower pans will let the batter run
over when the cake rises.
(See the photograph on page 44.)*

2¼ cups all-purpose flour
½ cup unsweetened cocoa
    powder
1½ tsp. baking powder
1 tsp. baking soda
½ tsp. ground cinnamon
¼ tsp. salt

◆◆◆

½ cup shortening
1¾ cups sugar
1 tsp. vanilla
3 eggs
1⅓ cups cold water

◆◆◆

1 recipe Chocolate Cream
    Cheese Frosting (see right)
1 recipe Chocolate Glaze (see
    right)

1 Grease and lightly flour two
9×1½-inch round cake pans or
one 13×9×2-inch baking pan; set
pan(s) aside. In a medium mixing
bowl stir together the flour, cocoa
powder, baking powder, baking
soda, cinnamon, and salt; set mixture aside.

2 In a large mixing bowl beat
the shortening with an electric
mixer on medium to high speed
for 30 seconds. Add sugar and
vanilla; beat until well combined,
scraping the sides of bowl. Add
eggs, one at a time, beating well
after each. Add the dry mixture
and cold water alternately to the
beaten mixture, beating on low

speed after each addition just
until combined.

3 Spoon batter into prepared
pan(s), spreading evenly. Bake in a
350° oven for 30 to 35 minutes or
until a wooden toothpick inserted
near the center comes out clean.
Cool round layer cakes in pans on
wire racks for 10 minutes.
Remove from pans. Cool thoroughly on wire racks. Or, place
13×9×2-inch cake in pan on a
wire rack; cool thoroughly.

4 To assemble: Frost tops and
sides of layers or top of 13×9×2-
inch cake with Chocolate Cream
Cheese Frosting, reserving 1 cup
of frosting to make chocolate
"drops." Drizzle Chocolate Glaze
in a zigzag pattern atop cake.
Spoon reserved Chocolate Cream
Cheese Frosting into a pastry bag
fitted with a large round tip. Pipe
chocolate "drops" around base of
cake. Then pipe "drops" on top of
cake. Cover and store cake in the
refrigerator for up to 3 days. Makes
12 to 16 servings.

Nutrition facts per serving: 707 cal., 29 g
total fat (14 g sat. fat), 104 mg chol.,
359 mg sodium, 107 g carbo., 1 g fiber, 7 g
pro. *Daily values:* 20% vit. A, 12% calcium,
17% iron.

CHOCOLATE CREAM
CHEESE FROSTING

Start to finish: 20 min.

1 8-oz. pkg. cream cheese,
    softened
½ cup margarine or butter,
    softened
2 tsp. vanilla

6½ cups sifted powdered sugar
⅓ cup unsweetened cocoa
    powder
1 to 2 Tbsp. milk

1 In a large mixing bowl beat
together the cream cheese, margarine or butter, and vanilla with
an electric mixer on medium to
high speed until light and fluffy.
Gradually add 2 cups of the sifted
powdered sugar and the cocoa
powder, beating well. Gradually
beat in remaining powdered sugar
until smooth. Beat in milk, if
needed, to reach spreading consistency. Makes about 3½ cups.

CHOCOLATE GLAZE

Start to finish: 15 min.

2 oz. semisweet chocolate
    pieces
1 Tbsp. margarine or butter
¼ cup whipping cream
1 tsp. light-colored corn syrup

1 In a heavy small saucepan
melt chocolate pieces and margarine or butter over low heat,
stirring constantly until chocolate
begins to melt. Immediately
remove from heat and stir until
smooth; set aside.

2 In another saucepan stir
together the whipping cream and
corn syrup. Bring mixture to a
gentle boil; reduce heat. Cook,
uncovered, for 2 minutes.
Remove from heat. Stir the
chocolate mixture into whipping
cream mixture. Cool to room
temperature before using. Makes
about ⅔ cup.

THE CLEVER COOK

RECIPES AS GIFTS

My family and friends always ask for my latest and greatest recipes. A few years ago I decided to enclose a recipe in each Christmas or birthday card I sent throughout the year.

In order to get ready for the Christmas season, I start early in the fall and handwrite each recipe on a card. I try to suit the recipe to the person it's being sent to. I've found that these recipes are not only well received, but also result in a surprising phone call.

Vicki Alberts
Rogers, Arizona

HOT FUDGE SAUCE
Prep: 10 min. ◆ Cook: 5 min.

With a sauce this wonderful, it's easy to get impatient while cooking. But don't try to rush it; keeping the heat low eliminates the danger of scorching the chocolate. To build a sophisticated sundae, top coffee ice cream with coconut curls, crystallized ginger, whipped cream, and mint leaves.
(See the photograph on page 44.)

½ cup unsweetened cocoa powder
⅓ cup granulated sugar
⅓ cup packed dark brown sugar
3 Tbsp. margarine or butter
½ cup whipping cream

1 In a small bowl stir together cocoa powder, granulated sugar, and brown sugar; set aside. In a heavy small saucepan melt margarine or butter together with whipping cream over low heat, stirring constantly. Cook and stir over medium heat about 3 minutes or until mixture bubbles around edges. Add sugar mixture. Cook, stirring constantly, for 1 to 2 minutes more or until sugar is dissolved and mixture is smooth and thickened. Serve immediately. Or, cover and store in the refrigerator up to 1 week.* Use sauce for sundaes, cakes, pastries, or other desserts. Makes 1 cup.

*Note: To reheat on stovetop, in a heavy small saucepan stir sauce frequently over low heat. To reheat in microwave, place chilled topping in a 2-cup measure. Microcook, uncovered, on 100 percent power (high) for 1 to 2 minutes or until heated.

Nutrition facts per 1 tablespoon sauce: 89 cal., 5 g total fat (3 g sat. fat), 16 mg chol., 34 mg sodium, 10 g carbo., 0 g fiber, 1 g pro. *Daily values:* 5% vit. A, 3% calcium, 2% iron.

CHOCOLATE-RASPBERRY CHEESECAKE
Prep: 30 min. ◆ Bake: 50 min.
Cool: 1¾ hours ◆ Chill: 4 hours

1½ cups finely crushed graham crackers
¼ cup sifted powdered sugar
⅓ cup butter, melted

2 cups fresh or frozen loose-pack raspberries, thawed
½ tsp. granulated sugar
3 8-oz. pkgs. cream cheese, softened
1 14-oz. can (1¼ cups) sweetened condensed milk
4 eggs
1 tsp. vanilla
1 cup semisweet chocolate pieces (6 oz.), melted and cooled

1 For crust, combine crushed crackers and powdered sugar; stir in melted butter. Press onto bottom and 2 inches up sides of a 9-inch springform pan; set aside.

2 In a small bowl combine 1 cup of the raspberries and the granulated sugar; set aside. For filling, in a large mixing bowl beat cream cheese and condensed milk with an electric mixer until combined. Add eggs and vanilla; beat just until combined. Divide batter in half. Stir melted chocolate into half of the batter. Pour chocolate batter into crust-lined pan. Stir raspberry-sugar mixture into remaining batter. Spoon raspberry batter over chocolate batter.

3 Place pan on a shallow baking pan. Bake in 350° oven 50 to 60 minutes or until center appears nearly set when pan is gently shaken. Cool in pan on wire rack 15 minutes. Loosen crust from sides of pan. Cool 30 minutes. Remove sides; cool 1 hour. Cover; chill at least 4 hours. Serve with remaining raspberries. Serves 16.

Nutrition facts per serving: 382 cal., 26 g total fat (14 g sat. fat), 119 mg chol., 257 mg sodium, 32 g carbo., 0 g fiber, 8 g pro. *Daily values:* 27% vit. A, 7% vit. C, 10% calcium, 9% iron.

◆◆◆

$\mathcal{M}$ARCH
Say Cheese!

$\mathcal{M}$arch is winter's homestretch. Celebrate by rediscovering something you may be overlooking—cheese. Take a good look at the cheese in your grocer's deli case, at specialty stores, or through mail order. Bet you'll see some you've never tried. Tips in this chapter will help you find some cheese treasures. Challenge your taste buds with fun and easy recipes like Savory Feta Cheesecake, Choose-a-Cheese Soufflé, Fettuccine with Four Cheeses, or Field Greens with Quesadilla "Croutons." And save room for dessert—either creamy, decadent Classic New York-Style Cheesecake or Sweet Cheese Blintzes.

30-minute recipes indicated in RED.
Low-fat and no-fat recipes indicated
with a ♥.
Photographs indicated in italics.
*Bonus recipe

MEDITERRANEAN WALNUT SPREAD

Start to finish: 15 min.

Whether served on bread or pita slices, this spread is an ideal, not-too-filling appetizer.

1 cup canned garbanzo beans (about ½ of a 15-oz. can)
½ cup chopped walnuts
½ cup lightly packed basil leaves
2 Tbsp. olive oil
2 to 3 tsp. lemon juice
⅛ tsp. salt
⅛ tsp. pepper

♦♦♦

Toasted thin baguette slices or pita bread slices

1 Drain garbanzo beans, reserving the liquid. In a blender container or food processor bowl combine beans and 2 tablespoons of the reserved liquid, the walnuts, basil leaves, olive oil, lemon juice, salt, and pepper. Cover and blend or process until nearly smooth. (Scrape down sides and add additional reserved liquid if mixture appears stiff.)

2 Serve spread on toasted baguette slices or pita slices. Or, place in an airtight container and store in the refrigerator up to 5 days. Makes about 1¼ cups.

Nutrition facts per serving: 34 cal., 3 g total fat (0 g sat. fat), 0 mg chol., 25 mg sodium, 1 g carbo., 0 g fiber, 1 g pro.
Daily values: 1% iron.

DRIED TOMATO AND WHITE BEAN DIP

Prep: 25 min. ♦ Cook: 5 min.
Bake: 10 min. (Pita Crisps)

If there's extra, spread this hummus-style dip on a toasted bagel.

2 15-oz. cans white kidney beans, rinsed and drained
4 tsp. lemon juice

♦♦♦

1 cup sliced green onions
3 cloves garlic, minced
1 Tbsp. olive oil
¼ cup oil-pack dried tomatoes, drained and finely chopped
1 Tbsp. snipped fresh oregano or ½ tsp. dried oregano, crushed
½ tsp. ground cumin
¼ tsp. salt
Several dashes bottled hot pepper sauce
1 recipe Pita Crisps (see below)

1 In a food processor bowl or blender container combine half of the beans and the lemon juice. Cover and process or blend until nearly smooth; set aside.

2 In a large skillet cook green onions and garlic in olive oil until just tender. Stir in processed beans, whole beans, chopped tomatoes, oregano, cumin, salt, and hot pepper sauce. Heat through. Serve warm with Pita Crisps. Makes 16 servings.

Pita Crisps: Split 3 pita bread rounds in half horizontally, separating into two rounds. Cut each round into 8 wedges (48 total). Stir together 2 tablespoons olive oil, ½ teaspoon chili powder, and ¼ teaspoon garlic salt. Brush mixture lightly over rough surfaces of pita wedges. Arrange wedges, brushed side up, in a single layer on ungreased baking sheets. Bake in a 350° oven for 10 to 12 minutes or until crisp; cool. Store in an airtight container at room temperature for up to 1 week.

Nutrition facts per serving: 90 cal., 3 g total fat (0 g sat. fat), 0 mg chol., 214 mg sodium, 14 g carbo., 3 g fiber, 4 g pro.
Daily values: 1% vit. A, 6% vit. C, 2% calcium, 7% iron.

CELEBRATION CHEESE PLATTER

Prep: 30 min. ♦ Bake: 5 min.
Chill: 1 hour

The ultimate party tray lets cheese be its own raison d'être.

¼ cup finely chopped pecans or walnuts
½ tsp. dried thyme, crushed
⅛ tsp. ground red pepper

♦♦♦

1 lb. Boursin, soft goat cheese (chèvre), or other soft white cheese, chilled
2 Tbsp. finely snipped radicchio or fresh purple basil
2 Tbsp. finely chopped pistachio nuts
2 Tbsp. finely chopped almonds
2 Tbsp. snipped fresh chervil
2 Tbsp. snipped fresh thyme

♦♦♦

Assorted cut-up fresh fruit (optional)
Assorted crackers, breadsticks, pita chips, and/or melba toast

1 In a small mixing bowl stir together pecans or walnuts, thyme, and pepper. Spread nut mixture evenly on a baking sheet. Bake in a 350° oven 5 minutes, stirring once. Remove from oven; cool completely.

2 Roll and form cheese into assorted shapes using several teaspoons at a time for smaller shapes and 1 to 2 tablespoons for larger shapes. Roll some of the cheese shapes in cooled toasted nut mixture. Roll remaining cheese shapes in radicchio, pistachios, almonds, chervil, and/or fresh thyme. Place coated cheeses on a wax-paper-lined baking sheet. Cover; chill at least 1 hour.

3 To serve, arrange assorted shaped cheeses on chilled serving platters. Surround with cut fresh fruits, if desired. Serve with assorted crackers. Serves 12.

Nutrition facts per each 2-oz. serving: 182 cal., 19 g total fat (12 g sat. fat), 1 mg chol., 227 mg sodium, 2 g carbo., 0 g fiber, 3 g pro. *Daily values:* 1% iron.

JUST-RIGHT CHEESE BITES

Start to finish: 30 min.

For another entertaining version of this four-ingredient appetizer, use purchased chutney to fill these bite-size cheese cups.

♦♦♦

1 lb. mild, semifirm cheese, such as Colby, Monterey Jack, Edam, and/or provolone

♦♦♦

½ **cup chunk-style crabmeat or crab-flavored, salad-style fish, chopped**
2 Tbsp. prepared pesto
1 Tbsp. pine nuts, toasted

1 Using hors d'oeuvres cutters, cut cheese into 1¼- to 1½-inch pieces. Or, using a sharp knife, cut cheese into 1½-inch cubes. Using the small end of a melon baller, hollow out each cheese piece, taking care not to cut through the bottom. Refrigerate removed cheese for another use, such as a soufflé, soup, or fondue.

2 In a small mixing bowl gently stir together crabmeat, pesto, and pine nuts. Spoon 1 to 1½ teaspoons crabmeat mixture into each cheese piece. Makes 16.

Nutrition facts per piece (average): 112 cal., 9 g total fat (5 g sat. fat), 26 mg chol., 165 mg sodium, 1 g carbo., 0 g fiber, 7 g pro. *Daily values:* 7% vit. A, 13% calcium, 1% iron.

30 MIN. LOW FAT

ITALIAN CHEESE CUPS

Prep: 15 min. ♦ Bake: 10 min.

2 **2.1-oz. (15 count) pkg. 1¾-inch baked miniature phyllo shells**
½ **cup oil-packed dried tomatoes, drained and finely chopped**
4 **oz. fresh mozzarella cheese, cut into 30 pieces**
3 **Tbsp. refrigerated pesto sauce**

1 Place phyllo shells on a large baking sheet. Place ¼ teaspoon of the chopped tomato in the bottom of each shell. Top with a piece of mozzarella and

MAIL-ORDER CHEESE SOURCES

There are dozens of mail-order sources for cheeses. The following is a short list of some companies that can provide you with information about different cheeses and that will ship to you the cheeses used in these recipes—or any other cheese you may want to try. Be sure to ask them which cheeses are newly available or on special. Different companies have different ordering requirements, so be sure to ask for details.

1. DiBruno Bros. House of Cheese—888/322-4337, or visit their Internet site at www.dibruno.com.
2. Formaggio Kitchen, Boston—888/212-3224.
3. Ideal Cheese Shop — 800/382-0109.
4. The Mozzarella Company—800/798-2954, or e-mail at MozzCo@aol.com.
5. Murray's by Mail— 888/692-4339 or 212/243-3289, or e-mail at murrays_cheese@msn.com.
6. Zingerman's—888/636-8162, or e-mail at zing@ chamber.ann-arbor.mi.us.

about ¼ teaspoon of the pesto sauce. Bake in a 350° oven about 10 minutes or until cheese is melted. Serve warm. Makes 30 appetizers.

Nutrition facts per serving: 47 cal., 3 g total fat (0 g sat. fat), 2 mg chol., 44 mg sodium, 3 g carbo., 0 g fiber, 2 g pro. *Daily values:* 3% vit. C, 2% calcium, 1% iron.

Savory Feta Cheesecake

Prep: 20 min. ◆ Bake: 40 min.
Cool: 45 min. ◆ Chill: 3 hours

Feta, dill, and olives add a Greek touch to this full-flavored cheesecake. Cut in small wedges and serve with crisp, raw vegetables.

- 1 cup ground walnuts
- ½ cup finely crushed zwieback
- 2 Tbsp. margarine or butter, melted

◆◆◆

- 1 15-oz. carton ricotta cheese
- 1½ cups finely crumbled feta cheese flavored with basil and tomato (6 oz.)
- 3 eggs
- ¾ cup finely chopped fresh mushrooms
- ⅓ cup finely chopped pitted ripe olives
- ¼ cup milk
- ½ tsp. pepper

◆◆◆

Sliced ripe olives (optional)
Fresh oregano (optional)
Fresh sliced vegetables (optional)

1 For crust, combine ground walnuts, crushed zwieback, and melted margarine or butter. Press onto bottom of a 9-inch springform pan.

2 For filling, in a large bowl beat ricotta and feta cheeses with an electric mixer on medium speed until well combined. Add eggs, beating on low speed until just combined. Stir in mushrooms, chopped olives, milk, pepper, and ⅛ teaspoon *salt*.

3 Place springform pan on a baking sheet. Pour filling into pan. Bake in a 325° oven for 40 to 45 minutes or until the center appears nearly set when shaken. Cool for 15 minutes on a wire rack. Run a spatula around inside of the pan. Cool for 30 minutes more. Remove the sides of pan. Cover; refrigerate at least 3 hours.

4 To serve, using a knife, cut cheesecake into wedges. Garnish cheesecake with sliced ripe olives and fresh oregano, if desired. Serve with fresh sliced vegetables. Makes 20 appetizer servings.

Nutrition facts per serving: 152 cal., 12 g total fat (5 g sat. fat), 59 mg chol., 292 mg sodium, 5 g carbo., 0 g fiber, 7 g pro. *Daily values:* 8% vit. A, 13% calcium, 3% iron.

Cheesecake Olé

Prep: 20 min. ◆ Bake: 35 min.
Cool: 45 min. ◆ Chill: 3 hours

No need to mince and chop the snappy veggies that spark this robust south-of-the-border cheesecake; just stir in purchased salsa.

Nonstick spray coating
- 2 Tbsp. fine dry bread crumbs
- 1 8-oz. pkg. cream cheese, softened
- 1 8-oz. carton dairy sour cream
- ½ tsp. ground cumin
- 1 egg
- ½ cup chunky red salsa
- 2 Tbsp. milk
- ¾ cup shredded co-jack or Monterey Jack cheese
- ¼ cup sliced green onions

◆◆◆

Sliced tomato, sour cream, and sliced green onions (optional)

1 Spray a 7- or 8-inch springform pan with nonstick coating. Sprinkle bottom of pan evenly with bread crumbs; set aside. For filling, in a large mixing bowl beat the cream cheese, sour cream, and cumin with an electric mixer on medium speed until smooth. Add egg; beat on low speed just until combined. Stir in salsa and milk. Stir in the shredded cheese and ¼ cup sliced green onions.

2 Place springform pan on a baking sheet. Pour filling into pan. Bake in a 350° oven for 35 to 45 minutes or until center appears nearly set when shaken. Cool for 15 minutes on a wire rack. Run a spatula around inside of pan. Cool 30 minutes more. Remove the sides of pan. Cover and refrigerate at least 3 hours. Garnish with chopped tomato, sour cream, and sliced green onions, if desired. Makes 12 servings.

Nutrition facts per serving: 150 cal., 14 g total fat (8 g sat. fat), 54 mg chol., 159 mg sodium, 3 g carbo., 0 g fiber, 5 g pro. *Daily values:* 17% vit. A, 6% vit. C, 8% calcium, 4% iron.

Fresh Mozzarella Salad

Prep: 15 min. ◆ Roast: 20 min.

If you've never tasted fresh mozzarella before, you're in for a treat. This delicate cheese has a light flavor and soft texture, unlike the more familiar shreddable "pizza" mozzarella. (See the photograph on page 81.)

- 2 medium red and/or yellow sweet peppers

◆◆◆

- 8 oz. smoked fresh mozzarella cheese or fresh mozzarella cheese, thinly sliced

2 cups fresh arugula or
   spinach
¼ cup olive oil
¼ cup balsamic vinegar
¼ tsp. coarsely ground black
   pepper
⅛ tsp. salt (optional)
2 small fresh hot peppers,
   halved (optional)*

1 Halve sweet peppers lengthwise; remove stems, seeds, and membranes. Place peppers, cut side down, on a foil-lined baking sheet. Roast in a 425° oven for 20 to 25 minutes or until skins are blistered and dark. Remove peppers from oven; immediately cover tightly with foil. Let stand about 30 minutes to steam. Remove skin from peppers; discard. Cut roasted sweet peppers into 3×1½-inch strips.

2 On chilled salad plates, loosely overlap sweet pepper strips, mozzarella slices, and half of the arugula or spinach. Drizzle with oil and vinegar. Sprinkle with black pepper and, if desired, salt. Surround with remaining arugula or spinach. Garnish with hot pepper halves, if desired. Makes 4 side-dish servings.

*Note: Hot peppers contain oils that can burn eyes, lips, and sensitive skin, so wear plastic gloves while preparing them and be sure to wash your hands thoroughly afterward.

Nutrition facts per serving: 306 cal., 26 g total fat (9 g sat. fat), 44 mg chol., 218 mg sodium, 8 g carbo., 0 g fiber, 12 g pro. *Daily values:* 43% vit. A, 108% vit. C, 26% calcium, 5% iron.

FIELD GREENS WITH QUESADILLA "CROUTONS"

Prep: 25 min. ◆ Cook: 15 min.

Shrimp-and-cheese-filled tortilla triangles enliven this crisp, Tex-Mex salad with yellow-gold accents. (See the photograph on page 79.)

3 Tbsp. olive oil
3 Tbsp. vinegar
1 Tbsp. lime juice
½ tsp. dried thyme, crushed
⅛ tsp. ground red pepper
8 cups torn mixed greens
2 Tbsp. chopped tomatoes
2 Tbsp. chopped tomatillos or
   green sweet pepper

◆◆◆

1½ cups shredded Mexican
   cheese, such as Queso
   Añejo, Queso Blanco, or
   Ancho Chili Caciotta
1½ cups shredded Monterey
   Jack cheese (6 ounces)
8 8-inch flour tortillas or
   whole wheat flour tortillas
   Ground cumin
2 Roma tomatoes, thinly sliced
1 cup frozen peeled, cooked
   tiny shrimp
2 large poblano peppers,
   seeded and finely chopped
1 small onion, finely chopped
   Nonstick spray coating

1 In a screw-top jar combine olive oil, vinegar, lime juice, thyme, ground red pepper, and ⅛ teaspoon *salt*. Cover and shake well. Place greens in a large bowl; toss with dressing, chopped tomatoes, and tomatillos. Arrange greens on 8 plates; set aside.

2 Using half the cheese, divide evenly over 4 of the tortillas; sprinkle lightly with cumin. Layer

with Roma tomatoes, shrimp, peppers, and onion. Top with remaining cheese and tortillas. Spray nonstick coating in heavy skillet or griddle; place over medium heat. Cook each quesadilla 2 minutes or until golden; turn carefully. Cook 2 minutes more or until cheese melts and bottom is golden. Repeat with remaining quesadillas. Cut each quesadilla into 6 wedges. Arrange 3 wedges on top of each plate of greens. Makes 8 main-dish servings.

Nutrition facts per serving: 346 cal., 22 g total fat (6 g sat. fat), 74 mg chol., 450 mg sodium, 20 g carbo., 2 g fiber, 17 g pro. *Daily values:* 16% vit. A, 52% vit. C, 30% calcium, 16% iron.

SHERRIED ARTICHOKE AND SHRIMP SOUP

30 MIN.

Start to finish: 30 min.

½ cup coarsely chopped onion
1 Tbsp. butter
1 Tbsp. sugar
1 9-oz. pkg. artichoke hearts, thawed and coarsely chopped
3 cups chicken broth
2 Tbsp. white wine Worcestershire sauce
8 oz. cooked, peeled, and deveined shrimp
1 cup half-and-half or light cream
2 Tbsp. dry sherry

1 In a medium saucepan cook onion in butter over medium heat until tender. Stir in sugar. Continue cooking about 10 minutes more or until onions are caramelized, stirring occasionally. Stir artichokes, broth, Worcestershire sauce, and ⅛ teaspoon *pepper* into onion mixture. Bring to boiling; stir in shrimp, half-and-half, and sherry. Heat through. To serve, ladle soup into bowls. Makes 4 servings.

Nutrition facts per serving: 254 cal., 12 g total fat (7 g sat. fat), 141 mg chol., 886 mg sodium, 17 g carbo., 3 g fiber, 20 g pro. *Daily values:* 15% vit. A, 15% vit. C, 11% calcium, 21% iron.

WILD RICE AND CHEESE SOUP

Start to finish: 40 min.

2 cups shredded smoked Gouda or smoked cheddar cheese (8 oz.)
4 tsp. all-purpose flour

2 tsp. margarine or butter
2 Tbsp. finely chopped onion
1 medium cooking apple, cored and chopped (1 cup)
½ cup cooked wild rice
1¼ cups reduced-sodium chicken broth
½ cup brown ale or amber beer
¼ tsp. ground white pepper
⅔ cup half-and-half or light cream

1 In a medium mixing bowl toss shredded cheese with flour; set aside. In a 2-quart saucepan melt margarine or butter; add onion. Cook and stir over medium-high heat 4 minutes or until tender. Add ¾ cup of the apple, cooked rice, chicken broth, beer, and pepper. Bring mixture to boiling; reduce heat. Simmer, uncovered, 10 minutes. Slowly stir in cheese mixture until melted. Stir in half-and-half or light cream. Cook over medium-low heat until just heated through.

2 To serve, ladle into warmed bowls; top with remaining chopped apple. Garnish with *fresh thyme sprigs,* if desired. Makes 4 main-dish servings.

Nutrition facts per serving: 343 cal., 23 g total fat (14 g sat. fat), 86 mg chol., 713 mg sodium, 15 g carbo., 1 g fiber, 18 g pro. *Daily values:* 17% vit. A, 3% vit. C, 38% calcium, 3% iron.

UP-AND-COMING CHEESES

These interesting cheeses are making inroads into American supermarkets and specialty stores. They are well worth looking for, or ask your local cheese purveyor to order them.

1. Scamorze (ska-MORZ) This mildly smoked cheese from Italy is similar in flavor and texture to provolone.

2. Fresh Mozzarella (maht-suh-REHL-lah) A delicate cheese with a pure, milky flavor that goes with almost anything. The small balls are "bocconcini," Italian for "little bites."

3. Aged Gouda (GOO-dah) This venerable Dutch cheese, which is given a long time to ripen, has a rich flavor with notes of caramel.

4. Chaource (sha-OORS) This ripened cheese from France has a milder, creamier flavor than Brie or Camembert.

5. Madrigal (mah-dri-GAHL) France's answer to Swiss cheese with a taste that's slightly deeper than that of its more familiar relative.

6. Banon (bah-NON) From Indiana, this delicate goat cheese wrapped in brandied chestnut leaves has a full flavor without being too overpowering.

7. Manchego (mon-CHAY-go) This Spanish sheep's-milk grating cheese is enjoying a welcome surge in popularity. Use manchego as you would a Parmesan.

8. Humboldt An ash-veined goat cheese from California that's known for its slightly sweet, nutty flavor.

9. Ancho Chili Caciotta (kah-chee-OH-tah) A Texas original; goat cheese flavored with cilantro and ancho.

10. Vela Jack Cheese This full-bodied, dried Monterey Jack from California is perfect for grating or enjoying on its own.

CORN AND SAUSAGE CHOWDER

Start to finish: 20 min.

After you've spent a blustery day dashing around, you want a dinner solution, not a dinner problem. That's where this hearty meal-in-a-bowl comes in—it's delicious, nutritionally balanced, and ready in 20 minutes.

1 20-oz. pkg. refrigerated shredded potatoes

1 14½-oz. can reduced-sodium chicken broth

1 10-oz. pkg. frozen whole kernel corn

2 cups skim milk

1 12-oz. 97 percent fat-free cooked link sausage, halved lengthwise and sliced

⅓ cup sliced green onions

¼ tsp. black pepper

❖❖❖

Salt

Cilantro sprigs

Green or red bottled hot pepper sauce

1 In a 4-quart Dutch oven combine the potatoes, chicken broth, and corn. Bring mixture just to boiling; reduce heat. Simmer, covered, about 10 minutes or until potatoes are just tender, stirring occasionally. Using a potato masher, slightly mash potatoes. Stir in milk, sausage, green onions, and black pepper; heat through. Season to taste with salt, cilantro, and green or red hot pepper sauce. Makes 5 servings.

Nutrition facts per serving: 264 cal., 3 g total fat (0 g sat. fat), 26 mg chol., 1,243 mg sodium, 42 g carbo., 3 g fiber, 19 g pro. *Daily values:* 8% vit. A, 186% vit. C, 10% calcium, 6% iron.

FOND OF FONDUE

Start to finish: 30 min.

In France, the flavor of a savory fondue is enhanced by rubbing the inside of the pot with a cut garlic clove.

12 1-inch-thick slices French, Italian, sourdough, and/or rye bread, cut into 1-inch cubes; and/or cooked vegetables, such as parsnip, daikon, potatoes, fennel, and/or carrots, cut into sticks*

1¼ lb. process Gruyère or Swiss cheese, shredded (about 5 cups)

2 tsp. cornstarch

¼ tsp. ground white pepper

1½ cups sweet white wine, such as Riesling; or sparkling wine or apple cider

❖❖❖

¼ cup half-and-half or light cream

1 Toast bread cubes, if desired**; set aside. In a large mixing bowl toss cheese with cornstarch and pepper; set aside. In a large saucepan heat wine over medium heat just until it simmers; reduce heat to low. Simmer, uncovered, for 5 minutes.

2 Whisk cheese mixture, ½ cup at a time, into wine until nearly melted. Whisk in half-and-half or light cream; heat through. Transfer to fondue pot. Keep mixture warm over fondue burner. As fondue stands, it may thicken. Stir in 1 to 2 tablespoons of warmed half-and-half or light

Fond of Fondue (see left)

❖❖❖

Salad of fresh greens, dried cranberries, toasted pine nuts, and a fruit vinaigrette

❖❖❖

White wine or sparkling water

❖❖❖

Assorted fresh fruit

cream. Use bread cubes and/or vegetable pieces for dipping. Makes 12 main-dish servings.

*Note: To make dipping vegetables: Clean and peel 2 pounds root vegetables, such as parsnips, daikon, potatoes, fennel, and/or carrots. Cut into ½-inch-thick slices. Cook, covered, in a small amount of salted boiling water about 8 minutes or until crisp-tender. Drain; rinse with cold water. Drain on paper towels. Serve immediately or cover vegetables and chill. Let stand at room temperature for 20 minutes before serving.

**Note: To toast bread cubes: Spread bread cubes in a shallow roasting pan. Bake, uncovered, in a 350° oven about 10 minutes or until golden, stirring once.

Nutrition facts per serving: 293 cal., 17 g total fat (9 g sat. fat), 53 mg chol., 314 mg sodium, 14 g carbo., 0 g fiber, 16 g pro. *Daily values:* 18% vit. A, 42% calcium, 5% iron.

GREATER THAN GRATE

Hard cheeses merit more than a beeline trip to the grater. Wedges of aged goat cheese, Parmigiano-Reggiano, Vela Jack, aged Gouda, and other hard cheeses are a treat served with fruity red wines, dessert wines and sparkling wines, or ciders. These cheeses also are great mates with nuts or fruits, such as apples, pears, figs, or dates. Serve them as appetizers or try them after desserts.

When you grate a hard cheese, prepare only what you need. Wrap the remaining piece tightly in plastic wrap and refrigerate. The rind of many hard cheeses, such as Parmigiano-Reggiano, is edible. Simmer the rind in soup until it softens. Remove and cut into bite-size pieces to serve with the soup.

FETTUCCINE WITH FOUR CHEESES

Prep: 20 min. ◆ Cook: 14 min.

Three Italian cheeses (Parmigiano-Reggiano, Asiago, and Montasio) and one Spanish cheese (Manchego) provide the flourish to a simple dish of pasta and herbs. Use the cheeses suggested or any combination of hard grating cheese. (See the photograph on page 81.)

5　oz. packaged dried fettuccine
3　cloves garlic, minced
1　Tbsp. olive oil
⅛　to ¼ tsp. freshly ground
　　white pepper

◆◆◆

2　Tbsp. shaved Parmigiano-
　　Reggiano cheese
2　Tbsp. shaved Asiago cheese
2　Tbsp. shaved Montasio
　　cheese
2　Tbsp. shaved Manchego
　　cheese
　　Snipped fresh oregano
　　(optional)

1 Prepare fettuccine according to package directions, adding minced garlic during last minute of cooking. Drain fettuccine; toss with oil and pepper.

2 Divide fettuccine into 4 bowls. Top each serving with ½ tablespoon of each of the cheeses. Garnish with snipped oregano, if desired. Makes 4 side-dish servings.

Nutrition facts per serving: 227 cal., 8 g total fat (3 g sat. fat), 10 mg chol., 176 mg sodium, 29 g carbo., 1 g fiber, 9 g pro. *Daily values:* 1% vit. A, 1% vit. C, 11% calcium, 9% iron.

Alfredo-Style Fettuccine: Prepare the 5 oz. dried fettuccine according to package directions. In a large skillet heat oil. Cook garlic for 30 seconds. Add ⅓ cup dry white wine and ⅓ cup chicken broth. Bring to boiling. Simmer, uncovered, about 4 minutes or until liquid is reduced by half. Add ⅔ cup whipping cream, ⅛ to ¼ tsp. white pepper, and ⅛ tsp. ground mace or nutmeg. Simmer, uncovered, about 6 minutes or until cream thickens. Drain fettuccine. Toss pasta with sauce. Divide into 4 bowls. Top each serving with ½ tablespoon of each of the cheeses. Garnish with snipped fresh oregano, if desired.

CHOOSE-A-CHEESE SOUFFLÉ

Prep: 30 min. ◆ Bake: 40 min.

The cheese you use is yours to choose. (We provide a few suggestions below.) Harder cheeses will make a slightly firmer, lower-volume soufflé that will hold up a little longer before serving. (See the photograph on page 80.)

4　eggs
2　cups shredded cheese (such
　　as aged goat cheese,
　　Havarti, or Montasio)
2　tsp. snipped fresh thyme or
　　½ tsp. dried thyme,
　　crushed

◆◆◆

¼　cup butter or margarine
¼　cup all-purpose flour
⅛　tsp. ground red pepper
1　cup milk
1　recipe Pear and Shallot
　　Condiment (see page 55)
　　(optional)

1 Separate eggs; cover both bowls with plastic wrap. Set aside at room temperature for 30 minutes. Toss shredded cheese with thyme; cover and set aside.

2 In medium saucepan melt butter; stir in flour and pepper. Add milk. Cook and stir over medium heat just until thickened and bubbly. Remove from heat.

3 Add cheese mixture, a little at a time, stirring just until melted. In a bowl beat egg yolks with a fork until smooth. Gradually stir cheese sauce into yolks. Set aside to cool (about 5 minutes).

4 In a large mixing bowl beat egg whites until stiff peaks form (tips stand straight). Gently fold about half of the beaten egg whites into the cheese mixture to lighten it, then gently fold that mixture into remaining egg whites in the large bowl.

5 Pour into an ungreased 1½-quart soufflé dish. Bake in a 350° oven 40 minutes or until a knife inserted near center comes out clean. Serve immediately. Pass Pear and Shallot Condiment, if desired. Makes 6 servings.

Nutrition facts per serving: 306 cal., 24 g total fat (14 g sat. fat), 205 mg chol., 374 mg sodium, 7 g carbo., 0 g fiber, 16 g pro. *Daily values:* 28% vit. A, 28% calcium, 7% iron.

30 MIN. LOW FAT

PEAR AND SHALLOT CONDIMENT

Start to finish: 15 min.

This mild, fruity compote pairs perfectly with the Choose-a-Cheese Soufflé.

1 Tbsp. margarine or butter
2 medium firm, ripe pears, cored and thinly sliced
2 large shallots, very thinly sliced (¼ cup)
1 Tbsp. cider vinegar
½ tsp. honey

1 In a medium skillet heat the margarine or butter over medium heat. Cook pears and shallots, uncovered, 4 to 5 minutes or until shallots are tender, stirring often. Add vinegar, honey, and dash *salt;* cook and stir 2 minutes more. Serve as a condiment to soufflés. Makes 6 servings.

Nutrition facts per serving: 56 cal., 2 g total fat (0 g sat. fat), 0 mg chol., 46 mg sodium, 10 g carbo., 2 g fiber, 0 g pro. *Daily values:* 10% vit. A, 4% vit. C, 1% iron.

EIGHT O'CLOCK MACARONI AND CHEESE

Prep: 25 min. ◆ Cook: 25 min. ◆ Stand: 10 min.

The quintessential comfort favorite gets upgraded for dinner at eight.

6 oz. dried tomato penne, rigatoni, and/or other short tubular pasta (1½ to 2 cups)
1 Tbsp. margarine or butter
2 cloves garlic, minced
2 Tbsp. all-purpose flour
2 cups milk
2 cups shredded Port Salut or other semisoft cheese (8 oz.)
1 cup shredded American cheese (about 4 oz.)
2 Tbsp. snipped fresh oregano or 1 tsp. dried oregano, crushed
1 cup soft light rye or wheat bread crumbs

◆◆◆

2 Tbsp. chopped pistachio nuts (optional)
¼ cup crumbled or grated Shropshire, Stilton, and/or Parmesan cheese (optional)
Green onion tops (optional)

1 Cook pasta according to package directions; drain.

2 Meanwhile, in a large saucepan heat margarine or butter over medium heat. Add garlic; cook and stir for 30 seconds. Stir in flour. Add milk all at once. Cook and stir until mixture is thickened and bubbly; reduce

heat. Add shredded cheeses. Stir until melted. Remove from heat. Stir in cooked pasta and oregano. Spoon mixture into an ungreased 1½-quart casserole. Sprinkle bread crumbs evenly over top.

3 Bake, uncovered, in a 350° oven for 20 minutes. Sprinkle with pistachios and crumbled cheese, if desired. Bake about 5 minutes more or until bubbly. Let stand 10 minutes before serving. Garnish individual servings with green onion tops, if desired. Makes 6 servings.

Nutrition facts per serving: 395 cal., 21 g total fat (11 g sat. fat), 71 mg chol., 574 mg sodium, 31 g carbo., 1 g fiber, 20 g pro. *Daily values:* 29% vit. A, 1% vit. C, 39% calcium, 11% iron.

MORE UP-AND-COMING CHEESES

The cheeses listed here are worth seeking out for their distinct flavors yet comfortingly familiar textures. Use them in your favorite cheese recipes or serve them on their own.

1. Shropshire (SHROP-sher) This English cheese looks like a cross between cheddar and blue cheese but has a softer texture and stronger flavor than most blue cheeses.

2. Teleme (TEH-luh-may) A mild cheese that resembles a large, square Brie but tastes like sweet butter.

3. Shaped Goat Cheeses Fresh goat cheeses that are shaped and rolled in spices.

4. Raclette (rah-KLET) A French cheese with the texture of Gruyère, the appearance of Swiss, and a flavor that's a combination of the two.

5. Aged Goat Cheese Firm cheese from New York that boasts a mellow flavor comparable to Romano cheese.

6. Queso Añejo (KAY-so on-YAY-ho) Aged, white, Mexican-style cheese from Texas with a mild flavor.

7. Buffalo Mozzarella Made with buffalo milk, this fresh mozzarella is slightly sweeter than its cow's-milk cousin.

8. Oka This cheese from Canada was developed by Trappist monks, and is similar in flavor to a creamy Havarti but with a smoother texture.

PISTACHIO PASTA

Start to finish: 20 min.

12 oz. wide egg noodles
2 cups small broccoli florets

♦♦♦

1¼ cups shelled pistachio nuts
1 12-oz. can (1½ cups) evaporated milk
½ cup cubed provolone cheese
½ tsp. bottled minced roasted garlic
1 tsp. finely chopped, seeded jalapeño pepper (see recipe note, page 51)

♦♦♦

½ cup shredded carrot
1 tsp. snipped fresh thyme or ¼ tsp. dried thyme, crushed
1 tsp. snipped fresh basil or ¼ tsp. dried basil, crushed
½ tsp. finely shredded lemon peel
Cracked black pepper

1 Cook noodles according to package directions adding ¼ teaspoon *salt* to the boiling water. Add broccoli to noodles the last 2 minutes of cooking time; drain and return to saucepan.

2 In a blender or food processor bowl combine 1 cup of the nuts, milk, cheese, garlic, jalapeño pepper, and ¼ teaspoon *salt*. Cover; blend or process until smooth. Add blended mixture to noodle mixture in saucepan; add carrot, thyme, basil, and lemon peel. Heat through. Transfer to a serving dish. Sprinkle with remaining nuts and black pepper. Makes 6 main-dish servings.

Nutrition facts per serving: 489 cal., 24 g total fat (7 g sat. fat), 74 mg chol., 355 mg sodium, 53 g carbo., 6 g fiber, 19 g pro. *Daily values:* 37% vit. A, 36% vit. C, 24% calcium, 24% iron.

PORK AND MANGO PICADILLO

Start to finish: 20 min.

This South American-inspired classic is a tantalizing blend of sweet and spicy.

1 lb. lean ground pork
⅓ cup thinly sliced green onions
2 cloves garlic, minced
1 tsp. ground cinnamon
1 tsp. ground coriander
1 tsp. ground cumin
1 tsp. dried oregano, crushed
1 tsp. dried thyme, crushed
1 cup thick-and-chunky salsa
1 mango, peeled, pitted, and cubed

♦♦♦

Hot cooked white or yellow rice (optional)
2 Tbsp. smoked almonds or whole almonds, chopped
2 Tbsp. snipped fresh cilantro

1 In a large skillet cook the ground pork until no longer pink. Drain off fat. Stir in green onions, garlic, cinnamon, coriander, cumin, oregano, and thyme. Cook and stir for 2 minutes more. Gently stir in salsa and mango. Cook, covered, 1 to 2 minutes or until heated through.

2 To serve, spoon mixture over hot cooked rice, if desired. Sprinkle with chopped almonds and cilantro. Makes 4 servings.

Nutrition facts per serving: 223 cal., 12 g total fat (4 g sat. fat), 53 mg chol., 268 mg sodium, 16 g carbo., 2 g fiber, 16 g pro. *Daily values:* 30% vit. A, 58% vit. C, 5% calcium, 20% iron.

THREE-GRAIN RISOTTO
Prep: 30 min. ◆ Cook: 32 min.

If Caciotta cheese with sage is not available, use plain Caciotta or other semisoft cheese and add ½ teaspoon of dried, crushed sage leaves.

2 **medium fennel bulbs with tops**

◆◆◆

1 **Tbsp. olive oil**
1 **small onion, finely chopped**
3 **cloves garlic, minced**
½ **tsp. ground white pepper**
½ **cup Arborio or short grain rice**
½ **cup quick-cooking barley**
¼ **cup quinoa (well rinsed) or quick-cooking brown rice**

◆◆◆

1 **14½-oz. can reduced-sodium chicken broth**
¼ **cup dry white wine or water**
1 **Tbsp. snipped fresh rosemary or 1 tsp. dried rosemary, crushed**
1 **tsp. snipped fresh marjoram or ½ tsp. dried marjoram, crushed**

◆◆◆

1 **cup shredded Caciotta with sage, provolone, and/or mozzarella cheese**
½ **cup half-and-half or light cream**
Fresh rosemary sprigs (optional)

1 Remove any tough or brown outer layers of fennel bulb. Rinse whole fennel with cold water; gently shake dry. Remove and discard the top 2 inches of fennel stalks, reserving green fronds. Snip fronds; set aside. Remove and finely chop remaining fennel stalks. Cut 1 bulb into six ¼-inch-thick slices; set aside. Pull apart leaf and stalk sections of remaining bulb. Chop and set aside (should have about 1 cup).

2 In a 1-quart saucepan cook fennel bulb slices, covered, in a small amount of lightly salted water for 5 minutes or just until tender. Drain; set aside. In a large saucepan heat oil. Add chopped fennel, onion, garlic, and pepper. Cook over medium heat for 4 to 5 minutes or until tender, stirring often. Add grains; cook and stir for 3 minutes more.

3 Stir in 1 cup *water,* the chicken broth, white wine, rosemary, and marjoram. Return to boiling; reduce heat. Simmer, covered, 20 minutes or until grains are tender, stirring often.

4 Remove grain mixture from heat. Stir in cheese and half-and-half or light cream until cheese is melted. Sprinkle with fennel leaves. Garnish each serving with reserved cooked fennel slice and fresh rosemary sprigs, if desired. Makes 6 main-dish servings.

Nutrition facts per serving: 283 cal., 11 g total fat (5 g sat. fat), 21 mg chol., 386 mg sodium, 35 g carbo., 9 g fiber, 10 g pro. *Daily values:* 7% vit. A, 7% vit. C, 16% calcium, 12% iron.

STORING CHEESE

Airtight packaging is the key to proper cheese storage. If the cheese has a rind, leave it on to keep the cheese fresh. Wrap unused cheese tightly in foil or plastic wrap, then seal it in a plastic bag or a container with a tight-fitting lid. Store cheese in refrigerator.

Most cheese comes stamped with a "sell by" date on the package. In general, the softer the cheese, the shorter the storage life. If there is no date on the container, cheeses such as cottage and ricotta should be stored no longer than 5 days after purchase. Firm and hard cheese have less moisture and can be stored for longer periods. For instance, sharp cheddar may keep for weeks in your refrigerator, if properly wrapped. For longer storage, cheese can be frozen, but semisoft and hard cheese will be more crumbly and soft cheeses may separate slightly. Because of these texture changes, it's best to use thawed cheeses for casseroles and sauces.

As cheese ages, it naturally develops more flavor and may develop surface mold. Most surface mold looks unappealing but is harmless. For firm cheese, cut away at least 1 inch around the moldy area and use the remaining cheese. Discard soft cheeses, such as cottage cheese, ricotta, and cream cheese, that have mold.

MUSHROOM AND ASPARAGUS STRATA

Prep: 25 min. ◆ Chill: 2 to 24 hours
Bake: 45 min. ◆ Stand: 10 min.

A layered baked strata for brunch celebrates the rich warmth of spring promised by the month of March. This recipe works great as an overnight make-ahead, too.

1 lb. thin asparagus spears

◆◆◆

1 Tbsp. olive oil
4 cups sliced fresh variety mushrooms, such as button, portobello, and/or shiitake (about 12 oz.)
2 cloves garlic, minced
¼ tsp. salt
¼ tsp. freshly ground white or black pepper

◆◆◆

2 cups shredded Swiss and/or Edam cheese (8 oz.)
2 Tbsp. snipped fresh dill weed or 1 tsp. dried dill weed

◆◆◆

6 slices French or Italian bread, cut into 4×1×1-inch sticks

◆◆◆

6 eggs
2¼ cups half-and-half, light cream, or whole milk
¼ cup grated Romano, Parmesan, or other hard grating cheese

◆◆◆

Fresh dill sprigs (optional)

1 Clean asparagus. Snap off woody bases. If spears are thick, cut in half lengthwise. Cut spears into 3-inch pieces. In a large saucepan bring a small amount of water to boiling. Add asparagus. Cook, uncovered, for 1 minute. Drain and rinse immediately with cold water. Set aside to drain on paper towels.

2 In a large skillet heat oil. Add mushrooms, garlic, salt, and pepper. Cook over medium-high heat for 4 to 5 minutes or until nearly all of the liquid has evaporated, stirring often; set aside.

3 In a medium mixing bowl toss together the shredded Swiss and/or Edam cheese and the dill weed.

4 Arrange half the bread pieces in the bottom of a lightly greased 2-quart rectangular baking dish. Top with half of the mushrooms, half of the cheese mixture, and half of the asparagus. Repeat with remaining mushrooms, cheese mixture, and asparagus. Top with remaining bread pieces.

5 In a mixing bowl beat together eggs and half-and-half. Pour mixture over layers in dish. Press lightly with back of a spoon to thoroughly moisten bread. Sprinkle desired cheese over top. Cover and chill for 2 to 24 hours.

6 Bake strata, uncovered, in a 325° oven about 45 minutes or until a knife inserted near the center comes out clean. Remove from oven. Let stand for 10 minutes. To serve, cut into 6 to 8 squares or rectangles. Garnish each serving with dill sprigs, if desired. Makes 6 to 8 main-dish servings.

Nutrition facts per serving: 484 cal., 31 g total fat (16 g sat. fat), 284 mg chol., 521 mg sodium, 27 g carbo., 2 g fiber, 27 g pro. *Daily values:* 35% vit. A, 26% vit. C, 48% calcium, 23% iron.

THE CLEVER COOK

SAVE YOUR LEMONS

If you have a couple of lemons in the refrigerator, save them from spoiling. Simply slice, place in a single layer on a baking sheet, and freeze. Then, transfer the frozen lemon slices to a self-sealing plastic freezer bag and store in the freezer. Use frozen lemon slices to float in drinks or to garnish fish or chicken dinners.

Virginia Henry
Encinitas, California

OLYMPIA CHICKEN

Prep: 15 min. ◆ Roast: 1¼ hours
Stand: 10 min.

You can substitute herbed feta cheese for the plain feta and dried oregano, if desired.
(See the photograph on page 81.)

1 cup crumbled feta cheese (about 4 oz.)
1 Tbsp. dried oregano, crushed
1 lemon
1 Tbsp. olive oil
¼ tsp. coarsely ground black pepper

◆◆◆

1 3- to 4-lb. whole broiler-fryer chicken

1 Combine feta and oregano; set aside. Juice the lemon; measure 2 tablespoons lemon juice.

Olympia Chicken
(see left)

❖❖❖

Roasted new potatoes

❖❖❖

Sautéed greens
sprinkled with Kalamata
olives

❖❖❖

Multigrain dinner rolls
with butter

❖❖❖

Classic New York-Style
Cheesecake
(see page 60)

Quarter squeezed lemon; set aside. Stir together lemon juice, olive oil, and pepper; set aside.

2 Rinse chicken; pat dry. Starting at the edge of the breast, slip your fingers between skin and meat, loosening skin as you work toward the neck end. With your entire hand under the skin, carefully free skin around the thigh and leg area up to, but not around, the tip of the drumsticks. Using your hands or a tablespoon, carefully stuff the cheese mixture under skin, filling the drumstick-thigh area first, working up to the breast. Press gently to distribute cheese mixture throughout the space underneath chicken skin.

3 Place lemon quarters inside chicken cavity. Skewer neck skin to back; tie legs to tail. Twist wings under back. Rub lemon-oil mixture over entire bird. Place chicken, breast side up, on a rack in a shallow pan. Insert a meat

thermometer into the center of an inside thigh muscle. Do not allow thermometer to touch bone.

4 Roast, uncovered, in a 375° oven 1¼ to 1¾ hours or until drumsticks move easily and meat is no longer pink and thermometer registers 180° to 185°. Remove chicken from oven. Loosely cover; let stand 10 minutes. Serve with *lemon wedges,* if desired. Serves 6.

Nutrition facts per serving: 192 cal., 13 g total fat (5 g sat. fat), 61 mg chol., 259 mg sodium, 1 g carbo., 0 g fiber, 16 g pro. *Daily values:* 5% vit. A, 9% calcium, 6% iron.

LOW FAT TURKEY-COUSCOUS PHYLLO TRIANGLES

Prep: 30 min. ◆ Bake: 15 min.

8 oz. ground raw turkey
¼ cup finely chopped onion
1 clove garlic, minced
½ cup chicken broth
¼ tsp. ground cinnamon
¼ tsp. ground cumin
¼ tsp. pepper
   Dash ground nutmeg
⅓ cup quick-cooking couscous
¼ cup chopped almonds

❖❖❖

12 sheets frozen phyllo dough (18×14-inch rectangles), thawed
½ cup butter or margarine, melted

❖❖❖

1 recipe Cucumber Yogurt Sauce (see right)

1 For filling, in a large skillet cook turkey, onion, and garlic until no longer pink; drain. Stir in broth, cinnamon, cumin, pepper, and nutmeg. Bring to boiling. Stir in couscous and almonds.

Remove from heat. Cover and let stand 5 minutes.

2 Meanwhile, lightly brush a sheet of phyllo with some of the melted butter. Place another sheet of phyllo on top; brush with butter. Cover remaining phyllo with plastic wrap to prevent it from becoming dry and brittle.

3 Cut the 2 layered sheets crosswise into six equal strips (each 14 inches long). Spoon a rounded teaspoon of filling about 1 inch from a short side of each strip. For each strip, bring a corner over filling so the short side lines up with a long side of the strip, forming a triangle. Continue folding strip in a triangular shape. Repeat with remaining phyllo, butter, and filling.

4 Place triangles on a baking sheet; brush with butter. Bake in a 375° oven 15 minutes or until golden. Serve with Cucumber Yogurt Sauce. Makes 36.

Cucumber Yogurt Sauce: In a small bowl stir together one 8-ounce carton plain low-fat yogurt and ½ cup chopped, seeded cucumber. Serve immediately.

TO MAKE AHEAD

Prepare triangles, except do not bake. Place in a freezer container for up to 1 month. To serve, place frozen phyllo triangles on a baking sheet. Brush with butter. Bake in a 375° oven about 15 minutes or until golden.

Nutrition facts per serving: 67 cal., 4 g total fat (2 g sat. fat), 10 mg chol., 74 mg sodium, 5 g carbo., 0 g fiber, 2 g pro. *Daily values:* 2% vit. A, 1% calcium, 2% iron.

EASY SAUERBRATEN-STYLE MEAT LOAF

Prep: 20 min. ◆ Bake: 1 hour

Here's a delicious, quick-to-assemble alternative to the German specialty.

2 eggs, beaten
1 cup gingersnap crumbs
½ cup chopped onion
½ cup shredded carrot
3 Tbsp. dried parsley flakes
3 Tbsp. balsamic vinegar
1 tsp. salt
½ tsp. caraway seed, crushed
1 lb. ground beef
1 lb. bulk pork sausage

◆◆◆

1 large tomato, thinly sliced

1 In a large mixing bowl combine eggs, gingersnap crumbs, chopped onion, shredded carrot, parsley flakes, balsamic vinegar, salt, and caraway seed. Add ground beef and pork sausage; mix well.

2 Pat meat mixture into a 9×5×3-inch loaf pan. Arrange tomato slices atop loaf.

3 Bake, uncovered, in a 400° oven for 60 to 70 minutes or until a meat thermometer inserted into center of loaf registers 170°. Cool in pan 10 minutes. Using a large spatula, lift loaf from pan. Slice to serve. Makes 8 servings.

Nutrition facts per serving: 299 cal., 17 g total fat (7 g sat. fat), 111 mg chol., 734 mg sodium, 15 g carbo., 1 g fiber, 18 g pro. *Daily values:* 23% vit. A, 10% vit. C, 2% calcium, 18% iron.

FILLED-AND-GRILLED CHEESE SANDWICH

Prep: 35 min. ◆ Grill: 12 min. (onions); 4 min. (sandwiches)

(See the photograph on page 81.)

8 dried tomato halves (not oil-packed)
1 small sweet onion, cut crosswise into ½-inch-thick slices
2 Tbsp. purchased basil-flavored olive oil or olive oil

◆◆◆

1 4½-inch wheel Brie cheese, chilled (8 oz.)
4 ½-inch-thick slices sourdough bread
2 Tbsp. sliced almonds

1 Place tomatoes in a bowl. Cover with boiling water. Soak for 30 minutes. Brush onion with some of the olive oil. Place onion slices on a grill rack directly over medium-hot coals 12 to 16 minutes or until both sides are slightly charred, turning once; set aside.

2 Using a serrated knife, thinly slice chilled Brie. Drain and rinse tomatoes. Brush 1 side of each bread slice with remaining oil, placing slices oiled sides down on waxed paper. Arrange half of cheese slices on 2 of the bread slices (oiled sides down). Top cheese with onion, tomatoes, and nuts. Top with remaining cheese and bread slices (oiled sides up). Press gently to keep ingredients from spilling out during grilling.

3 Carefully place sandwiches on grill rack directly over medium-hot coals. Grill 2 to 3 minutes

per side or until the cheese is just melted and the bread is toasted.

4 To serve, cut each large sandwich in half. Garnish with *fresh basil sprigs,* if desired. Serve immediately. Makes 2 large sandwiches (4 servings).

Nutrition facts per serving: 364 cal., 26 g total fat (11 g sat. fat), 56 mg chol., 650 mg sodium, 19 g carbo., 1 g fiber, 16 g pro. *Daily values:* 12% vit. A, 5% vit. C, 12% calcium, 7% iron.

CLASSIC NEW YORK-STYLE CHEESECAKE

Prep: 1¼ hours ◆ Bake: 65 min.
Cool: 2 hours ◆ Chill: 4 hours

½ cup butter, softened
¼ cup packed brown sugar
4 eggs
1¼ cups all-purpose flour

◆◆◆

4 8-oz. pkg. cream cheese, softened
1½ cups granulated sugar
¼ cup all-purpose flour
4 tsp. vanilla
2 8-oz. cartons dairy sour cream

1 In a large mixing bowl beat butter on medium to high speed for 30 seconds. Add brown sugar. Beat until fluffy. Add 1 of the eggs; beat well. Slowly beat in the 1¼ cups flour until combined. Divide dough in half. Cover and refrigerate 1 portion.

2 Spread remaining portion onto the bottom of an ungreased 10-inch springform pan with sides removed. Place on baking sheet. Bake in a 350° oven for

10 minutes. Let cool completely. When bottom crust has cooled, attach sides of pan. Press chilled dough onto sides to a height of about 1¾ inches; set aside.

3 Increase oven temperature to 450°. In a large mixing bowl beat cream cheese and 1¼ cups of the granulated sugar until fluffy. Beat in the ¼ cup flour on low speed until smooth. Add the remaining 3 eggs and 3 teaspoons of the vanilla all at once, beating on low speed until just combined. Stir in ½ cup of the sour cream.

4 Pour batter into crust-lined pan. Place on a shallow baking pan in oven. Bake for 10 minutes. Reduce oven temperature to 300°. Bake about 30 minutes more or until center appears nearly set when gently shaken. Remove from oven. Stir together remaining sour cream, remaining granulated sugar, and the remaining vanilla. Using a spoon, spread mixture evenly over top of baked cheesecake. Return to oven and bake for 15 minutes more. Remove from oven. Cool on wire rack for 15 minutes. Loosen crust from sides of pan. Cool for 30 minutes more. Remove sides of pan; cool completely. Cover and chill at least 4 hours or overnight. Let stand at room temperature for 15 minutes before slicing. Makes 16 servings.

TO MAKE AHEAD

Prepare and bake cheesecake. Cool as directed. Place cooled cake in a freezer container or bag and freeze for up to 1 month. To thaw, place in refrigerator for 24 hours, or thaw individual pieces at room temperature for 30 minutes.

Nutrition facts per serving: 455 cal., 33 g total fat (20 g sat. fat), 144 mg chol., 260 mg sodium, 33 g carbo., 0 g fiber, 8 g pro. *Daily values:* 38% vit. A, 7% calcium, 9% iron.

PRIZE TESTED RECIPE WINNER

HAZELNUT PAVLOVA WITH COFFEE CREAM

Prep: 45 min. ◆ Bake: 35 min.
Stand: 1 hour

Dazzling, yes, but practical, too: It can be made a day ahead and it tastes better that way.

> 4 **egg whites (room temperature)**
> 1 **tsp. vanilla**
> ¼ **tsp. cream of tartar**
> 1⅓ **cups sugar**
> 1 **cup ground hazelnuts (filberts)**
>
> ◆◆◆
>
> 2 **oz. semisweet chocolate**
> 3 **Tbsp. margarine or butter, softened**
> 1 **3-oz. pkg. cream cheese, softened**
> ⅓ **cup sugar**
> 1 **cup whipping cream**
> 3 **Tbsp. coffee liqueur**
> ¼ **cup coarsely chopped hazelnuts (filberts)**

1 Draw two 8-inch circles on a foil-lined baking sheet; set aside. In a large mixing bowl combine egg whites, vanilla, and cream of tartar. Beat egg white mixture with an electric mixer on medium speed until soft peaks form (tips curl). Gradually add the 1⅓ cups sugar, a tablespoon at a time, beating about 7 minutes on high speed until stiff peaks form (tips stand straight) and sugar is almost dissolved. Gently fold in the 1 cup nuts.

2 Spread half of egg white mixture over each circle on baking sheet. Bake in a 300° oven for 35 minutes. Turn off oven. Let meringues dry in oven, with door closed, for 1 hour.

3 Just before ready to assemble, in a small saucepan melt chocolate and 1 tablespoon of the margarine or butter over low heat, stirring constantly. Set aside to cool. In a medium mixing bowl beat cream cheese with remaining margarine until smooth; beat in the ⅓ cup sugar. Gradually add whipping cream, beating on low speed until combined, then on medium speed just until soft peaks form. Stir in coffee liqueur.

4 To assemble, carefully peel meringues from foil. Place a meringue on a serving plate. Drizzle with the chocolate. Spread with half of whipped cream mixture. Place second meringue on top. Spread with remaining whipped cream mixture. Sprinkle with the ¼ cup chopped nuts. Cover loosely and chill for 2 to 24 hours. Serves 12 to 16.

Nutrition facts per serving: 355 cal., 23 g total fat (10 g sat. fat), 43 mg chol., 77 mg sodium, 36 g carbo., 2 g fiber, 4 g pro. *Daily values:* 14% vit. A, 4% calcium, 6% iron.

ON, WISCONSIN!

If you think Wisconsin means only Cheddar, think again. Some great European-style cheeses are coming out of the Dairy State. The six cheeses featured here are:

1. **Stravecchio (strah-VECK-ee-oh)** Wisconsin's answer to Parmesan, this version has a pleasant, slightly sweet and nutty flavor.

2. **Wild Morel and Leek Jack** Mellow Jack cheese laced with wild mushrooms and leeks.

3. **Pepato** Softer and milder than Parmesan, with an added bite of whole peppercorns.

4. **Kasseri (kuh-SEHR-ee)** A semifirm Greek-style cheese similar in flavor to a white cheddar.

5. **Gruyère (groo-YEH)** This full-flavored domestic version of the famed fondue cheese is still a little bit milder than its imported cousins.

6. **Brie** Like the imported French Brie cheeses, this creamy cheese grows stronger with age.

SWEET CHEESE BLINTZES

Prep: 40 min. ◆ **Cook: 10 min.**

(See the photograph on page 78.)

1 8-oz. carton mascarpone or cottage cheese
1 Tbsp. honey
1 Tbsp. milk
½ tsp. finely shredded lemon peel or snipped lemon verbena
¼ tsp. anise seed, crushed

◆◆◆

¾ cup all-purpose flour
½ tsp. baking powder
1 egg white
¾ cup milk
1 egg yolk
2 tsp. walnut oil or hazelnut oil
1½ tsp. granulated sugar
½ tsp. vanilla

◆◆◆

Nonstick spray coating

◆◆◆

1 cup seedless green grapes, sliced
Powdered sugar

1 For filling, in a mixing bowl beat together mascarpone cheese, honey, the 1 tablespoon milk, shredded lemon peel or verbena, and anise seed. Cover; set aside.

2 For blintzes, stir together flour and baking powder; set aside. In a small mixing bowl beat egg white with an electric mixer on medium to high speed until soft peaks form. In a large mixing bowl combine the ¾ cup milk, egg yolk, walnut or hazelnut oil, granulated sugar, and vanilla. Beat with electric mixer until well combined. Add flour mixture; beat just until mixture is smooth. Fold in beaten egg white (texture should be that of a milk shake).

3 Spray a nonstick griddle or skillet with nonstick spray coating. Heat over medium heat 1 to 2 minutes. For each blintz, pour about 2 tablespoons batter onto griddle. Quickly spread batter to 4- to 5-inch circle. Cook blintz pancake about 30 seconds or until light brown. Gently turn with a spatula; cook second side for 15 seconds. Invert blintz onto a plate lined with paper towels.

THE CLEVER COOK

PLASTIC LIDS MAKE GREAT CUTTING BOARDS

Recycle the plastic lids from yogurt cartons, margarine tubs, or whipped topping containers, by washing them thoroughly, then using them as I do—miniature cutting boards. They work really great for small cutting jobs such as mincing a tablespoon or two of onion or cutting lemon wedges for iced tea.

M. Ryland Koppenhoefer
Cincinnati, Ohio

Repeat with remaining batter to make 10 to 12 blintzes. (You may cook up to 3 or 4 blintzes at a time in a large skillet.) Place a dry paper towel between each layer of blintzes. Cover; keep warm.

4 To serve, spoon 1 slightly rounded tablespoon of cheese mixture across pancake just below center. Fold bottom of pancake over filling. Fold in sides; roll up. Arrange blintzes, seam-side down, on dessert plates or in a serving bowl. Top with grapes. Sprinkle with powdered sugar. Serve warm or at room temperature. Makes 10 to 12.

Nutrition facts per blintz: 150 cal., 10 g total fat (5 g sat. fat), 43 mg chol., 40 mg sodium, 12 g carbo., 0 g fiber, 6 g pro. *Daily values:* 1% vit. A, 2% vit. C, 3% calcium, 3% iron.

APRIL
Spring Flavors

*S*pring toward the first flavors of the season with asparagus, radishes, tiny new potatoes, rhubarb, strawberries, and even mushrooms. Mushrooms are the unheralded harbingers of spring. Enjoy their earthy goodness in a Mushroom-Crepe Lasagna appetizer or Mushroom Relish. Or experience an exotic taste treat with Mushroom-Coconut Soup. Spring also is the time for Easter brunches. Popover Egg Nests with a tender Asparagus Bouquet and Blushing Pink Compote on the side bring warm, fresh colors to your table.

30-minute recipes indicated in RED.
Low-fat and no-fat recipes indicated
with a ♥.
Photographs indicated in italics.
*Bonus recipe

MUSHROOM-CREPE LASAGNA

Prep: 40 min. ◆ Bake: 20 min.

Layered bliss: For this elegant appetizer, round or square crepes work equally well.

1 7-oz. jar roasted red sweet peppers, rinsed and drained
⅓ cup half-and-half or light cream
1 tsp. balsamic vinegar

◆◆◆

1 8-oz. pkg. cream cheese, softened
3 Tbsp. snipped fresh parsley
1 tsp. bottled minced roasted garlic
3 cups sliced crimini, button, and/or shiitake mushrooms
½ cup chopped onion
2 Tbsp. margarine or butter
4 oz. thinly sliced prosciutto or ham, chopped (about ¾ cup)

◆◆◆

½ of a 4½-oz. pkg. prepared crepes (5 crepes)

1 For sauce, in a blender container or food processor bowl combine roasted peppers, half-and-half, and vinegar. Cover; blend or process until smooth. Pour into a bowl. Cover; set aside.

2 In a second bowl stir together cream cheese, parsley, garlic, and ¼ teaspoon *black pepper;* set aside. In a large skillet cook mushrooms and onion in hot margarine or butter over medium-high heat for 4 to 5 minutes or until mush-

rooms are tender and most liquid evaporates. Remove from heat; stir in prosciutto or ham.

3 Place a crepe in the bottom of a lightly greased 9-inch pie plate. Spread about one-fifth of the cream cheese mixture over crepe; sprinkle with about one-fifth of the mushroom mixture. Add a second crepe, setting it at a slight angle to first crepe so points are staggered (if using square crepes). Add another one-fifth of the cream cheese and the mushroom mixtures as before. Repeat with the remaining crepes, cream cheese, and mushroom mixtures, ending with a mushroom layer. Cover loosely with foil.

4 Bake in a 350° oven about 20 minutes or until heated through. To serve, cut into wedges. Pass pepper sauce. Makes 6 to 8 appetizer servings.

Nutrition facts per serving: 285 cal., 24 g total fat (12 g sat. fat), 65 mg chol., 509 mg sodium, 9 g carbo., 1 g fiber, 10 g pro. *Daily values:* 35% vit. A, 122% vit. C, 5% calcium, 11% iron.

Grilled chicken breasts served with Mushroom Relish
(see page 65)

◆◆◆

Hot cooked rice

◆◆◆

Stir-fried zucchini and yellow summer squash strips

◆◆◆

Sundae Pound Cake
(see page 87)

MUSHROOM AND LEEK TART

Prep: 25 min. ◆ Bake: 32 min.

½ of a 15-oz. pkg. folded refrigerated unbaked piecrust (1 crust)

◆◆◆

3 cups sliced fresh mushrooms
3 medium leeks, thinly sliced (white part only)
1 Tbsp. olive oil
1 8-oz. tub cream cheese with garden vegetables
1 egg
¼ cup milk
½ cup thinly sliced fresh basil

◆◆◆

⅓ cup chopped walnuts, toasted
2 hard-cooked eggs, finely chopped
⅓ cup well-drained and finely chopped roasted red sweet pepper or pimiento

1 Let piecrust stand at room temperature according to package directions. On a well-floured surface, roll the unfolded crust to a 12-inch circle. Loosely wrap pastry around rolling pin. Ease pastry into a 10-inch tart pan. Press edges of piecrust against edges of pan. Trim excess pastry. Line pastry shell with a double thickness of foil; press down firmly but carefully. Bake in a 450° oven for 5 minutes. Remove foil; bake for 7 to 9 minutes more or until pastry is nearly done. Place pastry in pan on a wire rack. Reduce the oven temperature to 325°.

2 Meanwhile, in a large skillet cook mushrooms and leeks in hot oil until tender; set aside. In a large mixing bowl beat cream cheese, egg, and milk with an electric mixer on low speed. Stir mushroom mixture and 1 tablespoon of the basil into cream cheese mixture. Spoon into the baked crust.

3 Bake in a 325° oven for 20 to 25 minutes or until set. Remove from oven. Arrange the remaining basil, walnuts, hard-cooked eggs, and red pepper atop tart in alternating strips. Cut into wedges; serve warm. Serves 12.

Nutrition facts per serving: 215 cal., 16 g total fat (4 g sat. fat), 75 mg chol., 199 mg sodium, 14 g carbo., 1 g fiber, 4 g pro. *Daily values:* 7% vit. A, 22% vit. C, 4% calcium, 6% iron.

SPICY TERIYAKI MUSHROOMS

Start to finish: 10 min.

2 Tbsp. sugar
2 Tbsp. soy sauce
1 Tbsp. white wine vinegar
1 Tbsp. cooking oil
¼ to ½ tsp. crushed red pepper
¼ to ½ tsp. ground ginger
⅛ to ¼ tsp. garlic powder
24 small mushrooms, quartered
2 Tbsp. sliced green onion

1 In a saucepan combine first seven ingredients. Add mushrooms and green onion. Cook and stir over medium heat until heated through. Makes 4 appetizer servings.

Nutrition facts per serving: 178 cal., 4 g total fat (1 g sat. fat), 0 mg chol., 518 mg sodium, 33 g carbo., 1 g fiber, 4 g pro. *Daily values:* 1% vit. A, 4% vit. C, 1% calcium, 14% iron.

MUSHROOM-GARLIC SAUCE

Start to finish: 25 min.

Packed with flavor, this versatile sauce can be served over polenta, potatoes, chicken, or steak.

2 8-oz. pkg. fresh mushrooms, quartered
¼ cup finely chopped shallots
1 Tbsp. bottled minced garlic
½ tsp. curry powder
⅛ to ¼ tsp. crushed red pepper
2 Tbsp. olive oil
¾ cup chicken broth
2 tsp. soy sauce
¼ tsp. ground nutmeg
1 Tbsp. cornstarch
¼ cup dry white wine or chicken broth

1 In a large saucepan cook mushrooms, shallots, garlic, curry powder, and crushed red pepper in hot oil until the mushrooms are tender. Add ¾ cup chicken broth, soy sauce, and nutmeg; bring to boiling. Combine cornstarch and wine or broth; add to saucepan. Cook and stir until sauce is thickened and bubbly; cook and stir 2 minutes more. Makes 2½ cups sauce.

Nutrition facts per serving: 53 cal., 3 g total fat (0 g sat. fat), 0 mg chol., 129 mg sodium, 5 g carbo., 1 g fiber, 2 g pro. *Daily values:* 5% vit. A, 4% vit. C, 6% iron.

MUSHROOM RELISH

Prep: 30 min. ◆ Chill: 4 to 24 hours

1 cup chopped fresh button mushrooms
1 cup chopped fresh shiitake mushrooms
1 cup chopped fresh brown mushrooms

THE FACTS ON RICE VINEGAR

Rice vinegar, made from rice wine or sake, has a subtle tang and slightly sweet taste. Chinese rice vinegars are stronger than Japanese vinegars, although both are slightly milder than most vinegars. Chinese rice vinegar comes in three types: white (clear or pale yellow), used mainly in hot-and-sour or sweet-and-sour dishes; red, a typical accompaniment for boiled or steamed shellfish; and black, used mainly as a condiment.

½ cup chopped yellow and/or red sweet pepper
4 cloves garlic, minced
1 Tbsp. cooking oil
2 medium tomatoes, seeded and coarsely chopped
¼ cup sliced green onions
¼ cup rice vinegar
½ tsp. cumin seed, crushed
¼ tsp. chili oil

1 In a large skillet cook mushrooms, pepper, and garlic in hot oil for 8 to 10 minutes or until most of the liquid has evaporated. Transfer to a bowl; stir in tomatoes, onions, vinegar, cumin, and chili oil. Cover; chill for 4 to 24 hours. Let stand at room temperature for 30 minutes before serving. Using a slotted spoon, serve relish atop cooked chicken, turkey, or pork. Makes about 2½ cups.

Nutrition facts per serving: 28 cal., 2 g total fat (0 g sat. fat), 0 mg chol., 3 mg sodium, 3 g carbo., 1 g fiber, 1 g pro. *Daily values:* 2% vit. A, 25% vit. C, 40% iron.

MARVELOUS MUSHROOMS

There are many types of mushrooms available these days. Try experimenting with different varieties. It's easy to find the common white or brown mushrooms, often referred to as button mushrooms. They are very mild in flavor.

For a richer, earthier flavor try morels, shiitakes, or portobellos. The best way to clean mushrooms is to brush them off with a clean, soft vegetable brush and wipe them with a clean, damp cloth. Do not soak mushrooms because they're like a sponge and the water will ruin their firm texture.

INDIVIDUAL MUSHROOM QUICHES

Prep: 15 min. ◆ Bake: 20 min.

Nonstick spray coating

◆◆◆

3 cups chopped assorted fresh mushrooms such as oyster, crimini, and portobello
2 cloves garlic, minced
2 Tbsp. margarine or butter
½ cup shredded Swiss cheese (2 oz.)

◆◆◆

3 eggs, beaten
1½ cups half-and-half, light cream, or milk
2 tsp. snipped fresh thyme or ½ tsp. dried thyme, crushed
¼ tsp. salt
¼ tsp. pepper
1 medium tomato, chopped

1 Spray six 6-ounce custard cups or individual soufflé dishes with nonstick coating; set aside.

2 In a large skillet cook the mushrooms and garlic in hot margarine or butter over medium heat for 4 to 5 minutes until tender and most of the liquid evaporates. Divide the mushroom mixture evenly among custard cups. Sprinkle with cheese.

3 In a medium mixing bowl stir together the eggs, half-and-half, thyme, salt, and pepper. Pour over cheese and mushrooms in custard cups.

4 Bake in a 350° oven for 20 to 25 minutes or until slightly puffed and a knife inserted near center comes out clean. Sprinkle with chopped tomato. Let stand 10 minutes before serving. Makes 6 servings.

Nutrition facts per serving: 207 cal., 16 g total fat (8 g sat. fat), 137 mg chol., 217 mg sodium, 7 g carbo., 1 g fiber, 9 g pro. *Daily values:* 21% vit. A, 11% vit. C, 14% calcium, 10% iron.

MUSHROOM-COCONUT SOUP

Start to finish: 30 min.

Coconut, curry, and lemon combine with a mélange of mushrooms in this simple soup to give it a taste of Thai.

3 cups coarsely chopped mushrooms such as button, shiitake, straw, and baby portobello
1 Tbsp. cooking oil
½ tsp. red curry paste
3 cups coarsely chopped cabbage
1 14½-oz. can vegetable or chicken broth
1 13½-oz. can reduced-fat coconut milk
1 Tbsp. white wine Worcestershire sauce
1 tsp. finely shredded lemon peel
2 green onions, finely chopped

1 In a large saucepan cook mushrooms in hot oil for 4 to 5 minutes or until tender. Stir in red curry paste and cabbage; cook and stir for 1 minute more. Carefully add broth, coconut milk, and Worcestershire sauce. Bring to boiling; reduce heat. Simmer, covered, for 10 minutes. Stir in lemon peel and green onions. Makes 4 side-dish servings.

Nutrition facts per serving: 126 cal., 10 g total fat (4 g sat. fat), 0 mg chol., 518 mg sodium, 10 g carbo., 2 g fiber, 2 g pro. *Daily values:* 3% vit. A, 60% vit. C, 3% calcium, 14% iron.

ITALIAN MUFFINS

Prep: 20 min. ◆ Bake: 20 min.

¼ cup oil-packed dried tomatoes
Olive oil

◆◆◆

1 cup fresh mushrooms, coarsely chopped

◆◆◆

1¾ cups all-purpose flour
½ cup finely shredded Asiago or Romano cheese (2 oz.)
2 Tbsp. sugar
2 tsp. baking powder
½ tsp. garlic salt
¼ tsp. baking soda

◆◆◆

1 egg, beaten
¾ cup milk

❖❖❖

2 to 3 Tbsp. finely shredded
  Asiago or Romano cheese
  (optional)

1 Grease twelve 2½-inch muffin cups or spray with *nonstick spray coating*. Drain tomatoes, reserving oil. Chop tomatoes; set aside. Add enough additional olive oil to reserved oil to equal ⅓ cup.

2 In a medium skillet cook mushrooms in 1 tablespoon of the oil until tender and most of the liquid has evaporated. Remove from heat; cool slightly.

3 In a medium mixing bowl stir together flour, the ½ cup Asiago or Romano cheese, the sugar, baking powder, garlic salt, baking soda, and ⅛ teaspoon *pepper*. Make a well in the center of the dry mixture; set aside.

4 In another bowl combine egg, milk, and remaining oil. Stir in mushrooms and chopped tomatoes. Add egg mixture to dry mixture. Stir just until moistened.

5 Spoon batter into prepared muffin cups, filling each two-thirds full. If desired, sprinkle with additional cheese. Bake in a 400° oven about 20 minutes or until golden. Cool in muffin cups on a wire rack for 5 minutes. Remove from muffin cups; serve warm. Makes 12 muffins.

Nutrition facts per serving: 165 cal., 9 g total fat (2 g sat. fat), 24 mg chol., 244 mg sodium, 17 g carbo., 1 g fiber, 4 g pro. *Daily values:* 2% vit. A, 4% vit. C, 9% calcium, 7% iron.

GARDENER'S TREAT BREAD

Prep: 40 min. ◆ Rise: 1¾ hours
Bake: 15 min.

Fresh chives, green onions, leeks, and parsley from your garden (or the grocer's shelves) add a touch of spring to the tops of these loaves.
(See the photograph on page 82.)

4 to 4½ cups all-purpose flour
1 pkg. active dry yeast

❖❖❖

1 cup milk
3 Tbsp. sugar
2 Tbsp. margarine or butter
½ tsp. salt
2 eggs
1 cup shredded Asiago or
  Parmesan cheese (4 oz.)
2 Tbsp. snipped fresh chives

❖❖❖

1 beaten egg white
1 Tbsp. water
1 whole green onion
1 leek, thinly sliced (white part
  only)
  Fresh chives
  Italian parsley sprigs
1 Tbsp. olive oil

1 In a large mixing bowl stir together 2 cups of the flour and the yeast; set aside.

2 In a medium saucepan heat and stir milk, sugar, margarine or butter, and salt just until warm (120° to 130°) and margarine almost melts. Add milk mixture to dry mixture along with the 2 whole eggs. Beat with an electric mixer on low to medium speed for 30 seconds, scraping sides of bowl constantly. Beat on high speed for 3 minutes. Using a wooden spoon, stir in cheese, snipped chives, and as much of the remaining flour as you can.

3 Turn dough out onto a lightly floured surface. Knead in enough remaining flour to make a moderately stiff dough that is smooth and elastic (6 to 8 minutes total). Shape dough into a ball. Place in a lightly greased bowl; turn once. Cover and let rise in a warm place until dough is double in size (about 1 hour).

4 Punch dough down. Turn dough out onto a lightly floured surface. Divide dough into 4 portions. Cover; let rest 10 minutes. Lightly grease 2 baking sheets.

5 Shape dough by gently pulling each portion of dough into a 10×4½-inch rectangle. Place on prepared baking sheets. In a small bowl stir together egg white and water. Brush loaves with egg white mixture. Gently press green onion onto one loaf. Arrange leek slices on a second loaf. Place several whole chives on a third loaf. Top remaining loaf with parsley sprigs. Gently brush onion, chives, leeks, and parsley with olive oil to prevent them from drying out. Cover and let rise in a warm place until dough is nearly double in size (about 45 minutes).

6 Bake in a 375° oven for 15 to 18 minutes or until golden. (If necessary, cover loosely with foil the last 5 minutes of baking to prevent overbrowning.) Remove loaves from baking sheets; cool on wire racks. Makes 4 loaves (16 servings).

Nutrition facts per serving: 187 cal., 6 g total fat (3 g sat. fat), 39 mg chol., 177 mg sodium, 26 g carbo., 1 g fiber, 6 g pro. *Daily values:* 4% vit. A, 1% vit. C, 7% calcium, 10% iron.

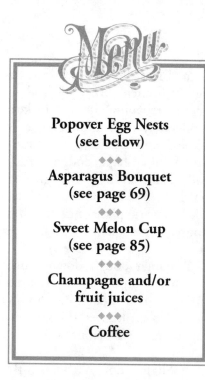

Popover Egg Nests
(see below)

◆ ◆ ◆

Asparagus Bouquet
(see page 69)

◆ ◆ ◆

Sweet Melon Cup
(see page 85)

◆ ◆ ◆

Champagne and/or
fruit juices

◆ ◆ ◆

Coffee

POPOVER EGG NESTS

Prep: 40 min. ◆ Bake (popovers):
40 min. ◆ Poach (eggs):
3 to 5 min.

These poached eggs tucked into popovers
and accented with Lime
Hollandaise Sauce add a magical touch
to a special Sunday brunch.
(See the photograph on page 82.)

1 recipe Spring Popovers (see
    right)
6 eggs
1 recipe Lime Hollandaise
    Sauce (see page 69)

◆ ◆ ◆

6 thin slices prosciutto,
    Canadian-style bacon, or
    cooked ham (about 4 oz.)
    Finely shredded lime peel
    (optional)
    Lime wedges (optional)

1 Prepare the Spring Popovers. Meanwhile, as the popovers
bake, poach the eggs and prepare
the Lime Hollandaise Sauce.

2 For the poached eggs, lightly grease a large skillet. Add water
to the skillet until it is half-full.
Bring water to boiling. Reduce
heat to simmering (bubbles
should begin to break the surface
of the water).

3 Break 1 of the eggs into a
measuring cup. Carefully slide the
egg into simmering water, holding the lip of the cup as close to
the water as possible. Repeat with
the remaining eggs, allowing each
egg to have an equal amount of
space in the pan's water.

4 Simmer the eggs, uncovered, for 3 to 5 minutes or until
the whites are completely set and
the yolks begin to thicken but are
not hard. Using a slotted spoon,
carefully remove the poached eggs
and place the eggs in a large shallow pan of hot water to keep them
warm while preparing the Lime
Hollandaise Sauce.

5 For each serving, split a
popover in half and place on a
plate. Top each popover with a
thin slice of prosciutto. Top the
prosciutto with a poached egg,
then spoon about 2 tablespoons
of the Lime Hollandaise Sauce
over egg. Garnish with lime peel
and serve with lime wedges,
if desired. Serve immediately.
Makes 6 main-dish servings.

Nutrition facts per serving: 452 cal., 35 g
total fat (14 g sat. fat), 434 mg chol., 730
mg sodium, 18 g carbo., 0 g fiber, 18 g pro.
Daily values: 45% vit. A, 1% vit. C, 8%
calcium, 14% iron.

SPRING POPOVERS
Prep: 10 min. ◆ Bake: 40 min.

Perfect as nests for poached eggs,
these crispy shells are equally delicious
slathered with butter or jam.

Shortening or nonstick spray
    coating

◆ ◆ ◆

2 eggs, beaten
1 cup milk
1 Tbsp. cooking oil
1 cup all-purpose flour
¼ tsp. salt

1 Using ½ teaspoon shortening for each cup, grease the
bottoms and sides of six 6-ounce
custard cups or cups of a popover
pan. Or, spray cups with nonstick
coating. If using, place the custard
cups on a 15×10×1-inch baking
pan; set aside.

2 In a medium mixing bowl,
use a wire whisk or a rotary beater to beat the eggs, milk, and oil
until combined. Add flour and
salt; beat until smooth.

3 Fill the prepared cups half-
full with batter. Bake in a 400°
oven about 40 minutes or until
popovers are very firm and golden
brown. Immediately after removing pan from oven, prick each
popover with a fork to let steam
escape. Turn off the oven. For
crisper popovers, return the
popovers to the still-warm oven
for 5 to 10 minutes or until
desired crispness is reached.
Remove popovers from cups.
Serve immediately as Popover Egg
Nests. Makes 6 popovers.

Nutrition facts per popover: 154 cal., 7 g
total fat (2 g sat. fat), 74 mg chol., 130 mg
sodium, 17 g carbo., 1 g fiber, 5 g pro.
Daily values: 5% vit. A, 5% calcium,
7% iron.

LIME
HOLLANDAISE SAUCE

Start to finish: 15 min.

It's best to use a double boiler when making this sauce to prevent overheating and curdling.

½ **cup butter**

♦♦♦

3 **egg yolks, beaten**
1 **Tbsp. water**
1 **Tbsp. lime juice**
⅛ **tsp. salt**

1 Cut the butter into thirds and bring it to room temperature.

2 In the top of a double boiler, combine egg yolks, water, lime juice, and salt. Add a piece of the butter. Place over boiling water (upper pan should not touch water). Cook, stirring rapidly with a whisk, until butter melts and sauce begins to thicken. Add the remaining butter, a piece at a time, stirring constantly until melted. Continue to cook and stir about 2 minutes more or until sauce thickens. Immediately remove from heat. If sauce is too thick or curdles, immediately whisk in 1 to 2 tablespoons hot water. Serve with Popover Egg Nests.* Makes ¾ cup sauce.

*Note: You also can serve this smooth, lime-accented sauce over steamed fresh spring vegetables.

Nutrition facts per serving (2 tablespoons): 164 cal., 18 g total fat (10 g sat. fat), 147 mg chol., 203 mg sodium, 0 g carbo., 0 g fiber, 2 g pro.
Daily values: 30% vit. A, 1% vit. C, 1% calcium, 2% iron.

RANCH EGGS

Prep: 10 min. ♦ Bake: 20 min.

Your taste buds will get a wake-up call with this Mexican-style casserole. If hot-and-spicy doesn't suit you in the morning, serve this meatless main dish for supper.

Nonstick spray coating
1 **large onion, halved and thinly sliced**

♦♦♦

1 **14½-oz. can chunky chili-style tomato sauce**
1 **jalapeño pepper, seeded and chopped***
3 **Tbsp. snipped fresh cilantro**
6 **eggs**
¼ **tsp. salt**
⅛ **tsp. black pepper**

♦♦♦

1 **cup shredded Monterey Jack or cheddar cheese (4 oz.)**
Flour tortillas or toast

1 Spray a 2-quart rectangular baking dish with nonstick spray coating. Separate onion into half-rings and place in dish.

2 In a small mixing bowl stir together the tomato sauce, jalapeño pepper, and cilantro. Pour sauce mixture over onions in dish. Break eggs, one at a time, atop tomato mixture. Sprinkle eggs with salt and black pepper.

3 Bake, uncovered, in a 400° oven for 20 to 25 minutes or until eggs are set. Sprinkle with cheese; bake 1 minute more. Serve with warmed flour tortillas or toast. Makes 6 servings.

*Note: Hot peppers contain oils that can burn eyes, lips, and sensitive skin. Wear plastic gloves while preparing peppers and be sure to thoroughly wash your hands afterward.

Nutrition facts per serving: 270 cal., 13 g total fat (6 g sat. fat), 230 mg chol., 736 mg sodium, 26 g carbo., 0 g fiber, 15 g pro.
Daily values: 23% vit. A, 19% vit. C, 19% calcium, 16% iron.

30 MIN.
LOW FAT
ASPARAGUS BOUQUET

Start to finish: 10 min.

1½ **lb. fresh asparagus spears**
2 **tsp. olive oil or melted margarine or butter**
2 **Tbsp. snipped fresh chervil or 2 tsp. snipped fresh tarragon**
Coarse salt or salt

1 Snap off and discard woody bases from asparagus. If desired, use a paring knife to scrape off scales. Combine oil and 1 tablespoon of the chervil or 1 teaspoon of the tarragon. Drizzle over asparagus. Toss gently to coat. In a greased 15×10×1-inch baking pan arrange asparagus in a single layer. Sprinkle lightly with salt.

2 Roast asparagus, uncovered, in a 475° oven for 4 to 6 minutes or until just tender, stirring once. To serve, place asparagus spears upright in a glass jar or flat on a serving platter. Sprinkle with the remaining 1 tablespoon snipped chervil or 1 teaspoon snipped tarragon. Garnish with *fresh chervil sprigs,* if desired. Makes 6 side-dish servings.

Nutrition facts per serving: 33 cal., 2 g total fat (0 g sat. fat), 0 mg chol., 48 mg sodium, 4 g carbo., 2 g fiber, 2 g pro.
Daily values: 6% vit. A, 35% vit. C, 1% calcium, 3% iron.

WILD RICE AND BULGUR SALAD

Prep: 10 min. ♦ Cook: 25 min.
Chill: 4 to 24 hours

1 6-oz. pkg. long grain and
   wild rice mix

◆◆◆

1½ cups water
½ cup bulgur

◆◆◆

1½ cups cherry tomatoes, halved
½ of a small jicama, peeled and
   cut into bite-size pieces
1 cup frozen sugar snap peas,
   thawed and halved
   diagonally
1 2¼-oz. can sliced pitted ripe
   olives, drained, or ½ cup
   sliced pitted kalamata
   olives
¼ cup finely chopped onion
2 Tbsp. snipped fresh basil
½ cup Italian salad dressing
¼ cup shelled sunflower seeds

1 Prepare rice mix according to package directions; omit seasoning packet. Cool rice.

2 Meanwhile, in a small saucepan bring water to boiling; add bulgur. Return to boiling; reduce heat. Simmer, covered, for 10 minutes. Drain well; cool.

3 In a large bowl combine cooked rice, cooked bulgur, tomatoes, jicama, peas, olives, onion, and basil. Add salad dressing; toss gently to coat. Cover and chill for 4 to 24 hours. Just before serving, sprinkle with sunflower seeds. Makes 8 side-dish servings.

Nutrition facts per serving: 241 cal., 12 g total fat (1 g sat. fat), 0 mg chol., 175 mg sodium, 31 g carbo., 4 g fiber, 6 g pro.
Daily values: 3% vit. A, 38% vit. C, 2% calcium, 13% iron.

PEAS-AT-EASE SALAD

Prep: 30 min. ♦ Chill: 30 to 60 min.

Don't fret over the pea pods that pop open during cooking. They add fun to the presentation of this spring salad.

3 medium carrots

◆◆◆

3 cups fresh sugar snap peas,
   ends trimmed (10 oz.)

◆◆◆

¼ cup thinly sliced shallots or
   green onions
3 Tbsp. snipped fresh cilantro

◆◆◆

3 Tbsp. white wine vinegar
1 Tbsp. olive oil
2 tsp. sugar
¾ tsp. Dijon-style mustard
½ tsp. finely shredded lemon
   peel
   Dash salt
   Fresh chives

1 Peel carrots. Using a vegetable peeler, carefully cut carrots into long, wide ribbons (see illustration, below). Place in cold water to crisp; set aside.

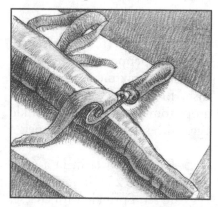

2 Cook peas, covered, in a small amount of boiling salted water for 2 to 4 minutes or until crisp-tender. Drain. Rinse with cold water; drain again.

3 Drain carrot ribbons. In a large bowl combine carrot ribbons, peas, shallots, and cilantro; set aside.

4 For dressing, in a screw-top jar combine white wine vinegar, olive oil, sugar, Dijon-style mustard, lemon peel, and salt. Cover and shake well. Pour dressing over peas and carrots mixture; toss lightly to coat. Cover and chill for 30 to 60 minutes before serving. Garnish with fresh chives. Serve with a slotted spoon. Makes 6 side-dish servings.

Nutrition facts per serving: 65 cal., 2 g total fat (0 g sat. fat), 0 mg chol., 64 mg sodium, 10 g carbo., 2 g fiber, 2 g pro.
Daily values: 94% vit. A, 38% vit. C, 2% calcium, 8% iron.

CURLY CUKES AND RADISH SALAD

Start to finish: 20 min.

*This simple salad becomes
a sensation when you include
watermelon radishes.*

10 radishes

◆◆◆

2 medium seedless cucumbers

◆◆◆

1 fresh jalapeño pepper, seeded
   and sliced into rings*
2 Tbsp. snipped fresh sorrel or
   snipped fresh basil
½ tsp. sugar
¼ tsp. salt
1 Tbsp. olive oil
1 Tbsp. white wine vinegar

1 Set aside 1 whole radish for garnish. Thinly slice 5 of the remaining radishes. Cut rest of radishes into halves or quarters.

2 Use a vegetable peeler to cut thin lengthwise ribbons from cucumbers, discarding first slice (see photo, page 70). (You should have about 2 cups.)

3 In a bowl combine radish slices, halves, and quarters; cucumber ribbons; jalapeño pepper; sorrel or basil; sugar; and salt. Drizzle with olive oil and white wine vinegar. Toss gently to coat. Garnish with reserved whole radish. Makes 6 side-dish servings.

*Note: Hot peppers contain oils that can burn eyes, lips, and sensitive skin. Wear plastic gloves while preparing peppers and be sure to thoroughly wash your hands afterward.

Nutrition facts per serving: 36 cal., 2 g total fat (0 g sat. fat), 0 mg chol., 93 mg sodium, 4 g carbo., 1 g fiber, 1 g pro.
Daily values: 2% vit. A, 18% vit. C, 1% calcium, 2% iron.

PARISIAN CHICKEN

Prep: 20 min. ◆ Marinate: 6 to 8
hours ◆ Broil: 12 min.

Here's a light main-dish salad to see you through the hottest months.

4 **skinless, boneless chicken breast halves (1 lb.)**
2 **tsp. finely shredded orange peel**
⅓ **cup orange juice**
4 **cloves garlic, minced**
2 **Tbsp. honey**

1½ **tsp. dried thyme, crushed**
◆◆◆
¼ **tsp. salt**
⅛ **tsp. black pepper**
◆◆◆
¼ **cup olive oil**
2 **Tbsp. white wine vinegar**
2 **Tbsp. orange juice**
2 **cloves garlic, minced**
1½ **tsp. finely chopped shallots**
¼ **tsp. salt**
⅛ **tsp. black pepper**
◆◆◆
4 **cups torn baby greens**
1 **medium yellow sweet pepper, seeded and thinly sliced**
2 **medium oranges, peeled and sectioned**

1 Rinse chicken; pat dry with paper towels. Place chicken in a plastic bag set in a shallow dish. For marinade, combine orange peel, the ⅓ cup orange juice, the 4 cloves minced garlic, honey, and thyme. Pour over chicken. Close bag. Marinate chicken in refrigerator 6 to 8 hours, turning the bag occasionally.

2 Drain chicken; discard marinade. Place chicken on unheated rack of a broiler pan. Season with the ¼ teaspoon salt and ⅛ teaspoon black pepper. Broil 4 to 5 inches from heat for 12 to 15 minutes or until chicken is no longer pink, turning it once halfway through.

3 Meanwhile, for dressing, in a screw-top jar combine olive oil, vinegar, the 2 tablespoons orange juice, the 2 cloves of garlic, shallots, the ¼ teaspoon salt, and ⅛ teaspoon pepper. Cover and shake well.

THE CLEVER COOK

PLANTING A PIZZA GARDEN

A great springtime family project is planting a "pizza garden." Do this by sectioning a round garden plot into wedges and planting tomato plants, sweet pepper plants, yellow onions, oregano, and basil. When the garden is ready to harvest, round up the kids and gather your fresh pizza ingredients. Top your favorite crust with the fresh garden ingredients and other toppings of your choice.

Doris R. Craigo
Austin, Texas

4 To serve, divide greens among 4 individual plates. Scatter one-fourth of yellow sweet pepper slices on top of greens. Cut chicken into ½-inch slices. Arrange chicken and orange sections on top of each salad. Drizzle some of the dressing over each salad. Makes 4 main-dish servings.

Nutrition facts per serving: 305 cal., 17 g total fat (3 g sat. fat), 59 mg chol., 261 mg sodium, 16 g carbo., 1 g fiber, 23 g pro.
Daily values: 6% vit. A, 190% vit. C, 4% calcium, 9% iron.

The Mexican Potato

Jicama (*HE kuh muh*) often is referred to as the Mexican potato. This large, bulbous root vegetable has a thin brown skin and white crunchy flesh. Unlike regular potatoes, jicama has a sweet, nutty flavor and is good both raw and cooked. It is available from November through May and can be purchased in Mexican markets and most large supermarkets. Jicama will last up to 5 days when stored in the refrigerator. The thin skin should be peeled just before using. When cooked, jicama retains its crisp, water chestnut-type texture.

---

30 MIN. LOW FAT

SPRINGTIME SPINACH AND SMOKED CHICKEN SALAD

Start to finish: 25 min.

Bake some blueberry muffins to go alongside and you've got lunch.

- 8 cups torn fresh spinach
- 12 oz. cooked smoked chicken breast, cut into ½-inch cubes (about 2½ cups)
- 1 medium red onion, thinly sliced and separated into rings
- ½ of a small jicama, peeled and cut into thin strips
- ½ cup sliced radishes
- ¼ cup sliced almonds, toasted

♦♦♦

- 3 Tbsp. olive oil
- 2 Tbsp. lemon juice
- 2 Tbsp. pure maple syrup or maple-flavored syrup

1 In a large salad bowl combine the spinach, chicken, red onion, jicama, radishes, and almonds; set aside.

2 For dressing, in a screw-top jar combine the olive oil, lemon juice, and maple syrup. Cover and shake well. Pour dressing over spinach mixture. Toss gently to coat. Serve immediately. Makes 6 main-dish servings.

Nutrition facts per serving: 205 cal., 10 g total fat (1 g sat. fat), 47 mg chol., 640 mg sodium, 14 g carbo., 3 g fiber, 16 g pro. *Daily values:* 51% vit. A, 50% vit. C, 8% calcium, 21% iron.

COMPANY CHICKEN SALAD

Prep: 20 min. ♦ Marinate: 4 to 24 hours ♦ Grill: 12 min. Chill: 1 to 4 hours

While the grill is hot, roast a few sweet pepper halves. Use these shells as individual bowls for this festive salad. (See the photograph on page 77.)

- 1 lb. skinless, boneless chicken breast halves
- ¼ cup water
- ¼ cup low-fat red wine and herb vinaigrette
- ¼ cup teriyaki sauce
- 4 tsp. lemon juice
- 1 Tbsp. honey
- ½ tsp. ground ginger
- ⅛ tsp. garlic pepper

♦♦♦

- ½ cup light dairy sour cream
- ½ cup light mayonnaise dressing or salad dressing
- 2 Tbsp. milk
- ½ tsp. ground ginger
- ⅛ tsp. garlic pepper

♦♦♦

- 6 oz. rotini pasta, cooked and drained

- 1 cup small broccoli florets
- 4 green onions, thinly sliced
- 4 radishes, shredded
- 1½ cups chopped yellow and/or red sweet peppers

1 Rinse chicken; pat dry with paper towels. Place chicken in a plastic bag set in a shallow dish. For marinade combine water, vinaigrette, teriyaki sauce, lemon juice, honey, ½ teaspoon ground ginger, and ⅛ teaspoon garlic pepper; pour mixture over chicken in bag. Seal bag. Marinate in refrigerator for 4 to 24 hours, turning the bag occasionally.

2 Drain chicken; discard marinade. Place the chicken on the rack of an uncovered grill. Grill directly over medium coals for 12 to 15 minutes or until tender and no longer pink, turning once halfway through grilling. Cool slightly; cut into strips.

3 Meanwhile, for dressing, in a small mixing bowl stir together the sour cream, mayonnaise or salad dressing, milk, ½ teaspoon ground ginger, and ⅛ teaspoon garlic pepper; set aside.

4 In a large bowl combine the cooked pasta, broccoli, green onions, radishes, and sweet peppers. Add grilled chicken strips. Toss to mix. Pour dressing over salad mixture. Toss lightly to coat. Chill for 1 to 4 hours. If needed, add additional milk to moisten dressing before serving. Makes 6 main-dish servings.

Nutrition facts per serving: 324 cal., 12 g total fat (3 g sat. fat), 43 mg chol., 508 mg sodium, 32 g carbo., 2 g fiber, 21 g pro. *Daily values:* 34% vit. A, 101% vit. C, 4% calcium, 13% iron.

APRICOT-BASIL CHICKEN

Prep: 30 min. ◆ Grill: 18 min.

The sweetness of the apricots makes a striking contrast to the herbiness of the pesto.

- 1 **cup loosely packed fresh basil leaves**
- ⅓ **cup dried apricot halves**
- ¼ **cup chopped pecans**
- 2 **Tbsp. grated Parmesan cheese**
- 2 **Tbsp. olive oil**
- 2 **cloves garlic, quartered**

◆◆◆

- 4 **skinless, boneless chicken breast halves (1 lb.)**
- ½ **tsp. salt**

◆◆◆

- ¼ **cup apricot preserves, melted**

1 For pesto, in a blender container or food processor bowl combine basil, apricot halves, pecans, Parmesan cheese, olive oil, and garlic. Cover and blend or process with several on-off turns until a paste forms, stopping the machine several times and scraping the sides.

2 Rinse chicken; pat dry with paper towels. Place each chicken breast half between 2 pieces of plastic wrap. Working from the center to the edges, pound lightly with the flat side of a meat mallet to ⅛-inch thickness. Remove plastic wrap. Sprinkle chicken with salt. Spread pesto on each chicken breast. Fold in sides of each piece;

roll up from short end into a spiral, pressing edges to seal. Secure with wooden toothpicks.

3 Place the chicken on the rack of an uncovered grill. Grill directly over medium coals for 18 to 20 minutes or until chicken is tender and no longer pink, turning once halfway through grilling time. Brush with preserves the last 5 minutes of grilling. Makes 4 servings.

Nutrition facts per serving: 324 cal., 16 g total fat (3 g sat. fat), 62 mg chol., 382 mg sodium, 23 g carbo., 1 g fiber, 24 g pro. *Daily values:* 9% vit. A, 2% vit. C, 7% calcium, 11% iron.

CHILI RELLENOS CHICKEN

Prep: 25 min. ◆ Bake: 40 min.

We've taken the classic cheese-stuffed chili pepper one step further; here it's rolled up in chicken. Slice the chicken rolls and serve atop Spanish-style rice. (See the photograph on page 79.)

- 4 **large skinless, boneless chicken breast halves (about 1¼ lb.)**

◆◆◆

- ½ **cup shredded taco cheese blend or cheddar cheese (2 oz.)**
- 2 **Tbsp. finely chopped onion**
- 2 **Tbsp. snipped fresh cilantro (optional)**
- 1 **tsp. chili powder**
- 4 **whole canned green chilies, drained**

◆◆◆

- 1 **egg, beaten**
- 1 **Tbsp. milk**
- ¼ **cup fine dry bread crumbs**
- 1 **tsp. chili powder**
- ½ **tsp. salt**

1 Rinse chicken; pat dry with paper towels. Place each chicken breast half between 2 pieces of plastic wrap. Working from the center to the edges, pound lightly with the flat side of a meat mallet to ¼-inch thickness; set aside.

2 In a small bowl combine the cheese, onion, cilantro (if using), and 1 teaspoon chili powder. Stuff one-fourth of the cheese mixture into each whole chili pepper.

3 Place a stuffed pepper on top of each flattened chicken breast. Roll up chicken around chili, folding in sides. If necessary, secure with wooden toothpicks.

4 In a shallow dish combine the egg and milk. In another shallow dish stir together the bread crumbs, 1 teaspoon chili powder, and salt. Dip the chicken rolls in the milk mixture, and then in the crumb mixture.

5 Place chicken rolls in an ungreased 2-quart square baking dish. Bake, uncovered, in a 375° oven about 40 minutes or until chicken is no longer pink. Serve immediately. Makes 4 servings.

TO MAKE AHEAD

Prepare chicken as directed, except do not bake. Cover and chill for up to 2 hours. Then bake as directed.

Nutrition facts per serving: 262 cal., 11 g total fat (2 g sat. fat), 141 mg chol., 570 mg sodium, 7 g carbo., 1 g fiber, 34 g pro. *Daily values:* 10% vit. A, 16% vit. C, 14% calcium, 12% iron.

WALKING THE PROTEIN TIGHTROPE

Protein is popular. People are devouring giant steaks in restaurants across the country, high-protein fad diet books are best-sellers, plus serious athletes and weekend warriors alike are guzzling protein shakes and chomping away at protein bars. Wherever you turn, protein is being pushed as an all-powerful health panacea.

There's no denying that protein is important. Second only to water, it makes up the greatest percentage of our body weight. This key nutrient provides the building blocks kids and adults need for growing, maintaining, and repairing worn-out cells. Without protein, our bodies couldn't regulate fluids and our immune systems would shut down. In fact, if it weren't for protein there would be no hormones or enzymes—the protein compounds that take part in every single physical function.

However, most Americans eat more protein than they need. "In this country, true protein deficiency is rare except under strange circumstances," says Paul Reeds, Ph.D., researcher with the United States Department of Agriculture (USDA) and professor at Baylor College of Medicine, Houston. According to the USDA, the average American consumes about 90 grams of protein daily, significantly more than the 50 grams per day average recommended for healthy adults.

BE A PROTEIN PRO

More is not better when it comes to protein. If we eat too much of it, the excess is converted to fat and waste. Breaking down more protein than you need strains the kidneys and liver and can also increase your risk of osteoporosis. High levels of protein increase your requirement for vitamin B6, too. Additional dangers are associated with popular high-protein, low-carbohydrate fad diets.

The theory behind these diets is that our bodies inefficiently burn carbohydrates, turning too many into fat. Eat fewer carbohydrates, reduce fat production, and lose weight, the dieters say. But the truth is, carbohydrates are an efficient fuel and when the body doesn't have enough, it scavenges muscle for fuel. This leads to ketosis, a toxic condition resulting from disrupted metabolism.

These fad diets go against what most health professionals advise: To enjoy balance and variety, and to eat more vegetables, fruits, and grains. The majority of evidence indicates that high-protein diets only work—when they work—for the same reason all diets work: They limit calories. Fewer calories from any source—protein, fat, or carbohydrates—will lead to weight loss, healthy or not (see "Protein and Insulin Resistance," page 75).

BEST PROTEIN BET

The key to being a protein pro (and staying slim) is to satisfy your body's needs without going overboard. Your best bet: Get protein every day from a varied selection of foods. Moderately active, healthy adults need about 45 to 65 grams of protein a day—a little less than 0.3 grams for every pound you weigh. This is the amount in two glasses of milk plus two 3-ounce servings of cooked meat, fish, or poultry. Pregnant? Add 10 more grams daily. If you're a nursing mother, add 15 grams.

Although eating more than twice the recommended daily amounts of protein is where you start to increase health risk, there are some cases where the recommended amounts won't be enough. Traumatic events—such as injuries, surgery, or emotional upsets—increase your protein needs because the body makes special proteins for the immune system and cell repair.

"During times of injury and stress the body can lose up to 30 or more grams of protein a day," says Reeds. Physical stress also includes exercise. Research shows that athletes (both weight lifters and people involved in aerobic exercise, such as running) will need about 50 percent more protein than the recommended average to help repair and build tissues.

THANKS FOR THE COMPLEMENT

Meat, milk, eggs, poultry, and seafood are considered high-quality, "complete" proteins because they have all the essential amino acids (protein's building blocks) in just the right proportion. Except for soy, plant sources—nuts, beans, seeds, and grains—are deficient in one or more of the essential amino acids. But don't give up beans for burgers. Plant foods contain other vital nutrients (such as phytochemicals and fiber) not found in animal foods.

It was once believed that "complementary" amino acid sources—beans and rice, peanut butter and bread—had to be eaten together to yield usable proteins. Most experts now agree that such foods can be divided throughout the day. Adding animal protein to plant foods completes the amino acid collection, too—something we do when we pour milk on cereal, add cheese to pasta, or toss a little meat into a stir-fry.

Meeting protein needs from a variety of different foods is easy. Three cooked ounces of meat, fish, or poultry contain 21 grams of protein, and milk has 8 grams of protein in every cup. A tablespoon of peanut butter, an egg, or ½ cup cooked beans provides 7 grams of protein. You'll get 6 grams in a cup of bean soup or a large bagel, while one slice of bread, ½ cup of pasta, and ⅓ cup of rice give you 3 grams each. Count on approximately 2 grams of protein for every ½ cup serving of vegetables.

While the average American gets most of his or her daily protein in a single meal, it's better to spread your enjoyment of protein foods throughout the day. Keep your protein balance by eating one protein-rich food at each meal and throwing in a protein-packed snack or two between meals.

—*Ellen Albertson, M.S., R.D., is an author and journalist who specializes in nutrition communication.*

PROTEIN BASICS

Proteins are made up of separate compounds called amino acids—and it's these amino acids that our bodies actually need, not the entire protein molecule. Some amino acids are essential—they must be obtained from the diet—and others can be made in the body from pieces of other amino acids. Powder and tablet forms of amino acids have become popular as health supplements. But their prolonged, excessive use can upset your natural amino acid balance and lead to kidney, liver, and nervous system damage. Don't take these supplements without first consulting a registered dietitian or physician.

PROTEIN AND INSULIN RESISTANCE

Lately, a condition called insulin resistance has been used as the basis for popular weight-loss diets that condemn carbohydrates and push protein. Some experts believe 8 in 10 obese people are insulin resistant. Insulin helps the body burn sugar. When sugar levels rise after a meal, insulin production increases. In insulin-resistant people, the body loses its ability to use insulin, so unused sugar gets stored as fat, leading to obesity.

The "chicken or the egg" question is, which comes first, obesity or insulin resistance? Research results are mixed, although most studies only looked at persons who were already obese and/or had diabetes. Because it's not clear whether insulin resistance precedes obesity or obesity worsens insulin response, the best diet is one of balance and moderation.

Below are four simple suggestions to help you maintain your body's insulin balance:

◆ **Eat small, frequent meals** (five to six each day), rather than three large meals. This can prevent large swings in blood sugar.

◆ **Choose foods high in fiber and complex carbohydrates,** such as whole-grain breads, bran cereals, legumes, beans, and vegetables, rather than refined, easily digested carbohydrates.

◆ **Eat small amounts of lean protein** (fish, poultry, lean cuts of meat, tofu, etc.) with each meal. The protein in these foods helps to slow the digestion of carbohydrates.

◆ **Exercise** is one of the best prescriptions available to treat insulin resistance. Regular daily exercise, such as a brisk 45- to 60-minute walk, will effectively reduce insulin levels.

—*Kathy McManus is the Clinical Nutrition Manager at Brigham and Women's Hospital, Harvard Medical School, Boston.*

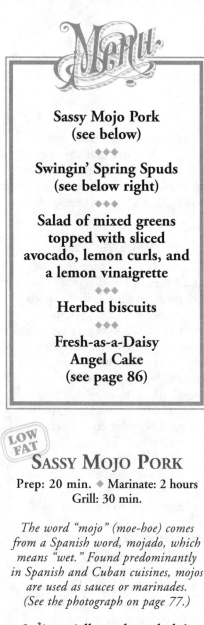

Sassy Mojo Pork
(see below)

◆◆◆

Swingin' Spring Spuds
(see below right)

◆◆◆

Salad of mixed greens
topped with sliced
avocado, lemon curls, and
a lemon vinaigrette

◆◆◆

Herbed biscuits

◆◆◆

Fresh-as-a-Daisy
Angel Cake
(see page 86)

SASSY MOJO PORK

Prep: 20 min. ◆ **Marinate:** 2 hours
Grill: 30 min.

The word "mojo" (moe-hoe) comes from a Spanish word, mojado, which means "wet." Found predominantly in Spanish and Cuban cuisines, mojos are used as sauces or marinades. (See the photograph on page 77.)

2   ¾- to 1-lb. pork tenderloins
4   canned chipotle peppers in
    adobo sauce, rinsed (2 oz.)
½   cup orange juice
¼   cup coarsely chopped onion
2   Tbsp. snipped fresh oregano
    or 2 tsp. dried oregano,
    crushed
2   Tbsp. lime juice
1   Tbsp. honey
1   Tbsp. cooking oil
3   cloves garlic, minced

1 Place meat in a large plastic bag set in a shallow dish. For marinade, in a food processor bowl or blender container com-

bine peppers, orange juice, onion, oregano, lime juice, honey, oil, garlic, and ½ teaspoon *salt.* Cover; process until nearly smooth. Pour over meat. Close bag. Marinate in refrigerator for 2 hours. (Do not marinate more than 2 hours because the citrus juices cause meat to become too tender and mushy.) Drain meat; discard marinade.

2 In a grill with a cover, arrange preheated coals around drip pan. Test for medium heat where meat will cook. Insert a meat thermometer near the center of one of the tenderloins. Place the meat on a rack in a roasting pan on the grill rack. Cover and grill for 30 to 45 minutes or until meat thermometer registers 160°.

3 Remove pork from grill. Cover with foil; let stand 5 minutes before carving. Serve with Swingin' Spring Spuds, if desired (see recipe, below). Garnish with *fresh oregano leaves,* if desired. Makes 6 main-dish servings.

Nutrition facts per serving: 164 cal., 5 g total fat (2 g sat. fat), 81 mg chol., 153 mg sodium, 3 g carbo., 0 g fiber, 25 g pro. *Daily values:* 4% vit. A, 7% vit. C, 1% calcium, 9% iron.

SWINGIN' SPRING SPUDS

Prep: 10 min. ◆ **Cook:** 10 min.
Grill: 20 min.

If you can find fresh morel mushrooms, they're heavenly. If not, use button mushrooms, which add their own flavor to this citrusy grilled potato packet. (See the photograph on page 77.)

1½ lb. tiny new potatoes, halved
    (or quartered if large)
16 pearl onions

1   cup fresh morel mushrooms
    and/or fresh button
    mushrooms
2   Tbsp. olive oil
1   tsp. finely shredded orange
    peel
¼ to ½ tsp. salt

1 Cook potatoes, covered, in a small amount of boiling salted water for 7 minutes. Add the onions. Cook, covered, for 3 minutes more. Drain well. Remove potatoes and onions from pan.

2 Fold a 36×18-inch piece of heavy foil in half to make a double thickness of foil that measures 18×18 inches. Cut any large mushrooms in half lengthwise. Place potatoes, onions, and mushrooms in center of foil. Drizzle vegetables with olive oil. Sprinkle with orange peel and salt. Bring up 2 opposite edges of foil and seal with a double fold. Then fold remaining ends to completely enclose the vegetables, leaving space for steam to build.

3 In a grill with a cover, arrange preheated coals around drip pan. Test for medium heat where vegetables will cook. Place foil packet on grill rack over drip pan. (If serving with Sassy Mojo Pork, place foil packet on grill next to roasting pan during the last 20 minutes of grilling time.) Cover and grill about 20 minutes or until potatoes are tender. Serve with Sassy Mojo Pork, if desired (see recipe, left). Makes 6 side-dish servings.

Nutrition facts per serving: 161 cal., 5 g total fat (1 g sat. fat), 0 mg chol., 98 mg sodium, 28 g carbo., 2 g fiber, 3 g pro. *Daily values:* 27% vit. C, 1% calcium, 14% iron.

Top: *Company Chicken Salad (page 72)*
Above: *Sassy Mojo Pork* and *Swingin' Spring Spuds (page 76)*

Page 78: *Sweet Cheese Blintzes (page 62)*
Right: *Chili Rellenos Chicken (page 73)*
Below: *Field Greens with Quesadilla "Croutons" (page 51)*

Page 80: *Choose-a-Cheese Soufflé (page 54)*
Top left: *Olympia Chicken (pages 58-59)*
Above: *Filled-and-Grilled Cheese Sandwich (page 60)*

Top right: *Fresh Mozzarella Salad (page 50)*
Above: *Fettuccine with Four Cheeses (page 54)*

Page 83: *Easter Egg Cookies (page 88)*
Above: *Popover Egg Nests (page 68)*
Right: *Gardener's Treat Bread (page 67)*

Right: *Sweet Melon Cup (page 85)*
Below: *Good-Thyme Lemon Ice in Blushing Pink Compote (page 85)*

GOOD-THYME LEMON ICE

Prep: 30 min. ◆ Cook: 5 min.

Freeze: 8 to 24 hours

You'll avoid last-minute fuss when you make this frosty confection up to a week in advance. (See the photograph on page 84.)

3 cups water

1 cup sugar

1 tsp. finely shredded lemon peel

◆◆◆

½ cup fresh lemon juice

1 Tbsp. snipped fresh lemon thyme or thyme, or ½ tsp. dried thyme, finely crushed

4 drops yellow food coloring (optional)

◆◆◆

1 recipe Blushing Pink Compote (see right)

1 In a medium saucepan combine the water, sugar, and, if using, dried thyme (not the fresh). Bring just to boiling to dissolve sugar; remove from heat. Stir in lemon peel. Cool thoroughly. Cover and chill.

2 In a 2-quart square baking dish combine the chilled syrup mixture, lemon juice, and, if using, fresh lemon thyme or thyme. Add yellow food coloring, if desired. Cover and freeze for 3 to 4 hours or until almost firm.

3 Break the frozen mixture into small chunks. Transfer chunks to a chilled mixing bowl. Beat with an electric mixer on medium speed until mixture is fluffy but not melted. Return quickly to chilled dish. Cover and freeze until firm. Store, covered, in freezer up to 1 week.

4 To serve, if mixture is very firm, let stand at room temperature for 5 minutes. Scrape across top of ice with a tablespoon, forming ice into 2-inch balls. Place a ball of the ice on top of a serving of Blushing Pink Compote (see recipe, below). Garnish with *lemon thyme sprigs,* if desired. Makes 9 servings.

Nutrition facts per serving for ice without compote: 89 cal., 0 g total fat, 0 mg chol., 3 mg sodium, 23 g carbo., 0 g fiber, 0 g pro. *Daily values:* 10% vit. C.

BLUSHING PINK COMPOTE

Prep: 20 min. ◆ Cook: 10 min.

A touch of vanilla flavors this fruity combo, which pairs well with our Good-Thyme Lemon Ice (see recipe, left). You also can serve the compote solo or spooned on top of pancakes. (See the photograph on page 84.)

½ to ⅔ cup sugar

¼ cup water

3 cups sliced fresh rhubarb

2 cups strawberries (halved if large)

1 tsp. vanilla

1 recipe Good-Thyme Lemon Ice (see left)

1 In a medium saucepan stir together sugar and water. Bring to boiling, stirring to dissolve sugar. Stir in rhubarb. Return to boiling; reduce heat. Simmer, covered, 5 minutes or until rhubarb is tender. Stir in strawberries and vanilla. Cool to room temperature.

2 To serve, spoon compote into dessert dishes. Top with a ball of Good-Thyme Lemon Ice and garnish with *lemon thyme sprigs,* if desired. Or, cover and chill compote up to 24 hours. Makes 9 servings.

Nutrition facts per serving compote without ice: 63 cal., 0 g total fat, 0 mg chol., 2 mg sodium, 15 g carbo., 1 g fiber, 1 g pro. *Daily values:* 36% vit. C, 3% calcium, 1% iron.

SWEET MELON CUP

Prep: 20 min. ◆ Cook: 8 min.

Chill: 2 to 24 hours

A whisper of ginger in the dressing accents the freshness of the melons. (See the photograph on page 84.)

1 cup dry white wine or white grape juice

¼ cup sugar

½ tsp. grated fresh ginger

◆◆◆

4 cups cantaloupe balls

2 cups honeydew balls Crystallized ginger (optional)

1 In a small saucepan combine wine or grape juice, sugar, and fresh ginger. Bring to boiling; reduce heat. Simmer, covered, for 5 minutes. Remove from heat. Strain ginger from mixture. Discard ginger. Cover and chill for 2 to 24 hours.

2 Before serving, in a medium mixing bowl combine cantaloupe, honeydew, and wine or juice mixture. Toss gently to coat. To serve, divide mixture evenly among 6 cups or bowls. Garnish with strips of crystallized ginger, if desired. Makes 6 servings.

Nutrition facts per serving: 116 cal., 0 g total fat, 0 mg chol., 17 mg sodium, 23 g carbo., 1 g fiber, 1 g pro. *Daily values:* 34% vit. A, 98% vit. C, 1% calcium, 2% iron.

FLOWERS FOR NIBBLING

Unless you're positive they're edible, please don't eat the daisies. Colorful English daisies are edible and can be used to decorate Fresh-as-a-Daisy Angel Cake (see recipe, below). Most daisies aren't edible, however.

Here are a few flowers that are safe to nibble: calendula, dianthus, lilac, Johnny-jump-up, lavender, and violet. You can find packaged edible flowers near the fresh herbs in major grocery stores. Or, you can even pick some posies from your own back yard if you're sure they are an edible variety and haven't been sprayed with chemicals. Do not use flowers from a florist.

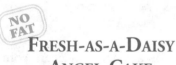

FRESH-AS-A-DAISY ANGEL CAKE

Prep: 50 min. ◆ Bake: 40 min.
Cool: 2 hours

For a shortcut to this impressive dessert, start with a purchased angel food cake mix. Prepare according to package directions, adding the orange flower water and chopped edible flowers to the batter before baking.

1½ **cups egg whites (10 to 12 large)**
1½ **cups sifted powdered sugar**
1 **cup sifted cake flour or sifted all-purpose flour**
♦ ♦ ♦
1½ **tsp. cream of tartar**
1 **tsp. orange flower water or orange extract**
1 **cup granulated sugar**
♦ ♦ ♦

1 **cup chopped edible flowers or ½ cup dried edible flower confetti***
♦ ♦ ♦
1 **recipe Orange Flower Icing (see right)**
  Edible flowers, such as calendula, dianthus, and lavender

1 In an extra-large mixing bowl, allow egg whites to stand at room temperature 30 minutes. Meanwhile, sift the powdered sugar and flour together 3 times; set aside.

2 Add cream of tartar and orange flower water or orange extract to egg whites. Beat with an electric mixer on medium speed until soft peaks form (tips curl). Gradually add granulated sugar, about 2 tablespoons at a time, beating until stiff peaks form (tips stand straight).

3 Sift about one-fourth of the flour mixture over beaten egg whites; fold in gently. Repeat, folding in remaining flour mixture by fourths, along with chopped edible flowers. Pour into an ungreased 10-inch tube pan. Gently cut through batter with a narrow metal spatula or knife to remove large air pockets.

4 Bake on the lowest rack in a 350° oven for 40 to 45 minutes or until top of cake springs back when lightly touched. Immediately invert cake (leave in pan); cool thoroughly. Using a narrow metal spatula, loosen sides of cake from pan; remove cake.

5 To frost cake, lightly brush off any excess crumbs. Place cake on wire rack over a 15×10×1-inch baking pan. Use a spoon or ladle to pour Orange Flower Icing over cake to cover completely. Let stand 20 minutes. Repeat with a second layer of icing. Let dry 20 minutes. Repeat with a third layer of icing. If necessary, reuse icing that has dripped on pan, straining it to remove crumbs. Let icing dry completely. Place edible flowers in a circle around bottom edge of cake. If desired, place English daisies or other edible flowers in a tiny vase in center hole of cake. Makes 12 servings.

***Note:** For a more colorful effect in the cake, use dried flower confetti. Spread 3 cups edible flower petals in a single layer on two 15×1×1-inch baking pans or cookie sheets. (Nasturtiums tend to darken and brown when dried, so you might want to avoid using them in the dried confetti.)

Let stand 2 to 3 days until completely dry, stirring occasionally to help the drying process. Snip dried petals into small pieces and measure ½ cup to use in cake. Store remaining petals in an airtight container in a cool, dark place.

Orange Flower Icing: In a large mixing bowl combine 2 tablespoons light-colored corn syrup and ½ teaspoon orange flower water. Stir in 2 cups sifted powdered sugar and 2 tablespoons orange juice. Stir in an additional 2 cups sifted powdered sugar and enough hot water (1 to 2 tablespoons) to make an icing of drizzling consistency.

Nutrition facts per serving: 301 cal., 0 g total fat, 0 mg chol., 49 mg sodium, 73 g carbo., 0 g fiber, 4 g pro.
Daily values: 2% vit. C, 5% iron.

SUNDAE POUND CAKE

Prep: 20 min. ◆ Bake: 50 min.

½ cup butter
3 eggs
⅔ cup dairy sour cream

◆◆◆

½ of a 4-oz. bar sweet baking
    chocolate, cut up
2 Tbsp. milk
1 Tbsp. water
1⅓ cups all-purpose flour
¼ tsp. baking powder
⅛ tsp. baking soda

◆◆◆

1¼ cups sugar
1 tsp. vanilla
1 tsp. finely shredded lemon
    peel

◆◆◆

1 recipe Dark Chocolate Glaze
    (see right)
1 recipe Milk Chocolate
    Drizzle and/or White
    Chocolate Drizzle (see
    right)(optional)

1 Let butter, eggs, and sour cream stand at room temperature for 30 minutes. Grease and flour a 6-cup fluted tube pan or 9×5×3-inch loaf pan; set aside.

2 In a small heavy saucepan melt the sweet baking chocolate with milk and water over low heat, stirring until smooth. Remove from heat; cool slightly. In a small mixing bowl combine flour, baking powder, and baking soda; set aside.

3 In a large mixing bowl beat butter with an electric mixer on medium to high speed until softened. Gradually add sugar, beating until very light and fluffy. Add vanilla. Add eggs, 1 at a time, beating on low to medium speed for 1 minute after each addition.

Alternately add flour mixture and sour cream, beating on low speed just until combined. Stir in peel.

4 Spread half of the batter in prepared pan. Drizzle with the chocolate mixture; top with remaining batter. Bake in a 325° oven for 50 to 60 minutes or until a wooden toothpick inserted into the center of the cake comes out clean. Cool cake in pan on a wire rack for 10 minutes. Remove cake from pan and cool completely.

5 Spoon Dark Chocolate Glaze over cake. If desired, using a pastry bag with a small tip, pipe Milk Chocolate Drizzle and/or White Chocolate Drizzle over glaze. Serve with fresh *strawberries* and *vanilla ice cream,* if desired. Makes 12 servings.

Dark Chocolate Glaze: In a small saucepan combine 1 ounce unsweetened chocolate, 2 tablespoons butter, and 2 tablespoons milk, stirring over low heat until chocolate is melted. Remove from heat. Stir in 1 cup sifted powdered sugar and ½ teaspoon vanilla. Beat until smooth.

Milk Chocolate Drizzle: In a small saucepan combine ½ ounce milk chocolate, 1 tablespoon butter, and 1 tablespoon milk, stirring over low heat until melted. Remove from heat. Stir in ½ cup sifted powdered sugar and ¼ teaspoon vanilla. Beat until smooth.

White Chocolate Drizzle: In a small saucepan combine ½ ounce white baking bar, 1 tablespoon butter, and 1 tablespoon milk, stirring over heat until melted. Remove from heat. Stir in ½ cup

TEST KITCHEN TIP

NOW OR LATER? STORING AND FREEZING CAKES

How far in advance can you make a cake? Once made, should the cake be stored in the refrigerator? Can it be frozen? The answers depend on the cake. Here are some guidelines.

Cakes filled or frosted with whipped cream should be assembled no more than 2 hours before serving to prevent them from getting soggy.

If your cake filling or frosting contains whipped cream, cream cheese, yogurt, or eggs, store it in the refrigerator. As an alternative to a cake cover, invert a bowl over the cake.

To freeze an unfrosted layer cake, place the cooled cake on a baking sheet and freeze just until firm. Place the frozen cake in a freezer bag or airtight freezer container and freeze for up to 4 months.

Angel food, sponge, and chiffon cakes are best frozen unfrosted. Place them in a large freezer bag and freeze for up to 3 months. Don't store them any longer than that or the delicate sponge texture may deteriorate. Thaw at room temperature for several hours before serving.

sifted powdered sugar and ¼ teaspoon vanilla. Beat until smooth.

Nutrition facts per serving: 329 cal., 17 g total fat (10 g sat. fat), 85 mg chol., 143 mg sodium, 44 g carbo., 1 g fiber, 4 g pro. *Daily values:* 14% vit. A, 3% calcium, 7% iron.

NO-SLIP-GRIP BANANAS

Does your toddler have trouble getting a grip on slippery banana pieces? Here's an easy fix: Simply smash a handful of cornflakes in a self-sealing plastic bag, add some banana chunks, and shake. The cereal makes the pieces easy to grip, and they taste good, too.

L. Shahan
Allen, Maryland

EASTER EGG COOKIES

Prep: 50 min. ◆ Bake: 8 min.
per batch

Edible wheat grass makes a cozy resting spot for these spring sweets. Find the grass in the produce section of major supermarkets. Or, check at large health-food stores where the grass is blended to make a good-for-you beverage.
(See the photograph on page 83.)

1 cup butter, softened
1 cup sifted powdered sugar
1 egg
2¼ cups all-purpose flour
1 Tbsp. finely shredded lemon peel
　 Food coloring paste

1 In a large mixing bowl beat butter with an electric mixer on medium to high speed for 30 seconds. Add powdered sugar; beat on low speed until combined, scraping sides of bowl. Beat in egg. Beat in as much flour as you

can with mixer. Using a wooden spoon, stir in lemon peel and any remaining flour. Tint portions of dough as desired.

2 Snip a pencil-size hole in a corner of a 1-quart heavy plastic bag or a disposable pastry bag (or use a #12 tip in a pastry bag). Fill bag with dough. Force unchilled dough through bag to pipe about 18 oval shapes (each about 4×3 inches) onto ungreased cookie sheets (see illustration below). Pipe designs inside each oval shape, making sure designs connect to the sides of the oval to resemble a decorated Easter egg.

3 Bake in a 375° oven for 8 to 10 minutes or until edges are firm but not browned. Cool on cookie sheets for 1 minute. Transfer cookies to a wire rack; let cool. Makes about 18 cookies.

Nutrition facts per cookie: 167 cal., 11 g total fat (6 g sat. fat), 39 mg chol., 107 mg sodium, 17 g carbo., 0 g fiber, 2 g pro. *Daily values:* 9% vit. A, 4% iron.

Almond Cookies: Prepare cookies as directed at left, except omit the shredded lemon peel and beat in ¾ teaspoon almond extract with the egg.

TOP BANANA BARS

LOW FAT

Prep.: 15 min. ◆ Bake: 20 min.

½ cup all-purpose flour
½ cup whole wheat flour
1 Tbsp. toasted wheat germ
1 tsp. baking powder
½ tsp. ground cinnamon
◆◆◆
1 egg, beaten
½ cup packed brown sugar
⅓ cup milk
¼ cup cooking oil
½ tsp. vanilla
1 ripe medium banana, mashed
⅓ cup mixed dried fruit bits
1 recipe Vanilla Icing (see below)

1 Grease an 11×7×1½-inch baking pan; set aside. In a mixing bowl combine flours, wheat germ, baking powder, cinnamon, and ⅛ teaspoon *salt;* set aside.

2 In another bowl stir together egg, sugar, milk, oil, and vanilla. Stir in banana and fruit bits. Add banana mixture to flour mixture, stirring to combine. Spread batter evenly in the prepared pan.

3 Bake in a 350° oven for 20 to 25 minutes or until a wooden toothpick inserted near center comes out clean. Cool in pan on a wire rack. Drizzle Vanilla Icing over top. Cut into bars. Makes 20.

Vanilla Icing: Combine ⅓ cup sifted powdered sugar and ¼ teaspoon vanilla. Add milk (1 to 2 teaspoons) until icing is of drizzling consistency.

Nutrition facts per bar: 91 cal., 3 g total fat (1 g sat. fat), 11 mg chol., 27 mg sodium, 15 g carbo., 1 g fiber, 1 g pro. *Daily values:* 1% vit. A, 1% vit. C, 2% calcium, 3% iron.

M AY
Fast Fish

30-minute recipes indicated in RED.
Low-fat and no-fat recipes indicated with a ♥.
Photographs indicated in italics.
*Bonus recipe

*S*chool's ending and summer's beginning. Who has time to cook during this busy transition time? Here comes quick-cooking fish to the rescue! You can have Thai-Style Shrimp and Cucumbers, Salmon and Feta Pita, or Halibut with Two-Pepper Sauce on the table in 30 minutes or less. Or whip up an Asian Shrimp and Millet Salad—ready in the refrigerator when you come home. With all your extra time, you can eat dessert, too. There's no secret to how good Secret Strawberry-Rhubarb Pie is. And White Chocolate and Berries Shortcake and Frozen Berry Yogurt will get you dreaming of summer's lazy days ahead.

Wild Mushroom Tart
(see below)

♦ ♦ ♦

Steamed fresh asparagus spears drizzled with lemon or orange butter

♦ ♦ ♦

Assorted melon wedges and fresh berries

♦ ♦ ♦

Fruit juices and/or coffee

WILD MUSHROOM TART

Prep: 35 min. ♦ Bake: 12 min. (crust), 20 min. (tart)

A mix of fresh mushrooms fills a delicate cornmeal crust. This quichelike tart is just right for brunch.

2 **cups sliced onions**
1 **Tbsp. olive oil**
2 **cups sliced shiitake, chanterelle, and/or oyster mushrooms**

♦ ♦ ♦

⅔ **cup yellow cornmeal**
⅔ **cup all-purpose flour**
¼ **tsp. salt**
3 **Tbsp. butter**
4 **to 5 Tbsp. water**

♦ ♦ ♦

4 **eggs**
½ **cup dairy sour cream**
½ **cup chopped roasted red sweet peppers (½ of a 7¼-oz. jar)**
2 **Tbsp. yellow cornmeal**
¼ **tsp. dried thyme, crushed**
½ **tsp. salt**
¼ **tsp. black pepper**
⅓ **cup grated Parmesan cheese**

1 In a large skillet cook onions in hot oil about 10 minutes or until onions are golden, stirring occasionally. Add mushrooms and cook about 5 minutes more or until mushrooms are tender, stirring occasionally. Set aside.

2 In a medium mixing bowl stir together the ⅔ cup cornmeal, the flour, and ¼ teaspoon salt. Using a pastry blender, cut in the butter until pieces are the size of small peas. Sprinkle 1 tablespoon of the water over part of the mixture; gently toss with a fork. Push the moistened dough to the side of the bowl. Repeat moistening dough, using 1 tablespoon of the water at a time until all of the dough is moistened. Form dough into a ball.

3 Press the dough onto the bottom and up the sides of an 11×8-inch rectangular or a 10-inch round tart pan with removable bottom. Bake in a 350° oven for 12 minutes.

4 Meanwhile, in the same mixing bowl combine the eggs and sour cream. Stir in the roasted red pepper, 2 tablespoons cornmeal, the thyme, ½ teaspoon salt, and ¼ teaspoon black pepper.

5 Spread mushroom mixture over prebaked crust. Carefully pour egg mixture over mushroom mixture. Sprinkle cheese over top of tart. Bake in the 350° oven for 20 to 25 minutes or until center is set. Cool on a wire rack for 10 minutes. Remove the sides of the tart pan. Serve warm. Makes 6 main-dish servings.

Nutrition facts per serving: 328 cal., 18 g total fat (9 g sat. fat), 170 mg chol., 483 mg sodium, 32 g carbo., 3 g fiber, 11 g pro. *Daily values:* 24% vit. A, 62% vit. C, 11% calcium, 17% iron.

PECAN POTATO BALLS

Prep: 30 min. ♦ Chill: 2 to 4 hours
Cook: 1½ min. per batch

Crispy pecan-coated on the outside and bacon-and-jalapeño-studded on the inside, these little bites can be served as an appetizer or a side dish.

2 **cups unseasoned mashed potatoes**
4 **slices bacon or turkey bacon, crisp-cooked, drained, and crumbled**
¼ **cup margarine or butter, melted and cooled**
1 **jalapeño pepper, seeded and finely chopped***
1 **Tbsp. snipped fresh chives**
½ **tsp. salt**
½ **tsp. ground cumin**
⅛ **tsp. ground red pepper**

♦ ♦ ♦

1 **egg, slightly beaten**
1 **Tbsp. water**
½ **cup all-purpose flour**
2 **cups finely chopped pecans**

♦ ♦ ♦

Cooking oil or shortening for deep-fat frying

1 In a medium mixing bowl stir together potatoes, bacon, margarine, jalapeño, chives, salt, cumin, and ground red pepper. Cover and chill for 2 to 4 hours.

2 Shape the potato mixture into 1½-inch balls. In a small bowl combine the egg and water. Roll balls in flour, then egg-water mixture, and finally in pecans.

3 In a heavy saucepan or deep-fat fryer heat 2 inches of cooking oil or melted shortening to 375°. Fry potato balls, a few at a time, for 1½ to 2 minutes or until golden, turning once. Using a slotted spoon, remove potato balls from hot oil. Drain on paper towels. Serve immediately. Makes 15 balls.

*Note: Hot peppers contain oils that can burn eyes, lips, and sensitive skin. Wear plastic gloves while preparing peppers and be sure to thoroughly wash your hands afterward.

Nutrition facts per ball: 225 cal., 19 g total fat (2 g sat. fat), 16 mg chol., 140 mg sodium, 13 g carbo., 1 g fiber, 3 g pro. *Daily values:* 4% vit. A, 11% vit. C, 1% calcium, 5% iron.

ROASTED POTATOES WITH ARTICHOKES

Prep: 10 min. ♦ Bake: 55 min.

2 lb. whole tiny new potatoes
1 6½-ounce jar marinated artichoke hearts
¼ cup coarsely chopped, pitted kalamata olives
1 medium red onion, cut into thin wedges
2 Tbsp. drained capers
¼ tsp. salt
¼ tsp. pepper
½ cup crumbled feta cheese (2 oz.)

1 Scrub potatoes; quarter and set aside. Drain artichoke hearts, reserving marinade; set aside.

2 In a large bowl combine the potatoes, reserved marinade, olives, onion wedges, capers, salt, and pepper. Toss gently to coat potatoes. Transfer mixture to a greased 3-quart rectangular baking dish.

3 Bake, uncovered, in a 350° oven for 50 minutes, stirring occasionally. Stir in artichokes. Bake for 5 to 10 minutes more or until potatoes are tender. Transfer to a serving dish. Sprinkle with feta. Makes 6 side-dish servings.

Nutrition facts per serving: 208 cal., 5 g total fat (1 g sat. fat), 8 mg chol., 406 mg sodium, 38 g carbo., 2 g fiber, 5 g pro. *Daily values:* 3% vit. A, 44% vit. C, 6% calcium, 18% iron.

WILTED CHARD

Start to finish: 20 min.

Sometimes known as "chard," Swiss chard is a mild salad green that is a member of the beet family. Its crinkly dark green leaves have a hearty spinach flavor and either a white or scarlet stem with a celerylike taste. Swiss chard is available all year, but peak time is summer through early fall.

1 lb. Swiss chard
♦♦♦
1 small onion, finely chopped
1 small red sweet pepper, finely chopped
2 cups sliced button, oyster, crimini and/or shiitake mushrooms
1 tsp. grated fresh ginger
2 Tbsp. olive oil
2 Tbsp. white wine vinegar
1 Tbsp. honey
¼ tsp. salt
¼ cup toasted chopped walnuts

1 Trim Swiss chard. Remove center ribs; chop ribs and set aside. Thinly slice the leafy greens and place in a large salad bowl.

2 In a large skillet cook the chard ribs, onion, red sweet pepper, mushrooms, and ginger in hot olive oil about 5 minutes or until chard is just tender. Remove from heat; stir in vinegar, honey, and salt. Pour over greens in bowl; add walnuts. Toss mixture until coated. Serve immediately. Makes 8 side-dish servings.

Nutrition facts per serving: 83 cal., 6 g total fat (1 g sat. fat), 0 mg chol., 169 mg sodium, 7 g carbo., 1 g fiber, 2 g pro. *Daily values:* 22% vit. A, 36% vit. C, 3% calcium, 12% iron.

WHITE CORN AND BABY PEA SALAD

Prep: 20 min. ◆ Chill: 2 hours

This crunchy, refreshing salad is fat free. For a healthy supper, serve it alongside grilled fish or chicken.

- 1 16-oz. pkg. frozen white whole kernel corn (shoe peg), thawed
- 1 16-oz. pkg. frozen baby peas, thawed
- 1 cup chopped, peeled jicama
- ⅔ cup chopped celery
- ½ cup thinly sliced green onions
- ¼ cup chopped red and/or orange sweet pepper

◆◆◆

- ½ cup seasoned rice vinegar
- 2 Tbsp. brown sugar
- 1 Tbsp. snipped fresh parsley
- ½ tsp. salt
- ¼ tsp. ground white pepper
- 1 Tbsp. snipped fresh mint

1 In a large salad bowl combine corn, peas, jicama, celery, green onions, and sweet pepper.

2 For dressing, in a screw-top jar combine vinegar, brown sugar, parsley, salt, and white pepper. Cover and shake well. Pour over salad; toss gently to coat. Sprinkle with fresh mint. Cover and chill up to 2 hours. Makes 10 to 12 side-dish servings.

Nutrition facts per serving: 90 cal., 0 g total fat, 0 mg chol., 151 mg sodium, 21 g carbo., 2 g fiber, 4 g pro.
Daily values: 10% vit. A, 34% vit. C, 1% calcium, 9% iron.

SAVORY POLENTA SKILLET

Prep: 25 min. ◆ Broil: 6 min.
Bake: 22 min.

- 1 16-oz. tube refrigerated cooked polenta (plain or flavored), sliced about ¼ inch thick
- 1 Tbsp. cooking oil

◆◆◆

- ½ of a 10-oz. pkg. frozen chopped spinach, thawed and well drained
- 1½ cups chopped cooked chicken or turkey
- ½ cup crumbled feta cheese (2 oz.)
- 1 cup meatless spaghetti sauce
- ½ cup shredded Monterey Jack cheese (2 oz.)

1 Place polenta slices in a well-greased 15×10×1-inch baking pan. Brush slices with oil. Broil 4 to 5 inches from heat for 6 to 8 minutes or until tops are lightly browned and crisp. Let hot polenta slices cool slightly before removing from pan. Adjust oven to 400°.

2 Arrange half of the polenta slices in the bottom of a 2-quart square baking dish. Sprinkle with spinach, chicken, and feta. Top with remaining polenta slices. Spoon spaghetti sauce over polenta. Bake, uncovered, in 400° oven about 20 minutes or until heated through. Sprinkle with Monterey Jack cheese. Bake 2 to 3 minutes more or until melted. Makes 6 main-dish servings.

Nutrition facts per serving: 240 cal., 11 g total fat (6 g sat. fat), 50 mg chol., 770 mg sodium, 18 g carbo., 3 g fiber, 16 g pro.
Daily values: 19% vit. A, 9% vit. C, 18% calcium, 5% iron.

CAJUN BEER BURGERS

Prep: 20 min. ◆ Grill: 14 min.

Add a side of seasoned grilled potato wedges and a frosty beer for a brew-pub-style meal.

- 1 egg, slightly beaten
- ½ cup finely chopped onion
- ¼ cup fine dry bread crumbs
- ¼ cup beer
- 1 Tbsp. Worcestershire sauce
- ½ tsp. dried thyme, crushed
- ¼ tsp. dry mustard
- ¼ tsp. ground red pepper
- 1 lb. lean ground beef

◆◆◆

- 1 recipe Cajun Beer Sauce (see below)

◆◆◆

- 6 hamburger buns, split and toasted
  Romaine leaves (optional)
  Tomato slices (optional)

1 In a large mixing bowl combine the egg, onion, bread crumbs, beer, Worcestershire sauce, thyme, mustard, and pepper. Add ground beef; mix well. Shape meat mixture into six ¾-inch-thick patties.

2 Grill patties on the rack of an uncovered grill directly over medium coals for 14 to 18 minutes or until no pink remains, turning once. Meanwhile, prepare Cajun Beer Sauce.

3 Serve burgers on toasted buns with romaine and tomato slices, if desired. Top each burger with Cajun Beer Sauce. Makes 6 servings.

Cajun Beer Sauce: In a small saucepan cook ¼ cup chopped onion and ¼ cup chopped green or red sweet pepper in 1 tablespoon cooking oil until tender. Stir together ½ cup beer, ½ cup water, 1 tablespoon cornstarch, and 1 teaspoon cajun seasoning. Add to saucepan. Cook and stir over medium heat until thickened and bubbly. Cook and stir for 2 minutes more. Serve over burgers.

Nutrition facts per serving: 349 cal., 16 g total fat (5 g sat. fat), 82 mg chol., 390 mg sodium, 30 g carbo., 1 g fiber, 19 g pro. *Daily values:* 3% vit. A, 16% vit. C, 7% calcium, 21% iron.

GLAZED MEAT LOAF

Prep: 30 min. ◆ Bake: 45 min.

Finally, even those counting calories and watching fat can enjoy a true blue plate special. These lighter and spunkier versions of an old-fashioned meat loaf and Sour Cream Smashed Potatoes (see recipe, right) taste like they're direct from the diner.

Nonstick spray coating
⅓ cup sliced green onions
¼ cup finely chopped red and/or yellow sweet pepper
¼ cup finely chopped carrot
◆◆◆
2 slightly beaten egg whites
½ cup finely crushed saltine crackers (14 crackers)
2 Tbsp. fat-free milk
2 Tbsp. bottled chili sauce
1 Tbsp. snipped fresh basil or oregano or ½ teaspoon dried basil or oregano, crushed
¼ tsp. ground black pepper
1 lb. extra-lean ground beef
◆◆◆
¼ cup bottled chili sauce
1 Tbsp. brown sugar
1 tsp. vinegar
1 recipe Sour Cream Smashed Potatoes (see right)

1 Spray a small skillet with nonstick spray coating. Add the green onions, sweet pepper, and carrot. Cook over medium heat 5 to 8 minutes or until vegetables are tender, stirring occasionally. Remove from heat; cool slightly.

2 In a large mixing bowl combine egg whites, crackers, milk, the 2 tablespoons chili sauce, basil or oregano, and black pepper. Add the cooked vegetables and the ground beef; mix well.

3 Pat meat mixture firmly into a 7½×3½×2-inch loaf pan. Invert pan with meat mixture into a shallow baking pan; remove loaf pan. Bake the meat loaf in a 350° oven for 30 minutes.

4 Meanwhile, for glaze, in a small mixing bowl stir together the ¼ cup chili sauce, brown sugar, and vinegar. Spoon glaze over meat loaf. Bake for 15 to 20 minutes more or until no pink remains. Transfer meat loaf to a platter. To serve, cut into slices. Pass remaining sauce, if desired. Makes 6 servings.

TO MAKE AHEAD

Prepare meat loaf as directed, except do not shape and bake. Cover bowl; chill meat mixture up to 24 hours. Shape meat loaf as directed. Bake in a 350° oven about 40 minutes or until meat loaf is nearly done. Spoon the glaze over meat loaf and bake about 15 minutes more or until done. Serve as directed.

Nutrition facts per serving: 190 cal., 8 g total fat (3 g sat. fat), 48 mg chol., 352 mg sodium, 12 g carbo., 16 g pro. *Daily values:* 19% vit. A, 16% vit. C, 2% calcium, 13% iron.

SOUR CREAM SMASHED POTATOES

Prep: 20 min. ◆ Cook: 25 min.

4 medium baking potatoes (about 1⅓ lb. total)
4 cloves garlic, peeled
◆◆◆
½ cup light dairy sour cream
2 to 3 Tbsp. fat-free milk (optional)
1 Tbsp. finely shredded Parmesan cheese (optional)
Fresh basil sprigs (optional)

1 If desired, peel potatoes. Cook potatoes and garlic cloves, covered, in boiling water for 20 to 25 minutes or until potatoes are tender; drain.

2 Using a potato masher, mash potatoes and garlic; add sour cream. If necessary, beat in enough milk to make fluffy. Season to taste with *salt* and *pepper.* Return potatoes to pan and heat through. Sprinkle with Parmesan cheese and garnish with basil, if desired. Makes 6 side-dish servings.

TO MAKE AHEAD

Prepare potatoes as directed, except place in a greased 1½-quart casserole before heating through. Do not sprinkle with Parmesan mixture. Cover and chill for up to 24 hours. Bake, covered, in a 350° oven about 55 minutes or until heated through. Just before serving, sprinkle with the Parmesan cheese.

Nutrition facts per serving: 127 cal., 1 g total fat (1 g sat. fat) 3 mg chol., 209 mg sodium, 26 g carbo., 1 g fiber, 4 g pro. *Daily values:* 2% vit. A, 22% vit. C, 3% calcium, 11% iron.

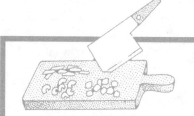

COMING CLEAN ON CUTTING BOARDS

Plastic or wood? Several years ago, health authorities suggested using plastic cutting boards instead of wood when handling raw meat and poultry. A study then questioned this recommendation after discovering that more bacteria survive on plastic than on wood. However, after reviewing other research, the United States Department of Agriculture (USDA) determined that cutting boards made of non-porous material (such as plastic or glass) are less likely to form the deep scars or nicks that provide a haven for harmful microbes. Therefore, they are better to use with meats, poultry, and fish. USDA food safety specialists suggest you follow these protective measures to make sure all cutting boards are safe from contamination:

◆ Designate one nonporous board, preferably plastic, tempered glass, or a dishwasher-safe hard wood, for cutting raw meat and poultry.
◆ Wash all boards in the dishwasher after each use. If your board cannot go in the dishwasher, wash it thoroughly with hot, soapy water.
◆ Sanitize all cutting boards often in a mild bleach solution. Use 2 teaspoons of bleach per quart of water.
◆ Immediately replace cutting boards that have become overly nicked or scarred.

ROASTED TENDERLOIN WITH TRICOLOR POTATOES

Prep: 15 min. ◆ Roast: 35-45 min.

Beef tenderloin is a most reliable cut; it has little fat, no bones, and cooks evenly.

- **3 Tbsp. bottled minced garlic**
- **4 tsp. dried marjoram, crushed**
- **1 Tbsp. finely shredded lemon peel**
- **2 tsp. cracked black pepper**
- **½ tsp. salt**
- **1 2- to 3-lb. center-cut beef tenderloin**
- **1 Tbsp. olive oil**

◆◆◆

- **1½ lb. tiny white, purple, and/or red potatoes, scrubbed and quartered**
- **2 Tbsp. olive oil**
- **½ tsp. salt**

◆◆◆

Fresh marjoram sprigs (optional)
Fresh rosemary sprigs (optional)
Lemon wedges (optional)

1 In a small bowl stir together garlic, marjoram, lemon peel, cracked black pepper, and the ½ teaspoon salt. Brush tenderloin with the 1 tablespoon olive oil. Sprinkle half the garlic-pepper mixture evenly over roast, patting to coat.

2 Place meat on a rack in a shallow roasting pan. Insert a meat thermometer into the center

of the meat (see illustration, above). Roast tenderloin in a 425° oven for 35 to 40 minutes for medium-rare (145°) or 45 to 50 minutes for medium (160°).

3 Meanwhile, toss potatoes with the 2 tablespoons olive oil, the remaining garlic-pepper mixture, and ½ teaspoon salt. Add potato mixture to the roasting pan during the last 30 minutes of roasting.

4 Remove tenderloin and potatoes to serving platter. Cover loosely with foil. Let stand for 15 minutes (the meat's temperature will rise 5° during standing). With a sharp knife carve beef into ½-inch slices. Garnish with marjoram and rosemary sprigs and lemon wedges, if desired. Makes 8 servings.

Nutrition facts per serving: 290 cal., 12 g total fat (3 g sat. fat), 64 mg chol., 322 mg sodium, 20 g carbo., 1 g fiber, 24 g pro. *Daily values:* 22% vit. C, 2% calcium, 30% iron.

CHICKEN WITH ORZO

Prep: 20 min. ◆ Bake: 10 min.

This Greek-style dinner goes together in a matter of minutes.

Nonstick spray coating
1½ cups orzo pasta (8 oz.)
◆◆◆
2 cups shredded fresh spinach leaves
¼ cup crumbled feta cheese (1 oz.)
1 tsp. finely shredded lemon peel
◆◆◆
1 hot rotisserie chicken, cut into serving-size pieces
1 medium tomato, cut in wedges
¼ cup crumbled feta cheese (1 oz.)

1 Spray a 2-quart rectangular baking dish with nonstick coating; set aside. Prepare orzo according to package directions. Drain well. Return orzo to saucepan. Add spinach, ¼ cup feta cheese, and lemon peel to saucepan, tossing to mix.

2 Spread orzo mixture in the prepared baking dish. Arrange chicken pieces and tomato wedges atop. Sprinkle with ¼ cup feta cheese. Bake, uncovered, in a 450° oven about 10 minutes or until heated through. Makes 4 to 6 main-dish servings.

Nutrition facts per serving: 459 cal., 14 g total fat (6 g sat. fat), 96 mg chol., 446 mg sodium, 48 g carbo., 2 g fiber, 35 g pro. *Daily values:* 25% vit. A, 23% vit. C, 17% calcium, 27% iron.

CHICKEN DINNERS IN MINUTES

Try these additional ideas for a rotisserie chicken:
◆ Fill an omelet with shredded chicken, sliced avocado, diced tomato, and snipped fresh cilantro.
◆ Whip up a chicken club salad by topping mixed salad greens with chopped chicken, tomato wedges, shredded Swiss cheese, bagel chips or croutons, and creamy buttermilk ranch dressing with bacon.
◆ Make barbecue chicken sandwiches by removing the chicken from the bone and stirring into some warm barbecue sauce. Spoon the barbecued chicken on hoagie buns and top with sliced dill pickles and onion.
◆ Toss together shredded chicken, refrigerated pesto sauce, and hot cooked pasta. Sprinkle on your favorite chopped, cooked vegetables.
◆ Layer an Italian bread shell with pizza sauce, shredded chicken, sliced red onion, and mozzarella cheese. Or, use your own favorite pizza toppings on the bread shell and bake according to the package directions.
◆ Make a quesadilla by layering chopped chicken, sliced ripe olives, snipped dried tomatoes, and shredded Monterey Jack cheese on one side of a large flour tortilla. Fold tortilla in half, pressing down gently. Cook the tortilla in a large skillet until cheese melts, turning it over once.
◆ Roll shredded chicken in flour tortilla with canned black beans that have been rinsed and drained, diced green chilies, cheddar cheese, chopped tomatoes, and snipped fresh cilantro.
◆ Feature sliced chicken on your next submarine sandwich. For toppings, use sliced cucumber, sprouts, and blue cheese dressing.

CHICKEN TORTILLA ROLL-UPS

Start to finish: 25 min.

To lower the fat in each serving, substitute low-fat salad dressing.

8 oz. shredded cooked chicken
½ cup shredded mozzarella cheese (2 oz.)
¼ cup finely shredded carrot
¼ cup pine nuts, toasted
½ cup blue cheese or ranch salad dressing
8 large spinach leaves, stems removed
4 7- to 8-inch flour tortillas

1 In a mixing bowl combine chicken, mozzarella cheese, carrot, and pine nuts. Toss gently to mix. Add the salad dressing; stir gently to coat.

2 To assemble, place 2 spinach leaves on each flour tortilla. Divide filling among the tortillas; roll up. Slice each into thirds. Secure with wooden picks. Makes 4 servings.

Nutrition facts per serving: 444 cal., 30 g total fat (7 g sat. fat), 77 mg chol., 582 mg sodium, 20 g carbo., 1 g fiber, 26 g pro. *Daily values:* 34% vit. A, 8% vit. C, 14% calcium, 19% iron.

ORIENTAL CHICKEN BITES

Prep: 20 min. ♦ Bake: 10 min.

A coating of crushed sesame crackers and peanuts gives these family favorites their Oriental flavor.

1 lb. skinless, boneless chicken breast halves
¼ cup all-purpose flour
½ tsp. garlic salt
½ tsp. five-spice powder
¼ tsp. pepper

♦♦♦

1 egg, beaten
2 Tbsp. milk
⅔ cup finely crushed toasted sesame crackers
⅓ cup finely ground peanuts

♦♦♦

⅓ cup bottled sweet-and-sour sauce
2 Tbsp. bottled barbecue sauce

1 Rinse chicken; pat dry with paper towels. Cut chicken into 1½-inch cubes. In a self-sealing plastic bag combine the flour, garlic salt, five-spice powder, and pepper; add chicken. Seal bag and shake to coat evenly. Remove chicken cubes.

2 In a shallow bowl combine egg and milk. In another bowl combine sesame crackers and peanuts. Dip flour-coated chicken chunks in egg mixture and then roll in cracker-peanut mixture.

3 Spread the coated chicken chunks in a 15×10×1-inch baking pan. Bake in a 400° oven for 10 to 12 minutes or until chicken is no longer pink.

4 Meanwhile, stir together sweet-and-sour sauce and barbecue sauce. Serve as a dipping sauce for chicken chunks. Makes 4 main-dish servings.

Nutrition facts per serving: 338 cal., 15 g total fat (2 g sat. fat), 113 mg chol., 688 mg sodium, 26 g carbo., 1 g fiber, 27 g pro. *Daily values:* 4% vit. A, 54% vit. C, 3% calcium, 12% iron.

CHICKEN WITH SKILLET TOMATO SAUCE

Prep: 10 min. ♦ Cook: 1 hour

Feel free to skip the blending step if you've a mind to—that's the cook's prerogative. Just combine all the sauce ingredients in the skillet and boil gently for 10 minutes, and you'll wind up with an invitingly chunky sauce. (See the photograph on page 121.)

2 to 2½ lb. meaty chicken pieces (breasts, thighs, and drumsticks)
¼ tsp. salt
¼ tsp. black pepper
¼ cup slivered almonds

♦♦♦

2 Tbsp. olive oil

♦♦♦

6 oz. packaged dried rigatoni

♦♦♦

½ cup sliced onion
3 cloves garlic, minced
4 medium tomatoes, seeded and cut up (1½ lb.)
¼ cup tomato paste
1 Tbsp. red wine vinegar
½ tsp. sugar
¼ tsp. salt
⅛ tsp. crushed red pepper
¼ cup coarsely chopped, pimiento-stuffed green olives

♦♦♦

Fresh marjoram sprigs (optional)

1 Skin chicken, if desired. Rinse chicken; pat dry with paper towels. Sprinkle with ¼ teaspoon salt and the black pepper; set aside. Place almonds in a 12-inch skillet. Cook over medium heat for 5 to 7 minutes or until almonds are lightly toasted, stirring often; remove from pan and set aside.

2 In the same 12-inch skillet heat olive oil. Add chicken to the skillet, placing meaty pieces toward the center. Cook, uncovered, over medium heat about 15 minutes or until lightly browned, turning to brown evenly. Reduce heat. Cook, covered, for 30 to 35 minutes more or until chicken is tender and no longer pink.

3 Meanwhile, cook pasta according to package directions; drain and keep warm. Remove chicken from skillet; drain off all but 2 tablespoons drippings. Cover chicken and keep warm while preparing sauce.

4 For sauce, cook onion and garlic in the reserved drippings until tender; transfer to a blender container or food processor bowl. Add the tomatoes, tomato paste, vinegar, sugar, ¼ teaspoon salt, and red pepper. Cover and blend or process until nearly smooth. Return mixture to skillet. Stir in olives. Bring to boiling; reduce heat. Boil gently, uncovered, about 10 minutes or until of desired consistency.

5 To serve, divide pasta among 4 bowls or plates. Top with a piece of chicken. Spoon sauce over chicken and pasta. Sprinkle with toasted almonds.

Garnish with marjoram sprigs, if desired. Makes 4 servings.

Nutrition facts per serving: 599 cal., 27 g total fat (5 g sat. fat), 104 mg chol., 426 mg sodium, 49 g carbo., 6 g fiber, 43 g pro. *Daily values:* 19% vit. A, 68% vit. C, 6% calcium, 31% iron.

PRIZE
TESTED
RECIPE
WINNER

LEMONY ITALIAN SALAD
Prep: 35 min. ◆ Chill: 1 to 2 hours

There's something to please everyone in this easy Mediterranean buffet-table star.

⅔ **cup dry lentils**
1⅓ **cups water**

◆◆◆

5 **plum tomatoes, chopped (about 1¾ cups)**
¾ **cup finely shredded Parmesan cheese (3 oz.)**
¾ **cup finely shredded Asiago cheese (3 oz.)**
2 **cups baby fresh spinach leaves or torn fresh spinach**
8 **oz. thinly sliced prosciutto or ham (about 12 slices)**

◆◆◆

⅓ **cup vinegar**
⅓ **cup olive oil**
2 **Tbsp. lemon juice**
1 **Tbsp. Dijon-style mustard**
2 **tsp. snipped fresh rosemary**
¼ **tsp. salt**

1 Rinse lentils; place in a small saucepan with water. Bring to boiling; reduce heat. Simmer, covered, for 20 to 25 minutes or until just tender. Drain and chill.

2 Arrange the tomatoes, cheeses, spinach leaves, cooked

Chicken with Skillet Tomato Sauce
(see page 96)

◆◆◆

Salad of torn romaine, artichoke hearts, thinly sliced onion, shaved Parmesan cheese, and an Italian vinaigrette

◆◆◆

Crusty Italian bread with butter or olive oil

◆◆◆

Double-Rich Pound Cake with Mascarpone Topper
(see page 108)

lentils, and prosciutto in rows on a large square or rectangular platter, or a serving dish.

3 For dressing, in a screw-top jar combine vinegar, olive oil, lemon juice, mustard, rosemary, salt, and ⅛ teaspoon *pepper*. Cover and shake well. Drizzle over salad. Makes 8 to 10 main-dish servings.

TO MAKE AHEAD

Prepare salad and dressing as directed, except do not drizzle on dressing. Cover salad and dressing separately and chill in the refrigerator for up to 2 hours. Before serving, let dressing stand at room temperature for 30 minutes. Drizzle dressing over salad.

Nutrition facts per serving: 340 cal., 23 g total fat (4 g sat. fat), 19 mg chol., 869 mg sodium, 15 g carbo., 1 g fiber, 20 g pro. *Daily values:* 14% vit. A, 26% vit. C, 17% calcium, 16% iron.

SHRIMP POTATO SALAD WITH CANDIED WALNUTS

Prep: 30 min. ◆ Chill: 1 hour.

⅓ cup sugar
¾ cup walnut pieces

❖❖❖

2 medium red potatoes, cut into ¾-inch pieces
12 oz. fresh or frozen medium shrimp, peeled and deveined

❖❖❖

⅓ cup mayonnaise or salad dressing
¼ cup vinegar
5 cups torn mixed salad greens
1 cup torn radicchio

1 For candied walnuts, butter a large piece of foil; set aside. Place the sugar in a small heavy skillet. Cook, without stirring, over medium-high heat until the sugar begins to melt, shaking skillet occasionally. Reduce heat to low. Stir with a wooden spoon until the sugar is golden brown and completely melted. Add walnuts, stirring to coat. Spread walnuts on buttered foil; cool. Break walnuts apart; set aside.

2 In a large saucepan cook potatoes, covered, in lightly salted boiling water for 10 minutes. Add shrimp. Cook, uncovered, about 2 minutes more or until shrimp turn pink and potatoes are tender; drain and chill.

3 For dressing, in a large mixing bowl stir together the mayonnaise and vinegar. Add potatoes and shrimp; toss to coat. Gently stir in nuts. Line 4 salad plates with greens. Top with potato mixture. Makes 4 main-dish servings.

Nutrition facts per serving: 495 cal., 31 g total fat (4 g sat. fat), 137 mg chol., 258 mg sodium, 41 g carbo., 2 g fiber, 20 g pro. *Daily values:* 8% vit. A, 26% vit. C, 6% calcium, 28% iron.

ASIAN SHRIMP AND MILLET SALAD

Prep: 25 min. ◆ Chill: 4 to 24 hours

1 Tbsp. cooking oil
1 cup millet

❖❖❖

2 cups cooked, peeled, and deveined shrimp
1 mango, seeded, peeled, and chopped
1 8-oz. can sliced water chestnuts, drained
½ cup chopped red onion
¼ cup snipped fresh cilantro
¼ cup rice vinegar
¼ cup salad oil
1 Tbsp. finely shredded orange peel
1 tsp. toasted sesame oil

1 In a large saucepan heat the cooking oil over medium heat. Add the millet; cook and stir for 2 minutes. Carefully add 2 cups *water.* Bring to boiling; reduce heat. Simmer, covered, about 25 minutes or until millet is fluffy and water is absorbed.

2 Transfer millet to a large bowl. Add shrimp, mango, water chestnuts, onion, and cilantro; toss to combine. Stir together vinegar, salad oil, orange peel, sesame oil, and ¼ teaspoon *salt.* Pour over millet mixture; toss to coat. Cover; chill 4 to 24 hours. Makes 5 to 6 main-dish servings.

Nutrition facts per serving: 395 cal., 17 g total fat (3 g sat. fat), 133 mg chol., 267 mg sodium, 42 g carbo., 7 g fiber, 19 g pro. *Daily values:* 20% vit. A, 26% vit. C, 3% calcium, 24% iron.

THAI-STYLE SHRIMP AND CUCUMBERS

Start to finish: 30 min.

Choose the type and the amount of hot chili peppers that best suit your palate.

1 lb. fresh or frozen medium shrimp in shells

❖❖❖

1 Tbsp. cooking oil
1 small onion, coarsely chopped
4 cloves garlic, minced
1 to 3 Thai* or serrano peppers, finely chopped
2 medium cucumbers, halved lengthwise, seeded, and sliced ¼ inch thick

1 cup fresh pea pods, stems removed
2 Tbsp. rice vinegar
2 tsp. toasted sesame oil

♦♦♦

Hot cooked rice noodles or rice
3 Tbsp. chopped honey-roasted peanuts
2 Tbsp. fresh snipped cilantro
Thai or serrano peppers (optional)

1 Thaw shrimp, if frozen. Peel, devein, and rinse shrimp; pat dry with paper towels. Set aside.

2 In a large nonstick skillet heat cooking oil over medium heat. Add onion, garlic, and chopped peppers and cook for 2 to 3 minutes or until onions are tender. Add cucumbers. Cook, covered, for 5 minutes, stirring occasionally. Add shrimp and cook, uncovered, about 3 minutes or until shrimp turn pink. Stir in pea pods. Cook and stir 1 minute more or until pea pods are heated. Stir in vinegar and sesame oil.

3 To serve, spoon shrimp mixture over cooked rice noodles or rice. Sprinkle peanuts and cilantro over each serving. Garnish with extra Thai or serrano peppers, if desired. Makes 4 servings.

*Note: Thai peppers resemble serrano peppers, but are smaller, slightly crooked, and somewhat hotter than serranos. Like all hot peppers, Thai peppers contain oils that can burn eyes, lips, and sensitive skin, so wear plastic gloves while preparing them and be sure to wash your hands thoroughly afterward.

HOT AS A CUCUMBER

Forget "cool as a cucumber." Cooking cucumbers brings out the sweetness that reveals their relation to berries and squashes. You'll find cooked cucumbers most often in Asian cuisine, but their delicate flavor can also augment your favorite pasta, casserole, or soup recipe.

For a quick accompaniment to fish or chicken, steam sliced cucumbers with a little dill and black pepper. Or, stir-fry cucumbers with toasted sesame oil and cayenne pepper.

Nutrition facts per main-dish serving: 462 cal., 12 g total fat (2 g sat. fat), 131 mg chol., 196 mg sodium, 72 g carbo., 3 g fiber, 19 g pro. *Daily values:* 9% vit. A, 45% vit. C, 6% calcium, 32% iron.

FISH FILLETS WITH BABY SPINACH, RED PEPPER, AND ONION WEDGES

Prep: 20 min. ♦ Cook: 9 min.

4 cups chopped baby spinach
1 medium onion, cut in thin wedges
3 Tbsp. olive oil or cooking oil
¼ cup red jalapeño jelly
1 small red or yellow sweet pepper, cut into thin strips

♦♦♦

1 lb. mahi mahi or cod fillets, ¾ to 1 inch thick
1 Tbsp. balsamic vinegar

1 Place baby spinach in a large bowl; set aside. In a large skillet cook onion in 1 tablespoon of the oil over medium heat until tender and slightly golden. Stir in 1 tablespoon of the jalapeño jelly. Add sweet pepper; cook and stir for 1 minute more. Remove from heat. Stir onion mixture into spinach; cover and set aside.

2 Meanwhile, cut fish into 4 serving-size pieces; sprinkle with ¼ teaspoon *salt* and ¼ teaspoon *black pepper*. In same large skillet heat remaining 2 tablespoons oil over medium-high heat. Add fish; cook 2 minutes on each side to sear. Steady fish when turning it in pan so fish doesn't break (see illustration, below). Reduce heat to medium—cook 5 minutes more or until fish just flakes easily when tested with a fork. Transfer fish to a platter; cover to keep warm.

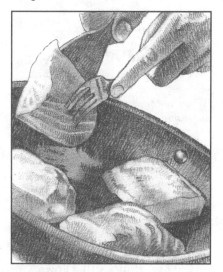

3 Add remaining jelly to skillet. Cook and stir until melted. To serve, toss spinach mixture with the vinegar. Serve fish atop spinach mixture. Spoon melted jelly over fish. Makes 4 servings.

Nutrition facts per main-dish serving: 264 cal., 11 g total fat (2 g sat. fat), 83 mg chol., 282 mg sodium, 19 g carbo., 2 g fiber, 23 g pro. *Daily values:* 46% vit. A, 64% vit. C, 5% calcium, 22% iron.

OPEN-FACED SALMON MELT

Prep: 10 min. ◆ Broil: 1½ min.

When you find yourself fishing around for a quick-to-fix lunch, reach into the pantry for a can of salmon and toss together this calcium-packed treat.

- 1 6-oz. can skinless, boneless salmon, drained and flaked
- 3 Tbsp. creamy Dijon-style mustard blend
- 1 Tbsp. thinly sliced green onion
- ½ tsp. lemon juice
- ⅛ tsp. pepper
- 2 bagels or English muffins, cut in half and toasted

◆◆◆

- 4 slices mozzarella cheese

1 In a small mixing bowl stir together salmon, mustard blend, green onion, lemon juice, and pepper. Spread the salmon mixture on toasted bagel or English muffin halves.

2 Top each sandwich with a slice of mozzarella cheese. Broil about 4 inches from heat for 1½ to 2 minutes or until the cheese is melted and bubbly. Serve immediately. Makes 4 servings.

Nutrition facts per serving: 278 cal., 11 g total fat (4 g sat. fat), 39 mg chol., 765 mg sodium, 22 g carbo., 0 g fiber, 22 g pro. *Daily values:* 8% vit. A, 1% vit. C, 28% calcium, 12% iron.

SALMON BURGERS

Prep: 10 min. ◆ Cook: 6 min.

This salmon and carrot combination is a great change from beef burgers.

- 1 egg white, beaten
- 1 Tbsp. milk
- 4 tsp. snipped fresh basil or ¾ tsp. dried basil, crushed
- ⅛ tsp. pepper
- 1 6-oz. can skinless, boneless pink salmon, drained and flaked
- ½ cup finely crushed wheat crackers
- 1 small carrot, finely shredded
- 2 to 3 Tbsp. yellow cornmeal

◆◆◆

- 1 Tbsp. cooking oil
- 3 hamburger buns, split and toasted
  Tomato slices (optional)
  Red onion, thinly sliced (optional)
  Mayonnaise (optional)
  Lemon wedges (optional)

1 In a small mixing bowl combine egg white, milk, basil, and pepper. Add salmon, crackers, and shredded carrot; mix well. Shape salmon mixture into three ¾-inch-thick patties. Coat patties with cornmeal.

2 In a skillet cook the patties in hot oil over medium-low heat about 6 minutes or until golden brown, turning once. Serve on toasted buns with tomato, onion, and mayonnaise, if desired. Serve with lemon wedges, if desired. Makes 3 servings.

Nutrition facts per serving: 303 cal., 12 g total fat (2 g sat. fat), 32 mg chol., 602 mg sodium, 31 g carbo., 2 g fiber, 16 g pro. *Daily values:* 35% vit. A, 2% vit. C, 13% calcium, 12% iron.

SALMON AND FETA PITA

Start to finish: 20 min.

- 2 6-oz. cans skinless, boneless salmon, drained and flaked
- ⅔ cup crumbled feta cheese (3 oz.)
- ½ cup cucumber ranch or buttermilk ranch salad dressing
- ¼ cup thinly sliced green onions
- 1½ tsp. snipped fresh dill or ½ tsp. dried dillweed, crushed

◆◆◆

- 4 large pita bread rounds, halved crosswise
- 1½ cups shredded spinach or romaine
- 1 cup chopped tomatoes

1 In a small mixing bowl stir together the salmon, feta cheese, dressing, green onions, and dill.

2 Spoon salmon mixture into each pita bread half. Top each pita with spinach and tomatoes. Makes 4 servings.

Nutrition facts per serving: 520 cal., 27 g total fat (9 g sat. fat), 92 mg chol., 1,484 mg sodium, 40 g carbo., 1 g fiber, 30 g pro. *Daily values:* 28% vit. A, 29% vit. C, 39% calcium, 23% iron.

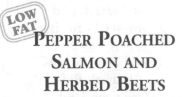

PEPPER POACHED SALMON AND HERBED BEETS

Prep: 20 min. ◆ Cook: 4 min.

Poaching means cooking in simmering liquid. It's one of the best ways to cook fish because the fish will never dry out.

1 to 1½ lb. fresh or frozen salmon fillets

◆◆◆

1 cup loosely packed watercress leaves
2 Tbsp. snipped fresh tarragon
½ of a lemon, cut into thick slices
2 tsp. whole peppercorns
3 bay leaves

◆◆◆

½ cup light dairy sour cream
1 tsp. snipped fresh tarragon
1 Tbsp. snipped fresh chives
1 recipe Herbed Beets (see right)
  Watercress and fresh tarragon sprigs (optional)

1 Thaw fish, if frozen. Measure thickness of fish. Cut into 4 serving-size pieces, if necessary. In a large skillet combine 1 cup *water* and ½ teaspoon *salt*.

2 For the bouquet garni, place ½ cup of the watercress, the

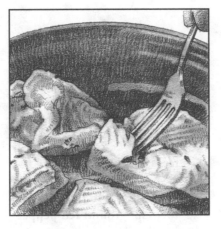

2 tablespoons tarragon, lemon slices, peppercorns, and bay leaves in the center of a double-thick, 9-inch-square piece of 100-percent-cotton cheesecloth. Bring the corners of the cheesecloth together and tie with clean 100-percent cotton string. Place the bouquet garni in the skillet. Bring water to boiling; reduce heat. With a slotted spatula, gently lower the fish fillets into the water. Simmer, covered, for 4 to 6 minutes for each ½ inch of thickness or until fish just flakes when tested with a fork (see illustration, above). Using a slotted spoon, carefully remove the fish fillets to a platter. Cover fish; keep it warm while preparing sauce.

3 For sauce, in a blender container or food processor bowl combine sour cream, remaining ½ cup watercress, the 1 teaspoon tarragon, ½ teaspoon *ground pepper,* and ¼ teaspoon *salt.* Cover and blend or process until smooth. Stir in chives. Spoon sauce onto plates and top with fish. Serve with Herbed Beets. Garnish with additional watercress and tarragon, if desired. Makes 4 servings.

Nutrition facts per serving (for salmon and sauce): 149 cal., 6 g total fat (2 g sat. fat), 24 mg chol., 507 mg sodium, 5 g carbo., 0 g fiber, 19 g pro. *Daily values:* 10% vit. A, 11% vit. C, 5% calcium, 8% iron.

HERBED BEETS

Prep: 10 min. ◆ Cook: 20 min.

It's best to peel cooked beets under a running faucet so the beet juice is rinsed away before it can stain.

1 lb. fresh baby beets (about 12) or small beets, quartered

◆◆◆

1 Tbsp. olive oil
1 Tbsp. red wine vinegar
⅛ tsp. salt
2 Tbsp. snipped fresh watercress
1 Tbsp. snipped fresh tarragon

1 Cut green tops off the beets; discard. Wash beets; do not peel.

2 In a small saucepan bring a small amount of lightly salted water to boiling. Add beets. Cook, covered, over medium heat about 20 minutes or until crisp-tender; drain. Allow beets to stand about 10 minutes or until cool enough to handle. Under a running faucet, slip skins off beets.

3 In a serving bowl combine beets, olive oil, vinegar, and salt Toss gently to coat beets. Sprinkle with watercress and tarragon. Serve with Pepper Poached Salmon (see recipe, left). Makes 4 servings.

Nutrition facts per serving (beets): 55 cal., 3 g total fat (0 g sat. fat), 0 mg chol., 106 mg sodium, 6 g carbo., 3 g fiber, 1 g pro. *Daily values:* 8% vit. C, 3% iron.

HOOKED ON HALIBUT

Halibut is especially rich in omega-3 fatty acids, the compounds that help reduce your risk of heart disease and make fish a great, healthful food. This giant, flounderlike fish is caught in the icy waters off Alaska from late spring through fall. It's available fresh during this time, but most of the catch is processed and flash-frozen on the boats, so you can get halibut most of the year.

Halibut has a mild flavor and a firm texture, which holds up well during cooking. Grill or broil halibut and serve it with a simple sauce to complement the delicate flavor.

If you're buying fish fresh, look for firm, translucent flesh that springs back when touched. Fresh fish should have virtually no odor and should be kept at 38 degrees or less, for no more than two days.

Because it's a hardy cold-water fish, halibut freezes well. If buying frozen fish, look for packages with no frost buildup under the wrapper. Frozen fish, held at 0 degrees, will keep for up to three months.

HALIBUT WITH TWO-PEPPER SAUCE

Start to finish: 30 min.

Adjust the heat on this dish by using either mild or hot banana peppers.

4 fresh or frozen halibut steaks, cut 1 inch thick (about 1½ lb.)
½ to 1 tsp. ground red pepper
2 small yellow sweet peppers, seeded and chopped
1 medium onion, chopped
2 fresh banana peppers, seeded and chopped
4 cloves garlic, minced
1 Tbsp. cooking oil
1 cup chicken broth

♦♦♦

2 Tbsp. lime juice
⅛ tsp. salt

♦♦♦

1 Tbsp. cooking oil

♦♦♦

Banana pepper rings (optional)
Italian parsley sprigs (optional)

1 Thaw fish, if frozen; rinse and pat dry. Rub fish with ground red pepper; set aside.

2 For sauce, in a medium saucepan cook chopped peppers, onion, and garlic in 1 tablespoon oil over medium heat for 10 minutes, stirring occasionally. Carefully add the broth and bring just to boiling; reduce heat. Boil mixture gently, uncovered, about 5 minutes or until it is reduced to 1½ cups.

3 Cool pepper mixture slightly. Pour cooled mixture into a

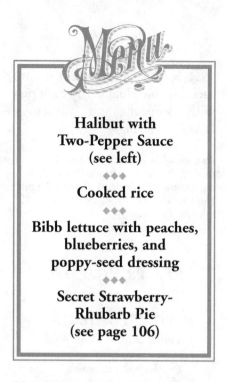

Menu

Halibut with Two-Pepper Sauce (see left)

♦♦♦

Cooked rice

♦♦♦

Bibb lettuce with peaches, blueberries, and poppy-seed dressing

♦♦♦

Secret Strawberry-Rhubarb Pie (see page 106)

blender container; add lime juice and salt. Cover and blend until smooth. Press mixture through a sieve and discard solids. Return sauce to saucepan and heat through without boiling. Remove sauce from heat and keep it warm while cooking fish.

4 In a large skillet cook fish steaks in 1 tablespoon oil over medium heat until fish just flakes when tested with a fork, carefully turning once. Allow 4 to 6 minutes per ½-inch thickness. (Add additional oil, if necessary, to prevent sticking.) Remove steaks from skillet.

5 To serve, spoon sauce onto warm dinner plates. Top each plate with a halibut steak. Garnish with banana pepper rings and parsley, if desired. Makes 4 servings.

Nutrition facts per serving: 284 cal., 11 g total fat (2 g sat. fat), 55 mg chol., 356 mg sodium, 7 g carbo., 1 g fiber, 38 g pro. *Daily values:* 10% vit. A, 159% vit. C, 8% calcium, 12% iron.

ORANGE ROUGHY WITH MUSTARD SAUCE

Prep: 20 min. ♦ Broil: 8 min.
Chill: 1 hour (sauce)

The cool yogurt sauce tempers this slightly spicy fish dish.

1 lb. fresh or frozen orange roughy fillets
1 Tbsp. curry powder
1 Tbsp. cooking oil

♦♦♦

   Nonstick spray coating

♦♦♦

1 recipe Yogurt-Mustard Sauce (see below, right)
1 ½-inch-piece fresh ginger, peeled, cut into matchsticks
   Fresh lime peel, cut into strips

1 Thaw fish, if frozen; rinse and pat dry. Cut fillets into 4 serving-size portions. In a small bowl stir together curry powder and cooking oil; brush on both sides of the fish.

2 Spray the unheated rack of a broiler pan with nonstick spray coating. Place fish on rack. Broil 4 inches from the heat until fish just flakes easily with a fork. Turn halfway through broiling if fish is 1 inch or more thick. (Allow 4 to 6 minutes total per ½-inch thickness of fish.)

3 Serve fish with Yogurt-Mustard Sauce. Garnish with ginger and lime peel. Makes 4 main-dish servings.

FISH STORIES

When you've chosen the best-quality fish or shellfish for a meal, your next decision is how much to buy. Aim for satisfying, reasonably sized portions for main dishes using the following guidelines.

AMOUNT OF FISH PER SERVING

The amount you buy depends on the form you choose:
Drawn. The internal organs and maybe some scales have been removed.
Dressed. Fish that's ready for the pan with organs, scales, head, tail, and fins removed.
Steak. A crosscut slice, ready to cook; may contain bones.
Fillet. A boneless piece cut from the side and away from the backbone, skinned or not, but ready to cook.

Drawn fish	12	ounces
Dressed or pan-dressed	8	ounces
Steaks or fillets	4	to 5 ounces
Frozen fish sticks	4	to 5 pieces

AMOUNT OF SHELLFISH PER SERVING

Generally there are three to four ounces of meat per pound. Count on larger portion sizes if the shellfish comes with shells and/or cartilage.

Clams in shell (large)	6	
Clams in shell (littleneck)	6	to 8
Crabs, live blue	1	pound
Crabmeat, cooked	4	to 5 ounces
Crawfish in shell	1	pound
Lobster, live, whole	1	to 1½ pounds
Lobster tail in shell, frozen	1	(about 8 ounces)
Mussels in shells	12	
Oysters in shells	6	
Oysters, shucked	½	pint
Scallops	4	to 6 ounces
Shrimp in shells	4	to 6 ounces
Shrimp, peeled and deveined	3	to 4 ounces
Surimi (imitation seafood)	4	to 5 ounces

Yogurt-Mustard Sauce: In a small mixing bowl stir together ⅓ cup plain fat-free yogurt, 1 tablespoon lime juice, and 2 teaspoons Dijon-style mustard. Cover and chill the sauce for 1 hour before serving.

Nutrition facts per serving: 153 cal., 5 g total fat (1 g sat. fat), 61 mg chol., 171 mg sodium, 3 g carbo., 1 g fiber, 23 g pro. *Daily values:* 1% vit. A, 2% vit. C, 5% calcium, 5% iron.

NUTS TAKE THE PRIZE

Squirrels have the right idea. Not the loud chattering in the treetops thing, but the nut-eating habit. New research proves that nuts are a lot more than just a tasty source of protein.

Nuts are also loaded with heart-protecting compounds and B vitamins, especially B6 and folate. Phytochemicals, the natural substances in plant foods thought to fend off cancer, are in abundance, too. And few foods can boast as much vitamin E. Just an ounce of hazelnuts contains more than two-thirds of the recommended dietary allowance of vitamin E, which fights cancer and heart disease.

There's also a mother lode of essential trace minerals in nuts that the body needs in minute amounts, including zinc, magnesium, iron, potassium, selenium, and calcium. Iron and zinc, two minerals that most Americans don't get enough of in their diet, are crucial for blood and enzyme function. Selenium, an antioxidant, helps ward off heart disease and was shown in a recent study to decrease the risk of prostate cancer. An ounce of mixed nuts—about a handful tossed into your oatmeal in the morning—has between 5 and 18 percent of an entire day's needs for all these minerals (see chart, page 105).

STRIKING OIL

The monosaturated oils in nuts protect against heart disease in several ways. As a major source of vitamin E, nut oils protect our circulatory systems, where the vitamin works as an antioxidant to inhibit cell and tissue damage. Nut oils also help keep desired HDL-cholesterol levels stable while lowering LDL-cholesterol and triglycerides. Packing a peanut butter sandwich instead of eating fast food laden with saturated fat is another way nuts can help protect against vascular disease.

NUTS TO THE BABY

Many nuts also include generous amounts of omega-3 fatty acids in their healthful oil arsenal. Omega-3 has been shown in dozens of studies to play a role in protecting the heart and circulatory system. But new studies indicate that omega-3s may play a significant role in combating symptoms associated with rheumatoid arthritis, diabetes, and depression—conditions that affect millions of Americans.

Omega-3 oils also are crucial for brain and eye development in growing fetuses, notes Oregon Health Sciences University nutrition professor William E. Connor, M.D. Although fish, especially deep-water types such as cod and tuna, are the best omega-3 sources, less than one-tenth of Americans eat fish daily. Nuts come to the rescue here, too: Most nuts are about 50 percent oil, with about a tenth of that amount omega-3 oils.

Walnuts have one of the highest concentrations of omega-3s of any plant food. Connor recommends pregnant women increase their intake of omega-3s to between 20 to 30 calories (½ to 1 percent of their total daily need). Says Connor, "Pregnant women can add one ounce of shelled English walnuts to their daily diet for 10 to 15 calories toward that amount."

A NUT BY ANY OTHER NAME

Poor little peanut. It's actually a legume, not a "true" nut. However, everybody thinks it's a nut and, in fact, peanuts account for nearly half of the "nuts" consumers report eating. The nutrition profile of the peanut is impressive. Peanuts have as much or more of the monosaturated oils and the protein and minerals that tree nuts have. But more than that, peanuts have the highest amount of niacin of any "nut" and more than double the amount of folate as nuts that grow on trees. Folate is the B vitamin that has earned accolades for preventing neural-tube birth defects, such as spina bifida, as well as helping to prevent strokes and heart attacks.

Fiber on the Half Shell

Throwing an extra ounce of mixed nuts into your trail mix or munching a handful of nuts at your desk does more than give you a midday boost of energy—it helps you keep cancer away, too. Diets high in fiber have been shown to reduce the risk of cancer of the stomach, esophagus, and colon. Most nuts boast about 2 to 3 grams of fiber per ounce—about 10 percent of your fiber needs for the entire day. Fiber also helps digestion and provides a feeling of fullness. In one study, the high fiber content of almonds fed to subjects as extra calories was thought to keep those extra calories from causing weight gain.

Won't Nuts Make Me Fat?

Some people avoid nuts because nuts are rich in calories. But eating nuts did not seem to lead to an increase in weight during a recent short-term (four weeks) controlled study at the Health Research and Studies Center in Los Angeles. Although the study focused on the effects of monosaturated fats on cholesterol levels, volunteers who ate 3 ounces of almonds a day in addition to the control diet did not have significant weight gain. The evidence suggests that the body compensates by favoring a natural reduction in overall daily calorie intake.

"Let's put one nutrition myth to rest: It's not eating fat that makes you fat," says Dr. Penny Kris-Etherton, a professor of nutrition and a dietary fat researcher at Pennsylvania State University. "Eating more calories than you burn up with activity is what adds on the unwanted pounds. In fact, continued research supports the evidence that diets high in monosaturated fats are preferable to low-fat diets for helping to prevent certain cardiovascular diseases. Nuts, especially nuts that are high in monosaturated fat, such as peanuts, can occupy a major place in heart-healthy diets."

Nuts by the Numbers

Here are the approximate percentages of the Daily Values* for selected minerals, fiber, and vitamin E in each 1-ounce serving.

	iron	zinc	calcium	potassium	fiber	vit. E
almonds	6	7	8	6	12	20
brazil nuts	6	9	5	5	8	20
cashews	11	11	1	5	4	10
hazelnuts	7	5	6	4	8	70
peanuts	5	7	2	6	8	20
pecans	6	11	1	3	12	10
pistachios	6	3	2	8	12	20
walnuts	6	5	3	4	4	10

*averaged from various sources

SECRET STRAWBERRY-RHUBARB PIE

Prep: 30 min. ◆ Bake: 50 min.

What's the secret? Almond cake-and-pastry filling adds a pleasing hint of nuttiness.

1 recipe Pastry for Double-Crust Pie (see right)

◆◆◆

⅔ cup sugar
¼ cup cornstarch
½ of a 12½-oz. can almond cake-and-pastry filling (not almond paste) (about ½ cup)
1 Tbsp. lemon juice
½ tsp. ground nutmeg
¼ tsp. salt
3 cups fresh or frozen sliced rhubarb
2½ cups sliced fresh strawberries
1 Tbsp. margarine or butter

◆◆◆

1 slightly beaten egg white
2 Tbsp. sliced almonds

1 Prepare pastry for double-crust pie. On a lightly floured surface roll out half the pastry to a 12-inch circle. Line a 9-inch pie plate with the pastry; set aside.

2 In a large bowl stir together sugar, cornstarch, almond filling, lemon juice, nutmeg, and salt. Stir in rhubarb and strawberries. (If using frozen fruit, let mixture stand about 30 minutes or until fruit is partially thawed, but still icy.) Transfer mixture to pastry-lined pie plate. Trim pastry to edge of pie plate. Dot filling with margarine or butter.

3 Roll out remaining pastry to a 12-inch circle. Cut slits in remaining pastry; place on filling and seal. Crimp edge. To prevent overbrowning, cover edge of pie with foil. Place pie plate on a baking sheet to catch any drips.

4 Bake in a 375° oven for 25 minutes for fresh fruit (50 minutes for frozen fruit). Remove foil. Bake pie for 25 to 30 minutes more or until top is golden. During last 10 minutes of baking, quickly brush top with egg white; sprinkle with almonds. Cool on a wire rack. Makes 8 servings.

Pastry for Double-Crust Pie: In a medium mixing bowl stir together 2 cups all-purpose flour and ½ teaspoon salt. Using a pastry blender, cut in ⅔ cup shortening until pieces are pea-size. Sprinkle 1 tablespoon water over part of the mixture; gently toss with a fork. Push moistened dough to side of bowl. Repeat, using 1 tablespoon water at a time, until all the dough is moistened (using 6 to 7 tablespoons water total). Divide in half. Form each half into a ball. Use as directed for individual pie recipes.

Nutrition facts per serving: 461 cal., 22 g total fat (5 g sat. fat), 4 mg chol., 253 mg sodium, 62 g carbo., 5 g fiber, 5 g pro. *Daily values:* 1% vit. A, 51% vit. C, 4% calcium, 13% iron.

CHERRY-APPLE BREAD PUDDING

Prep: 25 min. ◆ Bake: 45 min.

9 slices firm textured white bread
3 Tbsp. butter, softened

3 medium Golden Delicious apples, peeled and very thinly sliced
2 Tbsp. lemon juice
½ cup dried tart red cherries
6 eggs, beaten
3 cups milk
½ cup sugar

1 Lightly butter 1 side of the bread slices; cut bread into quarters. Arrange half of the bread pieces, buttered side down, in a 3-quart rectangular baking dish.

2 Toss together apples and lemon juice. Sprinkle the apples and cherries atop bread in baking dish. Top with remaining bread, buttered side up. Combine eggs, milk, and sugar; pour atop bread in dish. Press mixture down lightly with back of a large spoon to be sure that all bread is moistened.

3 Bake in a 350° oven for 45 to 50 minutes or until set and a knife inserted off center comes out clean. Cool 30 minutes on a rack. Serve warm. Serves 8 to 10.

Nutrition facts per serving: 315 cal., 11 g total fat (5 g sat. fat), 178 mg chol., 270 mg sodium, 45 g carbo., 2 g fiber, 10 g pro. *Daily values:* 21% vit. A, 8% vit. C, 13% calcium, 9% iron.

WHITE CHOCOLATE AND BERRIES SHORTCAKE

Prep: 20 min. ◆ Bake: 15 min.
Stand: 10 min.

1½ cups whipping cream
½ of a 6-oz. pkg. white chocolate baking squares, chopped (3 oz.)

◆◆◆

2 cups all-purpose flour
¼ cup sugar

2 tsp. baking powder
1 tsp. finely shredded orange
   peel
¼ tsp. ground nutmeg
½ cup cold butter
1 egg, beaten
⅔ cup orange juice

◆◆◆

3 cups sliced strawberries

1 In a small saucepan heat and stir ¾ cup of the whipping cream and white chocolate until chocolate is melted. Place in a mixing bowl; cover and chill thoroughly.

2 Meanwhile, for shortcake, in a large mixing bowl stir together flour, sugar, baking powder, orange peel, and nutmeg. Using a pastry blender, cut in butter until mixture resembles coarse crumbs. Combine egg and orange juice; add to dry mixture. Stir just to moisten. Spread batter into a greased 8×1½-inch round baking pan. Bake in a 450° oven for 15 to 18 minutes or until a wooden toothpick inserted near center comes out clean. Cool in pan for 10 minutes. Remove from pan. While still warm, split into 2 layers.

3 Add remaining whipping cream to white chocolate mixture. Beat with an electric mixer until soft peaks form. Place bottom shortcake layer on a serving platter; spread with half of the white chocolate mixture and top with 2 cups of the berries. Add top layer, remaining white chocolate mixture, and remaining berries. Makes 8 to 10 servings.

Nutrition facts per serving: 480 cal., 33 g total fat (20 g sat. fat), 122 mg chol., 244 mg sodium, 42 g carbo., 2 g fiber, 6 g pro. *Daily values:* 31% vit. A, 43% vit. C, 12% calcium, 12% iron.

PINEAPPLE-LEMON CHIFFON PIE

Prep: 1¼ hours ◆ Chill: 4 hours

⅓ cup butter
¼ cup sugar
1 cup finely crushed graham
   crackers
¼ cup finely chopped toasted
   almonds

◆◆◆

2 envelopes unflavored gelatin
1 8¼-oz. can crushed
   pineapple (syrup pack)
1¼ cups sugar
1½ cups refrigerated or frozen
   egg product, thawed
2 tsp. finely shredded lemon
   peel
¾ cup lemon juice

◆◆◆

¾ cup whipping cream

1 Melt butter; stir in ¼ cup sugar. Add graham cracker crumbs and almonds. Press onto bottom and sides of a 9-inch pie plate to form a firm, even crust. Bake in a 375° oven for 4 to 5 minutes or until edge is lightly browned. Cool on wire rack.

2 Meanwhile, in a small saucepan soften gelatin in ⅔ cup *water.* Cook and stir over low heat just until gelatin dissolves. Remove from heat; transfer to a large mixing bowl. Stir in undrained pineapple, 1¼ cups sugar, egg product, lemon peel, and lemon juice (mixture may appear curdled). Chill until mixture mounds when spooned, stirring occasionally.

3 Beat gelatin mixture with an electric mixer on medium to high speed for 4 to 5 minutes or until mixture becomes light and frothy.

DON'T DESERT DESSERT

Even when you don't have time to make the simplest recipe, dessert doesn't have to be a lost prospect. Try one of these super-simple dessert ideas that will satisfy the craving for just a little something sweet after a delicious dinner:

◆ Fresh fruit sliced and tossed with a little honey and sprinkled with toasted almonds. Ripe, juicy peaches, nectarines, or plums are great choices.

◆ A tea bar set up with several kinds of teabags (a selection of herbal, decaffeinated, and black tea among them), lemon, milk, honey, and sugar—along with purchased tea biscuits.

◆ A cheese course featuring a selection of cheeses and fresh fruit. Some perfect pairings include ripe pears with a blue cheese such as Roquefort or Gorgonzola; berries and apples with brie; oranges (particularly blood oranges, which are super-juicy and sweet) with thin wedges of Parmesan or Romano.

In a clean bowl with clean beaters, immediately beat whipping cream until soft peaks form. Fold whipped cream into gelatin mixture. Chill again until mixture mounds when spooned. Transfer filling to crust. Sprinkle with *toasted coconut,* if desired. Cover and chill about 4 hours or until firm. Makes 8 servings.

Nutrition facts per serving: 409 cal., 19 g total fat (10 g sat. fat), 51 mg chol., 207 mg sodium, 55 g carbo., 1 g fiber, and 8 g pro. *Daily values:* 39% vit. A, 26% vit. C, 4% calcium, and 11% iron.

WHY SIFT POWDERED SUGAR?

Unlike flour, which needs only stirring before measuring, powdered sugar must be sifted either through a sieve or a sifter because it can pack down or lump during shipping. If you use the sugar when it's packed down, you will wind up with too much of the sugar in your frosting. Plus, lumpy sugar makes lumpy icing.

How to sift: Spoon powdered sugar into a sifter or a sieve. Holding it over a bowl, operate the handle of the sifter or push through sieve with a wooden spoon, stirring, if necessary, to break up any lumps. Then gently spoon it into a dry measuring cup or a measuring spoon. Level off excess with straight edge of a metal spatula or knife.

COMPANY CAKE EXPRESS

Prep: 30 min. ◆ Bake: 15 min.

Geometry lesson: Make something in an unexpected size or shape—like these cakes—and the everyday becomes infinitely more appealing. (See the photograph on page 123.)

1¼ cups all-purpose flour
1¼ tsp. baking powder
¼ tsp. salt

◆◆◆

⅓ cup butter, softened
¾ cup granulated sugar
1 tsp. vanilla
1 egg
⅔ cup milk

1 recipe Butter Frosting (see right)
Edible flowers, such as nasturtium petals and scented geranium leaves

1 Grease and flour twelve 2½-inch muffin pans, thirty-six 1¾-inch muffin pans, or a combination of both sizes, shaking out excess flour. Set aside. Combine flour, baking powder, and salt.

2 In a medium mixing bowl beat butter with an electric mixer 30 seconds. Add sugar and vanilla; beat until combined. Add egg; beat well. Add flour mixture and milk alternately to beaten mixture, beating on low speed after each addition just until combined. Fill muffin cups two-thirds full with batter.

3 Bake in a 375° oven about 15 minutes or until a wooden toothpick inserted near the center comes out clean. Let cool in pans for 5 minutes. Remove from pans. Cool completely on wire racks.

4 To decorate, invert cupcakes. Using a pastry bag fitted with a round tip, pipe dots or swirls of Butter Frosting on bottoms of cupcakes. (Or, using a table knife or small spatula, spread frosting on bottom of each inverted cupcake.) To serve, arrange on a cake stand with small cupcakes to outside of plate if using both 2½- and 1¾-inch sizes. Garnish with edible flowers. Makes 12 (or 36) cupcakes.

Nutrition facts per cupcake with frosting (for 12 cupcakes): 302 cal., 10 g total fat (6 g sat. fat), 43 mg chol., 185 mg sodium, 52 g carbo., 0 g fiber, 2 g pro. Daily values: 9% vit. A, 4% calcium, 4% iron.

BUTTER FROSTING

Start to finish: 20 min.

¼ cup butter
3½ cups sifted powdered sugar
2 Tbsp. rum (or ¼ tsp. rum flavoring plus 2 Tbsp. milk)
Milk

1 In a mixing bowl beat butter with an electric mixer until fluffy. Gradually add 2 cups of the powdered sugar, beating well. Slowly beat in the rum or rum flavoring and 2 tablespoons milk. Slowly beat in remaining powdered sugar. Beat in additional milk, if needed, to reach desired consistency. Makes 1⅔ cups.

DOUBLE-RICH POUND CAKE WITH MASCARPONE TOPPER

Prep: 1 hour ◆ Bake: 60 to 70 min.

To serve fruit with the cake, count on about ¾ cup for each person. (See the photograph on page 122.)

1 8-oz. pkg. cream cheese
¾ cup butter
6 eggs
2 cups all-purpose flour
1 tsp. baking powder
2 cups sugar
2 tsp. vanilla

◆◆◆

Assorted fresh fruit, such as kiwi, carambola (star fruit), blueberries, raspberries, blackberries, and sliced strawberries (optional)
1 recipe Mascarpone Topper (see page 109)

1 Allow cream cheese, butter, and eggs to stand at room temperature for 30 minutes. Grease and lightly flour a 10-inch fluted tube pan or two 8×4×2-inch loaf pans; set aside. Combine flour and baking powder; set aside.

2 Beat cream cheese and butter with an electric mixer for 30 seconds. Gradually add sugar, beating about 6 minutes or until very light and fluffy. Beat in vanilla. Add eggs, 1 at a time, beating 1 minute after each addition. Add flour mixture, beating just until combined. Pour batter into prepared pan, spreading, if necessary, to form an even layer.

3 Bake in a 325° oven for 60 to 65 minutes for tube pan or 65 to 70 minutes for loaf pans or until done. Cool in pan(s) on wire rack 10 minutes. Remove from pan(s); cool on rack. Cut triangles of cake. Arrange cake in bowls with fruit, if desired. Top with Mascarpone Topper. Serves 20.

Nutrition facts per serving: 306 cal., 19 g total fat (10 g sat. fat), 109 mg chol., 149 mg sodium, 31 g carbo., 0 g fiber, 7 g pro. *Daily values:* 14% vit. A, 3% calcium, 6% iron.

MASCARPONE TOPPER

Start to finish: 5 min.

- 1 8-oz. carton mascarpone cheese, softened
- ¼ cup chopped walnuts
- 2 Tbsp. milk
- 1 Tbsp. honey

1 Stir together cheese, walnuts, milk, and honey. Serve with Double-Rich Pound Cake. Store,

tightly covered, in the refrigerator up to 2 days. Makes 1¼ cups.

FLOWER PETAL CHEESECAKE

Prep: 25 min. ◆ Bake: 50 min.
Chill: 4 hours

- 1¾ cups finely crushed graham crackers
- 3 Tbsp. all-purpose flour
- ⅓ cup butter, melted
- ½ cup chopped edible flowers

◆◆◆

- 3 8-oz. pkg. cream cheese, softened
- ¾ cup sugar
- ¼ cup honey
- 1 tsp. finely shredded lemon peel
- 3 Tbsp. lemon juice
- 2 8-oz. cartons dairy sour cream
- 3 eggs
- 2 Tbsp. sugar

◆◆◆

- 2 cups strawberries, hulled
- 1 Tbsp. honey

1 For crust, combine graham crackers, 1 tablespoon of the flour, and melted butter. Press onto bottom and 2 inches up sides of an 8-inch springform pan. Reserve 2 tablespoons of the chopped flowers for garnish; cover and chill until needed.

2 Beat cream cheese, ¾ cup sugar, ¼ cup honey, ½ teaspoon of the lemon peel, 2 tablespoons of the lemon juice, the remaining 2 tablespoons flour, and 1 carton dairy sour cream until combined. Add eggs, beating on low speed just until combined. Stir in remaining edible flowers. Pour filling into crust-lined pan. Place

on a shallow baking pan. Bake in a 375° oven 45 to 50 minutes or until center appears nearly set when shaken. Combine remaining sour cream and 2 tablespoons sugar; spread atop cheesecake. Bake 5 minutes more. Cool in pan for 15 minutes. Loosen crust from sides of pan; cool 30 minutes. Remove sides of pan; cool cheesecake completely. Cover and chill at least 4 hours.

3 In a blender container combine strawberries, remaining ½ teaspoon lemon peel and 1 tablespoon lemon juice, and 1 tablespoon honey. Cover and process until smooth. Spoon some of sauce onto plates; add cheesecake and sprinkle with reserved edible flowers. Makes 12 to 16 servings.

Nutrition facts per serving: 499 cal., 35 g total fat (21 g sat. fat), 146 mg chol., 326 mg sodium, 39 g carbo., 1 g fiber, 9 g pro. *Daily values:* 40% vit. A, 27% vit. C, 9% calcium, 10% iron.

FROZEN BERRY YOGURT

Prep: 20 min. ◆ **Chill:** 8 to 24 hours
Freeze: 25 min. ◆ **Ripen:** 4 hours

*Kick off the ice-cream-making season
with this frosty treat.
(See the photograph on page 123.)*

1¼ cups sugar
1 cup water

◆◆◆

3 cups fresh raspberries,
   blackberries, and/or
   strawberries
3 8-oz. containers vanilla yogurt
1 tsp. vanilla

◆◆◆

   **Fresh melon or other fruit,
   cut into thin slices
   (optional)**

1 In a medium saucepan combine sugar and water. Cook and stir over high heat until mixture comes to a boil and sugar dissolves. Remove from heat; cool.

2 In a blender container combine half the sugar mixture and berries; cover and blend until almost smooth. Pour into a fine mesh sieve set over a bowl. Repeat with remaining sugar mixture and berries. Press berry mixture through sieve; discard seeds. Transfer berry mixture to a large mixing bowl. Stir in yogurt and vanilla; mix until well combined. Cover and chill for 8 to 24 hours.

3 Freeze mixture in a 2-quart ice-cream freezer according to manufacturer's directions. Ripen 4 hours. Cut melon or other fruit into long, thin ribbons with a vegetable peeler, if desired. Serve with

scoops of frozen yogurt. Makes 6 to 8 servings.

Nutrition facts per serving: 298 cal., 2 g total fat (1 g sat. fat), 6 mg chol., 67 mg sodium, 67 g carbo., 3 g fiber, 5 g pro. *Daily values:* 3% vit. A, 27% vit. C, 13% calcium, 3% iron.

ORANGE SHERBET WITH MINTED ORANGE SLICES

Prep: 20 min. ◆ **Freeze:** 8 hours

2 8-oz. containers lemon low-
   fat yogurt
1 6-oz. can frozen orange juice
   concentrate, thawed
1 8-oz. can crushed pineapple
   (juice pack)
¼ cup sugar

◆◆◆

2 medium oranges, peeled and
   thinly sliced
2 Tbsp. sugar
2 Tbsp. finely snipped fresh
   mint

1 Stir together yogurt, orange juice concentrate, pineapple, and the ¼ cup sugar. Pour into a 9×5×3-inch loaf pan. Cover and freeze about 8 hours or until firm.

2 Meanwhile, in a bowl combine oranges, the 2 tablespoons sugar, and mint; gently toss. Cover; chill until serving time.

3 Let sherbet stand at room temperature for 15 to 20 minutes before serving. Divide orange slices among dessert dishes; place scoops of sherbet atop oranges.

Nutrition facts per serving: 216 cal., 1 g total fat (0.5 g sat. fat), 3 mg chol., 46 mg sodium, 49 g carbo., 2 g fiber, 5 g pro. *Daily values:* 3% vit. A, 120% vit. C, 12% calcium, 4% iron.

GINGERED ORANGE-RHUBARB PUNCH

Start to finish: 20 min.

*When fresh rhubarb is in
abundance, stir together a batch of
this chilling refresher.*

5 cups cut-up rhubarb
1 1-inch piece ginger, thinly
   sliced
⅔ cup sugar

◆◆◆

2 6-oz. cans or one 12-oz. can
   frozen orange juice
   concentrate, thawed
1 6-oz. can frozen lemonade
   concentrate, thawed
1 1-liter bottle ginger ale,
   chilled

1 In a large saucepan combine rhubarb, ginger, and 1 cup *water.* Bring to boiling; reduce heat. Simmer, covered, for 5 minutes. Remove from heat and cool slightly. Pour mixture into a fine mesh sieve set over a bowl. Strain rhubarb mixture, pressing rhubarb gently to get out as much liquid as you can. Discard pulp. Return the strained liquid to saucepan; add sugar. Cook and stir until sugar is dissolved. Cover and chill, if desired.

2 Just before serving, stir the orange juice and lemonade concentrates into rhubarb liquid. Transfer to a large punch bowl. Add 4 cups *water.* Gradually pour ginger ale down sides of punch bowl. Serve over ice. Makes 14 (6-ounce) servings.

Nutrition facts per serving: 106 cal., 0 g total fat, 0 mg chol., 10 mg sodium, 27 g carbo., 1 g fiber, 1 g pro. *Daily values:* 32% vit. C, 3% calcium, 1% iron.

JUNE
Salads and Steaks

30-minute recipes indicated in RED.
Low-fat and no-fat recipes indicated
with a ♥.
Photographs indicated in italics.
*Bonus recipe

Summer's here, so why wait to start feasting on salads and steaks on the grill? Kaleidoscope Potato Salad features tender, thin green beans (haricots vert) and Pineapple-Spinach Salad uses baby spinach—one of the first of summer's great garden foods. Grill ears of corn for a fun, fresh-tasting Corn-on-the-Cob Salad. And while that grill is fired up, toss on a few steaks for recipes like Sizzling Beef Salad, Marinated Steak with Blue Cheese, Cilantro Pesto Steak, or Salsa-Topped Rosemary Rib Eyes. And to cool off after all that grilling, finish with a big bowl of the best summer has to offer—Old-Fashioned Vanilla Bean Ice Cream!

A MATTER OF TASTE

Shiitakes (shee-TAH-kee) are prized for their meaty flavor and texture.

The buttery-flavored **chanterelle** mushroom is best in simple recipes.

Wispy **enoki** (eh-NOH-kee) mushrooms come vacuum-packed. Show off their delicate flavor raw in salads.

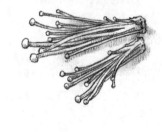

Portobellos are velvety brown behemoths boasting a deep mushroom flavor.

Savory **morels** (more-EL), once a rare treat, have an intense mushroom flavor and aroma.

Criminis (creh-MIN-nee), close relatives of the button mushroom, have a similar, but stronger, flavor.

Try a handful of small, lemony **beech** mushrooms in your next stir-fry.

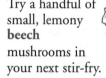

Trumpet mushrooms have a mellow, woodsy taste.

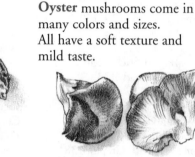

Oyster mushrooms come in many colors and sizes. All have a soft texture and mild taste.

Wood ear mushrooms are favored for their yielding, crunchy texture.

(30 MIN.)

WILD-ABOUT-MUSHROOMS PASTA

Start to finish: 25 min.

Luckily, many once-wild mushrooms, such as oyster, shiitake, and trumpet, are now grown on farms. Wild in name only, they still retain their unfettered mushroom flavor.

- 8 oz. assorted cultivated mushrooms, or about 1 cup assorted dried wild mushrooms
- 3 oz. mafalda, pappardelle, or medium shell pasta
- 2 Tbsp. butter or margarine
- 1 Tbsp. olive oil
- ¼ tsp. cracked black pepper
- ⅛ tsp. salt
- 1 to 2 tsp. snipped fresh herbs, such as thyme, basil, or rosemary (optional)

1 Clean fresh mushrooms, if using. If using dried mushrooms, place in a medium bowl and pour boiling water over to cover; let stand 30 minutes. Rinse and drain well; discard tough stems, if present. Thinly slice mushrooms and set aside. (You should have about 3 cups if using fresh mushrooms and about 1½ cups if using dried mushrooms.)

2 Prepare the mafalda, pappardelle, or the shell pasta according to the package directions.

3 Meanwhile, in a large skillet heat butter or margarine and oil over medium heat. Add mushrooms, pepper, and salt. Cook, uncovered, about 8 minutes or until tender, stirring occasionally. Remove from heat; stir in herbs, if desired. Let stand 3 minutes. Drain pasta; toss with mushroom mixture. Makes 4 side-dish servings.

*Note: Leave the picking of true wild mushrooms to the experts. Many wild varieties—including some that appear identical to familiar edible types—are poisonous and can be harmful, even fatal, to eat.

Nutrition facts per serving: 147 cal., 6 g total fat (4 g sat. fat), 15 mg chol., 126 mg sodium, 19 g carbo., 2 g fiber, 4 g pro. *Daily values:* 5% vit. A, 3% vit. C, 1% calcium, 12% iron.

SAUCY SKILLET MUSHROOMS

Start to finish: 25 min.

4 slices turkey bacon, chopped

♦♦♦

1 Tbsp. olive oil
1 lb. large button mushrooms (about 1½ to 2 inches in diameter)
2 Tbsp. stone-ground mustard

♦♦♦

2 Tbsp. snipped fresh Italian parsley

1 In a large, heavy skillet cook bacon over medium heat until crisp. Transfer bacon to paper towels; set aside.

2 Add olive oil to the same skillet. Cook and stir mushrooms in hot oil over medium heat for 1 to 2 minutes or until mushrooms just begin to brown. Cover and cook mushrooms about 8 minutes or until tender, stirring occasionally. Stir in cooked bacon and mustard; heat through.

3 To serve, transfer mushroom mixture to a serving bowl. Sprinkle parsley over mushrooms. Makes 4 side-dish servings.

Nutrition facts per serving: 101 cal., 7 g total fat (2 g sat. fat), 9 mg chol., 310 mg sodium, 6 g carbo., 2 g fiber, 6 g pro. *Daily values:* 11% vit. C, 2% calcium, 15% iron.

ORZO WITH ROOT VEGETABLES

Start to finish: 30 min.

Just right for the summer months when quick-to-fix, light suppers are the order of the day. Strips of mellow tasting carrot and turnip keep the dish bright and colorful. (See the photograph on page 120.)

1 large onion, halved and thinly sliced
2 cloves garlic, minced
1 Tbsp. olive oil
1 14½-oz. can chicken or vegetable broth
¼ cup water
½ tsp. dried thyme, crushed
⅛ tsp. ground red pepper
¾ cup orzo (rosamarina)
2 medium carrots, cut into matchstick strips

♦♦♦

1 medium turnip, cut into matchstick strips
1 medium red sweet pepper, cut into matchstick strips

TEST KITCHEN TIP

COMING CLEAN

The flavor of mushrooms is in their delicate spores, so clean gently. Lightly brush large mushrooms, such as portobellos, with a square of cheesecloth or a paper towel. Morel and trumpet mushrooms have many places for dirt to hide. These mushrooms can be washed by gently swirling them around in a bowl of cold water. (Remove them from the water immediately or they will become saturated.) Gently shake the mushrooms and pat dry with paper towels. Use cleaned fresh mushrooms immediately.

1 15-oz. can red beans, rinsed and drained

1 In a large saucepan cook onion and garlic in hot oil until just tender. Stir in broth, water, thyme, and ground red pepper. Bring to boiling. Add orzo and carrots. Simmer, covered, for 10 minutes.

2 Stir turnip, sweet pepper, and red beans into mixture in saucepan; return to boiling. Simmer, covered, for 2 to 3 minutes more or until orzo is tender. Makes 4 main-dish servings.

Nutrition facts per serving: 329 cal., 5 g total fat (1 g sat. fat), 5 mg chol., 335 mg sodium, 59 g carbo., 10 g fiber, 14 g pro. *Daily values:* 82% vit. A, 57% vit. C, 7% calcium, 29% iron.

Menu

Grilled pork tenderloin

◆◆◆

Kaleidoscope Potato Salad
(see below)

◆◆◆

Sliced ripe red and/or
yellow tomatoes

◆◆◆

Sourdough rolls

◆◆◆

Fruit Bowl Sundae
(see page 139)

KALEIDOSCOPE POTATO SALAD

Prep: 25 min. ◆ Cook: 15 min.

When available, use thin, sweet French green beans (haricots vert) in place of regular green beans. Be sure to cook the delicate haricots for no longer than 2 minutes or just until crisp-tender. (See the photograph on page 118.)

8 oz. whole tiny, red new
   potatoes
8 oz. purple potatoes
8 oz. green beans, trimmed

◆◆◆

3 Tbsp. olive oil
3 Tbsp. white wine vinegar
1 Tbsp. snipped fresh
   rosemary or ½ tsp. dried
   rosemary, crushed
¼ tsp. salt
¼ tsp. ground white pepper
¼ cup sliced green onions or
   3 Tbsp. snipped fresh
   chives

1 Scrub potatoes with a stiff brush under running water. Cut potatoes in quarters. In a Dutch oven cook potatoes in a small amount of boiling, lightly salted water, covered, for 10 to 15 minutes or until tender. Add beans the last 3 to 5 minutes of cooking. Drain; rinse with cold water until vegetables are cooled. Drain.

2 In a medium bowl stir together oil, vinegar, rosemary, salt, and pepper. Add potato mixture and onions or chives. Toss mixture gently. Serve immediately. Makes 6 to 8 side-dish servings.

Nutrition facts per serving: 146 cal., 7 g total fat (1 g sat. fat), 0 mg chol., 96 mg sodium, 20 g carbo., 2 g fiber, 2 g pro. *Daily values:* 3% vit. A, 23% vit. C, 2% calcium, 12% iron.

CORN-ON-THE-COB SALAD

Prep: 15 min. ◆ Grill: 20 min.

This fun approach to corn salad is a great excuse to break out the decorative corn holders. Make it the night before and present it at a backyard picnic. (See the photograph on page 118.)

6 fresh ears of corn
½ of an 8-oz. bottle Italian
   salad dressing
3 Tbsp. snipped fresh
   rosemary

◆◆◆

4 medium Roma tomatoes,
   sliced ½ inch thick

◆◆◆

3 cups fresh baby spinach or
   spinach leaves

1 Remove husks and silk from corn. Break or cut each ear of corn in half. Brush corn with some of the dressing; sprinkle with rosemary. Grill corn on the rack of an uncovered grill directly over medium to medium-hot coals about 20 minutes or until tender, turning often. Cool slightly. (Or, preheat oven to 425°. Brush husked corn with dressing. Bake for 30 minutes, turning once.)

2 Place corn and tomatoes in a 1½- to 2-quart pitcher or a self-sealing, 1-gallon plastic bag set in a large, shallow bowl. Pour the remaining dressing over vegetables; cover or seal. If desired, chill for 4 to 24 hours, turning once or twice. Let stand for 20 minutes before serving.

3 To serve, arrange spinach on 6 chilled plates. Using a slotted spoon, remove corn and tomatoes from marinade, reserving any remaining dressing. Place 2 pieces of corn on top of spinach; garnish with tomato slices. Pass any remaining dressing. Makes 6 side-dish servings.

Nutrition facts per serving: 199 cal., 12 g total fat (2 g sat. fat), 0 mg chol., 188 mg sodium, 24 g carbo., 4 g fiber, 4 g pro. *Daily values:* 23% vit. A, 33% vit. C, 2% calcium, 9% iron.

PINEAPPLE-SPINACH SALAD

Start to finish: 30 min.

Pretrimmed fresh pineapple is a time-saver in this simple salad. But it's easy to trim and prepare a whole pineapple yourself, if you prefer. Just cut off the pineapple's top and base. Cut the pineapple lengthwise into quarters. Trim away the core, then the shell. Remove any remaining "eyes." Cut the pineapple into wedges, if desired.

4 cups fresh baby spinach or
   torn spinach
2 cups watercress*
¼ of a small fresh pineapple,
   peeled, cored, and cut into
   wedges
½ of a small red onion, cut into
   wedges
1 recipe Citrus Vinaigrette (see
   below)
⅓ cup broken walnut pieces,
   toasted**

1 In a salad bowl toss together spinach, watercress, pineapple, and onion. Just before serving, pour Citrus Vinaigrette over salad. Toss lightly to coat. Sprinkle with walnuts. Arrange in 6 individual glass bowls or cups. Makes 6 side-dish servings.

*Note: For tips on choosing and storing watercress, see page 132.

**Note: Toasting heightens the flavor of nuts. To toast walnuts, place them in a small skillet. Cook over medium heat, stirring often, for 5 to 7 minutes or until light golden, watching carefully to prevent burning.

Citrus Vinaigrette: In a small mixing bowl whisk together 1 tablespoon walnut oil or salad oil, 1 tablespoon vinegar, 1 tablespoon frozen orange juice concentrate, and 2 teaspoons honey. Drizzle over Pineapple-Spinach Salad.

Nutrition facts per serving: 99 cal., 7 g total fat (1 g sat. fat), 0 mg chol., 35 mg sodium, 9 g carbo., 2 g fiber, 3 g pro.
Daily values: 30% vit. A, 40% vit. C, 5% calcium, 8% iron.

CITRUS VEGGIE SALAD

Start to finish: 10 min.

Score a hole in one for nutrition with this crunchy, fresh salad. At 10 minutes prep from start to finish, you'll get twice your daily vitamin A, nearly a full-day's measure of vitamin C, and one-fifth of your vitamin E needs in just one refreshing serving.

1 10-oz. pkg. julienne,
   matchstick, or coarsely
   shredded carrots
1 medium green sweet pepper,
   cut into matchstick strips

◆◆◆

3 Tbsp. orange juice
1 Tbsp. lime juice
1 Tbsp. salad oil
½ tsp. toasted sesame oil
¼ cup chopped dry-roasted
   peanuts

1 In a large salad bowl gently toss together the shredded carrots and sweet pepper.

2 Add the orange juice, lime juice, salad oil, and sesame oil to mixture in salad bowl. Toss gently to coat. Sprinkle salad with the dry-roasted peanuts. Makes 4 side-dish servings.

Nutrition facts per serving: 137 cal., 9 g fat, (1 g sat. fat), 0 mg chol., 26 mg sodium, 13 g carbo., 3 g fiber., 3 g pro.
Daily values: 202% vit. A, 85% vit C, 20% vit. E, 2% calcium, 5% iron.

NEW WALDORF SALAD

Prep: 15 min. ◆ Chill: 2 to 24 hr.

By using lower-fat ingredients, this version of Waldorf Salad saves you 80 calories and 10 grams of fat per serving.

½ of a fresh pineapple, peeled,
   cored, and cut up (2 cups),
   or two 15¼-oz. cans
   pineapple chunks (juice
   pack), drained
1 medium apple, cored and
   coarsely chopped (1 cup)
½ cup thinly sliced celery
½ cup halved seedless red
   grapes
½ cup walnut pieces, toasted
2 kiwifruit, peeled, halved
   lengthwise, and sliced

◆◆◆

½ cup light mayonnaise
   dressing or salad dressing
⅓ cup lemon yogurt
1 Tbsp. honey
   Lettuce leaves (optional)

1 In a large bowl gently toss together the pineapple, apple, celery, grapes, walnuts, and kiwifruit. Set aside.

2 In a small bowl stir together the mayonnaise or salad dressing, yogurt, and honey. Fold dressing gently into fruit mixture. Cover and chill for 2 to 24 hours. Serve on lettuce leaves, if desired. Makes 6 to 8 side-dish servings.

Nutrition facts per serving: 210 cal., 13 g total fat (2 g sat. fat), 7 mg chol., 146 mg sodium, 23 g carbo., 3 g fiber, 3 g pro.
Daily values: 59% vit. C.

THAT'S FOH-KAH-CHEE-AH!

Focaccia is a flatbread—akin to deep-dish pizza crust—that originated in the Italian region of Liguria. Olive oil often is incorporated into the dough, as well as being generously brushed on top before the focaccia is finished with the desired toppings, such as minced garlic, onions, fresh herbs, tomatoes, olives, or a dusting of cheese. Generally, the best focaccia is to be found at artisanal or Italian bakeries, but your grocery store might make its own version, too. If you don't plan to eat your focaccia the day it is purchased, place it in a heavy-duty freezer bag and freeze for up to 3 months.

MILE-HIGH MUFFULETTA

Start to finish: 25 min.

We opted for a lively sour cherry relish instead of a traditional olive relish to better enhance the thinly sliced meats. (See the photograph on page 117.)

- 2 Tbsp. cooking oil
- 1½ cups dried tart red cherries
- ¾ cup chopped red onion
- ¾ cup red wine vinegar
- 5 cups finely shredded savoy, napa, or green cabbage
- ½ to ¾ cup light mayonnaise dressing

- 1 12-inch loaf Italian flatbread (focaccia)
- 1 lb. thinly sliced, cooked, smoked ham, turkey, and/or turkey ham

1 In a medium skillet heat oil. Cook cherries and onion in hot oil about 5 minutes or until just softened, stirring often. Stir in vinegar; set mixture aside. In a medium bowl combine shredded cabbage and mayonnaise dressing; cover and set aside.

2 Using a long, serrated knife, carefully split flatbread horizontally. Spoon cherry relish on bottom slice of bread. Layer meat on top of relish. Spoon cabbage mixture on top of meat. Cover with top half of bread. Cut into wedges before serving. Makes 8 servings.

Nutrition facts per serving: 380 cal., 14 g total fat (4 g sat. fat), 30 mg chol., 797 mg sodium, 48 g carbo., 4 g fiber, 18 g pro. *Daily values:* 19% vit. A, 42% vit. C, 7% calcium, 9% iron.

LEMON-PEPPER PASTA AND CHICKEN

Start to finish: 20 min.

Serve this light linguine as a fast after-work meal, or enjoy it the next day as a cool tote-along lunch. (See the photograph on page 117.)

- 8 oz. dried lemon-pepper linguine or penne pasta*
- 1 cup shelled fresh or frozen baby peas
- 3 Tbsp. olive oil
- 12 oz. skinless, boneless chicken breast halves, cut into thin, bite-size strips

- 1 medium red onion, cut into thin wedges
- 1 Tbsp. snipped fresh marjoram or 1 tsp. dried marjoram, crushed
- 4 cloves garlic, sliced
- ½ tsp. salt
- 1 Tbsp. lemon juice

1 Prepare pasta according to package directions, adding peas during the last 1 minute of cooking. Drain pasta mixture; toss with 1 tablespoon of the olive oil. Set aside.

2 Meanwhile, in a large skillet heat remaining olive oil over medium heat. Cook chicken, onion wedges, dried marjoram, if using, garlic, and salt in hot oil for 3 to 4 minutes or until no pink remains in chicken, stirring often.

3 Stir lemon juice into mixture in skillet. Cook and stir for 1 minute more, scraping up browned bits. Gently toss pasta with chicken mixture and fresh marjoram, if using. Serve immediately. Makes 4 servings.

*Note: If lemon-pepper pasta is not available, add ¼ teaspoon freshly ground black pepper and ¼ teaspoon grated lemon peel to 2 cups plain cooked pasta just before tossing with chicken.

Nutrition facts per serving: 446 cal., 14 g total fat (2 g sat. fat), 45 mg chol., 311 mg sodium, 54 g carbo., 4 g fiber, 26 g pro. *Daily values:* 2% vit. A, 14% vit. C, 3% calcium, 23% iron.

Left: *Lemon-Pepper Pasta and Chicken (page 116)*
Below: *Mile-High Muffuletta (page 116)*

Top: *Orzo with Root Vegetables (page 113)*
Above: *Sweet and Tangy Fish (page 127)*
Right: *Chicken with Skillet Tomato Sauce (page 96)*

Top: *Frozen Berry Yogurt (page 110)*
Above: *Company Cake Express (page 108)*
Page 122: *Double-Rich Pound Cake with Mascarpone Topper (page 108)*

Left: *Bistro Burger (page 125)*
Below: *Tuna and Avocado Stuffed Shells (page 125)*

TUNA AND AVOCADO STUFFED SHELLS

Start to finish: 25 min.

To cut prep time, substitute a 9-ounce can of water-pack, solid white tuna, drained and broken into small chunks, for the cooked fresh tuna.
(See the photograph on page 124.)

8 jumbo shell macaroni
8 oz. tuna fillet, cooked and broken into small chunks*
1 medium avocado, halved, seeded, peeled, and coarsely chopped
3 Tbsp. walnut oil or cooking oil
3 Tbsp. lemon juice
2 Tbsp. snipped fresh chives
1 Tbsp. Dijon-style mustard
1 medium cantaloupe, cut into wedges

1 Cook the jumbo shells according to package directions. Drain; rinse with cold water. Drain and set aside.

2 In a large mixing bowl gently stir together the tuna, avocado, walnut or cooking oil, lemon juice, chives, and mustard. Carefully spoon about ¼ cup of the tuna salad mixture into each cooked shell.

3 To serve, arrange 2 filled shells with a cantaloupe wedge on each of 4 dinner plates. Makes 4 main-dish servings.

*Note: To cook tuna fillet, rub with cooking oil. Grill fish on rack of an uncovered grill directly over medium to medium-hot coals for 8 to 12 minutes or until fish just flakes with a fork, turning once. Cover and refrigerate until cool enough to handle.

Nutrition facts per serving: 354 cal., 22 g total fat (2 g sat. fat), 24 mg chol., 134 mg sodium, 22 g carbo., 8 g fiber, 19 g pro. *Daily values:* 76% vit. A, 102% vit. C, 2% calcium, 11% iron.

BISTRO BURGERS

Prep: 20 min. ◆ Grill: 14 min.

The ground pork and chicken combination makes for a tasty grilled treat. Served open-faced and topped with Brie cheese, this burger is fancy enough to serve as white cloth napkin fare.
(See the photograph on page 124.)

2 Tbsp. dry white wine or water
¼ tsp. salt
¼ tsp. pepper
¾ lb. ground pork
¾ lb. ground raw chicken or turkey breast
2 Tbsp. creamy Dijon-style mustard blend
1 Tbsp. snipped fresh chives
1 to 2 garlic cloves, minced
1 4½-oz. round Brie cheese, rind removed and cut into 12 slices
6 slices French bread or bagel halves, toasted
8 ripe yellow and/or red tomato slices
    Raddichio or leaf lettuce

1 In a medium bowl combine the wine or water, salt, and pepper. Add the ground pork and chicken; mix well. Shape meat mixture into six ½-inch-thick patties. Cover and chill for at least 30 minutes.

CHILL OUT!

Quick chilling saves time and locks in flavor. For fastest chilling, use an ice bath. Fill a Dutch oven or deep roasting pan halfway with ice. Add cold water to the same level. Set the container holding the hot food, covered, in the ice bath with the rim well above the level of the ice water. Stir occasionally until cooled. Refrigerate at once.

2 Meanwhile, in a small bowl stir together the mustard blend, chives, and garlic. Set aside.

3 Grill patties on the rack of an uncovered grill directly over medium coals for 14 to 18 minutes or until no pink remains, turning once halfway through. Top each burger with 2 slices of cheese. Grill, uncovered, about 3 minutes more or until cheese begins to melt.

4 To serve, spread sauce on one side of the toasted bread slices. Add tomato slices and raddichio or leaf lettuce. Place a meat patty atop. Makes 6 servings.

Nutrition facts per serving: 297 cal., 15 g total fat (7 g sat. fat), 69 mg chol., 551 mg sodium, 16 g carbo., 1 g fiber, 22 g pro. *Daily values:* 7% vit. A, 12% vit. C, 6% calcium, 13% iron.

A Nice Return

I was always taught that when a dish was borrowed, it should be returned in cleaner or better condition than it was before. So, I started a new tradition in my home. When I borrow a dish or when someone comes to my home with a dish of food, later, after the food is eaten and the dish cleaned, I return it filled with home-made baked goods or fresh produce from my garden. The response is pure delight.

Patricia Dake
Quincy, California

LOW FAT

OPEN-FACE SHRIMP "TAMALES"

Prep: 20 min. ◆ Bake: 15 min.

To add some heat to this cool tamale, stir one or two finely chopped jalapeño or serrano peppers into the tomato mixture just before serving.

3 **large fresh ears of corn (with husks)**

◆◆◆

1 **16 oz.-tube refrigerated cooked polenta**
   Nonstick spray coating

◆◆◆

4 **medium Roma tomatoes, chopped (about 1½ cups)**
3 **Tbsp. balsamic vinegar**

1 **Tbsp. snipped fresh thyme or 1 tsp. dried thyme, crushed**
¾ **tsp. cumin seed, crushed**
¼ **tsp. salt**
18 **cooked large shrimp, peeled and deveined (tails on, if desired) (about 8 oz.)**

◆◆◆

Fresh cilantro leaves

1 Carefully remove husks from corn, keeping husks whole. Wash husks and set aside to dry. Set aside 12 of the larger husks (about 6×4 inches). Cut corn kernels from cobs. You should have about 2 cups kernels. Discard cobs and set corn aside.

2 Cut polenta crosswise into 12 slices. Spray a 15×10×1-inch baking pan with nonstick coating. Lay polenta slices in single layer in pan. Bake in a 450° oven for 15 to 20 minutes or until golden brown, turning after 10 minutes.

3 Meanwhile, spray a large skillet with nonstick coating. Cook corn, uncovered, over medium heat 5 minutes or until lightly browned, stirring occasionally. Stir in tomatoes, vinegar, thyme, cumin seed, and salt. Cook 1 to 2 minutes. Stir in shrimp; cover and heat through.

4 To serve, arrange 2 corn-husks on each of 6 dinner plates. Place 2 polenta slices on corn-husks; spoon the shrimp and corn mixture onto husks. Garnish with cilantro leaves. Serves 6.

Nutrition facts per serving: 177 cal., 1 g total fat (0 g sat. fat), 74 mg chol., 481 mg sodium, 31 g carbo., 4 g fiber, 12 g pro. *Daily values:* 7% vit. A, 20% vit. C, 1% calcium, 13% iron.

LOW FAT

SALMON CON SALSA-FRESCA

Prep: 25 min. ◆ Cook: 12 min.

Jicama (pronounced HEE-ka-mah), a Mexican tuber with a thick, tan skin and a crunchy, slightly sweet flesh, is low in calories and high in vitamin C. Look for one that is firm and smooth. (See the photograph on page 118.)

½ **of a small jicama, peeled and shredded**
1 **small cucumber, seeded and finely diced**
1 **small red sweet pepper, cut into matchstick strips**
3 **Tbsp. white vinegar or rice vinegar**
½ **tsp. sugar**

◆◆◆

12 **oz. skinless salmon fillet, cut into eight 1½-inch-thick pieces**
1 **Tbsp. cooking oil**
¼ **tsp. salt**
¼ **to ½ tsp. ground red pepper**

◆◆◆

1 **head Bibb lettuce**

1 In a large mixing bowl stir together jicama, cucumber, sweet pepper, vinegar, and sugar. Cover and chill.

2 Rub salmon with oil; sprinkle with salt and red pepper. Heat a large cast-iron skillet or heavy, nonstick skillet. Cook fish, uncovered, over medium heat for 6 minutes per side or until fish just flakes with a fork. Serve immediately, or cover and chill before serving.

3 To serve, overlap 2 or 3 lettuce leaves on each of 4 dinner plates. Top with 2 salmon pieces. Spoon about 2 tablespoons of the jicama and sweet pepper salsa over the fish. Makes 4 main-dish servings.

Nutrition facts per serving: 134 cal., 6 g total fat (1 g sat. fat), 15 mg chol., 188 mg sodium, 6 g carbo., 1 g fiber, 13 g pro. *Daily values:* 21% vit. A, 56% vit. C, 2% calcium, 7% iron.

SWEET AND TANGY FISH

Start to finish: 40 min.

See the photograph on page 120.

4 fresh or frozen skinless fish fillets (1 lb.)

♦♦♦

¾ cup chopped onion
1 Tbsp. cooking oil
2 medium tomatoes, seeded and chopped (1 cup)
¾ cup frozen whole kernel corn
2 Tbsp. white balsamic vinegar or white wine vinegar
1 Tbsp. sugar

♦♦♦

2 cups hot cooked couscous
¼ cup finely chopped walnuts
2 Tbsp. fine dry bread crumbs
2 Tbsp. snipped fresh parsley
1 Tbsp. margarine or butter, melted

1 Thaw fish, if frozen. Rinse fish; pat dry. Measure thickness of fillets; set aside.

2 In a large skillet cook onion in hot oil until tender but not brown. Add tomatoes, corn, vinegar, and sugar. Bring to boiling. Carefully add fish fillets. Return to boiling; reduce heat. Simmer, covered, for 4 to 6 minutes per ½-inch thickness of fish or until fish just flakes with a fork.

3 To serve, place couscous on a platter; arrange fish mixture atop. In a small bowl stir together the walnuts, bread crumbs, parsley, and melted margarine or butter; sprinkle over fish. Makes 4 servings.

Nutrition facts per serving: 381 cal., 13 g total fat (2 g sat. fat), 53 mg chol., 162 mg sodium, 42 g carbo., 5 g fiber, 26 g pro. *Daily values:* 11% vit. A, 37% vit. C, 4% calcium, 13% iron.

SIZZLING BEEF SALAD

Prep: 20 min. ♦ Marinate: 30 min. Grill: 12 min.

Red chili paste is very pungent. If oven-broiling this recipe, be sure you have a working ventilation system.

12 oz. boneless beef sirloin steak, cut 1 to 1½ inches thick
Salt
1 to 2 Tbsp. purchased red chili paste* (sambal)

♦♦♦

⅓ cup lime juice
3 Tbsp. cooking oil
2 Tbsp. hoisin sauce

♦♦♦

6 cups shredded romaine
1 medium fresh papaya, seeded, peeled, and sliced
2 Tbsp. chopped honey-roasted peanuts

1 Sprinkle both sides of meat lightly with salt. Spread 1 or both sides of steak with chili paste. Place in a sealable plastic bag or shallow dish. Seal bag or cover dish; let stand for 30 minutes. (Or, refrigerate for several hours or overnight.)

2 Grill steak on an uncovered grill directly over medium-hot

Sizzling Beef Salad (see left)

♦♦♦

Warm pita bread wedges

♦♦♦

Poached Summer Peaches with Cherries (see page 138)

coals for 12 to 15 minutes or until medium doneness, turning once. (Or, place steak on the unheated rack of a broiler pan. Broil 3 to 4 inches from the heat for 12 to 15 minutes or until medium doneness, turning once.) Cool. Wrap in foil; set aside or chill.

3 To make dressing, in a screw-top jar combine lime juice, oil, and hoisin sauce. Cover and shake well.

4 To serve, arrange romaine on 4 chilled plates. Thinly slice steak. Arrange steak slices on shredded romaine; add papaya slices. Drizzle with dressing; sprinkle with peanuts. Makes 4 main-dish servings.

*Note: Hot peppers and products made from them, such as chili paste, contain volatile oils that can burn eyes, lips, and sensitive skin. Wear plastic gloves while working with peppers and be sure to wash your hands thoroughly afterward.

Nutrition facts per serving: 369 cal., 20 g total fat (5 g sat. fat), 57 mg chol., 259 mg sodium, 25 g carbo., 4 g fiber, 22 g pro. *Daily values:* 26% vit. A, 173% vit. C, 5% calcium, 23% iron.

MARINATED STEAK WITH BLUE CHEESE

Prep: 20 min. ◆ Marinate: 6 to 24 hrs.
Grill: 8 min.

- 1 **lb. boneless beef top sirloin steak, cut 1 inch thick**
- ¼ **cup olive oil**
- ¼ **cup dry red wine**
- 2 **cloves garlic, minced**
- 1 **tsp. coarse ground pepper**
- ½ **tsp. salt**
- ½ **tsp. Dijon-style mustard**

◆◆◆

- ¼ **cup thinly sliced green onions**
- ¼ **cup crumbled blue cheese (1 oz.)**
- 2 **Tbsp. soft goat cheese (chèvre)**
- 1 **clove garlic, minced**

1 Trim fat from meat. Place meat in a plastic bag set in a shallow dish. For marinade, stir together olive oil, red wine, the 2 cloves garlic, pepper, salt, and mustard. Pour marinade over steak. Close bag. Marinate in the refrigerator for 6 to 24 hours, turning bag occasionally.

2 Drain steak, discarding the marinade. Grill steak on the rack of an uncovered grill directly over medium coals to desired doneness, turning once halfway through. (Allow 8 to 12 minutes for medium-rare and 12 to 15 minutes for medium.) Meanwhile, in a small bowl combine green onions, blue cheese, goat cheese, and the 1 clove garlic.

3 Transfer meat to serving platter. Spoon some of the blue cheese mixture over steak. To serve, thinly slice meat across the grain. Pass remaining blue cheese mixture. Makes 4 servings.

Nutrition facts per serving: 315 cal., 21 g total fat (7 g sat. fat), 89 mg chol., 345 mg sodium, 1 g carbo., 0 g fiber, 29 g pro. *Daily values:* 4% vit. A, 3% vit. C, 5% calcium, 20% iron.

SPICY PANBROILED STEAK

Start to finish: 25 min.

*If you like fajitas, you'll love
this variation that highlights smoky-
spicy chipotle peppers.*

- 1 **tsp. garlic salt**
- 1 **tsp. ground cumin**
- 1 **tsp. dried oregano, crushed**
- 2 **Tbsp. olive oil**
- 1 **medium red sweet pepper, cut into thin, bite-size strips (1 cup)**
- ½ **cup chopped onion**
- 1 **or 2 chipotle peppers in adobo sauce, drained and chopped**

◆◆◆

- 1 **lb. boneless beef top loin steaks, cut ¾ inch thick**

◆◆◆

- 1 **medium tomato, seeded and chopped (½ cup)**
- **Warm tortillas**
- **Guacamole**

1 Combine garlic salt, cumin, and oregano. In a large skillet heat 1 tablespoon of the oil over medium-high heat. Add 2 teaspoons of the spice mixture, the red sweet pepper, onion, and chipotle peppers. Cook and stir 2 to 3 minutes or until vegetables are just tender, stirring occasionally. Using a slotted spoon, remove vegetables from skillet; keep warm.

2 Add remaining oil, remaining spice mixture, and meat to same skillet. Cook over medium-high heat about 4 minutes on each side or until meat is slightly pink in the center. Transfer meat to a serving platter, reserving drippings in skillet. Thinly slice meat; keep warm.

3 Return vegetables to skillet. Stir in tomato; heat through. Spoon vegetables over meat. To serve, fill tortillas with meat mixture; roll up. Serve with guacamole. If desired, garnish with *fresh cilantro.* Makes 4 servings.

Nutrition facts per serving: 341 cal., 15 g total fat (3 g sat. fat), 65 mg chol., 772 mg sodium, 25 g carbo., 1 g fiber, 26 g pro. *Daily values:* 20% vit. A, 62% vit. C, 6% calcium, 31% iron.

BRANDIED STEAK

Start to finish: 30 min.

Fresh porcini mushrooms are a rare find in most grocery stores. If you're lucky enough to find them, choose those with firm, large caps and pale undersides.

- 2 6-oz. beef tenderloin steaks, cut 1 inch thick
- 1 Tbsp. cooking oil
  ◆◆◆
- 1 Tbsp. butter or margarine
- 1 cup sliced fresh porcini or button mushrooms
- ½ cup chopped onion
- 2 cloves garlic, minced
- 3 Tbsp. brandy
- 2 tsp. fresh snipped rosemary or ½ tsp. dried rosemary, crushed
- 1 tsp. Dijon-style mustard
- 1 tsp. Worcestershire sauce
- 4 cups fresh spinach leaves, stems removed

1 In a large skillet cook steaks in hot oil over medium heat to desired doneness, turning once. (Allow 8 to 11 minutes for medium-rare or 12 to 14 minutes for medium.) Remove steaks from skillet; keep warm.

2 In same skillet heat butter or margarine over medium heat. Add mushrooms, onion, and garlic. Cook and stir mushrooms and onion about 5 minutes or until just tender. Remove mixture from skillet; keep warm.

3 In a small bowl stir together the brandy, rosemary, mustard, and Worcestershire sauce. Carefully add mixture to skillet; stir in spinach. Cook, covered, for 1 to 2 minutes or until spinach is wilted.

4 To serve, spoon spinach mixture onto 2 dinner plates. Place steaks and mushrooms atop. Makes 2 servings.

Nutrition facts per serving: 452 cal., 24 g total fat (9 g sat. fat), 111 mg chol., 308 mg sodium, 10 g carbo., 4 g fiber, 37 g pro. *Daily values:* 80% vit. A, 66% vit. C, 11% calcium, 53% iron.

STEAK WITH MADEIRA MUSHROOM SAUCE

Prep: 15 min. ◆ Cook: 20 min.

Positively perfect for company, the rich cream sauce studded with mushrooms and served over steak is one to be savored.

- 1 lb. boneless beef top sirloin steak, cut 1 inch thick
  Salt and pepper
- 2 Tbsp. olive oil
  ◆◆◆
- 2 Tbsp. lemon juice
  ◆◆◆
- 1 lb. assorted sliced fresh mushrooms, such as oyster, shiitake, porcini, portobello, and/or button
- 2 medium leeks, sliced
- 4 cloves garlic, minced
- ¼ cup Madeira wine
- ½ cup whipping cream
- 2 Tbsp. snipped fresh basil
- ¼ tsp. salt
- ⅛ tsp. pepper

1 Cut meat into 4 portions. Sprinkle with salt and pepper. In a large skillet heat 1 tablespoon of the oil over medium heat. Add steak; cook to desired doneness, turning once. (Allow 8 to 11 minutes for medium-rare or 12 to 14 minutes for medium.) Transfer steak to a serving platter.

2 Carefully add the lemon juice to the skillet. Bring to boiling, scraping up any crusty browned bits. Spoon mixture over meat; keep warm.

3 In same skillet heat remaining oil over medium-high heat. Add mushrooms, leeks, and garlic. Cook and stir for 4 to 5 minutes or until tender and most of the liquid is evaporated. Stir in Madeira; bring to boiling. Boil gently for 2 minutes more. Stir in whipping cream, basil, the ¼ teaspoon salt, and ⅛ teaspoon pepper. Bring to boiling; cook and stir 3 to 4 minutes or until mixture thickens slightly. Serve sauce over steaks. Makes 4 servings.

Nutrition facts per serving: 434 cal., 28 g total fat (12 g sat. fat), 116 mg chol., 277 mg sodium, 13 g carbo., 4 g fiber, 30 g pro. *Daily values:* 13% vit. A, 19% vit. C, 5% calcium, 37% iron.

WHAT'S IN A NAME?

Several cuts of beef have intriguing names, but few cooks know why. Sirloin likely comes from the French word surlonge (over the loin). Filet mignon is French for small and boneless; the name first appeared in a book by O. Henry in 1906. It is cut from the small end of the beef tenderloin. London Broil is actually the name of a recipe, not a cut—but some markets sell an appropriate cut (flank, top round, or chuck shoulder) by that name anyway. The recipe is named after England's capital city.

CILANTRO PESTO STEAK

Prep: 20 min. ◆ Marinate: 1 hr.
Grill: 12 min.

As an alternative, serve the steak alongside roasted new potato and garlic kabobs.

1 1- to 1½-lb. beef flank steak
½ tsp. salt
¼ tsp. pepper
3 cloves garlic, minced
◆◆◆
½ cup firmly packed cilantro leaves

½ of a small red onion, cut up
1 tsp. finely shredded lime peel
2 Tbsp. lime juice
2 tsp. Worcestershire sauce
¼ tsp. ground cumin
¼ tsp. dried oregano, crushed
◆◆◆
4 flour tortillas
1 tomato, chopped
1 cup shredded lettuce
¼ cup dairy sour cream

1 Score meat by making shallow diagonal cuts at 1-inch intervals in a diamond pattern. Repeat on other side. Sprinkle meat with salt and pepper and rub garlic over both sides, pushing garlic into the shallow cuts. Place meat in a shallow dish; set aside.

2 In a blender container or food processor bowl combine the cilantro, onion, lime peel and juice, Worcestershire sauce, cumin, and oregano. Cover and blend or process with a few pulses just until coarsely chopped. Pour mixture over meat in dish. Cover and chill for 1 hour, turning once.

3 Drain meat; discard marinade. Grill steak on the rack of an uncovered grill directly over medium coals for 12 to 14 minutes for medium or to desired doneness, turning once.

4 To serve, thinly slice meat across the grain. Place strips of meat atop flour tortillas. Top with tomatoes, lettuce, and sour cream; roll up. Makes 4 to 6 servings.

Nutrition facts per serving: 332 cal., 14 g total fat (6 g sat. fat), 60 mg chol., 538 mg sodium, 25 g carbo., 1 g fiber, 26 g pro. *Daily values:* 6% vit. A, 26% vit. C, 7% calcium, 26% iron.

SALSA-TOPPED ROSEMARY RIB EYES

Prep: 15 min. ◆ Grill: 12 min.

The simple treatment of rubbing steaks with a blend of herbs and seasonings brings bursts of flavor once grilled.

1 Tbsp. snipped fresh rosemary or 1 tsp. dried rosemary, crushed
1 tsp. snipped fresh thyme or ¼ tsp. dried thyme, crushed
¼ tsp. salt
⅛ tsp. black pepper
2 12-oz. beef rib eye steaks, cut 1 inch thick
◆◆◆
1 medium tomato, seeded and chopped
¼ cup chopped red onion
¼ cup chopped yellow and/or green sweet pepper
1 clove garlic, minced
Dash salt
Dash black pepper
Dash bottled hot pepper sauce

1 Combine rosemary, thyme, salt, and black pepper. Rub over steaks. Grill steaks on rack of an uncovered grill directly over medium coals 12 to 15 minutes for medium doneness, turning once.

2 Meanwhile, for salsa, in a medium bowl stir together the tomatoes, onion, sweet pepper, garlic, salt, black pepper, and hot pepper sauce. Serve with steaks. Makes 4 servings.

Nutrition facts per serving: 309 cal., 17 g total fat (7 g sat. fat), 100 mg chol., 262 mg sodium, 3 g carbo., 1 g fiber, 34 g pro. *Daily values:* 2% vit. A, 30% vit. C, 1% calcium, 22% iron.

SEASON FOR GOOD TASTE

Beyond salt, pepper, and parsley there's a whole world of spices and herbs—tiny purveyors of flavor that can transform an ordinary dinner into a standout creation. All you need are simple seasoning skills and a dash of imagination.

HELP WITH HERBS

If you're in the getting-acquainted stage, approach ad-lib additions gingerly. Taste the recipe after adding the seasoning, and add more as needed.

You just can't beat the flavor of fresh herbs. But when fresh herbs aren't available or you're too busy to clean and snip them, then dried herbs make convenient stand-ins.

Substitute dried herbs for fresh (and vice versa) by using 1 teaspoon dried mild-flavored herb (basil, mint, oregano, and savory) for 1 tablespoon snipped fresh herb. For stronger flavored herbs, such as dillweed, marjoram, rosemary, sage, tarragon, and thyme, use ½ teaspoon dried for each tablespoon fresh. If you're adding a ground form of a dried herb, use even less.

For maximum flavor, add dried herbs to hot mixtures early in the cooking process; add fresh herbs toward the end of cooking.

THE BEAUTY OF BLENDS

Ready-to-measure blends of herbs and spices, available in the spice section of your grocery store, offer an easy way to familiarize yourself with different seasonings. Popular combinations include:

◆ Barbecue seasoning: A zippy mingling of ground peppers, herbs, and spices, just right for grilled meats.

◆ Beau Monde: A mixture of salt, onion, and celery. Try it on eggs, seafood, and vegetables.

◆ Cajun seasoning: A hot fusion of onion, garlic, and salt with the classic Cajun trio of white, black, and red peppers.

◆ Fines herbes (feenz ERB): A classic French mix of finely chopped herbs, typically chervil, parsley, chives, and tarragon. Use it in sauces, gravies, and soups.

◆ Herbes de Provence: A blend of lavender, sage, fennel, basil, rosemary, marjoram, and thyme that's considered another French classic. Try it sprinkled in poultry or pasta dishes and stirred into salad dressings.

◆ Jamaican jerk seasoning: A Caribbean favorite containing salt, sugar, red pepper, onion, cinnamon, thyme, and allspice. Substitute it for Cajun seasoning or chili powder.

◆ Mexican seasoning: A blend of cumin, chili peppers, salt, onion, sweet peppers, garlic, oregano, and hot red pepper.

◆ Old Bay seasoning: A medley of cassia, cardamom, mace, ginger, pimiento, cloves, bay leaves, pepper, mustard, and celery salt. Ideal for fish and shellfish dishes.

SEASONING GUIDE

Like pairing foods with wine, matching seasonings with foods comes with experience and experimentation. No strict rules prevail, but veteran cooks favor certain combinations.

BEAN, SPLIT PEA, AND LENTIL DISHES:
Beans: thyme, coriander, oregano, red pepper, cumin
Split peas: sage, Italian seasoning, savory
Lentils: basil, oregano, rosemary, sage, red pepper

CHEESE DISHES:
Sauces and soufflés: red pepper, paprika, basil, fines herbes
Cheese casseroles: marjoram, paprika, sage

EGGS:
Omelets and frittatas: basil, thyme, oregano, rosemary, lemon pepper
Scrambled: savory, thyme, chervil, herbes de Provence

FISH AND SHELLFISH:
Fish: marjoram, tarragon, curry, thyme, rosemary, lemon pepper, dill, coriander, Jamaican jerk seasoning
Shellfish: red pepper, paprika, marjoram, savory, lemon pepper

MEATS:
Ground beef: curry, basil, marjoram, savory, chili powder
Beef roasts, steaks, and chops: basil, caraway seed, oregano, red pepper, thyme
Veal: lemon pepper, basil, rosemary, oregano
Pork: sage, ginger, cloves (for ham), curry, rosemary
Lamb: rosemary, mint, oregano

POULTRY:
Baked or fried chicken: marjoram, sage, paprika, thyme, lemon pepper, oregano
Ground turkey: tarragon, nutmeg, Italian seasoning, chervil

WATERCRESS

Watercress should be dark green and crisp. Discard any pale, yellowing, or limp leaves. Watercress will last for up to a week in the refrigerator. To store, in a tall plastic container or cup place cleaned cress, stems down, in 1 inch of clean water. Cover loosely with a plastic bag.

LAMB CHOP SANDWICH

Prep: 15 min. ◆ Grill: 8 min.

This recipe is also a great way to use leftover cooked beef or pork.

- 8   3- to 4-oz. lamb rib chops, cut ½ inch thick
   Garlic salt
   Pepper

   ◆◆◆

- 2   tsp. cooking oil
- 1   large apple, peeled, cored, and finely chopped
- 3   Tbsp. minced shallots
- 2   tsp. brown sugar
- ⅛   tsp. ground cloves
- 1   cup blackberries

   ◆◆◆

- 4   kaiser rolls, split and toasted
- 1⅓ cups watercress sprigs

1 Trim fat from chops; discard fat. Season chops with garlic salt and pepper. Grill lamb chops on rack of an uncovered grill directly over medium coals 8 to 10 minutes or until medium doneness, turning once. (Or, in a large skillet cook chops in 1 tablespoon hot cooking oil over medium heat about 10 minutes or until medium doneness, turning once.) Transfer chops to a paper-towel-lined dish to drain; set aside.

2 For relish, in a medium skillet heat oil. Cook apple, shallots, brown sugar, and cloves in the hot oil over medium heat about 3 minutes or until just tender. Add blackberries; reduce heat. Cook mixture, uncovered, for 5 minutes, stirring often. Cool. Cover and chill, if desired.

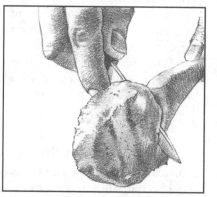

3 To serve, using a sharp knife carefully remove meat from bones (see photo, above). Spoon one-fourth of the blackberry relish onto cut side of each roll bottom. Top with watercress sprigs. Arrange 2 of the boned, cooked chops on top. Cover with roll tops. Makes 4 servings.

Nutrition facts per serving: 377 cal., 12 g total fat (3 g sat. fat), 52 mg chol., 365 mg sodium, 44 g carbo., 3 g fiber, 22 g pro. *Daily values:* 15% vit. A, 24% vit. C, 7% calcium, 23% iron.

GREEK RAVIOLI

Prep: 25 min. ◆ Cook: 2 min. per batch ravioli; 25 minutes for sauce

When cooking, don't crowd the ravioli or they'll stick together.

- 8   oz. ground lamb or beef
- 1   large clove garlic, minced, or ⅛ tsp. garlic powder
- 1   egg, beaten
- ½   cup crumbled feta cheese (2 oz.)
- ¼   cup shredded carrot
- 2   green onions, thinly sliced
- 2   tsp. snipped fresh oregano or ½ tsp. dried oregano, crushed
- ¼   tsp. pepper
- 48 wonton skins (about 12 oz.)

   ◆◆◆

- 1   Tbsp. cooking oil

   ◆◆◆

- 1   recipe Creamy Tomato Sauce (see page 133)
   Fresh oregano sprigs (optional)

1 In a large skillet cook lamb or beef with garlic until meat is brown and no pink remains. Drain and cool slightly. Stir in egg, feta, carrot, green onions, oregano, and pepper.

2 For each ravioli, place a rounded tablespoon of filling in the center of a wonton skin. Brush edges with water and place a second skin over the first, pressing down lightly with the tips of your fingers to force out air and seal edges. Repeat with remaining wonton skins and filling.

3 In a large pot bring a large amount of water and the cooking oil to a gentle boil. Cook ravioli, 6 at a time, for 2 to 2½ minutes or until just tender. (Don't let the water boil vigorously.) As ravioli are cooked, lift out with a slotted spoon. Drain and place in a single layer on a lightly greased baking sheet. Cover loosely with foil. Keep warm in a 300° oven for up to 10 minutes.

4 To serve, spoon some Creamy Tomato Sauce on 8 plates. Add 3 ravioli to each plate; spoon remaining sauce atop. Garnish with fresh oregano sprigs, if desired. Makes 24 ravioli (8 appetizer servings).

Creamy Tomato Sauce: In a medium saucepan cook ½ cup chopped onion and 2 cloves garlic, minced, in 1 tablespoon hot margarine or butter until onion is tender but not brown. Carefully stir in one 14½-ounce can diced tomatoes; one 8-ounce can tomato sauce; 1 tablespoon snipped fresh oregano or 1 teaspoon dried oregano, crushed; ½ teaspoon sugar; ¼ teaspoon salt; and ⅛ teaspoon pepper. Bring to boiling; reduce heat. Boil gently, uncovered, about 10 minutes or until sauce is thickened, stirring occasionally. Slowly add ½ cup whipping cream, stirring constantly. Cook and stir for 3 minutes more. Remove from heat. Keep warm. Makes about 2½ cups sauce.

Nutrition facts per serving: 313 cal., 14 g total fat (7 g sat. fat), 78 mg chol., 761 mg sodium, 35 g carbo., 1 g fiber, 13 g pro. *Daily values:* 26% vit. A, 18% vit. C, 8% calcium, 18% iron.

SUMMER SOLSTICE BREAD

Prep: 25 min. ◆ Bake: 25 min.

The alluring aroma of fresh bread fills the house from this easy, peasant-style quick bread. If desired, make one large flat loaf and use for the Mile-High Muffuletta (see recipe, page 116).

3 Tbsp. olive oil
¼ cup chopped onion

♦♦♦

1 cup all-purpose flour
1 cup whole wheat flour
½ cup shredded Romano or Parmesan cheese
¼ cup snipped fresh basil or 2 tsp. dried basil, crushed
1 tsp. baking powder
¼ tsp. baking soda
¼ tsp. salt
1 egg
½ cup buttermilk

♦♦♦

1 egg
1 Tbsp. water
2 to 3 Roma tomatoes, very thinly sliced

1 In a small skillet heat 1 tablespoon of the olive oil over medium heat. Cook and stir onion in hot oil about 5 minutes or until golden brown. Set aside.

2 In a large mixing bowl combine all-purpose flour, whole wheat flour, Romano or Parmesan cheese, basil, baking powder, baking soda, and salt. Make a well in the center of dry mixture.

3 Slightly beat 1 egg. In a small mixing bowl stir together remaining oil, buttermilk, and the beaten egg. Stir in onion mixture.

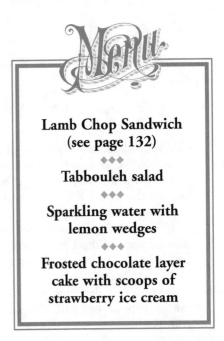

Lamb Chop Sandwich (see page 132)

♦♦♦

Tabbouleh salad

♦♦♦

Sparkling water with lemon wedges

♦♦♦

Frosted chocolate layer cake with scoops of strawberry ice cream

Add the buttermilk mixture to dry mixture, stirring until flour mixture is just moistened.

4 With floured hands, knead gently in bowl 2 to 3 times or until dough is nearly smooth. Shape into two 4-inch rounds. (Or, shape into one 6-inch round loaf.) Place on a lightly greased baking sheet.

5 Slightly beat 1 egg with 1 tablespoon water. Brush loaf with egg mixture. Arrange tomato slices on top. Bake in a 375° oven for 25 to 30 minutes or until golden. Cool slightly on a wire rack; serve warm or at room temperature. Keep for 2 or 3 days at room temperature in a paper bag. Makes 12 servings.

Nutrition facts per serving: 136 cal., 6 g total fat (1 g sat. fat), 39 mg chol., 177 mg sodium, 16 g carbo., 2 g fiber, 6 g pro. *Daily values:* 2% vit. A, 1% vit. C, 7% calcium, 6% iron.

KITCHEN CLEANUP CHECKLIST

Get your clipboard ready. It's time to conduct your own kitchen-safety inspection. If your home is typical, there are danger zones in your kitchen that could put your family at risk for acquiring a foodborne illness.

In fact, the kitchen is the most germ-infested spot in the house, according to a University of Arizona study led by micro-biologist Charles Gerba. Bacteria, which thrive in warm, dark, moist environments, can be kept at bay with this checklist as your guide.

PUT THE SQUEEZE ON SPONGES

Some 700 million microorganisms lurk in a typical damp household sponge, more than are found in any other spot in the kitchen or even the bathroom, according to the Arizona study, which was underwritten by The Clorox Co. One way to wipe out bacteria that thrive in sponges and dishcloths is to soak them in a diluted bleach solution (¾ cup bleach in 1 gallon of water) three times a week. The sponges should then be allowed to air dry.

Better yet, reach for a paper towel to clean up spills, especially juices from raw meat, advises Michael Doyle, director of the Center for Food Safety and Quality Enhancement at the University of Georgia. Then immediately dispose of the paper towels.

KEEP A SHARP EYE ON CUTTING BOARDS

More than one-third of foodborne illnesses in the home are caused by cross-contamination where "clean" food picks up bacteria from tainted cutting boards, knives, and other utensils. Avoid such cross-contamination by making sure boards and knives used to prepare raw meat, poultry, and fish don't come in contact

with ready-to-eat foods. Use two separate cutting boards—one for preparing raw meat, the other for foods that don't require cooking, such as fruit, vegetables, or cheese. After exposure to raw meat juices, wash boards and utensils in hot, soapy water; rinse; then allow them to air dry. Or run nonwooden cutting boards through the dishwasher, advises Bessie Berry, manager of the U.S. Department of Agriculture's (USDA) Meat and Poultry Hotline (800/535-4555). For an added measure of safety, use a sanitizing solution (see *A Solution for Germs,* page 135) on the board and tools after washing them. New boards touting antibacterial protection or boards with one side distinctly marked for "raw meat only" still need to be cleaned and sanitized after being used for raw meat or poultry.

HANDS UP

Although cutting boards and knives are cited as potential sources of cross-contamination of foods, hands also can spread microorganisms. When preparing food, wash your hands before and after handling it, as well as after touching pets, using the bathroom, or changing diapers. To really do a job on germs, wash your hands with warm water and soap for at least 20 seconds. That's about how long it takes to sing the Happy Birthday song—twice.

If you have an open wound or cut, prevent contamination by wearing rubber gloves when handling food.

COUNTER ATTACK

Countertops also harbor germs, according to Gerba's University of Arizona research. Gerba advises sanitizing kitchen counters with a commercial bleach-based cleanser. Or apply the same homemade sanitizing solution used to clean cutting boards (see below, right).

However, 99.9 percent of the time, cleaning the surfaces with hot soapy water takes care of the debris that could harbor organisms, says the USDA's Berry. Disposable paper towels are best to use for countertop cleanup.

HANDLE WITH CARE

Remember to clean handles on faucets and on refrigerator doors with hot, soapy water, or wipe them with a sanitizing solution. Handles may pick up germs from any hand that touches them. The Arizona study found an average of 229,000 germs per square inch on frequently touched kitchen faucet handles.

INSIDE THE FRIDGE

To keep food cold enough to slow bacterial growth, the temperature inside your refrigerator should be 40° or less. This temperature won't kill bacteria that are already present, but it will slow their growth. Use a thermometer to check your refrigerator's temperature, then adjust your fridge's control dial, if necessary. When reheating leftovers, be sure the food reaches a temperature of 165° to kill microorganisms.

Wipe up spills and drips with paper towels. Again, be careful of raw meat juices. To prevent juices from dripping onto other foods, raw meat, poultry, and fish should be isolated. Thaw these foods on plates on your refrigerator's bottom shelf or in a meat drawer used only for such uncooked products.

THE KITCHEN SINK

More breeding grounds for bacteria are the kitchen sink and drain. These two often are overlooked areas, according to the Food and Drug Administration's Center for Food Safety and Applied Nutrition. Trapped food particles in the drain's moist environment promote bacterial growth. To get rid of germs that might be dwelling there, use a sanitizing solution (see below) or a commercial cleanser on a daily basis. Gerba suggests sanitizing at least three times a week by filling the sink with 1 gallon of water and ¾ cup of bleach. Let the bleach solution soak in the sink for 10 minutes before draining.

AFTER-DINNER DISHES

To prevent contamination of freshly washed dishes, pots, and pans, allow them to air dry rather than using a dish towel to dry them. That goes for any dishes and pans in the dishwasher that may have a few drops of water on them when the cycle is finished. Because a tiny amount of standing water might contain bacteria, make sure bowls, cups, pans, and other dishes are completely dry before you store them.

A SOLUTION FOR GERMS

Using hot, soapy water to clean your countertops and cutting boards helps to reduce the chances that you or your family will contract a foodborne illness at home. As an added precaution, you can sanitize with a commercial antibacterial product or you can make your own. The USDA advises combining 1 teaspoon of household bleach with 1 quart of water. Countertops and cutting boards should be "flooded" with the bleach solution, then rinsed, and allowed to air dry, says Bessie Berry. Experts say the homemade bleach mixture's effectiveness begins to wear off if stored more than three days, so don't make more than you can use right away.

Why bother with the cleanliness routine? Bacteria can double every 20 minutes if given the right conditions. That means a single bacterium on a wet countertop can wildly reproduce to nearly 17 million in just eight hours. While that doesn't mean you have to disinfect your kitchen every 20 minutes, the goal is to minimize risk.

BUTTERMILK

The name may fool you, but there's really no butter in buttermilk. It was so-named because in days of yore, buttermilk actually was the liquid left over from churning butter. Since most buttermilk today is made from fat-free or light milk with added culture, buttermilk contains less than 100 calories a cup. If you see any golden flecks of butter in your buttermilk, they've been added by the manufacturer.

When used in baked goods, such as biscuits, the special culture in buttermilk creates a light, tender texture with a flavor touched with a subtle tang.

Are you out of buttermilk? You can easily create your own by mixing 1 tablespoon lemon juice or vinegar with enough milk to equal 1 cup. Let the mixture stand for 5 minutes before using.

BUTTERMILK BISCUIT STICKS

Prep: 20 min. ◆ Bake: 10 min.

Hints of lemon and tarragon come through in every bite of these flaky, savory sticks. For lunch on the porch, serve them alongside a fresh green salad and a glass of iced lemonade.

- 2 cups all-purpose flour
- 2 Tbsp. sugar
- 2 tsp. baking powder
- 2 tsp. finely shredded lemon peel
- 2 tsp. snipped fresh tarragon or ½ tsp. dried tarragon, crushed
- ¼ tsp. baking soda
- ¼ cup butter
- 1 egg, beaten
- ½ cup buttermilk

◆◆◆

Buttermilk
Poppy seed (optional)

1 In a medium mixing bowl stir together flour, sugar, baking powder, lemon peel, tarragon, and baking soda. Using a pastry blender, cut in butter until mixture resembles coarse crumbs. Make a well in center of mixture. Add egg and the ½ cup buttermilk all at once. Using a fork, stir until moistened.

2 Turn dough out onto a lightly floured surface. Quickly knead dough 10 to 12 strokes or until dough is nearly smooth. Lightly roll dough into a 12×6-inch rectangle. Cut into twenty-four 6-inch strips.

3 Place strips ½ inch apart on a lightly greased baking sheet. Brush with additional buttermilk. If desired, sprinkle sticks with poppy seed.

4 Bake sticks in a 425° oven about 10 minutes or until buttermilk sticks are golden. Cool slightly. Serve warm. Makes 24 biscuit sticks.

Nutrition facts per stick: 61 cal., 2 g total fat (1 g sat. fat), 14 mg chol., 71 mg sodium, 9 g carbo., 0 g fiber, 1 g pro.
Daily values: 2% vit. A, 3% calcium, 3% iron.

OLD-FASHIONED VANILLA BEAN ICE CREAM

Prep: 10 min. ◆ Chill: 4 hr.
Freeze: 20 min. ◆ Ripen: 4 hr.

This recipe makes 1½ quarts of ice cream, which is just right for the smaller iceless models and will work in larger ice-cream makers as well. Consider doubling the recipe and using a 4-quart freezer if you want to satisfy a hungry crowd.

- 2½ cups half-and-half, light cream, or whole milk
- ¾ cup sugar
- 1 4- to 6-inch vanilla bean or 1 Tbsp. vanilla extract*

◆◆◆

- 1¼ cups whipping cream

1 In a large saucepan heat and stir half-and-half, sugar, and vanilla bean (if using) just to a simmer. Remove from heat. Remove vanilla bean; let cool.

2 Using a paring knife, slit vanilla bean lengthwise. Scrape out seeds. Stir seeds (or vanilla extract, if using) and whipping cream into milk mixture. Cover and chill about 4 hours.

3 Freeze mixture in ice-cream freezer according to manufacturer's directions. Ripen 4 hours. Makes 1½ quarts.

***Note:** Omit heating the mixture if using vanilla extract.

Nutrition facts per ½-cup serving: 205 cal., 15 g total fat (9 g sat. fat), 54 mg chol., 30 mg sodium, 16 g carbo., 0 g fiber, 2 g pro. *Daily values:* 16% vit. A, 5% calcium.

MEMORY-MAKING VANILLA ICE CREAM

Funny how the icy-cold creaminess of homemade ice cream stirs up tasty images: Kids giggling on the porch stoop, ice cream melting lazily down their cones. Grown-ups savoring every rich spoonful.

It's easy to create summer memories with the recipe on page 136 for old-fashioned ice cream, speckled with the real McCoy—vanilla-bean flecks. (You can opt for vanilla extract if you prefer.) Scoop up spoonfuls of this yummy ice cream, or sandwich it between cookies for a kid-pleasing treat.

When it comes to ice-cream freezers, you've got two basic choices. One type requires salt and ice and comes in electric or hand-crank versions. Your second option is a smaller, iceless variety with a double-walled bowl you pop in the freezer overnight before using.

1. Bean There
Heating and stirring a whole vanilla bean with the half-and-half and sugar softens the bean, making it easier to split open.

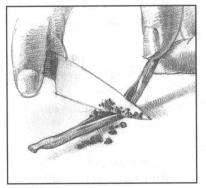

2. Seeds of Flavor
Use a paring knife to carefully slit open the vanilla bean from end to end; scrape out the tiny brown-black seeds loaded with concentrated flavor. Add the seeds to the ice-cream mixture.

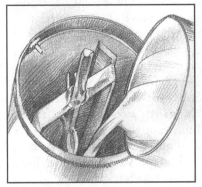

3. Dashing Experience
With the dasher in place, pour the chilled cream mixture into the container, filling it about half to three-quarters full. This allows plenty of space for the ice cream to expand as it freezes.

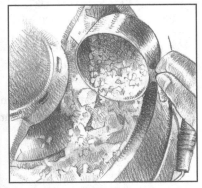

4. Cold Combination
After the lid is securely placed on the ice-cream container, fill the outer bucket with ice cubes and rock salt, according to the directions provided with your ice-cream freezer. Rock salt can be found at most supermarkets and hardware stores. Some directions call for the use of table salt.

5. It's Freezing in Here
When the mixture reaches the consistency of soft ice cream, the motor will strain or slow (or the crank handle will become difficult to turn). Stop machine; remove and scrape ice cream from dasher.

Pack and ripen ice cream as directed by freezer manufacturer. Ripening helps mixture harden slightly and develop a fuller flavor.

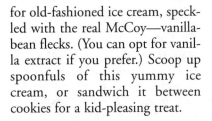

6. Frozen Fun
A no-ice, no-salt ice-cream maker has an insulated container that is placed in the freezer overnight. A liquid coolant in between its double-insulated walls helps keep the ice-cream mixture chilled while the machine is cranked by hand or by electricity. These machines typically make up to 1½ quarts of ice cream.

GREAT GRAPES!

SEEDLESS GRAPES

You can choose from green, red, and black seedless grape varieties year-round to decorate the tart.

GREEN

Perlette: These early-season grapes range from sweet to slightly tart in flavor. Domestic grapes are available from May to July, and imports arrive from December through February.

Superior: You'll find these firm, elongated sweet grapes from June through August.

Thompson: This popular sweet, oval grape variety is available almost year-round.

RED

Flame: Available almost all year long, these scarlet grapes are juicy and sweet.

Ruby: Slightly darker than flame seedless, ruby grapes have a tender skin and a bluish color. They're available from August to May, excluding February.

Emperatriz: This new variety is a fall grape, in the markets from September to December.

Crimson: Like the Emperatriz, this new red grape is available from September to December.

Champagne: These tiny sweet specialty grapes are available from September to November.

BLACK

New Fantasy: These crisp and mild-flavored blue-black grapes are in the market from June through October.

Black: Violet-black in color, these seedless grapes are available from December through April.

MASCARPONE TART WITH GRAPES

Prep: 40 min. ◆ Bake: 10 min.
Cool: 30 min.

Mascarpone (mas-kar-POHN-ay) is a rich, ivory-colored cream cheese from the Lombardy region of Italy. You may need to order it from the cheese counter of your supermarket.

½ **of a 17¼-oz. pkg. frozen puff pastry sheet, thawed**

◆◆◆

1 **egg white, beaten**
1 **Tbsp. water**

◆◆◆

1 **recipe Mascarpone Filling (see right)**
1 **cup halved seedless red and green grapes**
   Mint leaves (optional)

1 Let the folded pastry stand at room temperature for 20 minutes to thaw. On a lightly floured surface, unfold pastry and roll into a 13-inch square. Trim edges to make an even 12-inch square, reserving trimmings. Cut the square in half lengthwise to make two 12×6-inch rectangles. From each rectangle, cut two ¾-inch-wide strips crosswise, then cut two ¾-inch-wide strips lengthwise from each rectangle. Set the 8 pastry strips aside. Cut decorative designs from trimmings.

2 Place the 2 large pastry rectangles on an ungreased baking sheet. Combine egg white and water. Brush rectangles with the egg white mixture. Position 4 pastry strips atop each rectangle to build a rim on edges, trimming to fit. Brush rims with egg white mixture. Decorate with pastry cutouts. Brush again. Prick bottom of pastry with a fork. Bake in

a 375° oven for 10 to 15 minutes or until golden. Remove from oven. Cool on a wire rack.

3 Just before serving, prepare Mascarpone Filling. Spoon half the filling into each baked rectangle; spread to edges. Arrange grapes atop. If desired, garnish with mint leaves. Serves 8 to 12.

Mascarpone Filling: In a small mixing bowl stir together one 8-ounce carton mascarpone cheese or cream cheese (softened), 2 tablespoons sugar, 2 tablespoons cream sherry or orange juice, and ¼ teaspoon ground nutmeg.

Nutrition facts per serving: 291 cal., 23 g total fat (8 g sat. fat), 36 mg chol., 138 mg sodium, 19 g carbo., 0 g fiber, 8 g pro. *Daily values:* 3% vit. C.

POACHED SUMMER PEACHES WITH CHERRIES

Prep: 15 min. ◆ Cook: 20 min.

1½ **cups white Zinfandel, rosé wine, or cranberry-apple drink**
1 **2-inch piece stick cinnamon**
3 **medium peaches, halved and pitted**
½ **cup fresh sweet cherries, pitted**

◆◆◆

⅓ **of a 6-oz. pkg. (2 oz.) white baking bar**
½ **tsp. shortening**

1 In a 10-inch skillet bring wine or cranberry-apple drink and cinnamon just to boiling. Add peach halves and cherries; cover and simmer about 10 minutes or until peaches are just

tender. Remove peach halves and cherries with a slotted spoon to a shallow serving dish. Cook remaining wine mixture, uncovered, over medium heat about 10 minutes or until reduced to ½ cup. Remove and discard cinnamon. Spoon liquid mixture over peaches and cherries.

2 In a small, microwave-safe bowl melt baking bar and shortening in a microwave oven set on 100 percent power for 1 to 1½ minutes, stirring once. Let mixture cool slightly.

3 Using a spoon, transfer mixture to a sealable plastic bag. Snip a ¼-inch corner off the bag; squeezing gently, drizzle melted baking bar in threads over the poached peaches and cherries. Makes 6 servings.

Nutrition facts per serving: 142 cal., 4 g total fat (2 g sat. fat), 3 mg chol., 13 mg sodium, 17 g carbo., 2 g fiber, 1 g pro. *Daily values:* 4% vit. A, 10% vit. C, 1% calcium, 2% iron.

FRUIT BOWL SUNDAE

Start to finish: 15 min.

This "sundae" uses fruit instead of ice cream to satisfy your sweet tooth with a light, seasonal touch. (See the photograph on page 119.)

⅓ cup whipping cream
2 Tbsp. chocolate-flavored syrup
2 chocolate with white filling sandwich cookies, crushed
2 medium bananas, sliced
1 cup strawberries, sliced
2 Tbsp. shredded coconut, toasted

1 In a chilled medium mixing bowl beat whipping cream until soft peaks form (tips curl). Gradually fold in chocolate syrup until smooth; fold in cookie pieces. Arrange bananas and strawberries in 4 dessert dishes. Spoon chocolate mixture on top. Sprinkle with coconut. Serve immediately. Makes 4 servings.

Nutrition facts per serving: 188 cal., 10 g total fat (6 g sat. fat), 27 mg chol., 45 mg sodium, 27 g carbo., 2 g fiber, 2 g pro. *Daily values:* 9% vit. A, 43% vit. C, 2% calcium, 4% iron.

PRIZE TESTED RECIPE WINNER

CRANBERRY GINSENG TEA

Prep: 20 min. ◆ Cool: 2 hr.

A beguiling blend of flavors sets this ruby-hued beauty apart from traditional iced tea.

2 cups water
2 green tea bags
2 ginseng tea bags
1 mint tea bag
2 cups cranberry juice cocktail, chilled
1 cup carbonated water, chilled
    Edible flowers, such as nasturtiums or pansies

1 In a small saucepan bring the 2 cups water to boiling. Remove from heat. Add all tea bags. Cover; let steep 10 minutes. Remove tea bags. Cool at room temperature, covered, for 2 hours.

2 Transfer to a pitcher; add cranberry juice and carbonated water. Sprinkle with edible flowers. Serve over ice cubes. Store remaining tea, covered, in refrigerator up to 2 days. Makes 5 to 6 servings.

Nutrition facts per serving: 20 cal., 0 g total fat, 0 mg chol., 5 mg sodium, 5 g carbo., 0 g fiber, 0 g pro. *Daily values:* 19% vit. C.

TEA TRIVIA

◆ Discovered in China more than 5,000 years ago, tea is the second most widely consumed drink in the world (after water).

◆ Iced tea was invented in the United States by an English tea merchant and quite by accident. At the 1904 World's Fair in St. Louis, Richard Blechynden tried to peddle hot tea in the sweltering heat. When fair attendees balked, he dumped a block of ice into the brew, and the drink became an instant hit.

◆ According to the U.S. Tea Council, about 80 percent of all tea sipped by Americans is iced.

◆ Unsweetened, fresh-brewed tea has no fat, calories, sugar, or carbohydrates, and about half the caffeine found in a cup of coffee.

◆ The three types of true tea—green, black, and oolong—originate from the same plant, *Camellia sinensis.* The difference is in the processing of the leaves. Green tea leaves are steamed right after harvest. Black and oolong tea leaves are crushed and dried after harvest.

◆ Herbal teas are not true teas; they combine varying mixtures of herbs, berries, seeds, leaves, and roots of many different plants. Some herbal teas contain fruit peels and spices.

NO FAT

CITRUS SLUSH

Prep: 10 min. ◆ Freeze: 4 to 24 hr.

2 cups water
1 cup sugar
◆◆◆
1 15¼-oz. can crushed pineapple (juice pack)
1 6-oz. can frozen orange juice concentrate, thawed
¼ cup lime juice
◆◆◆
1 1-liter bottle lemon-lime carbonated beverage, chilled

1 In a large bowl stir together the water and sugar until sugar dissolves; set aside.

2 In a blender container or food processor bowl combine the undrained pineapple and orange juice concentrate. Cover and blend or process until smooth.

Add to sugar mixture; stir in lime juice. Transfer mixture to a 13×9×2-inch baking pan. Freeze for 4 to 24 hours.

3 To serve, let stand at room temperature for 20 minutes. Scrape a large spoon across frozen mixture; spoon into glasses; add carbonated beverage. Makes 12 servings.

Nutrition facts per serving: 154 cal., 0 g total fat, 0 mg chol., 12 mg sodium, 39 g carbo., 0 g fiber, 1 g pro. *Daily values:* 54% vit. C, 1% calcium, 1% iron.

NO FAT

RASPBERRY REFRESHER

Prep: 20 min. ◆ Chill: 4 to 24 hr.

Pink so bright, this summery thirst quencher is sure to delight.

3 cups water
1¼ cups sugar
◆◆◆
4 cups fresh raspberries
1 cup lemon juice
◆◆◆
1 33.8-oz. bottle club soda, chilled
Ice cubes

1 In a medium saucepan heat and stir the water and sugar over medium heat until sugar is dissolved. Remove from heat; cool.

2 Meanwhile, place the raspberries in a blender container or food processor bowl. Cover and blend or process until pureed. Sieve puree; discard seeds. (Should have about 1½ cups puree). Stir puree and lemon juice into sugar mixture. Cover and chill for 4 to 24 hours.

3 To serve, stir club soda into raspberry mixture. Serve over ice. Makes 8 to 10 servings.

Nutrition facts per serving: 159 cal., 0 g total fat, 0 mg chol., 29 mg sodium, 41 g carbo., 3 g fiber, 1 g pro. *Daily values:* 49% vit. C, 1% calcium, 2% iron.

WHITE SANGRIA PUNCH

Prep: 25 min. ◆ Chill: 2 to 4 hr.

Filled with fruit, this punch can double as a beverage and an appetizer at your next party. (See the photograph on page 119.)

1 small honeydew melon, halved, seeded, and cut into chunks
1 small pineapple, peeled and cut into chunks
4 medium peaches, cut into thin wedges
1 lemon, thinly sliced
1 lime, thinly sliced
2 750-ml bottles dry white wine, chilled
½ cup sugar
2 Tbsp. lime juice
1 32-oz. bottle sparkling water, chilled
1 cup loosely packed small fresh mint leaves

1 In a large punch bowl combine fruits and lemon and lime slices. Add wine, sugar, and lime juice. Stir well to dissolve sugar. Cover and chill. Just before serving, stir in carbonated water and mint leaves. Serve with additional *pineapple spears.* Serves 16.

Nutrition facts per serving: 123 cal., 0 g total fat, 0 mg chol., 20 mg sodium, 16 g carbo., 1 g fiber, 1 g pro. *Daily values:* 2% vit. A, 35% vit. C, 2% calcium, 9% iron.

JULY
Berry Bonanza

30-minute recipes indicated in RED.
Low-fat and no-fat recipes indicated
with a ♥.
Photographs indicated in italics.
*Bonus recipe

No matter where your berries of summer come from (see page 153)—your garden, the farmer's market, or the grocery store, get them when they're fresh and enjoy them for all kinds of meal occasions. For a weekend breakfast, glorify pancakes with raspberry-laced Berries to Pour. Weekday salads like The Blues Salad and Season's Finest Salad are made special with homemade Blueberry Vinegar or Strawberry Dressing. Gooseberries are the unexpected supper partner to bratwurst in Brats with Gooseberry Catsup. Of course, it almost goes without saying, berries really hit their stride in special desserts, like Pick-of-the-Crop Pie and Easy-Freezy Sorbet.

JUST PEACHES

Fresh peaches are at their prime between June and September. When selecting peaches, look for those that are firm to slightly soft when gently pressed. The skin color varies from golden yellow to dark reddish brown, but the peaches should have no tinges of green.

To ripen firm, fresh peaches, place them in a small, clean paper bag. (A plastic bag doesn't allow the fruit to breathe and can produce mold on fruit from moisture trapped in the bag.) Loosely close the bag and store it at room temperature. Check fruit daily and remove any that yields to gentle pressure. Use the ripe peaches immediately or transfer them to the refrigerator for a few days to retard further ripening.

30 MIN. LOW FAT

PEACH PANCAKES WITH PEACHY-BERRY SAUCE

Prep: 10 min. ◆ Cook: 3 to 4 min. per batch

Homemade peach puree perks up these cinnamon-touched pancakes.

- 1 **cup all-purpose flour**
- 2 **Tbsp. cornmeal**
- 1 **Tbsp. sugar**
- 1 **tsp. baking powder**
- ½ **tsp. baking soda**
- ½ **tsp. ground cinnamon**
- ¼ **tsp. salt**

- 1 **cup milk**
- ½ **cup peach puree***
- 1 **egg, beaten**
- 2 **Tbsp. cooking oil**

◆◆◆

- 1 **recipe Peachy-Berry Sauce (see right)**

1 In a bowl stir together flour, cornmeal, sugar, baking powder, baking soda, cinnamon, and salt. Make a well in center of flour mixture; set aside.

2 In another bowl combine milk, peach puree, egg, and cooking oil. Add the milk mixture all at once to the flour mixture. Stir just until moistened (batter should be lumpy).

3 For each 2-inch pancake, pour about 1 tablespoon batter onto a hot, lightly greased griddle or heavy skillet. (For 4-inch pancakes, use about ¼ cup batter.) Cook over medium heat about 2 minutes on each side or until pancakes are golden brown, turning to second sides when pancakes have bubbly surfaces and edges are slightly dry. Serve pancakes warm with Peachy-Berry Sauce. Makes about twenty 2-inch pancakes (5 servings).

***Note:** For peach puree, pit, peel, and quarter 1 large or 2 medium peaches. Place in a food processor bowl or blender container. Cover and process or blend until smooth.

Nutrition facts per serving without sauce: 209 cal., 8 g total fat (2 g sat. fat), 46 mg chol., 343 mg sodium, 29 g carbo., 1 g fiber, 6 g pro.
Daily values: 6% vit. A, 4% vit. C, 11% calcium, 10% iron.

30 MIN. NO FAT

PEACHY-BERRY SAUCE

Start to finish: 5 min.

Take care to avoid overcooking fruit if you want to preserve the freshness.

- ½ **cup pure maple syrup**
- 1 **cup fresh raspberries**
- ¾ **cup thinly sliced, peeled peaches**

1 In a saucepan bring maple syrup just to a simmer. Stir in raspberries and peaches; heat through. Serve over Peach Pancakes (see recipe, at left). Makes 2½ cups.

Nutrition facts per 2 tablespoons: 152 cal., 0 g total fat, 0 mg chol., 2 mg sodium, 13 g carbo., 1 g fiber, 0 g pro. *Daily values:* 1% vit. A, 7% vit. C, 2% iron.

BLUEBERRY RIPPLE COFFEE CAKE

Prep: 40 min. ◆ Bake: 50 min.

- ¼ **cup granulated sugar**
- 2 **Tbsp. cornstarch**
- 1 **cup blueberries**

◆◆◆

- ¼ **cup packed brown sugar**
- 3 **Tbsp. all-purpose flour**
- ¼ **tsp. ground cinnamon**
- 2 **Tbsp. cold butter**
- ½ **cup rolled oats**
- ¼ **cup sliced or slivered almonds**

◆◆◆

- 2 **cups all-purpose flour**
- 1 **Tbsp. baking powder**
- ¼ **tsp. baking soda**
- ¼ **tsp. salt**
- ½ **cup butter, softened**
- 1 **cup granulated sugar**
- 3 **eggs**
- 1 **8-oz. carton dairy sour cream**

1 Grease and flour a 10-inch fluted tube pan; set aside. In a small saucepan combine the ¼ cup granulated sugar and the cornstarch. Stir in ¼ cup *water* and the blueberries. Cook and stir over medium-low heat until the mixture is very thick and bubbly. Cook for 1 minute more. Remove mixture from heat; cover surface with plastic wrap. Cool without stirring.

2 In a medium bowl combine brown sugar, the 3 tablespoons flour, and the cinnamon. Using a pastry blender, cut in the 2 tablespoons butter until mixture is crumbly. Stir in rolled oats and almonds; set aside.

3 Stir together the 2 cups flour, baking powder, soda, and salt; set aside. In a large mixing bowl beat the ½ cup butter with an electric mixer on medium to high speed for 30 seconds. Beat in the 1 cup granulated sugar until fluffy. Add eggs, 1 at a time, beating for 1 minute after each. Alternately add flour mixture and sour cream to egg mixture, beating on low to medium speed after each addition just until combined. (Batter will be stiff.)

4 Sprinkle half of the oat mixture into prepared pan. Drop one-third of the batter by spoonfuls atop oat mixture; carefully spread to cover. Spoon the blueberry mixture atop the batter in pan. Repeat with another one-third of the batter; sprinkle the remaining oat mixture atop. Repeat with remaining batter.

5 Bake in a 350° oven about 50 minutes or until a wooden

toothpick inserted near center of cake comes out clean. Cool cake in pan for 10 minutes. If needed, loosen edges of cake using a table knife. Invert cake onto a wire rack. Cool cake at least 45 minutes before serving. Makes 12 servings.

Nutrition facts per serving: 355 cal., 17 g total fat (9 g sat. fat), 87 mg chol., 287 mg sodium, 47 g carbo., 1 g fiber, 6 g pro. *Daily values:* 15% vit. A, 2% vit. C, 11% calcium, 11% iron.

BAKED CRANBERRY-APPLE PANCAKE

Prep: 15 min. ◆ Bake: 15 min.

The beauty of this crowd-serving pancake is it bakes in the oven, so there's no tending the griddle.

2 Tbsp. margarine or butter
¼ cup dried cranberries
1 small apple, peeled, cored, and chopped
◆◆◆
¼ cup packed brown sugar
1 tsp. finely shredded orange peel (set aside)
¼ cup orange juice
◆◆◆
¾ cup all-purpose flour
4 tsp. granulated sugar
½ tsp. baking powder
½ tsp. baking soda
⅛ tsp. salt
1 egg, beaten
½ cup buttermilk
4 tsp. cooking oil

1 Preheat oven to 350°. Place margarine or butter in a 9-inch pie plate. Place pie plate in preheating oven just until margarine is melted. Remove from oven; add cranberries and apple.

Baked Cranberry-Apple Pancake (see left)

◆◆◆

Cooked sausage links or Canadian-style bacon

◆◆◆

Coffee and/or assorted fruit juices

2 Meanwhile, in a small saucepan combine brown sugar and orange juice. Bring to boil; reduce heat to medium. Boil gently, uncovered, for 5 minutes. Pour atop cranberries and apple in pie plate.

3 In a medium mixing bowl stir together flour, granulated sugar, baking powder, soda, and salt; set aside. In another mixing bowl combine egg, buttermilk, oil, and orange peel. Add egg mixture all at once to flour. Stir just until mixed. Pour batter evenly atop mixture in pie plate.

4 Bake in a 350° oven about 15 minutes or until top springs back when lightly touched. Cool in pie plate for 5 minutes. Carefully invert pancake onto a serving platter. Cut in wedges and serve warm. Makes 8 side-dish servings.

Nutrition facts per serving: 151 cal., 6 g total fat (1 g sat. fat), 27 mg chol., 195 mg sodium, 22 g carbo., 1 g fiber, 3 g pro. *Daily values:* 5% vit. A, 8% vit. C, 4% calcium, 5% iron.

30 MIN. NO FAT

BERRIES TO POUR

Start to finish: 15 min.

A cross between a syrup and a jam.

- **4 cups fresh red or black raspberries, or sliced fresh strawberries**
- **½ cup honey or ⅓ to ½ cup sugar**
- **2 Tbsp. water**
- **2 Tbsp. raspberry liqueur (optional)**

1 Using a potato masher, crush 3 cups of the berries. In a saucepan combine crushed berries, honey or sugar, and water. Cook and stir until bubbly. Cook and stir 2 minutes more or until slightly thickened. Cool slightly. Add remaining berries and, if desired, liqueur. Store, covered, in refrigerator up to 2 weeks. Serve warm or chilled as a dessert sauce or topper for pancakes. Makes 3 cups.

Nutrition facts per 2 tablespoon serving: 32 cal., 0 g total fat , 0 mg chol., 0 mg sodium, 8 g carbo., 1 g fiber, 0 g pro.
Daily values: 8% vit. C, 1% iron.

CHICKEN AND PEACH WONTONS

Prep: 30 min. ◆ Cook: 1½ min. per batch

- **Nonstick spray coating**
- **8 oz. ground raw chicken or turkey**
- **¼ cup pineapple juice**
- **3 Tbsp. finely chopped green onions**
- **1 Tbsp. soy sauce**
- **1 tsp. ground ginger**
- **½ cup finely chopped, peeled peaches**
- **⅛ tsp. ground red pepper**

◆◆◆

- **36 wonton wrappers**

◆◆◆

- **Cooking oil for deep-fat frying**

1 For filling, spray a large skillet with nonstick spray coating. Cook chicken in skillet until no longer pink; drain. Add pineapple juice, green onions, soy sauce, and ginger to skillet. Bring to boiling; reduce heat. Simmer, uncovered, about 4 minutes or until liquid has evaporated. Stir in peaches and red pepper. Cool slightly.

2 To fill, spoon 1 rounded teaspoon chicken mixture into center of each wonton wrapper. Brush edges with water. Fold wrapper diagonally in half over filling and press to seal.

3 Meanwhile, in a heavy saucepan or deep-fat fryer heat 2 inches oil to 365°. Fry wontons, 4 at a time, in hot oil for 1½ to 2 minutes or until golden brown, turning once. Remove wontons from oil; drain on paper towels. Place fried wontons on a baking sheet. Keep warm in a 300° oven while frying remaining wontons. Serve warm. Makes 36 wontons.

TO MAKE AHEAD

Fry the wontons, drain, and cool. Wrap in foil, label, and freeze for up to 1 month. To serve, place frozen wontons on a baking sheet. Bake, uncovered, in a 400° oven for 5 to 7 minutes or until hot.

Nutrition facts per wonton: 59 cal., 3 g total fat (1 g sat. fat), 0 mg chol., 78 mg sodium, 5 g carbo., 0 g fiber, 2 g pro.
Daily values: 2% iron.

SOUTHWESTERN PIEROGI

Prep: 40 min. ◆ Cook: 2 min. per batch

Similar to the Polish pierogi and the Chinese wonton, these half-moon-shaped appetizers have a tacolike filling encased in a crispy shell. (See the photograph on page 159.)

- **12 oz. ground beef**
- **½ cup chopped onion**
- **¼ cup drained, chopped, roasted red sweet peppers**
- **1 tsp. dried oregano, crushed**
- **½ tsp. ground cumin**
- **¼ tsp. ground black pepper**

◆◆◆

- **30 egg roll wrappers**
- **1 egg, slightly beaten**
- **1 Tbsp. water**

◆◆◆

- **¼ cup cooking oil**
- **Salsa, dairy sour cream, and/or guacamole (optional)**

1 For filling, in a large skillet cook ground beef and onion until meat is no longer pink; drain. Stir in sweet pepper, oregano, cumin, and ground black pepper.

2 Using a 4-inch round cutter, cut out the center of each egg roll wrapper. Spoon about 1 tablespoon of the meat mixture into the center of each circle. Brush edges with a mixture of egg and water. Fold wrapper in half over filling. Seal edges with the tines of a fork.

3 Heat oil in a large skillet over medium heat. Cook pierogi, six at a time, in hot oil for 2 to 3 minutes or until golden, turning once and adding more oil if necessary. Drain on paper towels. If desired, serve with salsa, sour cream, and/or guacamole. Makes 30 pierogi.

TO MAKE AHEAD

Fill pierogi as directed, but do not fry. Place in a single layer on a baking sheet; freeze. When frozen, place in a freezer container. Seal, label, and freeze for up to 1 month. To serve, thaw overnight in the refrigerator. Fry and serve as directed.

Nutrition facts per pierogi: 72 cal., 4 g total fat (1 g sat. fat), 22 mg chol., 10 mg sodium, 6 g carbo., 0 g fiber, 3 g pro. *Daily values:* 1% vit. A, 5% vit. C, 4% iron.

CHILLED SHRIMP AND DILL PÂTÉ

Prep: 30 min. ◆ Chill: 4 to 24 hr.

1 pkg. unflavored gelatin
⅓ cup water
1 8-oz. carton dairy sour cream or light dairy sour cream
1 8-oz. pkg. cream cheese or reduced-fat cream cheese (Neufchâtel), softened

¼ cup grated Romano or Parmesan cheese
¼ cup dry white wine
¼ cup snipped fresh dillweed
3 Tbsp. snipped fresh parsley
1 Tbsp. drained capers
2 cloves garlic, quartered
½ tsp. coarsely ground black pepper
8 oz. cooked, peeled, and deveined shrimp, finely chopped
Toasted baguette slices
Thin slices peeled cantaloupe and/or honeydew melon

1 In a small saucepan combine the gelatin and water; let stand 5 minutes. Cook and stir over low heat until gelatin is dissolved; set aside.

2 In a blender container or food processor bowl combine the sour cream, cream cheese, Romano cheese, wine, dillweed, parsley, capers, garlic, and pepper; add the gelatin mixture. Cover and blend or process until well-combined. Transfer mixture to a medium bowl; stir in the shrimp.

3 Place shrimp mixture in a 4-cup glass bowl. Cover and chill for 4 to 24 hours. To unmold, run a long knife or spatula around edges and sides of bowl to loosen pâté. Turn the shrimp mixture out onto a serving platter. Garnish with *fresh dill sprigs.* Serve with toasted baguette slices and thin slices of melon. Makes 12 appetizer servings.

Nutrition facts per serving: 174 cal., 12 g total fat (7 g sat. fat), 69 mg chol., 205 mg sodium, 8 g carbo., 0 g fiber, 8 g pro. *Daily values:* 23% vit. A, 22% vit. C, 6% calcium, 8% iron.

LOW FAT

DRIED CHERRY AND GOAT CHEESE ROLL-UPS

Prep: 25 min. ◆ Chill: 2 hr.

1 cup apple juice or water
1 cup dried tart red cherries, snipped

◆◆◆

½ of an 8-oz. pkg. cream cheese, softened
1 5.3-oz. pkg. soft goat cheese
¼ cup toasted, chopped slivered almonds or pine nuts
½ tsp. finely shredded lemon peel
¼ tsp. pepper
4 rounds of lefsa or four 7- or 8-inch flour tortillas

1 In a small saucepan bring apple juice or water to boiling. Remove saucepan from heat. Add cherries. Cover and let stand about 15 minutes or until cherries are softened. Drain cherries; pat dry with paper towels.

2 In a medium mixing bowl stir together the softened cherries, cream cheese, goat cheese, almonds, lemon peel, and pepper until well combined. Spread mixture evenly over lefsa or tortillas. Roll up each. Wrap in plastic wrap. Chill for up to 2 hours.

3 To serve, cut each roll into 1-inch slices. Arrange on a serving platter. Makes 24 to 28 slices.

Nutrition facts per slice: 74 cal., 4 g total fat (1 g sat. fat), 11 mg chol., 55 mg sodium, 8 g carbo., 0 g fiber, 2 g pro. *Daily values:* 5% vit. A, 1% calcium, 2% iron.

WATER WATER EVERYWHERE

Too many of us are missing out on an important nutrient. It's not a food. It's not a vitamin or mineral. But without it, vitamins and minerals—in fact, all the elements of food and nutrition—can't do their work. This overlooked nutrient is readily available, often free, and easy to take. The powerful player here is water, and most of us aren't drinking the eight 8-ounce glasses recommended daily for good health.

Not all liquids are created equal, and not all liquids are water. The average healthy adult should drink the equivalent of about two quarts of this most important liquid asset every day, or about 1 quart for every 1,000 calories-worth of food.

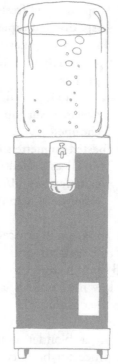

Although water is in all beverages, and in all foods, too, it is most beneficial to your body's thirsty cells when consumed without embellishment. To put it simply: Nothing beats a swig of plain, old-fashioned, crystal-clear drinking water, whether it's straight from the tap or bottled (see "A Bottle in Front of Me," page 147).

It's easy to draw water into your busy workday. Just follow these eight easy steps:

Seven a.m. Start your day with an 8-ounce glass of water. Your body's cells need water to provide structure, and the fluid cushions your organs, acting as a shock absorber to help minimize day-to-day stress damage. Water also is necessary for optimum lubrication of the joints. As a reminder to start the day with water, place a glass by the sink the night before.

Ten a.m. Take a breather from your morning workload and drink 8 ounces of water. It will help flush your kidneys and rid your body of toxic substances. Water also helps your body maintain its volume of blood. When you're dehydrated, blood volume drops and your energy level decreases.

In fact, a drop of as little as 1 percent of body-fluid volume can noticeably reduce your body's capacity to perform its functions. A 4-percent loss decreases this capacity to nearly a third less than normal. Drinking that midmorning glass of water could help you feel just a little more energetic.

Noon. Drink 8 ounces of water with lunch. Water balances electrolytes (minerals such as sodium, chloride, and potassium), which help regulate body temperature and control blood pressure.

Two p.m. Time for another break. And another 8 ounces of water. The body needs the precious fluid to transport water-soluble vitamins and nutrients, such as protein, minerals, and the B and C vitamins.

Four p.m. Hitting the road to pick up the kids from soccer practice or to run some afternoon errands? Or are you busy wrapping things up at the office? Either way, drink 8 ounces of water in the late afternoon. Don't wait until you feel thirsty—your body's feeling of thirst is not a reliable indicator of dehydration.

Sometimes dehydration signals are mistaken for hunger pangs. If you respond by eating, especially by snacking on sugary or salty munchies, you'll only aggravate your dehydration while adding unwanted calories. Water provides a feeling of fullness and is calorie-free, so it can help keep your energy intake balanced.

Six p.m. When you're settling in for the evening or getting ready for your supper, don't forget the water. It's time for another 8 ounces. Water is a significant source of vital ultratrace minerals, such as magnesium, cobalt, copper, and manganese.

Eight p.m. Drink another 8 ounces of water. Before you put the kids to bed, you might want to know this: Younger children have a poorly developed thirst mechanism. Make sure they're getting sufficient fluids throughout the day, especially water with fluoride (see story, below).

Ten p.m. End the day with a final 8-ounce glass of water. Water becomes more important as we age. The older you get, the less reliable your thirst mechanism is. After age 65, we start to lose our thirst "trigger" and are more susceptible to dehydration. Older persons should carefully monitor their daily fluid intake.

A BOTTLE IN FRONT OF ME

Each year Americans drink nearly 1 billion gallons of bottled water, divided among nearly 1,000 brands. Some brands are pure, mineral-rich water from underground sources, but other brands are nothing more than tap water with a fancy label. To make sure you are getting what you're after, read the labels. They should tell you the source of the water and whether or not any minerals have been filtered out.

A common concern with tap water is pollution from chemicals or heavy metals, such as lead. These pollutants can come from farm runoff or industrial pollution. Call your water company to check if the tap water in your area is approved as safe. You also may call the Environmental Protection Agency's Safe Drinking Water Hotline at 800/426-4791 for water information.

Houses older than five years, or in areas with soft water (which can be corrosive to pipes), may be susceptible to trace amounts of undesired metals leaching into the water. Use a purchased water filter or let the tap run for 5 to 30 seconds to flush the system before filling your glass.

In America, treated tap water is the leading source of dietary fluoride. This mineral is vital for building strong teeth and healthy bones. Consider a fluoride-added brand of water if your children drink nonfluoridated water from filtered, bottled, or well-water sources.

WHEN MORE IS BETTER

◆ Exercise and other activities increase water needs, especially when it's warm and humid out. It's best to drink a glass or two of water shortly before performing physical activity. Even if you only work out a few times per week, you'll need to boost your water intake. Add between one and three glasses, depending on the strenuousness and duration of the activity.

◆ Women who are pregnant or breast-feeding should add at least two extra glasses of water to the eight-glasses-per-day recommendation. This compensates for the increased body-fluid volume needed. Adequate water also can decrease symptoms associated with morning sickness.

◆ Winter weather can dehydrate you as thoroughly as any sweltering summer day. When the furnace in your house is running full blast and winter winds blow, the air turns bone-dry, drawing the moisture out of you. Keep up your eight-glasses-per-day regimen and add an extra glass or two following outdoor activities.

TRAVEL ADVISORY

◆ Travel, especially air travel, is a desiccating experience. Whether in the air or on the road, you should drink one glass of water for every hour you travel. Remember: To avoid dehydration you should drink before you feel thirsty.

DON'T LIKE PLAIN WATER?

Try these thirst-quenching fix-ups:

◆ Flavor water with a little fruit juice, about ¼ cup per 8 ounces of water.

◆ Add a slice of orange, lime, lemon, or other citrus fruit to a tall glass of ice water for a refreshing hint of flavor. Star fruit is also a fun, fruit enhancement for your ice water.

◆ Drink hot water with a slice of lemon as a hot-beverage alternative to coffee or tea.

SESAME BEEF KABOBS

Prep: 30 min. ◆ Marinate: 4 to 24 hr.
Grill: 12 min.

Inspired by Korean beef known as Bul-Kogi, these little skewers make a great grilled appetizer.

12 oz. beef flank steak

◆◆◆

2 Tbsp. soy sauce
2 Tbsp. toasted sesame oil
1 green onion, sliced
2 cloves garlic, minced
1½ tsp. sugar
1½ tsp. dry sherry (optional)
½ tsp. sesame seed
½ tsp. crushed red pepper

◆◆◆

¾ cup fresh pea pods, trimmed and halved diagonally crosswise (about 2 ounces)

◆◆◆

15 cherry tomatoes, halved

1 Score meat by making shallow cuts at 1-inch intervals in a diamond pattern. Repeat on other side. Place meat in a plastic bag set in a shallow dish.

2 For marinade, combine the soy sauce, oil, green onion, garlic, sugar, sherry (if desired), sesame seed, and crushed red pepper. Pour over meat; seal bag. Marinate in refrigerator for 4 to 24 hours, turning occasionally.

3 Drain meat; discard marinade. Grill meat on the rack of an uncovered grill directly over medium coals for 12 to 14 minutes or until medium doneness, turning once.

4 Meanwhile, cook pea pods in a small amount of boiling water for 2 to 4 minutes or until crisp-tender; drain. Cut meat into ¾-inch pieces.

5 To serve, place meat cubes and pea pods on wooden picks with cherry tomato halves. Makes about 30 appetizer servings.

Nutrition facts per serving: 23 cal., 1 g total fat (0 g sat. fat), 5 mg chol., 30 mg sodium, 1 g carbo., 0 g fiber, 2 g pro.
Daily values: 6% vit. C, 2% iron.

PRIZE TESTED RECIPE WINNER

TOMATO MELTS

Prep: 15 min. ◆ Bake: 15 min.

These tasty morsels are so irresistible, seconds are hard to refuse.

3 large tomatoes (about 8 oz. each) or a variety of smaller tomatoes (about 1½ lb. total)
1½ cups shredded Monterey Jack cheese with jalapeño peppers or Monterey Jack cheese (2 oz.)
1 small green, yellow, purple, or red sweet pepper, finely chopped (about ½ cup)
¼ cup sliced almonds, toasted

1 Cut each tomato into 4 slices, about ½ inch thick. If using smaller tomatoes, halve each one. For each of 4 servings, arrange 3 tomato slices, overlapping slightly, in a foil-lined, 15×10×1-inch baking pan. (Or, if using smaller tomatoes, arrange in a single layer in a foil-lined, 15×10×1-inch baking pan.) Sprinkle with shredded cheese, finely chopped pepper, and toasted almonds. Bake in a 350° oven about 15 minutes or until cheese is bubbly. Carefully lift with large metal spatula to individual plates, allowing excess juices to drain off. Makes 4 appetizer servings.

GRILL DIRECTIONS

Arrange ingredients as directed in a shallow disposable foil pan. In a grill with a cover arrange medium-hot coals around the edge of the grill; test for medium heat above the center of the grill. Place the pan with the tomatoes in the center of the grill rack. Grill, covered, for 12 to 15 minutes or until cheese is bubbly.

Nutrition facts per serving: 203 cal., 14 g total fat (6 g sat. fat), 25 mg chol., 172 mg sodium, 13 g carbo., 2 g fiber, 10 g pro.
Daily values: 21% vit. A, 79% vit. C, 20% calcium, 10% iron.

CHIPOTLE CATSUP

Start to finish: 1½ hr.

- 4 lb. ripe tomatoes (12 medium)
- ½ cup chopped onion
- 1 or 2 dried chipotle chili peppers, crumbled*
- ½ cup sugar

◆◆◆

- ½ cup white vinegar
- 1 Tbsp. snipped fresh marjoram or 1 tsp. dried marjoram, crushed
- 1 tsp. salt

1 Core and quarter tomatoes; drain. In a large saucepan combine tomatoes, onion, and chipotle chili peppers. Bring to boiling, stirring often; reduce heat. Simmer, covered, for 15 minutes. Press through food mill or sieve. Discard seeds and skins. Return to saucepan; stir in sugar. Bring to boiling; reduce heat. Simmer, uncovered, for 45 to 60 minutes or until reduced by half, stirring occasionally. (Use a clean wooden or metal ruler to measure depth of mixture before and after cooking to determine when it is reduced by half.)

2 Add vinegar, marjoram, and salt to tomato mixture. Simmer, uncovered, about 30 minutes or until desired consistency, stirring often. Makes 2 cups.

*Note: Hot peppers contain oils that can burn. Wear plastic gloves to crumble peppers. Do not touch eyes or face, and thoroughly wash hands.

Nutrition facts per tablespoon: 25 cal., 0 g total fat, 0 mg chol., 72 mg sodium, 6 g carbo., 1 g fiber, 1 g pro.
Daily values: 3% vit. A, 20% vit. C, 2% iron.

SPICY FRENCH FRIES

Prep: 10 min. ◆ Bake: 30 min.

Here's a baked version of America's favorite way to eat potatoes. Dip these spice-coated wedges into the peppery Chipotle Catsup (see recipe, left) for a spicy taste treat.

- 1 tsp. dried marjoram or oregano, crushed
- 1 tsp. unsweetened cocoa powder
- ½ tsp. onion powder or garlic powder
- ½ tsp. paprika
- ¼ tsp. salt
- ⅛ tsp. pepper
- ½ of a 24-oz. pkg. frozen potato wedges or 2 medium potatoes, each cut into 8 wedges (about 12 oz. total)
- Nonstick spray coating
- Lime wedges (optional)

1 In a small bowl combine marjoram or oregano, cocoa powder, onion or garlic powder, paprika, salt, and pepper. Spray potatoes with nonstick coating; place in a plastic bag. Add spice mixture and shake to coat. Place potatoes in a single layer on a baking sheet sprayed with nonstick coating.

2 If using fresh potatoes, bake in a 450° oven about 30 minutes or until potatoes are tender. If using frozen potatoes, bake according to package directions. Serve with Chipotle Catsup (see recipe, left) and, if desired, lime wedges. Makes 2 or 3 side-dish servings.

Nutrition facts per serving: 229 cal., 7 g total fat (0 g sat. fat), 0 mg chol., 317 mg sodium, 39 g carbo., 0 g fiber, 2 g pro.
Daily values: 3% vit. A, 9% vit. C, 1% calcium, 7% iron.

PRIZE TESTED RECIPE WINNER

SWISS CHARD BRUSCHETTA

Start to finish: 20 min.

Varicolored chard called Bright Lights adds interest to the topping of this Italian-style appetizer. Look for it in the produce aisle or grow your own.

- 2 Tbsp. olive oil
- 8 oz. Swiss chard, coarsely chopped (about 3 cups)
- 2 Tbsp. water
- Salt and pepper

◆◆◆

- 1 Tbsp. olive oil
- 1 Tbsp. balsamic vinegar
- 6 slices French bread, cut diagonally ¾ inch thick and toasted
- ½ cup torn arugula or small arugula leaves
- ½ cup crumbled garlic-and-herb feta cheese or plain feta cheese (2 oz.)

1 In a large skillet or wok heat the 2 tablespoons olive oil. Stir-fry Swiss chard over medium-high heat for 2 minutes. Add water; cook 2 minutes more. Add salt and pepper to taste. Remove from heat.

2 In a small bowl combine the 1 tablespoon oil and the vinegar; set aside. To serve, divide chard among the pieces of toast. Drizzle with the oil-and-vinegar mixture. Top with arugula and feta cheese. Serve immediately. Makes 6 side-dish servings.

Nutrition facts per serving: 164 cal., 10 g total fat (2 g sat. fat), 8 mg chol., 348 mg sodium, 16 g carbo., 1 g fiber, 4 g pro.
Daily values: 13% vit. A, 12% vit. C, 7% calcium, 11% iron.

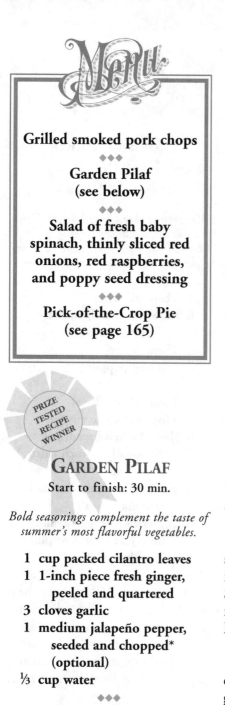

Menu

Grilled smoked pork chops

◆◆◆

Garden Pilaf
(see below)

◆◆◆

Salad of fresh baby spinach, thinly sliced red onions, red raspberries, and poppy seed dressing

◆◆◆

Pick-of-the-Crop Pie
(see page 165)

PRIZE TESTED RECIPE WINNER

Garden Pilaf

Start to finish: 30 min.

Bold seasonings complement the taste of summer's most flavorful vegetables.

1 cup packed cilantro leaves
1 1-inch piece fresh ginger, peeled and quartered
3 cloves garlic
1 medium jalapeño pepper, seeded and chopped* (optional)
⅓ cup water

◆◆◆

1 Tbsp. cooking oil
½ cup chopped onion
3 cups fresh vegetables, such as green beans, cut into 1-inch strips; carrots, cut into 1-inch strips; cauliflower florets; whole kernel corn; and/or peas
½ tsp. salt
¼ tsp. ground cinnamon
1½ cups cooked rice

3 green sweet peppers, halved (optional)**
½ cup coarsely chopped cashews
1 Tbsp. golden raisins
Cilantro sprigs

1 In a blender container or food processor bowl combine the 1 cup cilantro; fresh ginger; garlic; jalapeño pepper, if using; and water. Cover and blend or process until mixture is nearly smooth. Set aside.

2 In a large saucepan heat oil; cook and stir onion in hot oil over medium heat for 4 to 5 minutes or until onion is tender. Add vegetables, salt, cinnamon, and cilantro mixture. Bring to boiling; reduce heat. Simmer, covered, for 10 to 12 minutes or until vegetables are crisp-tender. Stir in cooked rice; heat through.

3 To serve, transfer mixture to a serving dish or if desired, spoon into halved green sweet peppers. Sprinkle with cashews and golden raisins; garnish with cilantro. Makes 6 side-dish servings.

*Note: Hot peppers contain oils that can burn. Wear plastic gloves to seed and chop pepper. Do not touch eyes or face, and thoroughly wash hands.

**Note: If desired, steam the sweet peppers for 6 to 7 minutes or until crisp-tender.

Nutrition facts per serving: 186 cal., 8 g total fat (1 g sat. fat), 0 mg chol., 263 mg sodium, 26 g carbo., 2 g fiber, 5 g pro. *Daily values:* 29% vit. A, 25% vit. C, 3% calcium, 13% iron.

30 MIN.
LOW FAT

Green Beans with Caramelized Onions

Start to finish: 30 min.

Seasoned golden onions and ripe red tomatoes turn beans beyond the basics.

1 lb. green beans, trimmed

◆◆◆

1 medium white or red onion, sliced
1 clove garlic, minced
1 Tbsp. olive oil

◆◆◆

1 medium tomato, seeded and chopped
1 tsp. snipped fresh oregano or ¼ tsp. dried oregano, crushed
¼ tsp. salt
⅛ tsp. pepper

1 In a medium saucepan cook beans in lightly salted boiling water for 12 to 15 minutes or until crisp-tender; drain.

2 Meanwhile, in a large skillet cook the onion and garlic, covered, in hot oil over medium-low heat for 12 to 15 minutes or until onions are tender, stirring occasionally. Uncover; cook and stir over medium-high heat for 3 to 5 minutes or until onions are golden, stirring once or twice. Remove from heat.

3 Add the tomato, oregano, salt, and pepper to mixture in skillet. Stir in beans. To serve, transfer to a serving dish. Makes 4 to 6 side-dish servings.

Nutrition facts per serving: 83 cal., 4 g total fat (1 g sat. fat), 0 mg chol., 140 mg sodium, 12 g carbo., 4 g fiber, 3 g pro. *Daily values:* 9% vit. A, 29% vit. C, 4% calcium, 10% iron.

CURRIED EGGPLANT KABOBS WITH MINT SAUCE

Prep: 35 min. ◆ Grill: 10 to 12 min.

Common to Indian cuisine, a cool and creamy mint sauce tames the spiciness of the curry mixture that's brushed on the vegetables.

¼ cup vegetable oil
¼ cup lemon juice
2 tsp. curry powder
¼ tsp. salt

◆◆◆

2 Japanese eggplants or 8 oz. eggplant, cut into 1-inch pieces
1 medium red sweet pepper, cut into 1-inch pieces
1 medium green sweet pepper, cut into 1-inch pieces
5 green onions, cut into 1-inch lengths

◆◆◆

2 8-oz. cartons plain low-fat yogurt
1 tsp. lemon juice
½ cup loosely packed fresh mint leaves, snipped

1 In a small bowl stir together the vegetable oil, the ¼ cup lemon juice, curry powder, and salt.

2 On six 12-inch or twelve 6-inch skewers thread eggplant, peppers, and onions, leaving ¼ inch between pieces. Brush curry mixture over vegetables.

3 Grill kabobs on rack of an uncovered grill directly over medium coals for 10 to 12 minutes or until vegetables are tender, turning kabobs occasionally.

4 Meanwhile, in a small bowl stir together the yogurt and 1 teaspoon lemon juice. Stir in the mint. Cover and chill until serving time. Serve with kabobs. Makes 6 side-dish servings.

Nutrition facts per serving: 127 cal., 10 g total fat (2 g sat. fat), 2 mg chol., 118 mg sodium, 8 g carbo., 2 g fiber, 3 g pro. *Daily values:* 14% vit. A, 70% vit. C, 7% calcium, 11% iron.

HELPING KIDS EAT RIGHT

Teaching your children to eat wisely is a precious gift that costs nothing but is worth everything—a longer, healthier life for them. To give your kids the positive guidance they need, try these techniques that have worked for other parents:

◆ Restock your pantry with foods that are low in fat and high in complex carbohydrates, such as fruits, vegetables, grains, pasta, and breads.

◆ Let your children plan dinner. Ask them to help in picking foods for dinner a couple of nights a week.

◆ Turn food shopping into a learning adventure. Show kids how to make the best choices for meals or snacks, using labels to explain why certain foods are good for them.

◆ Take your children to farmer's markets or to "pick your own" farms. Field trips are memorable, fun, and teach kids to appreciate where foods originate.

◆ Involve your children in making meals. For example, show them how to tear lettuce leaves for salads or how to rinse and clean vegetables.

◆ Have fresh fruit or nutritious snacks, such as yogurt or grain-filled muffins, available when your child gets hungry between meals. Have raw vegetables and a low-fat dip ready for dunking.

◆ Introduce your children to new foods, but don't force them to eat anything. They may want to try the foods another time.

◆ Try to make mealtime enjoyable. It may be the only time your family can sit down, relax, and enjoy each other's company. The memory of those times will last a lifetime.

◆ Avoid the "good food/bad food" mind-set. Allow your children to occasionally eat foods such as candy or desserts in reasonable amounts.

It's OK to eat a burger and fries or fried chicken now and then if you don't make a habit of it. Teach your children that balance in food choices is what counts throughout the day.

◆ Set a good example. If your children see you or your spouse turning up your nose at a food (or overindulging in one), they will probably do likewise.

CURIOUS FRUITS

What grows on a cactus and tastes like a watermelon? You'll soon know, once you try cactus pear. This little-known fruit and the others discussed here come to produce markets from southern climes during late winter and early spring. Served solo or combined with your favorite fruits, they're an easy way to give your meals an exotic flavor. Look for them in the produce section of your supermarket.

PICK SOME NEW FRUIT

Feijoa (fee-JO-ah) (or pineapple guava): Refresh with feijoa's minty pineapple flavor. This egg-shaped fruit has pale yellow to green flesh with a pearlike texture and tiny, edible seeds. Slice for salads or puree for drinks and sauces; discard the bitter skin. Ripen at room temperature until the skin yields when gently pressed, then store in the refrigerator for up to 1 week.

Guava (GWAH-vah): Guava tastes like a combo of lime, kiwifruit, banana, and berries. Its texture may remind you of a pear. Clustered in the center are small, edible seeds that usually are discarded. Peel, puree, and strain guavas for juices, sauces, or desserts. Choose guavas that are soft to the touch with an intense berry-like aroma.

Cactus pear (or prickly pear): This oval fruit tastes like watermelon but with a slight peach-pear flavor. Technically a berry of the cactus plant, the dethorned fruit may be spooned and eaten straight from its shell or peeled and cut up for salads. You can eat or discard the tiny seeds. Choose fruit that is tender to touch.

White sapote (sa-POH-tay): Expect a firm, avocado-like texture and a banana- or papaya-like flavor when you bite into this apple-shaped fruit. Serve sapote as you would apples—whole as a snack, pureed for shakes or sorbets, or cut up for fruit salads. Discard the large, flat seeds. Select hard fruit that has a yellow-green blush, and ripen at room temperature.

Pepino melon (puh-PEE-noh): You'll easily recognize this small, purple-striped yellow fruit as a member of the melon family. Its flavor is similar to cantaloupe, with a juiciness similar to watermelon. Serve pepinos as you would any melon—in fruit salads or compotes. To pick pepino melons, smell them. They should have a delicate, sweet aroma with firm, unbruised skin.

Cherimoya (cher-a-MOY-ya) (or custard apple): Expect a custardy creaminess and flavor reminiscent of vanilla, lime, banana, pineapple, and mango all rolled into this heart-shaped fruit. Halve and eat with a spoon, removing the inedible black seeds. When ripe, the skin will be dark and the fruit will yield to gentle pressure.

---

30 MIN. NO FAT

BLUEBERRY VINEGAR

Start to finish: 20 min.

Fresh blueberries should be used within a day or two of picking or purchasing.

- **3 cups fresh blueberries**
- **2 cups rice vinegar**
- **2 Tbsp. honey**

1 In a stainless-steel or enamel saucepan combine 1½ cups of the blueberries with rice vinegar. Bring to boiling; reduce heat. Simmer, uncovered, 3 minutes. Stir in honey. Remove from heat. Pour mixture through a fine-mesh strainer and let it drain into a bowl. Discard berries.

2 Transfer strained vinegar to a clean 1-quart jar or bottle. Add remaining 1½ cups blueberries to the jar or bottle. Cover tightly with a nonmetallic lid (or cover with plastic wrap and tightly seal with a metal lid). Store vinegar in a cool, dark place for up to 6 months. Before using vinegar, discard berries. Use the Blueberry Vinegar in The Blues Salad (see recipe, page 153). Makes about 3½ cups.

Nutrition facts per tablespoon: 4 cal., 0 g total fat, 0 mg chol., 0 mg sodium, 2 g carbo., 0 g fiber, 0 g pro.

THE BLUES SALAD

Start to finish: 20 min.

To toast walnuts, place them in a small skillet. Cook over medium heat, stirring often, for 5 to 7 minutes or until light golden. (See the photograph on page 161.)

¼ cup Blueberry Vinegar (see page 152)
2 Tbsp. walnut oil or olive oil
¼ tsp. salt
¼ tsp. coarsely ground pepper

♦♦♦

4 cups torn mixed greens
1 cup fresh blueberries
½ cup walnut halves, lightly toasted
¼ cup crumbled Stilton or blue cheese (1 oz.)
2 Tbsp. snipped fresh chives or thinly sliced green onion tops
   Fresh chives with blossoms (optional)

1 For dressing, in a screw-top jar combine Blueberry Vinegar, walnut or olive oil, salt, and pepper. Cover and shake well.

2 In a large bowl combine greens, blueberries, walnut halves, crumbled cheese, and snipped chives. Pour desired amount of dressing over salad. (Cover and refrigerate remaining dressing.) Toss lightly to coat. Divide salad mixture evenly among 4 individual bowls. If desired, garnish with fresh chives and blossoms. Makes 4 side-dish servings.

Nutrition facts per serving: 196 cal., 17 g total fat (3 g sat. fat), 6 mg chol., 215 mg sodium, 11 g carbo., 2 g fiber, 5 g pro. *Daily values:* 4% vit. A, 13% vit. C, 6% calcium, 5% iron.

BRATS WITH GOOSEBERRY CATSUP

Prep: 20 min. ♦ Cook: 10 min.
Chill: 2 hr. ♦ Grill: 7 min.

A make-your-own catsup adds spunk to your favorite grilled bratwursts.

1 cup fresh gooseberries, stems and blossom ends removed
½ cup tomato paste
¼ cup sugar
2 Tbsp. garlic-flavored wine vinegar or cider vinegar
2 Tbsp. finely chopped onion
1 Tbsp. Worcestershire sauce
⅛ tsp. salt

♦♦♦

6 fresh bratwursts
2 12-oz. cans beer (3 cups)
12 black peppercorns

♦♦♦

6 bratwurst or frankfurter buns
   Coarsely chopped onion (optional)

1 For catsup, in a saucepan combine gooseberries, tomato paste, sugar, vinegar, finely chopped onion, Worcestershire sauce, and salt. Bring to boiling; reduce heat. Simmer, uncovered, 10 minutes, stirring often. If desired, press mixture through a fine-mesh sieve; discard skins. Cover and chill for 2 hours or up to 2 weeks.

2 Meanwhile, pierce holes in skins of bratwursts. In a saucepan combine bratwursts, beer, and peppercorns. Bring to boiling; reduce heat. Simmer, covered, about 10 minutes or until no longer pink; drain.

3 Grill bratwursts on rack of an uncovered grill directly over medium coals for 7 to 8 minutes

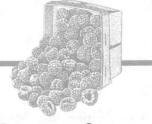

BERRIES OF SUMMER

Black raspberry: Smaller and a bit firmer than its red sister, this berry is a treat eaten fresh or baked in pies.

Blueberry: This versatile gem can be eaten like candy, frozen, baked in muffins, or used to flavor vinegars.

Golden raspberry: Fragile to the touch, the "golden" is a honey-sweet sister to the red raspberry. Best eaten fresh.

Gooseberry: Because it's so tart, the gooseberry shows off well in baked goods, jams, or jellies. Try it solo or with other fruits.

Loganberry: A cross between blackberries and raspberries, this tart jewel needs plenty of sweetening. Great in jams, jellies, and pies.

Marionberry: This blackberry holds an elongated shape and excellent mildly tart flavor, even after freezing.

Red raspberry: Refrigerate this perishable raspberry right away. Avoid mushy berries by washing just before using.

Strawberry: There's more vitamin C in eight strawberries than one orange. Don't wash or hull berries until ready to use.

or until skins are golden, turning often. Serve on buns with gooseberry catsup. If desired, top with coarsely chopped onion. Makes 6 servings.

Nutrition facts per serving: 444 cal., 25 g total fat (9 g sat. fat), 51 mg chol., 759 mg sodium, 39 g carbo., 2 g fiber, 16 g pro. *Daily values:* 6% vit. A, 36% vit. C, 7% calcium, 20% iron.

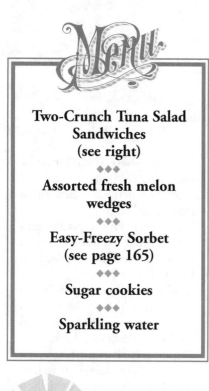

Menu

Two-Crunch Tuna Salad
Sandwiches
(see right)

◆◆◆

Assorted fresh melon
wedges

◆◆◆

Easy-Freezy Sorbet
(see page 165)

◆◆◆

Sugar cookies

◆◆◆

Sparkling water

PRIZE TESTED RECIPE WINNER

FIESTA SHRIMP SKEWERS

Prep: 20 min. ◆ **Marinate: 30 to 60 min.** ◆ **Grill: 6 min.**

Light up your palate with spicy shrimp, tempered by a flame-taming dip.

1 lb. large shrimp, peeled and deveined (about 24)
½ cup amber ale or other desired ale
½ tsp. finely shredded lime peel
¼ cup fresh lime juice
2 Tbsp. chopped cilantro
1 small jalapeño pepper, seeded and finely chopped*
1 clove garlic, minced
¼ tsp. ground cumin
⅛ tsp. ground red pepper
◆◆◆
2 poblano peppers, seeded and cut into 1-inch pieces*
2 limes, cut into 1-inch pieces
1 recipe Cool Cilantro Dip (see right)

1 Place shrimp in a plastic bag set in a shallow dish. For marinade, combine ale, lime peel, lime juice, cilantro, jalapeño pepper, garlic, cumin, and red pepper. Pour the marinade over shrimp. Close bag. Marinate in the refrigerator for 30 to 60 minutes, turning bag occasionally.

2 Drain shrimp, reserving marinade. On ten to twelve 6-inch skewers thread shrimp, poblano peppers, and lime pieces, leaving ¼ inch between pieces. Brush with marinade; discard remaining marinade. Grill skewers on the rack of an uncovered grill directly over medium coals for 6 to 8 minutes or until shrimp turn opaque, turning once. Serve with Cool Cilantro Dip. Makes 10 to 12 appetizer servings.

*****Note:** Hot peppers contain oils that can burn. Wear plastic gloves to seed and cut pepper. Do not touch eyes or face, and thoroughly wash hands.

Cool Cilantro Dip: In a small bowl stir together one 8-ounce carton light dairy sour cream, 2 tablespoons snipped fresh cilantro, 1 tablespoon salsa, ½ teaspoon finely shredded lime peel, and 1 garlic clove, minced. Cover and chill until serving time. Makes 1 cup.

Nutrition facts per serving: 69 cal., 2 g total fat (1 g sat. fat), 55 mg chol., 93 mg sodium, 6 g carbo., 0 g fiber, 7 g pro. *Daily values:* 5% vit. A, 42% vit. C, 3% calcium, 6% iron.

TWO-CRUNCH TUNA SALAD SANDWICHES

Start to finish: 35 min.

Toasted walnuts and crisp cucumbers give each bite a bit of crunch.

1 8-oz. fresh or frozen tuna steak
1 medium cucumber, thinly sliced
½ tsp. sugar
¼ tsp. salt
⅛ tsp. pepper
◆◆◆
⅓ cup mayonnaise or salad dressing
2 Tbsp. drained, snipped oil-packed dried tomatoes
⅛ tsp. salt
½ cup chopped toasted walnuts
◆◆◆
8 slices whole wheat bread (toasted, if desired)
1 cup loosely packed sprigs watercress

1 Thaw fish, if frozen; set aside. In a small mixing bowl combine cucumber, sugar, ¼ teaspoon salt, and pepper. Toss gently to coat cucumber. Let mixture stand for 15 minutes.

2 Meanwhile, place the fish on the unheated rack of a broiler pan. Broil 3 to 4 inches from the heat for 4 to 6 minutes per ½-inch thickness of fish, turning once. Remove from rack to a cutting board. Flake fish.

3 In a large medium mixing bowl stir together the mayonnaise or salad dressing, dried tomatoes, and the ⅛ teaspoon salt. Add tuna and walnuts to bowl. Toss gently to coat tuna.

4 To assemble sandwiches, drain cucumbers. Arrange cucumbers atop 4 of the bread slices. Add tuna mixture; top with watercress. Top with remaining bread slices. Makes 4 servings.

Nutrition facts per serving: 473 cal., 30 g total fat (4 g sat. fat), 34 mg chol., 641 mg sodium, 32 g carbo., 1 g fiber, 23 g pro. *Daily values:* 43% vit. A, 16% vit. C, 6% calcium, 21% iron.

LOW FAT
CREOLE SHRIMP AND BEANS

Prep: 20 min. ◆ Cook: 20 min.

There's little cleanup, as it takes just one skillet to make this hearty one-dish meal from start to finish. (See the photograph on page 163.)

- 1 **cup sliced fresh mushrooms**
- ½ **cup chopped celery**
- ½ **cup chopped red or green sweet pepper**
- ⅓ **cup chopped onion**
- 1 **clove garlic, minced**
- 1 **Tbsp. cooking oil**
- 3 **tomatoes, seeded and chopped**
- 1 **15-oz. can kidney beans, rinsed and drained**
- 12 **oz. fresh okra, trimmed and sliced, or one 10-oz. pkg. frozen cut okra**
- ½ **cup chicken broth**
- 1 **tsp. salt-free creole seasoning**
  ◆◆◆
- 12 **oz. frozen, peeled, and deveined shrimp**
- 1 **Tbsp. lemon juice Salt and pepper**
  ◆◆◆
- 2 **cups hot cooked rice Lemon wedges (optional)**

1 In a large skillet cook and stir mushrooms, celery, sweet pepper, onion, and garlic in hot oil about 4 minutes or until tender. Stir in tomatoes, kidney beans, okra, chicken broth, and creole seasoning. Bring to boiling; reduce heat. Simmer, covered, for 10 minutes.

2 Add shrimp and lemon juice to mixture in skillet. Return to boiling. Simmer, uncovered, for 2 to 3 minutes or until shrimp is opaque. Season to taste with salt and pepper.

3 To serve, divide rice among 4 individual bowls. Spoon shrimp mixture atop. If desired, serve with lemon wedges. Makes 4 servings.

Nutrition facts per serving: 351 cal., 5 g total fat (1 g sat. fat), 131 mg chol., 450 mg sodium, 54 g carbo., 9 g fiber, 27 g pro. *Daily values:* 27% vit. A, 97% vit. C, 11% calcium, 37% iron.

30 MIN. LOW FAT
SALMON IN A SNAP

Start to finish: 20 min.

Salmon stirs up excitement for its high scores in protein and heart-saving omega-3 fatty acids. The flavorful fish becomes a star player when teamed with crunchy broccoli and fluffy couscous in a super 20-minute meal.

- 4 **1-inch-thick salmon fillets (about 1 lb. total)**
- ½ **tsp. lemon-pepper seasoning or freshly ground black pepper**
  Nonstick spray coating
- 1 **to 2 tsp. reduced-sodium soy sauce**
- 1 **medium orange, halved lengthwise and thinly sliced**
  ◆◆◆
- 2 **cups small broccoli florets**
- 1 **cup reduced-sodium chicken broth**
- ¾ **cup water**
- 2 **tsp. bottled minced roasted garlic**
- ¼ **tsp. salt (optional)**
- 1 **cup quick-cooking couscous or quick-cooking whole wheat couscous**

1 Sprinkle the salmon fillets with lemon-pepper seasoning or black pepper.

2 Lightly spray a nonstick baking pan with nonstick spray coating. Arrange fish fillets in pan. Drizzle with the soy sauce. Arrange the orange slices atop the fish.

3 Bake, covered, in a 450° oven for 8 to 12 minutes or until fish flakes easily with a fork.

4 Meanwhile, in a 2-quart saucepan combine the broccoli florets, chicken broth, water, garlic, and, if desired, salt. Bring to boiling; reduce heat. Cook, covered, for 3 minutes. Stir in couscous. Remove from heat. Let stand, covered, for 5 minutes. Serve fish over hot couscous and broccoli. Makes 4 servings.

Nutrition facts per serving: 316 cal., 5 g total fat, (1 g sat. fat), 20 mg chol., 290 mg sodium, 43 g carbo., 10 g fiber, 25 g pro. *Daily values:* 9% vit. A, 85% vit. C, 5% calcium, 12% iron.

MANGO-BERRY "CHALSA" WITH PORK

Prep: 25 min. ◆ Grill: 1 hour for
pork, 10 min. for "chalsa"

*Pop this pork onto the grill and ignore
it until it's done. Serve it with our
chunky sauce that combines the best
qualities of chutney and salsa.
(See the photograph on page 160.)*

1 Tbsp. soy sauce
3 cloves garlic, minced
1 1½- to 2-lb. boneless pork
   top loin roast (single loin)
   ◆◆◆
1 mango, seeded, peeled, and
   chopped (1 cup)
¼ cup chopped onion
2 Tbsp. brown sugar
1 finely chopped small, fresh
   banana pepper (1 to
   2 Tbsp.)
½ tsp. finely shredded lime peel
1 Tbsp. lime juice
   ◆◆◆
1 cup fresh raspberries
   Lime wedges (optional)

1 Combine soy sauce, garlic,
and ¼ teaspoon *black pepper.* Trim
excess fat from meat. Use a sharp
knife to score top and bottom of
roast in a diamond pattern, making cuts ¼ inch deep. Rub garlic
mixture evenly onto all sides of
meat. Insert a meat thermometer
near center of roast.

2 In a grill with a cover
arrange preheated coals for
indirect cooking. Test for medium-slow heat in center of grill
where meat will cook. Place meat
on a rack in a roasting pan on grill
rack. Cover and grill about 1 hour
or until meat thermometer registers 155°. Remove meat from
grill. Cover meat with foil; let
stand 15 minutes before carving.

(The meat's temperature will rise
5° during standing.)

3 Meanwhile, combine half of
the mango, all of the onion,
brown sugar, banana pepper, lime
peel and juice, and ⅛ teaspoon
salt. Tear off a 24×18-inch piece
of heavy foil. Fold in half to make
a double thickness of foil that
measures 18×12 inches. Spoon
mixture onto center of foil. Bring
up 2 opposite edges; fold foil to
enclose the mixture, leaving space
for steam to build.

4 Place mango packet on rack
of uncovered grill directly over
medium coals about 10 minutes
or until heated through. Remove
from grill. Transfer grilled mango
mixture to a medium bowl.
Gently stir remaining chopped
mango and the raspberries into
grilled mango mixture. Serve with
pork and, if desired, lime wedges.
Makes 6 servings.

Nutrition facts per serving: 189 cal., 8 g
total fat (3 g sat. fat), 51 mg chol., 257 mg
sodium, 14 g carbo., 2 g fiber, 17 g pro.
Daily values: 13% vit. A, 34% vit. C, 1%
calcium, 6% iron.

SEASON'S FINEST SALAD

Prep: 35 min. ◆ Grill: 12 min.
Stand: 10 min.

*Packed with the flavors of summer,
this main-dish salad is a feast
for the eyes and the palate.
(See the photograph on page 157.)*

4 medium skinless, boneless
   chicken breast halves
3 cups lightly packed, torn
   spinach leaves
1 cup lightly packed, torn
   sorrel leaves or arugula
   leaves

1 small red onion, thinly sliced
   and separated into rings
2 Tbsp. snipped fresh basil
3 cups pitted, sliced golden
   plums and/or nectarines
2 cups sliced fresh strawberries
1 recipe Strawberry Dressing
   (see below)

1 Rinse chicken; pat dry with
paper towels. Place chicken on
lightly greased rack of an uncovered grill. Grill directly over medium coals for 12 to 15 minutes or
until tender and no longer pink,
turning once halfway through
grilling. Let chicken stand about
10 minutes or until cool enough
to handle. Cut chicken into irreg-
ular pieces, about 2×1 inches.

2 Meanwhile, in a large salad
bowl combine spinach, sorrel,
onion, and basil. To serve, divide
spinach mixture among 4 dinner-
size shallow wooden bowls or dinner plates. Arrange fruit and
chicken on greens. Drizzle
Strawberry Dressing on each serving. If desired, garnish with *strawberry blossoms.* Makes 4 servings.

Strawberry Dressing: In a
food processor bowl or blender
container combine ¾ cup cut-up
fresh strawberries, 2 tablespoons
Berries to Pour (see recipe, page
144) or purchased strawberry
pourable fruit, 2 tablespoons olive
oil, 4 teaspoons sherry vinegar or
wine vinegar, ½ teaspoon grated
fresh ginger, ¼ teaspoon salt, and
⅛ teaspoon pepper. Cover and
process or blend until smooth.

Nutrition facts per serving: 357 cal., 12 g
total fat (2 g sat. fat), 59 mg chol., 233 mg
sodium, 41 g carbo., 6 g fiber, 26 g pro.
Daily values: 45% vit. A, 161% vit. C, 8%
calcium, 20% iron.

Season's Finest Salad (page 156)

Above: *Mango-Berry "Chalsa"*
with Pork (page 156)
Right: *Lemon-Meringue*
Beehives (page 167)
Far right: *The Blues Salad*
(page 153)

Season's Finest Salad (page 156)

Top: *Cal-Mex Veggie Wraps (page 178)*
Above: *Grillside Potato Chips (page 177)*
Page 158: *Red River Burgers (page 184)*

Top: *Steak Sandwich, Apulian-Style (page 180)*
Above: *Southwestern Pierogi (page 144)*

Above: *Mango-Berry "Chalsa"*
with Pork (page 156)
Right: *Lemon-Meringue*
Beehives (page 167)
Far right: *The Blues Salad*
(page 153)

Page 162: *Zucchini Crab Cakes*
(page 184)
Left: *Coconut Chicken Spears (page 181)*
Below: *Creole Shrimp and Beans*
(page 155)
Bottom left: *S'more Banana Split*
(page 189)
Bottom Right: *Mango Blossom*
(page 190)

Left: *Easy-Freezy Sorbet*
(page 165)
Below: *Pick-of-the-Crop Pie*
(page 165)

BERRY PIE FILLINGS

Berries	Amount of Berries	Sugar	Thickener
Blackberries	5 cups	¾ to 1 cup	⅓ cup all-purpose flour
Blueberries	5 cups	⅔ to ¾ cup	3 Tbsp. all-purpose flour
Raspberries	5 cups	¾ to 1 cup	⅓ cup all-purpose flour
Mixed berries	2 cups halved strawberries, 2 cups blueberries, and 1 cup blackberries or raspberries	½ to ⅔ cup	⅓ cup all-purpose flour

30 MIN.
NO FAT

PICK-OF-THE-CROP PIE

Prep: 30 min. ◆ Bake: 50 min.

Our pie chart (above) takes the guesswork out of making the berry filling of your choice. (See the photograph on page 164.)

1 recipe Pastry for Lattice-Crust Pie (see page 166)

◆◆◆

Berry Filling (see above)
2 tsp. finely shredded lemon peel or ½ tsp. ground cinnamon

◆◆◆

Milk (optional)
Sugar (optional)

1 Prepare pastry for Lattice-Crust Pie. On a lightly floured surface flatten 1 dough ball. Roll into a 12-inch circle. To transfer pastry, wrap it around a rolling pin; unroll into a 9-inch pie plate. Ease pastry into pie plate, being careful not to stretch pastry.

2 In a large mixing bowl combine the sugar and flour for desired berries, according to the chart above. Stir in berries and lemon peel or cinnamon. Gently toss berries until coated. Transfer berry mixture to the pastry-lined pie plate. Trim bottom pastry to ½ inch beyond edge of pie plate.

3 On a lightly floured surface roll remaining dough into a 12-inch circle. Cut into ½-inch strips. (Or follow instructions for Pastry for Double-Crust Pie, page 166). Weave strips over filling (see photos, page 166). If desired, brush pastry top with a little milk and sprinkle with sugar.

4 To prevent overbrowning, cover edge of pie with foil. Bake in a 375° oven for 25 minutes. Remove foil. Bake pie for 25 to 30 minutes more or until top is golden. Cool on a wire rack. Makes 8 servings.

Nutrition facts per serving of raspberry pie: 384 cal., 18 g total fat (4 g sat. fat), 0 mg chol., 134 mg sodium, 53 g carbo., 4 g fiber, 4 g pro.
Daily values: 1% vit. A, 32% vit. C, 2% calcium, 13% iron.

EASY-FREEZY SORBET

Start to finish: 10 min.

(See the photograph on page 164.)

2 cups fresh blueberries
2 cups fresh raspberries
¼ cup frozen pineapple-orange-banana juice concentrate or citrus beverage concentrate
Sugar cones (optional)

1 Freeze berries as directed on page 144. In a large bowl combine the frozen berries, frozen concentrate, and ½ cup *cold water*. Place half of the mixture in a food processor bowl. Cover and process until almost smooth. Repeat with remaining mixture. Serve immediately. (Or, transfer mixture to a baking dish. Cover; freeze about 4 hours or until firm.) Use within 2 days. If desired, scoop frozen mixture into cones. Serves 6 to 8.

Nutrition facts per serving: 66 cal., 0 g total fat, 0 mg chol., 4 mg sodium, 16 g carbo., 3 g fiber, 1 g pro.
Daily values: 1% vit. A, 46% vit. C, 1% calcium, 5% iron.

THE PERFECT LATTICE-TOPPED PIE

Lay half of the pastry strips on top of the filling at 1-inch intervals.

Fold alternate pastry strips back halfway. Place another pastry strip in the center of the pie horizontally across the strips already in place. Unfold folded strips; fold back remaining strips. Place another pastry strip parallel to strip in center. Repeat weaving steps until lattice covers filling.

Use your fingers to press the ends of the strips into crust rim. Fold bottom pastry over strips; seal and crimp edge.

PASTRY FOR LATTICE-CRUST PIE

Start to finish: 15 min.

2 cups all-purpose flour
½ tsp. salt
⅔ cup shortening

◆◆◆

6 to 7 Tbsp. cold water

1 In a mixing bowl combine flour and salt. Using a pastry blender, cut in shortening until pieces are pea-size.

2 Sprinkle 1 tablespoon of the water over part of mixture; gently toss with a fork. Push moistened dough to side of bowl. Repeat, using 1 tablespoon of the water at a time, until all the dough is moistened. Divide in half. Form each half into a ball. Use to make the Pick-of-the-Crop Pie (see recipe, page 165).

Pastry for Double-Crust Pie: Prepare as directed, except trim bottom pastry to edge of pie plate. For top crust, roll remaining dough into a circle about 12 inches in diameter. Place pastry on filling; trim ½ inch beyond edge of plate. Fold top pastry under bottom pastry. Crimp edge. Cut slits in top crust for steam to escape. Bake as directed.

SPARKLING FRUIT GEMS

Start to finish: 15 min.

Be gentle when mixing fragile berries. Serve them with a summer breakfast, as a special salad, or as a simple dessert.

¼ cup honey
2 Tbsp. balsamic vinegar
2 tsp. snipped fresh lemon
    balm or ¼ tsp. finely
    shredded lemon peel
3 to 4 cups fresh berries (mix
    of red and golden
    raspberries, blackberries,
    blueberries, and/or small
    strawberries)
    Fresh lemon balm sprigs
    (optional)

1 In a small bowl stir the honey and balsamic vinegar until combined. Stir in the snipped lemon balm.

2 To serve, place fresh berries in a compote or serving bowl. Drizzle with the honey mixture. If desired, garnish with sprigs of lemon balm. Makes 4 servings.

Nutrition facts per serving: 118 cal., 1 g total fat (0 g sat. fat), 0 mg chol., 2 mg sodium, 29 g carbo., 4 g fiber, 1 g pro. *Daily values:* 1% vit. A, 40% vit. C, 1% calcium, 5% iron.

LEMON-MERINGUE BEEHIVES

Prep: 35 min. ◆ Bake: 30 min.
Dry in oven: 1 hr.

The secret to successful meringue is adding sugar gradually so it dissolves into the egg whites. (See the photograph on page 160.)

2 egg whites
◆◆◆
1 tsp. lemon juice
¼ tsp. cream of tartar
⅔ cup sugar
◆◆◆
½ cup purchased lemon curd
1 cup fresh loganberries,
    blackberries, or other
    berries

1 Let egg whites stand at room temperature in a large mixing bowl for 30 minutes. Meanwhile, line baking sheet with parchment paper or foil. Using a pencil, draw eight 2¼-inch circles and eight 1¾-inch circles about 1 inch apart on the paper.* Turn paper pencil-side down on baking sheet; set aside.

2 Add lemon juice and cream of tartar to egg whites. Beat with an electric mixer on medium speed until soft peaks form (tips curl). Add sugar, 1 tablespoon at a time, beating on high speed about 7 minutes or until very stiff peaks form (tips stand straight) and sugar is almost dissolved.

3 Using a pastry bag fitted with a medium (¼ inch) round tip, pipe a flat base of meringue onto all of the circles on the paper. Pipe a ring of meringue onto edges of each of the 8 larger meringue rounds, building the sides ¾ inch tall by piping a continuous coil of meringue to form a small shell. For tops, pipe a coil of meringue on smaller rounds to make a cone shape that resembles the top of a beehive.

BALMY IDEAS

A lemony-flavored member of the mint family, lemon balm grows well in kitchen gardens. You also may find it at the farmer's market or in the herb section of your grocery store. Use it to garnish salads, chicken dishes, or drinks. Fresh or dried lemon balm can be steeped in hot water to make tea.

4 Bake in a 300° oven for 30 minutes. Turn off oven. Let meringues dry in oven, with door closed, at least 1 hour. Remove dry meringues from paper. Place in an airtight container. Store in a cool, dry place for up to 1 week.

5 Just before serving, spoon 1 tablespoon of lemon curd into each bottom meringue shell. Place a few berries on lemon curd. Prop top of meringue beehive next to bottom. Makes 8 servings.

*Note: For free-form meringue shells without tops, make eight 3-inch circles on foil or parchment. Use back of a large spoon to spread meringue over circles, building up sides to form shells. Bake as directed.

Nutrition facts per serving: 144 cal., 1 g total fat (1 g sat. fat), 15 mg chol., 29 mg sodium, 21 g carbo., 3 g fiber, 1 g pro. *Daily values:* 5% vit. C.

SUMMERTIME QUENCHER

Start to finish: 15 min.

Go ahead and pack a lot of fruit into this white sangria-like drink. Stir gently to prevent the fruit from breaking apart.

1 lemon
1 orange

❖❖❖

1 750-ml bottle white
   zinfandel wine (3¼ cups),
   chilled
2 cups carbonated water or
   lemon-lime carbonated
   beverage, chilled
1 unpeeled kiwifruit, sliced
¼ cup fresh blackberries,
   raspberries, or other
   berries
8 dark sweet cherries, pitted
8 fresh strawberries

1 Cut lemon and orange in half crosswise. Cut 1 lemon half and 1 orange half into ¼-inch-thick slices. Squeeze juice from remaining halves.

2 Place juice in a 2-quart pitcher. Stir in wine, carbonated beverage, kiwifruit, blackberries, cherries, strawberries, and lemon and orange slices. Serve over ice. Makes 8 (5-ounce) servings.

Nutrition facts per serving: 25 cal., 0 g total fat, 0 mg chol., 13 mg sodium, 4 g carbo., 0 g fiber, 0 g pro.
Daily values: 36% vit. C, 1% iron.

CAFÉ AU LAIT FRAPPE

Prep: 10 min. ◆ Freeze: 4 hr.

When temperatures soar too high to enjoy a freshly brewed cup of coffee, try this chilly delight.

2 cups strong brewed espresso
   or 2 cups boiling water
   plus 2 Tbsp. instant
   espresso powder
1 14-oz. can (1¼ cups)
   sweetened condensed milk
2 tsp. vanilla

❖❖❖

1 cup milk

1 In a medium bowl stir together the espresso, sweetened condensed milk, and vanilla until combined. Pour the mixture into 2 ice cube trays or an 8×4×2-inch loaf pan. Cover and freeze about 4 hours or until firm.

2 Place half of the frozen mixture in a blender container. Add half of the milk to the blender container. Cover and blend until smooth. Repeat with remaining mixture. Makes 6 to 8 (6-ounce) servings.

Nutrition facts per serving: 239 cal., 7 g total fat (4 g sat. fat), 25 mg chol., 106 mg sodium, 39 g carbo., 0 g fiber, 7 g pro.
Daily values: 9% vit. A, 3% vit. C, 19% calcium, 1% iron.

TEH TARIK

Start to finish: 5 min.

If you like dunking, try crispy ginger cookies in this steamy sweet tea.

3½ cups strong brewed tea
½ of a 14-oz. (⅔ cup)
   sweetened condensed milk

A SWEET TEA TREAT

Treat your family to a cup of creamy hot tea at breakfast time or for dessert. Called Teh Tarik (TAY tair-ICK) in Malaysia, this drink recipe blends tea and sweetened condensed milk until foamy.

The Malaysians foam the hot beverage by pouring it back and forth between two cups. For pour fun, the farther apart the cups the better! The recipe below suggests using a blender to foam the tea and milk. This method makes sure your hands don't get burned from the hot liquid, and it's quicker too.

1 In a blender container combine the tea and sweetened condensed milk. Cover and blend on high for 30 seconds.

2 Pour mixture into a medium saucepan. Cook and stir over high heat until heated through. Carefully pour into mugs. Makes 4 (8-ounce) servings.

Nutrition facts per serving: 161 cal., 4 g total fat (3 g sat. fat), 17 mg chol., 69 mg sodium, 28g carbo., 0 g fiber, 0 g pro.
Daily values: 4% vit. A, 2% vit. C, 11% calcium.

AUGUST
The Mighty Spud

In many regions of the country, the first potatoes are being gently dug from the ground in August. Bring out the best from these tender spuds in new-style salads, like Lemon Prosciutto Potato Salad, Roasted Potato Salad, and Caesar-Style Potato Salad. Or, put potatoes at the heart of your main dish in Two-Potato Pie or Zucchini, Corn, and Potato Tacos. Take potatoes to the grill by making Grillside Potato Chips, a great accompaniment to Red River Burgers. And you can finish that meal-on-the-grill with grilled bananas to make S'More Banana Splits.

30-minute recipes indicated in RED.
Low-fat and no-fat recipes indicated
with a ♥.
Photographs indicated in italics.
*Bonus recipe

TEX-MEX BEAN AND POTATO SALAD

Prep: 35 min. ◆ Cook: 10 min.
Chill: 4 to 24 hr.

*When you've got something great
sizzling on the grill, lasso in
a bowl of this spunky potato salad
to serve alongside.*

2 **medium red sweet peppers
or one 12-oz. jar roasted
red sweet peppers, drained**
◆◆◆
2 **lb. red potatoes, cut into
1-inch cubes**
¼ **tsp. salt (optional)**
◆◆◆
1 **15-oz. can black beans,
rinsed and drained**
1½ **cups frozen whole kernel corn**
1 **green sweet pepper, chopped**
½ **cup chopped red onion**
¼ **cup snipped fresh cilantro**
◆◆◆
¼ **cup red wine vinegar**
2 **Tbsp. olive oil or cooking oil**
1 **clove garlic, halved**
½ **tsp. ground cumin**
¼ **tsp. salt**
⅛ **tsp. ground red pepper**

1 Halve red sweet peppers, if
using fresh. Remove stems, seeds,
and membranes. Place pepper
halves, cut side down, on a foil-
lined baking sheet. Bake in a
425° oven about 20 minutes or
until skins are charred. Wrap pepper halves in foil and let stand
about 10 minutes or until cool
enough to handle. Remove and discard skins from peppers; set aside.

2 Meanwhile, cook the potatoes in boiling water, adding
¼ teaspoon salt, if desired, for
10 to 15 minutes or until tender.
Drain and cool slightly.

3 In a large mixing bowl combine the potatoes, black beans,
corn, green pepper, red onion,
and cilantro; set aside.

4 For dressing, in a blender
container or food processor bowl
combine the roasted peppers,
vinegar, oil, garlic, cumin, salt,
and ground red pepper. Cover
and blend or process until
smooth. Add dressing to potato
mixture. Toss to coat. Cover and
chill for 4 to 24 hours. Makes
10 to 12 side-dish servings.

Nutrition facts per serving: 172 cal., 3 g
total fat (0 g sat. fat), 0 mg chol., 246 mg
sodium, 33 g carbo., 4 g fiber, 6 g pro.
Daily values: 12% vit. A, 90% vit. C, 2%
calcium, 16% iron.

LEMON PROSCIUTTO POTATO SALAD

Prep: 25 min. ◆ Cook: 15 min.
Chill: 2 to 24 hr.

*Prosciutto is a spicy, strongly flavored
ham, originally made in Italy. Look for
it at the deli counter in large
supermarkets or in Italian grocery
stores. Use paper-thin slices—its intense
flavor goes a long way.*

6 **medium (2 lb.) red potatoes,
sliced ⅛- to ¼-inch thick**
◆◆◆
⅓ **cup mayonnaise or salad
dressing**
1 **tsp. finely shredded lemon
peel**
3 **cloves garlic, minced**
½ **tsp. salt**
¼ **tsp. ground black pepper**
⅛ **to ¼ tsp. ground red pepper
(optional)**
◆◆◆

4 **plum tomatoes, cut
lengthwise into wedges**
3 **oz. thinly sliced prosciutto,
cut into thin strips
Romaine lettuce leaves**
2 **hard-cooked eggs, chopped
Snipped fresh parsley**

1 Cook the potatoes in boiling lightly salted water about
15 minutes or until just tender.
Drain and cool slightly.

2 In a large mixing bowl stir
together the mayonnaise or salad
dressing, lemon peel, garlic, salt,
black pepper, and, if desired, red
pepper. Add potatoes to mayonnaise mixture. Toss gently to
combine. Cover and chill for 2 to
24 hours.

3 To serve, add the tomatoes
and prosciutto to potato mixture.
Gently toss to combine. Line a
serving bowl with romaine leaves.
Spoon potato mixture into lined
bowl. Sprinkle with hard-cooked
eggs and parsley. Makes 10 to
12 side-dish servings.

Nutrition facts per serving: 185 cal., 9 g
total fat (1 g sat. fat), 32 mg chol., 312 mg
sodium, 22 g carbo., 1 g fiber, 5 g pro.
Daily values: 3% vit. A, 29% vit. C, 1%
calcium, 11% iron.

CAESAR-STYLE POTATO SALAD

Prep: 20 min. ◆ Roast: 25 min.
Chill: 2 to 24 hr.

*The classic salad gets a makeover when
roasted potatoes are tossed with a
balsamic vinegar dressing, olives,
romaine, and Parmesan.*

1 **lb. whole tiny new potatoes,
quartered**

1 medium onion, cut into thin
   wedges
2 Tbsp. olive oil
¼ tsp. salt
¼ tsp. pepper

◆◆◆

3 Tbsp. balsamic vinegar
2 cloves garlic, minced
2 tsp. sugar
¼ cup pitted kalamata olives,
   halved
2 cups torn romaine lettuce
¼ cup finely shredded
   Parmesan cheese

1 Place potatoes and onion in an 8×8×2-inch baking pan. Drizzle with oil; sprinkle with salt and pepper. Roast potatoes, uncovered, in a 450° oven about 25 minutes or until just tender, stirring twice. Cool slightly.

2 Meanwhile, for dressing, in a screw-top jar combine the vinegar, garlic, and sugar. Cover and shake until well combined.

3 In a large bowl combine the potato mixture and olives. Drizzle dressing over potato mixture, tossing to coat well. Cover and chill for 2 to 24 hours.

4 Just before serving, add romaine lettuce to potato mixture, tossing to mix. Sprinkle with Parmesan cheese. Makes 4 to 6 side-dish servings.

Nutrition facts per serving: 245 cal., 10 g total fat (2 g sat. fat), 5 mg chol., 357 mg sodium, 34 g carbo., 2 g fiber, 6 g pro. *Daily values:* 8% vit. A, 41% vit. C, 10% calcium, 18% iron.

PRIZE TESTED RECIPE WINNER

Roasted Potato Salad

Prep: 15 min. ◆ Roast: 35 min.
Stand: 30 min.

Yellow potatoes give an old favorite a new look; basil gives it a summer-fresh flavor.
(See the photograph on page 202.)

Nonstick spray coating
2½ lb. Yukon Gold, Yellow Finn,
   or russet potatoes
2 Tbsp. olive oil

◆◆◆

¼ cup olive oil
½ cup lightly packed, fresh
   basil leaves
4 cloves garlic, halved
1 tsp. finely shredded lemon
   peel
3 Tbsp. lemon juice
1 Tbsp. Dijon-style mustard
1 tsp. salt
¼ tsp. ground black pepper

◆◆◆

½ cup chopped shallots
½ cup roasted red sweet
   pepper, cut into thin strips

◆◆◆

¼ cup slivered, fresh basil
   leaves
¼ cup finely shredded
   Parmesan cheese

1 Spray a shallow 15×10×2-inch roasting pan with nonstick coating. Scrub potatoes; peel, if desired. Cut potatoes into 1-inch wedges or cubes. Toss with the 2 tablespoons olive oil. Place in prepared pan. Roast potatoes, uncovered, in a 425° oven for 35 to 40 minutes or until just tender and lightly browned, stirring after 20 minutes.

TEST KITCHEN TIP

BETTER HOMES AND GARDENS TEST KITCHEN

Salad Spuds

When buying potatoes to use in salads, it's important to select a variety that keeps its shape when cooked. Potatoes classified as waxy, such as long whites and round reds, have a moist, smooth texture and perform well for this purpose.

New potatoes are not a type of potato, but are just young, small potatoes—often the round red variety—making them another good choice for salads. Yellow potatoes, such as Yukon Gold or Yellow Finn, have a smooth, creamy texture with a pale yellow flesh, giving a bowl of salad a unique look.

2 Meanwhile, for dressing, in a blender container combine the ¼ cup olive oil, the ½ cup basil, garlic, lemon peel, lemon juice, mustard, salt, and black pepper. Cover and blend until mixture is nearly smooth.

3 In a large mixing bowl toss hot potatoes with dressing. Stir in shallots and pepper strips. Let stand at room temperature for 30 minutes. Just before serving, sprinkle with the ¼ cup slivered basil and Parmesan cheese. Store any leftover salad, covered, in the refrigerator. Makes 8 side-dish servings.

Nutrition facts per serving: 267 cal., 11 g total fat (1 g sat. fat), 2 mg chol., 367 mg sodium, 38 g carbo., 1 g fiber, 5 g pro. *Daily values:* 17% vit. A, 84% vit. C, 5% calcium, 13% iron.

TROPICAL SWEET POTATO SALAD

Prep: 15 min. ◆ Cook: 10 min.
Chill: 2 to 8 hr.

2 **lb. sweet potatoes, peeled and cubed**

◆◆◆

½ **cup mayonnaise or salad dressing**
1 **Tbsp. frozen orange juice concentrate, thawed**
2 **tsp. finely shredded lemon peel**
½ **tsp. grated fresh ginger**
1 **cup dried cranberries**
1 **cup thinly sliced celery**
1 **cup toasted chopped pecans**
2 **Tbsp. toasted coconut**

1 In a large saucepan cook potatoes in boiling salted water for 10 to 15 minutes or until just tender. Drain and cool slightly.

2 Meanwhile, for dressing, in a large bowl combine the mayonnaise, orange juice concentrate, lemon peel, and ginger. Stir in the cranberries and celery. Add sweet potatoes. Gently fold to mix and coat potatoes with dressing. Cover and chill for 2 to 8 hours.

3 To serve, stir nuts into salad. Sprinkle with coconut. Makes 8 to 10 side-dish servings.

Nutrition facts per serving: 340 cal., 22 g total fat (3 g sat. fat), 5 mg chol., 97 mg sodium, 38 g carbo., 5 g fiber, 3 g pro. *Daily values:* 193% vit. A, 45% vit. C, 3% calcium, 6% iron.

FIESTA CITRUS JICAMA SALAD

Prep: 20 min. ◆ Chill: 2 to 6 hr.

4 **cups packaged shredded cabbage with carrot (coleslaw mix)**
2 **cups jicama cut into thin bite-size strips (8 oz.)**
1 **small green sweet pepper, cut into thin bite-size strips**
1 **small red sweet pepper, cut into thin bite-size strips**
½ **cup chopped red onion**

◆◆◆

⅔ **cup Italian salad dressing**
1 **medium orange, peeled, cut up, and seeded**
1 **jalapeño pepper, seeded and chopped***
½ **tsp. chili powder**

1 In a bowl combine cabbage and carrot mix, jicama, sweet pepper strips, and onion; set aside.

2 In a blender container or food processor bowl combine dressing, orange, jalapeño pepper, and chili powder. Cover and blend or process until nearly smooth. Pour dressing over cabbage mixture; toss to combine. Cover; chill 2 to 6 hours. Serve with a slotted spoon. Makes 8 to 10 side-dish servings.

***Note:** Hot peppers contain oils that can burn. Wear plastic gloves to seed and chop peppers. Do not touch eyes or face, and thoroughly wash hands.

Nutrition facts per serving: 135 cal., 10 g total fat (1 g sat. fat), 0 mg chol., 172 mg sodium, 12 g carbo., 3 g fiber, 1 g pro. *Daily values:* 29% vit. A, 94% vit. C, 2% calcium, 4% iron.

PRIZE TESTED RECIPE WINNER

CRANBERRY-WALNUT CABBAGE SLAW

Prep: 20 min. ◆ Chill: 1 to 6 hr.

The moment we tasted this flavorful slaw, we knew it was destined to become a potluck classic. (See the photograph on page 200.)

¼ **cup mayonnaise or salad dressing**
1 **Tbsp. sweet-pickle relish**
1 **Tbsp. honey mustard**
1 **Tbsp. honey**
¼ **tsp. white or black pepper**
⅛ **tsp. celery seed**

◆◆◆

5 **cups shredded green cabbage**
⅓ **cup chopped walnuts**
¼ **cup finely chopped celery**
¼ **cup finely chopped onion**
¼ **cup finely chopped red sweet pepper**
¼ **cup dried cranberries**

1 In a small bowl stir together mayonnaise, pickle relish, honey mustard, honey, pepper, celery seed, and ⅛ teaspoon *salt*.

2 In a large mixing bowl combine cabbage, walnuts, celery, onion, sweet pepper, and cranberries. Add mayonnaise mixture to cabbage mixture and toss to coat. Cover and chill at least 1 hour or up to 6 hours. Makes 8 to 10 side-dish servings.

Nutrition facts per serving: 124 cal., 9 g total fat (1 g sat. fat), 4 mg chol., 104 mg sodium, 12 g carbo., 2 g fiber, 2 g pro. *Daily values:* 4% vit. A, 55% vit. C, 3% calcium, 4% iron.

CREAMY BEET SLAW

Start to finish: 25 min.

Vibrant colors of red and orange radiate through the lemony dressing.

- 4 **beets (1 lb.), peeled and shredded**
- 3 **medium carrots, peeled and shredded**
- ¼ **cup lemon juice**
- ¼ **cup dairy sour cream**
- 3 **Tbsp. plain yogurt**
- 2 **tsp. sugar**
- ½ **tsp. salt**
  Dash pepper

1 In a medium bowl combine the beets and carrots, tossing to mix. Set aside.

2 For dressing, in a small bowl stir together the lemon juice, sour cream, yogurt, sugar, salt, and pepper. Pour dressing over beet-carrot mixture. Gently toss mixture to combine. Serve immediately. Makes 4 to 6 side-dish servings.

Nutrition facts per serving: 117 cal., 3 g total fat (2 g sat. fat), 7 mg chol., 378 mg sodium, 20 g carbo., 5 g fiber, 3 g pro. *Daily values:* 119% vit. A, 39% vit. C, 5% calcium, 8% iron.

PICKLED GREEN TOMATOES

Prep: 20 min. ◆ Chill: 12 hr.

These crisp tomato pickles are easy to make. Serve with Red River Burgers (see recipe, page 184).

- ¾ **cup vinegar**
- ⅔ **cup water**
- 2 **Tbsp. sugar**
- ¼ **tsp. salt**

◆◆◆

- 1 **lb. green tomatoes**
- 1 **tsp. salt**
- 1 **Tbsp. dill seed**
- 3 **to 6 small serrano peppers, halved* (optional)**

1 For pickling liquid, in small saucepan combine vinegar, water, sugar, and the ¼ teaspoon salt. Bring to boiling; reduce heat and boil gently, uncovered, 5 minutes.

2 Cut tomatoes into ¼-inch-thick slices. In a large saucepan cook the tomatoes and the 1 teaspoon salt, covered, in a small amount of boiling water for 1 minute. Drain; rinse with cold water. Drain well; transfer to three hot, clean half-pint jars. In each jar, place 1 teaspoon of the dill seed and, if desired, 1 to 2 serrano peppers. Pour hot pickling liquid over tomatoes, leaving a ¼-inch headspace. Seal and refrigerate overnight or up to 2 weeks. Makes 3 half-pint jars.

*Note: Hot peppers contain oils that can burn. Wear plastic gloves when working with hot peppers. Do not touch eyes or face, and thoroughly wash hands.

Nutrition facts per slice: 12 cal., 0 g total fat, 0 mg chol., 152 mg sodium, 4 g carbo., 0 g fiber, 0 g pro. *Daily values:* 1% vit. A, 9% vit. C, 1% iron.

BENEDICT-STYLE EGGS AND MUSHROOMS

Start to finish: 25 min.

- 4 **cups shiitake or button mushrooms**
- 2 **Tbsp. olive oil or butter**

◆◆◆

- 4 **eggs**

◆◆◆

- 1 **recipe Easy Hollandaise Sauce (see below)**

1 Remove stems from shiitake mushrooms and discard; halve mushrooms. In a large skillet cook mushrooms in hot oil or butter until tender. Sprinkle with ¼ teaspoon *salt* and ⅛ teaspoon *pepper.*

2 Meanwhile, grease another large skillet. Add water to half-fill. Bring to boiling; reduce heat. Break 1 egg into a cup. Carefully slide egg into simmering water. Repeat with remaining eggs. Simmer, uncovered, for 3 to 5 minutes or until whites are completely set and yolks begin to thicken but are not hard.

3 To serve, divide mushrooms among 4 plates. Using a slotted spoon, remove eggs from water and place 1 atop each mushroom mound. Top with sauce. Serves 4.

Easy Hollandaise Sauce: In a small saucepan stir together ¼ cup plain lowfat yogurt, ¼ cup mayonnaise, 1 teaspoon lemon juice, and ½ teaspoon Dijon-style mustard. Cook and stir over low heat until warm; do not boil.

Nutrition facts per serving: 259 cal., 23 g total fat (4 g sat. fat), 222 mg chol., 302 mg sodium, 5 g carbo., 1 g fiber, 8 g pro. *Daily values:* 10% vit. A, 4% vit. C, 4% calcium, 12% iron.

SHIELD OF GREENS

Folate isn't just for protecting babies anymore. New research on folate—also known as folic acid and folacin—shows that it may help the heart and shield against many different cancers, too. Past research already has proven that pregnant women who consume generous amounts of folate decrease their risk of having babies born with spinal defects by about one-half.

The best thing about folate is that it's found in a wide variety of foods, especially strawberries, citrus fruits, lentils, soybeans, peas, and leafy greens. "Eat your vegetables!"—the classic line you tell your kids—is now better advice than ever.

TAKE HEART

Nutrition experts have known for a long time that folate enables the body to make new cells, including red blood cells. Getting enough of this B vitamin also appears to help cut your risk of heart attack and stroke—powerful reasons to eat a folate-rich diet. The folate and heart disease story centers around a body chemical called homocysteine.

Homocysteine is an amino acid the body uses in a protein-building system that relies on folate to work properly. Without folate, homocysteine levels increase in the blood, causing plaque to build up along blood vessel walls. People born with a disorder causing abnormally high levels of homocysteine develop hardening of the arteries—leading to heart attacks—at a very young age. This was the first clue that homocysteine and folate play a possible role in heart disease.

Researchers looked at other groups of people and found a strong relationship between folate, homocysteine, heart disease, and stroke. A major diet and health survey in Canada found that persons with a low level of folate were more likely to develop heart disease than those with more folate in their systems. In the United States, the National Heart and Nutrition Examination Survey showed that strokes were more likely in people with low blood levels of folate.

A CANCER FIGHTER

Research on folate and cancer is still at an early stage, but there appears to be a link between high folate intake and reduced risk of cancer, particularly colorectal and cervical cancers.

It's been known for a long time that people who eat more fruits and vegetables are less likely to get cancer. In fact, the National Cancer Institute has teamed up with the produce industry to promote "Five a Day for Better Health," a campaign to encourage people to eat five servings of fruits and vegetables each day. Dr. Peter Greenwald at the Institute suggests folate may be one reason these foods are protective.

Some scientists think that folate actually helps the body's DNA resist cancer-causing elements. Folate may also participate in rebuilding and repairing damaged cells that would trigger cancerous growth if left unchecked. This effect of folate could possibly influence cancerous agents in all tissues of the body.

FOLATE AND BIRTH DEFECTS

The best known effect of folate in disease prevention is reducing the risk of spina bifida, a birth defect in which the spine doesn't form correctly, leaving the spinal cord exposed. Years of study revealed that women in the first three months of pregnancy who received at least 400 micrograms of folate per day were less likely to have premature infants or infants born with spina bifida.

Studies over the last few years point to links between adequate folate intake and decreased risk of other birth defects, such as cleft palate, as well. Recent studies indicate that a significant number of pregnant women are still struggling to get sufficient folate in their diet.

Since many women are not certain they're pregnant until the second or third month, doctors recommend that all women of child-bearing years should consume at least 400 micrograms of the vitamin daily.

SOURCES AND SUPPLEMENTS

Last year marked the beginning of the folate fortification program by the Food and Drug Administration. This program requires that folate be added to breads, flours, pastas, and all other grain products.

Products with added folate manufactured from January 1, 1998, should show this information on their labels. This makes it much easier for you to be sure you get sufficient folate in your diet, without the need of supplements.

In addition to fruits, orange juice, vegetables, and legumes, other great sources of the vitamin are liver, oatmeal, and sunflower seeds.

Folate is not a stable vitamin, so fruits and vegetables are best eaten raw or lightly cooked. When cooking vegetables, steam them for several minutes, just until crisp-tender, to retain most of their folate.

Like anything, it's possible to have too much of a good thing. Folate supplementation over 1,000 micrograms per day (supplements usually come in 400 microgram amounts) can cause nausea, gastrointestinal problems, or sleep loss. Too much folate also can mask a deficiency in vitamin B_{12} or interfere with anticonvulsant and anticancer drugs.

GREAT FOLATE FOODS

Fruits and Vegetables	Amount	Micrograms
Spinach (steamed)	½ cup	130
Broccoli (steamed)	1 cup	100
Strawberries	1 cup	80
Orange	1 medium	40
Orange juice	½ cup	40
Cantaloupe (sliced)	1 cup	30

Protein Foods	Amount	Micrograms
Lentils (boiled)	1 cup	350
Beef liver	4 oz.	250

A FOLATE-RICH MENU

The U.S. Recommended Dietary Allowance for folate is 200 micrograms (mcg) daily for men, 180 mcg for women, and 400 mcg for women of childbearing age. This menu supplies over 500 mcg, with a total of about 1,850 calories (27 percent of calories from fat).

Breakfast
- ½ cup orange juice*
- 1 cup cornflakes
- 1 tsp. sugar
- ¼ cup light (1% fat) milk
- ½ cup strawberries*
- 1 slice whole wheat toast*
- 2 tsp. jam
- Coffee or tea

Lunch
- 1 tuna salad sandwich with lettuce and tomato on whole wheat bread*
- 1 cup tossed salad* with 1 Tbsp. fat-free dressing
- 1 cup milk
- 1 medium orange*
- 2 rye crackers
- 1 oz. cheese

Dinner
- 4 oz. baked chicken breast with 1 Tbsp. fruit chutney
- 1 cup lentil soup*
- ½ cup scalloped potatoes
- ½ cup steamed spinach*
- 1 multigrain dinner roll with 1 tsp. butter or margarine
- 1 slice pound cake

(*Main source of folate)

Menu

Zucchini, Corn, and Potato
Tacos
(see right)

◆◆◆

Salad of mixed greens,
diced tomato, sliced red
onion, jicama strips, and
lemon vinaigrette

◆◆◆

Margaritas or lemonade

◆◆◆

Chocolate pound cake
slices topped with
chocolate ice cream and
assorted fresh fruit

PRIZE
TESTED
RECIPE
WINNER

TWO-POTATO PIE

Prep: 45 min. ◆ **Bake: 45 min.**
Cool: 15 min.

*You'll never miss the meat
with this hearty combination of
veggies, cheese, and herbs.
(See the photograph on page 202.)*

2 medium potatoes (about
6 oz. each)

◆◆◆

2 cups all-purpose flour
¾ tsp. salt
½ cup butter
1 8-oz. pkg. shredded Italian-
blend cheese (2 cups)
6 to 8 Tbsp. cold water
1 tsp. dried Italian seasoning,
crushed
1 cup finely shredded carrots
(2 medium)
½ cup chopped onion
(1 medium)

1 small zucchini, thinly sliced
(about 1 cup)

1 Peel and cook whole potatoes, covered, in lightly salted
boiling water for 20 to 25 minutes or until just tender; drain,
cool slightly, and thinly slice.

2 Meanwhile, for crust, stir
together flour and ½ teaspoon of
the salt. Using a pastry blender,
cut in butter until pieces are pea-
size. Stir in 1 cup of the cheese.
Sprinkle 1 tablespoon of the water
over part of the mixture; gently
toss with a fork. Push moistened
dough to side of bowl. Repeat,
using 1 tablespoon of the water at
a time, until all dough is moistened. Divide in half. Form each
half into a ball.

3 On a lightly floured surface,
flatten 1 dough ball. Roll from
center to edges into a 12-inch circle. Ease pastry into a 9-inch pie
plate. Arrange potatoes in pastry-
lined pie plate. Sprinkle Italian
seasoning and remaining ¼ teaspoon salt over potatoes. Sprinkle
with ¼ cup of cheese. Sprinkle
with carrots and ¼ cup of cheese.
Sprinkle with onion and ¼ cup of
cheese. Top with zucchini and
remaining cheese. Trim pastry to
edge of pie plate.

4 Roll remaining dough into a
12-inch circle. Cut slits to allow
steam to escape. Place remaining
pastry on filling; trim ½ inch
beyond edge of plate. Fold top
pastry under bottom. Crimp
edges. Cover edge with foil.

5 Bake in a 375° oven for
25 minutes. Remove foil. Bake for
20 to 25 minutes more or until
golden. Cool 15 to 20 minutes
before serving. Cut into wedges.
Makes 6 main-dish servings.

Nutrition facts per serving: 460 cal., 25 g
total fat (15 g sat. fat), 68 mg chol., 683 mg
sodium, 44 g carbo., 3 g fiber, 15 g pro.
Daily values: 72% vit. A, 9% vit. C, 20%
calcium, 15% iron.

PRIZE
TESTED
RECIPE
WINNER

ZUCCHINI, CORN, AND
POTATO TACOS

Start to finish: 25 min.

*Even picky eaters will go for
tofu when it is accompanied by so
many flavorful ingredients.
(See the photograph on page 202.)*

1 medium potato, cut into
½-inch cubes (1 cup)
2 medium carrots, chopped
(1 cup)
12 taco shells

◆◆◆

1 Tbsp. olive oil or cooking oil
½ cup chopped onion
1 clove garlic, minced
1 small zucchini (about 6 oz.),
cut into matchstick strips
(about 1¼ cups)
1 cup fresh or frozen whole
kernel corn
1 Tbsp. chili powder
½ tsp. salt
⅛ tsp. pepper
8 oz. firm tofu, cut into
½-inch cubes (1½ cups)

◆◆◆

1 cup shredded cheddar
and/or Monterey Jack
cheese (4 oz.)

Salsa (optional)
Sliced green onion (optional)
Dairy sour cream (optional)
Peeled avocado slices
 (optional)

1 In a medium saucepan cook the potato and carrots, covered, in a small amount of boiling water for 7 to 8 minutes or until just tender. Drain vegetables and set aside. If desired, heat taco shells according to package directions.

2 Meanwhile, in a large skillet heat oil. Cook and stir onion and garlic in hot oil over medium-high heat for 2 minutes. Add zucchini and corn; cook and stir for 3 minutes more. Add chili powder, salt, and pepper. Cook and stir for 1 minute more. Add potato-carrot mixture and tofu. Stir gently to heat through.

3 To serve, fill taco shells with the vegetable mixture. Sprinkle with cheese. If desired, serve with salsa, green onion, sour cream, and/or avocados. Makes 6 main-dish servings.

Nutrition facts per serving: 315 cal., 16 g total fat (5 g sat. fat), 20 mg chol., 438 mg sodium, 34 g carbo., 3 g fiber, 11 g pro. *Daily values:* 64% vit. A, 12% vit. C, 17% calcium, 14% iron.

30 MIN. NO FAT

BEER-SIMMERED BLACK BEANS

Start to finish: 15 min.

Serve these with the Kabobs-n-Beans (see recipe, page 178) or as a side dish with any outdoor favorite.

2 15-oz. cans black beans
1 cup light beer or reduced-sodium chicken broth

2 small fresh jalapeño peppers
 or serrano peppers,
 minced (optional)*
2 cloves garlic, chopped
1½ tsp. ground cumin
¼ tsp. salt

1 Rinse and drain beans. In a large saucepan combine the beans, light beer or chicken broth, jalapeño or serrano peppers (if desired), garlic, cumin, and salt. Cook black bean mixture, covered, over low heat for 8 to 10 minutes or until the beans are just heated through, stirring often. Serve with a slotted spoon. Makes about 3½ cups.

***Note:** Hot peppers contain oils that can burn. Wear plastic gloves when working with peppers. Do not touch eyes or face and thoroughly wash hands.*

Nutrition facts per ½-cup serving: 91 cal., 0 g total fat, 0 mg chol., 379 mg sodium, 17 g carbo., 6 g fiber, 8 g pro. *Daily values:* 4% calcium, 12% iron.

GRILLSIDE POTATO CHIPS

Prep: 10 min. ◆ Grill: 15 min.
Stand: 8 min.

For the best results, use Idaho russet potatoes. They have a low water content and will make a crisper chip. (See the photograph on page 159.)

1 lb. potatoes (russet or long white), scrubbed and bias-cut into ¹⁄₁₆-inch-thick slices
3 Tbsp. cooking oil
½ tsp. dried thyme, crushed
½ tsp. coarse salt or seasoned salt

SALTS OF THE EARTH

As a seasoning, salt reigns supreme. But you have other options beyond table salt. Sea salt, from sea water, is favored by professional chefs for its fresh, complex, marine flavor, and comes coarse for grinding or finely ground. Coarse-grained kosher salt is less salty tasting than either sea salt or table salt and has a rough texture.

1 Place potato slices in a Dutch oven. Add enough water to cover. Bring just to boiling. Cook for 2 to 3 minutes or until crisp-tender. Drain; place in single layer on paper towels. Carefully brush both sides of potato slices with cooking oil. Sprinkle with thyme and salt or seasoned salt.

2 Grill potato slices on the rack of an uncovered grill directly over medium-hot coals for 15 to 20 minutes or until browned and crisp, turning slices occasionally. Remove from grill; let stand for 8 to 10 minutes on a paper-towel-lined baking sheet. (Chips will crisp as they stand.) Makes 4 side-dish servings.

Nutrition facts per serving: 209 cal., 10 g total fat (1 g sat. fat), 0 mg chol., 276 mg sodium, 27 g carbo., 1 g fiber, 3 g pro. *Daily values:* 28% vit. C, 1% calcium, 9% iron.

GRILLING TRAYS AND WOKS

Grilling trays and woks come in all shapes and sizes, with and without handles. Grilling trays are sheets of nonstick enamel-coated metal with small holes that allow heat and smoke to penetrate foods, but prevent foods from falling into the fire. Woks are similar to trays, except they have higher sides, allowing you to turn foods with greater abandon. Both are ideal for small items, foods that have been precut into small pieces, or foods that fall apart easily. To use, oil lightly and place them directly on the grill rack. Use tongs to turn and remove foods. You may need to allow a little extra time when grilling with trays or woks.

CAL-MEX VEGGIE WRAPS

Prep: 30 min. ◆ Grill: 9 min.

Meat lovers can add beef, chicken, or turkey to these tomato-flavored tortillas that are overflowing with sweet pepper and summer squash.
(See the photograph on page 159.)

1 large red sweet pepper, seeded and cut into ½-inch-wide strips
1 large green sweet pepper, seeded and cut into ½-inch-wide strips
2 medium yellow summer squash, cut lengthwise into ¼-inch-thick slices
1 large sweet onion, cut into 1-inch wedges
1 Tbsp. cooking oil

◆◆◆

6 12-inch tomato- and/or spinach-flavored flour tortillas (wraps)
⅓ cup ranch salad dressing
4 oz. Monterey Jack cheese with jalapeño peppers, cut into thin slices
½ cup snipped fresh cilantro
1 Tbsp. cooking oil

◆◆◆

Assorted tortilla chips (optional)

1 Brush sweet peppers, yellow summer squash, and onion with 1 tablespoon oil before grilling. Grill the sweet peppers in a grill wok, grill basket, or on a greased grilling tray on an uncovered grill directly over medium-hot coals for 3 minutes.

2 Add squash and onion to grill and grill all vegetables for 5 to 8 minutes more or until crisp-tender, turning occasionally. Remove vegetables from the grill as they are done; set aside and keep warm.

3 To assemble wraps, spread 1 side of a tortilla with some of the ranch dressing. Top with slices of cheese. Spoon one-sixth of grilled vegetables (about ¾ cup) over cheese just below center of the wrap. Top vegetables with some snipped cilantro. Fold bottom third of tortilla partially over the vegetables. Roll into a cone.

Repeat with remaining tortillas, dressing, cheese, vegetables, and cilantro. Lightly brush outside of wraps with the 1 tablespoon oil.

4 Grill filled wraps on rack of an uncovered grill directly over medium-hot coals for 1 to 2 minutes or until the tortillas are lightly toasted and cheese begins to melt, turning once. If desired, serve with tortilla chips. Makes 6 wraps.

Nutrition facts per wrap: 434 cal., 20 g total fat (5 g sat. fat), 22 mg chol., 815 mg sodium, 51 g carbo., 2 g fiber, 15 g pro. *Daily values:* 24% vit. A, 108% vit. C, 19% calcium, 19% iron.

KABOBS-N-BEANS

Prep: 25 min. ◆ Marinate: 6 to 24 hr. ◆ Grill: 16 min.

There's something here for everyone: chicken, lamb, beef, and seasoned veggies, all artfully presented on skewers.
(See the photograph on page 201.)

1 small sweet onion, minced
⅓ cup Worcestershire sauce
1 Tbsp. finely shredded lime peel
¼ cup lime juice
2 Tbsp. snipped fresh rosemary
1 Tbsp. olive oil
6 pieces chicken-wing drumettes (about 6 oz.)
6 oz. lean boneless lamb, cut into 1-inch cubes
6 oz. boneless beef sirloin steak, cut into 1-inch cubes

12 oz. assorted vegetables (such as whole baby squash; sweet peppers cut into 1-inch pieces; and mushrooms, whole or quartered), about 2½ cups total

1 recipe Beer-Simmered Black Beans (see recipe, page 177)

1 For marinade, in a small mixing bowl combine onion, Worcestershire sauce, lime peel, lime juice, rosemary, and oil. Place chicken, lamb, beef, and vegetables in a 1-gallon sealable plastic bag. Pour marinade over meat and vegetables; seal. Refrigerate for 6 to 24 hours, turning occasionally.

2 Drain meat and vegetables, reserving marinade. Thread chicken, lamb, beef, and vegetables on separate 8-inch skewers.*

3 On the rack of an uncovered grill, directly over medium-hot coals, cook chicken skewers for 16 to 18 minutes or until no pink remains, turning once. Cook the lamb and beef skewers for 12 to 16 minutes or until desired doneness, turning several times. Grill the vegetable skewers for 6 to 8 minutes or until they become lightly browned, turning several times. Brush with remaining marinade during the first half of grilling time.

4 To serve, divide chicken, lamb, beef, and vegetables among 6 individual plates. Serve with Beer-Simmered Black Beans. Makes 6 servings.

MATING BEERS AND WINES WITH GRILLED FOODS

With grilling's casual, fun style, pairing food and drink shouldn't be an intimidating prospect. Keep things carefree and easy, and drink whatever you and your guests like. Here are a few ideas that may help you find just the right union of food and drink.

Grilled dishes are complex concentrations of flavors and textures. There's so much going on—crispy crusts, juicy insides, spicy rubs, tart marinades, sweet flavorful sauces, and smoke—that beverages offering simple, straightforward refreshment make a good choice. Or, consider something robust and hearty enough to stand up to the foods.

Cold, crisp beers are naturally refreshing because they're about 95 percent water. Their lower alcohol content won't heap on complexity, which makes balancing them with a wide variety of foods a breeze. Most lagers and ales, and even intensely flavored beers, make a happy gustatory marriage with grilled foods.

When choosing wines, the best matches for balance are those with roughly the same intensity as, or slightly more weight than, the food. Delicate foods taste best with lighter wines, while heartier or richer dishes need heavier or richer wines. The tannins (a substance found in grapes that contributes an astringent, dry flavor characteristic to wines) in big reds, such as cabernet sauvignon, for example, meld with the fats and proteins in red meats to bring a delightful velvety texture. Avoid aggressive wines, which can compete with the flavors in grilled foods to create a harsh taste in your mouth. Full-bodied wines can be so intensely flavored, for instance, that they can make seafood taste metallic.

Summertime grilling is a great time to enjoy young, light, or medium-bodied wines lower in tannins and high in dry fruitiness. Try a delicate pink rosé, Zinfandel, white Zinfandel, Pinot Noir, Syrah, Sangiovese, soft Sauvignon Blanc, Chenin Blanc, Riesling, or a blend.

Another tactic is to pair opposites, such as a refreshing, cold, light, fruity wine with spicy, smoky grilled meats and poultry. The palate-cleansing power of bubbles makes many sparkling wines especially thrilling with grilled seafood. For foods infused with the spicy Asian flavors of ginger, soy, herbs, and spices, Gewürztraminer is a perfect wine.

Serve wines at a temperature that will heighten their flavors. White and rosé wines should be lightly chilled; and reds are typically served at room temperature (which means about 65-degree cellar temperature, not 90-degree summer patio temperature).

*****Note:** If using nonmetal skewers (such as bamboo), soak them in cold water for 30 minutes before grilling.

Nutrition facts per serving: 191 cal., 11 g total fat (3 g sat. fat), 62 mg chol., 182 mg sodium, 7 g carbo., 1 g fiber, 17 g pro. *Daily values:* 2% vit. A, 72% vit. C, 2% calcium, 15% iron.

A HOT TIP

For some folks, it isn't summer without the spice of hot chili peppers adding their piquant sizzle to favorite grilling recipes. But hot peppers—and salsas, spreads, or other recipes that use hot peppers—contain volatile oils in their seeds and inner membranes that can easily burn eyes, lips, and sensitive skin.

When preparing recipes that use hot peppers, wear plastic gloves and be sure to wash your hands thoroughly with soap and water afterward.

STEAK SANDWICH, APULIAN-STYLE

Prep: 45 min. ◆ Grill: 24 min.

Crisp greens and roasted mild peppers are popular in Apulia, a region of Italy famous for dishes made with fresh ingredients that are casually prepared. (See the photograph on page 159.)

1 small eggplant
¾ tsp. salt
1 Tbsp. olive oil

◆◆◆

1 medium onion, chopped
4 cloves garlic, minced
8 oz. fresh, mild red cherry peppers or mild banana peppers, halved and stems and seeds removed
2 Tbsp. balsamic vinegar

12 oz. beef flank steak or boneless beef sirloin steak, about 1 inch thick
2 tsp. dried Italian seasoning, crushed

◆◆◆

4 6-inch Italian sourdough rolls, split horizontally
Olive oil (optional)

◆◆◆

Salad greens or romaine leaves
2 oz. shaved Parmesan cheese

1 Trim ends off eggplant; discard. Cut eggplant lengthwise into ¼-inch-thick slices, discarding the outside "peel" slices. Spread the eggplant slices in a single layer on a baking sheet. Sprinkle with ½ teaspoon of the salt; cover and set aside for 30 minutes. Rinse eggplant; pat dry. Rub eggplant slices with half of the olive oil; set aside.

2 For pepper spread, in a large skillet heat remaining oil. Cook onion and garlic, uncovered, in hot oil over medium heat about 5 minutes or until onion turns golden, stirring often. Add the cherry or banana peppers, the balsamic vinegar, and the remaining ¼ teaspoon salt. Cook and stir for 2 minutes; reduce heat. Cover and cook over low heat about 10 minutes or until mixture is soft, stirring occasionally. Remove pepper mixture from heat; let cool.

3 In a food processor bowl or blender container cover and process or blend pepper mixture until nearly smooth. Set aside.

4 Score meat on both sides by making shallow diagonal cuts at 1-inch intervals in a diamond pattern. If desired, season with *salt* and *pepper*. Rub both sides of steak with Italian seasoning.

5 Grill steak on rack of an uncovered grill directly over medium coals for 18 to 22 minutes for medium doneness, turning once. Grill eggplant slices for 6 to 8 minutes or until cooked through, turning once. Set aside. If desired, brush cut sides of Italian roll halves with olive oil. Grill bread, cut side down, for 1 to 2 minutes or until toasted.

6 To assemble, spread about 1 tablespoon pepper spread on bottom half of each Italian roll. Top with salad greens and eggplant slices. Slice steak across grain into very thin strips. Arrange sliced steak on eggplant slices. Sprinkle Parmesan cheese shavings atop steak. Lightly spread top halves of Italian rolls with remaining pepper spread. Serve open-face with top halves of rolls on the side. If desired, garnish with *fresh thyme sprigs.* Makes 4 sandwiches.

Nutrition facts per sandwich: 616 cal., 18 g total fat (7 g sat. fat), 47 mg chol., 1,300 mg sodium, 75 g carbo., 7 g fiber, 37 g pro. *Daily values:* 8% vit. A, 236% vit. C, 32% calcium, 32% iron.

COCONUT CHICKEN SPEARS

Prep: 20 min. ◆ Grill: 10 min.

To crack a fresh coconut, pierce two of the three "eyes" with an ice pick or corkscrew. Drain the liquid and use as a beverage or in place of water in recipes. Using a hammer, gently tap around the middle of the shell until it cracks and splits on its own.

8 6-inch bamboo skewers
½ cup purchased unsweetened coconut milk*
2 Tbsp. coconut, toasted
1 tsp. brown sugar
1 tsp. green curry paste*
1 tsp. red curry paste*

◆◆◆

12 chicken breast tenderloins or 12 oz. skinless, boneless chicken breasts, cut lengthwise into 1-inch-wide strips
1 Tbsp. five-spice powder*
¼ tsp. salt

◆◆◆

1 Tbsp. peanut oil or cooking oil

◆◆◆

2 small lemons, halved crosswise

◆◆◆

2 coconuts, halved (optional)
2 Key limes or small regular limes, halved (optional)
   Kaffir lime leaves (optional)*
   Star anise (optional)

1 Soak skewers in water for 30 minutes. In a small bowl stir together coconut milk, toasted coconut, and brown sugar. Divide mixture in half. Stir green curry paste into 1 portion of coconut mixture. Stir red curry paste into remaining coconut mixture.

Cover sauces; refrigerate until serving time.

2 Rinse chicken; pat dry with paper towels. Combine five-spice powder and salt. Rub chicken with seasoning mixture. Place the chicken tenderloin strips or pieces between 2 sheets of plastic wrap. Gently pound with the back of a heavy spoon or flat side of a meat mallet to about ¼-inch thickness.

3 Gently thread flattened chicken strips lengthwise onto bamboo skewers, feeding the sharp end slowly through the entire length of meat, keeping chicken strips straight (see illustration, below). Brush chicken with oil.

4 Grill skewers on the rack of an uncovered grill, directly over medium-hot coals, for 10 to 12 minutes or until no pink remains, turning once. Grill the lemon halves for 1 to 2 minutes or until cut surface is slightly charred.

5 To serve, spoon one-fourth of the green curry-coconut sauce into each coconut half, if using, or into condiment dishes, then gently swirl one-fourth of the red coconut sauce into the green

coconut sauce. Serve chicken with sauces and lemon halves. If desired, garnish with lime halves, lime leaves, and star anise. Makes 8 appetizer servings.

Nutrition facts per serving: 107 cal., 7 g total fat (3 g sat. fat), 23 mg chol., 149 mg sodium, 6 g carbo., 1 g fiber, 9 g pro. *Daily values:* 35% vit. C, 3% calcium, 7% iron.

*Note: You can find the coconut milk, the green and red curry pastes, the five-spice powder, and the lime leaves in Asian specialty stores and some large supermarkets. However, to make your own Five-Spice Powder and Curry-Coconut Sauce, follow these simple recipes:

Five-Spice Powder: In a spice grinder or blender container combine 3 tablespoons ground cinnamon, 6 star anise or 2 teaspoons anise seed, 1½ teaspoons fennel seed, 1½ teaspoons whole Szechuan peppers or whole black pepper, and ¾ teaspoon ground cloves. Cover and blend spices to a fine powder. Store in a tightly covered container for up to 2 months. Makes ¼ cup.

Curry-Coconut Sauce: If red and green curry pastes are unavailable, you can make this sauce as a substitute for the coconut milk, brown sugar, toasted coconut, and red and green curry paste mixtures.

In a small mixing bowl stir together ½ cup of purchased unsweetened coconut milk, 2 tablespoons toasted coconut, 1½ teaspoons curry powder, and 1 teaspoon brown sugar. Cover and chill. Makes about ⅔ cup.

GRILLING BASICS

POULTRY

If desired, remove the skin from the poultry. Rinse poultry and pat dry with paper towels. Test for desired coal temperature. Place poultry on the grill rack, bone side up, directly over the preheated coals (for direct grilling) or directly over drip pan (for indirect grilling).

Grill (uncovered for direct grilling or covered for indirect grilling) for the time given below or until tender and no longer pink. (Note: White meat will cook slightly faster.) Turn poultry over halfway through the grilling time.

Type of Bird	Weight	Temperature	Doneness	Direct Grilling Time	Indirect Grilling Time
Chicken, broiler-fryer, half	1¼ to 1½ pounds	Medium	Tender; no longer pink	40 to 50 minutes	1 to 1¼ hours
Chicken breast half, skinned and boned	4 to 5 ounces each	Medium	Tender; no longer pink	12 to 15 minutes	15 to 18 minutes
Chicken quarters	2½ to 3 pounds total	Medium	Tender; no longer pink	40 to 50 minutes	50 to 60 minutes
Meaty chicken pieces	2 to 2½ pounds total	Medium	Tender; no longer pink	35 to 45 minutes	50 to 60 minutes
Turkey breast tenderloin steak	4 to 6 ounces each	Medium	Tender; no longer pink	12 to 15 minutes	15 to 18 minutes

FISH & SEAFOOD

Thaw fish or shellfish, if frozen. Test for desired temperature. For fish fillets, place in a well-greased grill basket. For fish steaks and whole fish, grease the grill rack. Place the fish on the rack directly over the preheated coals (for direct grilling) or over a drip pan (for indirect grilling). Grill (uncovered for direct grilling or covered for indirect grilling) for the time given below or until the fish just begins to flake easily when tested with a fork; scallops and shrimp should look opaque. Turn the fish over halfway through the grilling time. If desired, brush fish with melted margarine or butter.

Form of Fish	Weight, Size, or Thickness	Temperature	Doneness or Thickness	Direct Grilling Time	Indirect Grilling Time
Dressed fish	½ to 1½ pounds	Medium	Flakes	7 to 9 minutes per ½ pound	20 to 25 minutes per ½ pound
Fillets, steaks, cubes (for kabobs)	½ to 1 inch thick	Medium	Flakes	4 to 6 minutes per ½-inch thickness	4 to 6 minutes per ½-inch thickness
Sea scallops (for kabobs)	(12 to 15 per pound)	Medium	Opaque	5 to 8 minutes	5 to 7 minutes
Shrimp (for kabobs)	Medium (20 per pound)	Medium	Opaque	6 to 8 minutes	8 to 10 minutes
	Jumbo (12 to 15 per pound)	Medium	Opaque	6 to 8 minutes	10 to 12 minutes

BEEF, PORK, OR LAMB

Test for the desired temperature. Place the meat on the rack of a grill directly over the preheated coals (for direct grilling) or directly over a drip pan (for indirect grilling). Grill meat (uncovered for direct grilling or covered for indirect grilling) for the time given below or until done, turning the meat over halfway through the grilling time.

Cut	Thickness	Temperature	Doneness	Direct Grilling Time	Indirect Grilling Time
Beef					
Boneless sirloin steak	1 inch	Medium	Medium rare	14 to 18 minutes	22 to 26 minutes
			Medium	18 to 22 minutes	26 to 30 minutes
	1½ inches	Medium	Medium rare	32 to 36 minutes	32 to 36 minutes
			Medium	36 to 40 minutes	36 to 40 minutes
Flank steak	¾ to 1 inch	Medium	Medium	12 to 14 minutes	18 to 22 minutes
Ground meat patties	¾ inch (4 per pound)	Medium	No pink remains	14 to 18 minutes	20 to 24 minutes
Steak (blade, chuck, top round)	1 inch	Medium	Medium rare	14 to 16 minutes	45 to 55 minutes
			Medium	18 to 20 minutes	60 to 70 minutes
	1½ inches	Medium	Medium rare	19 to 26 minutes	50 to 60 minutes
			Medium	27 to 32 minutes	1 to 1¼ hours
Steak (porterhouse, rib, rib eye, sirloin, T-bone, tenderloin, top loin)	1 inch	Medium	Medium rare	8 to 12 minutes	16 to 20 minutes
			Medium	12 to 15 minutes	20 to 24 minutes
	1¼ to 1½ inches	Medium	Medium rare	14 to 18 minutes	20 to 22 minutes
			Medium	18 to 22 minutes	22 to 26 minutes
Pork*					
Chop	¾ inch	Medium	Medium	8 to 11 minutes	20 to 24 minutes
	1¼ to 1½ inches	Medium	Medium	25 to 30 minutes	35 to 40 minutes
Lamb					
Chop	1 inch	Medium	Medium rare	10 to 14 minutes	16 to 18 minutes
		Medium	Medium	14 to 16 minutes	18 to 20 minutes
Kabobs	1-inch cubes	Medium	Medium	12 to 14 minutes	

*Note: Pork should be cooked until juices run clear.

RED RIVER BURGERS

Prep: 15 min. ◆ Grill: 14 min.

Many supermarkets carry jars of pickled green tomatoes.
If you'd like to make your own, see the recipe on page 173.
(See the photograph on page 158.)

½ cup chopped green onions or finely chopped white onion
2 Tbsp. fine dry bread crumbs
2 red serrano peppers, seeded and finely chopped*
3 canned chipotle peppers in adobo sauce, chopped
½ tsp. salt
1 lb. lean ground beef

◆◆◆

8 1-inch-thick slices bread or 4 whole wheat hamburger buns, split

◆◆◆

Roasted red pepper catsup, roasted garlic catsup, or other purchased flavored catsup (optional)
4 slices pickled green tomatoes (see page 173)
Sliced red onion (optional)
Red serrano peppers (optional)

1 In a large mixing bowl combine onions, bread crumbs, serrano peppers, chipotle peppers, and salt. Add beef; mix well. Shape meat mixture into four ¾-inch-thick patties.

2 Grill hamburger patties on the rack of an uncovered grill directly over medium coals for 14 to 18 minutes or until no pink remains, turning once. Grill or toast bread or buns.**

3 To serve, place burgers on grilled or toasted bread or buns. If desired, serve with desired catsup, green tomato slices, red onion slices, and serrano peppers. Makes 4 servings.

*Note: Hot peppers contain oils that can burn. Wear plastic gloves when working with peppers. Do not touch eyes or face and thoroughly wash hands.

**Note: To grill bread or buns, brush lightly with olive oil or margarine. Grill directly over medium coals for 30 seconds to 1 minute or until just toasted, turning once.

Nutrition facts per serving: 352 cal., 13 g total fat (5 g sat. fat), 71 mg chol., 756 mg sodium, 32 g carbo., 1 g fiber, 25 g pro. *Daily values:* 18% vit. A, 20% vit. C, 5% calcium, 24% iron.

ZUCCHINI CRAB CAKES

Prep: 20 min. ◆ Grill: 6 min.

Be sure to clean crabmeat carefully, removing and discarding any small pieces of shell or cartilage. (See the photograph on page 162.)

6 tsp. cooking oil
1 cup coarsely shredded zucchini (about 5 oz.)
¼ cup thinly sliced green onions

◆◆◆

1 egg, beaten
½ cup seasoned fine dry bread crumbs
1 Tbsp. Dijon-style mustard
½ tsp. snipped fresh lemon thyme or snipped fresh thyme
⅛ to ¼ tsp. ground red pepper (optional)
8 oz. fresh cooked crabmeat,* chopped (1½ cups)

◆◆◆

2 large red and/or yellow tomatoes, cut into ¼-inch-thick slices
Red and/or yellow cherry tomatoes (optional)
1 large lemon or lime, cut into wedges (optional)
1 recipe Tomato-Sour Cream Dipping Sauce (see page 185)

1 In a large skillet heat 2 teaspoons of the cooking oil. Cook and stir the zucchini and green onions in hot oil for about 3 minutes or until the vegetables are just tender and the liquid is evaporated. Cool slightly.

2 In a large mixing bowl combine the egg, bread crumbs, Dijon-style mustard, lemon thyme, and, if desired, red pepper. Add the zucchini mixture and crabmeat; mix well. Using about ¼ cup of the mixture for each crab cake, shape into 8 patties, ½ inch thick and 2½ inches in diameter. Brush both sides of the crab cakes lightly with the remaining 4 teaspoons oil.

3 Place the crab cakes directly on a lightly oiled, preheated grill rack. Grill crab cakes on an uncovered grill directly over medium-hot coals for 6 to 8 minutes or until golden brown, turning once.

4 To serve, overlap 2 crab cakes on individual salad plates along with sliced tomatoes. If desired, garnish with cherry tomatoes and lemon or lime wedges. Serve with Tomato-Sour Cream Dipping Sauce. Makes 4 side-dish servings.

*Note: You need to purchase about 1¼ pounds crab legs to get 8 ounces crabmeat.

Tomato-Sour Cream Dipping Sauce: In a small mixing bowl stir together ½ cup dairy sour cream, 3 tablespoons minced yellow and red tomatoes, 1 to 2 tablespoons lemon or lime juice, and ⅛ teaspoon seasoned salt. Cover and chill. Serve with crab cakes.

Nutrition facts per serving with 2 Tbsp. sour cream dipping sauce: 277 cal., 16 g total fat (5 g sat. fat), 123 mg chol., 424 mg sodium, 16 g carbo., 2 g fiber, 17 g pro. *Daily values:* 17% vit. A, 39% vit. C, 10% calcium, 11% iron.

PIZZA-ON-THE-BEACH
Prep: 25 min. ◆ Grill: 9 min.

1 large fennel bulb

◆◆◆

2 tsp. olive oil

4 oz. medium shrimp, peeled, deveined, and tails removed

4 oz. sea scallops, rinsed and halved horizontally

◆◆◆

Nonstick spray coating

1 10-oz. pkg. refrigerated pizza dough

◆◆◆

½ of a 10-oz. container refrigerated light alfredo sauce (about ½ cup)

½ tsp. fennel seed, crushed (optional)

1 cup shredded provolone, scamorze, mozzarella, and/or other cheese (4 oz.)

1 Cut off and discard stalks and base of fennel. Wash bulb; remove any wilted outer layers. Halve, core, and cut fennel crosswise into thin slices; set aside.

2 In a large nonstick skillet heat oil. Cook and stir shrimp and scallops in hot oil over medium-high heat for 2 to 3 minutes or until opaque. Remove shrimp mixture from skillet; set aside. Add fennel slices and ½ cup *water* to skillet. Bring to boiling; reduce heat. Simmer, covered, for 2 to 3 minutes or until just tender; drain and set aside.

3 Spray a 16-inch grill pizza pan or 12- to 13-inch pizza pan with nonstick coating; set aside. Unroll pizza dough; divide into 4 pieces. If desired, shape each piece into a ball for round pizzas,

or leave as rectangles. On a lightly floured surface, roll each dough piece to ¼-inch thickness. Transfer to pan. (If necessary, cook 2 pizzas at a time.)

4 Place pan on rack of covered grill directly over medium coals (or medium heat if using gas grill) for 6 to 8 minutes or until bottoms of crusts turn slightly golden, giving pan a half turn after 4 minutes. Remove pan from grill; cool slightly (about 3 minutes). Carefully turn crusts over.

5 Spread alfredo sauce on pizza crusts to within about ½ inch of edge. Top each crust with shrimp, scallops, and fennel. Sprinkle with fennel seed, if using, and cheese. Return pizzas to grill. Cook, covered, for 3 to 4 minutes more or until cheese is melted and bottoms of crusts are golden. Remove from grill. Let stand 5 minutes. Makes 8 appetizer or 4 main-dish servings.

Nutrition facts per appetizer serving: 218 cal., 9 g total fat (4 g sat. fat), 38 mg chol., 524 mg sodium, 23 g carbo., 6 g fiber, 12 g pro. *Daily values:* 6% vit. A, 4% vit. C, 14% calcium, 8% iron.

Menu

Pizza-on-the-Beach (see left)

◆◆◆

Salad of Bibb lettuce, chopped fresh mozzarella, baby yellow pear tomatoes, and vinegar and oil

◆◆◆

S'More Banana Split (see page 189)

FOOD SAFETY: A MIXED BAG

Softball league is at seven, your spouse is late, and you have less than an hour to get home and put dinner on the table. The solution? Hit the store for a roasted chicken, a bag of mixed salad greens, and precut vegetables.

This scenario may sound familiar for a good reason: Nearly a third of Americans supplement their menu with prepared take-out meals at least once a week. These "home meal replacements" are great time-savers but, by definition, they've passed through several more hands than would meals made from scratch. With food safety a mounting concern, just how safe are convenience foods?

MEATY ISSUES

It's a mixed grill out there. Prestuffed chicken breasts, already-skewered kabobs, and marinated meat and poultry vie for attention with precooked roasts and rotisserie chickens. As supermarkets respond to consumer needs, they're increasing their own lines of convenience items. "We rely on the individual market to provide safe handling of these products," observes Karen Penner, a Ph.D. food science specialist at Kansas State University.

Fully cooked meat and poultry items may be easy on your schedule, but they must be handled correctly to avoid recontamination or growth of harmful bacteria. "Although harmful and harmless bacteria may be destroyed initially, bacteria introduced by handling after cooking can thrive, especially without competing harmless bacteria. Moreover, the sniff test won't work here," Penner says. "Manufacturer- and store-cooked meats won't quickly develop off odors if mishandled."

"It comes down to the consumer taking responsibility and following directions, whatever the product," says Marlys Bielunski, food communications director at the

National Cattleman's Beef Association. "If you follow the directions for reheating (and letting stand before serving) these products, you'll bring the serving temperature up to a safe 165°."

The safe way to prepare uncooked, stuffed meats and poultry depends on the type of meat. The United States Department of Agriculture (USDA) suggests cooking beef and pork to 160°, ground poultry to 165°, whole chicken to 180°, and other poultry items and roasts to 170°. Individual items, such as prestuffed chops and chicken breasts, should be cooked to an internal temperature of 165°. Using a meat thermometer, take the temperature at the center of meat, making sure the thermometer tip doesn't touch bone. Follow preparation instructions on prepackaged items, and don't thaw frozen foods before cooking unless stated on package.

SAFE PRODUCE

Sales of packaged salad greens exceed $1 billion annually. Despite a recent scare over bacteria in packaged salad mixes, the industry touts a clean slate with regard to food-borne illness. "Safety starts in the field," reports Robyn Sprague, of Fresh Express, Inc. "The federal Food and Drug Administration (FDA) sets guidelines for agricultural and manufacturing practices to help ensure safe and sanitary growing and handling conditions before prepared produce reaches the supermarket."

Still, consumers can do a number of things to further ensure safety of purchased, prepared produce. "Look for products labeled as 'washed.' Also, triple-washed products are not necessarily better than those products simply labeled as 'washed,'" says Sprague. "The greens or vegetables should be cold to the touch, and the colors should be bright. There should be no brown-tipped or slimy greens. Observe the 'use by' dates marked on the outside of precut-produce packages."

When supermarkets package precut vegetables on site, the packages should bear a "packaged on" date. Use these items within four to seven days. Salad mixes sold in bulk bins haven't always been washed, posing a risk of bacterial contamination. Even salad mixes from open bulk bins that are advertised as washed should be washed again once you get them home because they've been exposed to contact with other shoppers and the circulating store air.

Packages of prewashed, precut produce note that it is not necessary to rewash their products, but from the standpoint of safety, it never hurts to give produce a good rinsing yourself. Wash precut produce under cold running water, then drain and pat dry with clean paper towels. Wash whole fruits and vegetables in cool water, using a scrub brush to remove evident soil.

PREPARING TO PREPARE

The main priority in food safety, whether at home or anywhere else, is to prevent cross-contamination. When a food comes in contact with another food, a surface, your hands, or any other source of contamination by micro-organisms, it is said to be cross-contaminated.

The FDA recommends washing hands in warm soapy water for 20 seconds before and after handling food. Any interruption in preparation—a sneeze, a phone call, pet nuzzling—requires another washing before resuming work in the kitchen. When storing raw meat, poultry, and fish, keep them (and their juices) from coming in contact with any other food or food preparation surface.

AT HOME PLATE

Food safety doesn't stop once the foods are in your possession. Here are several tips to keep food safe during the "between time" from purchase to prep.

1. Time your purchases. When rotisserie chicken or precooked roast is on the list, make it the last purchase before checking out. Once home, slip the item into a 200° oven until serving time. Use a "quick-read" thermometer to check the temperature of the meat. If below 140°, heat to 165° before serving.

2. Hustle home. Make food shopping the last stop of the day. If the trip home takes 30 minutes or more, bring an ice chest for perishables. A 15-minute stop on a summer day—or even a warm spring or fall day—can push food temperatures quickly into the 40° to 140° danger zone.

3. Hold in the cold. Use a cold thermometer to ensure your refrigerator is 35° to 40° and your freezer is at 0° or less. A recent survey by Audits International, Inc., found that nearly half the households studied kept their refrigerators too warm, thus promoting bacterial growth.

FOOD SAFETY

When it comes to food safety in the home, we may "talk the talk," but do we "walk the walk"? An Audits International, Inc., survey inspected 106 households for food-safety practices. They observed meal preparation, service, cleanup, and leftover storage. The results? Only one home received an acceptable rating. Ninety-six percent of the homes had at least one critical food safety violation. The average was three violations. Surveys by the Centers for Disease Control, the Food and Drug Administration, state health departments, and other concerned groups show that one-fifth to one-third of people do not wash their hands with soap after handling raw meat or chicken. The same number of people don't wash their cutting boards with soap or sanitizer after preparing raw meat or poultry.

CHOOSING A CAKE PAN

All cake pans are not created equal. For even baking, we suggest sturdy, single-wall aluminum pans. When choosing cake pans, also consider the pan's depth and surface finish:

Depth: When a recipe calls for 8×1½-inch round pans, make sure the pans you choose are truly 1½ inches deep. Some pans can be as much as ¼ inch shallower than others—cake batters may run over when baked in these pans.

Surface finish: Bakeware is made in a range of materials that have different effects on a cake. Shiny bakeware, including aluminum, tin, and stainless steel, reflects heat and will result in a thinner cake crust. Dark or dull-finish bakeware, including tin, glass, and many nonstick pans, absorbs more heat, increasing the amount of browning and resulting in a thicker crust.

CRANBERRY-CARROT CAKE WITH GINGERED TOPPING

Prep: 25 min. ◆ Bake: 50 min.
Cool: 2 hr.

2 cups all-purpose flour
2 cups granulated sugar
1 tsp. baking powder
1 tsp. baking soda
1½ to 2 tsp. grated fresh ginger
½ tsp. salt
3 cups finely shredded carrots
1 cup cooking oil

4 eggs
¾ cup dried cranberries
½ cup chopped toasted walnuts

◆◆◆

1 3-oz. pkg. cream cheese, softened
2 Tbsp. butter, softened
1 cup sifted powdered sugar
2 to 3 Tbsp. half-and-half, light cream, or milk
3 Tbsp. snipped dried cranberries (optional)

1 Grease a 13×9×2-inch baking pan; set aside. In a large mixing bowl stir together flour, granulated sugar, baking powder, baking soda, 1 teaspoon of the ginger, and the salt. Add carrots, cooking oil, and eggs. Beat with an electric mixer on medium speed for 2 minutes. Stir in the ¾ cup dried cranberries and the walnuts. Pour batter into the prepared pan.

2 Bake in a 325° oven for 50 to 60 minutes or until top springs back when lightly touched. Cool thoroughly in pan on a wire rack.

3 Meanwhile, in a medium bowl beat cream cheese, butter, remaining ½ to 1 teaspoon ginger, and the powdered sugar, with an electric mixer until well combined. Beat in enough of the half-and-half to make soft dollops. Chill until ready to serve.

4 To serve, cut cake in squares. Top each piece with a spoonful of cream cheese topping. If desired, sprinkle with snipped dried cranberries. Serves 12 to 16.

Nutrition facts per serving: 528 cal., 28 g total fat (6 g sat. fat), 85 mg chol., 299 mg sodium, 67 g carbo., 2 g fiber, 6 g pro. *Daily values:* 85% vit. A, 4% vit. C, 5% calcium, 10% iron.

HAZELNUT TORTE

Prep: 45 min. ◆ Bake: 30 min.
Cool: 2 hr. ◆ Chill: 2 hr.

The cake layers may have a slight dip in the center after baking. Once assembled and frosted, the dip won't be noticeable.

6 eggs, separated
1 cup granulated sugar
1 to 2 Tbsp. finely shredded orange peel

◆◆◆

3 cups very finely ground hazelnuts (filberts) (2¾ cups whole)
½ cup fine dry bread crumbs
¾ tsp. ground cinnamon
½ tsp. baking powder

◆◆◆

2 Tbsp. Frangelico or other hazelnut liqueur
1 recipe Butter Frosting (see page 189)

◆◆◆

Unsweetened cocoa powder
Hazelnuts

1 Grease and lightly flour two 9×1½-inch round baking pans. In a medium mixing bowl beat egg yolks with an electric mixer on high speed about 4 minutes or until thick and light-colored. Gradually beat in ½ cup of the sugar, 1 tablespoon at a time, until completely dissolved. Stir in orange peel; set aside.

2 Thoroughly wash beaters. In a large mixing bowl beat egg whites on high speed until soft peaks form. Beat in remaining ½ cup sugar, 1 tablespoon at a time, until stiff peaks form.

3 Fold a small amount of the beaten egg whites into egg yolk mixture to lighten. Fold yolk mixture into remaining egg whites.

4 Stir together ground nuts, bread crumbs, cinnamon, and baking powder. Gently fold nut mixture, one-third at a time, into egg mixture, just until combined. Divide batter evenly between prepared pans.

5 Bake in a 325° oven about 30 minutes or until a wooden toothpick inserted in center comes out clean. Cool in pans on wire rack for 15 minutes. Loosen edges; gently remove cakes from baking pans. Cool completely on wire racks.

6 To assemble, invert a cake layer onto a large cake platter. Drizzle with half of the Frangelico. Spread with about ½ cup Butter Frosting. Invert the other cake layer onto the frosted cake layer. Drizzle with remaining liqueur. Spread with ½ cup of the Butter Frosting.

7 Cover top and sides of assembled torte with remaining frosting. Lightly sprinkle with sifted unsweetened cocoa powder. Garnish with whole hazelnuts. Cover; chill for 2 hours. Let stand at room temperature about 20 minutes before serving. Cut into wedges. Makes 16 servings.

Butter Frosting: In a large mixing bowl beat ½ cup softened butter with an electric mixer on medium to high speed until fluffy. Gradually add 2½ cups sifted powdered sugar, beating until combined. Slowly beat in ¼ cup Frangelico or other hazelnut liqueur and 2 teaspoons frozen

orange juice concentrate, thawed. Gradually beat in another 2½ cups sifted powdered sugar. If necessary, beat in enough milk, 1 teaspoon at a time, to reach spreading consistency.

Nutrition facts per serving: 420 cal., 21 g total fat (5 g sat. fat), 95 mg chol., 117 mg sodium, 53 g carbo., 2 g fiber, 6 g pro. *Daily values:* 9% vit. A, 3% vit. C, 6% calcium, 8% iron.

S'MORE BANANA SPLIT
Prep: 20 min. ◆ Grill: 8 min.

Grilling bananas right in the peel is easy and fun, plus it gives them an irresistible, puddinglike texture. (See the photograph on page 163.)

4 large bananas or plantains, unpeeled

◆◆◆

2 1½-oz. bars milk chocolate, coarsely chopped
⅓ cup miniature marshmallows
1 cup bite-size graham squares, or 8 graham crackers, broken into large pieces

◆◆◆

Assorted sliced fresh fruits (optional)
Powdered sugar (optional)
Ground cinnamon (optional)

1 Grill unpeeled bananas or plantains on the rack of an uncovered grill directly over medium-hot coals for 8 to 10 minutes for bananas or about 15 minutes for plantains (or until just heated through and softened), turning them once.

2 While bananas or plantains are still warm, hold with a clean dish towel and, using a sharp knife, make a deep lengthwise cut

down the center of the inside curve of each. Cut to, but not through, the bottom. Spread the sides open slightly. Gently press chocolate pieces and marshmallows into the cut side of each. Insert graham crackers into cut sides. Let stand several minutes.

3 Serve on dessert plates. If desired, garnish with assorted sliced fruits. Sift powdered sugar and cinnamon on top, if desired. Makes 4 servings.

Nutrition facts per serving: 287 cal., 9 g total fat (5 g sat. fat), 0 mg chol., 108 mg sodium, 53 g carbo., 2 g fiber, 4 g pro. *Daily values:* 2% vit. A, 17% vit. C, 5% calcium, 7% iron.

Mango Blossom

Prep: 30 min. ◆ Grill: 2 min. for cake;
4 min. for mango

*A mango is ripe when the
skin is bright in color and the fruit
yields very slightly to touch
and has a strong floral aroma.
(See the photograph on page 163.)*

4 **mangoes**

◆◆◆

4 **kiwifruit, peeled**

◆◆◆

½ **of a 15-oz. purchased angel
food cake**

¼ **cup margarine or butter,
melted**

◆◆◆

3 **Tbsp. molasses or honey**

◆◆◆

Vanilla ice cream (optional)

1 Using a sharp knife, cut
mangoes lengthwise down both
flat sides, keeping the blade about
¼ inch from the seed. Score
mango pieces, making cuts
through the fruit just to the peel
in a crosshatch fashion (see photos, right). Set aside.

2 Carefully remove and discard the peel remaining around
the mango seeds. Cut away as
much of the fruit remaining
around each mango seed as you
can; discard seeds. Place the
removed fruit portion in a food
processor bowl or blender container. Cover and process or blend
fruit pieces until smooth. Transfer
pureed fruit to a small covered
container or a clean squeeze bottle. Chill until ready to use.

3 Rinse the food processor
bowl or blender container. Place

peeled kiwifruit in bowl or container. Cover and process or blend
until smooth. If desired, strain the
kiwifruit puree through a large
strainer to remove seeds. Transfer
to a small covered container or
squeeze bottle. Chill until ready
to use.

4 Cut angel food cake in half
horizontally (forming 2 half-
rings). Brush all sides with half of
the melted margarine or butter.
Grill cake on rack of an uncovered
grill directly over medium coals
for 2 to 3 minutes or until lightly
browned, turning once. Cut angel
food cake into large, irregular-
shaped croutons.

5 Brush fruit side of reserved
mango pieces with molasses or
honey and remaining melted margarine or butter. Grill mangoes,
cut side down, on the rack of an
uncovered grill directly over
medium coals for 4 to 6 minutes
or until brown around the edges
and heated through.

6 To serve, spoon or drizzle
mango and kiwifruit sauces on
the bottom of 8 chilled, shallow
dessert bowls. Carefully bend the
peel back on each mango half,
pushing the inside up and out
until the mango cubes pop up and
separate. Place each mango "blossom" on sauces; surround with
several cake croutons and vanilla
ice cream, if desired. Makes
8 servings.

Nutrition facts per serving: 215 cal., 4 g
total fat (1 g sat. fat), 0 mg chol., 249 mg
sodium, 45 g carbo., 2 g fiber, 3 g pro.
Daily values: 44% vit. A, 119% vit. C, 6%
calcium, 5% iron.

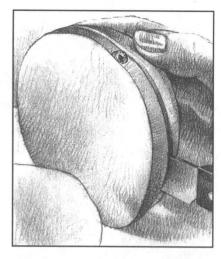

Using a sharp knife, make a
lengthwise cut, about ¼ inch
from the seed, down each side of
the mango. Cut away the pieces of
fruit remaining around the seed to
use for the mango sauce.

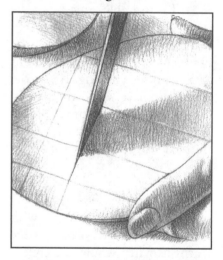

Make a series of crosshatch cuts
into the fruit, without cutting
through the peel. After grilling,
bend the mango back, carefully
pushing it inside-out to form a
decorative "blossom."

SEPTEMBER
Mealtime is Family Time

*S*eptember is when school activities kick into gear, placing family time at a premium. Set the tone for the coming months by keeping mealtime part of your family's routine. This chapter is filled with fast, doable recipes from two busy families like yours. When you're in a hurry, try Mad-Dash Dinner Salad, Pub Pork, or Mango-Sauced Snapper. Help with homework while Firehouse Meat Loaf bakes, then serve it up with Firehouse Potatoes. Or, let everyone get in on meal preparation with "Let Me Help" Kabobs or personalized Ham and Cheese Pizza Stacks.

30-minute recipes indicated in RED.
Low-fat and no-fat recipes indicated with a ♥.
Photographs indicated in italics.
*Bonus recipe

The Lecoqs:
Shop for what looks good, then decide how to cook it.

The ability to take decisive action in the face of chaos is the key to survival for a firefighter. It's a mind-set that also helps Renton, Washington, Fire Captain John Lecoq deftly carry out his cooking duties at home. Working around daughter Heather's after-school activities, wife Sandy's job, and a schedule that takes him away from home for 24 hours at a time, John has turned what many consider a chore into a relaxing activity. "Cooking at home—if done right—is a little luxury you can give yourself."

1 If using marinated chicken breast halves, cook according to package directions. Drain and cut into strips. If using frozen chicken breast strips, heat through according to package directions.

2 Divide greens among 6 salad bowls or plates. Arrange chicken strips, three-bean salad, cucumber, tomatoes, mozzarella cheese, olives, and onion atop lettuce. Drizzle salads with dressing. Makes 6 main-dish servings.

Nutrition facts per serving: 246 cal., 12 g total fat (3 g sat. fat), 30 mg chol., 840 mg sodium, 22 g carbo., 7 g fiber, 15 g pro. *Daily values:* 10% vit. A, 22% vit. C, 14% calcium, 10% iron.

MAD-DASH DINNER SALAD
Start to finish: 25 min.

Salads such as this invite improvisation; the only rule is to start with about 8 cups of lettuce to ensure a good ratio of greens to other ingredients. (See the photograph on page 198.)

8 to 10 oz. lemon-herb or lemon-pepper marinated skinless, boneless chicken breast halves or one 9-oz. pkg. frozen, cooked chicken breast strips

◆◆◆

8 cups torn mixed greens, such as red leaf lettuce, green leaf, curly endive, and/or romaine

1 15-oz. can three-bean salad, drained, or 2 cups three-bean salad from deli, drained

1 medium cucumber, halved lengthwise and sliced

3 medium plum tomatoes, cored and cut into wedges (6 oz.)

4 oz. mozzarella cheese, cut into cubes (about 1 cup)

1 cup pitted green, kalamata, ripe black, or niçoise olives

1 small red onion, thinly sliced and separated into rings (⅓ cup)

⅓ cup bottled balsamic vinaigrette salad dressing or red wine vinaigrette salad dressing

LOW FAT
OUT-OF-TOWN SALMON
Prep: 30 min. ◆ Bake: 30 min.

The packets will be very hot when they come out of the oven. Transfer them to individual plates before opening slowly to allow steam to escape. (See the photograph on page 199.)

4 4-oz. fresh or frozen skinless salmon fillets, ¾ inch thick

2 cups thinly bias-sliced carrots

◆◆◆

2 cups sliced fresh mushrooms

4 green onions, sliced

2 tsp. finely shredded orange peel

2 tsp. snipped fresh oregano or ½ tsp. dried oregano

4 cloves garlic, halved

¼ tsp. salt

¼ tsp. pepper

4 tsp. olive oil

Salt and pepper
2 medium oranges, thinly
   sliced
4 sprigs fresh oregano
   (optional)

1 Thaw fish, if frozen. Rinse fish; pat dry with paper towels. Set aside. In a small saucepan cook carrots, covered, in a small amount of boiling water for 2 minutes. Drain and set aside. Tear off four 24-inch pieces of 18-inch-wide heavy foil. Fold each in half to make four 18×12-inch pieces.

2 In a large bowl combine carrots, mushrooms, green onions, orange peel, snipped oregano, garlic, ¼ teaspoon salt, and ¼ teaspoon pepper; toss gently.

3 Divide vegetables among the 4 pieces of foil, placing in center. Place 1 piece of salmon on top of each stack of vegetables. Drizzle 1 teaspoon of the oil over each piece of salmon. Sprinkle each lightly with additional salt and pepper; top with orange slices and, if desired, a sprig of oregano. Bring together 2 opposite edges of foil and seal with a double fold. Fold remaining ends to completely enclose the food, allowing space for steam to build. Place the foil packets in a single layer on a baking pan.

4 Bake in a 350° oven about 30 minutes or until carrots are tender and fish flakes easily when tested with a fork. Transfer the packets to individual plates. Open

slowly to allow steam to escape. Makes 4 servings.

Nutrition facts per serving: 226 cal., 9 g total fat (1 g sat. fat), 20 mg chol., 288 mg sodium, 19 g carbo., 5 g fiber, 19 g pro. *Daily values:* 198% vit. A, 71% vit. C, 6% calcium, 14% iron.

REAL-WORLD RISOTTO
Prep: 15 min. ◆ Cook: 20 min.
Stand: 5 min.

Saffron serves to tie the flavors of this dish together in much the same way that garlic does in other dishes. It also lends a faintly nutty, almost cinnamonlike taste to the dish. (See the photograph on page 199.)

1 large onion, finely chopped
   (1 cup)
2 Tbsp. margarine or butter
1 cup Arborio or long grain
   rice

◆◆◆

2¾ cups reduced-sodium
   chicken broth
   Dash ground saffron, a
   pinch of thread saffron, or
   ⅛ tsp. ground turmeric

◆◆◆

½ cup grated Parmesan cheese
¼ cup half-and-half or light
   cream
2 Tbsp. pine nuts, toasted
1 Tbsp. snipped fresh Italian
   parsley or Italian parsley
   sprigs
   Parmesan cheese curls
   (optional)

1 In a large skillet cook onion in hot margarine or butter until tender but not brown. Add uncooked rice. Cook and stir for 2 minutes more.

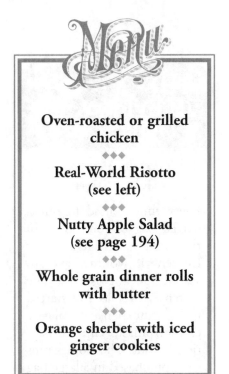

Menu

Oven-roasted or grilled chicken

◆◆◆

Real-World Risotto (see left)

◆◆◆

Nutty Apple Salad (see page 194)

◆◆◆

Whole grain dinner rolls with butter

◆◆◆

Orange sherbet with iced ginger cookies

2 Carefully stir in chicken broth and saffron or turmeric. Bring to boiling; reduce heat. Cover and simmer for 20 minutes (do not lift cover). Remove from heat. Let stand, covered, 5 minutes. Stir in cheese and half-and-half or light cream.

3 To serve, transfer rice mixture to a serving bowl. Sprinkle top with pine nuts and snipped parsley. Top with Parmesan cheese curls, if desired. Makes 6 to 8 side-dish servings.

Nutrition facts per serving: 234 cal., 10 g total fat (3 g sat. fat), 10 mg chol., 499 mg sodium, 29 g carbo., 1 g fiber, 8 g pro. *Daily values:* 8% vit. A, 3% vit. C, 11% calcium, 12% iron.

NUTTY APPLE SALAD

Prep: 20 min.

You can make the Herbed Nuts for this salad at the beginning of the week and have enough left over for topping such dishes as fried fish or sautéed mushrooms. They also taste great paired with blue cheeses, such as Roquefort or Stilton. (See the photograph on page 197.)

Romaine leaves
6 cups torn mixed greens
2 small tart green apples, cored and cut into wedges

♦♦♦

2 Tbsp. cider vinegar
2 Tbsp. olive oil
¼ tsp. pepper
⅛ tsp. salt
⅓ cup Herbed Nuts (see below)

1 Lay 2 or 3 romaine leaves on individual salad plates or bowls; top with torn greens and apple wedges.

2 In a small screw-top jar combine cider vinegar, olive oil, pepper, and salt. Cover and shake well. Drizzle dressing over salad. Top each plate with about 1 tablespoon of the Herbed Nuts. Makes 6 side-dish servings.

Nutrition facts per serving: 132 cal., 10 g total fat (1 g sat. fat), 0 mg chol., 66 mg sodium, 11 g carbo., 3 g fiber, 2 g pro. *Daily values:* 11% vit. A, 23% vit. C, 4% calcium, 8% iron.

HERBED NUTS

Prep: 5 min. ♦ Bake: 15 min.

Beyond sprinkling these savory nuts on salads, try them on vegetables, cheese platters, or alone as a snack.

2 Tbsp. margarine or butter
2 Tbsp. Worcestershire sauce
1½ tsp. poultry seasoning

♦♦♦

2 cups coarsely chopped mixed nuts

1 In a small saucepan melt the margarine or butter over low heat. Remove from heat; stir in the Worcestershire sauce and the poultry seasoning.

2 Spread nuts in an 8×8×2-inch baking pan. Drizzle margarine or butter mixture over nuts; toss to coat well.

3 Bake in a 350° oven about 15 minutes or until toasted, stirring twice. Spread on foil; cool. Store in airtight container in a cool place for up to 1 week. Makes 2 cups.

TO MAKE AHEAD

Prepare and bake nuts as directed; cool. Place the cooled nuts in a freezer container and freeze for up to 3 months.

Nutrition facts per tablespoon: 117 cal., 10 g total fat (1 g sat. fat), 0 mg chol., 37 mg sodium, 5 g carbo., 1 g fiber, 3 g pro. *Daily values:* 1% vit. A, 5% vit. C, 1% calcium, 5% iron.

GREEK-STYLE VEGETABLE SALAD

Start to finish: 20 min.

Pour the lemony dressing on this garden-fresh salad just before serving or the crunchy, toasted pita bread pieces will get soggy. If you'd like, add a little crumbed feta cheese.

1 6-inch pita bread round, cut into bite-size pieces

♦♦♦

2 Tbsp. olive oil
2 Tbsp. lemon juice
1 clove garlic, minced
¼ tsp. salt
¼ tsp. lemon-pepper seasoning
1 cup chopped tomatoes
¾ cup chopped cucumber
¼ cup thinly sliced radishes

3 Tbsp. sliced green onion
3 Tbsp. snipped fresh mint
2 Tbsp. snipped fresh parsley

1 Place pita bread pieces on a baking sheet. Bake in a 350° oven 8 to 10 minutes or until toasted.

2 Meanwhile, in a screw-top jar combine olive oil, lemon juice, garlic, salt, and lemon-pepper seasoning. Cover and shake well; set aside.

3 In a large salad bowl combine the toasted pita bread, tomatoes, cucumber, radishes, green onion, mint, and parsley. Pour dressing over all; toss to coat. Serve immediately. Makes 4 side-dish servings.

Nutrition facts per serving: 121 cal., 7 g total fat (1 g sat. fat), 0 mg chol., 290 mg sodium, 13 g carbo., 1 g fiber, 2 g pro. *Daily values*: 6% vit. A, 37% vit. C, 2% calcium, 10% iron.

BLT Salad with Crostini

Start to finish: 30 min.

BLTs have been a part of the American food experience for decades, but crostini, savory grilled bread slices topped with tomato and garlic, are a more recent addition to our dining experience, and an inspired sidekick to the legendary combo.

⅓ **cup fat-free mayonnaise dressing or salad dressing**
4 **Tbsp. milk**
2 **Tbsp. chopped oil-packed dried tomatoes**

1 **clove garlic**
12 **thin slices baguette-style French bread**
6 **cups torn mixed salad greens**
3 **plum tomatoes, seeded and chopped (1 cup)**
1 **small cucumber, halved lengthwise and thinly sliced**
½ **cup cubed Muenster or mozzarella cheese (2 oz.)**
8 **slices turkey bacon, crisp-cooked, drained, and crumbled**

1 For dressing, in a blender container or food processor bowl combine mayonnaise or salad dressing, milk, dried tomatoes, and garlic. Cover and blend or process until the tomatoes and garlic are finely chopped. Set dressing aside.

2 Place bread slices on a baking sheet. Bake in a 450° oven about 5 minutes or until toasted. Turn slices over; spread with some of the dressing. Bake 3 minutes more; set aside.

3 Meanwhile, in a large salad bowl toss together salad greens, chopped tomato, cucumber, Muenster or mozzarella cheese, and bacon. Drizzle with dressing; toss lightly to coat. Serve with toasted bread slices. Makes 4 main-dish servings.

Nutrition facts per serving: 236 cal., 12 g total fat (5 g sat. fat), 33 mg chol., 913 mg sodium, 22 g carbo., 2 g fiber, 13 g pro. *Daily values*: 12% vit. A, 31% vit. C, 14% calcium, 10% iron.

Guide to Great Menus

You're in for rave reviews when you serve a meal that's nutritious, attractive, and delicious. A bit of organizing can help harmonize all parts of the meal.

First, think about the flavor of your main course. Usually one highly seasoned food at lunch or dinner is enough. For example, alongside hot and spicy chili offer a mild accompaniment, such as corn bread. If you're serving a delicate fish, be sure the other dishes don't overpower it. With most dinners, one starchy dish (potatoes, rice, pasta, beans, or corn) is plenty. Bread can be served anytime.

Next, consider the texture and temperature of the foods. It's best to serve some hot foods and some cold foods as well as soft and crisp foods.

Think visually, too. How will the foods look together on the plate? This includes color and shapes of ingredients. An all-white meal of poached fish, mashed potatoes, and bread pales next to poached fish with steamed green beans and rye rolls. Also, a meal with all the same shapes is less interesting than one with varying shapes.

Even when two recipes aren't served at the same time, consider how each dish adds character to the meal. Plan a dessert that rounds out dinner—a light sweet following a hearty meal or a rich dessert after a light entrée.

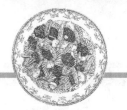

JOHN LECOQ'S
LOW-STRESS DINNERS

◆ Purchased pasta sauce with sautéed fresh vegetables stirred in and poured over pasta.

◆ An all-oven veggie meal that bakes potatoes together with such vegetables as squash, onions, turnips, and carrots.

◆ A frittata made with eggs gently cooked in a skillet with leftovers, such as ham, vegetables, or mushrooms.

FIREHOUSE MEAT LOAF

Prep: 20 min. ◆ Bake: 55 min.

*High-flavor ingredients—
such as prepared pasta sauce, sausage,
and provolone cheese—give
dishes depth and complexity without
requiring extra cooking time.
(See the photograph on page 197.)*

1 egg, beaten
1 cup soft bread crumbs
½ cup bottled pasta sauce with
   vegetables and/or herbs
1 to 2 cloves garlic, minced
½ tsp. dried rosemary, crushed
8 oz. Italian sausage or pork
   sausage links or ground
   beef
1 lb. ground beef
   ◆◆◆
2 oz. provolone or mozzarella
   cheese, cubed
   ◆◆◆
2 Tbsp. bottled pasta sauce
   with vegetables and/or
   herbs
2 Tbsp. shredded provolone or
   mozzarella cheese

1 In a large bowl combine egg, bread crumbs, the ½ cup pasta sauce, garlic, and rosemary. Remove casings from sausage, if using. Add ground beef and sausage; mix well. Press two-thirds of the mixture evenly in the bottom of an 8×4×2-inch loaf pan.

2 Make a ½-inch indentation down the center of the meat mixture. Place the cheese cubes in indentation. Pat remaining meat mixture evenly over top.

3 Bake, uncovered, in a 350° oven for 55 to 60 minutes until no pink remains and until a thermometer inserted in the thickest part of the loaf registers 170°. Let stand for 10 minutes.

4 To serve, transfer meat loaf to a platter. Drizzle top with the 2 tablespoons pasta sauce. Sprinkle with the 2 tablespoons shredded cheese. If desired, garnish with *fresh rosemary sprigs.* Makes 6 servings.

TO MAKE AHEAD

Prepare meat loaf as directed, except do not bake. Cover and chill for up to 24 hours. To serve, bake meat loaf, uncovered, about 1 hour or until no pink remains and a thermometer inserted into the thickest part of the meat loaf registers 170°.

Nutrition facts per serving: 328 cal., 21 g total fat (8 g sat. fat), 113 mg chol., 541 mg sodium, 8 g carbo., 0 g fiber, 25 g pro. *Daily values:* 9% vit. A, 9% vit. C, 10% calcium, 16% iron.

LOW FAT

FIREHOUSE POTATOES

Prep: 15 min. ◆ Cook: 20 min.

*Butter-browned onions give
the potatoes so much flavor that
gravy would be superfluous.
Heat the milk in a microwave oven
until hot, but do not boil.
(See the photograph on page 197.)*

2 lb. baking potatoes (such as
   russet, round white, or
   yellow), peeled and
   quartered
   ◆◆◆
1 cup chopped onion
4 cloves garlic, minced
2 Tbsp. margarine or butter
   ◆◆◆
½ tsp. salt
¼ tsp. coarsely ground black
   pepper
½ cup warmed milk

1 In a large saucepan cook potatoes, covered, in boiling, lightly salted water for 20 to 25 minutes or until tender; drain.

2 Meanwhile, in a saucepan cook onion and garlic in hot margarine or butter 10 to 12 minutes or until onion is lightly browned, stirring occasionally. Set aside.

3 Mash potatoes with a potato masher or beat with an electric mixer on low speed. Beat in browned onion-margarine mixture, salt, pepper, and enough warmed milk to make potatoes light and fluffy. If desired, season to taste with additional salt and pepper. Makes 6 servings.

Nutrition facts per serving: 213 cal., 4 g total fat (3 g sat. fat), 12 mg chol., 239 mg sodium, 40 g carbo., 2 g fiber, 5 g pro. *Daily values:* 4% vit. A, 40% vit. C, 4% calcium, 13% iron.

Top: *Nutty Apple Salad (page 194)*
Above: *Firehouse Meat loaf (page 196) and Firehouse Potatoes (page 196)*

Top: *Out-of-Town Salmon*
(page 192)
Right: *Real World Risotto*
(page 193)
Opposite page: *Mad-Dash Dinner*
Salad (page 192)

Top: *Corn Puffins (page 206)*
Above: *Fajita-Style Steak (page 206)*
Right: *Cranberry-Walnut Cabbage Slaw
(page 172)*
Opposite page: *Kabobs-N-Beans (page 179)*

Top: *Zucchini, Corn, and Potato Tacos (page 176)*
Above: *Banana-Chocolate Bites (page 220)*

Top: *Spicy Potato Pie (page 176)*
Above: *Roasted Potato Salad (page 171)*
Opposite page: *Almond Cake with Fresh Fruit (page 207)*

Left: *Roasted Summer Cherry Tomatoes (page 205)*
Below: *"Let Me Help" Kabobs (page 205)*

The Hopkins-Szostkowskis: Start with a BIG IDEA, then organize the details.

"I've always been a list maker," says Lynn Hopkins. It's a trait that serves her well, both in her architecture practice and in mealtime planning at her home in Lexington, Massachusetts. With two constantly-on-the-go daughters and an architect-husband who travels on business, the ability to plan and delegate dinner-hour tasks is essential.

"LET ME HELP" KABOBS
Prep: 30 min. ◆ Grill: 15 min.

A quick dip in fragrant herbs gives the vegetables the flavor benefits of a marinade in much less time. (See the photograph on page 204.)

12 oz. whole tiny new potatoes, halved, or small potatoes, quartered
⅓ cup finely snipped fresh parsley
2 Tbsp. finely snipped fresh oregano or 2 tsp. dried oregano
2 cloves garlic, minced
◆◆◆
2 medium yellow sweet peppers, seeded and cut into 2×1-inch strips (2 cups)
2 Tbsp. olive oil
◆◆◆
8 oz. cooked Polish sausage links, cut into 1½-inch bias slices
4 oz. cooked Italian sausage links, cut into 1½-inch bias slices

Honey mustard (optional)
Fresh oregano sprigs (optional)

1 In a medium saucepan cook potatoes, covered, in boiling salted water for 10 to 12 minutes or until just tender. Drain and set aside to cool slightly. Meanwhile, in a shallow dish stir together the snipped parsley, snipped oregano, and garlic; set aside.

2 Place potatoes and peppers in a bowl; drizzle with oil and toss to coat. Roll vegetables in the herb mixture, patting vegetables until lightly covered with herbs.

3 On six 12-inch skewers, alternately thread sausages, peppers, and potatoes, leaving about ¼ inch between the pieces.

4 In a grill with a cover, arrange preheated coals around a drip pan. Test for medium heat above the pan. Place kabobs on grill rack over drip pan. Cover and grill about 15 minutes or until sausage is heated through and peppers are just tender, turning once halfway through the grilling time. If desired, serve with honey mustard and garnish with oregano sprigs. Makes 6 servings.

Nutrition facts per serving: 293 cal., 22 g total fat (6 g sat. fat), 40 mg chol., 527 mg sodium, 16 g carbo., 1 g fiber, 9 g pro. *Daily values:* 2% vit. A, 136% vit. C, 3% calcium, 13% iron.

ROASTED SUMMER CHERRY TOMATOES
Prep: 20 min. ◆ Bake: 5 min.

See the photograph on page 204.

12 oz. cherry and/or other miniature tomatoes (such as plum or pear)
2 Tbsp. olive oil or cooking oil
¼ cup snipped fresh basil
1 Tbsp. minced garlic
¼ tsp. salt
⅛ tsp. pepper

1 Line a 13×9×2-inch baking pan with foil. Wash tomatoes; remove stems. Pat dry with paper towels. Pour the olive oil into prepared pan. Roll tomatoes in oil to coat. Sprinkle with snipped basil, garlic, salt, and pepper.

2 Bake in a 425° oven about 5 minutes or just until skins begin to split, stirring once. If desired, sprinkle with additional *snipped fresh basil* and garnish with *fresh basil sprigs.* Makes 4 to 6 servings.

Nutrition facts per serving: 85 cal., 7 g total fat (1 g sat. fat), 0 mg chol., 142 mg sodium, 6 g carbo., 1 g fiber, 1 g pro. *Daily values:* 5% vit. A, 29% vit. C, 1% calcium, 3% iron.

TESTING TEMPERATURE

To determine the temperature of the coals, carefully hold your hand, palm side down, above coals in the same location you plan to place the food for cooking. Count "one thousand one, one thousand two," etc., for as long as you can hold your hand there. Four seconds means coals are medium, as called for in the recipes below and on page 205.

FAJITA-STYLE STEAK

Prep: 15 min. ◆ Marinate: 30 min. Grill: 8 min.

You serve up double the flavor because the meat is marinated in lime, garlic, and cinnamon, then glazed with a sauce of red peppers, honey, mustard, and more garlic. (See the photograph on page 200.)

- 4 **boneless beef top sirloin steaks (2 lb. total)**
- ⅓ **cup lime juice**
- ¼ **cup cooking oil**
- 2 **cloves garlic, minced**
- 2 **tsp. ground cinnamon**

◆◆◆

- ½ **of a 7-oz. jar roasted red sweet peppers (½ cup), minced**
- ¼ **cup honey**
- ¼ **cup Dijon-style mustard**
- 2 **or 3 cloves garlic, minced**

1 Sprinkle meat with *salt* and *pepper.* Place in a plastic bag set in a shallow dish. For marinade, in a small bowl stir together lime juice, cooking oil, the 2 cloves garlic, and cinnamon. Pour over meat. Close bag. Marinate at room temperature for 30 minutes or in the refrigerator up to 6 hours, turning bag occasionally.

2 For glaze, in a small saucepan stir together red peppers, honey, Dijon-style mustard, and the 2 or 3 cloves garlic. Bring to boiling; reduce heat. Simmer, uncovered, for 5 to 7 minutes or until slightly thickened and reduced to ¾ cup. Remove from heat; set aside. Drain meat. Discard marinade.

3 Place steaks on the rack of an uncovered grill directly over medium coals; grill to desired doneness, turning once and brushing several times with glaze during the last half of the grilling time. (Allow 8 to 12 minutes for medium-rare and 12 to 15 minutes for medium.) To serve, slice and transfer the meat to dinner plates. Makes 4 servings.

TO BROIL

Place steaks on the unheated rack of a broiler pan. Broil 3 to 4 inches from the heat to desired doneness, turning once and brushing several times with glaze last half of broiling. (Allow 10 to 12 minutes for medium-rare or 12 to 15 minutes for medium.)

Nutrition facts per serving: 561 cal., 29 g total fat (10 g sat. fat), 151 mg chol., 188 mg sodium, 20 g carbo.,1 g fiber, 52 g pro. *Daily values:* 9% vit. A, 92% vit. C, 2% calcium, 42% iron.

30 MIN. LOW FAT

SESAME-TERIYAKI SEA BASS

Prep: 10 min. ◆ Cook: 8 min.

A simple teriyaki-flavored glaze and a sprinkling of sesame seed turns mild sea bass into an irresistible entrée. Add a rice pilaf and some buttered cooked carrots and you'll have a meal special enough for company.

- 4 **4-oz. fresh or frozen sea bass fillets, ½ to 1 inch thick**
- ¼ **tsp. pepper**

◆◆◆

- 3 **Tbsp. soy sauce**
- 3 **Tbsp. sweet rice wine (mirin)**
- 2 **Tbsp. dry white wine**
- 1½ **tsp. sugar**
- 1½ **tsp. honey**

◆◆◆

- 2 **tsp. cooking oil**
- 1 **Tbsp. toasted sesame seed or black sesame seed**

1 Thaw fish if frozen. Rinse fish; pat dry. Sprinkle fish with pepper; set aside.

2 In a small saucepan combine soy sauce, rice wine, white wine, sugar, and honey. Bring to boiling; reduce heat. Simmer, uncovered, for 10 minutes or until glaze is reduced to ¼ cup; set aside.

3 Meanwhile, in a large non-stick skillet heat the oil over medium heat. Add fillets. Fry fish on 1 side until golden. Allow 3 to 4 minutes per side for ½-inch- thick fillets (5 to 6 minutes per side for 1-inch-thick fillets). Turn carefully. Fry until second side is golden and fish flakes easily with a fork. Drain on paper towels.

4 To serve, transfer fish to a serving platter. Drizzle glaze over fillets. Sprinkle with sesame seed. Makes 4 servings.

Nutrition facts per serving: 185 cal., 6 g total fat (1 g sat. fat), 47 mg chol., 851 mg sodium, 6 g carbo., 0 g fiber, 22 g pro. *Daily values:* 5% vit. A, 4% vit. C, 1% calcium, 5% iron.

CORN PUFFINS

Prep: 15 min. ◆ Bake: 30 min.

Use nonstick cooking spray to ensure easy release of these airy muffins. In our Test Kitchen, oils and shortenings didn't work as well to prevent sticking. (See the photograph on page 200.)

Nonstick cooking spray
2 Tbsp. cornmeal
◆◆◆
3 eggs, beaten
1 cup milk
1 Tbsp. butter, melted
1 cup all-purpose flour
½ tsp. salt
¼ tsp. pepper
½ cup fresh* or frozen whole kernel corn, thawed
¼ cup thinly sliced green onions

1 Thoroughly spray twelve 2½-inch muffin cups with nonstick cooking spray. Sprinkle bottom and sides of each with cornmeal; set aside.

2 In a medium bowl beat eggs, milk, and butter with a rotary beater or wire whisk until combined. Add flour, salt, and pepper; beat until smooth. Stir in corn and green onions.

3 Spoon batter into prepared muffin cups, filling each two-thirds to three-fourths full. Bake in a 425° oven about 30 minutes or until deep golden brown. Remove from muffin cups and serve immediately. Makes 12.

*Note: If using fresh corn, remove husks from fresh ears. Scrub corn with a stiff brush to remove silks; rinse. Cut kernels from cob.

Nutrition facts per puffin: 85 cal., 3 g total fat (1 g sat. fat), 57 mg chol., 126 mg sodium, 11 g carbo., 1 g fiber, 4 g pro. *Daily values:* 5% vit. A, 1% vit. C, 2% calcium, 5% iron.

ALMOND CAKE WITH FRESH FRUIT

Prep: 10 min. ◆ Bake: 20 min.

One of our quickest, easiest cakes. (See the photograph on page 203.)

1 Tbsp. all-purpose flour
½ tsp. baking powder
½ tsp. finely shredded orange peel
◆◆◆
2 eggs
⅓ cup sugar
6 oz. whole unblanched almonds
◆◆◆
3 pears, peeled, cored, and halved, plus ½ cup chopped dried pears; or 2 cups fresh fruit and/or dried fruit

1 Grease and lightly flour one 8×1½-inch round baking pan; set pan aside. In a large bowl stir together the flour, baking powder, and orange peel; set aside.

LYNN HOPKINS' MUST-HAVES

◆ Fresh flowers add a special touch to any dinner table. In season, the girls, Alaina, 10, and Katherine, 8, are dispatched to the garden to pick a bouquet.
◆ Bottled teriyaki, barbecue, and other saucy kitchen helpers are brushed onto grilled meats.
◆ Refrigerated or frozen cheese-filled pastas, such as tortellini, make kid-pleasing additions to quick dinners.
◆ Pita bread takes to all kinds of fillings, from cold cuts to taco meat to summer veggies.

2 Place eggs and sugar in a blender container or food processor bowl. Cover and blend or process until smooth. Add nuts. Blend or process about 1 minute or until nearly smooth. Stir into the flour mixture. Spread batter evenly in prepared pan.

3 Bake in a 350° oven about 20 minutes or until lightly browned. Cool cake in pan on wire rack for 10 minutes. Remove cake from pan. Cool thoroughly on wire rack.

4 To serve, cut cake into wedges. Arrange fruit and cake in dessert bowls. Makes 6 servings.

Nutrition facts per serving: 272 cal., 17 g total fat (2 g sat. fat), 71 mg chol., 65 mg sodium, 26 g carbo., 4 g fiber, 8 g pro. *Daily values:* 3% vit. A, 4% vit. C, 9% calcium, 10% iron.

FOOD IN A FLASH

Families from all over the country share their secrets for subtracting stress and adding magic to mealtimes. Read on for some of their best tips on foods to fix quickly.

◆ Frozen pizzas, which are better than ever, are the favorite of Jill Witt Pertler, of Cloquet, Minnesota. She heaps a frozen pizza with vegetables and extra cheese. "I layer it with chopped sweet peppers, corn, and broccoli, and then top it with additional mozzarella."

◆ Boxes of pilaf mix figure prominently in the pantry of Milan, Illinois, resident Anne Colville; she mixes cubed raw skinless chicken breast meat with one of the mixes, and cooks for the time noted on the package. After adding a salad or vegetables, dinner is done.

◆ "When in doubt, do tacos," says Maryellyn Krantz, a Better Homes and Gardens® home economist and mother of two. "They're quick, easy, and everybody seems to like them. Whenever my kids have friends over who have iffy eating habits, tacos are a safe bet."

LOW FAT
CITRUS-HONEY SWORDFISH

Prep: 15 min. ◆ Marinate: 1 hr.
Grill: 8 min.

1 lb. fresh or frozen swordfish
   steaks, 1 inch thick
¼ cup orange juice
2 Tbsp. lemon juice

2 Tbsp. Dijon-style mustard
2 Tbsp. honey
1 Tbsp. soy sauce
◆◆◆
4 oz. vermicelli

1 Thaw fish if frozen. Rinse fish; pat dry. Cut fish into 4 portions. Place fish in a plastic bag set in a shallow dish. For marinade, combine orange juice, lemon juice, mustard, honey, and soy sauce. Pour over fish; close bag. Marinate in refrigerator 1 hour, turning bag occasionally.

2 Drain fish, reserving marinade. Lightly brush a grill rack with oil. Grill fish on the prepared rack of an uncovered grill directly over medium coals 8 to 12 minutes or until fish just begins to flake easily with a fork, turning once and brushing once with reserved marinade halfway through. Bring remaining marinade to boil; remove from heat.

3 Meanwhile, cook vermicelli according to package directions. Drain; toss with heated marinade. Serve with fish. Makes 4 servings.

Nutrition facts per serving: 303 cal., 6 g total fat (1 g sat. fat), 34 mg chol., 550 mg sodium, 34 g carbo., 1 g fiber, 27 g pro. *Daily values:* 3% vit. A, 20% vit. C, 1% calcium, 14% iron.

MANGO-SAUCED SNAPPER

Start to finish: 25 min.

4 fresh or frozen skinless red
   snapper fillets (about
   1½ lb. total)
¼ tsp. crushed red pepper

◆◆◆
1 Tbsp. margarine or butter
½ cup finely chopped onion
1½ tsp. cornstarch
¼ tsp. crushed red pepper
⅔ cup chicken broth
1 cup chopped, peeled, and
   seeded mango
¼ cup dried tart red cherries,
   cut up
◆◆◆
2 Tbsp. margarine or butter
◆◆◆
Lime wedges

1 Thaw fish if frozen. Rinse fish; pat dry. Sprinkle fish with the ¼ teaspoon crushed red pepper; set aside.

2 In a small saucepan melt the 1 tablespoon margarine or butter; add onion and cook until tender. Stir in cornstarch and ¼ teaspoon crushed red pepper. Add chicken broth all at once. Cook and stir until thickened and bubbly. Add mango and cherries; cook 2 minutes more. Remove from heat; set aside.

3 In a 12-inch nonstick skillet cook fish in the 2 tablespoons hot margarine over medium-high heat 2 to 3 minutes per side or until fish just begins to flake easily when tested with a fork.

4 To serve, arrange fish on a serving platter. Spoon fruit sauce atop fish. Serve with lime wedges. Makes 4 servings.

Nutrition facts per serving: 322 cal., 11 g total fat (2 g sat. fat), 18 mg chol., 309 mg sodium, 18 g carbo., 2 g fiber, 37 g pro. *Daily values:* 36% vit. A, 25% vit. C, 5% calcium, 3% iron.

Pecan Salmon with Sweet Pepper Mayo

Prep: 25 min. ◆ Chill: 30 min.
Cook: 6 min.

The fish cooks to moist, tender perfection in its crunchy cocoon of bread crumbs and nuts.

1½ lb. skinless salmon fillet
¾ cup finely chopped pecans
½ cup fine dry bread crumbs
½ to 1 tsp. black pepper
½ tsp. salt
1 egg
2 Tbsp. water
⅓ cup all-purpose flour

◆◆◆

½ of a 7-oz. jar roasted red
    sweet peppers (about
    ½ cup), drained
¼ cup mayonnaise or salad
    dressing
1 Tbsp. mango chutney, finely
    chopped
1 Tbsp. lemon juice
¼ tsp. garlic salt
⅛ tsp. ground red pepper

◆◆◆

2 Tbsp. cooking oil

1 Slice fish in half horizontally so that it is of nearly an even thickness (about ½ inch thick). Cut fish into 6 equal portions. In a shallow dish combine pecans, bread crumbs, black pepper, and salt. In another dish beat together egg and water; place flour in a third dish. Coat each fish portion with flour, then dip in egg mixture, and finally in pecan mixture. Place portions on a large plate; cover and chill for up to 30 minutes while preparing sweet pepper mayonnaise.

2 Meanwhile, pat the drained, roasted peppers dry on paper towels; chop coarsely. In a small serving bowl stir together chopped peppers, mayonnaise, chutney, lemon juice, garlic salt, and ground red pepper. Set aside.

3 In a 12-inch nonstick skillet heat cooking oil over medium-high heat. Add fish; cook 3 minutes. Turn fish; cook 3 to 4 minutes more or until fish just flakes easily when tested with a fork. (Reduce heat as necessary during cooking to prevent overbrowning.) Serve with sweet pepper mayonnaise. Makes 6 servings.

Nutrition facts per serving: 379 cal., 26 g total fat (4 g sat. fat), 61 mg chol., 457 mg sodium, 17 g carbo., 2 g fiber, 20 g pro. *Daily values:* 11% vit. A, 59% vit. C, 2% calcium, 13% iron.

Red Pepper and Snapper Soup

Start to finish: 50 min.

2 Tbsp. olive oil
3 medium red sweet peppers,
    coarsely chopped
1 cup chopped shallots or
    onions
3 14½-oz. cans reduced-
    sodium chicken broth

◆◆◆

¼ tsp. salt
¼ tsp. ground black pepper
⅛ tsp. ground red pepper
1¼ lb. skinless red snapper or
    orange roughy fillets, cut
    into 1-inch pieces
½ cup snipped fresh Italian
    parsley

Red Pepper and Snapper Soup
(see left)

◆◆◆

Crusty Italian bread

◆◆◆

Caesar salad

◆◆◆

White wine

1 In a large saucepan or Dutch oven heat oil. Cook sweet peppers and shallots in hot oil over medium heat for 5 minutes. Carefully add 1 can of the broth. Bring to boiling; reduce heat. Simmer, covered, about 20 minutes, until peppers are very tender. Remove from heat; cool slightly.

2 Pour half of the sweet pepper mixture into blender container. Cover and blend until nearly smooth. Pour into a medium bowl. Repeat with remaining pepper mixture. Return all to saucepan. Add remaining chicken broth, salt, ground black pepper, and ground red pepper. Bring mixture to boiling; reduce heat. Add fish to broth mixture. Simmer, covered, about 5 minutes or until fish just flakes easily with a fork, stirring once or twice. Stir in snipped parsley.

3 To serve, ladle soup into bowls. Garnish with *parsley sprigs*. Makes 5 main-dish servings.

Nutrition facts per serving: 223 cal., 8 g total fat (1 g sat. fat), 42 mg chol., 859 mg sodium, 10 g carbo., 0 g fiber, 27 g pro. *Daily values:* 76% vit. A, 142% vit. C, 5% calcium, 8% iron.

ADULT DIETS—NO KIDS ALLOWED

A diet perfect for a 40-year-old is not suitable for an energetic 3-year-old.

Getting little ones to eat right is a monumental task, and knowing just what to do may not always be clear. Understanding a few basic approaches to feeding small children will help you provide your kids with a nutritious diet, without making things needlessly—or unhealthily—complicated.

Many parents falsely assume all fat is bad. They go to painstaking lengths to eliminate it from their children's menus. Meanwhile, recent health surveys reveal that many of our children are making do on diets chronically deficient in vital nutrients. Yet childhood obesity in this country is continuing to climb at an appalling rate.

"Obesity isn't the same as overnutrition," explains Dr. Fima Lifshitz, child nutrition researcher and chief of staff at Miami Children's Hospital. "Kids can be overweight yet still be precariously short on important nutrients, such as iron, zinc, folate, and calcium. Basically, our children are eating plenty but not eating well."

WHAT'S GOOD FOR THE GOOSE MAY NOT BE GOOD FOR THE GOSLING

A diet plan perfect for an occasionally active 40-year-old is entirely unsuitable for a tirelessly energetic 3-year-old. Many infants and toddlers are not having their energy needs met because of their parents' fear of fat—a fear based on information never meant to apply to small children. Isabel Vazquez, clinical dietitian at Children's Hospital in Boston, frequently observes children failing to thrive because of restrictive, reduced-fat diets. "Such fat-modified diets can be lacking in total calories, protein, minerals, and other nutrients necessary for growth and development," says Vazquez.

Children, especially infants and toddlers, should eat a low-fat diet only if a diagnosed condition warrants it. The appropriate diet is one that includes a selection of different foods and has sufficient fat for developing nerve and brain tissues. Until they're toddlers (about 2 or 3 years of age), children need about 40 percent of their calories from fat, with most of the fat in the form of mono- and polyunsaturated fats (from vegetables, nuts, legumes, fish and their oils, and breast milk). After 3 years, fat calories can be gradually reduced to about one-third of the total. But if your kids are eating a variety of foods, especially fruits, vegetables, and grains, there's no need to be a kiddie calorie counter.

Because of the low-fat craze, hundreds of fat-modified products are pushed on kids. "Children can overindulge on fat-free products because there is little sense of fullness after eating," says Connie Roberts, a dietitian at Brigham and Women's Hospital in Boston. "Foods such as snack cakes, low-fat chips, and fat-free cookies replace more beneficial foods containing vitamins, minerals, protein, and fiber. Better selections would be fresh fruit, peanut butter, and other healthier items," she suggests.

Other common sources of non-nourishing calories are soft drinks and sugar-heavy juice drinks. Children are the most profuse consumers of these beverages. Richard Mattes, Ph.D., R.D., and professor of foods and nutrition at Purdue University, completed a 12-week study comparing the food intake and body weight of 15 people eating 450 extra calories a day—either from candy or soft drinks. The candy-eating group ate fewer calories later on in the day, while the soft-drink group did not adjust their intake and gained weight. Mattes says that although such research is preliminary, it indicates that drinking your calories may not give you the same feeling of fullness as eating them in the form of solid foods.

What to Do About Overweight Kids

"Lifestyle changes, such as restrictive diets or avoidance of certain foods, are rarely necessary for children. No one has proven that such approaches are helpful in reducing childhood obesity," says Dr. Lifshitz. More and more research is showing that low-fat diets don't necessarily lead to weight loss. Total calorie consumption and energy expenditure are keys to effectively reducing weight and keeping it off.

"With children, the goal is to grow the child into his or her size by increasing physical activity and keeping food intake normal," says Dr. Johanna Dwyer, director of the Frances Stern Nutrition Center at Tufts-New England Medical Center. "Don't think of your child as a miniature adult. Little children should not go on restricted, fat-phobic diets." The goal should be to maintain their current weight while they continue to grow taller.

Put emphasis on physical activity, such as biking or playing ball, with a goal of at least 30 minutes a day, five times per week. Getting kids outdoors and away from the television set is good for their health, plus it keeps them from being bombarded by ads for less nutritious foods. Seriously obese children should follow a moderate weight balance and exercise program under the supervision of a registered dietitian and pediatrician.

Broadening a child's eating and exercise horizons should be a gradual process. Begin with the easy changes, then follow with the harder ones. These steps will start you in the right direction.

◆ Make children active participants in menu choosing, food shopping, and meal preparation. Teach your kids how to clean vegetables, make salads, and safely use age-appropriate tools and appliances. Children who have basic cooking skills not only appreciate food more, they are more willing to experiment and try new foods.

◆ Kids need exercise throughout the day, so encourage—and make time for—fun physical activities. Join your children in hiking, biking, swimming, and other appropriate sports.

◆ If your child shuns vegetables or fruits, stock up your menu arsenal with fun and attractive vegetable or fruit dishes taken from kid-tested cookbooks.

◆ When you are faced with a picky eater or a tot who finds a food he or she likes and sticks to for days, don't cut off the favored foods. Instead of using a restrictive approach, try introducing new foods with the favored ones to increase variety. And be patient. Kids are just like adults—they have their own personal sets of likes and dislikes. Some children may need 8 to 12 exposures to a new food before they develop a taste for it.

◆ Communicate consistent and positive messages about food and specific food items. Adults, particularly parents, are a major influence on their kids' behavior. Avoid fad diets and food phobias, and your children will be more likely to do the same.

—Kathy McManus, M.S., R.D., is the clinical nutrition manager at Brigham and Women's Hospital/Harvard Medical School in Boston.

SURVIVAL STRATEGIES

Families share their ideas for preparing family meals, in short order and with great taste, while juggling work and recreation schedules.

◆ Put cooking first on your to-do list; you'll be surprised how quickly your meal will be ready. It's easy to burn up half an hour reading the mail, checking phone messages, and feeding the cat. But save those everyday chores for later.

◆ Forego the guilt. Jan Miller, *Better Homes and Gardens* magazine registered dietitian, notes that an occasional bowl of cereal for dinner is actually good for a child. "Cereals are fortified, and you're also providing them with a serving of milk. One day isn't going to make or break you nutritionally."

◆ Stock up on easy-cooking pantry staples to serve as the foundation for meals, such as frozen mashed potatoes, couscous, and boil-in-bag rice, says Helen Wolt, of Colorado Springs, Colorado.

◆ Unless you're already doing it successfully, don't bother trying to cook ahead and freeze meals that you think you'll thaw later. The busy, but organized, people we talked to said that the food just sat in their freezer. Many also said it was just too time-consuming. "I tried it for a couple of months, but I was using up my whole Sunday," says Daphne Knudson, of Bridgewater, Massachusetts.

◆ "Know thyself" when dividing cooking chores. If someone loves to show off his knife skills, give him chopping duty. Let the family organizer come up with menus. Get kids in the loop by giving them such simple tasks as setting the table—gradually adding to their responsibilities as their skill levels increase.

ITALIAN PASTA AND TUNA BAKE

Prep: 25 min. ◆ Bake: 20 min.

Move over, tuna noodle casserole. This new creamy pasta and tuna dish will soon become the family favorite.

12 oz. penne or rotini pasta
8 oz. tuna steaks, cut into ¾-inch cubes

◆◆◆

½ cup soft bread crumbs
¼ cup pine nuts
2 Tbsp. margarine or butter, melted
3 medium zucchini, sliced (1 lb.)
½ cup chopped onion
2 cloves garlic, minced
3 Tbsp. olive oil
⅓ cup all-purpose flour
1½ cups milk
1½ cups chicken broth

⅓ cup snipped dried tomatoes (not oil-packed)
1 tsp. dried rosemary, crushed
¼ tsp. salt

1 Cook pasta in boiling salted water according to package directions, adding tuna the last 6 minutes of cooking. Drain, return to saucepan, and set aside.

2 Meanwhile, in a small bowl combine the bread crumbs, pine nuts, and melted margarine or butter; set aside. For sauce, in a large saucepan cook the zucchini, onion, and garlic in hot oil until tender. Stir in flour. Add milk and broth all at once. Cook and stir until thickened and bubbly. Remove from heat. Stir in dried tomatoes, rosemary, and salt. Pour the sauce over pasta-tuna mixture in saucepan; stir to coat pasta.

Transfer to a 2-quart casserole. Sprinkle with crumb mixture.

3 Bake, uncovered, in a 375° oven about 20 minutes or until topping is golden. Serves 6.

Nutrition facts per serving: 502 cal., 19 g total fat (4 g sat. fat), 20 mg chol., 460 mg sodium, 60 g carbo., 3 g fiber, 24 g pro. *Daily values:* 24% vit. A, 9% vit. C, 9% calcium, 27% iron.

30 MIN.

PAN-SEARED SALMON WITH WARM RASPBERRY VINAIGRETTE

Prep: 20 min. ◆ Cook: 8 min.

4 4-oz. fresh or frozen skinless salmon fillets, ¾ inch thick
3 Tbsp. seedless raspberry jam
¼ tsp. salt

¼ tsp. dry mustard
¼ tsp. dried thyme, crushed
¼ tsp. garlic pepper

◆◆◆

6 cups torn mixed greens
1 small cucumber, halved
  lengthwise and thinly
  sliced (1 cup)
¼ cup shredded radishes

◆◆◆

3 Tbsp. olive oil
3 Tbsp. vinegar
2 Tbsp. chopped toasted
  pecans

1 Thaw fish, if frozen. Rinse fish; pat dry. In a small saucepan combine jam, salt, mustard, thyme, and garlic pepper. Heat and stir just until jelly is melted. Divide mixture in half. Set half of the mixture aside. Brush fish with remaining jelly mixture.

2 Divide greens, cucumber, and radishes among 4 salad plates; set aside.

3 In a large nonstick skillet heat 2 tablespoons of the oil over medium-high heat; add fish. Cook fish on 1 side for 4 to 5 minutes or until golden. Turn carefully. Cook for 4 to 5 minutes more or until fish flakes easily with a fork.

4 To serve, place 1 fish fillet atop greens on each plate. Add remaining 1 tablespoon oil, remaining raspberry mixture, and the vinegar to skillet; bring just to boiling. Drizzle dressing atop salads. Sprinkle with nuts. Serves 4.

Nutrition facts per serving: 273 cal., 16 g total fat, 20 mg chol., 212 mg sodium, 15 g carbo., 2 g fiber, 18 g pro.
Daily values: 5% vit. A, 9% vit. C, 3% calcium, 11% iron.

SEARED SCALLOP & SPINACH SALAD
Prep: 20 min. ◆ Cook: 7 min.

Give an old favorite a new lease on life by adding sea scallops to the usual lineup in a bacon-spinach salad. The scallops are dusted with chili powder and red pepper before searing—a guaranteed wake-up call for eaters.

8 oz. sea scallops
8 cups torn fresh spinach
2 cups sliced fresh mushrooms
1 cup shredded carrots

◆◆◆

4 slices bacon, cut into ½-inch
  pieces

◆◆◆

½ tsp. chili powder
⅛ to ¼ tsp. ground red pepper
¼ to ⅓ cup chutney, snipped
¼ cup water
1 to 2 tsp. Dijon-style mustard

1 Rinse scallops; pat dry. Set scallops aside. In a large bowl toss together spinach, mushrooms, and carrots; set aside.

2 In a large nonstick skillet cook bacon over medium heat until crisp. Drain bacon, reserving 1 tablespoon drippings in skillet.

3 In a medium bowl combine chili powder and ground red pepper; add scallops, tossing lightly to coat. Cook scallops in reserved bacon drippings over medium heat for 1 to 3 minutes or until scallops turn opaque. Remove scallops from skillet; set aside. Add chutney, water, and mustard to skillet. Cook over medium-high heat until hot and bubbly. Spoon chutney mixture over spinach mixture, tossing lightly.

THAT SPECIAL TOUCH

With only a few minutes to spare you can make a humdrum meal exciting while you also brighten someone's day. Read on for tips on little extras that make meals more enjoyable.

◆ Let family members know how much you care with little love notes tucked in lunch bags. Or personalize everyday objects—for instance, create instant place cards with dinner napkins.

◆ Take stock of what's in your pantry and the family's emotions before you plunge into dinner making. "I decide what to cook depending on what I've got on hand, and what mood everyone is in," says Holly Duttera, of Huron, Ohio. "If one of my kids has had a bad day at school, I don't want to complicate things by serving food he detests. It's less stress on me and on them to serve what they like."

◆ Give children ways to make the meal their own. Devon Delaney, of Princeton, New Jersey, gives each of her kids his own bottle of salad dressing. "For some reason that's gotten them to eat salad," she says. "Each gets their own thing, so I'm not the waitress."

4 Divide spinach mixture among 4 plates. Top with scallops and bacon. Makes 4 servings.

Nutrition facts per serving: 160 cal., 4 g total fat (1 g sat. fat), 22 mg chol., 324 mg sodium, 19 g carbo., 5 g fiber, 14 g pro.
Daily values: 154% vit. A, 63% vit. C, 13% calcium, 32% iron.

OF SPROUTING CONCERN

Alfalfa sprouts have a decades-old reputation as a health food. But all is not perfect in the world of sprouts. Alfalfa sprouts are now being associated with something far from healthy—foodborne illness.

Health officials have linked alfalfa sprouts to 10 foodborne illness outbreaks in the United States in the past few years alone. In 1997, contaminated alfalfa sprouts were responsible for four outbreaks, three of which involved E. coli 015:H7, a particularly dangerous strain of bacteria. This type of E. coli has killed scores of people in outbreaks involving other foods, such as ground beef. In 1998, salmonella-contaminated alfalfa sprouts made 60 people ill in California.

The Centers for Disease Control in Atlanta (CDC) and the Food and Drug Administration (FDA) advise that persons at risk for illness from contaminated food (such as children, the elderly, and those with compromised immune systems) should avoid eating raw alfalfa sprouts. The outbreaks have been associated only with alfalfa sprouts. But because some other leafy sprouts, such as radish and wheat sprouts, are grown in the same manner, they also may be vulnerable to the same safety issues.

Collectively, the FDA, the CDC, and the alfalfa sprout industry have kicked in a plan of action to solve the problem. They're looking into the ways sprouts are grown, washed, and packaged. Seed and sprout samples also are being randomly analyzed for their bacteria content.

The seeds from which the sprouts grow are often the source of contamination, so efforts to make sprouts safe are focused first on the sanitation of the seeds themselves. When tainted seeds sprout, the problem escalates. "The sprouting process generates nutrients and heat, providing an ideal environment for bacteria to flourish," says the CDC's Thomas Breuer, M.D.

The industry is hard at work to produce as safe a product as technology allows. Breuer notes, "The sprout industry has been 100 percent compliant with all that we have requested." A voluntary quality assurance program was initiated to ensure that sprout growers follow good growing and processing practices. This program—which includes a third-party audit or inspection—will certify the growers who sanitize their sprout seeds, according to The International Sprout Growers Association (ISGA). Growers who successfully participate can label their sprouts with an ISGA-certified grower's seal.

Rinsing sprouts thoroughly with clean water will minimize the growth of harmful bacteria, although it will not totally eliminate bacteria. But there are several precautions a wise consumer can take before buying and eating all varieties of sprouts.

◆ Pay attention to the sell-by date that is printed on the package.

◆ Check to see if the roots are clean. The stems should appear white or cream in color.

◆ Avoid any sprouts with yellowing or graying roots and signs of rot.

◆ Give sprouts the sniff test—fresh sprouts have a clean, fresh aroma.

Keep sprouts refrigerated, and use them within a few days. Finally, wash hands with warm, soapy water before and after handling all foods.

SWEET 'N' PEPPERY COUNTRY-STYLE RIBS

Prep: 15 min. ♦ Cook: 4 hr.

Although not hot enough to be considered Szechwan, three kinds of pepper give these Chinese-style ribs their kick.

3½ **lb. pork country-style ribs**

♦♦♦

6 **green onions, chopped**
¼ **cup reduced-sodium soy sauce**
¼ **cup molasses**
2 **Tbsp. hoisin sauce**
2 **Tbsp. packed brown sugar**
2 **Tbsp. white wine vinegar**
2 **tsp. toasted sesame oil**
2 **tsp. lemon juice**
½ **tsp. bottled hot pepper sauce**
½ **tsp. ground ginger**
½ **tsp. garlic powder**
½ **tsp. chili powder**
¼ **tsp. ground red pepper**
¼ **tsp. ground black pepper**

♦♦♦

2 **cups hot cooked rice**

1 Place ribs in a 3½- to 4-quart electric crockery cooker, cutting as necessary to fit.

2 For sauce, in a small bowl combine green onions, soy sauce, molasses, hoisin sauce, brown sugar, vinegar, toasted sesame oil, lemon juice, hot pepper sauce, ginger, garlic powder, chili powder, ground red pepper, and ground black pepper. Pour the sauce over the ribs in cooker, turning to coat.

3 Cover and cook on low-heat setting for 8 to 10 hours or on high-heat setting for 4 to 5 hours. Transfer ribs to serving platter. Strain sauce; skim off fat. Serve sauce over ribs and hot cooked rice. Makes 6 servings.

Nutrition facts per serving: 532 cal., 31 g total fat (11 g sat. fat), 69 mg chol., 511 mg sodium, 32 g carbo., 0 g fiber, 30 g pro. *Daily values:* 3% vit. A, 6% vit. C, 3% calcium, 18% iron.

Sweet 'n' Peppery Country-Style Rib Sandwiches: Prepare the ribs as directed at left, except omit the hot cooked rice. Remove the cooked meat from the bones. Using 2 forks, pull meat apart into shreds. To serve, add meat to split and toasted, large sesame buns or kaiser rolls. Serve the strained sauce on the side. Makes 8 to 10 sandwiches.

PUB PORK

Start to finish: 30 minutes

In England and Ireland, "pub grub" merits respect that bar food on this side of the Atlantic rarely achieves. The best pub grub is found in the countryside. Try this recipe using dark beer or stout.

4 **boneless pork loin chops, cut ¾ inch thick (1¼ lb.)**
1 **Tbsp. cooking oil**

♦♦♦

1 **cup dark beer**
2 **cups parsnips sliced ½ to 1 inch thick**
2 **cups sliced fresh button or crimini mushrooms**
2 **cloves garlic, minced**
1 **Tbsp. brown sugar**
1 **Tbsp. Dijon-style mustard**
¼ **tsp. salt**
⅛ **tsp. pepper**

♦♦♦

Hot cooked rice (optional)
Snipped fresh parsley (optional)

Pub Pork
(see left)

♦♦♦

Sauteed greens and garlic

♦♦♦

Rye bread with butter

♦♦♦

Dark beer

♦♦♦

Gingered Shortcake with Spiced Fruit
(see page 220)

1 In a large skillet cook pork chops in hot oil over medium-high heat for 8 to 10 minutes or until pork is just pink in center and juices run clear, turning once. Remove chops; keep warm. Drain off any fat from skillet.

2 Add the dark beer, parsnips, button or crimini mushrooms, garlic, brown sugar, Dijon-style mustard, salt, and pepper to the skillet. Bring just to boiling; reduce heat. Simmer, uncovered, about 15 minutes or until liquid is reduced to desired consistency and vegetables are tender. Return pork to skillet; heat through.

3 To serve, transfer a pork chop and a portion of the vegetables to each of 4 dinner plates. If desired, serve with hot cooked rice and sprinkle with parsley. Makes 4 servings.

Nutrition facts per serving: 315 cal., 13 g total fat (4 g sat. fat), 64 mg chol., 291 mg sodium, 23 g carbo., 4 g fiber, 22 g pro. *Daily values:* 1% vit. A, 24% vit. C, 3% calcium, 13% iron.

HAM AND CHEESE PIZZA STACKS

Prep: 15 min. ◆ Bake: 12 min.

Personalize these stacks as much as you please—substitute pepperoni, mushrooms, or other chopped veggies for the ham.

¼ cup purchased pesto
12 7- to 8-inch flour tortillas
8 oz. finely chopped cooked ham
2 cups shredded mozzarella cheese (8 oz.)
1 8-oz. can pizza sauce or ½ cup Alfredo pasta sauce

1 Spread the pesto over 4 of the tortillas. Top each with a second tortilla. Stir together the ham and half of the cheese. Sprinkle over second layer of tortillas. Top with remaining tortillas. Spread top layer with pizza sauce or Alfredo sauce and sprinkle with remaining cheese.

2 Place stacks on an ungreased baking sheet. Bake in a 425° oven for 12 to 15 minutes or until cheese is melted. To serve, cut stacks into wedges. Makes 8 main-dish servings.

Nutrition facts per serving: 354 cal., 15 g total fat (4 g sat. fat), 32 mg chol., 946 mg sodium, 34 g carbo., 0 g fiber, 19 g pro. *Daily values:* 11% vit. A, 21% vit. C, 21% calcium, 14% iron.

HAWAIIAN-STYLE BARBECUE PIZZA

Prep: 20 min. ◆ Bake: 10 min.

Deli-roasted chicken, a bread shell, and fresh pineapple chunks make assembling this pizza a breeze.

1 16-oz. Italian bread shell (Boboli)
½ cup bottled barbecue sauce
1 cup shredded pizza cheese
1 to 1½ cups deli-roasted chicken cut into strips or chunks (about ½ of a chicken)
1 cup fresh pineapple chunks*
1 papaya, peeled, seeded, and sliced
1 medium green sweet pepper, cut into thin strips
¼ of a small red or yellow onion, thinly sliced and separated into rings

1 Place bread shell on an ungreased baking sheet. Spread with barbecue sauce. Sprinkle with ½ cup of the cheese. Arrange chicken, pineapple, papaya, sweet pepper, and onion on top. Sprinkle with remaining cheese.

2 Bake in a 425° oven 10 minutes or until heated through. Cut into wedges. Serves 4.

*Note: To save time, buy peeled pineapple in the produce section of your supermarket. Or, use one 8-ounce can pineapple chunks, drained.

Nutrition facts per serving: 513 cal., 15 g total fat (4 g sat. fat), 55 mg chol., 1,040 mg sodium, 65 g carbo., 4 g fiber, 32 g pro. *Daily values:* 18% vit. A, 113% vit. C, 27% calcium, 22% iron.

PRIZE TESTED RECIPE WINNER

GREEK-STYLE PARTY PIZZAS

Prep: 15 min. ◆ Bake: 8 min.

If you can't find 6-inch pita rounds, use a larger size, but split them in half horizontally.

4 6-inch pita bread rounds
1 7-oz. container hummus
1 medium tomato, seeded and chopped
½ of a 6½-oz. jar marinated artichoke hearts, drained and chopped
½ cup crumbled feta cheese (2 oz.)
½ cup shredded mozzarella cheese (2 oz.)
2 tsp. olive oil (optional)
1 tsp. sesame seed (optional)

◆◆◆

8 pitted ripe olives, quartered (optional)
Fresh oregano leaves (optional)

1 Place pita rounds on a large baking sheet. Spread each with one-fourth of the hummus, leaving a 1-inch border. Sprinkle each with one-fourth of the tomatoes, artichoke hearts, feta, and mozzarella. If desired, drizzle with oil and sprinkle with sesame seed.

2 Bake in a 450° oven for 8 to 10 minutes or until cheese has melted and edges are lightly browned. If desired, top with olives and oregano. Cut in quarters. Makes 16 snack-size servings.

Nutrition facts per serving: 87 cal., 3 g total fat (1 g sat. fat), 5 mg chol., 184 mg sodium, 12 g carbo., 0 g fiber, 3 g pro. *Daily values:* 1% vit. A, 6% vit. C, 5% calcium, 4% iron.

PIZZAZZY LITTLE PIZZAS

One of the pizzazziest little party foods in town is bound to be the hit of your next gathering. Like magic, one sheet of purchased pizza dough turns into six petite pizzas. These single-serving pizzas are custom-made so family and friends pick their own toppings. Choose from the flavor combinations given here, or put on your creative cooking hat and design pizzettas all your own.

PIZZETTAS

1 **10-oz. pkg. refrigerated**
   pizza dough
   Desired toppings (see below and right)

1 Lightly grease a large baking sheet; set aside.

2 Unroll the pizza dough onto a lightly floured surface. Using a lightly floured rolling pin, roll dough into a 13½×9-inch rectangle. Cut dough into six 4½-inch squares. Place squares about 1 inch apart on the prepared baking sheet. Add a decorative edge to each pizza by using the tines of a fork or crimping the dough with your fingers.

3 Prebake the dough squares in a 425° oven for 4 to 5 minutes or until lightly browned. Top as suggested below or as desired. Bake about 5 to 6 minutes more or until toppings are heated through. Makes 6 pizzettas.

Shrimp, Tomato, and Cheese: For each pizzetta, place 4 or 5 thin slices of plum tomato on the prebaked crust. Top with 2 or 3 peeled and deveined, cooked medium shrimp, halved lengthwise; 1 teaspoon snipped fresh oregano; and, if desired, a dash of crushed red pepper. Sprinkle pizzetta with 2 tablespoons shredded four-cheese Italian blend cheese or mozzarella cheese.

Nutrition facts per pizzetta: 135 cal., 2 g total fat (1 g sat. fat), 11 mg chol., 287 mg sodium, 23 g carbo., 1 g fiber, 6 g pro. *Daily values:* 1% vit. A, 4% vit. C, 1% calcium, 8% iron.

Three Cheese and Herb: For each pizzetta, sprinkle 2 tablespoons shredded mozzarella cheese, 2 tablespoons shredded Gouda cheese or fontina cheese, 1 tablespoon crumbled blue cheese, and a dash of freshly ground pepper on prebaked crust. Top with 1 to 2 teaspoons snipped fresh herbs (such as basil, thyme, or sage) after baking.

Nutrition facts per pizzetta: 150 cal., 4 g total fat (2 g sat. fat), 8 mg chol., 333 mg sodium, 22 g carbo., 1 g fiber, 6 g pro. *Daily values:* 1% vit. A, 4% calcium, 6% iron.

Spicy Shredded Pork: For each pizzetta, spread 2 tablespoons salsa on the prebaked crust to within ½ inch of edges. Top with 2 tablespoons shredded cooked pork, 1 tablespoon rinsed and drained canned black beans, and 2 tablespoons shredded Chihuahua or Monterey Jack cheese. After baking, sprinkle with 1 teaspoon snipped fresh cilantro.

Nutrition facts per pizzetta: 138 cal., 3 g total fat (1 g sat. fat), 5 mg chol., 310 mg sodium, 23 g carbo., 6 g pro. *Daily values:* 2% vit. C, 7% iron.

Smoked Chicken and Roasted Pepper: For each pizzetta, spread 1 tablespoon cream cheese with chives on crust to within ½ inch of edges. Top with 2 tablespoons chopped smoked chicken, 1 tablespoon thinly sliced roasted red sweet pepper, 1 teaspoon snipped fresh basil, and 2 tablespoons shredded Gouda cheese.

Nutrition facts per pizzetta: 155 cal., 4 g total fat (2 g sat. fat), 11 mg chol., 333 mg sodium, 22 g carbo., 1 g fiber, 6 g pro. *Daily values:* 2% vit. A, 7% vit. C, 3% calcium, 7% iron.

TAMARIND EGGPLANT WITH ROASTED GARLIC

Start to finish: 50 min.

1 head garlic

♦♦♦

6 Japanese eggplants, cut into 1-inch pieces
1 large red sweet pepper, quartered, seeds and membranes removed
¼ cup olive oil

♦♦♦

1 tsp. finely shredded orange peel
¼ cup orange juice
1 Tbsp. tamarind paste or concentrate
2 tsp. sugar
1 tsp. grated fresh ginger
¼ tsp. salt

♦♦♦

½ cup chopped onion
1 jalapeño pepper, seeded, and finely chopped*
1 mango, seeded, peeled, and chopped
¼ cup snipped fresh cilantro

1 Cut off the pointed top portion of the garlic head, leaving the bulb intact but exposing the individual cloves. Wrap garlic head tightly in foil. Roast in a 425° oven for 25 to 30 minutes or until tender; set aside to cool.

2 Meanwhile, in a roasting pan toss eggplant and sweet pepper with 1 tablespoon of the oil. Roast, in the same oven about 20 minutes or until tender. Cool on wire rack. Cut pepper into thin bite-size strips.

3 Squeeze roasted garlic from skin into a bowl; discard skin. Stir in 2 tablespoons of the olive oil, orange peel, orange juice, tamarind, sugar, ginger, and salt. Set aside.

4 In a large nonstick skillet cook onion and jalapeño pepper in the remaining 1 tablespoon olive oil until tender. Add the garlic mixture. Bring to boiling; reduce heat. Simmer, uncovered, about 5 minutes or until slightly thickened. Stir in eggplant, red pepper strips, mango, and cilantro. Heat through. Makes 4 to 6 side-dish servings.

***Note:** Hot peppers contain oils that can burn. Wear plastic gloves when working with hot peppers. Do not touch eyes or face, and thoroughly wash hands.

Nutrition facts per serving: 250 cal., 14 g total fat (2 g sat. fat), 0 mg chol., 441 mg sodium, 32 g carbo., 7 g fiber, 3 g pro. *Daily values:* 24% vit. A, 106% vit. C, 46% calcium, 8% iron.

SPINACH RISOTTO WITH ACORN SQUASH

Start to finish: 30 min.

Stubby Italian Arborio rice—the key to authentic risottos—creates a luscious dish. During cooking, the grains not only soften, but their special starch transforms the broth into a creamy, unforgettable sauce.

1 1½- to 2-lb. acorn or butternut squash, halved lengthwise and seeded

♦♦♦

1 cup chopped red onion
4 cloves garlic, minced
1 Tbsp. olive oil
1 cup Arborio rice or short grain rice

♦♦♦

3 cups vegetable broth or
   chicken broth
3 cups packed, chopped
   fresh spinach
2 Tbsp. finely shredded
   Parmesan cheese

1 Cut each squash half cross-wise into 1-inch slices. Cook, covered, in a small amount of boiling water for 10 to 15 minutes or until tender. Drain; keep warm.

2 Meanwhile, in a large saucepan cook onion and garlic in hot oil over medium heat about 4 minutes or until onion is tender. Add uncooked rice; cook and stir for 1 minute more.

3 In a medium saucepan bring vegetable or chicken broth to boiling. Reduce heat and simmer. Slowly add 1 cup of the broth to the rice mixture, stirring constantly. Continue to cook and stir until liquid is absorbed. Add another ½ cup of the broth; continue to cook and stir until liquid is absorbed. Add another 1 cup broth, stirring constantly until broth has been absorbed. (This should take about 15 minutes.)

4 Stir in remaining ½ cup broth; cook and stir until rice is slightly creamy and just tender. Stir in chopped spinach and Parmesan cheese.

5 To serve, divide risotto evenly among 4 shallow bowls or plates. Top with squash slices. Makes 4 main-dish servings.

Nutrition facts per serving: 296 cal., 6 g total fat (1 g sat. fat), 2 mg chol., 778 mg sodium, 60 g carbo., 5 g fiber, 8 g pro.
Daily values: 129% vit. A, 59% vit. C, 12% calcium, 29% iron.

INDIAN SPICED SQUASH

Start to finish: 30 min.

Everyone's the cook when it comes to a curry, and this vegetarian version proves why. Its array of traditional condiments lets diners season to taste at the table, so no two mouthfuls are ever the same.

¼ cup shelled raw pumpkin
   seeds (pepitas)
   ◆◆◆
1 Tbsp. grated fresh ginger
2 Tbsp. olive oil
2 lb. winter squash, peeled,
   seeded, and cut into
   ½-inch pieces (about
   4 cups)
½ cup dried cranberries or
   raisins
1 tsp. ground cinnamon
1 tsp. ground coriander
½ tsp. ground cumin
½ tsp. curry powder
   ◆◆◆
1 14½-oz. can vegetable broth
   or chicken broth
   ◆◆◆
4 cups hot cooked brown rice
   Condiments such as sliced
   bananas, pineapple
   chunks, sliced green
   onions, and/or chutney
   (optional)

1 In a large skillet toast pumpkin seeds over medium heat 4 to 5 minutes or until puffed and lightly browned, stirring occasionally. (Watch carefully as pumpkin seeds may pop in skillet.) Remove seeds from skillet and set aside.

2 In the same skillet cook and stir ginger in hot oil over medium heat for 1 minute. Increase heat to medium-high; add winter squash

WHAT'S WINTER SQUASH?

Winter squashes are those that are hard-shelled, generally mature in the fall, and can be stored for winter use. Some varieties include acorn, banana, buttercup, butternut, delicata, hubbard, and turban. Winter squash needs to be cooked before eating.

To store, place the squash in a cool, dry place for up to 2 months. Do not refrigerate.

and cook for 3 to 5 minutes or until the squash starts to brown. Add the dried cranberries or raisins, cinnamon, coriander, cumin, and curry powder; cook for 1 minute more.

3 Carefully add vegetable broth or chicken broth to squash mixture. Bring to boiling; reduce heat. Cook, covered, for 10 to 15 minutes or until squash is tender, but not mushy.

4 To serve, divide the cooked brown rice evenly among 4 shallow bowls or plates. Spoon squash mixture over rice and sprinkle with toasted pumpkin seeds. If desired, pass condiments. Makes 4 main-dish servings.

Nutrition facts per serving: 450 cal., 13 g total fat (2 g sat. fat), 0 mg chol., 441 mg sodium, 81 g carbo., 9 g fiber, 9 g pro.
Daily values: 134% vit. A, 48% vit. C, 9% calcium, 27% iron.

BANANA-CHOCOLATE BITES

Prep: 20 min. ◆ Bake: 11 min.

See the photograph on page 202.

1 8-oz. pkg. refrigerated crescent rolls (8)
3 Tbsp. chocolate-hazelnut spread
2 medium bananas, cut into 16 slices (about ¾-inch pieces)
4 tsp. lemon juice

◆◆◆

1 egg yolk
1 Tbsp. water

1 Grease a baking sheet; set aside. Unroll crescent roll dough and separate into 8 triangles. Cut each triangle in half lengthwise, forming 16 long, narrow triangles. Place about ½ teaspoon of chocolate-hazelnut spread on wide end of each triangle. Brush each banana slice with some of the lemon juice. Place a banana slice on top of spread. Roll dough around bananas. Place bites on prepared baking sheet.

2 In a small bowl beat together egg yolk and water. Brush the egg yolk mixture onto dough of each bite. Bake in a 375° oven for 11 to 15 minutes or until golden brown. Transfer to a wire rack; cool 10 minutes before serving. Serve within 4 hours. Makes 16.

Nutrition facts per bite: 80 cal., 4 g total fat (1 g sat. fat), 13 mg chol., 118 mg sodium, 11 g carbo., 1 g fiber, 1 g pro.
Daily values: 2% vit. A, 3% vit. C, 1% iron.

GINGERED SHORTCAKE WITH SPICED FRUIT

Prep: 25 min. ◆ Bake: 18 min.
Cool: 40 min.

Shortcake isn't just for summer berries anymore! Enjoy this warming dessert with fall fruits such as apples, persimmons, or pears.

1 recipe Gingered Shortcake (see right)
1 cup whipping cream
2 Tbsp. granulated sugar
½ tsp. vanilla
3 Tbsp. butter
3 medium cooking apples, Fuyu persimmons, and/or pears, cored (if necessary) and thinly sliced
3 Tbsp. brown sugar
¼ tsp. ground nutmeg
1 cup blueberries

1 Prepare Gingered Shortcake. In a chilled bowl combine cream, granulated sugar, and vanilla. Beat with chilled beaters of an electric mixer until soft peaks form. Cover and refrigerate. In a large skillet melt butter over medium heat. Add apples, persimmons, and/or pears. Cook for 2 to 5 minutes or until almost tender. Stir in brown sugar and nutmeg. Cook for 1 to 3 minutes more or until fruit is tender. Stir in blueberries.

2 Place bottom cake layer on serving plate. Spoon about two-thirds of the fruit mixture and half of the whipped cream over cake. Top with second cake layer and remaining fruit mixture. Pass remaining whipped cream. Makes 8 servings.

FRUIT FINALES

Health experts recommend eating five or more servings of fruits or vegetables per day. Although that may seem like a lot, with a little planning you can easily meet the goal. One of the more pleasurable ways to serve fruits is in scrumptious desserts, such as those at left. If you like to close your meal with something sweet, plan on serving fruit-based desserts a couple of times a week. Don't forget that naturally sweet fresh fruit can stand on its own as a mealtime finale.

Gingered Shortcake: In a bowl combine 2 cups all-purpose flour, ¼ cup granulated sugar, and 2 teaspoons baking powder. Cut in ½ cup butter until mixture resembles coarse crumbs. Stir together 1 beaten egg, ⅔ cup milk, and 1 tablespoon grated ginger; add to dry mixture. Stir just to moisten. Spread in a greased 8×1½-inch round baking pan. Bake in a 450° oven for 18 to 20 minutes or until a wooden toothpick inserted near center comes out clean. Cool in pan for 10 minutes. Remove from pan; cool on a wire rack for 30 minutes. Split into 2 layers.

Nutrition facts per serving: 457 cal., 28 g total fat (17 g sat. fat), 111 mg chol., 280 mg sodium, 47 g carbo., 2 g fiber, 5 g pro.
Daily values: 30% vit. A, 6% vit. C, 12% calcium, 11% iron.

OCTOBER
Roots and Fruits

*A*utumn is the time to finish the harvest with root vegetables, squash, and fruit from the orchard. Fall fruits and vegetables like squash, potatoes, apples, and pears lend themselves to roasting, which brings out their natural sweetness. Try this easy cooking technique with Roasted Vegetables with Balsamic Vinegar, Roasted Fruit Soup, or Roasted Potato Soup. Apples show their versatility from breakfast to dessert in recipes like Double Apple Sweet Rolls, Chunky Apple Salsa, Sausage and Apple Pasta Bake, and Polenta-Pecan Apple Cobbler.

30-minute recipes indicated in RED.
Low-fat and no-fat recipes indicated
with a ♥.
Photographs indicated in italics.
*Bonus recipe

Happy Toppers

Here are some child-friendly ideas for topping the Warm and Fruity Breakfast Bowl (see recipe, below):
- ◆ Parade a row of animal crackers across the top of the cereal, or spell your child's name with cookie letters.
- ◆ Add a moon and stars with slices of star fruit (carambola) and a slice of peach.
- ◆ Make a silly face using grape halves for eyes, a mandarin orange for the mouth, a banana slice for a nose, and plain or toasted coconut for hair.
- ◆ Polka-dot the top with additional raisins or chopped pitted dates.
- ◆ Dollop with yogurt and sprinkle with brown sugar.
- ◆ Top with vanilla pudding, maple-flavored syrup, or honey.

30 MIN. LOW FAT

Warm and Fruity Breakfast Bowl

Prep: 5 min. ◆ Cook: 15 min.

- 1½ cups cracked wheat cereal
- ¾ cup quick-cooking brown rice
- ½ cup dried tart red cherries, cranberries, blueberries, or raisins
- ½ tsp. ground cinnamon
- ¼ tsp. salt
  Happy Toppers (see above) (optional)

1 In a self-sealing plastic bag combine wheat cereal, uncooked rice, dried fruit, cinnamon, and salt. Mix thoroughly to ensure dried fruit and seasonings are evenly distributed. (You may have to use your hands to separate pieces of fruit.) Close bag; store in refrigerator up to 1 month.

2 For 1 serving: In a small saucepan bring ⅔ cup *water* and ½ cup *milk* to boiling; reduce heat. Stir in ½ cup cereal mixture. Simmer, uncovered, for 15 to 20 minutes or until most of liquid is absorbed, mixture is creamy, and wheat is just tender,* stirring occasionally. Cool 3 to 5 minutes before serving to young children. If desired, add Happy Toppers. Makes 5 servings.

*Note: If mixture seems dry before wheat is tender, add additional water.

Nutrition facts per serving (without toppers): 233 cal., 3 g total fat (1 g sat. fat), 9 mg chol., 174 mg sodium, 45 g carbo., 1 g fiber, 9 g pro. *Daily values:* 14% vit. A, 2% vit. C, 13% calcium, 7% iron.

Double Apple Sweet Rolls

Prep: 40 min. ◆ Rise: 1½ hr. Bake: 25 min.

- 2 to 2½ cups all-purpose flour
- 1 pkg. active dry yeast
- ½ tsp. ground cinnamon
- ¼ tsp. ground nutmeg
- ½ cup milk
- 3 Tbsp. margarine or butter, cut up
- 3 Tbsp. granulated sugar
- ¼ tsp. salt
- 1 egg

◆◆◆

- 1 21-oz. can apple pie filling
- 1 Tbsp. margarine or butter, melted
- ½ cup raisins
- ⅓ cup chopped pecans
- ½ tsp. ground cinnamon
- ¼ tsp. ground nutmeg

◆◆◆

- 1 cup sifted powdered sugar
  Few drops almond extract
- 3 to 4 tsp. water

1 In a large mixing bowl combine 1 cup of the flour, the yeast, ½ teaspoon cinnamon, and ¼ teaspoon nutmeg. In a small saucepan combine milk, the 3 tablespoons margarine or butter, the granulated sugar, and salt. Heat and stir until warm (120° to 130°) and margarine almost melts. Add milk mixture to flour mixture; add egg. Beat with an electric mixer on low speed for 30 seconds, scraping the sides of the bowl constantly. Beat on high speed for 3 minutes more. Using a wooden spoon, stir in as much of the remaining flour as you can.

2 Turn the dough out onto a lightly floured surface. Knead in enough of the remaining flour to make a moderately soft dough that is smooth and elastic (3 to 5 minutes total). Shape the dough into a ball. Place dough in a lightly greased bowl, turning once to grease surface of the dough. Cover and let rise in a warm place until double (about 1 hour). Punch dough down. Turn dough out onto a lightly floured surface. Cover and let rest 10 minutes.

3 Meanwhile, generously grease the bottom of an 8×8×2-inch baking pan; set aside. Reserve ⅓ cup pie filling; set aside. Combine remaining pie filling and 1 tablespoon melted margarine; spread in the bottom of prepared pan. In a small mixing bowl, mash the ⅓ cup pie filling with a fork. Stir in raisins, pecans, ½ teaspoon cinnamon, and ¼ teaspoon nutmeg; set aside.

4 On a lightly floured surface, roll dough into a 9-inch square. Spread apple-raisin mixture evenly over dough to within ½ inch of edges. Roll up jelly-roll style. Slice roll into 9 equal pieces. Place, cut sides down, atop pie filling in pan. Cover; let rise in a warm place until nearly double (30 minutes).

5 Bake in a 375° oven for 25 to 30 minutes or until golden brown. Loosen edges. Carefully invert onto serving platter. Spoon on any filling that remains in pan. Cool 30 minutes.

6 Meanwhile, for icing, combine powdered sugar, almond extract, and enough water to make of drizzling consistency. Drizzle icing atop rolls. Serve warm. Makes 9 rolls.

Nutrition facts per roll: 333 cal., 9 g total fat (2 g sat. fat), 25 mg chol., 163 mg sodium, 61 g carbo., 2 g fiber, 5 g pro. *Daily values:* 15% vit. A, 12% vit. C, 3% calcium, 13% iron.

SWEET POTATO FRITTATA WITH FRESH CRANBERRY SALSA

Start to finish: 25 min.

Chutney, the traditional Indian relish that adds verve to this slightly sweet salsa, contains fruit (usually mangoes or limes), vinegar, sugar, and spices combined in proportions that play up contrasting flavors: sweet, sour, spicy, and piquant.

1 **cup cranberries, coarsely chopped**
¼ **cup sugar**
1 **Tbsp. water**
⅓ **cup chutney, snipped**
¼ **cup chopped red onion**

◆◆◆

1 **Tbsp. margarine or butter**
1½ **cups halved and sliced peeled sweet potato**
¼ **cup chopped red onion**
2 **oz. Canadian-style bacon, chopped (about ⅓ cup)**

◆◆◆

8 **eggs, beaten**

1 For cranberry salsa, in a small saucepan combine cranberries, sugar, and water. Bring to boiling, stirring occasionally. Remove from heat. Stir chutney and ¼ cup onion into cranberry mixture; set aside.

2 In a 10-inch skillet melt margarine or butter over medium heat. Add sweet potato and ¼ cup onion. Cook, covered, 4 to 5 minutes or until potatoes are almost tender, turning once. Sprinkle with Canadian bacon.

3 Pour eggs over potato mixture. Cook, uncovered, over medium heat. As eggs begin to set, run a spatula around edge of skillet, lifting eggs so uncooked portion flows underneath. Continue cooking and lifting edges until eggs are almost set (surface will be moist). Remove from heat. Cover and let stand for 3 to 4 minutes or until top is set. Cut into wedges. Serve with warm cranberry salsa. Makes 4 servings.

Nutrition facts per serving: 359 cal., 14 g total fat (4 g sat. fat), 431 mg chol., 308 mg sodium, 43 g carbo., 4 g fiber, 16 g pro. *Daily values:* 120% vit. A, 30% vit. C, 6% calcium, 12% iron.

APPLES STUFFED WITH COUSCOUS

Prep: 20 min. ◆ Bake: 25 min.
(See the photograph on page 279.)

4 **medium cooking apples, halved and cored**

◆◆◆

1 **Tbsp. butter**
½ **cup quick-cooking couscous**
¼ **cup raisins**
1 **Tbsp. chopped pecans**
1 **tsp. ground cinnamon**
⅛ **tsp. ground nutmeg**
2 **Tbsp. honey**
   Dash ground cloves

1 Hollow out apple halves, leaving a ½-inch shell and reserving ½ cup pulp. Arrange apples, cut sides down, in a 2-quart rectangular baking dish. Bake, covered, in a 350° oven 10 minutes.

2 Chop reserved apple pulp. Bring ¾ cup *water* and butter to boiling. Stir in chopped apple, couscous, raisins, nuts, cinnamon, and nutmeg. Remove from heat. Cover and let stand 5 minutes. In a small saucepan combine 2 tablespoons *water*, honey, and cloves. Bring to boiling; boil gently 1 minute. Remove from heat.

3 Fluff couscous mixture with a fork. Turn apple halves over. Fill halves with couscous mixture. Drizzle with honey mixture. Cover loosely with foil and bake 15 minutes more or until apples are tender. Makes 8 servings.

Nutrition facts per serving: 130 cal., 3 g total fat (1 g sat. fat), 4 mg chol., 84 mg sodium, 26 g carbo., 3 g fiber, 2 g pro. *Daily values:* 1% vit. A, 5% vit. C, 1% calcium, 2% iron.

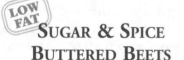

SUGAR & SPICE BUTTERED BEETS

Prep: 10 min. ◆ Cook: 40 min.
Bake: 20 min.

8 medium beets (2 lb.)

◆◆◆

¼ cup sugar
¼ tsp. salt
¼ tsp. ground cinnamon
¼ tsp. ground ginger
¼ tsp. ground allspice
⅛ tsp. pepper
2 Tbsp. butter or margarine, melted

1 Cut off all but 1 inch of fresh beet roots; wash. Do not peel. Cook, covered, in boiling lightly salted water 40 minutes or until barely tender. Drain and cool slightly. Slip skins off beets and cut into 1½-inch chunks.

2 Meanwhile, combine sugar, salt, and spices; set aside. Transfer cooked beets to a greased 2-quart rectangular baking dish. Drizzle melted butter over beets; toss. Sprinkle with sugar mixture; toss.

3 Bake, uncovered, in a 350° oven 20 to 25 minutes or until beets are tender, stirring once. Makes 6 side-dish servings.

Nutrition facts per serving: 99 cal., 4 g total fat, 10 mg chol., 180 mg sodium, 16 g carbo., 4 g fiber, 1 g pro. *Daily values:* 3% vit. A, 9% vit. C, 1% calcium, 4% iron.

ROASTED VEGETABLES WITH BALSAMIC VINEGAR

Prep: 15 min. ◆ Roast: 13 min.

These earthy and elegant roasted green beans and summer squash balance just about any entrée—steaks, chicken, pork chops, or salmon.

8 oz. green beans, ends trimmed
1 small onion, cut into thin wedges
1 clove garlic, minced
1 Tbsp. olive oil

◆◆◆

2 medium yellow summer squash, halved lengthwise and sliced ¼ inch thick

◆◆◆

⅓ cup balsamic vinegar

1 In a shallow roasting pan combine beans, onion, and garlic. Drizzle with olive oil; sprinkle with *salt* and *pepper.* Toss mixture until beans are evenly coated. Spread into a single layer.

2 Roast in a 450° oven for 8 minutes. Stir in squash and roast for 5 to 7 minutes more or until vegetables are tender and slightly browned.

3 Meanwhile, in a small saucepan bring the balsamic vine-gar to boiling over medium-high heat; reduce heat. Boil gently about 5 minutes or until reduced by half (vinegar will thicken slightly). Drizzle the vinegar over roasted vegetables; toss until veg-etables are evenly coated. Makes 4 to 6 side-dish servings.

Nutrition facts per serving: 81 cal., 4 g total fat (1 g sat. fat), 0 mg chol., 45 mg sodium, 12 g carbo., 1 g fiber, 1 g pro. *Daily values:* 4% vit. A, 19% vit. C, 3% calcium, 9% iron.

ROOT VEGETABLE RAGOUT

Start to finish: 30 min.

1 small fennel bulb
1 medium carrot
1 small beet

◆◆◆

2 cloves garlic, minced
2 Tbsp. olive oil or cooking oil
1 small onion, cut in thin wedges
½ cup chicken broth or vegetable broth
¼ tsp. dried thyme, crushed
1½ tsp. cornstarch
2 cups hot cooked couscous
2 Tbsp. finely shredded Parmesan cheese

1 Cut off and discard upper stalks of fennel; reserve some of the feathery tops for a garnish. Remove any wilted outer layers and discard; remove core. Chop remaining fennel into bite-size pieces. Peel carrot and beet; cut into bite-size pieces.

2 In a large skillet cook garlic in hot oil 30 seconds; add fennel, beets, carrots, and onion. Cook and stir over medium-high heat 3 minutes. Add ¼ cup of the broth, the thyme, ⅛ teaspoon *salt*, and ⅛ teaspoon *pepper*. Bring to boiling; reduce heat. Simmer, covered, 15 minutes or until vegetables are just tender.

3 Stir remaining ¼ cup broth into cornstarch; add to vegetables in skillet. Cook and stir until thickened and bubbly. Cook and stir 2 minutes more. Serve over couscous. Sprinkle with Parmesan and garnish with fennel tops. Makes 4 side-dish servings.

Nutrition facts per serving: 209 cal., 8 g total fat (1 g sat. fat), 3 mg chol., 241 mg sodium, 28 g carbo., 11 g fiber, 6 g pro. *Daily values:* 41% vit. A, 8% vit. C, 5% calcium, 5% iron.

BRAISED FALL VEGETABLES

Start to finish: 30 min.

A touch of cardamom adds a spicy-sweet taste to this flavorful autumn side dish that's cooked in a skillet. (See the photograph on page 237.)

2 Tbsp. margarine or butter
½ of a medium head red or green cabbage, cut into 6 wedges (about 1 lb.)

---

12 small whole carrots (about 8 oz. with tops) or 3 medium carrots, quartered lengthwise and halved crosswise
2 cups white and/or green cauliflower florets
1 medium red onion, cut in wedges
¼ cup water
2 Tbsp. vinegar
¼ tsp. salt
¼ tsp. pepper
¼ tsp. ground cardamom

1 In a large skillet melt margarine or butter. Cook cabbage wedges and carrots in hot margarine, covered, over medium heat for 3 minutes, stirring once or twice with a wooden spoon. Gently stir in the cauliflower, onion, water, vinegar, salt, pepper, and ground cardamom. Bring mixture to boiling; reduce heat. Simmer, covered, for 7 to 10 minutes or until the cabbage, carrots, and cauliflower florets are crisp-tender. Makes 6 to 8 side-dish servings.

Nutrition facts per serving: 74 cal., 4 g total fat (1 g sat. fat), 0 mg chol., 168 mg sodium, 9 g carbo., 4 g fiber, 2 g pro. *Daily values:* 74% vit. A, 59% vit. C, 3% calcium, 4% iron.

AUTUMN MEDLEY

Start to finish: 20 min.

The parsnips and carrots can be cut into ¼-inch slices if you prefer.

8 oz. parsnips, peeled and cut into matchstick strips (2¼ cups)

Menu

Oven-fried pork chops

♦♦♦

Baked sweet potatoes

♦♦♦

Autumn Medley (see below)

♦♦♦

Dinner rolls with butter

♦♦♦

Frosted spice cake

8 oz. carrots, peeled and cut into matchstick strips (2¼ cups)
¾ cup orange juice
⅓ cup dried cranberries
½ tsp. ground ginger

♦♦♦

3 Tbsp. brown sugar
2 Tbsp. margarine or butter
2 firm ripe pears, peeled and cut into ½-inch-thick slices
⅓ cup pecan halves

1 In a large nonstick skillet combine parsnips, carrots, orange juice, dried cranberries, and ginger. Bring to boiling; reduce heat to medium. Cook, uncovered, for 7 to 8 minutes or until vegetables are crisp-tender and most liquid is evaporated, stirring occasionally.

2 Add brown sugar, margarine or butter, pears, and pecans to mixture in skillet; stir. Cook, uncovered, for 2 to 3 minutes more or until vegetables are glazed. Makes 6 side-dish servings.

Nutrition facts per serving: 230 cal., 8 g total fat (1 g sat. fat), 0 mg chol., 77 mg sodium, 40 g carbo., 7 g fiber, 2 g pro. *Daily values:* 90% vit. A, 43% vit. C, 4% calcium, 7% iron.

CITRUS-SPLASHED SQUASH

Prep: 10 min. ◆ Roast: 35 min.

Like buttercup squash, kabocha squash has a sweet orange flesh that tastes even better with a splash of orange juice and a bit of thyme. The kabocha's shell is dark green with stripes of light green.
(See the photograph on page 239.)

1   1½-lb. kabocha, buttercup, and/or golden nugget squash, halved
4   small parsnips, peeled (about 12 oz. total)
¼   cup margarine or butter, melted
¼   cup orange juice
2   Tbsp. snipped fresh thyme or 1 tsp. dried thyme, crushed

1 In a greased 13×9×2-inch baking pan place squash halves, cut sides down, in half of the pan. Add parsnips to other half of pan. Combine melted margarine or butter, orange juice, and thyme. Drizzle ¼ cup of the mixture over parsnips; toss to coat.

2 Roast, uncovered, in a 350° oven for 35 to 50 minutes or until vegetables are tender, stirring parsnips once. Remove squash carefully and cut each half into 4 wedges. Remove seeds, if desired. (Seeds are edible, but fibrous.) To serve, place squash and parsnips in a shallow bowl or on a dinner plate. Drizzle with remaining orange juice mixture. Makes 4 side-dish servings.

Nutrition facts per serving: 228 cal., 12 g total fat (2 g sat. fat), 0 mg chol., 148 mg sodium, 30 g carbo., 7 g fiber, 4 g pro.
Daily values: 68% vit. A, 68% vit. C, 9% calcium, 11% iron.

MIXED GREENS SAUTÉ

Start to finish: 20 min.

Using a good-quality extra-virgin olive oil is worth the price in this recipe. The oil's subtle fruity flavor enhances the greens you choose. Take care to sauté over medium- to medium-high heat. Extra-virgin olive oil has a low "smoke point" compared to pure olive oil or other cooking oils. That means the extra-virgin oil will smoke and burn when cooked over high heat.
(See the photograph on page 239.)

2   to 2½ lb. Swiss chard, kale, mustard greens, and/or spinach
♦♦♦
¼   cup olive oil
5   medium cloves garlic, minced
4   oz. thinly sliced prosciutto (optional)
♦♦♦
Cider vinegar or lemon juice

1 Wash mixed greens thoroughly in cold water. Drain well. Pat greens dry with paper towels. Trim stems, if desired; trim any bruised leaves. Tear greens into 2-inch pieces.

2 In a 12-inch heavy, deep skillet heat olive oil over medium-high heat. Add garlic. Cook and stir for 30 to 60 seconds or until garlic is just brown. Add half of the mixed greens. Cook and stir greens for 1 minute. Add remaining greens. Cook and stir for 2 to 3 minutes more or until greens are slightly wilted. Remove from heat. If desired, stir in prosciutto.

3 To serve, transfer greens to a serving bowl. Pass cider vinegar or lemon juice. Makes 6 to 8 side-dish servings.

Nutrition facts per serving: 113 cal., 9 g total fat (1 g sat. fat), 0 mg chol., 323 mg sodium, 7 g carbo., 2 g fiber, 3 g pro.
Daily values: 50% vit. A, 77% vit. C, 8% calcium, 6% iron.

CREAMY VEGETABLE HASH

Start to finish: 30 min.

There are no potatoes in this hash. Instead, turnips, corn, apples, and onion are lightly coated with a horseradish cream sauce.

1¼   lb. turnips
♦♦♦
2   Tbsp. margarine or butter
1   cup frozen whole kernel corn, thawed
1   medium apple, cored and sliced
½   cup chopped onion
3   Tbsp. dairy sour cream
1   Tbsp. prepared horseradish
¼   tsp. salt
¼   tsp. ground nutmeg

1 Wash, peel, and cut turnips into ½-inch cubes (you should have 4 cups cubes). In a small saucepan cook turnips, covered, in a small amount of lightly salted boiling water for 10 to 12 minutes or until tender. Drain.

2 In a large skillet over medium heat melt the margarine or butter. Add the corn, apple, and onion to hot margarine and cook until apple is tender, stirring occasionally. Stir in the cooked turnip. Add the sour cream, horseradish, salt, and nutmeg, stirring to combine. Cook and stir until heated through (do not boil). Makes 6 side-dish servings.

Nutrition facts per serving: 103 cal., 6 g total fat (2 g sat. fat), 3 mg chol., 211 mg sodium, 14 g carbo., 4 g fiber, 2 g pro. *Daily values:* 6% vit. A, 22% vit. C, 2% calcium, 2% iron.

FIGS AND FRUIT SALAD

Start to finish: 40 min.

Blood oranges are not typically found during the fall months, but they make a colorful addition to this salad. If available, just substitute one deep-red blood orange for one of the oranges called for in the recipe. (See the photograph on page 242.)

¾ **cup dried Calimyrna (light or golden) figs (3 to 4 oz.)**

◆◆◆

1 **Tbsp. walnut oil**

◆◆◆

6 **cups torn fresh spinach**
⅓ **cup broken walnuts, toasted**
1 **recipe Walnut Oil Vinaigrette (see right)**
2 **oranges, peeled and sliced crosswise**
3 **oz. semisoft goat cheese, broken into large chunks (optional)**

1 Remove stems from figs; halve figs lengthwise. Pour enough boiling water over figs to cover; let figs stand for 30 minutes. Drain.

2 In a medium skillet heat walnut oil over medium heat for 15 seconds; add figs. Cook for 3 to 4 minutes or until lightly

browned, stirring gently to prevent burning. Remove from heat; set aside to cool.

3 In a large bowl combine the fresh spinach and toasted walnuts. Drizzle with Walnut Oil Vinaigrette; toss gently to coat.

4 To serve, divide spinach mixture among 6 individual bowls. Arrange the orange slices and figs atop spinach. If desired, add goat cheese to each salad. Makes 6 side-dish servings.

Walnut Oil Vinaigrette: In a blender container or food processor bowl combine 3 tablespoons rice vinegar; 3 tablespoons walnut oil; 1 small clove garlic, minced; 2 tablespoons snipped fresh mint; ¼ teaspoon pepper; and ⅛ teaspoon salt. Cover and blend or process until nearly smooth.

Nutrition facts per serving: 184 cal., 13 g total fat (1 g sat. fat), 0 mg chol., 74 mg sodium, 15 g carbo., 3 g fiber, 2 g pro. *Daily values:* 22% vit. A, 55% vit. C, 7% calcium, 8% iron.

CHUNKY APPLE SALSA

Prep: 10 min. ◆ Chill: 2 hr.

Not your typical peppery hot salsa, this triple apple combination is delicious served atop poultry or pork. Or, for a snack, add a spoonful atop a cream-cheese-slathered sweet cracker.

1 **medium Red Delicious apple, cored and chopped**
1 **medium Golden Delicious apple, cored and chopped**
1 **medium tart green apple, cored and chopped**

⅓ **cup dried cranberries, finely snipped**
1 **Tbsp. cider vinegar**
4 **tsp. maple syrup or maple-flavored syrup**
¼ **tsp. vanilla**

1 In a mixing bowl stir together apples, dried cranberries, cider vinegar, maple syrup, and vanilla. Cover and chill for up to 2 hours before serving. Serve with grilled or roasted meats or poultry. Makes 4 cups salsa.

Nutrition facts per ¼ cup: 24 cal., 0 g total fat, 0 mg chol., 1 mg sodium, 6 g carbo., 1 g fiber, 0 g pro. *Daily values:* 1% vit. C.

ROASTED FRUIT SOUP

Prep: 10 min. ◆ Roast: 35 min.

Roasting is perfect for fruit that is not quite ripe. The dry, high heat will caramelize the fruit's natural sugars, boosting sweetness. (See the photograph on page 240.)

1 cup cranberries
½ cup packed brown sugar
1 medium pear, cored and cut into wedges
1 medium cooking apple, such as Rome, Jonathan, or Fuji, cored and cut into wedges
3 plums, halved and pitted

◆◆◆

3 cups cranberry-apple juice
1 Tbsp. lemon juice
2 3-inch pieces stick cinnamon

1 In a 3-quart rectangular baking dish stir together cranberries and brown sugar. Add pear and apple wedges. Roast, uncovered, in a 450° oven about 20 minutes or until just tender. Add plum halves. Roast, uncovered, 15 minutes more or until fruit is tender and edges of fruit begin to brown or curl. Stir gently to combine.

2 Meanwhile, in a large saucepan combine cranberry-apple juice, lemon juice, and cinnamon sticks. Bring to boiling; reduce heat. Simmer, uncovered, for 10 minutes. Remove cinnamon sticks; discard. Gently stir roasted fruits and their juices into mixture in saucepan.

3 To serve, spoon fruit and juice mixture into 6 individual bowls. Makes 6 servings.

Nutrition facts per serving: 185 cal., 0 g total fat, 0 mg chol., 7 mg sodium, 47 g carbo., 3 g fiber, 1 g pro. *Daily values:* 1% vit. A, 81% vit. C, 3% calcium, 3% iron.

PRIZE TESTED RECIPE WINNER

ROOT VEGGIE SOUP WITH CURRY CROUTONS

Prep: 25 min. ◆ Cook: 30 min. Bake: 15 min.

Golden, crispy croutons bob merrily atop this hearty, satisfying vegetable soup.

1 medium fennel bulb (4 to 5 oz.)

◆◆◆

2 tsp. cooking oil
¼ cup chopped onion
1 clove garlic, minced
3 cups chicken broth
1 medium carrot, peeled and sliced
1 medium turnip, peeled and cubed
1 medium potato, peeled and cubed
¼ tsp. ground white or black pepper

◆◆◆

1 Tbsp. olive oil
½ tsp. curry powder
3 ¾-inch slices Italian-style bread, torn into bite-size pieces
¼ cup half-and-half or light cream
1 15-oz. can cannellini beans, rinsed and drained

1 Cut off and discard upper stalks of fennel, snipping and reserving feathery leaves for garnish. Remove any wilted outer layers of fennel and discard; remove core. Finely chop remaining fennel; set aside.

2 In a large saucepan heat cooking oil; cook onion and garlic in hot oil for 5 minutes or until onion is tender. Carefully add chicken broth, carrot, turnip, potato, chopped fennel, and white pepper. Bring to boiling; reduce heat. Simmer, covered, for 25 to 30 minutes or until vegetables are very tender. Cool slightly.

3 Meanwhile, in a medium bowl combine olive oil and curry powder. Add the torn bread pieces; toss until coated. Spread bread pieces in a single layer in a 15×10-inch baking pan. Bake in a 350° oven for 15 to 20 minutes or until croutons begin to brown, stirring once.

4 In a blender container or food processor bowl place one-third of the vegetable mixture. Cover and blend or process until smooth. Repeat twice with remaining mixture. Return all to saucepan. Stir in half-and-half or light cream and beans; heat through. Season to taste with *salt*.

5 To serve, ladle soup into 4 bowls. Float a few croutons atop each serving. If desired, garnish with snipped fennel leaves. Makes 4 main-dish servings.

Nutrition facts per serving: 282 cal., 10 g total fat (2 g sat. fat), 6 mg chol., 935 mg sodium, 42 g carbo., 16 g fiber, 14 g pro. *Daily values:* 42% vit. A, 20% vit. C, 8% calcium, 17% iron.

ROASTED POTATO SOUP

Prep: 20 min. ◆ Roast: 50 min.
Cook: 35 min.

Roasting the potatoes gives the soup a more intense, robust flavor.

6 medium baking potatoes
   (about 2 lb.)
1 large onion, quartered
6 cloves garlic, peeled
2 Tbsp. margarine or butter,
   melted
¼ to ½ tsp. cracked black
   pepper

◆◆◆

3 cups chicken broth
2 cups water

◆◆◆

1 cup whipping cream
   Salt and pepper (optional)
   Baked potato chips
   (optional)
   Snipped fresh sorrel
   (optional)

1 Scrub potatoes thoroughly with a brush. Pat dry with paper towels. Cut potatoes into 1-inch chunks. Place potatoes, onion, and garlic in a shallow roasting pan. Drizzle with the melted margarine or butter and sprinkle with the cracked pepper.

2 Roast, uncovered, in a 425° oven for 50 to 60 minutes or until potatoes are browned, stirring occasionally.

3 Transfer roasted potatoes and onion mixture to a large saucepan. Stir in chicken broth and water. Bring just to boiling; reduce heat. Simmer, covered, for 20 to 25 minutes or until potatoes are very tender.

4 Using a potato masher, mash potato mixture until nearly smooth. Simmer, uncovered, about 15 minutes more or until slightly thickened. Stir in whipping cream and heat through. If desired, season to taste with salt and pepper. If desired, for a smoother soup, carefully blend half of the soup at a time in a blender container.*

5 To serve, ladle soup into 6 bowls. If desired, sprinkle each serving with baked potato chips and snipped sorrel. Makes 6 side-dish servings.

*Note: When blending hot liquids, fill blender container only half-full. Cover tightly, leaving center slightly open to vent hot air; cover blender with a clean towel while operating.

Nutrition facts per serving: 361 cal., 19 g total fat (12 g sat. fat), 65 mg chol., 457 mg sodium, 41 g carbo., 2 g fiber, 7 g pro. *Daily values:* 21% vit. A, 41% vit. C, 5% calcium, 15% iron.

CATFISH WITH A CRUNCH

Prep: 20 min. ◆ Cook: 6 min.

If you're a real mustard fan, consider using pretzels flavored with honey-mustard in this crispy coating. (See the photograph on page 243.)

4 4-oz. fresh or frozen catfish
   fillets (about ½ inch thick)
1 egg, beaten
3 Tbsp. Dijon-style mustard
1 Tbsp. milk
¼ tsp. pepper
¼ cup all-purpose flour
1 cup coarsely crushed pretzels

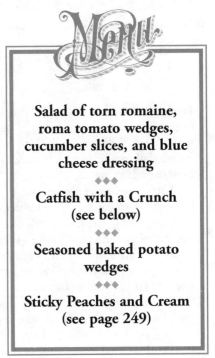

Salad of torn romaine, roma tomato wedges, cucumber slices, and blue cheese dressing

◆◆◆

Catfish with a Crunch
(see below)

◆◆◆

Seasoned baked potato wedges

◆◆◆

Sticky Peaches and Cream
(see page 249)

◆◆◆

2 Tbsp. cooking oil

1 Thaw fish, if frozen. Rinse fish; pat dry with paper towels. In a shallow dish combine the egg, Dijon-style mustard, milk, and pepper, beating with a whisk or fork until smooth. Place flour in another shallow dish. In a third shallow dish place the coarsely crushed pretzels.

2 Coat fish with flour. Dip fish in the mustard mixture, then in the crushed pretzels to coat both sides. In a large skillet cook fish in hot oil over medium heat for 3 to 4 minutes per side or until golden and fish just flakes easily with a fork. (Reduce heat as necessary to prevent burning.) If desired, serve with thick *lemon slices.* Makes 4 main-dish servings.

Nutrition facts per serving: 362 cal., 18 g total fat (4 g sat. fat), 107 mg chol., 537 mg sodium, 25 g carbo., 1 g fiber, 23 g pro. *Daily values:* 4% vit. A, 1% vit. C, 5% calcium, 13% iron.

ALTERNATIVE FUELS

by David Feder, R.D., and Jan Miller, R.D.

Picture yourself slim, trim, and on the go. Somewhere between tennis lessons and roller-blading you grab a "PowerFuelBar" or a can of "SlimEase" before dashing off to go horseback riding. At least that's how the ads show it.

What are you really getting when you buy one of these ready-to-eat meal replacements?

Some meal replacements are the concentrated sources of vitamins and protein they purport to be. But many are little more than sugar-filled, vitamin-added beverages or candy bars wearing a false badge of health. Before you peel the wrapper on an "energy" bar or pop the top on a liquid meal, look closely at the label for revealing clues to what's inside. Here's what to look for:

Energy: 1 Lump or 2? Those "energy-boosting carbos" emblazoned across a lot of meal-replacer labels are usually sugar, often listed as fructose, maltose, lactose, corn syrup, rice syrup, or barley syrup. Don't be fooled by the names; they're all used the same way by your body. For many of these products, sugars are the main ingredient. There's nothing wrong with sugar, but nutrition-wise it offers little more than short-term hunger satisfaction.

Protein Power Protein is hyped as a "power" nutrient. The truth is, protein, carbohydrates, and fat all power the body. Protein appears on ingredient labels as casein, milk protein, or soy protein. Do you need extra protein? Athletes, growing kids, and people with certain illnesses require a little more protein, but the average American already eats 2 to 3 times the daily need of one-half gram per pound of body weight. This is the amount in a few servings of meat, dairy foods, or beans.

Extra Options Phytochemicals—food compounds that can help prevent disease—are a selling point for some meal replacer products. So, too, are herbal additives, such as ginseng, gingko, Echinacea, and St. John's Wort. Research suggests that supplemental versions of phytochemicals are not as effective as those found naturally in food. In one recent study at Johns Hopkins University, scientists compared antioxidants (the most familiar phytochemicals) obtained from supplements to those found in fresh fruits and vegetables. The antioxidants were given to 123 people in a controlled, 11-week study. The scientists found that supplements did not provide the same benefits that fresh foods do.

Although the benefits of herbal supplements vary according to the plant, there is no regulation of purity and efficacy. Also, the cost of adding a few grams of an herb can be reflected by a substantial increase in the price of the item it's added to.

WHAT'S IN A CLAIM?

There are two types of claims on product labels: Health claims and structure/function claims. Health claims give information about a food or supplement's role in preventing a specific disease. Health claims are closely regulated by the United States Food and Drug Administration (FDA). Constance Geiger, Ph.D., R.D., says, "Look for words such as 'may reduce' and 'may prevent.' For example, 'Diets rich in calcium may help reduce your risk of osteoporosis.'"

Geiger, an assistant professor of nutrition at the University of Utah specializing in nutrition communications and labeling and health claims, points out, "Substantial research backs FDA-approved health claims, but structure/function claims are not well-regulated, don't have to be approved, and may not be backed by research. Look for words such as 'supports,' 'maintains,' and 'provides.' For example, 'supports memory,' or 'provides energy.'"

The good news is that the FDA is seeking to better regulate structure/function claims. If you want to know how that "memory-enhancing" herbal soda or health bar works, call the manufacturer (they usually have a toll-free number on the label) and request a copy of their research references.

ON THE BALANCE

A nutrition bar or drink can help in a pinch—like when you're dashing through the airport between flights and the only nourishment you're looking forward to is a lilliputian packet of pretzels. The replacer is better than doing without food or a meal altogether.

Replacer bars and beverages also are convenient, but the same could be said of a candy bar or a carton of milk and a daily multivitamin supplement. When it comes to fat content, energy bars may edge out the candy-and-supplement combination, but they also cost double or triple the price. Besides, nutritionally speaking, it's more important to monitor total calories, not fat.

Smart Comparison Shopping

The few minutes saved by swapping a meal with a replacer can get costly. The following compares cost and nutritional content of some meal replacements and their counterparts. (Percentages are averaged from several sources; vitamin values are for A, B 1-4, C, D, and E.)

Chocolate "Power" Drink vs. Chocolate 2% Milk + daily multivitamin and minerals supplement—both 8 oz.

	"Power" Drink	Chocolate Milk + Supplement
calories	240	192
grams protein	10	9
grams carbohydrates	40	27
grams fat/ saturated fat	4/1	6/3
%RDA vitamins	20 to 30	100 to 200
%RDA minerals	20 to 30	45 to 125
grams fiber	0	1
average cost	$1.38	30 cents

"Energy" Bar vs. Chocolate Candy Bar with Peanuts + daily multivitamin and minerals supplement—about 2.25 oz.

	"Energy Bar"	Candy Bar + Supplement
calories	240	280
grams protein	7	4
grams carbohydrates	45	35
grams fat/ saturated fat	5/1	14/5
%RDA vitamins	0 to 100	100
%RDA minerals	15	100 to 120
grams fiber	4	1
average cost	$1.55	70 cents

Best Bets

The best approach of all to "ultra-fast" food is to take 2 minutes to toss a homemade snack and a daily multivitamin into your backpack or briefcase, then enjoy them with juice or milk. Choose fruits and vegetables and whole grain bread or crackers. Here are two ideas to get you started:

One medium banana, one medium carrot, one ounce of whole grain crackers plus 8 ounces 2% milk and a daily multivitamin-and-minerals supplement

calories	387
grams protein	12
grams carbohydrates	67
grams fat/saturated fat	10/4
%RDA vitamins	100 to 200
%RDA minerals	100 to 125
grams fiber	7
average cost	75 cents

Peanut butter and fruit preserve sandwich on whole grain bread with 8 ounces orange juice and a daily multivitamin-and-minerals supplement

calories	384
grams protein	11
grams carbohydrates	68
grams fat/saturated fat	9/2
%RDA vitamins	100 to 200
%RDA minerals	100 to 125
grams fiber	5
average cost	80 cents

THE CLEVER COOK

MAKING GOOD USE OF ONE CASSEROLE DISH

When making a casserole to freeze and bake later, line the casserole dish with a few layers of foil. Prepare the casserole, then freeze. Once frozen, remove the foil-lined-casserole from the dish, securely wrap, label, and return to freezer. This will help empty your dish to use for other things.

When you're ready to bake the frozen casserole, simply remove the foil and slip the frozen mixture back into the dish and bake as directed.

Mrs. Perry Lewis
Neptune Beach, Florida

ENCHILADA CASSEROLE

Prep: 20 min. ◆ Bake: 30 min.

1 15-oz. can black beans, rinsed and drained
1 14½-oz. can Mexican-style stewed tomatoes, drained and cut up, reserving juice
1 cup frozen whole kernel corn
¼ cup sliced pitted ripe olives
◆◆◆
1 6-oz. can tomato paste
1 dried ancho chili pepper, seeded and finely chopped*
2 tsp. chili powder
¼ tsp. garlic powder
◆◆◆

10 to 12 (6-inch) corn tortillas
2 cups shredded taco cheese blend (8 oz.)

1 For filling, in a medium mixing bowl stir together the beans, tomatoes, corn, and olives; set aside.

2 For sauce, pour reserved tomato juice into a quart glass measure. Add *water* to equal 2½ cups. In a medium saucepan stir together the tomato juice-water mixture, tomato paste, chili pepper, chili powder, and garlic powder. Bring to boiling; reduce heat. Simmer, covered, for 5 minutes. Remove from heat.

3 To assemble, in a 2-quart rectangular baking dish arrange 3 to 4 corn tortillas. Top with half of the filling, a third of the sauce, and a third of the cheese. Top with 3 to 4 tortillas, remaining filling, a third of the sauce, and a third of the cheese. Top with remaining tortillas and sauce.

4 Bake, covered, in a 350° oven for 20 minutes. Uncover; sprinkle remaining cheese over casserole. Bake 10 minutes more or until heated through. Serves 8.

*Note: Hot peppers contain oils that can burn. Wear plastic gloves when working with peppers. Do not touch eyes or face, and thoroughly wash hands.

Nutrition facts per serving: 275 cal., 11 g total fat (1 g sat. fat), 27 mg chol., 739 mg sodium, 34 g carbo., 4 g fiber, 14 g pro. *Daily values:* 20% vit. A, 18% vit. C, 25% calcium, 16% iron.

GREEN CHILI PORK STEW

Prep: 20 min. ◆ Cook: 5 to 6 hr.

Chase away the chill of fall with a steamy bowl of this hearty stew. Add a wedge of fresh-baked corn bread to complete the meal.

1 lb. boneless pork sirloin, trimmed and cut into bite-size pieces
1 Tbsp. olive oil or cooking oil
2 medium potatoes, cut into bite-size pieces
1 cup chopped onion
3 cloves garlic, minced
1 tsp. ground cumin
1 tsp. dried oregano, crushed
1 tsp. fennel seed, crushed
1 14½-oz. can tomatoes, cut up, undrained
1 14½-oz. can chicken broth
◆◆◆
1 15-oz. can pinto beans, rinsed and drained
1 4½-oz. can diced green chili peppers or 2 Tbsp. chopped canned jalapeño peppers
2 Tbsp. snipped fresh cilantro
◆◆◆
Dairy sour cream (optional)
Fresh cilantro leaves (optional)

1 In a large skillet brown pork, half at a time, in hot oil. In a 3½- to 4-quart electric crockery cooker place potatoes, onion, garlic, cumin, oregano, and fennel seed. Top with browned meat. Add undrained tomatoes and chicken broth. Cover and cook on high-heat setting for 5 to 6 hours or on low-heat setting for 10 to 12 hours. Stir in the pinto beans, green chilies, and cilantro. Let stand 5 minutes before serving.

2 To serve, ladle stew into bowls. If desired, top each serving with a spoonful of sour cream and sprinkle with cilantro leaves. Makes 6 main-dish servings.

Nutrition facts per serving: 241 cal., 7 g total fat (2 g sat. fat), 32 mg chol., 696 mg sodium, 28 g carbo., 5 g fiber, 17 g pro. *Daily values:* 4% vit. A, 41% vit. C, 8% calcium, 24% iron.

SAUSAGE AND APPLE PASTA BAKE

Prep: 25 min. ◆ Bake: 40 min.

See the photograph on page 244.

- **8 oz. cooked smoked sausage, halved lengthwise and sliced**
- **3 medium tart apples, cored and chopped**
- **½ cup chopped onion**
- **½ cup chopped red or green sweet pepper**
- **½ cup chopped celery**
- **½ cup chopped carrot**
- **2 cups cooked and drained rotini pasta**
- **1 2-oz. jar diced pimiento, drained**

◆◆◆

- **1 8-oz. pkg. cream cheese, softened**
- **1 cup chicken broth**
- **1 tsp. dried sage, crushed**
- **¼ tsp. ground black pepper**

◆◆◆

- **¼ cup fine dry bread crumbs**
- **1 Tbsp. grated Parmesan cheese**
- **¼ tsp. paprika**
- **2 Tbsp. margarine or butter, melted**

1 In a large skillet cook sausage for 3 minutes. Add apples, onion, sweet pepper, cel-ery, and carrot. Cook and stir for 3 to 4 minutes or until vegetables are tender. Remove from heat. Stir in pasta and pimiento; set aside.

2 Meanwhile, in a small mixing bowl beat together cream cheese, broth, sage, and black pepper until smooth. Add to pasta mixture; toss to coat. Turn into a 2-quart rectangular baking dish.

3 Bake, uncovered, in a 375° oven for 30 minutes. Uncover and sprinkle with a mixture of bread crumbs, grated cheese, paprika, and melted margarine. Bake, uncovered, about 10 minutes more until heated through. Let stand 10 minutes. Makes 6 main-dish servings.

Nutrition facts per serving: 424 cal., 30 g total fat (14 g sat. fat), 68 mg chol., 704 mg sodium, 28 g carbo., 3 g fiber, 12 g pro. *Daily values:* 51% vit. A, 33% vit. C, 6% calcium, 13% iron.

CIDER-BRAISED PORK ROAST

Prep: 20 min. ◆ Braise: 55 min.

When the braising is done, you're left with plenty of fruity juices that make a wonderful base for the go-with cider sauce. (See the photograph on page 241.)

- **1 1½- to 2-lb. boneless pork shoulder roast**
- **2 Tbsp. cooking oil**
- **1¼ cups apple cider or apple juice**
- **½ cup chopped onion**

◆◆◆

- **2 medium cooking apples, such as Granny Smith or Jonathan, cored and cut into wedges**

WHAT IS BRAISING?

Braising means to cook food slowly in a small amount of liquid in a tightly covered pan on the range top or in the oven. This moist-heat method of cooking works well for less tender cuts of meat.

- **1 6-oz. pkg. dried apricot halves**
- **½ tsp. ground cardamom**
- **¼ tsp. ground cinnamon**

1 Trim fat from meat. In a 4-quart Dutch oven brown meat on all sides in hot oil. Drain off fat. Add apple cider, onion, and ½ teaspoon *salt* to Dutch oven. Bring to boiling; reduce heat. Simmer, covered, for 45 minutes.

2 Add apples, apricots, cardamom, and cinnamon. Bring to boiling; reduce heat. Simmer, covered, about 10 minutes more or until meat and fruit are tender. Using a slotted spoon, transfer meat, apples, and apricots to a serving platter, reserving juices in pot. Keep meat and fruit warm.

3 For cider sauce, boil remaining juices gently for 5 to 7 minutes or until reduced to ½ cup. Spoon over meat and fruit. If desired, garnish with *assorted fresh herbs*. Makes 6 servings.

Nutrition facts per serving: 321 cal., 11 g total fat (3 g sat. fat), 73 mg chol., 292 mg sodium, 32 g carbo., 4 g fiber, 24 g pro. *Daily values:* 21% vit. A, 9% vit. C, 3% calcium, 17% iron.

Foolproof Roasting

Timing is everything. So is temperature. That's about all it takes to turn a beef roast into a Sunday-dinner standout. Roasting, a method of oven-cooking food in an uncovered pan with no added liquid, is best reserved for tender cuts, like beef ribeye roast. Season it, pop it in the oven, and walk away. Then just try to ignore the aroma wafting about the kitchen. The beef itself is stunningly simple; spoon a few vegetables into the roasting pan for a company-special dinner. An added bonus: Any leftover meat makes a great start for another meal.

1. Here's the rub
Pat an herb mixture onto all surfaces of the meat.

2. Rack it up
Place roast onto a rack in a shallow roasting pan.

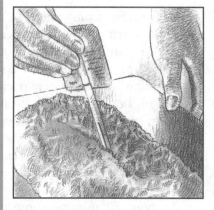

3. The right spot
Insert an ovenproof meat thermometer so the tip is centered in the thickest part of the roast.

4. The heat is on
Roasting the beef, uncovered, at 350° provides a deeply browned crust of flavor surrounding succulently tender meat.

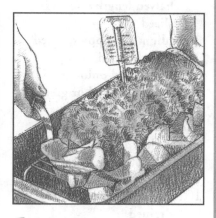

5. A finishing touch
About 45 minutes before the roast is finished, remove pan from oven and carefully spoon vegetables onto rack, surrounding the beef.

BEEF ROAST WITH VEGETABLES

Prep: 30 min. ◆ Roast: 1½ to 2 hr.

For a step-by-step roasting guide see the illustrations on page 234.

- 2 Tbsp. snipped fresh rosemary or 2 tsp. dried rosemary, crushed
- 1 tsp. salt
- 1 tsp. coarsely ground pepper
- 1 4- to 6-lb. boneless beef ribeye roast

◆◆◆

- 3 large sweet potatoes, peeled and cut into 1-inch pieces (about 1½ lb.)
- 3 turnips, peeled and cut into ½-inch cubes
- 3 medium onions, cut into thin wedges
- 2 cloves garlic, minced
- 2 Tbsp. olive oil or cooking oil

1 Combine the rosemary, salt, and pepper. Rub half of the mixture onto meat. Reserve remaining rosemary mixture. Place beef roast, fat side up, on a rack in a shallow roasting pan. Do not add any liquid. Do not cover. Insert a meat thermometer into center of roast.

2 Roast, uncovered, in a 350° oven for 1½ to 2 hours or until meat thermometer registers 135° for medium-rare, or 2 to 2½ hours or until thermometer registers 150° for medium.

3 Meanwhile, in a large Dutch oven cook sweet potatoes, turnips, and onions, covered, in enough boiling water to cover, for 3 minutes. Drain. Add garlic, olive oil or cooking oil, and remaining rosemary mixture to vegetables. Toss gently to combine. During last 45 minutes of roasting beef, arrange the vegetables around the meat in pan.

4 Remove roast from oven. Cover roast with foil; let stand 15 minutes before carving. (The meat's temperature will rise about 10° while it is standing.) Carve roast. Serve with roasted vegetables. Makes 8 main-dish servings plus leftovers.

Nutrition facts per serving: 328 cal., 15 g total fat (5 g sat. fat), 67 mg chol., 229 mg sodium, 24 g carbo., 5 g fiber, 25 g pro. *Daily values:* 144% vit. A, 42% vit. C, 4% calcium, 18% iron.

SWEET POTATO SHEPHERD'S PIE

Start to finish: 1¼ hr.

Here an old standard goes upscale as mashed sweets crown the top of this classic lamb stew. (See the photograph on page 243.)

- 1¼ lb. lean boneless lamb, cut into ½-inch cubes
- 1 Tbsp. olive oil or cooking oil
- 1 cup chopped onion
- 1 clove garlic, minced
- 1½ cups water
- ½ tsp. salt
- ½ tsp. dried savory, crushed
- ¼ tsp. ground cinnamon
- ¼ tsp. pepper
- 1 cup thinly sliced carrots
- 1 cup frozen cut green beans

◆◆◆

- 2 large sweet potatoes, peeled and cubed (about 1 lb.)
- 2 Tbsp. margarine or butter
- ¼ tsp. salt
- ⅛ tsp. ground nutmeg
  Milk (optional)

◆◆◆

- ¼ cup water
- 2 Tbsp. cornstarch

1 In a large skillet brown lamb, half at a time, in hot oil. Return all meat to pan. Stir in onion and garlic; cook for 1 minute more. Add the 1½ cups water, the ½ teaspoon salt, savory, cinnamon, and pepper. Bring to boiling; reduce heat. Simmer, covered, about 45 minutes or until meat is nearly tender. Add carrots and green beans. Cover and simmer about 10 minutes more or until vegetables are tender.

2 Meanwhile in a medium saucepan cook sweet potatoes in a small amount of boiling water for 20 to 25 minutes or until tender. Drain. Return to pan; add margarine or butter, the ¼ teaspoon salt, and nutmeg. Mash the cooked sweet potato mixture with a potato masher or with an electric mixer on low speed. If mixture seems dry, gradually stir in enough milk (about 2 to 3 tablespoons) to make potatoes fluffy. Set aside.

3 Combine the ¼ cup water and the cornstarch. Add water-cornstarch mixture to mixture in skillet. Cook and stir until thickened and bubbly. Spoon mashed sweet potato mixture in 6 mounds atop mixture in skillet. Simmer, uncovered, about 5 minutes more or until potatoes are heated through. Serve immediately. Makes 6 main-dish servings.

Nutrition facts per serving: 336 cal., 19 g total fat, 63 mg chol., 391 mg sodium, 23 g carbo., 3 g fiber, 18 g pro. *Daily values:* 191% vit. A, 30% vit. C, 5% calcium, 12% iron.

FRENCH COUNTRY CASSOULET

Prep: 20 min. ◆ Stand: 1 hr.
Cook: 2 hr.

1 lb. dry navy, great Northern, or cannellini beans

◆◆◆

1½ lb. lamb stew meat, cut into 1-inch cubes
1 large onion, cut into chunks
6 cloves garlic, minced
1 Tbsp. olive oil or cooking oil
4 cups reduced-sodium chicken broth
2 cups dry white wine
3 bay leaves

◆◆◆

4 medium carrots, peeled and cut into 1-inch pieces
6 oz. celery root, peeled and cut into ½-inch pieces
2 stalks celery, cut into 1-inch pieces
1½ tsp. dried rosemary, crushed

1 Rinse and sort beans, removing any pebbles or other foreign objects. In a 4-quart Dutch oven or pot combine beans and 8 cups *water*. Bring to boiling; reduce heat. Simmer 2 minutes. Remove from heat. Cover and let stand for 1 hour.

2 Drain soaked beans; rinse in a colander. In the same pot brown meat cubes, half at a time, with the onion and garlic in hot oil. Drain off fat. Add drained beans, broth, wine, and bay leaves to meat. Bring to boiling; reduce heat. Simmer, covered, for 1 hour, stirring occasionally.

3 Remove bay leaves. Stir in carrots, celery root, celery, rosemary, ½ teaspoon *salt*, and ¼ teaspoon *coarsely ground black pepper*.

CASSOULET ENCHANTÉ!

Simple French country cooking isn't just about sauces and cream. In fact, one of the best dishes France has to offer is the cassoulet (ka-soo-LAY), a slow-cooked stew of white beans, meat, and chunky root vegetables. Simmering allows the ingredients to steep together in an enchanting marriage of flavors. When served with warm, crusty bread and a carafe of your favorite wine, the result is an absolutely sublime meal in any country.

Return to boiling; reduce heat. Simmer, covered, 30 minutes more or until beans are nearly tender. Uncover and boil gently about 30 minutes more or until beans are tender and liquid has thickened, stirring occasionally. Makes 6 main-dish servings.

Nutrition facts per serving: 402 cal., 9 g total fat (3 g sat. fat), 50 mg chol., 552 mg sodium, 43 g carbo., 6 g fiber, 28 g pro. *Daily values:* 86% vit. A, 10% vit. C, 12% calcium, 35% iron.

FORK-TENDER LAMB SHANKS

Prep: 10 min.
Braise: 1 hr. and 35 min.

Ask your butcher for lamb foreshanks. They're smaller than hindshanks. (See the photograph on page 237.)

1 Tbsp. olive oil
4 meaty lamb foreshanks (about 4 lb.) or meaty veal shank crosscuts (about 3 lb.)

1 cup chicken broth
1 lb. boiling onions, peeled if desired
4 cloves garlic, minced
2 tsp. dried rosemary, crushed
¼ tsp. pepper

◆◆◆

½ cup pitted kalamata olives

◆◆◆

1¼ cups quick-cooking polenta mix

1 In a 6- to 8-quart Dutch oven heat oil. Brown meat on all sides in hot oil. Drain. Carefully stir in broth, onions, garlic, rosemary, and pepper. Bring to boiling; reduce heat. Simmer, covered, for 1½ to 2 hours or until meat is tender.

2 Remove shanks from pan.* Skim fat from the top of onion-broth mixture. Stir kalamata olives into mixture in Dutch oven. Bring to boiling; reduce heat. Simmer, covered, for 5 to 10 minutes more.

3 Meanwhile, prepare polenta according to package directions; set aside. Remove onions and olives from broth mixture with a slotted spoon. Serve meat, onions, and olives with polenta. Pass broth mixture. If desired, garnish with *fresh Italian parsley*. Makes 4 to 6 main-dish servings.

*****Note:** If desired, when meat is cool enough to handle, cut it off bones and coarsely chop. Discard fat and bones. Stir meat into onion-broth mixture along with the kalamata olives.

Nutrition facts per serving: 632 cal., 14 g total fat (3 g sat. fat), 99 mg chol., 460 mg sodium, 80 g carbo., 11 g fiber, 42 g pro. *Daily values:* 10% vit. C, 5% calcium, 26% iron.

Left: *Fork-Tender Lamb Shanks*
(page 236)
Below: *Braised Fall Vegetables*
(page 225)

Left: *Citrus-Splashed Squash*
(page 226)
Below: *Mixed Greens Sauté*
(page 226)
Page 238: *Roast Tarragon Chicken*
(page 247)

Top: *Sticky Peaches and Cream (page 249)*
Above: *Roasted Fruit Soup (page 228)*
Right: *Cider-Braised Pork Roast (page 233)*

Top: *Hazelnut-Mushroom Duckling (page 248)*
Page 242: *Figs and Fruit Salad (page 227)*

Above left: *Sweet Potato Shepherd's Pie (page 235)*
Above right: *Catfish with a Crunch (page 229)*

Above: *Venison with Juniper Berries (page 245)*
Left: *Sausage and Apple Pasta Bake (page 233)*

VENISON WITH JUNIPER BERRIES

Prep: 10 min. ◆ Chill: 1 to 2 hr.
Cook: 12 min.

See the photograph on page 244.

- **2 shallots, finely chopped**
- **4 cloves garlic, minced**
- **1 tsp. juniper berries, crushed**
- **2 8- to 12-oz. venison tenderloins or four 4-oz. beef tenderloin steaks, cut to 1-inch thickness**

◆◆◆

- **2 Tbsp. olive oil**

◆◆◆

- **1 recipe Tart-Sweet Cherry Relish (see right)**
  Waffle-style potato chips (optional)

1 In a small bowl combine shallots, garlic, juniper berries, ¼ teaspoon *salt*, and ⅛ teaspoon *pepper*. Rub mixture on all sides of meat; cover with plastic wrap. Refrigerate 1 to 2 hours, until ready to use.

2 In a large nonstick skillet heat oil. Cook venison in hot oil over medium-high heat for 12 to 14 minutes for medium-rare (145°), turning occasionally to brown evenly. Or, cook beef 4 to 6 minutes per side for medium-rare. (Reduce heat as necessary during cooking to prevent burning.)

3 To serve, cut venison or beef steaks into 1-inch-thick slices. Serve with Tart-Sweet Cherry Relish and, if desired, waffle-style potato chips. Makes 4 servings.

Nutrition facts per serving: 328 cal., 11 g total fat (2 g sat. fat), 93 mg chol., 195 mg sodium, 30 g carbo., 2 g fiber, 27 g pro. *Daily values:* 24% vit. A, 8% vit. C, 3% calcium, 21% iron.

TART-SWEET CHERRY RELISH

Start to finish: 10 min.

- **1 cup dried tart red cherries**
- **½ cup water**
- **2 Tbsp. lemon juice**
- **1 Tbsp. sugar**
- **2 Tbsp. slivered almonds, toasted**
- **1 Tbsp. fresh snipped cilantro**
- **1 tsp. juniper berries, finely crushed**

1 In a small saucepan combine dried cherries, water, lemon juice, and sugar. Bring to boiling; reduce heat. Simmer, uncovered, for 4 to 5 minutes or until most of the liquid is absorbed. Remove from heat. Stir in almonds, cilantro, and juniper berries. Cool. Serve with Venison with Juniper Berries (see recipe, left). Makes about 1 cup.

Nutrition facts per ¼ cup serving: 138 cal., 2 g total fat (0 g sat. fat), 0 mg chol., 2 mg sodium, 29 g carbo., 2 g fiber, 2 g pro. *Daily values:* 18% vit. A, 5% vit. C, 1% calcium, 1% iron.

VENISON FILLETS IN PORT

Start to finish: 20 min.

- **1 Tbsp. cooking oil**
- **1 lb. venison tenderloin, cut into 1-inch-thick fillets**
- **2 cups fresh mushrooms, quartered**
- **3 cloves garlic, minced**
- **¾ cup tawny port or dry red wine**

JUNIPER BERRY BITS

Often paired with game, tiny juniper berries have a pungent woodsy-pine taste that complements wild meat. The oil of the berries is distilled to give gin its prominent taste. When used in cooking, the dried berries are typically crushed to release their flavors. You can find the dried berries in the spice section of major markets or in specialty food stores.

- **1 tsp. snipped fresh rosemary or ¼ tsp. dried rosemary, crushed**

1 In a large skillet heat oil. Cook venison fillets 4 minutes or until browned, turning once. Remove from skillet. Season with *salt* and *coarsely ground pepper* to taste; set aside. Add mushrooms and garlic to hot skillet. Cook over medium heat until mushrooms are tender. Return fillets to skillet. Carefully add port or red wine and the 1 teaspoon rosemary. Cook, uncovered, over medium heat about 10 minutes or until liquid in skillet is reduced by more than half and fillets are cooked to medium doneness.

2 To serve, spoon mushroom sauce over fillets. If desired, garnish with *fresh rosemary sprigs.* Makes 4 servings.

Nutrition facts per serving: 273 cal., 6 g total fat (2 g sat. fat), 140 mg chol., 124 mg sodium, 7 g carbo., 1 g fiber, 38 g pro. *Daily values:* 3% vit. C, 2% calcium, 37% iron.

VENISON BY MAIL

You can order venison and other game by mail from companies such as Broken Arrow Ranch in Ingram, Texas (830/367-5875) and Millbrook Venison, Millbrook, New York (800/774-3337). Prices range from $4.98 to $25.98 per pound, and shipping takes about 2 to 3 working days. Some companies have a minimum order requirement.

HUNTSMAN'S CHILI

Prep: 40 min. ◆ Cook: 1 hr.

Set the heat level as high as you like by increasing the ground red pepper to suit your taste. Any cut of venison will do for this recipe.

2 **Tbsp. cooking oil**
1½ **lb. venison, cut into ½-inch cubes**
2 **medium onions, cut into ½-inch pieces**
2 **medium carrots, peeled and cut into ½-inch pieces**
2 **small parsnips, peeled and cut into ½-inch pieces**
¼ **cup currants or raisins**
4 **cloves garlic, minced**

◆◆◆

3 **Tbsp. chili powder**
2 **Tbsp. all-purpose flour**
½ **tsp. salt**
½ **tsp. ground cumin**
¼ **tsp. ground red pepper**
1 **15-oz. can dark red kidney beans, rinsed and drained**
1 **14½-oz. can diced tomatoes, undrained**
1 **12-oz. can beer or 1½ cups beef broth**
1 **cup water**

◆◆◆

Fresh cilantro sprigs, snipped

1 In a 4-quart Dutch oven or pot heat oil. Add half of the venison and the onion; cook until browned. Remove and set aside. Brown remaining venison; return all meat to pan. Add carrots, parsnips, currants or raisins, and garlic. Cook for 5 minutes.

2 Stir chili powder, flour, salt, cumin, and red pepper into mixture in pot. Add beans, undrained tomatoes, beer or broth, and water. Bring to boiling; reduce heat. Simmer, covered, for 1 hour, stirring often.

3 To serve, ladle chili into individual bowls. Sprinkle each serving with snipped cilantro. Makes 6 main-dish servings.

Nutrition facts per serving: 337 cal., 8 g total fat (1 g sat. fat), 93 mg chol., 575 mg sodium, 35 g carbo., 9 g fiber, 33 g pro. *Daily values:* 71% vit. A, 31% vit. C, 8% calcium, 37% iron.

QUICK CARIBBEAN CHICKEN

Start to finish: 20 min.

Sweet and savory flavors dance a rhythmic duet in this Caribbean-inspired meal. Let the rice cook while you prepare the chicken, and dinner is on the table in 20 minutes.

12 **oz. chicken tenderloin strips**
¼ **tsp. salt**
⅛ **to ¼ tsp. ground red pepper**

◆◆◆

1 **tsp. cooking oil**
1 **medium sweet potato, peeled, halved lengthwise, and thinly sliced**
1 **small banana pepper, seeded and chopped**

◆◆◆

¾ **cup unsweetened pineapple juice**
1 **tsp. cornstarch**
2 **unripe bananas, quartered lengthwise and cut into ¾-inch pieces**

◆◆◆

2 **cups hot cooked brown rice**

1 Season the chicken tenderloin strips with salt and ground red pepper.

2 In a large nonstick skillet heat oil. Cook chicken in hot oil for 3 to 4 minutes. Add the sweet potato and banana pepper. Cook and stir for 5 to 6 minutes more or until potatoes are just tender.

3 Meanwhile, in a small bowl stir together pineapple juice and cornstarch. Add juice-cornstarch mixture to mixture in skillet.

Cook, stirring gently, until bubbly. Add unripe banana pieces; cook and stir 2 minutes more.

4 To serve, in each of 4 shallow bowls, serve chicken mixture over cooked brown rice. Makes 4 main-dish servings.

Nutrition facts per serving: 326 cal., 5 g total fat (1 g sat. fat), 45 mg chol., 188 mg sodium, 50 g carbo., 4 g fiber, 20 g pro. *Daily values:* 73% vit. A, 48% vit. C, 3% calcium, 7% iron.

ROAST TARRAGON CHICKEN

Prep: 15 min. ◆ Roast: 1 hr. Stand: 10 min.

The cherry tomatoes and shallots roasted with the chicken create a sensational side dish. Or, try them as a topper for mashed potatoes, rice, or couscous and serve alongside the herbed poultry. (See the photograph on page 238.)

1 2½- to 3-lb. whole broiler-fryer chicken

◆◆◆

3 Tbsp. olive oil
2 cloves garlic, minced
2½ tsp. dried tarragon, crushed
½ tsp. coarsely ground pepper
¼ tsp. salt
1 lb. cherry tomatoes
8 small shallots, peeled

◆◆◆

1 recipe Mashed Potatoes (see right) (optional)
Fresh tarragon sprigs (optional)
Snipped fresh parsley (optional)

1 Rinse chicken; pat dry with paper towels. Skewer neck skin to back; tie legs to tail. Twist wings under back. Place chicken, breast side up, on a rack in a shallow roasting pan.

2 In a medium bowl stir together olive oil, garlic, tarragon, pepper, and salt. Add tomatoes and shallots. Toss to coat. Remove tomatoes and shallots from bowl; set aside. Brush chicken with remaining olive oil mixture.

3 Insert a meat thermometer into center of an inside thigh muscle of chicken. Do not allow thermometer tip to touch bone. Roast chicken, uncovered, in a 375° oven for 1 to 1¼ hours or until drumsticks move easily in their sockets, chicken is no longer pink, and meat thermometer registers 180°. During last 25 minutes of roasting time, arrange shallots around chicken in pan. During last 10 to 12 minutes of roasting time, arrange tomatoes around chicken in pan.

4 Remove tomatoes, shallots, and chicken from the roasting pan. Cover chicken and let stand 10 minutes before carving.

5 Serve chicken with shallots, tomatoes, and, if desired, Mashed Potatoes. If desired, garnish with fresh tarragon and parsley. Makes 6 main-dish servings.

Nutrition facts per serving: 227 cal., 13 g total fat (2 g sat. fat), 67 mg chol., 170 mg sodium, 5 g carbo., 1 g fiber, 23 g pro. *Daily values:* 7% vit. A, 26% vit. C, 2% calcium, 8% iron.

Menu

Figs and Fruit Salad (see page 227)

◆◆◆

Roast Tarragon Chicken (see left)

◆◆◆

Mashed Potatoes (see below)

◆◆◆

Crusty hard rolls with butter

◆◆◆

Fruit cobbler or crisp with ice cream

MASHED POTATOES

Start to finish: 35 min.

4 baking potatoes (1½ lb.)
2 Tbsp. margarine or butter
Salt
Pepper
3 to 5 Tbsp. milk.

1 Peel and quarter potatoes. Cook, covered, in a small amount of lightly salted boiling water for 20 to 25 minutes or until tender; drain. Mash with a potato masher or beat with an electric mixer on low speed. Add margarine or butter. Season to taste with salt and pepper. Gradually beat in enough milk to make light and fluffy. Makes 6 side-dish servings.

Nutrition facts per serving: 134 cal., 4 g total fat (1 g sat. fat), 1 mg chol., 143 mg sodium, 23 g carbo., 1 g fiber, 2 g pro. *Daily values:* 5% vit. A, 8% vit. C, 1% calcium, 2% iron.

THE DISH ON DUCKLING

Because duckling was once viewed as a fatty meat, the duckling industry went on a diet. By refining the breeding and feeding techniques, duckling producers developed a product that is lean and tender. Its nutritional content is comparable to chicken and turkey. The USDA recommends cooking duckling breasts to 160°, and whole poultry to 180°. Look for duckling in the poultry case or frozen food section of your neighborhood market, but if it's not available there you can order it by mail. Check with sources such as Culver Duck Farms in Middlebury, Indiana (800 825-9225, www. culverduck.com) and Maple Leaf Farms in Milford, Indiana (800 382-5546). Shipping takes about 2 to 3 working days.

HAZELNUT-MUSHROOM DUCKLING

Prep: 25 min. ◆ Cook: 16 min.

Pudgy-stemmed shimeji mushrooms can be found in Asian markets or in the ethnic section of major grocery stores. (See the photograph on page 243.)

8 oz. packaged dried mafalda or dried fettuccine

◆◆◆

1 cup fresh mushrooms, such as shimeji, enoki, or button

6 medium green onions, cut into 1-inch pieces (1 cup)
1 Tbsp. margarine or butter

◆◆◆

½ cup all-purpose flour
¼ tsp. ground black pepper
¼ tsp. dried thyme, crushed
⅛ tsp. salt
4 4-oz. skinless, boneless duckling breasts or boneless pork loin chops, cut ½ to ¾ inch thick, or skinless, boneless, chicken breast halves

◆◆◆

1 Tbsp. margarine or butter
⅔ cup reduced-sodium chicken broth
1 tsp. snipped fresh thyme or ¼ tsp. dried thyme, crushed
¼ tsp. ground black pepper

◆◆◆

Reduced-sodium chicken broth
¾ cup whipping cream

◆◆◆

¼ cup coarsely chopped toasted hazelnuts* (filberts)
Fresh thyme sprigs (optional)

1 Cook pasta according to package directions. Drain and set aside. Keep warm.

2 Meanwhile, in a large skillet cook and stir mushrooms and green onions in 1 tablespoon margarine or butter until tender. Remove mixture from skillet; set aside.

3 In a shallow dish combine the flour, ¼ teaspoon pepper, ¼ teaspoon dried thyme, and salt. Rinse duckling, pork, or chicken; pat dry with paper towels. Lightly press the flour mixture onto both sides of meat and shake off excess.

4 In the same skillet melt 1 tablespoon margarine. Cook meat in hot margarine over medium-high heat for 8 to 10 minutes, turning to brown evenly. Remove skillet from heat. Carefully add broth, the 1 teaspoon fresh thyme or ¼ teaspoon dried thyme, and ¼ teaspoon pepper. Bring to boiling; reduce heat. Simmer, uncovered, about 3 minutes or until meat is no longer pink and juices run clear, stirring sauce occasionally.

5 Transfer meat to a cutting board. Add additional broth to skillet to make ½ cup, if necessary. Return mushrooms and green onions to juices in skillet. Stir in whipping cream. Cook and stir about 5 minutes or until slightly thickened. Remove from heat.

6 To serve, divide pasta among 4 serving plates. Thinly slice the meat. Place on top of cooked pasta. Spoon mushroom mixture around meat. Sprinkle with hazelnuts. If desired, garnish with thyme sprigs. Makes 4 main-dish servings.

*To toast hazelnuts: Place nuts in a small skillet. Cook over medium-low heat, stirring or shaking skillet often, for 7 to 10 minutes or until skins begin to flake and nuts are light golden brown. Watch carefully to avoid over-browning. Remove nuts from skillet and place on a clean kitchen towel. When hazelnuts are cool enough to handle, rub the nuts together in the towel, removing as much of the brown skin as possible. Discard skin.

CINNAMON CREAM

Start to finish: 15 min.

A cross between pudding and whipped cream, this treat pairs well with sautéed fruit or a fresh-from-the-oven cobbler.

- **3 Tbsp. sugar**
- **2 tsp. cornstarch**
- **¼ tsp. ground cinnamon**
- **½ cup milk**
- **1 egg yolk, beaten**
- **2 tsp. margarine or butter**
- **½ tsp. vanilla**

❖❖❖

- **⅓ cup whipping cream**

1 In a small saucepan combine sugar, cornstarch, and cinnamon. Stir in milk. Cook and stir over medium heat until thickened and bubbly. Slowly stir hot mixture into egg yolk. Return mixture to pan. Cook and stir 2 minutes more or until bubbly. Remove from heat. Stir in margarine or butter and vanilla. Cover surface with plastic wrap; cool without stirring, then chill thoroughly.

2 Just before serving, in a small chilled bowl beat whipping cream until soft peaks form; fold into chilled mixture. Serves 6.

STICKY PEACHES AND CREAM

Start to finish: 8 min.

This sautéed standout is a delicious treat for the family, especially after a stroll in the brisk autumn air. The brown sugar-glazed peaches are yummy—with or without the cloud of Cinnamon Cream. (See the photograph on page 240.)

- **2 Tbsp. butter**
- **6 ripe medium peaches, peeled, pitted, and sliced, or 6 cups frozen unsweetened peach slices, thawed, drained, and patted dry**
- **2 Tbsp. brown sugar**
- **¼ tsp. ground ginger**

❖❖❖

- **6 amaretti cookies or oatmeal cookies**
- **1 recipe Cinnamon Cream (see left)**
- **3 Tbsp. crumbled amaretti cookies or oatmeal cookies**

1 In a large skillet melt butter over medium-high heat. Add peaches; cook and stir about 2 minutes or until heated through. Sprinkle with brown sugar and ginger. Cook and stir for 1 to 2 minutes more or until the peaches are coated and caramelized.

2 To assemble individual desserts, spoon about ½ cup of the caramelized peaches into each of 6 bowls. Place a whole amaretti or oatmeal cookie next to peaches.

THE CLEVER COOK

HANDY SPICE CONTAINERS

My husband and I vacation for extended periods of time and thus stay in resorts with kitchen facilities. Rather than pack large amounts of the spices and herbs I like to use when cooking, I put a small amount in empty and clean 35mm film containers. These containers store well, take up very little space in luggage, and help to reduce the vacation food budget. Once back home, the unused portion goes back into its original container with no loss or waste.

Betty E. Swain
Fairborn, Ohio

Dollop with about 3 tablespoons Cinnamon Cream. Sprinkle peaches in each bowl with about 1½ teaspoons cookie crumbles. Makes 6 servings.

WALNUT-PEAR SOUR CREAM CAKE

Prep: 30 min. ◆ Bake: 55 min.

For extra "wow," add whipped cream, edible flowers, fresh figs, and fresh bay leaf to each serving.

1 cup broken walnuts
⅓ cup packed brown sugar
1 tsp. ground cinnamon
¼ cup butter
⅓ cup all-purpose flour

◆◆◆

2 medium pears, peeled, cored, and sliced (about 2 cups)
2 tsp. lemon juice
1¾ cups all-purpose flour
¾ tsp. baking powder
½ tsp. baking soda
½ cup butter, softened
1 cup granulated sugar
1 tsp. vanilla
2 eggs
1 8-oz. carton dairy sour cream
½ cup broken walnuts (optional)

1 Grease a 9-inch springform pan or a 9×9×2-inch baking pan. Combine the 1 cup nuts, brown sugar, and cinnamon. For topping, cut ¼ cup butter into ⅓ cup flour to make coarse crumbs. Stir in ¾ cup of the nut mixture. Set nut mixture and topping aside.

2 Toss pears with lemon juice; set aside. Combine 1¾ cups flour, baking powder, soda, and ¼ teaspoon *salt;* set aside. Beat ½ cup butter with electric mixer 30 seconds. Beat in granulated sugar and vanilla. Add eggs, 1 at a time, beating after each. Add flour mixture and sour cream alternately to batter. Beat on low speed after each addition until combined.

3 Spread two-thirds batter into prepared pan. Sprinkle with reserved nut mixture. Layer pears over top. Gently spread remaining batter over pears. Sprinkle with reserved topping. Bake in a 350° oven for 10 minutes. If desired, for a chunky top, sprinkle with ½ cup more nuts. Bake 45 to 50 minutes more or until a wooden toothpick inserted in the center comes out clean. Cool in pan on a rack 10 minutes. Remove side of springform pan, if using. Cool 1 hour. Serve warm. Serves 12.

Nutrition facts per serving: 396 cal., 23 g total fat (10 g sat. fat), 75 mg chol., 260 mg sodium, 45 g carbo., 2 g fiber, 5 g pro. *Daily values:* 16% vit. A, 3% vit. C, 6% calcium, 10% iron.

PRIZE TESTED RECIPE WINNER

POLENTA-PECAN APPLE COBBLER

Prep: 25 min. ◆ Cook: 5 min.
Bake: 35 min.

If you've always wanted to try polenta, here's a homey way: pair it with fruit.

½ cup all-purpose flour
⅓ cup quick-cooking polenta mix or yellow cornmeal
2 Tbsp. granulated sugar
1 tsp. baking powder
⅛ tsp. salt
3 Tbsp. butter
½ cup chopped pecans
2 Tbsp. brown sugar
¼ tsp. ground cinnamon

◆◆◆

8 cups peeled, cored, cubed, cooking apples (8 medium)
½ cup dried tart red cherries
⅓ cup packed brown sugar
1 Tbsp. lemon juice

¼ tsp. ground cinnamon
¼ cup water
1 Tbsp. cornstarch

◆◆◆

⅓ cup half-and-half or light cream

1 For topping, in a bowl stir together flour, polenta, granulated sugar, baking powder, and salt. Cut in butter until mixture resembles coarse crumbs. Set aside. In another small bowl combine the pecans, 2 tablespoons brown sugar, and ¼ teaspoon cinnamon; set aside.

2 For filling, in a large saucepan combine the apples, cherries, ⅓ cup brown sugar, lemon juice, and ¼ teaspoon cinnamon. Bring to boiling, stirring constantly; reduce heat. Simmer, covered, about 5 minutes or until fruit is almost tender, stirring occasionally. Combine water and cornstarch; add to saucepan. Cook and stir until thickened and bubbly. Keep hot.

3 Add ⅓ cup half-and-half to flour mixture, stirring just to moisten. Transfer filling to a 2-quart square baking dish. Using a spoon, immediately drop topping into small mounds atop filling. Sprinkle with pecan mixture.

4 Bake in a 375° oven about 35 minutes or until a wooden toothpick inserted into topping comes out clean. If desired, serve with additional *half-and-half* or *light cream.* Makes 6 servings.

Nutrition facts per serving: 448 cal., 15 g total fat (6 g sat. fat), 24 mg chol., 180 mg sodium, 78 g carbo., 5 g fiber, 4 g pro. *Daily values:* 15% vit. A, 14% vit. C, 9% calcium, 9% iron.

NOVEMBER
No-Fuss Thanksgiving

Make this year's family Thanksgiving feast a celebration to remember. Ease the strain—and the gain—by following our suggestions for roasting the perfect bird (page 272) and creating a not-so-heavy dinner (page 274). Keep the meals before and after Thanksgiving easy, too. Pesto-Swirled Pasta and Vegetable Soup, Squash-Potato Chowder, Chicken and Pasta Primavera, Pork Medallions with Fennel and Pancetta, and Bistro Beef and Mushrooms are all hearty, delicious dishes that can be made in 30 minutes or less.

30-minute recipes indicated in RED.
Low-fat and no-fat recipes indicated
with a ♥.
Photographs indicated in italics.
*Bonus recipe

ITALIAN PEPPERONI-CHEESE PUFFS

Prep: 30 min. ◆ Bake: 15 min.

Fragrant and airy, these puffs are perfect for appetizers or snacks.

1¼ cups water
⅓ cup shortening
1½ cups all-purpose flour
4 eggs
¾ cup finely chopped pepperoni (3 oz.)
¾ cup finely shredded Pecorino Romano or Parmesan cheese (3 oz.)
2 Tbsp. snipped fresh parsley
⅛ tsp. garlic powder
⅛ tsp. pepper

1 Grease 2 large baking sheets; set aside. In a large saucepan combine water and shortening. Bring to boiling. Add flour all at once, stirring vigorously. Cook and stir until mixture forms a ball. Remove from heat. Cool for 10 minutes. Add eggs, 1 at a time, beating well with a wooden spoon after each addition. Stir in pepperoni, cheese, parsley, garlic powder, and pepper.

2 Drop dough by rounded teaspoons 2 inches apart onto prepared baking sheets. Bake in a 450° oven for 15 to 17 minutes or until golden. Transfer to a wire rack. Serve warm. Makes 48 puffs.

Nutrition facts per puff: 48 cal., 3 g total fat (1 g sat. fat), 21 mg chol., 62 mg sodium, 3 g carbo., 0 g fiber, 2 g pro.
Daily values: 1% vit. A, 1% calcium, 1% iron.

BAKED KASSERI CHEESE SPREAD

Prep: 20 min. ◆ Bake: 8 min.

When chilly winds blow, cozy up to the fire then linger over a glass of red wine, a loaf of crusty bread, and this creamy spread of kasseri cheese, piquant olives, and oregano.

12 oz. kasseri* or Scamorza cheese
⅔ cup kalamata olives, pitted and quartered
2 Tbsp. snipped fresh oregano
1 clove garlic, minced
¼ tsp. crushed red pepper

◆◆◆

French bread, apples, or crackers

1 Cut cheese into ½-inch-thick slices. Layer cheese in the bottom of a shallow 1-quart quiche dish or a 9-inch pie plate, overlapping if necessary. Toss together the olives, oregano, garlic, and crushed red pepper. Sprinkle over the cheese.

2 Bake in a 450° oven for 8 to 10 minutes or until cheese just begins to melt. Serve immediately on bread, apples, or crackers. Rewarm cheese as needed. Makes 12 appetizer servings.

***Note:** Traditionally Greek, kasseri cheese is made with either sheep's or goat's milk. Its sharp, salty flavor and meltability make it a natural for this dish.

Nutrition facts per serving (spread only): 141 cal., 12 g total fat (7 g sat. fat), 30 mg chol., 350 mg sodium, 1 g carbo., 0 g fiber, 7 g pro.
Daily values: 14% calcium.

TOASTED ALMONDS WITH ROSEMARY & CAYENNE

Start to finish: 15 min.

Sweet, hot, and crunchy. No wonder these herb-coated nuts disappear quickly. Make a bowl—maybe two—especially when you're serving cocktails. Then mix some martinis and kick back to the sounds of some cool jazz.

8 oz. unblanched almonds or pecan halves (about 2 cups)
1½ tsp. butter
1 Tbsp. finely snipped fresh rosemary
1½ tsp. brown sugar
¼ to ½ tsp. salt
¼ tsp. ground red pepper

1 Spread almonds or pecans in a single layer on a baking sheet. Bake in a 350° oven about 10 minutes or until nuts are lightly toasted and fragrant.

2 Meanwhile, in a medium saucepan melt butter over medium heat until sizzling. Remove from heat. Stir in rosemary, brown sugar, salt, and ground red pepper. Add nuts to butter mixture and toss to coat. Cool slightly before serving. Makes 16 appetizer servings.

TO MAKE AHEAD

Prepare nuts as directed; cool completely. Place cooled nuts in an airtight container and store up to 1 month in the refrigerator or up to 3 months in the freezer.

Nutrition facts per serving: 80 cal., 7 g total fat (1 g sat. fat), 1 mg chol., 37 mg sodium, 3 g carbo., 1 g fiber, 4 g pro.
Daily values: 4% calcium, 5% iron.

EASY DRESS-UPS

Spectacular-tasting holiday favorites deserve spectacular flourishes. Here are a dozen no-fuss frills to dress up your feast-time treasures. Happy eating!

1. Curl it. Using a large-hole zester, remove peel from an orange in long strips. Wind strips around a chopstick; let stand 30 minutes or until strips hold curls. Garnish dinner, salad, or dessert with the orange curls.

2. Adorn it. Brush tops of baked shortbread cookies with a mixture of 1 tablespoon dried egg whites dissolved in 2 tablespoons water. Place edible violas or other small flowers on top; brush on more egg-white mixture. Sprinkle with granulated sugar. Bake in a 325° oven for 5 minutes to dry tops of cookies.

3. Arrange it. Cut a round of brie into five wedges. Arrange wedges on a serving plate with points toward the rim of the plate. Top with kumquat slices, champagne grapes, edible flowers, and assorted fresh herbs.

4. Layer it. In a straight-edge, clear-glass dish, first layer olives, then marinated feta cubes, and finally marinated artichoke hearts. Ta da—great munching!

5. Top it. A long sprig or two of fresh rosemary or thyme adds easy style to a side of mashed sweets or regular potatoes.

6. Surround it. Go for glamour by surrounding your roasted holiday bird with ocher- and green-hued fresh apricots, figs, pears, apples, star fruit, and tufts of variegated fresh sage.

7. Herb it. Before baking a batch of yeast rolls, brush the unbaked risen rolls with a mixture of 1 egg white beaten with 1 tablespoon water. While egg-white mixture remains moist, place fresh Italian parsley or sage leaves on rolls. Brush again with egg-white mixture. Bake as directed.

8. Stuff it. A halved and baked butternut or acorn squash makes a fitting spot to pile a favorite stuffing or pilaf. For maximum effect, arrange the stuffed halves in a footed shallow bowl or compote.

9. Ribbon it. A dazzling ribbon does wonders when it comes to dressing up a plain cake or torte. Tie a wide ribbon around the outside and tuck in fresh herb sprigs for added flair.

10. Write it. Spoon melted chocolate into a pastry bag fitted with a #4 tip. Pipe a festive holiday message onto the border of a dessert plate; let stand until message is set.

11. Leaf it. On a floured surface roll pie pastry to ⅛-inch thickness. Using a small knife or cutters, cut pastry into leaf shapes. Transfer to an ungreased baking sheet. Make decorative marks in leaf shapes; brush with beaten egg. Bake in a 400° oven about 10 minutes or until leaves are golden.

12. Float it. Arrange crab apples in a circle slightly smaller than the diameter of a punch bowl. Link apples together using wooden toothpicks that have been halved crosswise. For a festive bow, top crab apple circle with fresh bay leaves.

SOUL OF THE SUN

The mystery of this sweet and crunchy root vegetable is not in how it's twice misnamed, but in why it gets less attention than it deserves.

Jerusalem artichokes, also called sunchokes, are impostors: They aren't artichokes at all. In fact, they're not even from Jerusalem. Jerusalem artichokes are actually the edible root of a variety of sunflower. They are tubers similar to the common potato. Their misnomer is derived from the Italian word for sunflower, girasole, which sounds a little like, Jerusalem.

Unlike potatoes, the Jerusalem artichoke is knobby with a crunchy texture and slightly sweet taste. To prepare, after washing and trimming, peel or scrub the vegetable. Shave raw Jerusalem artichokes into salads, or lightly cook slices or chunks to serve as a crisp and sunny side dish to herb-roasted chicken or beef pot roast.

GINGERED JERUSALEM ARTICHOKES

Start to finish: 15 min.

Wait until your dinner is just about ready to go on the table before you cook these slightly crunchy nibbles. Once cooked, they soften if not eaten right away.

1 Tbsp. margarine or butter
1 lb. Jerusalem artichokes, peeled, if desired, and cut up

2 tsp. grated fresh ginger
¼ cup marsala, sherry, or apple juice
Salt (optional)

1 In a large skillet heat the margarine or butter over medium-high heat. Cook artichokes in hot margarine for 5 to 6 minutes or until crisp-tender, stirring often. Add ginger; cook for 30 seconds. Remove from heat. Stir in marsala, sherry, or apple juice. If desired, add salt to taste. Makes 4 side-dish servings.

Nutrition facts per serving: 134 cal., 3 g total fat (2 g sat. fat), 0 mg chol., 35 mg sodium, 22 g carbo., 1 g fiber, 2 g pro. *Daily values:* 7% vit. C, 1% calcium, 26% iron.

CORN CAKES WITH FRESH CORN AND CHIVES

Prep: 20 min. ◆ Cook: 6 min.

Everything old is new again! That most traditional of American foods, the corn cake, has been updated with fresh corn and just-snipped herbs.

1 fresh ear of corn or ½ cup frozen whole kernel corn
2 Tbsp. all-purpose flour
1½ tsp. baking powder
1 tsp. sugar
½ tsp. salt

◆◆◆

1 cup boiling water
1 cup yellow cornmeal

¼ cup milk
1 egg, slightly beaten
1 Tbsp. snipped fresh chives
3 Tbsp. cooking oil

◆◆◆

1 tsp. snipped fresh chives or cilantro (optional)
⅓ cup dairy sour cream

1 Cut corn kernels from cob and measure ½ cup. Set aside. In a small bowl combine flour, baking powder, sugar, and salt. Set aside.

2 In a medium bowl stir boiling water into cornmeal to make a stiff mush. Stir in milk until smooth; then stir in fresh or frozen corn, egg, and the 1 tablespoon chives. Add flour mixture and stir just until combined.

3 In a large skillet heat 2 tablespoons of the oil over medium heat. Drop batter by rounded tablespoons into hot oil. Cook for 3 to 4 minutes or until golden brown, turning once. Transfer to a serving platter; cover and keep warm. Repeat with remaining batter, adding the remaining 1 tablespoon oil.

4 Meanwhile, if desired, stir the 1 teaspoon chives into sour cream. Serve with the corn cakes. Makes 6 side-dish servings.

Nutrition facts per serving: 215 cal., 11 g total fat (3 g sat. fat), 42 mg chol., 295 mg sodium, 25 g carbo., 2 g fiber, 4 g pro. *Daily values:* 6% vit. A, 2% vit. C, 10% calcium, 9% iron.

PESTO-SWIRLED PASTA AND VEGETABLE SOUP

Start to finish: 25 min.

A swirl of basil pesto provides the perfect flavor accent for this vegetable and pasta soup. Pesto can be purchased prepared at your supermarket or deli.

- 2 cloves garlic, minced
- 1 Tbsp. olive oil
- 2 14½-oz. cans vegetable broth
- ½ cup dried ditalini pasta or small shells pasta

❖❖❖

- 1 cup packaged frozen stir-fry vegetables
- 3 cups torn arugula, torn Swiss chard, or shredded Chinese cabbage
- 2 cups torn spinach
- 3 Tbsp. purchased pesto

1 In a large saucepan cook minced garlic in hot oil for 30 seconds. Add vegetable broth. Bring to boiling; add pasta. Return to boiling; reduce heat. Boil gently, uncovered, for 6 minutes, stirring occasionally.

2 Stir in stir-fry vegetables; return soup to boiling. Stir in arugula and spinach; cook and stir for 2 minutes more. Swirl pesto into each serving. Makes 3 side-dish servings.

Nutrition facts per serving: 261 cal., 17 g total fat (1 g sat. fat), 2 mg chol., 1,281 mg sodium, 29 g carbo., 1 g fiber, 7 g pro. *Daily values:* 63% vit. A, 40% vit. C, 7% calcium, 15% iron.

CREAMY CARROT & PASTA SOUP

Start to finish: 30 min.

Do you hear the reggae rhythms? Or is it just the hot Jamaican spices in this creamy pasta soup that dance in your mouth? It's a tropical trip via a dash of jerk seasoning—a unique island blend of spices, herbs, and fiery chilies that is Jamaica's own.

- 2 14½-oz. cans chicken broth (3½ cups)
- 2 cups sliced carrots
- 1 large potato, peeled and diced
- 1 cup chopped onion
- 1 Tbsp. grated fresh ginger
- ½ to 1 tsp. Jamaican jerk seasoning

❖❖❖

- 8 oz. dried tricolor radiatore or rotini

❖❖❖

- 1½ cups milk or one 12-oz. can evaporated skim milk
  Snipped fresh chives (optional)

1 In a large saucepan combine chicken broth, carrots, potato, onion, ginger, and Jamaican jerk seasoning. Bring to boiling; reduce heat. Simmer, covered, for 15 to 20 minutes or until vegetables are very tender. Cool slightly.

2 Meanwhile, cook pasta according to package directions; drain pasta.

SUNCHOKE SAVVY

You'll find Jerusalem artichokes (sunchokes) in the produce section of most supermarkets. They're usually available year-round, although their peak season is fall through winter. Look for firm roots without pits or blemishes. Jerusalem artichokes will keep, loosely wrapped, for up to one week in the refrigerator. They should not be cooked for more than a few minutes or they'll become mushy and lose their flavor.

3 Place one-fourth of the vegetable mixture in a food processor. Cover and process until smooth. Process remaining vegetable mixture one-fourth at a time. Return all to saucepan.

4 Add cooked pasta and milk to mixture in saucepan; heat through. To serve, ladle soup into bowls. If desired, sprinkle soup with fresh chives. Makes 4 main-dish servings.

Nutrition facts per serving: 363 cal., 4 g total fat (2 g sat. fat), 8 mg chol., 750 mg sodium, 65 g carbo., 3 g fiber, 16 g pro. *Daily values:* 91% vit. A, 10% vit. C, 12% calcium, 20% iron.

PEARL OF A GRAIN

The cultivation of barley can be traced back to ancient Mesopotamia, making it one of the oldest grains still grown. With a history this epic, you know these pearls of protein are good. Try barley in casseroles, salads, soups, and pilafs. For a cozy, nutritious cereal, stir a little maple syrup into some hot cooked barley.

HOT BARLEY CEREAL

Start to finish: 15 min.

Mild in taste, but rich in niacin, thiamine, selenium, and zinc, barley makes a great grain for breakfast.

½ **cup cooked barley**
⅓ **cup milk**
1 **Tbsp. maple syrup or honey**
1 **Tbsp. margarine or butter (optional)**

1 In a small saucepan combine cooked barley and milk. Bring to boiling; reduce heat. Simmer, uncovered, for 10 minutes, stirring occasionally. Stir in maple syrup or honey. Spoon into bowl. If desired, top with 1 teaspoon margarine or butter. Makes 1 serving.

Basic Barley: In a saucepan bring 3 cups water to boiling. Stir in ¾ cup pearl barley. Return to boiling; reduce heat. Simmer, covered, about 45 minutes or until the barley is tender. Drain, if necessary. Makes about 3 cups cooked barley.

For quick-cooking barley: In a saucepan bring 2 cups water to boiling. Stir in ¾ cup quick-cooking barley. Return to boiling; reduce heat. Simmer, covered, for 10 to 12 minutes or until tender. Drain, if necessary.

Nutrition facts per serving, with syrup and margarine: 206 cal., 6 g total fat (2 g sat. fat), 6 mg chol., 93 mg sodium, 34 g carbo., 3 g fiber, 6 g pro.
Daily values: 9% vit. A, 1% vit. C, 9% calcium, 7% iron.

LOW FAT

SCOTCH BARLEY BROTH

Prep: 15 min. ◆ Cook: 1 hr.

Scotch broth is one of the more familiar uses of barley in America. Stew beef can be substituted for lamb, if desired.

12 **oz. lamb stew meat, cut into 1-inch cubes**
½ **tsp. freshly ground pepper**
1 **Tbsp. cooking oil**
3 **14½-oz. cans beef broth**
1 **12-oz. bottle dark beer**
⅔ **cup pearl barley or quick-cooking barley**
◆◆◆
1 **large leek, halved lengthwise and sliced (about ½ cup)**
1 **large turnip, peeled and cut into ½-inch pieces (1 cup)**
2 **medium carrots, sliced ½ inch thick (about 1 cup)**
2 **Tbsp. snipped parsley**

1 In a 4-quart Dutch oven or pot cook lamb with pepper in hot oil for 5 minutes. Pour off fat; discard. Add broth and beer to meat in pan. Bring to boiling; add pearl barley, if using. Reduce heat. Simmer, covered, for 30 minutes.

2 Add leek, turnip, and carrots to mixture in pan. Return to boiling; reduce heat. Simmer, covered, about 30 minutes more or until tender. (If using quick-cooking barley, add it about 12 minutes before stew is finished.) Stir in parsley. Ladle into bowls. Makes 4 or 5 main-dish servings.

Nutrition facts per serving: 321 cal., 9 g total fat (2 g sat. fat), 43 mg chol., 1,089 mg sodium, 34 g carbo., 8 g fiber, 22 g pro.
Daily values: 86% vit. A, 14% vit. C, 5% calcium, 23% iron.

30 MIN. LOW FAT

WILD RICE, BARLEY, & MUSHROOM SOUP

Start to finish: 25 min.

It's hard to resist this enticing soup. The nutty flavor and chewy texture of wild rice and barley make pleasant contrasts to the earthy flavor and soft texture of the mushrooms. Add a splash of Madeira for a sophisticated accent.

1 **cup water**
¼ **cup quick-cooking barley**
◆◆◆
3 **medium leeks, washed, trimmed, and thinly sliced**
1 **medium carrot, sliced**
1 **small parsnip, finely chopped**
1 **clove garlic, minced**
1 **Tbsp. margarine or butter**
3 **cups sliced fresh mushrooms**
1 **Tbsp. snipped fresh sage or 1 tsp. dried sage, crushed**
2½ **cups vegetable broth**
¾ **cup cooked wild rice**
2 **Tbsp. Madeira wine or dry sherry (optional)**

1 In a small saucepan combine water and barley. Bring mixture to boiling; reduce heat. Simmer, covered, for 10 minutes.

2 Meanwhile, in a large saucepan cook leeks, carrot, parsnip, and garlic in hot margarine or butter for 5 minutes. Stir in the mushrooms and, if using, dried sage. Cook 5 to 10 minutes more or just until mushrooms are tender. Stir in the vegetable broth, cooked wild rice, cooked barley, and, if desired, Madeira. If using, stir in fresh sage. Cook and stir until heated through. Season to taste with *salt* and *pepper*. Ladle into bowls. Makes 3 main-dish or 6 side-dish servings.

Nutrition facts per serving: 223 cal., 6 g total fat (1 g sat. fat), 0 mg chol., 854 mg sodium, 45 g carbo., 9 g fiber, 7 g pro. *Daily values:* 60% vit. A, 20% vit. C, 5% calcium, 24% iron.

SQUASH-POTATO CHOWDER

Start to finish: 30 min.

Liven up a can of cream of potato soup with fresh vegetables.

1 **Tbsp. margarine or butter**
2 **cups cubed summer squash, such as zucchini, sunburst, pattypan, or crookneck**
1 **cup sliced carrot**
½ **cup chopped onion**
1 **clove garlic, minced**
¾ **tsp. dried thyme, crushed**
⅛ **to ¼ tsp. pepper**
1 **10¾-oz. can condensed cream of potato soup**
2 **cups milk**
 Fresh thyme sprigs or sliced green onions (optional)

1 In a large saucepan melt margarine or butter over medium-low heat. Add squash, carrot, onion, garlic, dried thyme, and pepper. Cover and cook for 15 to 20 minutes or until vegetables are crisp-tender, stirring occasionally. Stir in condensed soup and milk. Bring to boiling; reduce heat. Simmer, covered, 5 minutes. Ladle into soup bowls. If desired, garnish with thyme sprigs or sprinkle with green onions. Makes 6 side-dish servings.

Nutrition facts per serving: 118 cal., 5 g total fat (2 g sat. fat), 9 mg chol., 476 mg sodium, 16 g carbo., 2 g fiber, 4 g pro. *Daily values:* 93% vit. A, 13% vit. C, 11% calcium, 5% iron.

LOW FAT CHILI BLANC

Prep: 20 min. ◆ Cook: 25 min.

No tomatoes, but plenty of heat.

12 **oz. ground raw turkey**
½ **cup chopped onion**

◆◆◆

1 **12-oz. can or bottle beer**
½ **cup water**
2 **to 4 medium jalapeño peppers, seeded and finely chopped***
2 **tsp. instant chicken bouillon granules**
1½ **tsp. chili powder**
1 **tsp. ground cumin**
2 **15-oz. cans great Northern or cannellini beans, rinsed and drained**
1 **Tbsp. lime juice**

◆◆◆

 Dairy sour cream (optional)
 Snipped fresh cilantro (optional)
 Lime wedges (optional)
 Chili powder (optional)
 Bottled hot pepper sauce (optional)

1 In a saucepan cook turkey and onion until turkey is no longer pink. Drain fat.

TEST KITCHEN TIP

BARLEY BITS

Pearl barley is barley with the hull removed and the grain polished—the way most barley is sold. Rinse and soak unpolished barley before using. Allow 3 to 4 times the cooking time for unpolished barley as you would for pearl barley.

2 Stir beer, water, jalapeño peppers, bouillon granules, chili powder, and cumin into turkey-onion mixture in saucepan. Bring mixture to boiling; reduce heat. Simmer, uncovered, for 20 minutes, stirring occasionally. Stir in drained beans and lime juice. Cook for 5 minutes more.

3 If desired, mash half of the beans to thicken chili; stir. Ladle chili into bowls. If desired, garnish with sour cream, cilantro, and lime wedges. If desired, sprinkle with additional chili powder and pass pepper sauce. Makes 4 main-dish servings.

***Note:** Wear rubber gloves or plastic bags over your hands when chopping peppers; wash hands with soap and water immediately. Do not touch your eyes.

Nutrition facts per serving: 280 cal., 7 g total fat (2 g sat. fat), 32 mg chol., 818 mg sodium, 35 g carbo., 11 g fiber, 24 g pro. *Daily values:* 3% vit. A, 23% vit. C, 6% calcium, 27% iron.

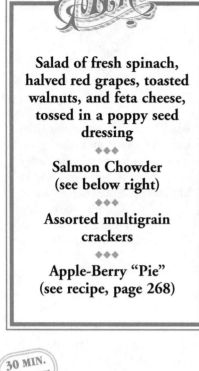

Salad of fresh spinach, halved red grapes, toasted walnuts, and feta cheese, tossed in a poppy seed dressing

◆◆◆

Salmon Chowder
(see below right)

◆◆◆

Assorted multigrain crackers

◆◆◆

Apple-Berry "Pie"
(see recipe, page 268)

30 MIN. LOW FAT

ROASTED GARLIC TURKEY CHOWDER

Start to finish: 30 min.

Opt for convenience by selecting this chowder. Count on the fresh vegetables, turkey, and basil to round out the roasted garlic flavor.

1 cup small broccoli florets
1 medium carrot, shredded
½ cup chopped peeled potato or ½ cup loose-pack frozen diced hash-brown potatoes
½ cup water
¼ cup chopped onion

◆◆◆

2 cups milk
1½ cups chopped cooked turkey or chicken

1 10½-oz. can condensed cream of roasted garlic soup
1½ tsp. snipped fresh basil or ½ tsp. dried basil, crushed

◆◆◆

Fresh basil leaves (optional)

1 In a large saucepan combine broccoli, carrot, potato, water, and onion. Bring to boiling; reduce heat. Simmer, covered, about 6 minutes or until vegetables are tender. Do not drain.

2 Stir milk, turkey, condensed soup, and snipped fresh basil into mixture in saucepan. Cook and stir over medium heat until heated through.

3 To serve, ladle soup into bowls. If desired, garnish with fresh basil leaves. Makes 4 main-dish servings.

Nutrition facts per serving: 269 cal., 9 g total fat (3 g sat. fat), 53 mg chol., 419 mg sodium, 24 g carbo., 4 g fiber, 22 g pro. *Daily values:* 53% vit. A, 56% vit. C, 15% calcium, 8% iron.

SALMON CHOWDER

Start to finish: 35 min.

The combination of caraway seed and dillweed simply seasons this fresh fish and vegetable chowder. (See the photograph on page 284.)

1 Tbsp. olive oil
½ cup thinly sliced celery
½ cup chopped onion
4 cups milk

1 10¾-oz. can condensed cream of celery soup
1 Tbsp. snipped fresh dillweed or 1 tsp. dried dillweed
¼ tsp. caraway seed
¼ tsp. pepper
⅛ tsp. salt
1 large potato, peeled, if desired, and cut into ½-inch cubes (about 1⅓ cups)

◆◆◆

8 oz. fresh or frozen skinless, boneless salmon fillets, cut into ¾-inch cubes

1 In a large saucepan heat oil over medium-high heat. Add celery and onion. Cook and stir about 4 minutes or until tender. Carefully stir in milk, condensed soup, dillweed, caraway seed, pepper, and salt. Stir in potato. Bring to boiling; reduce heat. Simmer, covered, for 10 to 15 minutes or until potato is tender.

2 Stir salmon into mixture in saucepan. Simmer, uncovered, for 2 to 3 minutes more or until salmon flakes easily with a fork.

3 To serve, ladle chowder into cups or bowls. Makes 6 main-dish servings.

Nutrition facts per serving: 215 cal., 9 g total fat (3 g sat. fat), 24 mg chol., 546 mg sodium, 21 g carbo., 1 g fiber, 13 g pro. *Daily values:* 12% vit. A, 12% vit. C, 19% calcium, 8% iron.

CHICKEN & PASTA PRIMAVERA

Start to finish: 25 min.

This almost effortless saucepan pasta gets fresh flavor from year-round market staples. A sour cream and mustard combo infused with fresh herbs wraps the meal in a creamy, tangy sauce.

1 9-oz. pkg. refrigerated spinach or plain fettuccine
2 medium carrots, thinly sliced
1 medium zucchini, halved lengthwise and thinly sliced
¾ cup frozen whole kernel corn
12 oz. deli-roasted chicken, cut into ½-inch strips (about 2½ cups)

❖❖❖

1½ cups chicken broth
4 tsp. cornstarch
1 Tbsp. snipped fresh tarragon or basil
2 tsp. finely shredded lemon peel
½ cup dairy sour cream
2 Tbsp. Dijon-style mustard

❖❖❖

Fresh tarragon sprigs or basil leaves (optional)

1 Cook pasta according to package directions, adding carrots, zucchini, and corn to the water with the pasta. Drain pasta and vegetables. Return all to pan; add chicken. (If chicken has been refrigerated, place it in a colander. Pour pasta, vegetables, and cooking liquid over chicken; drain.)

2 Meanwhile, in a medium saucepan combine chicken broth, cornstarch, snipped tarragon or basil, and lemon peel. Cook and stir over medium heat until thickened and bubbly. Cook and stir for 1 minute more. Remove from heat. Stir in sour cream and Dijon-style mustard. Pour over pasta mixture, tossing to coat.

3 To serve, divide pasta mixture among 6 dinner plates. If desired, garnish with fresh tarragon sprigs or basil leaves. Serve immediately. Makes 6 servings.

Nutrition facts per serving: 321 cal., 9 g total fat (4 g sat. fat), 97 mg chol., 425 mg sodium, 32 g carbo., 1 g fiber, 27 g pro. *Daily values:* 62% vit. A, 5% vit. C, 6% calcium, 19% iron.

CHICKEN WITH POACHED PEARS & FENNEL

Start to finish: 20 min.

No need to arduously plan for this perfectly autumnal meal. A fall fruit and anise-flavored fennel add seasonal flavor to this dish. Try serving it with hot, buttered egg noodles.

1 fennel bulb (about 1 lb.)

❖❖❖

12 oz. skinless, boneless chicken breast strips for stir-frying
1 Tbsp. cooking oil
¾ cup apple juice
1 tsp. five-spice powder
¼ tsp. salt
2 medium pears
¼ cup apple juice
1 Tbsp. cornstarch
2 Tbsp. white wine vinegar

1 Cut off and discard upper stalks of fennel, reserving a few leafy tops for garnish; wash and set aside. Remove any wilted outer layers; cut off a thin slice from base. Wash fennel and cut into thin slices (you should have about 1¼ cups). Rinse chicken; pat dry.

2 In a large skillet cook and stir chicken in hot oil over medium-high heat for 2 to 3 minutes or until no longer pink. Carefully stir in the sliced fennel, the ¾ cup apple juice, the five-spice powder, and salt. Bring to boiling; reduce heat. Simmer, covered, for 4 to 5 minutes or until fennel is crisp-tender, stirring occasionally. Meanwhile, core and slice pears; set aside.

3 In a small bowl stir together the ¼ cup apple juice and cornstarch. Add apple juice-cornstarch mixture to chicken mixture in skillet. Cook and stir until thickened and bubbly. Add vinegar; cook and stir for 1 minute more. Add pear slices; cook and stir mixture gently until pears are heated through.

4 To serve, transfer chicken mixture to a platter. Garnish with reserved fennel tops. Makes 4 servings.

Nutrition facts per serving: 217 cal., 6 g total fat (1 g sat. fat), 45 mg chol., 190 mg sodium, 25 g carbo., 10 g fiber, 17 g pro. *Daily values:* 12% vit. C, 3% calcium, 8% iron.

FENNEL REVIVAL

Bring home a bulb of fresh fennel and find out why this funny-looking vegetable has won the hearts of so many cooks. For centuries, Italian and other European cooks braised fennel, baked it with fish, and chopped it fresh for salads. The fennel attraction: a gentle, slightly sweet anise flavor that lends itself to almost any dish from soups to side dishes.

Fresh fennel season extends from fall until spring. Celerylike stalks and bright green fronds grow from the bulb, but these are often removed before the fennel reaches the supermarket produce section. Pick a firm, smooth bulb without cracks or brown spots. Fresh fennel loses its flavor quickly, so store it in a plastic bag in the refrigerator and use it within a few days.

When the stalks and fronds are still attached to the bulb, remove them and slice the bulb. You can snip the fronds and use them as an herb or a topper for soups. Reserve the tough stalks for making soup stock (in place of celery) or discard.

A simple way to enjoy raw fennel is sliced and munched like a carrot stick. Or, you can add chopped fennel to coleslaw or potato salad for extra crunch.

Cooking fennel mutes the flavor and softens the crisp texture. Italian cooks favor braising fennel as a side dish, but they include it in almost any course.

You can introduce fennel into your cooking as a substitute for celery. Chop or slice raw fennel for soups, stir-fries, and vegetable medleys. Or, substitute fennel wedges for another vegetable in a pot roast recipe. You also can use cooked fennel as a pizza topper.

To cook plain fresh fennel, cover it with a small amount of boiling water and cook for 6 to 10 minutes or until tender. Or, to steam it in your microwave oven, combine it with a little water. Cook it on 100% power (high) for 4 to 6 minutes or until tender, rearranging once.

To intensify the fennel flavor in cooked dishes, add a pinch of fennel seed. Fennel seed comes from a different variety of fennel plant and is sold in the spice aisle.

PORK MEDALLIONS WITH FENNEL AND PANCETTA

Start to finish: 30 min.

A little gourmet, a little down-home. Boneless chops and onions experience a bistro-style revival with fresh fennel, Italian bacon, and sage-cream sauce.

1 12-oz. pork tenderloin
¼ cup all-purpose flour
    Dash salt
    Dash pepper

♦♦♦

2 Tbsp. olive oil

♦♦♦

2 oz. pancetta (Italian bacon) or bacon, finely chopped

2 fennel bulbs, trimmed and cut crosswise into ¼-inch-thick slices
1 small onion, thinly sliced
2 cloves garlic, minced
2 Tbsp. lemon juice
½ cup whipping cream

1 Trim fat from meat. Cut meat crosswise into 1-inch-thick slices. Place each slice between 2 pieces of plastic wrap. Pound lightly with flat side of a meat mallet to ¼-inch thickness. Remove plastic wrap. Combine flour, salt, and pepper. Coat meat with flour mixture.

2 In a large heavy skillet heat olive oil over high heat. Add meat, half at a time, and cook for 2 to 3 minutes or until meat is slightly pink in center, turning once. (Add more oil if necessary.) Remove from skillet.

3 In the same skillet cook pancetta over medium-high heat until crisp. Add fennel, onion, and garlic and cook 3 to 5 minutes or until crisp-tender. Add lemon juice; stir in whipping cream. Bring to boiling; return meat to pan. Cook until meat is heated through and sauce is slightly thickened.

4 Transfer the meat to a serving platter. Spoon the sauce over the meat. Makes 4 servings.

Nutrition facts per serving: 341 cal., 23 g total fat (10 g sat. fat), 105 mg chol., 175 mg sodium, 12 g carbo., 12 g fiber, 22 g pro.
Daily values: 13% vit. A, 19% vit. C, 4% calcium, 10% iron.

LAMB CHOPS WITH SWEET POTATO CHUTNEY

Start to finish: 30 min.

Petite lamb chops make simple but pretty company fare—especially when they're crowned with a richly colored and flavor-packed homemade chutney.

8 lamb rib or loin chops, cut
    1 inch thick
⅓ cup finely chopped shallots
¼ tsp. crushed red pepper

◆◆◆

¼ cup packed brown sugar
¼ cup vinegar
2 Tbsp. dried cranberries or
    currants
½ tsp. grated fresh ginger
1 medium sweet potato, peeled
    and cubed

1 Trim fat from chops. In a small bowl combine shallots and red pepper. Reserve 2 tablespoons shallot mixture for chutney. Rub both sides of chops with the remaining shallot mixture. Place chops on the unheated rack of a broiler pan. Set aside.

2 For chutney, in a medium saucepan combine reserved shallot mixture, the brown sugar, vinegar, dried cranberries or currants, and ginger. Stir in sweet potato. Bring to boiling; reduce heat. Simmer, covered, for 10 minutes, stirring occasionally.

3 Meanwhile, broil chops 3 to 4 inches from the heat to desired doneness, turning once. (Allow 7 to 11 minutes for medium doneness.) Serve the chops with the chutney. Makes 4 servings.

Nutrition facts per serving: 317 cal., 11 g total fat (4 g sat. fat), 97 mg chol., 83 mg sodium, 24 g carbo., 1 g fiber, 30 g pro. *Daily values:* 81% vit. A, 13% vit. C, 3% calcium, 22% iron.

BISTRO BEEF & MUSHROOMS

Start to finish: 20 min.

Serve French bistro fare in a flash. The Burgundian flavors of Dijon mustard, red wine, and fresh thyme spark this hearty dish. Accompany the steaks with mashed potatoes and steamed and buttered haricots verts (tiny, slender green beans).

4 beef tenderloin steaks, cut
    ¾ inch thick (1 lb.)
1 Tbsp. Dijon-style mustard or
    coarse-grain brown
    mustard
1 Tbsp. olive oil or roasted
    garlic olive oil

◆◆◆

1 Tbsp. olive oil or roasted
    garlic olive oil
2 4-oz. pkg. sliced crimini,
    shiitake, or portobello
    mushrooms or one
    8-oz. pkg. sliced button
    mushrooms (about 3 cups)
⅓ cup dry red wine or sherry
1 Tbsp. white wine
    Worcestershire sauce
2 tsp. snipped fresh thyme

1 Trim fat from steaks. Spread mustard evenly over both sides of steaks. In a large skillet heat 1 tablespoon olive oil over medium heat. Add steaks; cook to desired doneness, turning once. (Allow 7 to 10 minutes for medium-rare or 10 to 12 minutes for medium.) Transfer steaks to a serving platter; keep warm.

2 Add 1 tablespoon olive oil to drippings in skillet. Add mushrooms; cook and stir for 4 minutes. Stir in wine, Worcestershire sauce, and thyme. Simmer, uncovered, for 3 minutes. Spoon over steaks. Makes 4 servings.

Nutrition facts per serving: 263 cal., 14 g total fat (4 g sat. fat), 64 mg chol., 176 mg sodium, 5 g carbo., 1 g fiber, 23 g pro. *Daily values:* 4% vit. C, 1% calcium, 25% iron.

LEMON-FILLED ANISE BRAID

Prep: 30 min. ◆ Rise: 1¼ hr.
Bake: 30 min.

*Purchased lemon curd and
cream cheese make a luscious filling
for the subtle anise-flavored,
rich sweet dough. You will need to use
a very large baking sheet as this
makes one long braid.*

3 to 3½ cups all-purpose flour
1 pkg. active dry yeast
1 cup water
⅓ cup sugar
2 Tbsp. margarine or butter
2 tsp. finely shredded lemon
  peel
1 tsp. anise seed, crushed
1 tsp. salt

◆◆◆

1 3-oz. pkg. cream cheese,
  softened
¼ cup purchased lemon curd

◆◆◆

1 egg, beaten

1 In a large mixing bowl combine 1¼ cups of the flour and the yeast. In a medium saucepan heat and stir the water, sugar, margarine or butter, lemon peel, anise seed, and salt until warm (120° to 130°) and margarine is almost melted. Add water mixture to flour mixture. Beat with an electric mixer on low speed for 30 seconds, scraping the sides of the bowl constantly. Beat on high for 3 minutes more. Using a spoon, stir in as much of the remaining flour as you can.

FREEZER SMARTS

Freezing preserves the fresh flavor of food, provided you follow a few guidelines:
 ◆ Freeze food in airtight containers or freezer wraps; otherwise it may get freezer burn, the grayish brown spots that form when food is exposed to cold air too long.
 ◆ Use moisture- and vapor-proof packaging, such as sealable plastic containers or freezer bags, plastic-coated freezer paper, and heavy-duty aluminum foil.
 ◆ Cool hot foods in the refrigerator before freezing them.
 ◆ Freeze foods in small portions so they freeze quickly.
 ◆ Quick-freeze packaged foods by placing them in a single layer against the freezer walls or on the quick-freeze shelf. After they've frozen, you may stack them.
 ◆ Don't overpack your freezer. Overloading it restricts the airflow, which can cause foods to defrost.
 ◆ Store foods at 0° F. or below to retain vitamins, flavor, and texture. Regularly check the freezer's temperature with a thermometer.
 ◆ Label items, noting the contents and date entered on the package. Use foods on a first-in, first-out basis. See chart for storage times.

Food	Storage (months)
Cooked meat	2 to 3
Cooked meat casseroles	3 to 6
Ground beef, veal, and lamb	3 to 4
Ground pork	1 to 3
Meat roasts	9 to 12
Meat chops and steaks	4 to 12
Poultry, cooked	4
Poultry, parts	9
Poultry, whole	12
Soups and stews	1 to 3
Vegetables	8

2 Turn the dough out onto a lightly floured surface. Knead in enough of the remaining flour to make a moderately soft dough that is smooth and elastic (3 to 5 minutes total). Shape the dough into a ball. Place dough in a lightly greased bowl, turning once to grease surface of the dough. Cover and let rise in a warm place until double (45 to 60 minutes).

3 Punch dough down. Turn dough out onto a lightly floured surface. Cover and let rest for 10 minutes. Grease a very large baking sheet; set aside.

4 Meanwhile, in a small bowl combine cream cheese and lemon curd. Beat with an electric mixer on low speed until smooth; set mixture aside.

5 On a lightly floured surface, roll dough into a 16×9-inch rectangle. Cut lengthwise to form three 16×3-inch strips. Spread one-third of the filling lengthwise down the center of each strip. Pinch edges and ends to seal, forming long ropes. Place ropes about 1 inch apart on the prepared baking sheet. Braid loosely, beginning in middle and working toward ends. Pinch ends together and tuck under. Cover and let rise in a warm place until almost double (30 to 45 minutes).

6 Brush braid with beaten egg. Bake in a 350° oven about 30 minutes or until golden brown. If necessary, cover loosely with foil last 5 to 10 minutes to prevent overbrowning. Remove to wire rack to cool. Cover and store any leftover braid in the refrigerator for up to 3 days. Makes 1 braid (10 to 12 servings).

Nutrition facts per serving: 238 cal., 7 g total fat (3 g sat. fat), 37 mg chol., 279 mg sodium, 34 g carbo., 2 g fiber, 5 g pro. *Daily values:* 7% vit. A, 1% calcium, 13% iron.

FLAX SEED CORN BREAD

Prep: 15 min. ◆ Bake: 25 min.

If a 10-inch cast iron skillet is not part of your pan pantry, use a greased 9×9×2-inch baking pan instead. Because the baking pan is thinner and penetrates heat more quickly, do not preheat it.

1 cup all-purpose flour
1 cup cornmeal
½ cup flax seed meal*
2 tsp. baking powder
1½ tsp. sugar
1 tsp. salt
¼ tsp. baking soda

◆◆◆

2 eggs, beaten
1 cup buttermilk
¼ cup olive oil

◆◆◆

1 Recipe Basil Butter (see right)

1 Place a well-greased 10-inch cast iron skillet in oven while preheating oven to 375°.

2 Meanwhile, in a large mixing bowl stir together flour, cornmeal, flax seed meal, baking powder, sugar, salt, and baking soda; set aside.

3 In another bowl combine eggs, buttermilk, and olive oil. Add buttermilk mixture to flour mixture. Stir just until moistened. Carefully spread batter into the preheated skillet.

4 Bake for 25 to 30 minutes or until golden and a wooden toothpick inserted in center

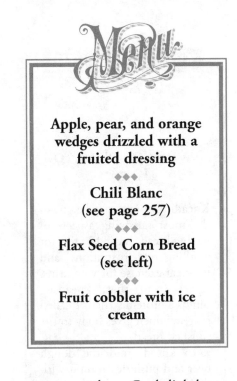

Apple, pear, and orange wedges drizzled with a fruited dressing

◆◆◆

Chili Blanc (see page 257)

◆◆◆

Flax Seed Corn Bread (see left)

◆◆◆

Fruit cobbler with ice cream

comes out clean. Cool slightly on a wire rack. Cut warm corn bread into wedges and serve with Basil Butter. Makes 8 servings.

*****Note:** If flax seed meal is not available at your supermarket or health food store, purchase flax seed. To make the meal, process the flax seed in a covered blender container for 1 to 2 minutes or until ground. One-third cup seed should make about ½ cup meal.

Basil Butter: In a small mixing bowl stir together ⅓ cup softened butter; 1 tablespoon finely snipped fresh basil or ¼ teaspoon dried basil, crushed; 1 clove minced garlic; and ¼ teaspoon black pepper.

Nutrition facts per serving corn bread with about 2 teaspoons Basil Butter: 303 cal., 18 g total fat (6 g sat. fat), 75 mg chol., 526 mg sodium, 29 g carbo., 2 g fiber, 7 g pro. *Daily values:* 10% vit. A, 12% calcium, 15% iron.

WHY YOU NEED TO KNEAD

Kneading dough may be one of the most satisfying aspects of baking bread. It can be great for working out frustrations, and it's great exercise for your arms. Apart from that, kneading builds a protein structure called gluten, which gives body to the finished bread.

To knead, fold the dough over and push down on it with the heels of your hands, curving your fingers over the dough. Give the dough a quarter turn and repeat the process of folding and pushing down until you have an elastic dough and the stiffness called for in a recipe. Here's how to tell:

Soft dough is very sticky and is used for breads that don't require kneading.

Moderately soft dough is slightly sticky and is used for rich, sweet breads. This dough is kneaded on a floured surface for about 3 to 5 minutes.

Moderately stiff dough is not sticky and is slightly firm to the touch. It usually requires 6 to 8 minutes of kneading on a lightly floured surface and is used for nonsweet breads.

Stiff dough is firm to the touch and will hold its shape after about 8 to 10 minutes of kneading. It's used for breads with a chewy texture, such as French bread.

CRANBERRY EGGNOG ROLLS

Prep: 35 min. ◆ Rise: 1¼ hr.
Bake: 30 min.

A holiday morning treat that's a great way to use up extra eggnog.

3 to 3¾ cups all-purpose flour
¼ cup whole wheat flour
1 pkg. active dry yeast
1¼ cups canned or dairy eggnog
¼ cup water
¼ cup granulated sugar
¼ cup butter
1 tsp. salt

◆◆◆

1 cup packed brown sugar
¼ cup butter
⅓ cup chopped fresh cranberries
¼ cup chopped walnuts

◆◆◆

2 Tbsp. butter, softened
¼ cup granulated sugar
¾ tsp. ground nutmeg
¼ tsp. ground cinnamon

1 In a large mixing bowl combine 1½ cups of the all-purpose flour, the whole wheat flour, and yeast; set aside. In a medium saucepan heat and stir 1 cup of canned or dairy eggnog, the water, ¼ cup granulated sugar, ¼ cup butter, and the salt until warm (120° to 130°) and butter almost melts. Add to flour mixture. Beat with an electric mixer on low speed for 30 seconds, scraping bowl constantly. Beat on high speed for 3 minutes more. Using a wooden spoon, stir in as much of the remaining all-purpose flour as you can.

2 Turn dough out onto a lightly floured surface. Knead in enough additional flour to make a moderately soft dough that is smooth and elastic (3 to 5 minutes total). Shape into a ball. Place in a greased bowl; turn once. Cover; let rise in a warm place until double (45 to 60 minutes).

3 Punch dough down. Turn out onto a lightly floured surface. Cover and let rest 10 minutes. Meanwhile, in a saucepan heat together brown sugar, ¼ cup butter, and the remaining ¼ cup eggnog until mixture bubbles. Pour into an ungreased 13×9×2-inch baking pan. Sprinkle with cranberries and walnuts.

4 On a lightly floured surface, roll dough to a 15×12-inch rectangle. Spread with 2 tablespoons softened butter. Sprinkle with mixture of ¼ cup granulated sugar, nutmeg, and cinnamon. Roll up loosely, starting at a short side. Moisten and seal edge. Cut roll into twelve 1-inch slices. Place, cut side down, on top of brown sugar mixture. Cover and let rise in a warm place until nearly double (30 to 40 minutes).

5 Bake in a 350° oven about 30 minutes or until golden brown. If necessary, cover loosely with foil the last 5 minutes of baking. Remove from oven. Let stand 5 minutes on a wire rack. Invert to remove from pan. Cool slightly or completely. Makes 12.

Nutrition facts per roll: 361 cal., 13 g total fat (2 g sat. fat), 0 mg chol., 314 mg sodium, 56 g carbo., 2 g fiber, 5 g pro. *Daily values:* 12% vit. A, 3% calcium, 13% iron.

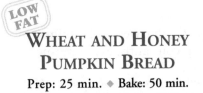

WHEAT AND HONEY PUMPKIN BREAD

Prep: 25 min. ◆ Bake: 50 min.

A drizzle of orange icing adds a festive touch to this nutty pumpkin loaf. The recipe makes two loaves, so keep one for yourself and give the other as a gift.

2 cups all-purpose flour
1⅓ cups whole wheat flour
2½ tsp. pumpkin pie spice or apple pie spice
1½ tsp. baking powder
1½ tsp. salt
1 tsp. baking soda

◆◆◆

1¾ cups granulated sugar
⅓ cup shortening
4 eggs
1 15-oz. can pumpkin
½ cup honey
⅓ cup water
1 cup chopped walnuts or pecans

◆◆◆

1 cup sifted powdered sugar
3 to 4 tsp. orange juice

1 Grease the bottom and ½ inch up the sides of two 8×4×2 or 9×5×3-inch loaf pans; set aside. In a large mixing bowl stir together the all-purpose flour, whole wheat flour, pumpkin or apple pie spice, baking powder, salt, and baking soda. Set aside.

2 In a very large mixing bowl beat granulated sugar and shortening with an electric mixer on medium speed until well combined. Beat in eggs, 1 at a time, beating well after each addition. On low speed, beat in pumpkin, honey, and water just until combined. Stir flour mixture into

beaten mixture just until combined. Fold in walnuts or pecans. Divide mixture evenly between the prepared pans.

3 Bake in a 350° oven for 50 to 60 minutes or until a wooden toothpick inserted near center comes out clean. Cool in pans on a wire rack for 10 minutes. Remove loaves from pans. Cool completely on a wire rack.

4 For icing, in a small mixing bowl stir together powdered sugar and enough orange juice to make of drizzling consistency. Drizzle icing over cooled loaves. Makes 2 loaves (32 servings).

THE TRADITION OF EGGNOG

Eggnog recalls Charles Dickens' tales of Victorian Christmases, when bell-ringers and carolers rode horse-drawn carriages through the snow to visit friends and neighbors. At each stop, guests hastened to the parlor to jovially toast one another with rich punches. Lively toasting with spirited drinks took center stage throughout the caroling and merry-making of the 12 days of Christmas.

Across Europe, various frothy beverages made with sweetened wine or ale had long been expressions of hospitality, and American immigrants brought the tradition with them. By the early 1700s, a partiality for strong drinks at festive gatherings was firmly established in Colonial America. Eggnog parties continued to set the holiday social scene in Washington, D.C., until World War II. They became especially popular in the South, and many homes still keep a jar of eggnog, made with Kentucky bourbon, in the refrigerator during the holiday season to welcome guests.

Most eggnogs today are rich blends of milk, cream, beaten eggs, sugar, nutmeg, and liquor. Instead of the brandy and sherry or Madeira used in the old English and pre-Civil War-era eggnogs, most American recipes now use locally made bourbon whiskeys, flavored liqueurs, and rums that arrived here by way of the West Indies spice trade. Regional recipes vary slightly, but all share the indulgent qualities we've come to love. This cheering libation is a holiday tradition worth preserving.

TO MAKE AHEAD

Prepare and bake bread as directed; cool completely. Do not ice. Place bread in a freezer container or bag and freeze up to 3 months. To serve, thaw the wrapped bread overnight in the refrigerator. Make icing and drizzle over bread.

Nutrition facts per serving: 171 cal., 5 g total fat (1 g sat. fat), 27 mg chol., 166 mg sodium, 29 g carbo., 1 g fiber, 3 g pro. *Daily values:* 30% vit. A, 1% vit. C, 2% calcium, 6% iron.

PRIZE TESTED RECIPE WINNER

BLACKBERRY GINGERBREAD

Prep: 20 min. ◆ Bake: 50 min.

Sprightly blackberries and a rich sauce bring a welcome taste of summer to winter days.

2 cups all-purpose flour
2 tsp. ground ginger
1 tsp. baking powder
1 tsp. ground cinnamon
¼ tsp. baking soda
⅓ cup butter, softened

½ cup packed brown sugar
1 egg
½ cup mild-flavored molasses
¾ cup warm water
1½ cups frozen blackberries or boysenberries
1 Tbsp. all-purpose flour

◆◆◆

1 recipe Pudding Sauce (see below)
Frozen blackberries or boysenberries, thawed

1 Grease and flour a 2-quart square glass baking dish; set aside. In a medium bowl combine 2 cups flour, ginger, baking powder, cinnamon, and soda.

2 In a large mixing bowl beat butter with an electric mixer on medium speed for 30 seconds. Add brown sugar and beat until combined. Add egg and molasses; beat 1 minute. Add the flour mixture and water alternately to beaten mixture, beating on low speed after each addition until combined. Toss frozen berries with the 1 tablespoon flour; fold into molasses mixture. Pour batter into prepared baking dish.

3 Bake in a 325° oven about 50 minutes or until a wooden toothpick inserted near the center comes out clean. Cool in dish on a wire rack for 5 minutes. Remove from dish. Cool 20 minutes more. Serve warm with Pudding Sauce and additional berries. Serves 9.

Pudding Sauce: In a small saucepan combine ⅓ cup granulated sugar, ¼ cup butter, and ¼ cup half-and-half or light cream. Bring to boiling, stirring constantly; reduce heat. Boil gently, uncovered, 2 minutes, stirring constantly. Serve warm.

Nutrition facts per serving with 1 tablespoon sauce: 350 cal., 14 g total fat (8 g sat. fat), 58 mg chol., 214 mg sodium, 55 g carbo., 2 g fiber, 4 g pro.
Daily values: 13% vit. A, 8% vit. C, 8% calcium, 18% iron.

DOUBLE-CHOCOLATE BUTTERMILK LOAF

Prep: 25 min. ◆ Bake: 1 hr.

Although this very rich loaf could be served as a sweet bread, it is more like a cake. Serve it with a dollop of whipped cream or crème fraîche.

1⅔ cups all-purpose flour
⅔ cup unsweetened cocoa powder
½ tsp. baking powder
½ tsp. baking soda
½ tsp. salt

◆◆◆

½ cup butter, softened
1 cup sugar
2 eggs
1 cup buttermilk
⅓ cup chopped pecans or walnuts
¼ cup miniature semisweet chocolate pieces

1 Grease the bottom and ½ inch up the sides of an 8×4×2-inch loaf pan; set aside. In a medium mixing bowl combine flour, cocoa powder, baking powder, baking soda, and salt; set aside.

2 In a large mixing bowl beat the butter with an electric mixer on medium speed for 30 seconds. Add sugar and beat until fluffy. Beat in eggs until well combined. Alternately add the flour mixture and buttermilk, beating just until combined after each addition. Stir in nuts. Spoon half of the batter into prepared pan. Sprinkle with chocolate pieces. Spoon on remaining batter.

3 Bake in a 350° oven for 60 to 65 minutes or until a wooden toothpick inserted near center comes out clean. Cool in pan on a wire rack for 10 minutes. Remove loaf from pan; cool on wire rack. Makes 1 loaf (16 servings).

Nutrition facts per serving: 200 cal., 9 g total fat (4 g sat. fat), 43 mg chol., 199 mg sodium, 26 g carbo., 0 g fiber, 4 g pro. *Daily values:* 6% vit. A, 6% calcium, 8% iron.

PINEAPPLE UPSIDE-DOWN CORNMEAL CAKE

Prep: 15 min. ◆ Bake: 30 min.

1 8-oz. can pineapple slices

◆◆◆

2 Tbsp. margarine or butter
⅓ cup packed brown sugar
1 Tbsp. water
¼ cup dried cranberries, tart red cherries, or blueberries
¼ cup broken pecans, toasted

◆◆◆

1½ cups all-purpose flour
½ cup yellow cornmeal
⅓ cup packed brown sugar
1 tsp. baking powder
¼ tsp. baking soda
¼ tsp. salt
2 eggs, beaten
½ cup dairy sour cream
¼ cup cooking oil

1 Drain pineapple, reserving 3 tablespoons juice. Halve pineapple slices.

2 Melt margarine or butter in a 9×1½-inch round baking pan.

Stir in ⅓ cup brown sugar and the water. Arrange pineapple slices, dried fruit, and pecans in the pan.

3 In a mixing bowl combine flour, cornmeal, ⅓ cup brown sugar, baking powder, soda, and salt. In another bowl combine eggs, sour cream, cooking oil, and reserved pineapple juice. Add egg mixture all at once to flour mixture; stir just until combined. Spoon mixture over fruit in pan.

4 Bake in a 350° oven for 30 to 35 minutes or until a wooden toothpick inserted near center comes out clean. Cool in pan on a wire rack for 5 minutes. Loosen sides; invert cake onto a plate. Serve warm. Makes 8 servings.

Nutrition facts per serving: 371 cal., 17 g total fat (4 g sat. fat), 60 mg chol., 217 mg sodium, 51 g carbo., 2 g fiber, 5 g pro. *Daily values:* 9% vit. A, 6% vit. C, 7% calcium, 14% iron.

PRIZE TESTED RECIPE WINNER

CANDY-SUGAR CRÈME TART

Prep: 25 min. ◆ Bake: 40 min.

Three types of candy swirled through a luscious cream cheese filling make for one indulgent dessert.

¾ cup finely crushed shortbread cookies (about 12 cookies)
¼ cup graham cracker crumbs
1 Tbsp. butter, melted

◆◆◆

1 8-oz. pkg. cream cheese, softened
3 Tbsp. butter, softened

½ cup half-and-half or light cream
3 eggs
¼ cup sugar
1 tsp. vanilla
3 1.4-oz. bars chocolate-covered English toffee, coarsely chopped
1 1.55-oz. bar white chocolate with crunchy chocolate cookie bits, coarsely chopped
15 malted milk balls (⅓ cup), coarsely chopped

1 For the crust, stir together crushed cookies, crushed graham crackers, and 1 tablespoon melted butter (mixture may be crumbly). Press crumb mixture onto bottom and up sides of a 9×1-inch tart pan with removable bottom. Bake in a 350° oven 10 minutes or until lightly browned. Set aside to cool slightly.

2 For the filling, in a blender container or food processor bowl combine the cream cheese, the 3 tablespoons softened butter, half-and-half, eggs, sugar, and vanilla. Cover and blend or process until smooth. In a bowl stir together chopped candy. Stir into cream cheese mixture. Pour filling into crust-lined pan. Place in a shallow baking pan to catch any drips.

3 Bake about 30 minutes or until center appears nearly set when shaken. Cool on a wire rack for 1 hour. Cover and chill at least 4 hours before serving. To serve, cut into wedges. Serves 12.

Nutrition facts per serving: 265 cal., 19 g total fat (8 g sat. fat), 93 mg chol., 195 mg sodium, 20 g carbo., 0 g fiber, 4 g pro. *Daily values:* 16% vit. A, 3% calcium, 4% iron.

Remember the last time you had a cold and a stuffed-up nose? Most likely you noticed the food you ate tasted fairly bland. The problem was not with the food or your taste buds but with your sense of smell. When you eat something, as much as 80 percent of the flavor you perceive comes from your sense of smell. The aroma of the food travels up your throat and into your nose.

For those with a cold, this loss of smell and taste is only temporary. But, for others, it can be a permanent condition. The loss of smell and taste can develop as we grow older. Fortunately, little tricks at mealtime can help you enjoy food whether you are experiencing a temporary or a permanent taste loss.

◆ To get the most flavor from your food, chew it well. The smaller the pieces of food, the greater the taste and aroma you'll experience as you eat.

◆ Try something new. Some foods that you used to enjoy may no longer taste as good to you. Instead of getting upset, venture out and discover new mealtime favorites.

◆ Boost flavors with herbs, spices, and condiments. Studies suggest that caffeine may enhance flavor, so try drinking coffee with your meal.

◆ Switch from one food to another while eating. After a couple of bites of the same food, its taste becomes less pronounced.

◆ Vary food textures and temperatures in each meal to add excitement.

◆ Make your meals look as appetizing as possible with colorful vegetables, salads, and even edible garnishes.

◆ Remember that although food is important, mealtime is also a great time to relax and enjoy the company of family and friends.

Cover and process until coarsely chopped. Remove from bowl. Repeat with the cranberries until coarsely chopped, then the walnuts. (Or, coarsely chop ingredients by hand.)

2 In a medium bowl combine apples, cranberries, walnuts, the ½ cup sugar, the raisins, and the 1 tablespoon orange peel. Spread mixture evenly in the bottom of pie plate; set aside.

3 For topping, in the food processor bowl or a mixing bowl combine egg, flour, melted butter, the ⅓ cup sugar, the 1½ teaspoons orange peel, the vanilla, salt, and almond extract. Cover and process or beat with an electric mixer until smooth. Spread batter evenly over fruit mixture.

4 Bake in a 350° oven about 40 minutes or until topping is browned and a wooden toothpick inserted in the center comes out clean. Cool slightly in pie plate on a wire rack. Serve warm. Makes 8 servings.

TO MAKE AHEAD

Bake pie as directed and cool completely. Cover with foil and refrigerate for up to 24 hours. To reheat, bake, covered, in a 350° oven for about 20 minutes or until warm.

Nutrition facts per serving: 290 cal., 15 g total fat (8 g sat. fat), 57 mg chol., 159 mg sodium, 40 g carbo., 2 g fiber, 2 g pro. *Daily values:* 12% vit. A, 9% vit. C, 1% calcium, 4% iron.

APPLE-BERRY "PIE"

Prep: 20 min. ◆ Bake: 40 min.

A bit like a pie (though far easier to make) and a bit like a cobbler—that's the fun of this homey baked fruit dessert. Serve it slightly warm and top it with a scoop of vanilla ice cream or a spoonful of cream. Your guests will eat it with gusto!

1 **lb. baking apples, quartered and cored (3 medium)**
1 **cup cranberries**
¼ **cup walnuts**
½ **cup sugar**
¼ **cup raisins**
1 **Tbsp. finely shredded orange peel**

◆◆◆

1 **egg**
½ **cup all-purpose flour**
½ **cup butter, melted**
⅓ **cup sugar**
1½ **tsp. finely shredded orange peel**
½ **tsp. vanilla**
⅛ **tsp. salt**
   Several drops almond extract

1 Generously butter a 9-inch pie plate; set aside. Place unpeeled apples in a food processor bowl.

MILE HIGH CRANBERRY-APPLE PIE

Prep: 50 min. ◆ **Bake:** 65 min.

Apple pie doesn't get any better than this. Tender, juicy apples and dried tart cranberries are layered in a flaky pastry, then topped with an ooey-gooey caramel and nut sauce. See the photograph on the cover.

¾ cup water
3 Tbsp. sugar
12 cups thinly sliced, peeled cooking apples, such as Jonathan or Granny Smith (about 4½ lb.)
1 cup dried cranberries

◆◆◆

¾ cup sugar
⅓ cup all-purpose flour
½ tsp. ground nutmeg
2 Tbsp. rum or frozen apple juice concentrate, thawed

◆◆◆

1 recipe Pastry for Double-Crust Pie (see below right)

◆◆◆

1 egg, beaten
1 Tbsp. water

◆◆◆

1 recipe Caramel Pecan Sauce (see far right) (optional)
Ice cream (optional)

1 In a very large saucepan or Dutch oven combine the ¾ cup water and the 3 tablespoons sugar. Bring to boiling over medium-high heat; add apples and dried cranberries. Cook fruit, covered, 4 minutes, stirring once. Drain well in a colander.

2 In a very large mixing bowl, combine the ¾ cup sugar, the flour, nutmeg, and rum or apple juice concentrate. Add apple mix-ture; toss gently to combine. Set aside while preparing pastry.

3 Prepare pastry for Double-Crust Pie. On a lightly floured surface, roll half of the dough into a 12-inch circle. Wrap the pastry around rolling pin; unroll onto a 9-inch pie plate. Ease pastry into pie plate, being careful not to stretch pastry.

4 Stir fruit filling. Fill the pas-try-lined pie plate with the fruit filling. Trim pastry to edge of pie plate. Roll remaining dough into a 12-inch circle. Cut slits for steam to escape. Place on top of fruit filling. Trim top crust to ½ inch beyond edge of pie plate. Fold top pastry under bottom pastry. Crimp edge as desired. Brush top with a mixture of beat-en egg and 1 tablespoon water. To prevent overbrowning, cover the edge of pie with foil. Place pie on a cookie sheet to catch any drips. Place pie and cookie sheet on low-est oven rack setting (to help bot-tom crust get done and prevent overbrowning of top crust).

5 Bake in a 375° oven for 30 minutes. Remove foil. Bake for 35 to 40 minutes more or until the top is golden. Cool on a wire rack. Serve slightly warm or at room temperature. If desired, spoon some Caramel Pecan Sauce atop and pass remaining sauce. If desired, serve with ice cream. Makes 8 servings.

Pastry for Double-Crust Pie: Stir together 2 cups all-purpose flour and ½ teaspoon salt. Using a pastry blender, cut in ⅔ cup shortening until pieces are the size of small peas. Using a total of 6 to 7 tablespoons cold water, sprinkle 1 tablespoon water at a time over part of the mixture; gently toss with a fork. Push to side of bowl. Repeat until all is moistened. Divide dough in half.

Caramel Pecan Sauce: In a medium skillet melt ¼ cup butter or margarine. Add ⅓ cup broken pecans. Cook and stir over medi-um-low heat for 3 to 5 minutes or until pecans are lightly toasted. Carefully add ½ cup light-colored corn syrup, ½ cup packed brown sugar, and 2 tablespoons water. Cook and stir with wooden spoon until bubbly and the brown sugar is dissolved. Add ¼ cup whipping cream. Bring to boiling; reduce heat. Boil gently, uncovered, over low heat for 5 minutes. Allow to cool slightly. Serve warm.

Nutrition facts per serving of pie (without sauce): 525 cal., 19 g total fat (5 g sat. fat), 27 mg chol., 145 mg sodium, 86 g carbo., 5 g fiber, 5 g pro.
Daily values: 2% vit. A, 15% vit. C, 1% calcium, 14% iron.

TEST KITCHEN TIP

APPLE MATH

Measuring up just the right amount of apples is as simple as 1-2-3.

1 pound apples equals:
2 large apples *or*
3 medium apples *or*
4 small apples *or*
2¾ cups sliced apples *or*
2 cups chopped apples

We Gather Together

Welcome noted cookbook author and cooking school teacher Betty Rosbottom into your kitchen and you'll reap the benefits of her two-decade quest to get the most out of traditional American ingredients. Each year, inspired by her passion for cooking, and a love of gathering friends and family, Betty reinvents Thanksgiving. The day, the menu, the decor—each is as quintessentially American as the other. Join us as we savor Betty's favorite holiday.

ORANGE- AND HERB-ROASTED TURKEY

Prep: 25 min. ◆ Roast: 3¾ hr.
Stand: 15 min.

This year's feast bird is gussied up with a glorious fruit ensemble—fresh and candied orange and pear slices and fresh and candied kumquats. You'll find both candied fruits (also known as glacé) in large supermarkets and specialty food shops.
(See the photograph on page 281.)

1   14-lb. turkey
    Salt
    Freshly ground black pepper
1   medium onion, cut into
      wedges
1   medium orange, cut into
      wedges
6   fresh rosemary sprigs (4 to
      5 inches long)
4   fresh thyme sprigs (4 to
      5 inches long)

◆◆◆

1   to 2 Tbsp. cooking oil

◆◆◆

1   6-oz. can frozen orange juice
      concentrate, thawed
¾   cup reduced-sodium chicken
      broth

¼   cup margarine or butter,
      melted

◆◆◆

    Reduced-sodium chicken
      broth
4   tsp. finely snipped fresh
      rosemary or 2 tsp. dried
      rosemary, crushed
3   Tbsp. cornstarch
¼   cup reduced-sodium chicken
      broth

◆◆◆

    Candied fruit slices and/or
      fresh fruit, such as pears,
      oranges, and kumquats
      (optional)

1 Rinse turkey well and pat dry. Season cavity generously with salt and pepper. Place onion and orange wedges in cavity along with the rosemary sprigs and thyme sprigs.

2 Pull turkey neck skin to back; fasten with skewer. If a band of skin crosses the tail, tuck the drumsticks under the band. If there is no band, tie drumsticks securely to tail. Twist wing tips under the back.

3 Place bird, breast side up, on rack in a shallow roasting pan. Brush skin lightly with oil. Insert a meat thermometer into center of one of the inside thigh muscles, but not touching bone. Cover bird loosely with foil, leaving air space between bird and foil. Roast in a 325° oven about 3¾ hours total: After 2½ hours, cut band of skin or string between drumsticks so thighs will cook evenly. Continue to roast, covered with foil, about 20 minutes more or until thermometer registers 160°.

4 Stir together orange juice concentrate, the ¾ cup chicken broth, and the melted margarine or butter. Remove foil; brush some of the orange mixture over bird. Continue roasting, uncovered, until meat thermometer registers 180°, brushing some of the remaining orange mixture over bird every 15 minutes. Reserve any remaining orange mixture for gravy. (When bird is done, the drumsticks should move easily in their sockets and the thickest parts of the drumsticks should be very soft when pressed.)

5 Remove turkey from oven and discard ingredients from cavity. Transfer turkey to a platter and let stand, covered with foil to keep warm, for 15 to 20 minutes before carving.

6 Meanwhile, to make the gravy, strain juices from roasting pan into a large glass measure. (Also scrape the browned bits into the cup.) Skim off and discard fat. Add the remaining orange mixture to juices in measuring cup. Measure liquid and add additional chicken broth, if necessary, to equal 3 cups. Pour juices into a medium saucepan. Add snipped or crushed rosemary. Combine cornstarch and the remaining ¼ cup chicken broth. Add to saucepan. Cook and stir over medium heat until thickened and bubbly; cook and stir for 2 minutes more. Season to taste with additional *salt* and *pepper*. Remove from heat.

7 Just before serving, garnish platter with candied fruit slices and/or fresh fruit, if desired. Pass gravy with turkey. Makes 10 to 12 servings.

Nutrition facts per serving: 469 cal., 23 g total fat (8 g sat. fat), 185 mg chol., 261 mg sodium, 10 g carbo., 0 g fiber, 52 g pro. *Daily values:* 17% vit. A, 49% vit. C, 4% calcium, 25% iron.

ROASTED CORN AND PEPPER SOUP

Start to finish: 1 hr.

If you're really strapped for time, you can skip roasting the corn for this luscious meal starter. But roasting intensifies the corn's flavor, lends a savory sweetness to the soup, and builds in layers of mouthwatering appeal. (See the photograph on page 277.)

1 16-oz. pkg. frozen whole
    kernel corn
1 Tbsp. cooking oil
    ♦♦♦
2 cups chopped onions
1½ cups seeded and coarsely
    chopped red sweet peppers
4 14½-oz. cans chicken broth
    (7¼ cups)
½ tsp. dried thyme, crushed
⅛ to ¼ tsp. ground red pepper
    ♦♦♦

⅓ cup all-purpose flour
½ cup whipping cream
    ♦♦♦
⅔ cup cooked crabmeat, cut
    into bite-size pieces,
    cartilage removed (4 oz.)
  Fresh thyme sprigs
    (optional)

1 Thaw frozen corn and pat dry with paper towels. Line a 15×10×1-inch baking pan with foil; use a little of the cooking oil to lightly grease the pan.

2 Spread corn in prepared pan. Roast, uncovered, in a 450° oven for 10 minutes; stir. Continue to roast about 10 minutes more until golden brown, stirring once or twice. Remove pan from oven and set aside.

3 In a 4-quart Dutch oven, cook onions and sweet peppers in remaining oil over medium heat for 3 to 4 minutes or until nearly tender. Add the corn, 3 cans of the broth (about 5½ cups), thyme, and ground red pepper. Bring to boiling; reduce heat. Simmer, uncovered, 15 minutes.

4 In a screw-top jar combine remaining 1 can chicken broth and the flour; cover and shake well. Add to soup; cook and stir until slightly thickened and bubbly. Cook and stir for 1 minute more. Stir whipping cream into soup; heat through.

5 To serve, ladle soup into 12 soup bowls. Divide crabmeat among bowls. If desired, garnish with fresh thyme sprigs. Makes 12 side-dish servings.

TO MAKE AHEAD

Prepare soup as directed, except after simmering soup for 15 minutes, cool, cover, and refrigerate soup mixture up to 2 days. When ready to serve, reheat mixture, thicken with flour, and add cream. Serve as above.

Nutrition facts per serving: 133 cal., 6 g total fat (3 g sat. fat), 22 mg chol., 496 mg sodium, 14 g carbo., 1 g fiber, 7 g pro. *Daily values:* 14% vit. A, 39% vit. C, 2% calcium, 5% iron.

STUFFED WHOLE TURKEY ROASTING GUIDE

Ready-to-cook turkey weight	Oven temperature	Roasting time
8 to 12 lb.	325°	3 to 3¾ hr.
12 to 14 lb.	325°	3¼ to 4½ hr.
14 to 18 lb.	325°	4 to 5 hr.
18 to 20 lb.	325°	4½ to 5¼ hr.
20 to 24 lb.	325°	4¾ to 5¾ hr.

For unstuffed turkeys of the same weight, reduce the total cooking time by 15 to 45 minutes.

THE SIMPLE SOLUTION

Decades of testing in our kitchens—and the experiences of great home cooks all across the country—have confirmed that simplicity is the surest route to a tender, perfectly bronzed bird.

Steady heat, a little basting if you wish, and a helping of patience are all you need to make your meal a success. Read on for everything you need to know.

◆ **Buying the turkey:** With birds that weigh 12 pounds or less, allow 1 pound per adult family member. With birds that weigh more than 12 pounds, count on ¾ pound for each serving. If you're serving boneless turkey breast, figure ½ pound per person. To allow for plenty of leftovers, calculate the size bird you need, then buy one that is 2 to 4 pounds larger.

In the store, look for the "sell by" date on the label of fresh turkey. This date is the last day the turkey should be sold. The unopened turkey should maintain its quality and be safe to use for 1 or 2 days after the sell by date. For frozen turkey products, look for packaging that is clean, undamaged, and free of frost.

◆ **Thawing safely:** Allow plenty of time to thaw the bird. For a whole frozen turkey, leave the bird in its wrapping and place it on a tray in the refrigerator for 2 to 5 days. Plan on at least 24 hours for every 5 pounds. Remember, don't count the day you will be roasting the bird. For a bird of 12 pounds, you would need to start thawing the bird Monday night if you were going to roast it on Thursday. For a 15-pounder—the average size purchased at the holidays—start Sunday night. Thawed birds will keep 1 or 2 days in the refrigerator.

If your turkey is not completely thawed on the day you plan to roast it, place the wrapped bird in a clean sink full of cold water. Change the water every 30 minutes. Do not thaw at room temperature, in the microwave, or in warm water; those methods will allow harmful bacteria to grow quickly to dangerous levels.

The bird is thawed and ready for roasting if the giblets can be removed easily and there are no ice crystals in the body and neck cavities. If the center is still frozen, the bird will cook unevenly. After thawing, remove the giblets and neck from the interior cavity. Rinse bird and pat dry with paper towels.

◆ **Safe stuffing:** If you don't have an accurate meat thermometer, consider cooking the stuffing in a covered casserole alongside the bird. Mix the stuffing just before you stuff and roast the bird.

To stuff, first measure out the amount of stuffing that will go into the bird, allowing about ¾ cup per pound of bird. Release drumsticks from band of skin, unhooking tail or leg clamp if one is provided. The clamp may be removed if you prefer not to use it. Spoon stuffing loosely into neck cavity. Pull neck skin over stuffing; fasten to turkey's back with a skewer.

Loosely spoon stuffing into the body cavity; do not pack or stuffing may not be fully cooked and safe to eat by the time the turkey is done. Spoon any remaining stuffing into a casserole; cover and chill until ready to bake. (If you prefer not to stuff your turkey, place quartered onions and celery in the body cavity to add flavor to drippings used in gravy. Pull the neck skin to back; fasten with a short skewer.)

Tuck drumsticks under the band of skin that crosses the tail or reset into leg clamp. If there isn't a band or if you've removed the clamp, tie drumsticks with kitchen string to tail. Twist wing tips under the back.

◆ **Oven roasting:** Place oven rack in its lowest position and preheat oven to 325°. Place turkey, breast side up, on a rack in a shallow pan. To enhance browning, brush with cooking oil. Push a meat thermometer into the center of an inside thigh muscle. Cover turkey loosely with foil, pressing it over drumsticks and neck. Roast, using timings in chart (see page 271) as a guide. Since most turkeys are self-basting, it is not necessary to baste, but it will add flavor to the turkey.

When the bird has been in the oven for two-thirds of the time, cut skin between drumsticks. Remove foil the last 30 to 45 minutes. When done, thigh meat should be 180° and stuffing should be at least 165°. The temperature of meat will rise about 5° after bird comes out of oven.

When turkey is done, drumsticks should move easily in their sockets, and their thickest parts should feel soft when pressed. In addition, juices from the thigh should run clear when pierced deeply with a long-tined fork. Remove turkey from oven; cover loosely with foil. Let stand 20 minutes. Release legs from leg clamp, if present. Remove stuffing before carving.

◆ **Leftovers:** Do not allow turkey to remain at room temperature more than 2 hours after it comes out of the oven. Cooked turkey and stuffing may be covered and refrigerated separately up to 2 days.

BETTY'S FAVORITE CORN BREAD

Prep: 15 min. ◆ Bake: 15 min.

2 Tbsp. cooking oil

◆◆◆

3 eggs, beaten
1 cup buttermilk
1½ tsp. baking powder
¼ tsp. baking soda
1½ cups yellow cornmeal

1 Pour oil into a 9-inch cast iron skillet or a 9×1½-inch round baking pan. Place pan in oven while preheating oven to 450°.

2 Meanwhile, in a large bowl combine eggs and buttermilk with a wire whisk. Mix in baking powder, soda, and ½ teaspoon *salt*. Pour hot oil from pan into batter; mix well. Stir in cornmeal.

3 Pour batter into prepared pan. Bake 15 to 20 minutes or until a wooden toothpick inserted into center comes out clean. Cool in pan 5 minutes. Loosen edges. Carefully invert to remove from pan. Turn bread browned side up; cool on wire rack. Makes 1 loaf (9 servings).

| TO MAKE AHEAD |

Prepare and bake corn bread as directed. Cool completely, then tightly wrap. Store at room temperature up to 24 hours. Or, place cooled corn bread in moisture- and vapor-proof plastic freezer bag; freeze up to 1 week. Open bag and thaw corn bread before using.

Nutrition facts per serving: 133 cal., 5 g total fat (1 g sat. fat), 65 mg chol., 238 mg sodium, 18 g carbo., 1 g fiber, 4 g pro. *Daily values:* 3% vit. A, 7% calcium, 7% iron.

CHUNKY CORN BREAD DRESSING

Prep: 35 min. ◆ Bake: 35 min.

See the photograph on page 283.

1 recipe Betty's Favorite Corn Bread (see left)
5 thick slices firm-textured white bread

◆◆◆

4 Tbsp. butter
2 cups sliced leeks (6 medium)
1½ cups sliced celery with tops
1 Tbsp. dried leaf sage, crushed, or 3 Tbsp. snipped fresh sage
2 tsp. dried thyme, crushed, or 1 Tbsp. snipped fresh thyme
½ tsp. freshly ground black pepper

◆◆◆

8 oz. crimini mushrooms, sliced ¼ inch thick (about 3 cups)
8 slices crisp-cooked bacon, drained and broken into 1-inch pieces

◆◆◆

3 eggs, beaten
2½ to 3 cups reduced-sodium chicken broth

◆◆◆

Fresh thyme and sage sprigs (optional)

1 Cut corn bread and white bread into ½-inch cubes. (You should have about 7 cups corn bread cubes and 4 cups white bread cubes.) Spread corn bread cubes on 1 or 2 shallow baking pans and white bread cubes on another baking pan. Bake in a 325° oven for 15 to 20 minutes or until lightly toasted, stirring once. Remove and place in a very large mixing bowl.

2 In a large skillet melt 2 tablespoons of the butter over medium heat. Add leeks and celery; cook, stirring occasionally, about 5 minutes or until tender. Stir in sage, thyme, and pepper. Add to bread cubes in bowl.

3 In same skillet melt remaining 2 tablespoons butter over medium-high heat. Add mushrooms. Cook, stirring occasionally, for 4 to 5 minutes or until most of the liquid is evaporated. Add to bread mixture in bowl. Stir in bacon pieces.

4 In a medium mixing bowl combine eggs and 2 cups of the broth. Pour over ingredients in very large mixing bowl, tossing lightly to coat. Add enough additional broth to make a stuffing of desired moistness.

5 Lightly grease a 3-quart rectangular baking dish. Place dressing in prepared dish. Bake, covered, for 20 minutes. Uncover and bake for 15 to 20 minutes more or until top is lightly browned and dressing is heated through. If desired, garnish with fresh thyme and sage sprigs. Makes 10 to 12 side-dish servings.

| TO MAKE AHEAD |

Prepare the dressing as directed, up through the addition of the bacon pieces. Cover and refrigerate up to 24 hours. Add eggs and broth. Bake dressing 25 minutes after uncovering or until it is heated through.

Nutrition facts per serving: 308 cal., 15 g total fat (5 g sat. fat), 145 mg chol., 656 mg sodium, 34 g carbo., 5 g fiber, 11 g pro. *Daily values:* 11% vit. A, 12% vit. C, 12% calcium, 21% iron.

TURKEY DAY TUNE-UP

Our Thanksgiving dinner tips and tricks will help you carve away calories and boost nutrition, while preserving the traditional tastes you love. Refuse to tamper with a favorite calorie-laden dessert? Don't panic: Sweet treats are no problem when enjoyed in moderation. Let's start the overhaul with the basics—the turkey and the stuffing.

BETTER-THAN-EVER TURKEY AND GRAVY

Though it's one of the leanest meats you can gobble up, you can run afoul with turkey if you're not careful. An 8-ounce helping of light and dark meat with skin, topped with a generous half-cup of gravy, weighs in at 535 calories. To save about half of the calories of a traditional turkey dinner, first drop the turkey portion to about 6 ounces. Choose light meat, dark meat, or a mix—dark meat has about 9 calories more than the light meat per ounce. And by going skinless you can cut the calories by almost 20 percent. Removing the fat from the drippings before making the gravy skims about two-thirds of the calories from the finished product. Finally, drizzle—don't pour—the gravy.

SMART STUFFING

Many stuffing recipes call for cooking the vegetables in butter or oil. It's no wonder a puny half-cup of bread stuffing adds up to 200 calories. Putting a pound of pork sausage into the mix adds 160 calories and 14 grams of fat per serving. You don't need butter or oil—at up to 120 calories per tablespoon—to make a moist, succulent stuffing. Instead, cook the vegetables in cooking spray. Moisten the mixture with fat-free chicken broth. Use smoked turkey sausage for the same traditional flavor, but less than half the calories, of pork sausage.

NOW TO THE SIDES

Creamy mashed potatoes are often a staple on the Thanksgiving table. Plenty of butter and whole milk give this dreamy favorite 220 calories per one-cup serving. Instead, make Simply Smashing Garlic Mashed Potatoes: Cook your potatoes in chicken broth seasoned with roasted garlic. Drain, reserving the broth. Then beat the potatoes with enough of the hot broth to make them light and fluffy. Serve topped with snipped green onions for just 160 calories per cup.

A quarter-cup of cranberry relish can slide as many as 100 deceptive calories onto your plate. But appealingly trim and tangy Orange-Cranberry Relish—less than 70 calories per quarter cup—is a cinch to make: In a food processor bowl or food grinder combine one 12-ounce package fresh cranberries; one unpeeled orange, sliced and seeded; ⅔ cup of sugar; and 2 teaspoons snipped rosemary. Process or grind together until of desired consistency.

Candied sweet potatoes are the second-most traditional dish of the Thanksgiving feast, right next to the turkey itself. Instead of smothering those beta-carotene-rich sweet potatoes in butter, sugar, and marshmallows (at 235 calories per ¾-cup), how about tossing chunks of sweet potatoes and carrots with a tablespoon of walnut oil, then roasting them until caramel-brown? You'll get rich, intense flavors at about half the calories. And don't forget the green vegetables: Gently steam fresh green beans or seasonal leafy greens, then flavor them with a sprinkling of herbs. You won't even miss the butter or cream.

THE PIE THAT BINDS

Nobody wants to deny you dessert after a festive meal. It's just a matter of perspective. Keep the portions on the thin side by cutting pies into ten slices instead of eight. Depending on the filling, one-eighth of a 9-inch pie with a scoop of premium vanilla ice cream can round off your feast with up to 630 calories. To help pumpkin pie, leave off the topping. Or, instead of fruit pie, simmer sliced apples, pears, and quinces in apple juice with brown sugar, cinnamon, and cloves. Serve the poached fruit warm, drizzled with just a little fresh cream. You'll enjoy a sweet finish to the meal without getting a meal's worth of calories from just one piece of pie.

Diane Quagliani, M.B.A., R.D., is a Chicago-based nutrition writer and educator.

TWEAK THAT TURKEY DINNER

◆ **Baste your turkey with fat-free chicken broth,** wine, or apple cider instead of butter or drippings. Give stuffing a fiber boost by using whole wheat bread cubes instead of white. Or, break out of the bread mold and try a stuffing recipe that calls for wild rice, brown rice, or bulgur wheat.

◆ **Add extra sweetness, fiber,** and health benefits to your sweet potatoes or stuffing by tossing in a handful of raisins or chopped prunes. These fruits scored the highest in antioxidant power in a recent USDA test on several fruits and vegetables.

◆ **For a low-cal bread spread,** use fruit butter or pumpkin butter. They're tasty calorie-savers that contribute a meager 10 calories per teaspoon.

◆ **Slice 200 calories** and nearly 30 grams of fat from a pumpkin pie filling by using a can of fat-free evaporated milk instead of whole evaporated milk.

AWAY FROM HOME

◆ **Don't arrive on empty.** Starving all day to "save up" for Thanksgiving dinner can backfire when your appetite careens out of control. Prepare to calmly face the big feast by eating light at usual mealtimes.

◆ **Moderate the alcohol.** Alcohol contains 7 calories per gram and lowers your resistance to how much you eat. Slash the calories in half by alternating between an alcoholic drink and sparkling water.

◆ **Nix the predinner nibbles.** Taste a few nuts here, a little cheese and crackers there and before you can say "Mayflower," you've got several hundred calories under your belt buckle, with the main event yet to begin. Socialize with some humorous anecdotes and light beverages rather than more munching.

◆ **Prioritize your plate.** Before filling up, survey all the offerings. Choose only foods you like best, and skip the rest.

◆ **Pick petite portions.** A typical Thanksgiving spread can hold over a dozen selections. Start out with half-size portions. If you're still hungry (yeah, right!) you can always go back for more.

◆ **Make room for exercise.** Taking a long walk before or after the celebratory dinner will burn off—at the rate of over 100 calories per half hour—some of those high-calorie indulgences.

◆ **Don't gobble your food.** Eat slowly, savor every bite, and be satisfied, not stuffed.

BISCUIT BASICS

Light, tender, flaky biscuits and scones are a breeze to make when you follow these basic techniques:

Stir dry ingredients well to distribute the leavening agent.

When a recipe calls for butter, make sure it's cold when you begin.

Mix butter or shortening and flour only until mixture resembles coarse crumbs.

Stir in the liquid just until the mixture is moistened.

Very gently knead the dough by folding and pressing—10 to 12 strokes should be enough to distribute the moisture.

Cut out as many of the biscuits as possible from a single rolling of the dough (the second rolling and the additional flour will make them a bit tougher than the first batch).

Place biscuits and scones close together on the baking sheet for a soft crust; for a crispy crust, place them about 1 inch apart.

Remove from the oven when top and bottom crusts are an even golden brown.

Store in a sealed plastic bag at room temperature for 2 or 3 days, or freeze them for up to 3 months.

Reheat foil-wrapped biscuits or scones in a 300° oven 10 to 12 minutes; reheat frozen biscuits for 20 to 25 minutes.

PEPPERY WHITE CHEDDAR BISCUITS

Prep: 25 min. ◆ Bake: 13 min.

See the photograph on page 277.

  4 cups all-purpose flour
  2 Tbsp. baking powder
  ½ cup shortening
  ¼ cup butter
  1½ cups finely crumbled or shredded sharp white cheddar cheese (6 oz.)
  2 to 3 tsp. coarsely ground black pepper
  1½ cups milk

  ◆◆◆

  1 egg, beaten

1 Lightly grease a large baking sheet; set aside. Combine flour, baking powder, and ½ teaspoon *salt.* Cut in shortening and butter until mixture resembles coarse crumbs. Add cheese and pepper; mix well. Make a well in center of the dry mixture. Add milk all at once; stir until just moistened.

2 Turn dough out onto a lightly floured surface. Quickly knead dough 10 to 12 strokes until almost smooth. Divide dough in half. Roll or pat each half into a 6-inch square, about 1 inch thick. Using a sharp knife, cut dough into 2-inch squares. Combine egg and 1 teaspoon *water;* brush tops of biscuits. Place on prepared baking sheet.

3 Bake in a 400° oven 13 to 15 minutes or until golden on top. Transfer to a wire rack. Serve warm. Makes 18.

▮ TO MAKE AHEAD ▮

Prepare and bake biscuits as directed; cool completely. Place biscuits in a freezer container or bag and freeze up to 3 months. To serve, wrap frozen biscuits in foil and bake in a 300° oven about 20 to 25 minutes or until warm.

Nutrition facts per biscuit: 247 cal., 14 g total fat (6 g sat. fat), 34 mg chol., 314 mg sodium, 24 g carbo., 1 g fiber, 7 g pro. *Daily values:* 8% vit. A, 19% calcium, 11% iron.

30 MIN. NO FAT

CRANBERRY AND APRICOT CHUTNEY

Prep: 10 min. ◆ Cook: 15 min.

See the photograph on page 280.

  1¼ cups granulated sugar
  1 12-oz. pkg. cranberries
  ¾ cup snipped dried apricots
  3 Tbsp. cider vinegar
  3 Tbsp. brown sugar
  1 Tbsp. minced fresh ginger

1 In a heavy large saucepan combine granulated sugar and ½ cup *water.* Cook and stir over medium-high heat until sugar is dissolved. Bring to boiling without stirring. Stir in cranberries, apricots, vinegar, brown sugar, and ginger; reduce heat. Simmer, uncovered, 5 minutes or until berries have popped and mixture starts to thicken. Remove from heat; cool. Cover and chill up to 4 days. Before serving, let stand at room temperature 30 minutes.

2 To serve, spoon chutney into a serving bowl. Makes about 3½ cups.

Nutrition facts per ¼-cup serving: 106 cal., 0 g total fat, 0 mg chol., 2 mg sodium, 28 g carbo., 2 g fiber, 0 g pro. *Daily values:* 5% vit. A, 5% vit. C, 3% iron.

Top: *Roasted Corn and Pepper Soup (page 271)*
Above: *Peppery White Cheddar Biscuits (page 276)*

Left: *Apples Stuffed with Couscous (page 223)*
Below: *Party Grapes (page 290)*
Page 278: *Mashed Sweets and Turnips (page 285)*

Above: *Cranberry and Apricot Chutney (page 276)*
Right: *Orange- and Herb-Roasted Turkey (page 270)*

Above: *Chunky Corn Bread Dressing (page 273)*
Left: *Ginger- and Honey-Glazed Carrots (page 286)*

Left: *Salmon Chowder (page 258)*
Below: *Pumpkin Spice Loaves (page 285)*

Pumpkin Spice Loaves

Prep: 40 min. ◆ Bake: 1 hr.

See the photograph on page 284.

2 cups coarsely chopped black
    walnuts or a mixture of
    chopped walnuts and
    hazelnuts (filberts)
3 cups all-purpose flour
2 tsp. baking powder
1 tsp. ground cinnamon
¾ tsp. freshly grated nutmeg
    or ground nutmeg
½ tsp. baking soda
¼ tsp. salt
◆◆◆
¾ cup butter, softened
1 cup granulated sugar
1 cup packed brown sugar
1 tsp. vanilla
4 eggs
1 15-oz. can pumpkin
½ cup milk
◆◆◆
¼ cup maple-flavored syrup
1 cup whipping cream
½ tsp. freshly grated nutmeg
    or ground nutmeg

1 Butter two 8×4×2 or 9×5×3-inch loaf pans. Place nuts in bottom of prepared pans; set aside. Stir together flour, baking powder, cinnamon, ¾ teaspoon nutmeg, soda, and salt. Set aside.

2 In a very large mixing bowl beat butter with an electric mixer on medium speed for 30 seconds. Add granulated and brown sugars and vanilla; beat 1 to 2 minutes or until well combined. Add eggs, 1 at a time, beating just until combined after each. (Mixture may look curdled.) Beat in pumpkin. Add flour mixture and milk alternately, beating on low speed until well blended after each addition; scrape sides of bowl.

3 Pour batter into prepared pans and smooth tops with a rubber spatula. Bake in a 350° oven about 1 hour or until a wooden toothpick inserted near center comes out clean. Cool loaves in pans on wire rack for 15 minutes. Loosen edges with a narrow metal spatula and remove from pans. Cool completely on wire racks, nut side up. Store in an airtight container in a cool place up to 2 days.

4 To serve, place cakes, nut side up, on a serving plate. Brush tops with 2 tablespoons of the maple-flavored syrup. In a chilled bowl beat whipping cream, remaining 2 tablespoons syrup, and ½ teaspoon nutmeg just until stiff peaks form. Serve the cream in a bowl with the cake. Makes 2 loaves (16 to 20 servings).

Nutrition facts per serving: 446 cal., 25 g total fat (10 g sat. fat), 97 mg chol., 238 mg sodium, 51 g carbo., 2 g fiber, 9 g pro. *Daily values:* 76% vit. A, 3% vit. C, 8% calcium, 16% iron.

Mashed Sweets and Turnips

Start to finish: 55 min.

It's great to know you can get a head start on this inventive sweet potato recipe. Simply cook and mash the sweet potatoes and turnips one day ahead and reheat them in the microwave just before serving.
(See the photograph on page 278.)

3 lb. sweet potatoes, peeled
    and cut into 1-inch cubes
    (about 9½ cups)
2½ lb. turnips, peeled and cut
    into 1-inch cubes
    (8½ cups)
3 Tbsp. unsalted butter or
    regular butter
◆◆◆
2 Tbsp. unsalted butter or
    regular butter
2 tart, medium red cooking
    apples, cored and coarsely
    chopped
½ cup whole dates, pitted and
    snipped
¼ cup brown sugar
1 Tbsp. lemon juice

1 In a 6- to 8-quart Dutch oven combine sweet potatoes, turnips, and enough water to cover. Bring to boiling; reduce heat. Simmer, covered, for 12 to 15 minutes or until tender. Drain well in a very large colander. Return vegetables to the Dutch oven and add the 3 tablespoons butter and 1 teaspoon *salt*. Mash vegetables with a potato masher until nearly smooth.

2 For the relish, in a medium skillet melt the 2 tablespoons butter. Add apples, dates, and brown sugar. Cook and stir until sugar is dissolved and apples are just tender. Stir in lemon juice.

3 To serve, mound hot vegetables in a serving bowl and garnish center with the relish. Makes 10 to 12 side-dish servings.

▮ TO MAKE AHEAD ▮

Prepare vegetables as directed. Place in a 2- to 2½-quart microwave-safe dish; cool slightly, then cover, and refrigerate. To reheat, microwave, covered, on 70% power (medium-high) for 20 to 25 minutes or until heated through, stirring twice. Make relish before serving.

Nutrition facts per serving: 238 cal., 6 g total fat (4 g sat. fat), 16 mg chol., 304 mg sodium, 46 g carbo., 9 g fiber, 3 g pro. *Daily values:* 236% vit. A, 67% vit. C, 5% calcium, 6% iron.

GREEN BEANS AND FENNEL

Prep: 20 min. ◆ Cook: 12 min.

No matter how they were prepared, green beans were one of Betty Rosbottom's childhood favorites. With subtle lemon accents and only 77 calories per serving, this Thanksgiving update of the treasured side dish is irresistible.

2 Tbsp. butter, softened
1½ tsp. fennel seeds, crushed
1½ tsp. finely shredded lemon peel
¾ tsp. coarsely ground black pepper

◆◆◆

3 fennel bulbs (3 lb.)

◆◆◆

1¾ lb. green beans, trimmed, if desired

1 In a large mixing bowl stir together butter, fennel seeds, lemon peel, pepper, and ¼ teaspoon *salt;* set aside.

2 To prepare fennel, cut off and discard upper stalks. Remove any wilted outer layers; cut off a thin slice from fennel base. Wash fennel and cut into quarters. Remove cores. Cut fennel lengthwise into ¼-inch-wide strips.

3 In a 4-quart Dutch oven, cook beans, covered, in boiling salted water 4 to 5 minutes. Add fennel to beans and cook for 6 to 10 minutes more or until tender. Drain. Toss vegetables in bowl with seasoned butter. Transfer to a serving dish. Serves 10 to 12.

Nutrition facts per serving: 77 cal., 3 g total fat (1 g sat. fat), 6 mg chol., 126 mg sodium, 13 g carbo., 26 g fiber, 3 g pro. *Daily values:* 7% vit. A, 31% vit. C, 7% calcium, 7% iron.

GINGER- AND HONEY-GLAZED CARROTS

Prep: 45 min. (15 min. with prepeeled carrots) ◆ Cook: 15 min.

A side dish for all ages and all holidays: Fresh, tender-sweet carrots lightly coated in a buttery glaze accented with fresh ginger. (See the photograph on page 282.)

6 cups water
¾ tsp. salt
3 lb. young, small carrots with tops trimmed to 2 inches, peeled or scrubbed; or 3 lb. packaged peeled baby carrots

◆◆◆

2 Tbsp. butter
2 Tbsp. honey
4 tsp. minced fresh ginger

1 Line a baking sheet with paper towels. In a 12- or 14-inch heavy skillet combine water and salt. Bring to boiling over high heat. Add carrots. Return to boiling; reduce heat. Cover and simmer about 10 to 12 minutes or until carrots are just tender. Drain carrots. Carefully turn out onto prepared baking sheet. (When green tops are left on carrots during cooking, they become fragile. As the carrots cook, some of the tops may come off.) Pat dry with additional paper towels.

2 To glaze carrots, in the same heavy skillet combine butter, honey, and fresh ginger. Stir constantly over medium heat until the butter is melted. Carefully add the carrots. Toss gently for 2 to 3 minutes or until carrots are thoroughly coated with glaze and heated through completely.

3 To serve, arrange carrots in a shallow bowl or on a platter; drizzle carrots with remaining glaze from the pan. Makes 10 to 12 side dish servings.

TO MAKE AHEAD

Carrots may be cooked, cooled, covered, and refrigerated up to one day ahead. Bring to room temperature (about 1 hour) when ready to glaze. Heat carrots in glaze for 4 to 5 minutes.

Nutrition facts per serving: 90 cal., 3 g total fat (1 g sat. fat), 6 mg chol., 266 mg sodium, 17 g carbo., 4 g fiber, 1 g pro. *Daily values:* 309% vit. A, 4% vit. C, 3% calcium, 5% iron.

AUTUMN FRUIT TARTLETS

Prep: 45 min. ◆ Bake: 10 min. Chill: 2 hr.

We added a bit of whimsy to these wee tarts with pineapple, pear, and kumquat slices. You can use the harvest fruits of your choice. From apples to berries, they're yours for the picking.

½ cup butter
1½ cups all-purpose flour
1 egg yolk, slightly beaten
2 to 3 Tbsp. ice water

◆◆◆

¾ cup sugar
¼ cup cornstarch
3 cups milk
5 egg yolks, beaten
1 Tbsp. butter
1½ tsp. vanilla

◆◆◆

1 recipe Crackly Caramel
   Spikes (see below right)
   (optional)

❖❖❖

Assorted fresh fruits such as
   small pear halves,
   pineapple wedges, and
   kumquats
Lemon juice
1 recipe Crackly Caramel
   Sauce (see below right)
   (optional)

1 For tart shells, in a mixing bowl cut ½ cup butter into flour until pieces are pea-size, using a pastry blender. Stir together 1 egg yolk and 1 tablespoon of the ice water. Gradually stir egg yolk mixture into flour mixture. Add remaining water, 1 tablespoon at a time, until dough is moistened. Gently knead the dough just until a ball forms. If necessary, cover dough with plastic wrap and refrigerate for 30 to 60 minutes or until dough is easy to handle.

2 Cut dough into 8 equal pieces and flatten each into a disk. On a lightly floured surface, roll each disk into a 5½-inch-diameter circle. Gently ease each circle of dough into a 4-inch-diameter tart pan with removable bottom. Press pastry into sides of pans and trim edges. Do not prick pastry. Line each tart with a double thickness of foil and place on baking sheet.

3 Bake in a 450° oven for 6 minutes. Remove foil and bake for 4 to 5 minutes more or until light golden brown. Remove from oven. Cool tart shells in pans on wire racks.

4 For filling, in a heavy medium saucepan combine sugar and cornstarch. Stir in milk. Cook and stir over medium heat until bubbly. Cook and stir for 2 minutes more. Remove from heat. Gradually stir 1 cup of the milk mixture into 5 beaten egg yolks. Add egg mixture to milk mixture in saucepan. Bring to a gentle boil; reduce heat. Cook and stir for 2 minutes more. Remove from heat. Stir in 1 tablespoon butter and the vanilla. Pour pudding into a bowl. Cover surface with plastic wrap; chill thoroughly. Do not stir while chilling. If desired, prepare Crackly Caramel Spikes.

5 To assemble, spoon pudding into tart shells. Cut pears into wedges; core. Brush cut surfaces with lemon juice. Stand assorted fruits up and, if desired, arrange Caramel Spikes on top of tartlets. If desired, prepare and drizzle each tartlet with Crackly Caramel Sauce. Makes 8 servings.

Crackly Caramel Spikes: Line a baking sheet with foil. Butter the foil; set pan aside. In a 12-inch nonstick skillet heat ¾ cup sugar over medium-high heat until sugar begins to melt, shaking skillet occasionally. Do not stir. Reduce heat; cook and stir about 3 minutes more or until sugar is melted and medium caramel in color. Remove from pan heat and stir in ½ teaspoon hot water. Immediately pour mixture onto foil-lined baking sheet, spreading caramel mixture as thin as possible. Cool about 30 minutes. When cool, tap gently with a wooden spoon to break into large shards; store tightly covered.

Crackly Caramel Sauce: Just before serving tartlets, prepare

THE CLEVER COOK

CLIP ON YOUR SHOPPING LIST

When I go to the supermarket I take along a clothespin or a metal clip. I use the pin or clip to clip my shopping list and coupons to the front of the shopping cart (the part that opens and goes back). This way my shopping list and coupons are visible and it helps me to remember the items I need.

Zelda Band
Forest Hills, New York

Crackly Caramel Spikes as directed, except omit foil-lined and buttered baking sheet and reduce sugar in the skillet to ½ cup. Immediately drizzle caramel sauce over tarts (mixture will harden).

TO MAKE AHEAD

Pudding can be made 2 days ahead. Pastry shells can be made and filled with pudding up to 1 day ahead. Store in refrigerator. Just before serving, add Crackly Caramel Spikes and fruit, then prepare and drizzle with Crackly Caramel Sauce.

Nutrition facts per tartlet: 394 cal., 19 g total fat (10 g sat. fat), 201 mg chol., 183 mg sodium, 50 g carbo., 2 g fiber, 8 g pro. *Daily values:* 41% vit. A, 9% vit. C, 11% calcium, 11% iron.

BETTY'S HOLIDAY CENTERPIECE

Putting together an eyecatching centerpiece is simple if you take a cue from the abundant harvest. Following are a few of Betty's quick and easy seasonal favorites:

◆ Load up an oversize pewter, wooden, or crystal bowl with a mélange of bountiful produce such as pumpkins, squashes, gourds, pears, and persimmons.

◆ Hollow out a medium-size pumpkin or squash and fill it with a fresh mum bouquet in a fitting harvest hue. A small amount of water will keep the flowers fresh for a few days.

◆ Line a shallow basket or wooden bowl with fresh cabbage or kale leaves. In the center, mound pomegranates, red pears, and red grapes.

◆ Arrange fresh bittersweet vines, Bosc pears, petite orange or ivory pumpkins, and ivory candles down the center of the table.

LEMON CHEESECAKE

Prep: 25 min. ◆ Bake: 5 min.
Chill: 6 hr.

(See the photograph on page 1.)

1½ **cups pure butter packed**
    shortbread cookie crumbs
    (5½ oz.)
2 **Tbsp. butter, melted**
    ◆◆◆
¼ **cup half-and-half or light**
    cream
1 **envelope unflavored gelatin**
    ◆◆◆
3 **8-oz. pkg. cream cheese,**
    softened

1 **cup lemon curd (about one**
   10-oz. jar)
2 **tsp. finely shredded lemon**
   peel
    ◆◆◆
1 **cup fresh pomegranate seeds**
   or 2 cups fresh raspberries

1 For crust, in a medium mixing bowl stir together the shortbread cookie crumbs and the melted butter. Press the cookie crumbs onto the bottom only of an 8-inch springform pan with a removable bottom. Bake in a 350° oven for 5 minutes. Cool crust on a wire rack.

2 To make the filling, pour half-and-half or cream into a small saucepan. Sprinkle gelatin over half-and-half; let stand for 3 minutes to soften. Heat gently over medium heat about 1 minute or just until gelatin dissolves. Remove pan from heat and cool.

3 Meanwhile, place cream cheese in a large mixing bowl. Beat with an electric mixer on medium speed until smooth. Add lemon curd and lemon peel. Add half-and-half mixture and beat about 1 minute more until combined. Pour filling into crumb-lined springform pan. Smooth top with a spatula. Cover with plastic wrap and chill for 6 or up to 48 hours or until firm.

4 To serve, use a narrow metal spatula or knife to loosen the cheesecake from sides of springform pan. Remove sides of pan. Top cheesecake with pomegranate seeds or raspberries. Cut into wedges. Makes 10 to 12 servings.

TEST KITCHEN TIP

SELECTING, STORING AND SEEDING POMEGRANATES

Pomegranates should have a shiny, bright red skin with no signs of shriveling. Buy the largest fruits you can find. Pomegranates should feel heavy for their size.

Pomegranates found in the supermarket should be ready to eat. Because they keep well, you can store them in the refrigerator for several weeks. Or, you can freeze the pomegranate seeds in freezer containers or bags for up to 1 year.

To remove the seeds without staining your hands or countertops, score pomegranate skin from end to end in quarters; gently break fruit apart along these lines. Immerse fruit in a bowl of water, bend back the rind and rub the seeds free. The skin and white membrane will float to the top; remove with slotted spoon and discard. Drain seeds.

TO MAKE AHEAD

Prepare cheesecake as directed. Cover cheesecake well and store in the refrigerator for up to 2 days. Serve as directed.

Nutrition facts per serving: 451 cal., 32 g total fat (19 g sat. fat), 109 mg chol., 322 mg sodium, 17 g carbo., 3 g fiber, 7 g pro. *Daily values:* 32% vit. A, 3% vit. C, 5% calcium, 9% iron.

DECEMBER
Holiday Fun

30-minute recipes indicated in RED.
Low-fat and no-fat recipes indicated
with a ♥.
Photographs indicated in italics.
*Bonus recipe

*T*he holidays are filled with the fancy, fun, and colorful. This is one time of year that celebrates the art of going all-out, from festive drinks, like Stained Glass Splash, to easy-but-appealing desserts, like Wintery Ice Cream Balls or Pear-Tree Wonders. For an open house or party, present a selection of appetizers, such as Endive-Mango Appetizers, Lemony-Herbed Olives, and Pistachio-Salmon Nuggets. And show off at a Christmas or New Year's Eve dinner by serving our elegant Festive Salad with Celebration Roast or Walnut-Encrusted Pork Roast.

CRANBERRY VODKA

Prep: 10 min. ◆ Stand: 2 weeks

This holiday season surprise your neighbors, friends, or relatives with a jar of this spirited drink. For an easy presentation, tie a wide ribbon around the rim of the jar and attach a little card.

2 cups cranberries
2 cups vodka

1 Wash cranberries; pat dry with paper towels. Place cranberries in a clean 1-quart jar. Pour vodka over cranberries. Cover jar tightly with a nonmetallic lid (or cover the jar with plastic wrap and tightly seal with a metal lid). Let stand in a cool, dark place for 2 weeks. Can be kept up to 2 months.

2 To serve, pour the vodka into a small glass. Makes 16 (1-ounce) servings.

Nutrition facts per serving: 80 cal., 0 g total fat, 0 mg chol., 0 mg sodium, 2 g carbo., 1 g fiber, 0 g pro.
Daily values: 3% vit. C.

STAINED GLASS SPLASH

Prep: 10 min.

Bright red shimmers through the ice in this layered cranberry drink. Have the ingredients on hand so you can make this pour-and-serve beverage when unexpected guests stop by.

¼ cup apple-cranberry, cherry-cranberry, or cranberry juice
1 tsp. cherry-flavored syrup (for coffee) or grenadine syrup

¾ cup small ice cubes or coarsely crushed ice
¼ cup carbonated water or lemon-lime carbonated beverage, chilled
2 Tbsp. chopped maraschino cherries, drained

1 Combine the cranberry juice and syrup and pour into a 10-ounce glass. Gently spoon ice on top. Carefully pour the carbonated beverage over the ice. Top with the cherries. Serve immediately. Makes 1 serving.

Nutrition facts per serving: 86 cal., 0 g total fat, 0 mg chol., 5 mg sodium, 20 g carbo., 0 g fiber, 0 g pro.
Daily values: 33% vit. C, 1% calcium.

CHERRY MARTINI

Prep: 10 min.

Here's a merry little drink to toast holiday cheer. It's so very cherry that even those who traditionally pass on martinis may enjoy this fruity version.

½ tsp. cherry-flavored syrup (for coffee)
1 maraschino cherry
2 tsp. chopped papaya or mango
1 oz. vodka
Small ice cubes

1 Pour syrup in the bottom of a martini glass. Place cherry on top. Top with chopped papaya or mango. Carefully pour vodka over the fruit. Top with a few ice cubes. Makes 1 serving.

Nutrition facts per serving: 92 cal., 0 g total fat (0 g sat. fat), 0 mg chol., 1 mg sodium, 4 g carbo., 0 g fiber, 0 g pro.
Daily values: 6% vit. C.

PARTY GRAPES

Prep: 10 min. ◆ Roast: 40 min.

Red and green grapes are slowly roasted to boost their sweetness, then splashed with sherry vinegar and served with prosciutto.
(See the photograph on page 279.)

2 lb. red grapes (with stems)
2 lb. green grapes (with stems)
½ cup sherry vinegar or balsamic vinegar
◆◆◆
4 oz. thinly sliced prosciutto, cut into thin shreds
Sherry vinegar or balsamic vinegar (optional)

1 Line a 15×10×1-inch baking pan with heavy foil. Arrange bunches of grapes on foil and bring up sides of foil slightly. Drizzle vinegar over grapes.

2 Roast grapes, uncovered, in a 450° oven for 40 to 50 minutes or until lightly browned, turning bunches over after 20 minutes. (Open oven door carefully as vinegar fumes may cause eyes to sting.) Place grapes on a serving platter with prosciutto next to grapes. If desired, drizzle grapes with additional vinegar. Makes 12 appetizer servings.

Nutrition facts per serving: 148 cal., 3 g total fat (0 g sat. fat), 0 mg chol., 172 mg sodium, 29 g carbo., 2 g fiber, 3 g pro.
Daily values: 1% vit. A, 29% vit. C, 1% calcium, 5% iron.

CRISPY SWEET ROSEMARY

Prep: 5 min. ◆ **Cook: 5 min.**

As a centerpiece for your plate, set off the simple beauty of the aromatic herbs by tucking them into a silver cup. The container acts as a mirror, reflecting other foods you have on the plate.

¼ **cup olive oil or cooking oil**
12 **2-inch fresh rosemary sprigs**
¼ **tsp. sea salt or coarse kosher salt**

1 In a medium skillet heat oil over medium heat. Cook a few sprigs of herb at a time for 1 to 1¼ minutes or until crisp but not browned, turning once. Use a slotted spoon or tongs to carefully turn and remove sprigs from hot oil. Drain on paper towels. Sprinkle with salt. Use as garnish for roasted onions, Lemony-Herbed Olives (see recipe, page 292), or other vegetables. Makes 12 sprigs.

Nutrition facts per sprig: 10 cal., 1 g total fat (0 g sat. fat), 0 mg chol., 49 mg sodium, 0 g carbo., 0 g fiber, 0 g pro.
Daily values: 1% vit. A, 1% vit. C, 1% calcium, 1% iron.

HOLIDAY APPETIZER TIER

Assembly: 20 min

Pull out your grandmother's three-tiered platter and arrange a festive variety of appetizers upon it.

Assorted cheeses
Purchased vegetable terrine
1 **recipe Endive-Mango Appetizers (see right)**

1 **recipe Lemony-Herbed Olives (see page 292)**
1 **recipe Pistachio-Salmon Nuggets (see page 292)**
Lavosh chips, flatbread chips, and/or crackers
Fresh herb sprigs (optional)

1 On a 3-tiered stand arrange a variety of cheeses, some cut into wedges and/or slices, along with the Endive-Mango Appetizers, Lemony-Herbed Olives, and Pistachio-Salmon Nuggets. Serve with lavosh chips, flatbread, and/or crackers. If desired, garnish with herb sprigs.

ENDIVE-MANGO APPETIZERS

Prep: 20 min.

Although these make a stunning appetizer, you also could serve a few filled endive as a salad.
(See the photograph on page 319.)

1 **3-oz. pkg. cream cheese, softened**
¼ **cup coarsely chopped macadamia nuts**
2 **to 3 medium Belgian endives, separated into individual leaves**
1 **large mango and/or papaya, peeled, and cut into thin strips about 2×¾ inches**

1 In a small bowl combine softened cream cheese and macadamia nuts. Spread about 1 teaspoon cream cheese mixture into each endive leaf.* Top with sliced mango and/or papaya.

THE CLEVER COOK

TIMELY ADVICE

When using a recipe that calls for a time-consuming step, such as marinating or chilling overnight, highlight that step with a colored marker. This way, you can tell at a glance if a recipe needs extra time and can plan accordingly.

Lenore Felpel
East Killingly, Connecticut

Arrange on Holiday Appetizer Tier (see left). Makes about 24 appetizers.

*Note: If desired, endive leaves may be spread with cheese mixture up to 2 hours before serving. Cover loosely with plastic wrap and chill. Just before serving, top with mango and/or papaya and arrange on platter.

Nutrition facts per appetizer: 29 cal., 2 g total fat (1 g sat. fat), 4 mg chol., 11 mg sodium, 2 g carbo., 0 g fiber, 0 g pro.
Daily values: 5% vit. A, 5% vit. C.

LEMONY-HERBED OLIVES

Prep: 15 min. ◆ Marinate: 4 to 24 hr.

Once the crushed red pepper is stirred in, the mixture of kalamata and green olives goes from mellow to merry. If you like things spicy hot, use the 1 teaspoon crushed red pepper. (See the photograph on page 319.)

1 lb. pitted kalamata and/or green olives (3½ cups)
1 Tbsp. olive oil
½ tsp. finely shredded lemon peel
1 Tbsp. lemon juice
2 tsp. snipped fresh oregano or ½ tsp. dried oregano, crushed
½ to 1 tsp. crushed red pepper

◆◆◆

Lemon peel curls (optional)

1 Place olives in a plastic bag set in a bowl. For marinade, combine olive oil, lemon peel, lemon juice, oregano, and crushed red pepper. Pour over olives. Close the bag. Marinate in the refrigerator for 4 to 24 hours.

2 To serve, let stand at room temperature for 30 minutes. Drain and serve on Holiday Appetizer Tier (see page 291). If desired, garnish olives with curled strips of lemon peel. Makes about 56 appetizer servings.

Nutrition facts per 1 tablespoon olives: 15 cal., 1 g total fat (0 g sat. fat), 0 mg chol., 94 mg sodium, 1 g carbo., 0 g fiber, 0 g pro.

PISTACHIO-SALMON NUGGETS

Prep: 15 min. ◆ Marinate: 30 min.
Cook: 3 min.

See the photograph on page 319.

1 lb. fresh or frozen skinless salmon fillets, cut 1 inch thick
2 Tbsp. water
2 Tbsp. soy sauce
1 Tbsp. grated fresh ginger or 1 tsp. ground ginger
2 tsp. toasted sesame oil or cooking oil

◆◆◆

1 Tbsp. cooking oil
1 Tbsp. finely chopped pistachio nuts

1 Thaw fish, if frozen. Rinse fish; pat dry with paper towels. Cut fish into 1-inch chunks. Place fish in a plastic bag set in a shallow dish. For marinade, combine water, soy sauce, ginger, and sesame oil. Pour over the salmon chunks. Close the bag. Marinate at room temperature for 30 minutes, turning the bag occasionally.

2 In a large nonstick skillet or wok heat the 1 tablespoon cooking oil over medium-high heat. Drain salmon, discarding marinade. Cook and stir half of the salmon chunks for 3 to 5 minutes or until fish flakes easily with a fork; remove from skillet. Cook and stir remaining fish; remove. Sprinkle with pistachio nuts. Serve warm on Holiday Appetizer Tier (see page 291). Makes 20 to 24 appetizer servings.

Nutrition facts per serving: 32 cal., 2 g total fat (0 g sat. fat), 4 mg chol., 65 mg sodium, 0 g carbo., 0 g fiber, 3 g pro.
Daily values: 1% iron.

FESTIVE SALAD

Start to finish: 45 min.

Simple salad ingredients go from everyday to dazzling. Thin slices of cucumber create a "bowl" around crunchy root vegetables and baby greens in this styled salad. (See the photograph on page 319.)

2 large English (seedless) cucumbers (about 2 lb.)
3 oz. daikon (optional)

◆◆◆

6 cups torn baby red-tipped lettuce and/or mixed baby greens
1 cup coarsely shredded, peeled celeriac (celery root)
1 small red onion, cut into thin wedges (⅓ cup)
1 recipe Basil Vinaigrette (see page 293) or ¼ cup bottled red wine vinaigrette

◆◆◆

Fresh dill sprigs and/or oregano sprigs (optional)
1 recipe Crouton Stars (see page 293)
Fresh chives (optional)

1 Use a mandoline to cut lengthwise slices from cucumbers. (You should have about 4 cups cucumber slices.) Place cucumber slices in cold water to crisp; set aside. If desired, use the mandoline to cut daikon into lengthwise slices about ¼ inch thick. Cut the daikon slices into 3-inch wedges; set aside.

2 In a large bowl combine greens, celeriac, and red onion. Drizzle 2 tablespoons Basil Vinaigrette over salad mixture. Toss lightly to coat.

3 Drain cucumber slices; pat dry with paper towels. Create a cucumber bowl on each of 6 salad plates by wrapping and overlapping cucumber slices, turban-style. Divide the greens evenly and mound in center of each cucumber bowl. If desired, tuck a slice of daikon and dill and/or oregano sprigs into greens. Top with Crouton Stars and a whole chive, if desired. Pass remaining vinaigrette. Makes 6 servings.

Basil Vinaigrette: In a screw-top jar combine 2 tablespoons olive oil; 2 tablespoons red wine vinegar or balsamic vinegar; 1 teaspoon honey mustard; 1 tablespoon snipped fresh basil or 1 teaspoon dried basil, crushed; ¼ teaspoon salt; and ⅛ teaspoon pepper. Cover and shake well. If desired, chill up to 2 days.

Nutrition facts per serving (without croutons): 85 cal., 5 g total fat (1 g sat. fat), 0 mg chol., 124 mg sodium, 10 g carbo., 3 g fiber, 2 g pro.
Daily values: 13% vit. A, 34% vit. C, 6% calcium, 9% iron.

Crouton Stars

Prep: 30 min. ◆ Bake: 15 min.

Small celestial cookie cutters are used to make these crunchy bites. For other occasions, try using small cutters such as hearts, shamrocks, and leaves.

- **1 16-oz. loaf sourdough bread, cut into ¾-inch slices (about 13 slices)**

◆◆◆

- **2 Tbsp. margarine or butter**
- **½ tsp. coarsely ground pepper (optional)**
- **Salt (optional)**

1 Use 1- to 2-inch star-shaped cookie cutters to cut stars from white portion of bread. (Or use a knife to cut bread into 1-inch cubes.) Set aside.

2 In a large skillet melt margarine or butter. Remove from heat. If desired, stir in pepper and salt. Add the bread cutouts, stirring until coated with the margarine mixture.

3 Arrange crouton stars in a single layer in a shallow baking pan. Bake, uncovered, in a 300° oven for 10 minutes; turn croutons over. Bake 5 minutes more or until croutons are dry and crisp. Cool completely. Store, tightly covered, up to 1 week. Serve with Festive Salad (see recipe, page 292). Makes about 36 star croutons (2 to 3 cups).

Nutrition facts per serving (3 croutons): 121 cal., 3 g total fat (1 g sat. fat), 0 mg chol., 252 mg sodium, 20 g carbo., 0 g fiber, 3 g pro.
Daily values: 2% vit. A, 2% calcium, 6% iron.

Pear-Endive Salad With Honey Vinaigrette

Start to finish: 20 min.

Made with pears and embellished with crunchy walnuts, this endive salad takes on a simple hint of Christmas with a sprinkling of pomegranate seeds.

- **2 ripe red Bartlett pears, Bosc pears, and/or apples, cored and thinly sliced**
- **2 Tbsp. lemon juice**

- **8 oz. Belgian endive, leaves separated (2 medium heads)**
- **¼ cup coarsely chopped walnuts**
- **Dash salt**
- **Dash pepper**

◆◆◆

- **3 Tbsp. olive oil or salad oil**
- **2 Tbsp. sherry vinegar or white wine vinegar**
- **1 shallot, finely chopped, or 1 Tbsp. finely chopped onion**
- **1 Tbsp. honey**
- **½ tsp. ground cinnamon**

◆◆◆

- **Pomegranate seeds (optional)**

1 In a small bowl gently toss pear or apple slices with the lemon juice to prevent darkening. Set aside.

2 Place the endive leaves in each of 4 salad bowls or salad plates. Arrange the sliced pears and/or apples over top. Sprinkle with walnuts, salt, and pepper.

3 For vinaigrette, in a small bowl combine olive oil or salad oil, sherry vinegar or white wine vinegar, shallot or onion, honey, and cinnamon; whisk until thoroughly blended.

4 To serve, drizzle the vinaigrette over the salads. If desired, sprinkle with pomegranate seeds. Makes 4 servings.

Nutrition facts per serving: 216 cal., 15 g total fat (2 g sat. fat), 0 mg chol., 39 mg sodium, 22 g carbo., 3 g fiber, 2 g pro.
Daily values: 3% vit. A, 21% vit. C, 1% calcium, 6% iron.

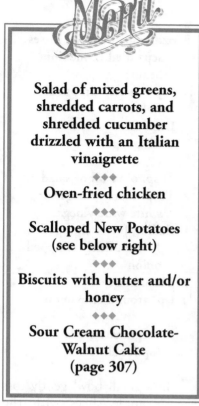

Salad of mixed greens, shredded carrots, and shredded cucumber drizzled with an Italian vinaigrette

♦♦♦

Oven-fried chicken

♦♦♦

Scalloped New Potatoes (see below right)

♦♦♦

Biscuits with butter and/or honey

♦♦♦

Sour Cream Chocolate-Walnut Cake (page 307)

---

30 MIN. LOW FAT

HEAVENLY PEAS WITH MASHED POTATOES

Start to finish: 15 min.

Sour cream gives the potatoes their richness; pureed peas gives them their hue of Christmas green. (See the photograph on page 318.)

1 10-oz. pkg. frozen peas
¼ cup chopped onion
1 Tbsp. margarine or butter
¼ tsp. salt
⅛ tsp. pepper
2 Tbsp. chicken broth

♦♦♦

½ cup dairy sour cream
4 to 5 cups prepared hot mashed potatoes*
   Fresh rosemary sprigs (optional)

1 Cook peas and onion in margarine or butter for 5 minutes

or until tender, stirring occasionally. Remove from heat; stir in salt and pepper. Remove ½ cup of the pea-onion mixture; set aside.

2 Place remaining pea-onion mixture in a blender container or food processor bowl along with broth. Cover and blend or process until smooth. (If necessary, add an additional 1 tablespoon broth to make mixture whirl in machine.) Stir together pureed peas and reserved ½ cup whole pea-onion mixture; set aside.

3 In a large bowl, stir sour cream into hot mashed potatoes. Add pea mixture to potatoes and fold gently to combine. If desired, garnish each serving with fresh rosemary sprigs. Makes 8 side-dish servings.

*Note: If desired, use two 20-ounce packages of refrigerated mashed potatoes heated according to package directions.

Nutrition facts per serving: 151 cal., 5 g total fat (3 g sat. fat), 8 mg chol., 448 mg sodium, 24 g carbo., 2 g fiber, 4 g pro. *Daily values:* 7% vit. A, 17% vit. C, 4% calcium, 5% iron.

30 MIN. LOW FAT

SAUTÉED BROCCOLI RABE

Start to finish: 20 min.

Broccoli rabe, also known as rapini, has a leafy green stalk with small clusters of broccoli-like florets. Find it at many supermarkets and specialty foods stores.

2 lb. broccoli rabe or 6 cups coarsely chopped broccoli florets
3 cloves garlic, minced

¼ tsp. salt
4 tsp. olive oil
   Crushed red pepper (optional)

1 Wash broccoli rabe; remove and discard woody stems. Cut into 2-inch pieces. In a very large skillet cook and stir broccoli rabe or broccoli, garlic, and salt in hot oil over medium-high heat for 3 to 4 minutes or until broccoli rabe is crisp-tender. (If using broccoli florets, cook and stir for 5 to 6 minutes or until crisp-tender). If desired, sprinkle with crushed red pepper. Makes 6 side-dish servings.

Nutrition facts per serving: 71 cal., 4 g total fat (0 g sat. fat), 0 mg chol., 128 mg sodium, 8 g carbo., 5 g fiber, 5 g pro. *Daily values:* 21% vit. A, 188% vit. C, 6% calcium, 8% iron.

PRIZE TESTED RECIPE WINNER

SCALLOPED NEW POTATOES

Prep: 25 min. ♦ Bake: 20 min.

This recipe has all the cheesy-creamy goodness of scalloped potatoes but about half the fat.

   Nonstick cooking spray
2 lb. whole tiny new potatoes, sliced

♦♦♦

1 cup chopped onion
3 cloves garlic, minced
3 Tbsp. margarine or butter
3 Tbsp. all-purpose flour
1¼ tsp. dried rosemary, crushed
1 tsp. dried parsley
½ tsp. salt
¼ tsp. pepper
1¾ cups milk

6 cups torn spinach or 4 cups
broccoli rabe, cut into
1½-inch pieces
1 small red sweet pepper, cut
into matchstick strips

◆◆◆

¾ cup shredded white cheddar
cheese
¼ cup fine dry bread crumbs

1 Spray a 2-quart oval or rectangular baking dish with nonstick coating; set aside. In a large saucepan cook potatoes, covered, in a moderate amount of boiling salted water about 5 minutes or until just tender. Drain and transfer to an extra-large mixing bowl.

2 In same saucepan cook onion and garlic in 2 tablespoons of the margarine over medium heat 5 minutes or until just tender. Stir in flour, rosemary, parsley, salt, and pepper. Stir in milk. Cook and stir over medium heat until thickened and bubbly.

3 Add spinach or broccoli rabe and sweet pepper to potatoes. Toss gently to combine. Pour sauce over potato mixture. Stir gently until coated. Transfer potato mixture to prepared baking dish (dish will be very full).

4 Sprinkle cheese evenly over top. Melt the remaining 1 tablespoon of margarine. Add bread crumbs, tossing to coat. Sprinkle over cheese. Bake in a 375° oven 20 minutes or until edges are bubbly and crumbs are golden. Makes 10 to 12 side-dish servings.

Nutrition facts per serving: 214 cal., 8 g total fat (3 g sat. fat), 12 mg chol., 274 mg sodium, 30 g carbo., 2 g fiber, 8 g pro. *Daily values:* 35% vit. A, 54% vit. C, 14% calcium, 16% iron.

PRIZE TESTED RECIPE WINNER

BULGUR-WILD RICE CASSEROLE

Prep: 25 min. ◆ Bake: 30 min.

If you use dried herbs rather than fresh, add them along with the chicken broth.

¼ cup margarine or butter
1 cup bulgur
1 cup chopped celery
½ cup chopped onion

◆◆◆

3 cups chicken broth
1½ cups cooked wild rice
½ cup snipped fresh parsley
2 cups sliced fresh mushrooms
1 cup chopped toasted walnuts
1 Tbsp. snipped fresh basil or
1 tsp. dried basil, crushed
2 tsp. snipped fresh oregano or
½ tsp. dried oregano,
crushed

1 In a large saucepan melt margarine over medium heat. Add bulgur; cook 2 minutes. Stir in celery and onion. Cook and stir 3 minutes more or until vegetables are just tender.

2 Stir in broth, cooked wild rice, parsley, and ¼ teaspoon *pepper.* Bring to boiling; reduce heat. Simmer, covered, for 10 minutes. Stir in mushrooms, walnuts, basil, and oregano. Transfer mixture to a 2-quart casserole.

3 Bake, covered, in a 350° oven for 30 minutes or until liquid is absorbed. Serves 8 to 10.

Nutrition facts per serving: 266 cal., 16 g total fat (2 g sat. fat), 0 mg chol., 381 mg sodium, 26 g carbo., 6 g fiber, 8 g pro. *Daily values:* 9% vit. A, 12% vit. C, 3% calcium, 12% iron.

MAPLE RUTABAGA-APPLE CASSEROLE

Prep: 40 min. ◆ Bake: 40 min.

1 medium rutabaga, peeled
and chopped (about
4 cups)
2 large cooking apples, peeled
and chopped (about
2½ cups)

◆◆◆

2 eggs, beaten
⅔ cup half-and-half, light
cream, or milk
⅓ cup maple or maple-flavored
syrup
½ tsp. salt
¼ tsp. pepper
¾ cup soft bread crumbs
(1 slice)
1 Tbsp. margarine or butter,
melted

1 In a large saucepan cook rutabaga and apples, covered, in a moderate amount of boiling water for 20 to 25 minutes or until rutabaga is tender. Drain.

2 Mash rutabaga-apple mixture with a potato masher until nearly smooth. Stir in eggs, half-and-half, maple syrup, salt, and pepper. Transfer to a 1½-quart casserole. Combine bread crumbs and melted margarine; sprinkle over rutabaga mixture.

3 Bake, uncovered, in a 350° oven for 40 to 45 minutes or until a knife inserted near the center comes out clean. Let stand 5 minutes before serving. Makes 6 to 8 side-dish servings.

Nutrition facts per serving: 203 cal., 7 g total fat (3 g sat. fat), 81 mg chol., 281 mg sodium, 32 g carbo., 4 g fiber, 5 g pro. *Daily values:* 9% vit. A, 42% vit. C, 7% calcium, 7% iron.

COASTAL BEND TEXAS BEEF TENDERLOIN

Prep: 25 min. ◆ Marinate: 2 to 12 hr.
Roast: 30 min.

*Time is the secret ingredient; as
the hours pass, the spicy rub imbues
the meat with flavor.*

4 shallots, peeled and halved
8 cloves garlic, peeled
2 Tbsp. brown sugar
2 Tbsp. coriander seed
4 tsp. cracked black
    peppercorns
1 2- to 3-lb. beef tenderloin

◆◆◆

1 15-oz. can black beans,
    rinsed and drained
1 cup chopped mango
1 medium red sweet pepper,
    chopped
1 medium green, yellow, or
    orange sweet pepper,
    chopped
½ cup frozen whole kernel
    corn, thawed
2 to 3 fresh jalapeño peppers,
    seeded and finely
    chopped*
½ cup snipped fresh cilantro
3 Tbsp. lime juice
2 Tbsp. Italian salad dressing

1 For rub, in a food processor
bowl or blender container combine shallots, garlic, brown sugar,
coriander seed, peppercorns, and
2 teaspoons *coarse salt.* Cover;
process or blend until coriander
and peppercorns are coarsely
chopped and mixture is combined. Spread over top and sides
of meat. Place meat in a plastic bag
set in a dish. Close bag. Marinate
in refrigerator 2 to 12 hours.

2 For salsa, in a mixing bowl
combine black beans, mango,
sweet peppers, corn, jalapeño
peppers, and cilantro. Stir together lime juice, salad dressing, and
½ teaspoon *coarse salt;* add to
bean mixture. Stir gently to combine. Cover and refrigerate for
2 hours or overnight.

3 To prepare meat, remove
meat from bag. Place meat on
rack in a shallow roasting pan.
Replace any shallot mixture that
may have fallen off. Insert a meat
thermometer into center of meat.
Roast, uncovered, in a 425° oven
for 30 to 45 minutes or until
meat thermometer registers 140°.
Cover meat with foil; let stand
15 minutes. (Meat temperature
will rise 5° during standing.) Slice
meat and serve with salsa. Makes
8 to 10 servings.

*Note: Hot peppers contain
oils that can burn eyes, lips, and
sensitive skin. Wear plastic gloves
while preparing peppers and be
sure to thoroughly wash your
hands afterward.

Nutrition facts per serving: 267 cal., 9 g
total fat (3 g sat. fat), 64 mg chol., 880 mg
sodium, 23 g carbo., 4 g fiber, 26 g pro.
Daily values: 24% vit. A, 76% vit. C, 4%
calcium, 28% iron.

SOUTHWEST ROAST WITH ZESTY SAUCE

Prep: 20 min. ◆ Roast: 20 min.
(tomato and peppers); 1½ hr. (meat)

2 plum tomatoes, halved
1 fresh poblano pepper,
    halved and seeded
4 cloves garlic, halved
¼ cup chopped onion
2 Tbsp. olive oil
1 Tbsp. lime juice
1 tsp. ground cumin
¾ tsp. salt
¼ tsp. pepper

◆◆◆

1 4- to 6-lb. boneless beef
    ribeye roast

◆◆◆

1 10-oz. can enchilada sauce
½ cup dairy sour cream

1 Place tomato and poblano
pepper halves, cut side down, on
a foil-lined baking sheet. Roast in
a 425° oven for 20 to 25 minutes
or until skin is blackened. Wrap
in foil and cool. Remove and discard peel from tomatoes and
poblano. In a blender container
or food processor bowl combine
tomatoes, poblano, garlic, onion,
oil, lime juice, cumin, salt, and
pepper. Cover and blend or
process until nearly smooth.

2 Cut 1-inch-wide pockets
into beef roast at 3-inch intervals.
Rub tomato mixture onto roast
and into pockets. Place meat, fat
side up, on rack in a shallow
roasting pan. Insert a meat thermometer into center of meat.
Roast, uncovered, in a 350° oven
for 1½ to 2 hours or until meat
thermometer registers 135° or to
desired doneness. Cover roast
with foil; let stand 15 minutes.
(Meat temperature will rise 10°
during standing.)

3 In a saucepan combine
enchilada sauce and sour cream;
heat through (do not boil). Slice
meat; pass sauce. Serves 12 to 14.

Nutrition facts per serving: 324 cal., 20 g
total fat (8 g sat. fat), 93 mg chol., 326 mg
sodium, 4 g carbo., 0 g fiber, 31 g pro.
Daily values: 3% vit. A, 17% vit. C, 2%
calcium, 29% iron.

THERMOMETERS ARE HOT

Peanut brittle and French fries just wouldn't be the same without 'em. Cooking thermometers are a necessity in candy-making and in deep-frying. They're also essential in determining when foods are cooked to a safe temperature. Let this round-up be a guide to some basic, easy-to-use thermometers and their functions.

1. Meat Thermometer
Typically used to check the internal temperature of large cuts of meats such as roasts and whole poultry, this thermometer should be inserted at least 2 inches in the center of the meat (not touching bone).

2. Candy/Deep-Frying Thermometers
Relied on when making candy, some frostings, and syrups, this thermometer also helps when frying foods in a large quantity of cooking oil or shortening. The thermometer is marked with the stages of candy making, such as soft-ball and hard-crack. It's also marked for deep-fat frying.

3. Digital Instant-Read Thermometer
Insert this thermometer into food and the temperature pops up on its face within 10 seconds or so. Because the probe is placed ½ inch deep, it's great for checking the doneness of thin foods—hamburger patties, chicken breasts, or fish—as well as thick cuts. Remove the thermometer while the food is cooking. A pen-like storage case protects its point.

4. Electronic Thermometer
Like the basic meat thermometer (above), this works best on roasts or large cuts of meat. A built-in timer alerts you when food reaches the desired temperature. A stay-cool cord lets you attach the magnet-backed unit to your oven door while the probe does the work.

5. Instant-Read Thermometers
Both the large-type (left) and small-type (right) versions of this thermometer perform the same function. They are used near the end of cooking time to check the internal temperature of food. The thermometer stem should be inserted about halfway into the food. Do not allow the thermometer to remain in food that is in the oven or microwave oven. When not in use, the unit can be safely stored in a protective case.

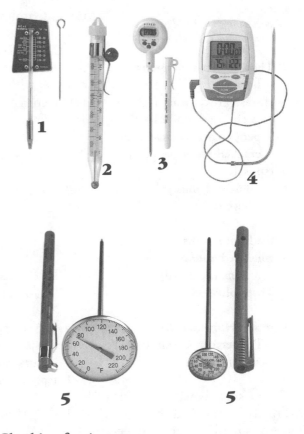

Checking for Accuracy
Most thermometers are accurate within a few degrees, but you should double-check for accuracy so you know exactly when your food reaches the right temperature. Because water boils at 212° Fahrenheit, test your thermometer by immersing the stem in at least two inches of boiling water for 30 seconds. The dial should read 212°. If it doesn't, take any inaccuracies into account when using the thermometer. For instance, if the thermometer reads 215° in boiling water, subtract 3° when taking the temperature of a food. Unfortunately, this method won't work at high altitudes where water boils at a lower temperature. As an alternate method, plunge the thermometer stem into a glass filled with ice water for 30 seconds. The temperature should read 32°.

CELEBRATION ROAST

Prep: 25 min. ◆ Roast: 1½ hr.

Accented by a horseradish-peppercorn rub, this beef roast is a stunning choice to carve for your holiday dinner. (See the photograph on page 318.)

- 2 **Tbsp. cream-style prepared horseradish**
- 4 **cloves garlic, minced**
- 4 **to 5 tsp. pink and black peppercorns, cracked; or cracked black pepper**
- ½ **tsp. salt**
- 1 **4- to 6-lb. boneless beef ribeye roast**
  ◆◆◆
- 8 **medium onions**
- 6 **small red and/or white onions (optional)**
- 1 **Tbsp. olive oil**
  ◆◆◆
- 1 **recipe Horseradish-Peppercorn Cream (see right) (optional)**

1 In a small bowl stir together cream-style horseradish, garlic, 3 teaspoons of the cracked peppercorns, and the salt. Rub horseradish mixture onto meat. Place beef roast, fat side up, on a rack in a shallow roasting pan. Insert a meat thermometer into center of roast. Roast, uncovered, in a 350° oven for 1½ to 2 hours or until thermometer registers 135° for medium-rare, or 2 to 2½ hours or until thermometer registers 150° for medium. Cover meat with foil; let meat stand 15 minutes. (Meat temperature will rise 10° during standing.)

2 Meanwhile, slice root ends from the medium and small onions (so they'll stand upright). If desired, leave about 1 inch of onion top. Brush onions with olive oil. Sprinkle with remaining 1 to 2 teaspoons cracked peppercorns. During the last 1¼ hours of roasting time, arrange onions upright, around meat.

3 To serve, slice meat. If desired, serve meat and roasted onions with the Horseradish-Peppercorn Cream. Makes 12 to 16 servings.

Nutrition facts per serving: 294 cal., 16 g total fat (7 g sat. fat), 89 mg chol., 199 mg sodium, 5 g carbo., 1 g fiber, 31 g pro. Daily values: 4% vit. C, 1% calcium, 20% iron.

HORSERADISH-PEPPERCORN CREAM

Start to finish: 10 min.

- ½ **cup whipping cream**
- 2 **Tbsp. cream-style prepared horseradish**
- 1 **tsp. Dijon-style mustard**
  ◆◆◆
- 1 **to 2 Tbsp. pink and black peppercorns, cracked**

1 In a mixing bowl beat whipping cream with an electric mixer on medium speed just until soft peaks form. Fold in cream-style horseradish and Dijon-style mustard. If not using immediately, cover and store horseradish mixture in the refrigerator for up to 6 hours.

2 Serve with Celebration Roast (see left). Sprinkle each serving of cream with cracked peppercorns. Makes about 1 cup.

Nutrition facts per tablespoon: 28 cal., 3 g total fat (2 g sat. fat), 10 mg chol., 31 mg sodium, 1 g carbo., 0 g fiber, 0 g pro. Daily values: 3% vit. A, 2% vit. C, 1% calcium, 1% iron.

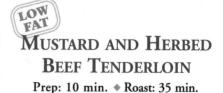

MUSTARD AND HERBED BEEF TENDERLOIN

Prep: 10 min. ◆ Roast: 35 min.

For last-minute, hassle-free entertaining, serve quick-to-roast, melt-in-your-mouth beef tenderloin. It's a guest-pleaser every time.

- 2 **Tbsp. Dijon-style mustard**
- 1 **Tbsp. snipped fresh rosemary or ½ tsp. dried rosemary, crushed**
- 1 **Tbsp. snipped fresh thyme or ½ tsp. dried thyme, crushed**
- 1 **Tbsp. snipped fresh basil or 1 tsp. dried basil, crushed**
- 1 **2-lb. beef tenderloin**
  ◆◆◆
- ¾ **cup soft bread crumbs (1 slice)**
- 1 **Tbsp. margarine or butter, melted**

1 In a small bowl combine Dijon-style mustard and half each of the rosemary, thyme, and basil. Place tenderloin on a rack in a shallow roasting pan. Spread mustard-herb mixture over the tenderloin. Insert meat thermometer into center of meat. Roast, uncovered, in a 425° oven for 30 to 40 minutes or until thermometer registers 135°.

2 Meanwhile, combine bread crumbs, melted margarine or butter, and remaining herbs. Remove roast from oven and sprinkle with crumb mixture, pressing lightly and carefully into mustard. Bake for 5 to 10 minutes more or until thermometer registers 140°. Cover meat with foil; let stand for

15 minutes. (The meat temperature will rise 5° during standing.) Slice meat. Serves 8.

Nutrition facts per serving: 184 cal., 9 g total fat (3 g sat. fat), 64 mg chol., 181 mg sodium, 2 g carbo., 0 g fiber, 22 g pro. *Daily values:* 1% vit. A, 1% calcium, 18% iron.

30 MIN. LOW FAT

PORK MEDALLIONS WITH PEAR-MAPLE SAUCE

Start to finish: 25 min.

1   12- to 16-oz. pork tenderloin
2   tsp. snipped fresh rosemary or ½ tsp. dried rosemary, crushed
1   tsp. snipped fresh thyme or ¼ tsp. dried thyme, crushed
¼   tsp. salt
¼   tsp. pepper
1   Tbsp. olive oil or cooking oil
♦♦♦
2   medium pears, peeled, cored, and coarsely chopped
¼   cup maple syrup or maple-flavored syrup
2   Tbsp. dry white wine or apple juice
2   Tbsp. dried tart red cherries, halved

1 Slice tenderloin crosswise into ¼-inch-thick slices. Combine rosemary, thyme, salt, and pepper. Sprinkle herb mixture over pork slices. In a large skillet heat oil. Cook pork, half at a time, in hot oil for 2 to 3 minutes or until no longer pink, turning meat slices once. Remove meat from skillet and set aside.

2 In same skillet combine pears, maple syrup, white wine or apple juice, and dried cherries. Heat to boiling; reduce heat. Boil gently, uncovered, about 3 minutes or until pears are just tender. Return meat to skillet with pears; heat through.

3 To serve, transfer pork medallions to a warm serving platter. Spoon pear sauce over. Makes 4 servings.

Nutrition facts per serving: 255 cal., 7 g total fat (2 g sat. fat), 60 mg chol., 179 mg sodium, 29 g carbo., 3 g fiber, 19 g pro. *Daily values:* 2% vit. A, 6% vit. C, 1% calcium, 10% iron.

ROAST PORK WITH APPLE PUFF STUFFING

Prep: 20 min. ♦ Roast: 1¼ hr.

1   2½- to 3-lb. boneless pork top loin roast (single loin)
    Salt
    Pepper
♦♦♦
1   cup thinly sliced celery
2   Tbsp. sugar
1½ tsp. apple pie spice or pumpkin pie spice
½   tsp. finely shredded lemon peel
⅓   cup margarine or butter
3   large red apples, coarsely chopped (3 cups)
♦♦♦
3   cups dry bread cubes (4 slices)
3   egg yolks, beaten
½   cup applesauce

1 Place roast on a rack in a shallow roasting pan. Season with salt and pepper. Insert a meat thermometer into center of meat. Roast in a 325° oven 35 minutes.

Menu

Mixed green salad

♦♦♦

Roast Pork with Apple Puff Stuffing (see left)

♦♦♦

Buttered corn or hominy

♦♦♦

Meringue-topped vanilla cream pie

2 Meanwhile, in a large skillet cook celery, sugar, spice, and lemon peel in 1 tablespoon of the margarine or butter until celery is just tender. Remove from heat. Stir in apples. Spoon mixture around pork in bottom of roasting pan. Roast for 20 minutes.

3 Melt remaining margarine; remove from heat Stir in dry bread cubes, egg yolks, and applesauce. Spoon over apple mixture in roasting pan. Roast 20 to 40 minutes more or until meat thermometer registers 155° and stuffing temperature is 160°. Cover meat with foil; let meat stand for 15 minutes before carving. (Meat temperature will rise 5° during standing.)

4 To serve, slice meat. Serve apple stuffing with meat. Makes 8 servings.

Nutrition facts per serving: 346 cal., 19 g total fat (5 g sat. fat), 144 mg chol., 224 mg sodium, 20 g carbo., 2 g fiber, 23 g pro. *Daily values:* 22% vit. A, 7% vit. C, 3% calcium, 11% iron.

DREAMING OF A LIGHT CHRISTMAS

It's back. The annual holiday onslaught of food situations that tempt and allure us, stretching our willpower to the limit—and beyond—is here again.

Perhaps the treadmill you got last year is still being used as a towel rack, or the sweet siren song of Aunt Mae's pumpkin pie is beckoning you to take seconds. Instead of caving in, take charge: Here are strategies to help you through the weak moments. This year, get wrapped up in a happy, guilt-free season.

THROUGHOUT THE HOLIDAYS

◆ A profusion of hurdles springs up this time of year that makes you feel like eating: stress, shopping, and the omnipresent sweets freely given out by well-meaning "elves." These contribute more to winter girth-gain than anything else. Instead of satisfying these urges, learn to anticipate them. Then counteract them before they jump out at you.

◆ When a houseful of guests is expected and you haven't even got the roast in yet, stress levels will ratchet up several notches—and so will the urge to eat for the sake of eating. Keep a pot of hot cinnamon, ginger, or mint beverage on hand when you anticipate hectic periods; without sweeteners, such soothing drinks satisfy and are virtually calorie-free.

◆ It's a given not to visit the supermarket on an empty stomach. But that's not always possible. Here's a tip: Keep a low-calorie granola bar, fruit bar, or other healthful and filling (but nonperishable) snack in the car. At stoplights, munch away. By the time you reach the supermarket, you will be pushing the shopping cart, not your hunger pangs.

◆ At the grocery store, beat the compulsion to try all the free samples. Remember, there's no such thing as a free lunch, especially when it rings up an extra 500 calories.

◆ Curtail aisle-side snacking by making a list and checking it twice. A shopping list, that is. As basic as it seems, shopping lists help you to focus on what's needed and nothing else. Then you can move on to your next task.

◆ When gift shopping, bring along a snack. Single-serve packages of dried fruits, nuts, or 100-percent fruit juice in your purse or backpack are handy choices. These snacks deliver greater energy and have longer staying power than much of the high-calorie food-court fodder.

LITTLE THINGS ADD UP

◆ Take active resistance against rote eating—the eating you do to fill your time, not your tummy. Instead of snacking while cooking, stop to write out a note or card or even wrap a gift or two once the roast is in the oven.

◆ Take exercise breaks. Facing a barely surmountable task load brings stress, and that leads to nervous noshing. If you're cleaning the house for the inevitable rush of relatives, take a quick stroll once around the block between vacuuming and dusting. Exercise does wonders to relieve both stress and hunger.

◆ Break up larger jobs into small parts, taking a short break between them. By dividing the day's work into discrete parcels, you can focus on your accomplished goals instead of food.

◆ Avoid stocking up on seasonal treats. Keeping them out of the house reduces the temptation to munch away while doing holiday chores. There will be plenty of food to enjoy when the actual festivities are under way.

◆ Eat only in the kitchen or dining room. Move candies, chips, and other snack foods out from in front of the television and away from the family room.

TREAD ON OLD TRADITIONS

◆ Tweak those generations-old recipes with some updated approaches to calories and fat. For instance, zip up fluffy mashed potatoes with low-fat yogurt and a dash of nutmeg instead of margarine or butter. Rather than using high-fat nuts in stuffing recipes, substitute equal amounts of toasted cooked wheat berries, crushed pretzel bits, or small amounts of dried fruits (such as apricots, apples, cherries, and cranberries).

◆ When it comes to vegetables, let their natural flavors speak for themselves. Don't hide fresh and fluffy yams under buttery sauces or layers of molasses and marshmallows. And instead of cooking your greens in oils, steam them lightly, then sprinkle with a pinch of ground anise seed and freshly ground pepper.

PORTIONS, SECONDS, AND SAMPLING

◆ Yes, there are almost too many tasty dishes to try at the big dinner. It's OK, you can try them all—if you reduce portion sizes and think twice about seconds.

◆ Keep your meat serving to a total of 3 ounces (about the size of the palm of your hand). When choices are available, such as ham, turkey, and beef, accept the equivalent of two forkfuls of each. A few bites each of stuffing, sweet potatoes, and mashed potatoes will be nicely filling too.

◆ Share that pie! If the desserts have been precut, go halves—or even thirds—with a friend or cousin.

◆ Pause between sampling. Give your stomach time to tell your brain you've had enough.

STRATEGIES FOR PARTYING

◆ Gear up for the goody gauntlet. Calorie control often gets broadsided when you're away from home. Here's how to stay in focus when visiting relatives:

◆ Savor the socializing over the snacking. Position yourself near a friend or relative to catch up, not next to your favorite treat to fill up. Talk more, eat less. Besides, it's impolite to talk with your mouth full, so bring several humorous stories and favorite jokes to every event.

◆ Alcohol adds empty calories to your diet—about 150 calories per drink. Three drinks can equal an entire meal's worth of calories. Keep the numbers in mind as you toast the holidays. Some more refreshing, yet lower-calorie, alternatives are: equal parts cranberry juice cocktail and ginger ale, or lemon-lime soft drink (top with a slice of orange or lime for a festive lift). Or, sip on a tall vegetable juice cocktail on the rocks with just a dash of hot pepper sauce and a celery stick stirrer.

◆ Finally, during all your "running around," remember to do some actual running—or at least walking. A brisk, 30-minute walk every day burns off up to 150 calories. Do that throughout the holidays—without adding extra munchies—and you might even lose a pound or two.

—Linda Nebeling is a registered dietitian and public health nutritionist for the "5 A Day for Better Health" program at the National Cancer Institute.

WINE FOR THE OCCASION

Selecting the ideal wines to accompany the bounty of your holiday dinner need not be an intimidating prospect. The old tenets are passé—what matters most is that everyone enjoys the gathering. So, serve whatever wines you and your guests prefer.

That said, there are a few guidelines, based on tradition and experience, that will help enhance the pleasures of both the foods and wines that you serve.

Generally, wines and foods belonging to the same culture are the most compatible. Because Thanksgiving is an all-American feast, this is the perfect time to serve American wines. For Christmas, try wines from any wine region of your choice.

As you eat and drink, your palate becomes fatigued, so lighter and more delicate foods and wines are more appreciated when served before heavier and more pungent ones.

If you're serving hors d'oeuvres, soft, light-bodied wines that are simple and fruity, such as Chenin Blanc, are usually suitable accompaniments. For appetizer courses that are especially stylish, consider serving a sparkling wine.

Intensely flavored wines or foods can obliterate your palate's ability to taste milder ones. Holiday dinners typically include an abundance of rich, flavorful foods, so wines need to be able to stand up to the challenge.

Don't even try to perfectly match wines to the myriad disparately flavored dishes on your menu—keep it simple. You can't go wrong with the conventional white wine selections, like Sauvignon Blancs or slightly oaky Chardonnays.

If you feel that reds are more festive, there are several good choices. Lighter, fruitier Pinot Noirs, served slightly chilled, usually appeal to everyone. For red wine enthusiasts, Cabernet Sauvignons or Zinfandels that aren't too tannic also can be good choices.

Remember to serve wines at a temperature that will heighten their flavors. White and rosé wines should be lightly chilled, and reds should be around 65 degrees.

Gathering loved ones around the table to share inviting foods is a pleasurable tradition. Enjoying a favorite wine makes the feast all the more memorable.

PRIZE TESTED RECIPE WINNER

WALNUT-ENCRUSTED PORK ROAST

Prep: 20 min. ◆ Roast: 1¼ hr.
Stand: 15 min.

Lingonberries are tiny sweet-tart berries; find them in the preserves section.

1 2- to 2¼-lb. boneless pork
   top loin roast (single loin)
⅓ cup finely chopped walnuts
1 Tbsp. snipped fresh
   rosemary
   Salt
   Pepper

◆◆◆

1 cup canned lingonberries
   (about ⅔ of a 14.5-oz. jar)
   or 1 cup whole cranberry
   sauce (about ½ of a 16-oz.
   can)
½ cup Merlot or other dry red
   wine
1 Tbsp. lemon juice
1 6-inch sprig fresh rosemary

1 Place roast on a rack in a shallow roasting pan. Combine walnuts and snipped rosemary. Press nut-rosemary mixture over top and sides of roast. Sprinkle with salt and pepper. Insert a meat thermometer into center of meat. Roast, uncovered, in a 325° oven for 1¼ to 1½ hours or until meat thermometer reaches 155°. Cover meat with foil and let stand for 10 minutes before carving. (Meat temperature will rise 5° during standing.)

2 Meanwhile, in a small saucepan combine lingonberries or whole cranberry sauce, red wine, lemon juice, and rosemary sprig. Bring to boiling; reduce heat. Boil gently, uncovered, about 15 minutes or until sauce is reduced to 1 cup. Allow sauce to cool 15 minutes. Remove rosemary sprig. (Sauce thickens slightly as it cools.)

3 To serve, slice meat. Serve fruit sauce over meat. Makes 8 servings.

Nutrition facts per serving: 265 cal., 11 g total fat (3 g sat. fat), 57 mg chol., 92 mg sodium, 19 g carbo., 1 g fiber, 19 g pro. *Daily values:* 2% vit. C, 5% iron.

ROAST LOIN OF PORK WITH FRUITED RICE STUFFING

Prep: 35 min. ◆ Roast: 1¾ hr.

Apple juice slightly sweetens the demi-glace-like sauce. Drizzle a couple tablespoons of sauce over each slice of stuffed pork.

½ cup chopped onion
2 Tbsp. margarine or butter
2¼ cups water
1 cup long grain rice
½ cup snipped pitted prunes
½ tsp. salt
½ tsp. dried leaf sage, crushed
⅛ tsp. pepper
⅓ cup chopped toasted walnuts

◆◆◆

1 3-lb. boneless pork top loin roast (double loin tied)

◆◆◆

Apple juice
4 tsp. cornstarch
1 Tbsp. balsamic vinegar
⅛ tsp. salt

1 In a medium saucepan cook onion in hot margarine until tender. Stir in water, uncooked rice, prunes, the ½ teaspoon salt, sage, and pepper. Bring to boiling; reduce heat. Simmer, covered, for 15 minutes. Remove from heat; let stand, covered, 5 minutes. Stir in walnuts.

2 Untie the roast; separate into halves. Trim fat from meat. Season meat with *salt* and *pepper*. Spoon about 1 cup of stuffing over half of the meat. Spoon remaining stuffing into a 1-quart casserole; cover and chill until ready to bake. Reassemble roast. Tie with string to secure.

3 Place roast on a rack in a shallow roasting pan. Insert meat thermometer into center of meat. If desired, cover the stuffing with foil to prevent drying out. Roast, uncovered, in a 325° oven for 1¾ to 2¼ hours or until meat thermometer registers 155°. Add the stuffing casserole for the last 35 minutes of roasting. Cover meat and let stand 15 minutes. (Meat temperature will rise 5° during standing.)

4 Measure pan drippings; add apple juice to equal 1¼ cups. In a small saucepan combine drippings, cornstarch, balsamic vinegar, and the ⅛ teaspoon salt. Cook and stir over medium-high heat until thickened and bubbly; cook and stir 2 minutes more.

5 To serve, slice meat. Pass the sauce with the roast and stuffing. Makes 10 servings.

Nutrition facts per serving: 303 cal., 14 g total fat (4 g sat. fat), 61 mg chol., 211 mg sodium, 23 g carbo., 1 g fiber, 22 g pro. *Daily values:* 4% vit. A, 2% vit. C, 1% calcium, 12% iron.

WARM SWEET POTATO, APPLE, AND SAUSAGE SALAD

Start to finish: 30 min.

Leafy raw spinach provides a nutrient-rich base for a hearty salad that includes spicy turkey sausage.

1 lb. sweet potatoes or yams, peeled and cut into ½-inch pieces (3 cups)
1 small onion, cut into thin wedges
2 Tbsp. margarine or butter
1 lb. cooked smoked turkey sausage, cut diagonally into ½-inch-thick slices
2 medium cooking apples, cut into wedges
½ cup bottled sweet-and-sour sauce
½ tsp. caraway seed

◆◆◆

6 cups torn fresh spinach

1 In a large skillet cook sweet potatoes and onion in margarine over medium heat 10 minutes or until tender, stirring occasionally. Stir in sausage, apples, sweet-and-sour sauce, and caraway seed. Cook, covered, over medium heat about 3 minutes or until apples are tender and sausage is heated through, stirring occasionally. (If mixture seems thick, add water, 1 tablespoon at a time, to make desired consistency.)

2 Place spinach on a large serving platter. Top with sweet potato mixture. Makes 4 servings.

Nutrition facts per serving: 415 cal., 14 g total fat (3 g sat. fat), 72 mg chol., 196 mg sodium, 50 g carbo., 7 g fiber, 24 g pro. *Daily values:* 257% vit. A, 89% vit. C, 17% calcium, 31% iron.

CHRISTMAS LIMAS WITH PESTO BULGUR

Start to finish: 20 min.

Dappled red over pale green, Christmas limas are aptly named and easy to spot, but it's their nutty flavor that makes them a standout in this Italian-inspired meal. Cook the beans ahead or use canned beans when dinner is really last minute.

1⅓ **cups vegetable broth or chicken broth**
⅔ **cup bulgur**

◆◆◆

2 **cups cooked Christmas lima beans, pinto beans, or cranberry beans* or one 15-oz. can pinto beans, rinsed and drained**
1 **medium red sweet pepper, chopped**
⅓ **cup refrigerated pesto sauce**
¼ **cup thinly sliced green onions**
   Freshly ground pepper
   Toasted bread slices

1 In a medium saucepan bring broth to boiling; add bulgur. Return to boiling; reduce heat. Simmer, covered, for 10 minutes. Remove from heat.

2 Stir beans, sweet pepper, pesto sauce, and green onions into bulgur in saucepan. Season with ground pepper. Serve with toasted bread slices. Makes 6 servings.

*Note: To cook beans, rinse ¾ cup dried beans and combine with 5 cups water in a large Dutch oven. Bring to boiling; reduce heat. Simmer, uncovered, for

CAPER CAPERS

From Spain to China grows a lowly, spiny shrub that would remain largely ignored were it not for its unripened flower buds, called capers. These tiny titans of taste bring sauces, salads, or main dishes into unexpected territory.

The taste of a caper can best be described as a marriage of citrus and olive, heightened with a tanginess achieved by preserving in salt or vinegar—the way most capers are prepared and packaged.

The pungent and spicy flavor of capers should be applied to taste. Try capers and caper berries in the following ways:

Add a teaspoon or two of capers to each cup of your favorite pasta or spaghetti sauce, then serve on cooked noodles or in lasagna.

For a light caper pizza, cover a large Italian bread shell with shredded low-fat mozzarella cheese, thinly sliced tomatoes, and capers or sliced caper berries. Sprinkle with a little oregano, then bake according to bread directions.

To make a zesty spread for bagels or crackers, mix capers or chopped caper berries with softened light cream cheese, very finely chopped onion, dried thyme, and freshly ground black pepper.

2 minutes. Remove from heat. Cover and let stand for 1 hour. Drain and rinse beans. Return beans to pan. Add 5 cups fresh water. Bring to boiling; reduce heat. Simmer, covered, for 1¼ to

1½ hours or until tender; drain. (Or, place beans in 5 cups cold water in a Dutch oven. Cover and let soak in a cool place overnight.)

Nutrition facts per serving: 288 cal., 11 g total fat (0 g sat. fat), 2 mg chol., 542 mg sodium, 41 g carbo., 5 g fiber, 9 g pro. *Daily values:* 10% vit. A, 36% vit. C, 3% calcium, 10% iron.

A LIGHTER REMOULADE

Prep: 15 min. ◆ Chill: 2 hr.

This classic condiment tastes as great on seafood today as it did a century ago, when the recipe was first recorded. We've lowered the fat with light mayonnaise dressing.

1 **cup light mayonnaise dressing**
¼ **cup rinsed and drained capers**
2 **Tbsp. chopped dill pickle**
2 **Tbsp. lemon juice**
1 **Tbsp. finely chopped onion**
1 **Tbsp. finely chopped fresh chervil or parsley**
2 **tsp. pickle juice**
1 **tsp. finely chopped anchovies or anchovy paste (optional)**

1 In a medium mixing bowl combine mayonnaise dressing, capers, dill pickle, lemon juice, onion, chervil or parsley, pickle juice, and if desired, anchovies. Before serving, cover and chill for 2 hours. Store in a tightly sealed container in refrigerator for up to 1 week. Serve with fish or seafood. Makes 1¼ cups sauce.

Nutrition facts per tablespoon: 41 cal., 4 g total fat (1 g sat. fat), 0 mg chol., 137 mg sodium, 1 g carbo., 0 g fiber, 0 g pro. *Daily values:* 1% vit. C.

ONION CORN CAKE

Prep: 15 min. ◆ Bake 25 min.

½ cup chopped sweet onion
1 clove garlic, minced
1 Tbsp. margarine or butter

◆◆◆

1 8½-oz. pkg. corn muffin mix
1 egg
⅓ cup milk
Several dashes bottled hot pepper sauce

◆◆◆

1 8-oz. container dairy sour cream
1 cup shredded smoked cheddar or cheddar cheese
¼ tsp. dried leaf sage, crushed

1 Grease an 8×8×2-inch baking pan; set aside.

2 In a medium skillet cook onion and garlic in margarine or butter over medium heat until onion just begins to brown. Remove from heat and set aside.

3 Meanwhile, in a large mixing bowl stir together muffin mix, egg, milk, and bottled hot pepper sauce. Spread mixture evenly into prepared pan.

4 Stir sour cream, half of the cheese, and sage into onion mixture. Spoon mixture evenly over batter in pan. Sprinkle with remaining cheese.

5 Bake in a 425° oven about 25 minutes or until golden brown. Cool slightly in pan on a wire rack. Serve warm. Serves 9.

Nutrition facts per serving: 239 cal., 14 g total fat (6 g sat. fat), 49 mg chol., 305 mg sodium, 21 g carbo., 0 g fiber, 7 g pro. *Daily values:* 13% vit. A, 1% vit. C, 11% calcium, 4% iron.

SCANDINAVIAN SPICED RYE ROLLS

LOW FAT

Prep: 45 min. ◆ Rise: 1½ hr.
Bake: 12 min.

1 cup water
1 egg
3 Tbsp. full-flavored molasses
1 tsp. fennel seed
1 tsp. finely shredded orange peel
¾ tsp. salt
½ tsp. caraway seed
1 Tbsp. margarine or butter, softened
½ cup rye flour
3¼ cups bread flour
1 pkg. active dry yeast

◆◆◆

Golden raisins (optional)

◆◆◆

2 Tbsp. full-flavored molasses, warmed (optional)
Fennel seed and/or caraway seed (optional)

1 To mix the dough in a bread machine, add all of the ingredients except the golden raisins, 2 tablespoons warmed molasses, and the fennel seed to the pan of a 2-pound loaf bread machine according to manufacturer's directions. Select the dough cycle.

2 When bread machine cycle is complete, remove dough. Turn out onto a lightly floured surface. Divide the dough into 12 equal portions. Shape as desired.

3 To shape an S: Roll 1 portion of the dough into a rope about 12 inches long. Place on greased baking sheet; curl the ends tightly to make an S shape. Repeat with remaining portions of dough to make 12 rolls. Cover rolls loosely; let rise until nearly double (30 to

45 minutes). If desired, press a raisin into the curl of each roll.

4 Bake in a 375° oven for 12 to 15 minutes or until rolls are lightly browned. If desired, brush hot rolls with warm molasses to glaze, and sprinkle lightly with fennel seed. Cool on a wire rack. Makes 12 rolls.

CONVENTIONAL DIRECTIONS

Heat the water to lukewarm (105° to 115°). Pour into a large mixing bowl; sprinkle the yeast over water and stir to dissolve. Let stand for 5 minutes. Add the egg, the 3 tablespoons molasses, the fennel seed, orange peel, salt, caraway seed, margarine, rye flour, and 1 cup of the bread flour. Beat with electric mixer on low to medium speed 30 seconds, scraping sides of bowl. Beat on high speed 3 minutes. Stir in as much of the remaining bread flour as you can with a wooden spoon.

Turn dough out onto a lightly floured surface; knead in enough remaining bread flour to make a moderately stiff dough that is smooth and elastic (6 to 8 minutes total). Place dough into a lightly greased bowl; turn once to grease surface. Cover and let rise until double (about 1 hour). Punch dough down; cover and let rest 10 minutes.

Turn dough out onto a lightly floured surface. Divide the dough into 12 equal portions. Shape and bake as directed above.

Nutrition facts per roll: 180 cal., 2 g total fat (1 g sat. fat), 20 mg chol., 151 mg sodium, 34 g carbo., 2 g fiber, 6 g pro. *Daily values:* 1% vit. A, 1% calcium, 13% iron.

ITALY'S CHRISTMAS BREAD

Originating in Milan, Italy, panettone (pahn-EHT-tohn) is a Christmastime treat, but is served for other special occasions, too, such as weddings and christenings.

Traditionally this sweet yeast bread that's baked in a cylindrical mold is loaded with raisins, citron, pine nuts, and anise. Because it is so rich and wonderful, it can be served for breakfast or for dessert.

FESTIVE FRUIT-AND-NUT PANETTONE

Prep: 15 min. ◆ Rise: 45 min.
Bake: 55 min.

Dried cherries add a tasty new touch to a long-held Italian bread tradition. (See the photograph on page 317.)

 1 **cup milk**
 2 **eggs**
 ½ **cup butter, cut up**
3¾ **cups bread flour**
 ½ **cup granulated sugar**
 1 **Tbsp. finely shredded lemon peel**
 1 **tsp. anise seed**
 ½ **tsp. salt**
 2 **pkg. active dry yeast**
 1 **cup dried tart cherries**
 ¾ **cup pine nuts**

◆◆◆

Nonstick cooking spray

◆◆◆

 ½ **cup golden raisins**

◆◆◆

 1 **egg, slightly beaten**
 1 **Tbsp. pine nuts**

◆◆◆

Powdered sugar (optional)

1 To mix the dough in a bread machine, add first 9 ingredients to the pan of a 2-pound loaf bread machine according to manufacturer's directions. Select dough cycle. About 20 minutes into the cycle of the machine (or when the machine signals); add the dried cherries and ¾ cup pine nuts.

2 Meanwhile, spray an 8×3-inch springform pan or soufflé dish with nonstick spray. Cut a piece of clean brown wrapping paper into a 25×6-inch strip. Fit the 6-inch collar on the inside of the greased pan, overlapping slightly. Spray the inside of the paper collar with nonstick coating. (It is not necessary to tape or paper-clip the collar, as the weight of the dough will hold it in place.)

3 When bread-machine cycle is complete, remove dough. Punch dough down. On a lightly floured surface, gently knead in the raisins. Shape dough into a ball. Transfer dough to the collared pan and flatten slightly to cover bottom of pan. Cover and let rise until almost double (45 to 60 minutes).

4 Mix egg and 1 tablespoon *water;* brush on top of loaf. Sprinkle with the 1 tablespoon pine nuts. Bake in a 350° oven for 45 minutes. Cover top of bread with foil; bake for 10 to 15 minutes more or until a wooden skewer inserted into the center of the bread comes out clean. Cool for 10 minutes in pan on a wire rack. Remove from pan. Cool bread completely.

5 If desired, dust the panettone with powdered sugar. Makes 1 large loaf (12 to 16 servings).

CONVENTIONAL DIRECTIONS

In a small saucepan heat milk just until lukewarm (105° to 115°). Pour into a large mixing bowl. Sprinkle the yeast over the milk and stir to dissolve. Let stand for 5 minutes. Add the eggs, butter, 1½ cups of the flour, sugar, lemon peel, anise seed, and salt. Beat with an electric mixer on low to medium speed for 30 seconds scraping sides of bowl constantly. Beat on high speed 3 minutes. Stir in cherries, ¾ cup pine nuts, raisins, and 3 to 3½ cups bread flour with a wooden spoon. Dough should be just stiff enough to knead. Turn dough out onto a floured surface; knead in enough of the remaining flour to make a moderately soft dough (about 3 to 5 minutes total). Cover; let rise in warm place until double (about 1 hour).

Punch dough down and shape into a ball. Transfer dough to the collared pan and flatten slightly to cover bottom of pan. Cover and let rise until almost double (45 to 60 minutes). Bake, cool, and serve as directed at left.

Nutrition facts per serving: 386 cal., 15 g total fat (6 g sat. fat), 57 mg chol., 189 mg sodium, 56 g carbo., 2 g fiber, 10 g pro. *Daily values:* 15% vit. A, 1% vit. C, 3% calcium, 20% iron.

WINTERY ICE CREAM BALLS

Prep: 25 min. ◆ Freeze: 1 hr.

See the photograph on page 320.

 2 **cups coconut**
 1 **qt. vanilla or cinnamon-flavored ice cream**

1 Place coconut in a shallow dish. Use an ice cream scoop and a large melon baller to create ice cream balls of varying sizes. Roll ice cream balls in coconut, pressing firmly, until coated. Place coated ice cream balls on a cookie sheet and return to freezer for 1 to 2 hours or until firm.

2 To serve, make a mountain of ice cream balls in serving dishes. Makes 25 (2-inch) balls.

Nutrition facts per ice cream ball: 70 cal., 4 g total fat (3 g sat. fat), 9 mg chol., 18 mg sodium, 7 g carbo., 0 g fiber, 1 g pro. *Daily values:* 2% vit. A, 2% calcium.

SOUR CREAM CHOCOLATE-WALNUT CAKE

Prep: 40 min. ◆ Bake: 35 min.
Cool: 1 hr.

You better take a wedge of this dense and double-chocolaty cake on your first trip to the dessert table—it's so-o-o delicious there won't be any left for a second trip.

½ **cup unsweetened cocoa powder**
¾ **cup boiling water**
◆◆◆
½ **cup butter, softened**
2 **cups granulated sugar**
1 **8-oz. carton dairy sour cream**
1 **tsp. vanilla**
½ **tsp. baking soda**
⅛ **tsp. salt**
2 **cups all-purpose flour**
½ **cup chopped walnuts**
3 **egg whites**
1½ **cups semisweet chocolate pieces**

⅓ **cup butter**
3½ **to 4 cups sifted powdered sugar**
½ **cup walnut halves, toasted**

1 Grease and flour two 8×1½- or 9×1½-inch round baking pans; set aside. In a small bowl stir together the cocoa powder and water until smooth; let cool 15 minutes.

2 In a large mixing bowl beat ½ cup butter with an electric mixer on medium to high speed for 30 seconds. Add granulated sugar and beat until well combined. Add cocoa mixture, ½ cup of the sour cream, vanilla, baking soda, and salt; beat until combined. Using a spoon, stir in the flour and ½ cup chopped walnuts.

3 Wash beaters thoroughly. In a medium bowl beat egg whites until stiff peaks form (tips stand straight). Fold egg whites into sour cream mixture. Turn into prepared pans.

4 Bake in a 350° oven about 35 minutes for 8-inch pans or about 25 minutes for 9-inch pans or until a wooden toothpick inserted near center comes out clean. Cool in pans on a wire rack for 10 minutes. Remove cakes from pans and cool completely.

5 Meanwhile, for frosting, in a saucepan melt semisweet chocolate and the ⅓ cup butter over low heat, stirring frequently. Remove from heat. Cool 5 minutes. Stir in the remaining sour cream (about ⅓ cup). Gradually beat in enough of the powdered sugar to make frosting of spreading consistency.

THE CLEVER COOK

AND THE FORK RAN AWAY WITH THE SPOON

In our house, table-setting duties fall to our children. Here's a fun rhyme we discovered for teaching children how to set the table: "The silverware had a fight; the knife and spoon were right, so the fork left." Another way to teach them would be the words knife and spoon have five letters, just like the word "right." "Fork" and "left" both have four letters.

Karen Ann Bland
Gove, Kansas

6 To assemble, place a cake layer, top side down, on a cake plate. Spread about ⅔ cup frosting over cake. Place the second cake layer, top side up, on top of the frosted layer. Spread remaining frosting evenly on top and sides of cake. Garnish with walnut halves. Store cake in the refrigerator. Makes 16 servings.

Nutrition facts per serving: 485 cal., 22 g total fat (8 g sat. fat), 32 mg chol., 173 mg sodium, 72 g carbo., 1 g fiber, 5 g pro. *Daily values:* 12% vit. A, 5% calcium, 11% iron.

APRICOT CREAM PUFFS

Prep: 50 min. ♦ Bake: 35 min.

1 cup water
½ cup butter
1 cup all-purpose flour
4 eggs

♦♦♦

⅔ cup whipping cream
1 8-oz. tub soft cream cheese
⅓ cup sifted powdered sugar
⅓ cup apricot preserves
½ cup semisweet chocolate
    pieces
1 tsp. shortening

♦♦♦

Sifted powdered sugar

1 Grease a large baking sheet; set aside. In a medium saucepan combine water and butter. Bring to boiling. Add flour all at once, stirring vigorously. Cook and stir until mixture forms a ball. Remove from heat. Cool for 10 minutes. Add eggs, 1 at a time, beating well with a wooden spoon after each addition.

2 Drop the dough into 12 equal mounds on the prepared baking sheet. Bake in a 400° oven for 35 to 40 minutes or until golden brown. Cool on a wire rack. (Wrap and freeze 6 cream puffs for another use.)

3 For filling, in a medium mixing bowl beat the whipping cream with an electric mixer on medium speed just until soft peaks form. Add the cream cheese, the ⅓ cup powdered sugar, and the preserves. Beat until fluffy; set aside. In a small saucepan heat and stir the chocolate and shortening over very low heat until melted.

HANUKKAH COOKIE FEAST

During Hanukkah, the annual Jewish celebration of freedom, families gather each evening to light candles and exchange small gifts. It's also traditional to partake of sweet homemade treats to commemorate the miraculous victory hard won by the Israelites nearly 2,200 years ago. Holiday Pistachio Cutouts (see below), specially shaped shortbread-style cookies with decorative icing, help pass the venerated tradition from generation to generation.

4 To serve, cut tops from puffs; remove soft dough from inside. Fill with cheese mixture. Replace tops. Drizzle with chocolate mixture. Sprinkle with additional powdered sugar. Makes 6.

Nutrition facts per cream puff: 499 cal., 37 g total fat (18 g sat. fat), 168 mg chol., 247 mg sodium, 38 g carbo., 0 g fiber, 7 g pro. *Daily values:* 28% vit. A, 4% calcium, 8% iron.

HOLIDAY PISTACHIO CUTOUTS

Prep: 20 min. ♦ Chill: 1 hr.
Bake: 18 min. per batch

Be sure the nuts are finely chopped so when you cut through the nutty dough with a cookie cutter, you get a nice straight edge.

1¼ cups all-purpose flour
3 Tbsp. sugar
½ cup margarine (at least
    70 percent vegetable oil)

⅓ cup finely chopped pistachio
    nuts

♦♦♦

1 recipe Powdered Sugar
    Frosting (see below)

1 In a medium mixing bowl stir together flour and sugar. Using a pastry cutter, cut in margarine until mixture resembles fine crumbs and starts to cling. Stir in pistachios. Form mixture into ball. Knead just until smooth. Wrap dough. Chill for 1 hour or until easy to handle.

2 On a lightly floured surface, roll the dough into a 10×6-inch rectangle. Cut the dough with decorative 2-inch cookie cutters or slice into thirty 2×1-inch strips. Place cut shapes or strips 1 inch apart on an ungreased cookie sheet.

3 Bake in a 325° oven for 18 to 22 minutes or until bottoms are lightly browned. Cool on sheet 5 minutes. Transfer to wire racks; cool completely. Decorate as desired with Powdered Sugar Frosting. Store in a tightly covered container. Makes 30 cookies.

Powdered Sugar Frosting: In a large mixing bowl combine 1 cup sifted powdered sugar, 1 tablespoon milk or orange juice, and ¼ teaspoon vanilla.

Stir in additional milk or juice, 1 teaspoon at a time, until the icing reaches a piping consistency. If desired, tint a portion of the icing with food coloring.

Nutrition facts per cookie: 71 cal., 4 g total fat (1 g sat. fat), 0 mg chol., 36 mg sodium, 9 g carbo., 0 g fiber, 1 g pro. *Daily values:* 3% vit. A, 2% iron.

GINGERBREAD TREES

Prep: 15 min. ◆ Bake: 5 min.

- 1½ cups all-purpose flour
- ¾ tsp. ground cinnamon
- ¾ tsp. ground ginger
- ½ tsp. baking powder
- ½ tsp. baking soda

◆◆◆

- ⅓ cup butter
- ⅓ cup packed brown sugar
- 1 egg
- ½ cup boiling water
- ⅓ cup mild-flavored molasses

1 Grease eighteen 3½×½-inch tree-shaped cookie molds or 2½-inch muffin cups. Set pans aside. Combine flour, cinnamon, ginger, baking powder, and baking soda; set aside.

2 In a mixing bowl beat butter with an electric mixer on medium speed for 30 seconds. Add brown sugar and beat until fluffy. Add egg and beat until combined. In a small bowl combine boiling water and molasses; add to brown sugar mixture. Beat on low speed until combined. Add flour mixture, beating until combined. Spoon batter into prepared pans, filling each half- to two-thirds full.

3 Bake in a 350° oven about 5 minutes if using the tree molds or 9 minutes if using the muffin cups or until a wooden toothpick inserted near center comes out clean. Cool in pans on wire racks for 5 minutes. Remove from pans. Cool completely. Use to make Pear-Tree Wonders (see right). Makes 18.

TO MAKE AHEAD

Prepare and bake trees as directed; cool completely. Wrap in heavy foil and freeze for up to 3 months. Thaw and serve at room temperature.

Nutrition facts per tree: 99 cal., 4 g total fat (2 g sat. fat), 21 mg chol., 85 mg sodium, 15 g carbo., 0 g fiber, 1 g pro.
Daily values: 3% vit. A, 2% calcium, 5% iron.

PEAR-TREE WONDERS

Prep: 20 min. ◆ Cook: 8 min.

See the photograph on page 2.

- 1 recipe Gingerbread Trees (see left)
- 6 firm ripe pears
- 2 Tbsp. butter
- ⅓ cup packed brown sugar
- ⅓ cup caramel ice-cream topping
- 1 recipe Armagnac Whipped Cream (see below right) or sweetened whipped cream

1 Prepare Gingerbread Trees; set aside. Peel pears, if desired. Cut ½ inch off stem end of each pear, leaving stems intact; set aside. Cut each pear crosswise into ½-inch-thick slices. In a very large skillet melt butter over medium heat. Add brown sugar; cook and stir for 1 to 2 minutes or until sugar is dissolved. Add pear slices and stem ends. Cook, covered, over medium heat about 8 minutes or until pears are just tender. Remove pears from skillet.

2 For each serving carefully stack pear slices into a shallow dessert bowl to reform a pear shape. Place a Gingerbread Tree next to pear. Drizzle about 1 tablespoon caramel ice-cream topping over each pear. Top Gingerbread Tree with a spoonful of Armagnac Whipped Cream. Makes 6 servings.

IT'S A MATTER OF DEGREES

For all kinds of baking—cookies included—it's important that your oven temperature is accurate. If you've noticed that your cookies brown too fast or that they seem to take forever to bake and are pale, coarsely textured, and dry when they do come out of the oven, your oven may be a little off.

To be certain, set your oven at 350° and let it heat for at least 10 minutes. Place an oven thermometer (available at hardware stores) in the oven and close the door for at least 5 minutes.

If the thermometer reads higher than 350°, reduce the oven setting specified in the recipe by the number of degrees between 350° and the thermometer reading. If it's lower, increase the temperature.

If it's off by more than 50 degrees in either direction, have your thermostat adjusted.

Armagnac Whipped Cream: In a chilled bowl combine ½ cup whipping cream, 3 tablespoons powdered sugar, and 2 teaspoons Armagnac or apple brandy. Beat with chilled beaters of an electric mixer until soft peaks form. Cover; chill up to 1 hour.

Nutrition facts per serving: 418 cal., 16 g total fat (9 g sat. fat), 58 mg chol., 185 mg sodium, 70 g carbo., 5 g fiber, 2 g pro.
Daily values: 16% vit. A, 11% vit. C, 6% calcium, 10% iron.

CUTOUT COOKIE KNOW-HOW

There's no end to the versatility and fun of making cutout cookies. Here are a few ways to ensure their success:

When rolling and cutting, work with half of the cookie dough at a time. Keep the other half of the dough refrigerated until you're ready to roll it out.

Keep the cookie dough from sticking to the countertop by lightly sprinkling the surface with all-purpose flour. A pastry stocking and pastry cloth also can help prevent the dough from sticking.

Dip the cutter in flour between uses to keep dough from sticking to it.

Leave little space between cutouts to get the greatest number of cookies from the dough.

After you've cut out your cookies, combine any scraps and reroll on a very lightly floured surface. Handle and roll the dough as little as possible to keep the cookies tender.

Cutout cookies are done when the bottoms are very lightly browned and the edges are firm.

Cool cookies completely before storing them so they retain their shape.

GINGERBREAD CUTOUTS

Prep: 35 min. ◆ Chill: 3 hr.
Bake: 6 to 15 min. per batch

This classic gingerbread dough is great for making ginger people. Use a variety of cutter sizes and make papa-, mama-, and child-size cookies.

½ cup shortening
½ cup sugar
1 tsp. baking powder
1 tsp. ground ginger
½ tsp. baking soda
½ tsp. ground cinnamon
½ tsp. ground cloves
½ cup molasses
1 egg
1 Tbsp. vinegar
2½ cups all-purpose flour

◆◆◆

1 recipe Orange Icing (see right)

1 In a mixing bowl beat shortening with an electric mixer on medium to high speed 30 seconds. Add sugar, baking powder, ginger, baking soda, cinnamon, and cloves. Beat until combined, scraping bowl. Beat in the molasses, egg, and vinegar until combined. Beat in as much of the flour as you can with the mixer. Stir in remaining flour. Divide dough in half. Cover and chill 3 hours or until easy to handle.

2 Grease a cookie sheet; set aside. On a lightly floured surface, roll half of the dough at a time to ¼-inch thickness. Cut into cookies using a 5- or 7½-inch cookie cutter or a 12-inch pattern.* Place 1 inch apart on the prepared cookie sheet.

3 Bake in a 375° oven for 6 to 8 minutes for 5-inch cookies, 10 to 12 minutes for 7½-inch cookies, and 13 to 15 minutes for 12-inch cookies or until edges are lightly browned. Cool on cookie sheet 1 minute. Transfer cookies to a wire rack and let cool. Decorate cookies with Orange Icing. Makes about twenty-four 5-inch cookies, eleven 7½-inch cookies, or four 12-inch cookies.

*Note: For 12-inch cookies, roll dough directly on prepared cookie sheet. Cut out cookies and remove excess dough from cookie sheet. Bake as directed.

Orange Icing: In a mixing bowl combine 2 cups sifted powdered sugar, 2 tablespoons orange juice or milk, and ½ teaspoon vanilla. Stir in additional juice or milk, 1 teaspoon at a time, until it reaches drizzling consistency.

TO MAKE AHEAD

Prepare and bake cookies as directed; cool completely. Do not decorate with Orange Icing. Place cookies in a freezer container or bag and freeze for up to 1 month. Before serving, thaw for 15 minutes. Prepare Orange Icing and decorate cookies.

Nutrition facts per 5-inch cookie: 151 cal., 5 g total fat (1 g sat. fat), 9 mg chol., 45 mg sodium, 26 g carbo., 0 g fiber, 2 g pro. *Daily values:* 1% vit. C, 2% calcium, 6% iron.

UNDER-THE-BIG-TOP COOKIES

Prep: 30 min. ◆ Chill: 3 hr.
Bake: 6 min. per batch

Half the fun of this edible circus is the decorating. Go for the au naturel look by topping them with nuts, pretzels, toasted coconut, and wheat biscuits.

½ cup butter
¾ cup granulated sugar
¼ cup packed dark brown
   sugar
1 tsp. baking powder
¼ tsp. salt
1 egg
1 Tbsp. milk
1 tsp. vanilla
2 cups all-purpose flour

◆◆◆

1 recipe Powdered Sugar
   Frosting (see right)
Chopped nuts, crushed
   shredded wheat biscuits,
   coconut, pretzel pieces,
   white oblong sprinkles,
   raw sugar, and/or
   multicolored coarse sugar

1 In a large mixing bowl beat butter with an electric mixer on medium to high speed for 30 seconds. Add granulated sugar, brown sugar, baking powder, and salt. Beat until combined, scraping bowl. Beat in egg, milk, and vanilla. Beat in as much of the flour as you can with the mixer. Using a wooden spoon, stir in any remaining flour. Divide dough in half. If necessary, cover and chill dough about 3 hours or until easy to handle.

2 On a lightly floured surface, roll half the dough at a time to ¼-inch thickness. Using a 6- to 8-inch cookie cutter, cut into de-sired shapes. Place on an ungreased cookie sheet.

3 Bake in a 375° oven for 6 to 8 minutes or until edges are firm and bottoms are very lightly browned. Transfer cookies to a wire rack and let cool. Frost with Powdered Sugar Frosting and sprinkle with decorations before frosting dries. Makes about twenty 6- to 8-inch cookies.

Powdered Sugar Frosting: In a medium mixing bowl combine 2 cups powdered sugar, 2 table-spoons milk, and ½ teaspoon vanilla. Stir in additional milk, 1 teaspoon at a time, until frost-ing reaches drizzling consistency. Makes about 1 cup.

Nutrition facts per cookie: 215 cal., 10 g total fat (4 g sat. fat), 23 mg chol., 97 mg sodium, 30 g carbo., 0 g fiber, 2 g pro.
Daily values: 4% vit. A, 2% calcium, 4% iron.

SHORTBREAD BUNDLES

Prep: 20 min. ◆ Bake: 20 min.

Be a Santa's helper: Package bundles of five cookies of each flavor in a clear cello wrap tied with festive ribbons, and deliver them to family and friends.

1¼ cups all-purpose flour
3 Tbsp. sugar
2 tsp. ground coriander
½ cup butter

1 In a medium mixing bowl combine the flour, sugar, and coriander. Using a pastry cutter, cut in butter until mixture resem-bles fine crumbs and starts to cling together. Form the mixture into a ball and knead gently just until smooth.

2 On an ungreased cookie sheet pat or roll the dough to a 9×4-inch rectangle, about ½ inch thick. Using a knife, cut dough into ½-inch squares, but do not separate squares.

3 Bake in a 325° oven for 20 to 25 minutes or until bottoms just start to brown. Remove from oven. Cut into squares on cookie sheet again while warm. Cool on the cookie sheet for 5 to 8 min-utes. Transfer cookies to a wire rack and cool completely. Makes 144 cookies.

▌TO MAKE AHEAD▐

Prepare and bake cookies as directed; cool completely. Place cookies in a freezer container or bag and freeze for up to 1 month. Before serving, thaw 15 minutes.

Nutrition facts per 5 cookies: 52 cal., 3 g total fat (2 g sat. fat), 9 mg chol., 32 mg sodium, 5 g carbo., 0 g fiber, 1 g pro.

Tangerine Shortbread Bites: Prepare Shortbread Bundles as directed, except substitute 2 tea-spoons finely shredded tangerine peel for the coriander.

Chocolate-Mocha Cookies: Prepare Shortbread Bundles as directed, except reduce flour to 1 cup, increase the sugar to ⅓ cup, omit the coriander, and add 3 tablespoons unsweetened cocoa powder to dry ingredients before cutting in the butter. Dissolve ½ teaspoon instant cof-fee crystals in 1 teaspoon water. Stir coffee into dough after cut-ting in the butter.

Springtime Brunch

As the first crop of fruits and vegetables appears in the garden, celebrate the season with these special creations.

Mushroom and Asparagus Strata (page 58)

◆◆◆

Baked ham slices

◆◆◆

Assorted miniature muffins or other bakery-fresh pastries

◆◆◆

Sweet Melon Cup (page 85)

◆◆◆

Gingered Orange-Rhubarb Punch (page 110) or fruit juice

The day before:
◆ Assemble strata; cover and chill.
◆ Prepare syrup for melon cup; cover and chill.

◆ Prepare rhubarb mixture for punch; cover and chill.

1 hour before:
◆ Bake strata; let stand and cut into squares or rectangles.

30 minutes before:
◆ Heat ham slices.
◆ Assemble melon cups.
◆ Finish punch.

Just before serving:
◆ Arrange muffins or pastries in baskets or on platters.
◆ Pour punch over ice in fluted glasses.

A Farmer's Market Lunch

Enjoy the morning by gathering nature's bounty; then retreat to the kitchen to feature the freshest of lunches.

Season's Finest Salad (page 156)

◆◆◆

Sliced seed bread or hard rolls

◆◆◆

Homemade lemonade or iced tea

◆◆◆

Lemon-Meringue Beehives (page 167)

Up to 1 week before:
◆ Make and bake meringue beehives; cover and store.

1 hour before:
◆ Prepare salad and dressing (do not dress).
◆ Prepare and chill lemonade or iced tea.

Just before serving:
◆ Slice bread.
◆ Dress salad.
◆ Serve lemonade or tea over ice.

Between courses:
◆ Assemble beehives.

Picnic in the Park

Ahh . . . the stuff simple afternoons in the park are made of. Spread out your blanket and unpack the cooler to enjoy this pure picnic pleasure.

Mile-High Muffuletta (page 116)

◆◆◆

Potato chips

◆◆◆

Fresh fruit bowl

◆◆◆

Chocolate Chip Cookie Sticks (page 32)

◆◆◆

Raspberry Refresher (page 140)

The day before:
◆ Make and bake cookie sticks; cover and store.
◆ Prepare raspberry mixture for punch; cover and chill.

1 hour before:
◆ Make sandwich; place in an airtight container and pack on ice.
◆ Prepare fruit bowl; cover and pack on ice.
◆ Pack punch mixture and club soda on ice.

Just before serving:
◆ Add club soda to raspberry mixture and serve punch over ice.

A "Big Catch" Meal

A salad-style salmon entrée is the star, but watch out—light and airy Chiffon Pie is a scene-stealer!

Pepper Poached Salmon and Herbed Beets (page 101)

◆◆◆

Country-style Italian bread

◆◆◆

Chiffon Pie (page 36)

6 hours before:
◆ Prepare pie; cover and chill.

4 hours before:
◆ Prepare Glazed Shredded Lime Peel, if using.

30 minutes before:
◆ Poach fish and make sauce.
◆ Prepare beets.

Just before serving:
◆ Slice bread.
◆ Arrange salmon and beets on plates.

Between courses:
◆ Slice bread.
◆ Cut pie into wedges; garnish with lime peel.

Back-to-School Dinner

Indulge the kids with a summer dinner finale—these homespun dishes they'll love.

Hamburger Pie (page 29)

◆◆◆

Salad of mixed greens, shredded carrots, sliced fresh mushrooms, and vinaigrette.

◆◆◆

Sundae Pound Cake (page 87)

◆◆◆

Milk

2 days before:
◆ Assemble Hamburger Pie; cover and chill.

Up to 8 hours before:
◆ Make, bake, and cool cake. Glaze cake and cover and store.

45 minutes before:
◆ Bake Hamburger Pie; let stand, then serve.
◆ Prepare salad (except vinaigrette)

Just before serving:
◆ Add vinaigrette to salad.

Between courses:
◆ Slice cake into wedges and serve with ice cream and strawberries, if desired.

Autumn's-in-the-Air Dinner

As the cool, crisp air of autumn begins to blow, gather around the table for this hearty meal of satisfying comfort dishes.

Figs and Fruit Salad (page 227)

◆◆◆

Braised Fall Vegetables (page 225)

◆◆◆

Roasted pork

◆◆◆

Multigrain bread with butter

◆◆◆

Polenta-Pecan Apple Cobbler (page 250)

2 hours before:
◆ Prepare and roast a 2 to 3 pound boneless top loin pork roast (single loin); let stand and slice.

1½ hours before:
◆ Prepare and bake cobbler.

45 minutes before:
◆ Prepare salad and arrange in bowls.
◆ Prepare vegetables.
◆ Prepare and bake cobbler.

Just before serving:
◆ Arrange meat and vegetables on a platter.

Between courses:
◆ Spoon cobbler into bowls.

Supper on the Quick

*Moms will love this one—a nutritious meal that's quick enough
to squeeze in between evening events.*

**Lemon-Pepper Pasta and Chicken
(page 116)**

♦♦♦

**Salad of romaine hearts, tomato wedges,
and Italian dressing**

♦♦♦

Bakery-fresh focaccia

♦♦♦

Fruit Bowl Sundae (page 139)

40 minutes before:
♦ Prepare salad (except dressing).
♦ Prepare pasta.

Just before serving:
♦ Dress salad.
♦ Slice bread.

Between courses:
♦ Prepare sundaes.

Old-Fashioned Barbecue

Croquet, horseshoes, hand-cranked ice cream, and barbecue recreate a "back when" Sunday afternoon.

Smoked Ribs and Ginger Sauce (page 27)

♦♦♦

Curly Cukes and Radish Salad (page 70)

♦♦♦

Potato salad

♦♦♦

Corn-on-the-cob

♦♦♦

Onion Corn Cake (page 305)

♦♦♦

**Old-Fashioned Vanilla Bean Ice Cream
(page 136)**

♦♦♦

Purchased brownies

8½ hours ahead:
♦ Prepare, chill, freeze, and ripen ice cream.

1½ hours before:
♦ Grill ribs; cut into serving-size pieces.

1 hour before:
♦ Make and bake corn cake.

30 minutes before:
♦ Prepare cucumber salad.

Just before serving:
♦ Cook corn.
♦ Arrange ribs on a platter.

The day before:
♦ Prepare barbecue rub; rub on ribs; cover and chill.
♦ Make Ginger Sauce; cover and chill.

Between courses:
♦ Arrange brownies on a platter.
♦ Scoop ice cream into bowls.

Thanksgiving Dinner

Quintessentially American, here's a feast that's beyond compare! Prepare the entire menu or choose a dish or two to add to your traditional fare.

Roasted Corn and Pepper Soup (page 271)

◆◆◆

Orange- and Herb-Roasted Turkey (page 270)

◆◆◆

Chunky Corn Bread Dressing (page 273)

◆◆◆

Peppery White Cheddar Biscuits (page 276)

◆◆◆

Mashed Sweets and Turnips (page 285)

◆◆◆

Green Beans and Fennel (page 286)

◆◆◆

Ginger and Honey-Glazed Carrots (page 286)

◆◆◆

Cranberry and Apricot Chutney (page 276)

◆◆◆

Lemon Cheesecake (page 288)

◆◆◆

Pumpkin Spice Loaves (page 285)

◆◆◆

Autumn Fruit Tartlets (page 286)

Up to 4 days ahead:
◆ Prepare chutney; cover and chill.
◆ Make corn bread for dressing; wrap and freeze.

2 days ahead:
◆ Prepare soup up to the thickening step; cover and chill.
◆ Make cheesecake; cover and chill.
◆ Prepare pudding for tartlets; cover and chill.
◆ Make and bake spice loaves.

The day before:
◆ Make dressing through adding bacon; cover and chill.
◆ Prepare and bake shells for tartlets; fill with pudding.
◆ Make caramel spikes for tartlets.
◆ Prepare Mashed Sweets and Turnips (except for relish).
◆ Prepare and boil carrots; cover and chill.

4¼ hours before.
◆ Prepare and roast turkey.

45 minutes before:
◆ Complete the corn bread dressing and bake.
◆ Prepare green beans.
◆ Make and bake biscuits.
◆ Reheat and thicken soup.
◆ Reheat Mashed Sweets and Turnips; prepare relish.

Just before serving:
◆ Glaze carrots.
◆ Make gravy.

Between courses:
◆ Top tartlets with fruits and caramel spikes; prepare Crackly Caramel Sauce; drizzle over tartlets.
◆ Prepare whipped cream for spice loaves; cut loaves.
◆ Unmold cheesecake.

Above: *Festive Fruit-and-Nut Panettone (page 306)*

Left: *Endive-Mango Appetizers*
(page 291),
Lemony-Herbed Olives (page 292),
Pistachio-Salmon Nuggets (page 292)
Below: *Festive Salad (page 292)*
Page 318: *Celebration Roast*
(page 298) and
Heavenly Peas with Mashed Potatoes
(page 294)

Wintery Ice Cream Balls (page 306)

EMERGENCY SUBSTITUTIONS

IF YOU DON'T HAVE:	SUBSTITUTE:
1 teaspoon baking powder	½ teaspoon cream of tartar plus ¼ teaspoon baking soda
1 tablespoon cornstarch (for thickening)	2 tablespoons all-purpose flour
1 package active dry yeast	1 cake compressed yeast
1 cup buttermilk	1 tablespoon lemon juice or vinegar plus enough milk to make 1 cup (let stand 5 minutes before using); or 1 cup plain yogurt
1 cup whole milk	½ cup evaporated milk plus ½ cup water; or 1 cup water plus ⅓ cup nonfat dry milk powder
1 cup light cream	1 tablespoon melted butter or margarine plus enough whole milk to make 1 cup
1 cup dairy sour cream	1 cup plain yogurt
1 whole egg	2 egg whites, 2 egg yolks, or 3 tablespoons frozen egg product, thawed
1 cup margarine	1 cup butter; or 1 cup shortening plus ¼ teaspoon salt, if desired
1 ounce semisweet chocolate	3 tablespoons semisweet chocolate pieces; or 1 ounce unsweetened chocolate plus 1 tablespoon granulated sugar
1 ounce unsweetened chocolate	3 tablespoons unsweetened cocoa powder plus 1 tablespoon cooking oil or shortening, melted
1 cup corn syrup	1 cup granulated sugar plus ¼ cup liquid
1 cup honey	1¼ cups granulated sugar plus ¼ cup liquid
1 cup molasses	1 cup honey
1 cup granulated sugar	1 cup packed brown sugar or 2 cups sifted powdered sugar
1 cup beef broth or chicken broth	1 teaspoon or 1 cube instant beef or chicken bouillon plus 1 cup hot water
2 cups tomato sauce	¾ cup tomato paste plus 1 cup water
1 cup tomato juice	½ cup tomato sauce plus ½ cup water
¼ cup fine dry bread crumbs	¾ cup soft bread crumbs, ¼ cup cracker crumbs, or ¼ cup cornflake crumbs
1 small onion, chopped (⅓ cup)	1 teaspoon onion powder or 1 tablespoon dried minced onion
1 clove garlic	½ teaspoon bottled minced garlic or ⅛ teaspoon garlic powder
1 teaspoon lemon juice	½ teaspoon vinegar
1 teaspoon poultry seasoning	¾ teaspoon dried sage, crushed, plus ¼ teaspoon dried thyme or marjoram, crushed
1 teaspoon dry mustard (in cooked mixtures)	1 tablespoon prepared mustard
1 tablespoon snipped fresh herb	½ to 1 teaspoon dried herb, crushed
1 teaspoon dried herb	½ teaspoon ground herb
1 teaspoon grated fresh ginger	¼ teaspoon ground ginger
1 teaspoon apple pie spice	½ teaspoon ground cinnamon plus ¼ teaspoon ground nutmeg, ⅛ teaspoon ground allspice, and dash ground cloves or ginger
1 teaspoon pumpkin pie spice	½ teaspoon ground cinnamon plus ¼ teaspoon ground ginger, ¼ teaspoon ground allspice, and ⅛ teaspoon ground nutmeg